W9-BJP-451

More praise for
THE GREAT LEVELER

"Very powerful."
—MARTIN WOLF, *Financial Times*

"[Scheidel] puts the discussion of increased inequality found in the recent work of Thomas Piketty, Anthony Atkinson, Branko Milanovic and others into a broad historical context and examines the circumstances under which it can be reduced."
—*The Economist*

"Stanford's Walter Scheidel should be heard."
—GEORGE WILL, *Washington Post*

"A scholarly and ambitious book."
—PAUL MASON, *Guardian*

"One by one Scheidel dismisses the non-catastrophic alternatives that have been the focus of virtually every peaceful movement for social justice: democracy, the extension of the franchise, education, economic growth, social democracy, trade unionism and the welfare state."
—JAMES C. SCOTT, *London Review of Books*

"[M]agisterial."
—AARON REEVES, *Nature*

"He is a formidable global historian for whom no place or period is beyond reach."
—AVNER OFFER, *Times Literary Supplement*

"[E]xcellent."
—BEN COLLYER, *New Scientist*

"An important and thought-provoking contribution to the academic and societal debate on inequality."
—BAS VAN BAVEL, *Economic History Review*

"Depressing and thought-provoking."
—ISAAC CHOTINER, *Slate*

"The year's best and most striking economics book."
—RYAN AVENT, *strategy+business*

"A fantastic piece of social science."
—MARK KOYAMA, *Public Choice*

"A very brave attempt to say very important things backed up by enormous empirical research. . . . Fascinating . . . and important book."
—MICHAEL MANN, *Millennium*

"Fascinating."
—GLENN ALTSCHULER, *Huffington Post*

"In his remarkable new book, *The Great Leveler*, historian Walter Scheidel shows that . . . reducing inequality has always been a miserable business. . . . Magisterial."
—IAN MORRIS, *BBC History Magazine*

"A thoroughly unsunny . . . but fascinating look at the engines of our discontent."
—*KIRKUS*

"A new history of wealth inequality from primitive times to the present that is provoking wide debate."
—DAVID TALBOT, *San Francisco Chronicle*

"If you think you've heard it all about economic inequality, think again. Walter Scheidel's analysis of what really reduces inequality is provocative, but he makes the case with reason, evidence, and style."
—STEVEN PINKER, author of *The Better Angels of Our Nature: Why Violence Has Declined*

"Brilliant, erudite, and chock-full of historical detail, *The Great Leveler* has a powerful message and asks a big question for the twenty-first century: Can we find a cure for inequality that isn't worse than the disease?"
—BRANKO MILANOVIC, author of *Global Inequality: A New Approach for the Age of Globalization*

"This is the best book on the history of income inequality. And the central message is that most significant reductions in inequality come through violence and destruction. Have a nice day!"
—TYLER COWEN, author of *The Complacent Class: The Self-Defeating Quest for the American Dream*

WALTER SCHEIDEL

Walter Scheidel is the Dickason Professor in the Humanities, Professor of Classics and History, and a Kennedy-Grossman Fellow in Human Biology at Stanford University. The author or editor of seventeen previous books, he has published widely on premodern social and economic history, demography, and comparative history. He lives in Palo Alto, California.

THE GREAT
LEVELER

Albrecht Dürer, *The Four Horsemen of the Apocalypse*, from *The Apocalypse*, 1497–1498. Woodcut, 15¼ × 11 in. (38.7 × 27.9 cm).

THE GREAT LEVELER

VIOLENCE AND THE HISTORY OF
INEQUALITY
FROM THE STONE AGE TO THE
TWENTY-FIRST CENTURY

WALTER SCHEIDEL

Princeton University Press
Princeton and Oxford

Copyright © 2017 by Princeton University Press
Published by Princeton University Press, 41 William Street, Princeton, New Jersey 08540
In the United Kingdom: Princeton University Press, 6 Oxford Street, Woodstock, Oxfordshire OX20 1TR

press.princeton.edu

Cover art: Albrecht Dürer, *The Four Horsemen of the Apocalypse*, from *The Apocalypse*, 1497–1498.
Woodcut, 15¼ × 11 in. (38.7 × 27.9 cm).

First paperback printing, 2018

Paper ISBN 978-0-691-18325-1
Cloth ISBN 978-0-691-16502-8

Library of Congress Control Number: 2016953046

British Library Cataloging-in-Publication Data is available

This book has been composed in Garamond Premier Pro

Printed on acid-free paper. ∞

Printed in the United States of America

For My Mother

"So distribution should undo excess,
And each man have enough."
Shakespeare, *King Lear*

"Get rid of the rich and you will find no poor."
De Divitiis

"How often does God find cures for us worse than our perils!"
Seneca, *Medea*

CONTENTS

FIGURES AND TABLES

TABLES

ACKNOWLEDGMENTS

The gap between the haves and the have-nots has alternately grown and shrunk throughout the course of human civilization. Economic inequality may only recently have returned to great prominence in popular discourse, but its history runs deep. My book seeks to track and explain this history in the very long run.

One of the first to draw my attention to this very long run was Branko Milanovic, a world expert on inequality who in his own research has reached all the way back to antiquity. If there were more economists like him, more historians would be listening. About a decade ago, Steve Friesen made me think harder about ancient income distributions, and Emmanuel Saez further piqued my interest in inequality during a shared year at Stanford's Center for Advanced Study in the Behavioral Sciences.

My perspective and argument have been inspired in no small measure by Thomas Piketty's work. For several years before his provocative book on capital in the twenty-first century introduced his ideas to a wider audience, I had read his work and pondered its relevance beyond the last couple of centuries (also known as the "short term" to an ancient historian such as myself). The appearance of his magnum opus provided much-needed impetus for me to move from mere contemplation to the writing of my own study. His trailblazing has been much appreciated.

Paul Seabright's invitation to deliver a distinguished lecture at the Institute for Advanced Studies in Toulouse in December 2013 prompted me to fashion my disorganized thoughts on this topic into a more coherent argument and encouraged me to go ahead with this book project. During a second round of early discussion at the Santa Fe Institute, Sam Bowles proved a fierce but friendly critic, and Suresh Naidu provided helpful input.

When my colleague Ken Scheve asked me to organize a conference on behalf of Stanford's Europe Center, I seized the opportunity to gather a group of experts from different disciplines to discuss the evolution of material inequality in the long run of history. Our meeting in Vienna in September 2015 was both enjoyable and educational: my thanks go to my local co-organizers, Bernhard Palme and Peer Vries, as well as to Ken Scheve and August Reinisch for their financial support.

I further benefited from feedback at presentations at the Evergreen State College, the Universities of Copenhagen and Lund, and the Chinese Academy of Social Sciences in Beijing. I am grateful to the organizers of these events: Ulrike Krotscheck, Peter Bang, Carl Hampus Lyttkens, Liu Jinyu, and Hu Yujuan.

David Christian, Joy Connolly, Peter Garnsey, Robert Gordon, Philip Hoffman, Branko Milanovic, Joel Mokyr, Reviel Netz, Şevket Pamuk, David Stasavage, and Peter Turchin very kindly read and commented on the whole manuscript. Kyle Harper, William Harris, Geoffrey Kron, Peter Lindert, Josh Ober, and Thomas Piketty also read parts of the book. A group of historians at the Saxo Institute in Copenhagen met to discuss my manuscript, and I am particularly grateful to Gunner Lind and Jan Pedersen for their extensive input. I received valuable expert advice on specific sections and questions from Anne Austin, Kara Cooney, Steve Haber, Marilyn Masson, Mike Smith, and Gavin Wright. It is entirely my own fault that I have not been as receptive to their comments as I surely ought to have been.

I am extremely grateful to a number of colleagues who generously shared their unpublished work with me: Guido Alfani, Kyle Harper, Michael Jursa, Geoffrey Kron, Branko Milanovic, Ian Morris, Henrik Mouritsen, Josh Ober, Peter Lindert, Bernhard Palme, Şevket Pamuk, Mark Pyzyk, Ken Scheve, David Stasavage, Peter Turchin, and Jeffrey Williamson. Brandon Dupont and Joshua Rosenbloom very helpfully generated and shared statistics on wealth distribution in the United States during the Civil War period. Leonardo Gasparini, Branko Milanovic, Şevket Pamuk, Leandro Prados de la Escosura, Ken Scheve, Mikael Stenkula, Rob Stephan, and Klaus Wälde kindly sent me data files. Stanford economics major Andrew Granato provided valuable research assistance.

I completed this project during a Stanford Humanities and Arts Enhanced Sabbatical Fellowship granted for the academic year of 2015/2016: my thanks go to my deans, Debra Satz and Richard Saller, for their support in this matter (in addition to many others). This sabbatical allowed me to spend the spring of 2016 as a visitor at the Saxo Institute of the University of Copenhagen when I was putting the finishing touches on my manuscript. I am grateful to my Danish colleagues for their warm hospitality—and above all to my good friend and serial collaborator Peter Bang. I also owe a somewhat awkward word of thanks to the John Simon Guggenheim Memorial Foundation for awarding me a fellowship to pursue this project. Having somehow managed to finish this book before I had a chance to take up this fellowship, I will be sure to make the most of it in my future endeavors.

As my project approached completion, Joel Mokyr kindly offered to include this title in his series and helped shepherd it through the review process. I have greatly appreciated his support and judicious comments. Rob Tempio has been a splendid instigator and editor, a true book lover and author's advocate. I am also in his debt for his having suggested the main title of this book. His colleague Eric Crahan granted me timely access to the page proofs of two related Princeton books. Further thanks are due to Jenny Wolkowicki, Carol McGillivray, and Jonathan Harrison for having ensured an exceptionally smooth and swift production process, and to Chris Ferrante for his striking cover design.

Introduction

THE CHALLENGE OF INEQUALITY

"A DANGEROUS AND GROWING INEQUALITY"

How many billionaires does it take to match the net worth of half of the world's population? In 2015, the richest sixty-two persons on the planet owned as much private net wealth as the poorer half of humanity, more than 3.5 billion people. If they decided to go on a field trip together, they would comfortably fit into a large coach. The previous year, eighty-five billionaires were needed to clear that threshold, calling perhaps for a more commodious double-decker bus. And not so long ago, in 2010, no fewer 388 of them had to pool their resources to offset the assets of the global other half, a turnout that would have required a small convoy of vehicles or filled up a typical Boeing 777 or Airbus A340.[1]

But inequality is not created just by multibillionaires. The richest 1 percent of the world's households now hold a little more than half of global private net wealth. Inclusion of the assets that some of them conceal in offshore accounts would skew the distribution even further. These disparities are not simply caused by the huge differences in average income between advanced and developing economies. Similar imbalances exist within societies. The wealthiest twenty Americans currently own as much as the bottom half of their country's households taken together, and the top 1 percent of incomes account for about a fifth of the national total. Inequality has been growing in much of the world. In recent decades, income and wealth have become more unevenly distributed in Europe and North America, in the former Soviet bloc, and in China, India, and elsewhere. And to the one who has, more will be given: in the United States, the best-earning 1 percent of the top 1 percent (those in the highest 0.01 percent income bracket) raised their share to almost six times what it had been in

---

[1] Hardoon, Ayele, and Fuentes-Nieva 2016: 2; Fuentes-Nieva and Galasso 2014: 2.

the 1970s even as the top tenth of that group (the top 0.1 percent) quadrupled it. The remainder averaged gains of about three-quarters—nothing to frown at, but a far cry from the advances in higher tiers.[2]

The "1 percent" may be a convenient moniker that smoothly rolls off the tongue, and one that I repeatedly use in this book, but it also serves to obscure the degree of wealth concentration in even fewer hands. In the 1850s, Nathaniel Parker Willis coined the term "Upper Ten Thousand" to describe New York high society. We may now be in need of a variant, the "Upper Ten-Thousandth," to do justice to those who contribute the most to widening inequality. And even within this rarefied group, those at the very top continue to outdistance all others. The largest American fortune currently equals about 1 million times the average annual household income, a multiple twenty times larger than it was in 1982. Even so, the United States may be losing out to China, now said to be home to an even larger number of dollar billionaires despite its considerably smaller nominal GDP.[3]

All this has been greeted with growing anxiety. In 2013, President Barack Obama elevated rising inequality to a "defining challenge":

> And that is a dangerous and growing inequality and lack of upward mobility that has jeopardized middle-class America's basic bargain—that if you work hard, you have a chance to get ahead. I believe this is the defining challenge of our time: Making sure our economy works for every working American.

Two years earlier, multibillionaire investor Warren Buffett had complained that he and his "mega-rich friends" did not pay enough taxes. These sentiments are widely shared. Within eighteen months of its publication in 2013, a 700-page academic tome on capitalist inequality had sold 1.5 million copies and risen to the top of the *New York Times* nonfiction hardcover bestseller list. In the Democratic

---

[2] Global wealth: Credit Suisse 2015: 11. U.S. top income shares according to WWID: the top 0.01, 0.1, and 1 percent shares, including capital gains, rose from 0.85, 2.56, and 8.87 percent in 1975 to 4.89, 10.26, and 21.24 percent in 2014, which represents increases of 475 percent, 301 percent, and 139 percent, respectively, and of 74 percent for those between the top 0.1 percent and 1 percent.

[3] Bill Gates's fortune of $75.4 billion in February 2016 equals roughly 1 million times average and 1.4 million times median U.S. household income, while Daniel Ludwig's assets of $2 billion in the first Forbes 400 list, published in 1982, equaled about 50,000 times average and 85,000 times median household income at the time. For China's billionaires, see www.economist.com/news/china/21676814-crackdown-corruption-has-spread-anxiety-among-chinas-business-elite-robber-barons-beware.

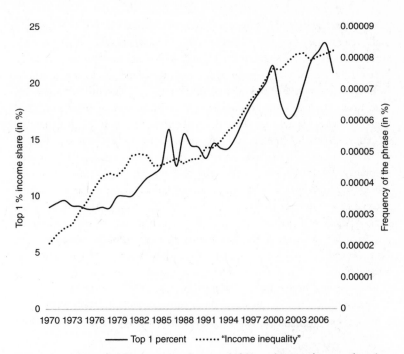

Figure I.1 Top 1 percent income share in the United States (per year) and references to "income inequality" (three-year moving averages), 1970–2008

Party primaries for the 2016 presidential election, Senator Bernie Sanders's relentless denunciation of the "billionaire class" roused large crowds and elicited millions of small donations from grassroots supporters. Even the leadership of the People's Republic of China has publicly acknowledged the issue by endorsing a report on how to "reform the system of income distribution." Any lingering doubts are dispelled by Google, one of the great money-spinning disequalizers in the San Francisco Bay Area, where I live, which allows us to track the growing prominence of income inequality in the public consciousness (Fig. I.1).[4]

---

[4] "Remarks by the President on Economic Mobility," December 4, 2013, https://www.whitehouse.gov/the-press-office/2013/12/04/remarks-president-economic-mobility. Buffett 2011. Bestseller: Piketty 2014. China: State Council 2013. Fig. I.1: WWID (including capital gains); https://books.google.com/ngrams. The prominence of this meme has most recently been underscored by the publication of a collection of poems fashionably entitled *Widening income inequality* (Seidel 2016).

So have the rich simply kept getting richer? Not quite. For all the much-maligned rapacity of the "billionaire class" or, more broadly, the "1 percent," American top income shares only very recently caught up with those reached back in 1929, and assets are less heavily concentrated now than they were then. In England on the eve of the First World War, the richest tenth of households held a staggering 92 percent of all private wealth, crowding out pretty much everybody else; today their share is a little more than half. High inequality has an extremely long pedigree. Two thousand years ago, the largest Roman private fortunes equaled about 1.5 million times the average annual per capita income in the empire, roughly the same ratio as for Bill Gates and the average American today. For all we can tell, even the overall degree of Roman income inequality was not very different from that in the United States. Yet by the time of Pope Gregory the Great, around 600 CE, great estates had disappeared, and what little was left of the Roman aristocracy relied on papal handouts to keep them afloat. Sometimes, as on that occasion, inequality declined because although many became poorer, the rich simply had more to lose. In other cases, workers became better off while returns on capital fell: western Europe after the Black Death, where real wages doubled or tripled and laborers dined on meat and beer while landlords struggled to keep up appearances, is a famous example.[5]

How has the distribution of income and wealth developed over time, and why has it sometimes changed so much? Considering the enormous amount of attention that inequality has received in recent years, we still know much less about this than might be expected. A large and steadily growing body of often highly technical scholarship attends to the most pressing question: why income has frequently become more concentrated over the course of the last generation. Less has been written about the forces that caused inequality to fall across much of the world earlier in the twentieth century—and far less still about the distribution of material resources in the more distant past. To be sure, concerns about growing income gaps in the world today have given momentum to the study of inequality in the longer run, just as contemporary climate change has encouraged analysis of pertinent historical data. But we still lack a proper sense of the big picture, a global survey that covers the broad sweep of observable

---

[5] U.S.: WWID, and herein, chapter 15, p. 409. England: Roine and Waldenström 2015: 579 table 7.A4. For Rome, see herein, chapter 2, p. 78 (fortunes), chapter 9, p. 266 (handouts), and Scheidel and Friesen 2009: 73–74, 86–87 (GDP and income Gini coefficient). For overall levels of inequality, see herein, appendix, p. 455. For the Black Death, see herein, chapter 10, pp. 300–306.

history. A cross-cultural, comparative, and long-term perspective is essential for our understanding of the mechanisms that have shaped the distribution of income and wealth.

THE FOUR HORSEMEN

Material inequality requires access to resources beyond the minimum that is needed to keep us all alive. Surpluses already existed tens of thousands of years ago, and so did humans who were prepared to share them unevenly. Back in the last Ice Age, hunter-gatherers found the time and means to bury some individuals much more lavishly than others. But it was food production—farming and herding—that created wealth on an entirely novel scale. Growing and persistent inequality became a defining feature of the Holocene. The domestication of plants and animals made it possible to accumulate and preserve productive resources. Social norms evolved to define rights to these assets, including the ability to pass them on to future generations. Under these conditions, the distribution of income and wealth came to be shaped by a variety of experiences: health, marital strategies and reproductive success, consumption and investment choices, bumper harvests, and plagues of locusts and rinderpest determined fortunes from one generation to the next. Adding up over time, the consequences of luck and effort favored unequal outcomes in the long term.

In principle, institutions could have flattened emerging disparities through interventions designed to rebalance the distribution of material resources and the fruits from labor, as some premodern societies are indeed reputed to have done. In practice, however, social evolution commonly had the opposite effect. Domestication of food sources also domesticated people. The formation of states as a highly competitive form of organization established steep hierarchies of power and coercive force that skewed access to income and wealth. Political inequality reinforced and amplified economic inequality. For most of the agrarian period, the state enriched the few at the expense of the many: gains from pay and benefactions for public service often paled next to those from corruption, extortion, and plunder. As a result, many premodern societies grew to be as unequal as they could possibly be, probing the limits of surplus appropriation by small elites under conditions of low per capita output and minimal growth. And when more benign institutions promoted more vigorous economic development, most notably in the emergent West, they continued to sustain high inequality. Urbanization, commercialization, financial sector innovation, trade on an increasingly global scale, and, finally, industrialization generated rich returns for holders of capital. As rents from the naked exercise of power declined, choking off a traditional source of elite enrichment, more secure property rights and state commitments strengthened the protection of hereditary private wealth. Even as economic structures, social norms, and political systems changed, income and wealth inequality remained high or found new ways to grow.

For thousands of years, civilization did not lend itself to peaceful equalization. Across a wide range of societies and different levels of development, stability favored economic inequality. This was as true of Pharaonic Egypt as it was of Victorian England, as true of the Roman Empire as of the United States. Violent shocks were of paramount importance in disrupting the established order, in compressing the distribution of income and wealth, in narrowing the gap between rich and poor. Throughout recorded history, the most powerful leveling invariably resulted from the most powerful shocks. Four different kinds of violent ruptures have flattened inequality: mass mobilization warfare, transformative revolution, state failure, and lethal pandemics. I call these the Four Horsemen of Leveling. Just like their biblical counterparts, they went forth to "take peace from the earth" and "kill with sword, and with hunger, and with death, and with the beasts of the earth." Sometimes acting individually and sometimes in concert with one another, they produced outcomes that to contemporaries often seemed nothing short of apocalyptic. Hundreds of millions perished in their wake. And by the time the dust had settled, the gap between the haves and the have-nots had shrunk, sometimes dramatically.[6]

Only specific types of violence have consistently forced down inequality. Most wars did not have any systematic effect on the distribution of resources: although archaic forms of conflict that thrived on conquest and plunder were likely to enrich victorious elites and impoverish those on the losing side, less clear-cut endings failed to have predictable consequences. For war to level disparities in income and wealth, it needed to penetrate society as a whole, to mobilize people and resources on a scale that was often only feasible in modern nation-states. This explains why the two world wars were among the greatest levelers in history. The physical destruction wrought by industrial-scale warfare, confiscatory taxation, government intervention in the economy, inflation, disruption to global flows of goods and capital, and other factors all combined to

---

[6] Revelation 6:4, 8.

wipe out elites' wealth and redistribute resources. They also served as a uniquely powerful catalyst for equalizing policy change, providing powerful impetus to franchise extensions, unionization, and the expansion of the welfare state. The shocks of the world wars led to what is known as the "Great Compression," massive attenuation of inequalities in income and wealth across developed countries. Mostly concentrated in the period from 1914 to 1945, it generally took several more decades fully to run its course. Earlier mass mobilization warfare had lacked similar pervasive repercussions. The wars of the Napoleonic era or the American Civil War had produced mixed distributional outcomes, and the farther we go back in time, the less pertinent evidence there is. The ancient Greek city-state culture, represented by Athens and Sparta, arguably provides us with earliest examples of how intense popular military mobilization and egalitarian institutions helped constrain material inequality, albeit with mixed success.

The world wars spawned the second major leveling force, transformative revolution. Internal conflicts have not normally reduced inequality: peasant revolts and urban risings were common in premodern history but usually failed, and civil war in developing countries tends to render the income distribution more unequal rather than less. Violent societal restructuring needs to be exceptionally intense if it is to reconfigure access to material resources. Similarly to equalizing mass mobilization warfare, this was primarily a phenomenon of the twentieth century. Communists who expropriated, redistributed, and then often collectivized leveled inequality on a dramatic scale. The most transformative of these revolutions were accompanied by extraordinary violence, in the end matching the world wars in terms of body count and human misery. Far less bloody ruptures such as the French Revolution leveled on a correspondingly smaller scale.

Violence might destroy states altogether. State failure or systems collapse used to be a particularly reliable means of leveling. For most of history, the rich were positioned either at or near the top of the political power hierarchy or were connected to those who were. Moreover, states provided a measure of protection, however modest by modern standards, for economic activity beyond the subsistence level. When states unraveled, these positions, connections, and protections came under pressure or were altogether lost. Although everybody might suffer when states unraveled, the rich simply had much more to lose: declining or collapsing elite income and wealth compressed the overall distribution of resources. This has happened for as long as there have been states. The earliest known examples reach back 4,000 years to the end of Old Kingdom Egypt and the Akkadian empire in Mesopotamia. Even today, the experience of Somalia suggests that this once potent equalizing force has not completely disappeared.

State failure takes the principle of leveling by violent means to its logical extremes: instead of achieving redistribution and rebalancing by reforming and restructuring existing polities, it wipes the slate clean in a more comprehensive manner. The first three horsemen represent different stages, not in the sense that they are likely to appear in sequence—whereas the biggest revolutions were triggered by the biggest wars, state collapse does not normally require similarly strong pressures—but in terms of intensity. What they all have in common is that they rely on violence to remake the distribution of income and wealth alongside the political and social order.

Human-caused violence has long had competition. In the past, plague, smallpox, and measles ravaged whole continents more forcefully than even the largest armies or most fervent revolutionaries could hope to do. In agrarian societies, the loss of a sizeable share of the population to microbes, sometimes a third or even more, made labor scarce and raised its price relative to that of fixed assets and other nonhuman capital, which generally remained intact. As a result, workers gained and landlords and employers lost as real wages rose and rents fell. Institutions mediated the scale of these shifts: elites commonly attempted to preserve existing arrangements through fiat and force but often failed to hold equalizing market forces in check.

Pandemics complete the quartet of horsemen of violent leveling. But were there also other, more peaceful mechanisms of lowering inequality? If we think of leveling on a large scale, the answer must be no. Across the full sweep of history, every single one of the major compressions of material inequality we can observe in the record was driven by one or more of these four levelers. Moreover, mass wars and revolutions did not merely act on those societies that were directly involved in these events: the world wars and exposure to communist challengers also influenced economic conditions, social expectations, and policymaking among bystanders. These ripple effects further broadened the effects of leveling rooted in violent conflict. This makes it difficult to disentangle developments after 1945 in much of the world from the preceding shocks and their continuing reverberations. Although falling income inequality in Latin America in the early 2000s might be the most promising candidate for nonviolent equalization, this trend has remained relatively modest in scope, and its sustainability is uncertain.

Other factors have a mixed record. From antiquity to the present, land reform has tended to reduce inequality most when associated with violence or the threat of violence—and least when not. Macroeconomic crises have only short-lived effects on the distribution of income and wealth. Democracy does not of itself mitigate inequality. Although the interplay of education and technological change undoubtedly influences dispersion of incomes, returns on education and skills have historically proven highly sensitive to violent shocks. Finally, there is no compelling empirical evidence to support the view that modern economic development, as such, narrows inequalities. There is no repertoire of benign means of compression that has ever achieved results that are even remotely comparable to those produced by the Four Horsemen.

Yet shocks abate. When states failed, others sooner or later took their place. Demographic contractions were reversed after plagues subsided, and renewed population growth gradually returned the balance of labor and capital to previous levels. The world wars were relatively short, and their aftereffects have faded over time: top tax rates and union density are down, globalization is up, communism is gone, the Cold War is over, and the risk of World War III has receded. All of this makes the recent resurgence of inequality easier to understand. The traditional violent levelers currently lie dormant and are unlikely to return in the foreseeable future. No similarly potent alternative mechanisms of equalization have emerged.

Even in the most progressive advanced economies, redistribution and education are already unable fully to absorb the pressure of widening income inequality before taxes and transfers. Lower-hanging fruits beckon in developing countries, but fiscal constraints remain strong. There does not seem to be an easy way to vote, regulate, or teach our way to significantly greater equality. From a global historical perspective, this should not come as a surprise. So far as we can tell, environments that were free from major violent shocks and their broader repercussions hardly ever witnessed major compressions of inequality. Will the future be different?

WHAT THIS BOOK IS NOT ABOUT

Disparities in the distribution of income and wealth are not the only type of inequality of social or historical relevance: so are inequalities that are rooted in gender and sexual orientation; in race and ethnicity; and in age, ability, and beliefs, and so are inequalities of education, health, political voice, and life chances. The title of this book is therefore not as precise as it could be. Then again, a subtitle such as "violent shocks and the global history of income and wealth inequality from the Stone Age to the present and beyond" would not only have stretched the publisher's patience but would also have been needlessly exclusive. After all, power inequalities have always played a central role in determining access to material resources: a more detailed title would be at once more precise and too narrow.

I do not endeavor to cover all aspects even of economic inequality. I focus on the distribution of material resources *within* societies, leaving aside questions of economic inequality *between* countries, an important and much-discussed topic. I consider conditions within particular societies without explicit reference to the many other sources of inequality just mentioned, factors whose influence on the distribution of income and wealth would be hard, if not impossible, to track and compare in the very long run. I am primarily interested in answering the question of why inequality fell, in identifying the mechanisms of leveling. Very broadly speaking, after our species had embraced domesticated food production and its common corollaries, sedentism and state formation, and had acknowledged some form of hereditary property rights, upward pressure on material inequality effectively became a given—a fundamental feature of human social existence. Consideration of the finer points of how these pressures evolved over the course of centuries and millennia, especially the complex synergies between what we might crudely label coercion and market forces, would require a separate study of even greater length.[7]

Finally, I discuss violent shocks (alongside alternative mechanisms) and their effects on material inequality but do not generally explore the inverse relationship, the question of whether—and if so, how—inequality helped generate these violent shocks. There are several reasons for my reluctance. Because high levels of inequality were a common feature of historical societies, it is not easy to explain specific shocks with reference to that contextual condition. Internal stability varied widely among contemporaneous societies having comparable levels of material inequality. Some societies that underwent violent ruptures were not particularly unequal: prerevolutionary China is one example. Certain shocks were largely or entirely exogenous, most notably pandemics that

---

[7] Milanovic 2005; 2012; Lakner and Milanovic 2013; and, most recently, Milanovic 2016: 10–45, 118–176 are among the most important studies of international income inequality. Anand and Segal 2015 survey scholarship in this area. Ponthieux and Meurs 2015 provide a massive overview of work on economic gender inequality. See also Sandmo 2015 on income distribution in economic thought.

leveled inequality by altering the balance of capital and labor. Even human-caused events such as the world wars profoundly affected societies that were not directly involved in these conflicts. Studies of the role of income inequality in precipitating civil war highlight the complexity of this relationship. None of this should be taken to suggest that domestic resource inequality did not have the potential to contribute to the outbreak of wars and revolutions or to state failure. It simply means that there is currently no compelling reason to assume a systematic causal connection between overall income and wealth inequality and the occurrence of violent shocks. As recent work has shown, analysis of more specific features that have a distributional dimension, such as competition within elite groups, may hold greater promise in accounting for violent conflict and breakdown.

For the purposes of this study, I treat violent shocks as discrete phenomena that act on material inequality. This approach is designed to evaluate the significance of such shocks as forces of leveling in the very long term, regardless of whether there is enough evidence to establish or deny a meaningful connection between these events and prior inequality. If my exclusive focus on one causal arrow, from shocks to inequality, encourages further engagement with the reverse, so much the better. It may never be feasible to produce a plausible account that fully endogenizes observable change in the distribution of income and wealth over time. Even so, possible feedback loops between inequality and violent shocks are certainly worth exploring in greater depth. My study can be no more than a building block for this larger project.[8]

HOW IS IT DONE?

There are many ways of measuring inequality. In the following chapters, I generally use only the two most basic metrics, the Gini coefficient and percentage shares of total income or wealth. The Gini coefficient measures the extent to which the distribution of income or material assets deviates from perfect equality. If each member of a given population receives or holds exactly the same amount of resources, the Gini coefficient is 0; if one member controls everything and everybody else has nothing, it approximates 1. Thus the more unequal the distribution, the higher the Gini value. It can be expressed as a fraction of 1 or as a percentage; I prefer the former so as to distinguish it more

---

[8] For more on this issue, see herein, chapter 14, pp. 392–394.

clearly from income or wealth shares, which are generally given as percentages. Shares tell us which proportion of the total income or wealth in a given population is received or owned by a particular group that is defined by its position within the overall distribution. For example, the much-cited "1 percent" represent those units—often households—of a given population that enjoy higher incomes or dispose of greater assets than 99 percent of its units. Gini coefficients and income shares are complementary measures that emphasize different properties of a given distribution: whereas the former compute the overall degree of inequality, the latter provide much-needed insight into the shape of the distribution.

Both indices can be used for measuring the distribution of different versions of the income distribution. Income prior to taxes and public transfers is known as "market" income, income after transfers is called "gross" income, and income net of all taxes and transfers is defined as "disposable" income. In the following, I refer only to market and disposable income. Whenever I use the term *income inequality* without further specification, I mean the former. For most of recorded history, market income inequality is the only type that can be known or estimated. Moreover, prior to the creation of extensive systems of fiscal redistribution in the modern West, differences in the distribution of market, gross, and disposable income were generally very small, much as in many developing countries today. In this book, income shares are invariably based on the distribution of market income. Both contemporary and historical data on income share, especially those at the very top of the distribution, are usually derived from tax records that refer to income prior to fiscal intervention. On a few occasions, I also refer to ratios between shares or particular percentiles of the income distribution, an alternative measure of the relative weight of different brackets. More sophisticated indices of inequality exist but cannot normally be applied to long-term studies that range across highly diverse data sets.[9]

The measurement of material inequality raises two kinds of problems: conceptual and evidential. Two major conceptual issues merit attention here. First,

---

[9] Despite what is often said, the Gini coefficient G can never quite reach 1, because $G = 1-1/n$, where n is the size of the population. See Atkinson 2015: 29–33 for a pithy summary of the different types of income and related metrics, noting complications arising from the need to control for the value of public services in addition to transfers and the difference between accrued and realized losses. For the purposes of this broad survey, such distinctions can safely be left aside. For ratios of income shares, see, most recently, Palma 2011 (top 10 percent/bottom 40 percent) and Cobham and Sumner 2014. For the methodology of inequality measurement, see Jenkins and Van Kerm 2009 and, in a more technical vein, Cowell and Flachaire 2015.

most available indices measure and express *relative* inequality based on the *share* of total resources captured by particular segments of the population. *Absolute* inequality, by contrast, focuses on the difference in the *amount* of resources that accrue to these segments. These two approaches tend to produce very different results. Consider a population in which the average household in the top decile of income distribution earns ten times as much as an average household in the bottom decile—say, $100,000 versus $10,000. National income subsequently doubles while the distribution of income remains unchanged. The Gini coefficient and income shares remain the same as before. From this perspective, incomes have gone up without raising inequality in the process. Yet at the same time, the income gap between the top and bottom deciles has doubled, from $90,000 to $180,000, ensuring much greater gains for affluent than for low-income households. The same principle applies to the distribution of wealth. In fact, there is hardly any credible scenario in which economic growth will fail to cause absolute inequality to rise. Metrics of relative inequality can therefore be said to be more conservative in outlook as they serve to deflect attention from persistently growing income and wealth gaps in favor of smaller and multidirectional changes in the distribution of material resources. In this book, I follow convention in prioritizing standard measures of relative inequality such as the Gini coefficient and top income shares but draw attention to their limitations where appropriate.[10]

A different problem stems from the Gini coefficient of income distribution's sensitivity to subsistence requirements and to levels of economic development. At least in theory, it is perfectly possible for a single person to own all the wealth that exists in a given population. However, nobody completely deprived of income would be able to survive. This means that the highest feasible Gini values for income are bound to fall short of the nominal ceiling of ~1. More specifically, they are limited by the amount of resources in excess of those needed to meet minimum subsistence requirements. This constraint is particularly powerful in the low-income economies that were typical of most of human history and that still exist in parts of the world today. For instance, in a society having a GDP equivalent to twice minimal subsistence, the Gini coefficient could not rise above 0.5 even if a single individual somehow managed to monopolize all income beyond what everybody else needed for bare survival.

---

[10] See Atkinson and Brandolini 2004, esp. 19 fig. 4, and also Ravaillon 2014: 835 and herein, chapter 16, p. 424. Milanovic 2016: 27–29 offers a defense of relative inequality measures.

At higher levels of output, the maximum degree of inequality is further held in check by changing definitions of what constitutes minimum subsistence and by largely impoverished populations' inability to sustain advanced economies. Nominal Gini coefficients need to be adjusted accordingly to calculate what has been called the extraction rate, the extent to which the maximum amount of inequality that is theoretically possible in a given environment has been actualized. This is a complex issue that is particularly salient to any comparisons of inequality in the very long run but that has only very recently begun to attract attention. I address it in more detail in the appendix at the end of this book.[11]

This brings me to the second category: problems related to the quality of the evidence. The Gini coefficient and top income shares are broadly congruent measures of inequality: they generally (though not invariably) move in the same direction as they change over time. Both are sensitive to the shortcomings of the underlying data sources. Modern Gini coefficients are usually derived from household surveys from which putative national distributions are extrapolated. This format is not particularly suitable for capturing the very largest incomes. Even in Western countries, nominal Ginis need to be adjusted upward to take full account of the actual contribution of top incomes. In many developing countries, moreover, surveys are often of insufficient quality to support reliable national estimates. In such cases, wide confidence intervals not only impede comparison between countries but also can make it hard to track change over time. Attempts to measure the overall distribution of wealth face even greater challenges—not only in developing countries, where a sizeable share of elite assets is thought to be concealed offshore, but even in data-rich environments such as the United States. Income shares are usually computed from tax records, whose quality and characteristics vary greatly across countries and over time and that are vulnerable to distortions motivated by tax evasion. Low participation rates in lower-income countries and politically driven definitions of what constitutes taxable income introduce additional complexities. Despite these difficulties, the compilation and online publication of a growing amount of information on top income shares in the "World Wealth and Income Database" has put our understanding of income inequality on a more solid footing and redirected attention from somewhat opaque

---

[11] See herein, pp. 445–456; for the example, see p. 445.

single-value metrics such as the Gini coefficient to more articulated indices of resource concentration.[12]

All these problems pale in comparison to those we encounter once we seek to extend the study of income and wealth inequality farther back in time. Regular income taxes rarely predate the twentieth century. In the absence of household surveys, we have to rely on proxy data to calculate Gini coefficients. Prior to about 1800, income inequality across entire societies can be estimated only with the help of social tables, rough approximations of the incomes obtained by different parts of the population that were drawn up by contemporary observers or inferred, however tenuously, by later scholars. More rewarding, a growing number of data sets that in parts of Europe reach back to the High Middle Ages have shed light on conditions in individual cities or regions. Surviving archival records of wealth taxes in French and Italian cities, taxes on housing rental values in the Netherlands, and income taxes in Portugal allow us to reconstruct the underlying distribution of assets and sometimes even incomes. So do early modern records of the dispersion of agricultural land in France and of the value of probate estates in England. In fact, Gini coefficients can fruitfully be applied to evidence that is much more remote in time. Patterns of landownership in late Roman Egypt; variation in the size of houses in ancient and early medieval Greece, Britain, Italy, and North Africa and in Aztec Mexico; the distribution of inheritance shares and dowries in Babylonian society; and even the dispersion of stone tools in Catal Höyük, one of the earliest known proto-urban settlements in the world, established almost 10,000 years ago, have all been analyzed in this manner. Archaeology has enabled us to push back the boundaries of the study of material inequality into the Paleolithic at the time of the last Ice Age.[13]

---

[12] For the relationship between Ginis and top income shares, see Leigh 2007; Alvaredo 2011; Morelli, Smeeding, and Thompson 2015: 683–687; Roine and Waldenström 2015: 503–606, esp. 504 fig. 7.7. For Gini adjustments, see esp. Morelli, Smeeding, and Thompson 2015: 679, 681–683 and herein, chapter 15, p. 409. Palma 2011: 105, Piketty 2014: 266–267, and Roine and Waldenström 2015: 506 stress the probative value of top income shares. For Gini comparisons, see, e.g., Bergh and Nilsson 2010: 492–493 and Ostry, Berg, and Tsangarides 2014: 12. Both prefer the Gini values reported in the Standardized World Income Inequality Database (SWIID), which I use throughout the book except when I cite references by other scholars. Confidence intervals are visualized at the SWIID website, http://fsolt.org/swiid/; see also herein, chapter 13, pp. 377–378. For the concealment of wealth, see Zucman 2015. Kopczuk 2015 discusses the difficulties of measuring U.S. wealth shares. For the nature and reliability of top income data, see esp. Roine and Waldenström 2015: 479–491 and the very extensive technical discussions in the many contributions to Atkinson and Piketty 2007a and 2010. The World Wealth and Income Database (WWID) can be accessed at http://www.wid.world/.

[13] All these and additional examples are discussed throughout Part I and in chapter 9, pp. 267–269, and chapter 10, pp. 306–310.

We also have access to a whole range of proxy data that do not directly document distributions but that are nevertheless known to be sensitive to changes in the level of income inequality. The ratio of land rents to wages is a good example. In predominantly agrarian societies, changes in the price of labor relative to the value of the most important type of capital tend to reflect changes in the relative gains that accrued to different classes: a rising index value suggests that landlords prospered at the expense of workers, causing inequality to grow. The same is true of a related measure, the ratio of mean per capita GDP to wages. The larger the nonlabor share in GDP, the higher the index, and the more unequal incomes were likely to be. To be sure, both methods have serious weaknesses. Rents and wages may be reliably reported for particular locales but need not be representative of larger populations or entire countries, and GDP guesstimates for any premodern society inevitably entail considerable margins of error. Nevertheless, such proxies are generally capable of giving us a sense of the contours of inequality trends over time. Real incomes represent a more widely available but somewhat less instructive proxy. In western Eurasia, real wages, expressed in grain equivalent, have now been traced back as far as 4,000 years. This very long-term perspective makes it possible to identify instances of unusually elevated real incomes for workers, a phenomenon plausibly associated with lowered inequality. Even so, information on real wages that cannot be contextualized with reference to capital values or GDP remains a very crude and not particularly reliable indicator of overall income inequality.[14]

Recent years have witnessed considerable advances in the study of premodern tax records and the reconstruction of real wages, rent/wage ratios, and even GDP levels. It is not an exaggeration to say that much of this book could not have been written twenty or even ten years ago. The scale, scope, and pace of progress in the study of historical income and wealth inequality gives us much hope for the future of this field. There is no denying that long stretches of human history do not admit even the most rudimentary quantitative analysis of the distribution of material resources. Yet even in these cases we may be able to identify signals of change over time. Elite displays of wealth are the most promising—and, indeed, often the only—marker of inequality. When archaeological evidence

---

[14] Once again, I employ these approaches in much of this book, especially in Parts I and V. Evidence for real wages going back to the Middle Ages has been gathered at "The IISH list of datafiles of historical prices and wages" hosted by the International Institute of Social History, http://www.iisg.nl/hpw/data.php. Scheidel 2010 covers the earliest evidence. For historical GDP data, estimates, and conjectures, see the "Maddison project," http://www.ggdc.net/maddison/maddison-project/home.htm.

of lavish elite consumption in housing, diet, or burials gives way to more modest remains or signs of stratification fade altogether, we may reasonably infer a degree of equalization. In traditional societies, members of the wealth and power elites were often the only ones who controlled enough income or assets to suffer large losses, losses that are visible in the material record. Variation in human stature and other physiological features can likewise be associated with the distribution of resources, although other factors, such as pathogen loads, also played an important role. The more we move away from data that document inequality in a more immediate manner, the more conjectural our readings are bound to become. Yet global history is simply impossible unless we are prepared to stretch. This book is an attempt to do just that.

In so doing we face an enormous gradient in documentation, from detailed statistics concerning the factors behind the recent rise in American income inequality to vague hints at resource imbalances at the dawn of civilization, with a wide array of diverse data sets in between. To join all this together in a reasonably coherent analytical narrative presents us with a formidable challenge: in no small measure, this is the true challenge of inequality invoked in the title of this introduction. I have chosen to structure each part of this book in what seems to me the best way to address this problem. The opening part follows the evolution of inequality from our primate beginnings to the early twentieth century and is thus organized in conventional chronological fashion (chapters 1–3).

This changes once we turn to the Four Horsemen, the principal drivers of violent leveling. In the parts devoted to the first two members of this quartet, war and revolution, my survey starts in the twentieth century and subsequently moves back in time. There is a simple reason for this. Leveling by means of mass mobilization warfare and transformative revolution has primarily been a feature of modernity. The "Great Compression" of the 1910s to 1940s not only produced by far the best evidence of this process but also represents and indeed constitutes it in paradigmatic form (chapters 4–5). In a second step, I look for antecedents of these violent ruptures, moving from the American Civil War all the way back to the experience of ancient China, Rome, and Greece, as well as from the French Revolution to the countless revolts of the premodern era (chapters 6 and 8). I follow the same trajectory in my discussion of civil war in the final part of chapter 6, from the consequences of such conflicts in contemporary developing countries to the end of the Roman Republic. This approach allows me to establish models of violent leveling that are solidly grounded in modern data before I explore whether they can also be applied to the more distant past.

In Part V, on plagues, I employ a modified version of the same strategy by moving from the best documented case—the Black Death of the Late Middle Ages (chapter 10)—to progressively less well known examples, one of which (the Americas after 1492) happens to be somewhat more recent whereas the others are located in more ancient times (chapter 11). The rationale is the same: to establish the key mechanisms of violent leveling brought about by epidemic mass mortality with the help of the best available evidence before I search for analogous occurrences elsewhere. Part IV, on state failure and systems collapse, takes this organizing principle to its logical conclusion. Chronology matters little in analyzing phenomena that were largely confined to premodern history, and there is nothing to be gained from following any particular time sequence. The dates of particular cases matter less than the nature of the evidence and the scope of modern scholarship, both of which vary considerably across space and time. I thus begin with a couple of well-attested examples before I move on to others that I discuss in less detail (chapter 9). Part VI, on alternatives to violent leveling, is for the most part arranged by topic as I evaluate different factors (chapters 12–13) before I turn to counterfactual outcomes (chapter 14). The final part, which together with Part I frames my thematic survey, returns to a chronological format. Moving from the recent resurgence in inequality (chapter 15) to the prospects of leveling in the near and more distant future (chapter 16), it completes my evolutionary overview.

A study that brings together Hideki Tojo's Japan and the Athens of Pericles or the Classic Lowland Maya and present-day Somalia may seem puzzling to some of my fellow historians, although less so, I hope, to readers from the social sciences. As I said, the challenge of exploring the global history of inequality is a serious one. If we want to identify forces of leveling across recorded history, we need to find ways to bridge the divide between different areas of specialization both within and beyond academic disciplines and to overcome huge disparities in the quality and quantity of the data. A long-term perspective calls for unorthodox solutions.

DOES IT MATTER?

All this raises a simple question. If it is so difficult to study the dynamics of inequality across very different cultures and in the very long run, why should we even try? Any answer to this question needs to address two separate but related issues—does economic inequality matter today, and why is its history worth exploring? Princeton philosopher Harry Frankfurt, best known for his earlier disquisition *On Bullshit*, opens his booklet *On Inequality* by disagreeing with

Obama's assessment quoted at the beginning of this introduction: "our most fundamental challenge is not the fact that the incomes of Americans are widely *unequal*. It is, rather, the fact that too many of our people are *poor*." Poverty, to be sure, is a moving target: someone who counts as poor in the United States need not seem so in central Africa. Sometimes poverty is even defined as a function of inequality—in the United Kingdom, the official poverty line is set as a fraction of median income—although absolute standards are more common, such as the threshold of $1.25 in 2005 prices used by the World Bank or reference to the cost of a basket of consumer goods in America. Nobody would disagree that poverty, however defined, is undesirable: the challenge lies in demonstrating that income and wealth inequality *as such* has negative effects on our lives, rather than the poverty or the great fortunes with which it may be associated.[15]

The most hard-nosed approach concentrates on inequality's effect on economic growth. Economists have repeatedly noted that it can be hard to evaluate this relationship and that the theoretical complexity of the problem has not always been matched by the empirical specification of existing research. Even so, a number of studies argue that higher levels of inequality are indeed associated with lower rates of growth. For instance, lower disposable income inequality has been found to lead not only to faster growth but also to longer growth phases. Inequality appears to be particularly harmful to growth in developed economies. There is even some support for the much-debated thesis that high levels of inequality among American households contributed to the credit bubble that helped trigger the Great Recession of 2008, as lower-income households drew on readily available credit (in part produced by wealth accumulation at the top) to borrow for the sake of keeping up the with consumption patterns of more affluent groups. Under more restrictive conditions of lending, by contrast, wealth inequality is thought to disadvantage low-income groups by blocking their access to credit.[16]

---

[15] Frankfurt 2015: 3. Wearing my historian's hat I am happy to take it as a given that any and all history is worth exploring and that knowledge is its own reward. Then again, when it comes to the world we live in, some questions may be more equal than others.

[16] For the difficulties, see Bourguignon 2015: 139–140 and esp. Voitchovsky 2009: 569, who summarizes conflicting results (562 table 22.11). Studies that report negative consequences include Easterly 2007; Cingano 2014; and Ostry, Berg, and Tsangarides 2014, esp. 16, 19 (more and longer growth). Changes in the income share of the top quintile have an effect on the growth rate over the following five-year period: Dabla-Norris et al. 2015. Rising income inequality between 1985 and 2005 reduced cumulative growth in an average OECD country by 4.7 percent in the period from 1990 to 2010: OECD 2015: 59–100, esp. 67. A survey of 104 countries suggests that between 1970 and 2010, higher income inequality tended to raise per capita GDP (as well as human capital) in low-income countries but had the opposite effect in those with middle

Among developed countries, higher inequality is associated with less economic mobility across generations. Because parental income and wealth are strong indicators of educational attainment as well as earnings, inequality tends to perpetuate itself over time, and all the more so the higher it is. The disequalizing consequences of residential segregation by income are a related issue. In metropolitan areas in the United States since the 1970s, population growth in high- and low-income areas alongside shrinking middle-income areas has led to increasing polarization. Affluent neighborhoods in particular have become more isolated, a development likely to precipitate concentration of resources, including locally funded public services, which in turns affects the life chances of children and impedes intergenerational mobility.[17]

In developing countries, at least certain kinds of income inequality increase the likelihood of internal conflict and civil war. High-income societies contend with less extreme consequences. In the United States, inequality has been said to act on the political process by making it easier for the wealthy to exert influence, although in this case we may wonder whether it is the presence of very large fortunes rather than inequality per se that accounts for this phenomenon. Some studies find that high levels of inequality are correlated with lower levels of self-reported happiness. Only health appears to be unaffected by the distribution of resources as such, as opposed to income levels:

---

or high incomes: Brueckner and Lederman 2015. This is consistent with an earlier study that was unable to show negative consequences for growth beyond advanced economies: Malinen 2012. If we confine ourselves rather narrowly to inequality expressed through the relative size of billionaire fortunes, negative effects may even be limited to wealth inequality associated with political connections: Bagchi and Svejnar 2015. Van Treeck 2014 reviews the debate about the role of inequality in the financial crisis. Wealth inequality and access to credit: Bowles 2012a: 34–72; Bourguignon 2015: 131–132.

[17] Björklund and Jäntti 2009 and Jäntti and Jenkins 2015 are the most recent surveys. For the association between inequality and mobility, see Corak 2013: 82 fig. 1 and Jäntti and Jenkins 2015: 889–890, esp. 890 fig. 10.13. Large differences exist within the OECD: the United States and the United Kingdom report both high inequality and low mobility, whereas the inverse applies to Nordic countries: OECD 2010: 181–198. Björklund and Jäntti 2009: 502–504 find that family background has a stronger influence on economic status in America than in Scandinavia, although broader cross-country studies sometimes suggest only weak effects. Men who grew up in more unequal societies in the 1970s were less likely to have experienced social mobility by the late 1990s: Andrews and Leigh 2009; Bowles and Gintis 2002 (indicators); Autor 2014: 848 (self-perpetuation, education). Reardon and Bischoff 2011a and b discuss residential segregation. Kozol 2005 focuses on its consequences for schooling. See also Murray 2012 for a conservative perspective on this issue. Changes in economic inequality aside, the findings of Clark 2014 suggest that social mobility more generally tends to be modest across a wide range of different societies and in the long run.

whereas health differences generate income inequality, the reverse remains unproven.[18]

What all these studies have in common is that they focus on the practical consequences of material inequality, on instrumental reasons for why it might be deemed a problem. A different set of objections to a skewed distribution of resources is grounded in normative ethics and notions of social justice, a perspective well beyond the scope of my study but deserving of greater attention in a debate that is all too often dominated by economic concerns. Yet even on the more limited basis of purely instrumental reasoning there is no doubt that at least in certain contexts, high levels of inequality and growing disparities in income and wealth are detrimental to social and economic development. But what constitutes a "high" level, and how do we know whether "growing" imbalances are a novel feature of contemporary society or merely bring us closer to historically common conditions? Is there, to use Francois Bourguignon's term, a "normal" level of inequality to which countries that are experiencing widening inequality should aspire to return? And if—as in many developed economies— inequality is higher now than it was a few decades ago but is lower than a century ago, what does this mean for our understanding of the determinants of the distribution of income and wealth?[19]

Inequality either grew or held fairly steady for much of recorded history, and significant reductions have been rare. Yet policy proposals designed to stem or reverse the rising tide of inequality tend to show little awareness or appreciation of this historical background. Is that as it should be? Perhaps our age has become so fundamentally different, so completely untethered from its agrarian and undemocratic foundations, that history has nothing left to teach us. And indeed, there is no question that much has changed: low-income groups in rich economies are generally better off than most people were in the past, and even the most disadvantaged residents of the least developed countries live longer

---

[18] For inequality and civil war, see hereafter, chapter 6, pp. 202–203, and cf. briefly Bourguignon 2015: 133–134. Politics: Gilens 2012. Happiness: van Praag and Ferrer-i-Carbonell 2009: 374, and see also Clark and D'Ambrosio 2015 on inequality's effect on subjective well-being and attitudes. Health: Leigh, Jencks, and Smeeding 2009; O'Donnell, Van Doorslaer, and Van Ourti 2015. However, the gap in life expectancy between different socioeconomic groups has been growing both in the United States and in several Western European countries: Bosworth, Burtless, and Zhang 2016: 62–69.

[19] Atkinson 2015: 11–14 distinguishes between instrumental and intrinsic reasons for why inequality is a problem. See also Frankfurt 2015. In fairness, Bourguignon 2015: 163 himself cautiously applies quotation marks to the concept of "a 'normal' level of inequality" but nevertheless defines conditions "prior to the last two or three decades" in these terms.

than their ancestors lived. The experience of life at the receiving end of inequality is in many ways very different from what it used to be.

But it is not economic or more broadly human development that concerns us here—rather how the fruits of civilization are distributed, what causes them to be distributed the way they are, and what it would take to change these outcomes. I wrote this book to show that the forces that used to shape inequality have not in fact changed beyond recognition. If we seek to rebalance the current distribution of income and wealth in favor of greater equality, we cannot simply close our eyes to what it took to accomplish this goal in the past. We need to ask whether great inequality has ever been alleviated without great violence, how more benign influences compare to the power of this Great Leveler, and whether the future is likely to be very different—even if we may not like the answers.

Part I

A BRIEF HISTORY OF INEQUALITY

Chapter I

THE RISE OF INEQUALITY

PRIMORDIAL LEVELING

Has inequality always been with us? Our closest nonhuman relatives in the world today, the African great apes—gorillas, chimpanzees, and bonobos—are intensely hierarchical creatures. Adult gorilla males divide into a dominant few endowed with harems of females and many others having no consorts at all. Silverbacks dominate not only the females in their groups but also any males who stay on after reaching maturity. Chimpanzees, especially but not only males, expend tremendous energy on status rivalry. Bullying and aggressive dominance displays are matched by a wide range of submission behaviors by those on the lower rungs of the pecking order. In groups of fifty or a hundred, ranking is a central and stressful fact of life, for each member occupies a specific place in the hierarchy but is always looking for ways to improve it. And there is no escape: because males who leave their group to avoid overbearing dominants run the risk of being killed by males in other groups, they tend to stay put and compete or submit. Echoing the phenomenon of social circumscription that has been invoked to explain the creation of hierarchy among humans, this powerful constraint serves to shore up inequality.

Their closest relatives, the bonobos, may present a gentler image to the world but likewise feature alpha males and females. Considerably less violent and intent on bullying than chimpanzees, they nevertheless maintain clear hierarchical rankings. Although concealed ovulation and the lack of systematic domination of females by males reduce violent conflict over mating opportunities, hierarchy manifests in feeding competition among males. Across these species, inequality is expressed in unequal access to food sources—the closest approximation of human-style income disparities—and, above all, in terms of reproductive success. Dominance hierarchy, topped by the biggest, strongest, and most aggressive males, which consume the most and have sexual relations with the most females, is the standard pattern.[1]

It is unlikely that these shared characteristics evolved only after these three species had branched off from the ancestral line, a process that commenced about 11 million years ago with the emergence of gorillas and that continued 3 million years later with the split of the common ancestor of chimpanzees and bonobos from the earliest forerunners of what were to evolve into australopiths and, eventually, humans. Even so, marked social expressions of inequality may not always have been common among primates. Hierarchy is a function of group living, and our more distant primate relatives, who branched off earlier, are now less social and live either on their own or in very small or transient groups. This is true both of gibbons, whose ancestors split from those of the great apes some 22 million years ago, and of the orangutans, the first of the great apes to undergo speciation about 17 million years ago and now confined to Asia. Conversely, hierarchical sociality is typical of the African genera of this taxonomic family, including our own. This suggests that the most recent common ancestor of gorillas, chimpanzees, bonobos, and humans already displayed some version of this trait, whereas more distant precursors need not have done so.[2]

Analogy to other primate species may be a poor guide to inequality among earlier hominins and humans. The best proxy evidence we have is skeletal data on sexual size dimorphism, the extent to which mature members of one sex—in this case, males—are taller, heavier, and stronger than those of the other. Among gorillas, as among sea lions, intense inequality among males with and without harems as well as between males and females is associated with a high degree of male-biased size dimorphism. Judging from the fossil record, prehuman hominins—australopiths and paranthropi, reaching back more than 4 million years—appear to have been more dimorphic than humans. If the orthodox position, which has recently come under growing pressure, can be upheld, some of the earliest species, *Australopithecus afarensis* and *anamensis*, which emerged 3 to 4 million years ago, were defined by a male body mass advantage of more than 50 percent, whereas later species occupied an intermediate position between them and humans. With the

---

[1] Boehm 1999: 16–42 is a classic account. See esp. 130–137 on why social relations in all three of these species can be defined as (more or less) "despotic." Note that even among nonhuman primates, a violent shock in the form of mass mortality may soften hierarchies and reduce rank-based bullying: Sapolsky and Share 2004.
[2] For these speciation dates, see Pozzi et al. 2014: 177 fig. 2, the most recent and comprehensive study available at the time of writing. Future research may well alter these estimates: only three years earlier, Tinh et al. 2011: 4 had reported significantly later dates. Traits of common ancestor: Boehm 1999: 154.

advent of larger-brained *Homo erectus* more than 2 million years ago, sexual size dimorphism had already declined to the relatively modest amount we still observe today. Insofar as the degree of dimorphism was correlated with the prevalence of agonistic male-on-male competition for females or shaped by female sexual selection, reduced sex differences may be a sign of lesser reproductive variance among males. On this reading, evolution attenuated inequality both among males and between the sexes. Even so, higher rates of reproductive inequality for men than for women have persisted alongside moderate levels of reproductive polygyny.[3]

Other developments that may have begun as long as 2 million years ago are also thought to have fostered greater equality. Changes in the brain and in physiology that promoted cooperative breeding and feeding would have countered aggression by dominants and would have softened hierarchies in larger groups. Innovations in the application of violence may have contributed to this process. Anything that helped subalterns resist dominants would have curtailed the powers of the latter and thus diminished overall inequality. Coalition-building among lower-status men was one means to this end, use of projectile weapons another. Fights at close quarters, whether with hands and teeth or with sticks and rocks, favored stronger and more aggressive men. Weapons began to play an equalizing role after they could be deployed over a greater distance.

Some 2 million years ago, anatomical changes in the shoulder made it possible for the first time to throw stones and other objects in an effective manner, a skill unavailable to earlier species and to nonhuman primates today. This adaptation not only improved hunting abilities but also made it easier for gammas to challenge alphas. The manufacturing of spears was the next step, and enhancements such as fire-hardened tips and, later, stone tips followed. Controlled use of fire dates back perhaps 800,000 years, and heat treatment technology is at least 160,000 years old. The appearance of darts or arrow tips made of stone, first attested about 70,000 years ago in South Africa, was merely the latest phase in a drawn-out process of projectile weapons development. No matter how primitive they may seem to modern observers, such tools privileged skill over size, strength, and aggressiveness and encouraged first strikes and ambushes

---

[3] Orthodoxy: Klein 2009: 197. Plavcan 2012: 49–50 rejects the notion of lower dimorphism, comparable to modern human levels, already in *Australopithecus afarensis* proposed by Reno, McCollum, Meindl, and Lovejoy 2010; Reno and Lovejoy 2015. Cf. also Shultziner et al. 2010: 330–331. See Plavcan 2012: 47 fig. 1 for a comparison of dimorphism in humans and other apes and 50–58 for a discussion of its likely causes. Labuda et al. 2010 and Poznik et al. 2013: 565 present genetic evidence for moderate polygyny in modern humans. Bowles 2006 argues for a role of reproductive leveling in the evolution of human altruism.

as well as cooperation among weaker individuals. The evolution of cognitive skills was a vital complement necessary for more accurate throwing, improved weapons design, and more reliable coalition building. Full language capabilities, which would have facilitated more elaborate alliances and reinforced notions of morality, may date back as few as 100,000 or as many as 300,000 years. Much of the chronology of these social changes remains unclear: they may have been strung out over the better part of the last 2 million years or may have been more concentrated among anatomically modern humans, our own species of *Homo sapiens*, which arose in Africa at least 200,000 years ago.[4]

What matters most in the present context is the cumulative outcome, the improved ability of lower-status individuals to confront alpha males in ways that are not feasible among nonhuman primates. When dominants became embedded in groups whose members were armed with projectiles and capable of balancing their influence by forming coalitions, overt dominance through brute force and intimidation was no longer a viable option. If this conjecture—for this is all it can be—is correct, then violence and, more specifically, novel strategies of organizing and threatening violent action, played an important and perhaps even critical role in the first great leveling in human history. By that time, human biological and social evolution had given rise to an egalitarian equilibrium. Groups were not yet large enough, productive capabilities not yet differentiated enough, and intergroup conflict and territoriality not yet developed enough to make submission to the few seem the least bad option for the many. Whereas animalian forms of domination and hierarchy had been eroded, they had not yet been replaced by new forms of inequality based on domestication, property, and war. That world has been largely but not completely lost. Defined by low levels of resource inequality and a strong egalitarian ethos, the few remaining foraging populations in the world today give us a sense, however limited, of what the dynamics of equality in the Middle and Upper Paleolithic may have looked like.[5]

---

[4] Shoulder: Roach, Venkadesan, Rainbow, and Lieberman 2013. Fire: Marean 2015: 543, 547. Stone tips for projectiles: Henshilwood et al. 2001; Brown et al. 2012. Boehm 1999: 174–181 attributes considerable leveling effects to these developments, most recently followed by Turchin 2016b: 95–111. See also Shultziner et al. 2010: 329. Language: Marean 2015: 542. Boehm 1999: 181–183, 187–191 emphasizes the equalizing potential of language and morality. Timing: Boehm 1999: 195–196, 198, with a preference for relatively recent and sudden changes, whereas Dubreuil 2010: 55–90 and Shultziner et al. 2010: 329–331 give greater weight to earlier changes. The oldest known fossil remains of *Homo sapiens* date from about 195,000 years ago: McDougall, Brown, and Fleagle 2005. This is consistent with modern DNA analysis by Elhaik et al. 2014 that points to speciation probably a little more than 200,000 years ago.

[5] These terms conventionally refer to the period from about 300,000 years ago until the onset of agriculture. For the limitations of this perspective, see herein, p. 30.

Powerful logistical and infrastructural constraints help contain inequality among hunter-gatherers. A nomadic lifestyle that does not feature pack animals severely limits the accumulation of material possessions, and the small size and fluid and flexible composition of foraging groups are not conducive to stable asymmetric relationships beyond basic power disparities of age and gender. Moreover, forager egalitarianism is predicated on the deliberate rejection of attempts to dominate. This attitude serves as a crucial check to the natural human propensity to form hierarchies: active equalization is employed to maintain a level playing field. Numerous means of enforcing egalitarian values have been documented by anthropologists, graduated by severity. Begging, scrounging, and stealing help ensure a more equal distribution of resources. Sanctions against authoritarian behavior and self-aggrandizement range from gossip, criticism, ridicule, and disobedience to ostracism and even physical violence, including homicide. Leadership consequently tends to be subtle, dispersed among multiple group members, and transient; the least assertive have the best chances to influence others. This distinctive moral economy has been called "reverse dominance hierarchy": operative among adult men (who commonly dominate women and children), it represents the ongoing and preemptive neutralization of authority.[6]

Among the Hadza, a group of a few hundred hunter-gatherers in Tanzania, camp members forage individually and strongly prefer their own households in distributing the acquired food. At the same time, food sharing beyond one's own household is expected and common, especially when resources can readily be spotted by others. Hadza may try to conceal honey because it is easier to hide, but if found out, they are compelled to share. Scrounging is tolerated and widespread. Thus even though individuals clearly prefer to keep more for themselves and their immediate kin, norms interfere: sharing is common because the absence of domination makes sharing hard to resist. Large perishable items such as big game may even be shared beyond the camp group. Saving is not valued, to the extent that available resources tend to be consumed without delay and not even shared with people who happen to be absent at that moment. As a result, the Hadza have only minimal private possessions: jewelry, clothes, a digging stick, and sometimes a cooking pot for women and a bow and arrows, clothes and jewelry, and perhaps a few tools for men. Many of these goods are not particularly durable, and owners do not form strong attachments to them. Property

---

[6] Material constraints: e.g., Shultziner et al. 2010: 327. Leveling needed to combat natural hierarchies: Boehm 1999: 37, 39. Enforcement: Boehm 1999: 43–89; also, more briefly, Shultziner et al. 2010: 325–327; Kelly 2013: 243–244; Boix 2015: 46–51; Morris 2015: 33–43.

beyond these basic items does not exist, and territory is not defended. The lack or dispersion of authority makes it hard to arrive at group decisions, let alone enforce them. In all these respects, the Hadza are quite representative of extant foraging groups more generally.[7]

A foraging mode of subsistence and an egalitarian moral economy combine into a formidable obstacle to any form of development for the simple reason that economic growth requires some degree of inequality in income and consumption to encourage innovation and surplus production. Without growth, there was hardly any surplus to appropriate and pass on. The moral economy prevented growth, and the lack of growth prevented the production and concentration of surplus. This must not be taken to suggest that foragers practice some form of communism: consumption is not equalized, and individuals differ not just in terms of their somatic endowments but also with respect to their access to support networks and material resources. As I show in the next section, forager inequality is not nonexistent but merely very low compared to inequality in societies that rely on other modes of subsistence.[8]

We also need to allow for the possibility that contemporary hunter-gatherers may differ in important ways from our pre-agrarian ancestors. Surviving forager groups are utterly marginalized and confined to areas that are beyond the reach of, or of little interest to, farmers and herders, environments that are well suited to a lifestyle that eschews the accumulation of material resources and firm claims to territory. Prior to the domestication of plants and animals for food production, foragers were much more widely spread out across the globe and had access to more abundant natural resources. In some cases, moreover, contemporary foraging groups may respond to a dominant world of more hierarchical farmers and pastoralists, defining themselves in contradistinction to outside norms. Remaining foragers are not timeless or "living fossils," and their practices need to be understood within specific historical contexts.[9]

For this reason, prehistoric populations need not always have been as egalitarian as the experience of contemporary hunter-gatherers might suggest. Observable material inequalities in burial contexts that date from before the

---

[7] Marlowe 2010: 225–254, esp. 232–234, 237–238, 240–241, 248, 251–254. Typical character (on the Hadza as "median foragers"): 255–283. The !Kung bushmen are another well-known and much-cited case: Lee 1979; 1984.

[8] Growth and surplus: Boix 2015: 54–55 for the point about heterogeneous outcomes. Low inequality: Smith et al. 2010b, and see herein, pp. 37–39.

[9] Outside contacts: Sassaman 2004: 229, 236–238. Not "living fossils": Marlowe 2010: 285–286; and Kelly 2013: 269–275 on hunter-gatherers as a proxy for prehistory, a complex yet useful analogy.

onset of the Holocene, which began about 11,700 years ago, are rare but do exist. The most famous example of unearned status and inequality comes from Sungir, a Pleistocene site 120 miles north of Moscow whose remains date from about 30,000 to 34,000 years ago, a time corresponding to a relatively mild phase of the last Ice Age. It contains the remains of a group of hunters and foragers who killed and consumed large mammals such as bison, horse, reindeer, antelope, and especially mammoth alongside wolf, fox, brown bear, and cave lion. Three human burials stand out. One features an adult man who was buried with some 3,000 beads made of mammoth ivory that had probably been sewn onto his fur clothing as well as around twenty pendants and twenty-five mammoth ivory rings. A separate grave was the final resting place of a girl of about ten years and a roughly twelve-year-old boy. Both children's clothing was adorned with an even larger number of ivory beads, about 10,000 overall, and their grave goods included a wide range of prestige items such as spears made of straightened mammoth tusk and various art objects.

Massive effort must have been expended on these deposits: modern scholars have estimated that it would have taken anywhere from fifteen to forty-five minutes to carve a single bead, which translates to a total of 1.6 to 4.7 years of work for one person carving forty hours a week. A minimum of seventy-five arctic foxes needed to be caught to extract the 300 canines attached to a belt and headgear in the children's grave, and considering the difficulty of extracting them intact, the actual number may well have been higher. Although a substantial spell of relative sedentism would have given the members of this group enough spare time to accomplish all this, the question remains why they would have wished to do so in the first place. These three persons do not appear to have been buried with everyday clothing and objects. That the beads for the children were smaller than those for the man implies that these beads had been manufactured specifically for the children, whether in life or, more likely, just for their burial. For reasons unknown to us, these individuals were considered special. Yet the two children were too young to have earned their privileged treatment: perhaps they owed it to family ties to someone who mattered more than others. The presence of possibly fatal injuries in both the man and the boy and of femoral shortening that would have disabled the girl in life merely add to the mystery.[10]

---

[10] Trinkaus, Buzhilova, Mednikova, and Dobrovolskaya 2014 is now the authoritative treatment of the Sungir finds: see esp. 3–33 on the site, date, and mortuary behavior and 272–274, 282–283, 287–288 on the injuries and disorders. Bead size: Formicola 2007: 446. Inherited status: Anghelinu 2012: 38.

Although the splendor of the Sungir burials has so far remained without parallel in the Paleolithic record, other rich graves have been found farther west. In Dolní Věstovice in Moravia, at roughly the same time, three individuals were buried with intricate headgear and resting on ocher-stained ground. Later examples are somewhat more numerous. The cave of Arene Candide on the Ligurian coast housed a deep pit grave for a lavishly adorned adolescent male put to rest on a bed of red ocher about 28,000 or 29,000 years ago. Hundreds of perforated shells and deer canines found around his head would originally have been attached to some organic headgear. Pendants made of mammoth ivory, four batons made of elk antlers, and an exceptionally long blade made of exotic flint that had been placed in his right hand added to the assemblage. A young woman buried in Saint-Germaine-la-Rivière some 16,000 years ago bore ornaments of shell and teeth: the latter, about seventy perforated red deer canines, must have been imported from 200 miles away. About 10,000 years ago, in the early Holocene but in a foraging context, a three-year-old child was laid to rest with 1,500 shell beads at the La Madeleine rock shelter in the Dordogne.[11]

It is tempting to interpret these findings as the earliest harbingers of inequalities to come. Evidence of advanced and standardized craft production, time investment in highly repetitive tasks, and the use of raw materials sourced from far away offers us a glimpse of economic activities more advanced than those found among contemporary hunter-gatherers. It also hints at social disparities not normally associated with a foraging existence: lavish graves for children and adolescents point to ascribed and perhaps even inherited status. The existence of hierarchical relations is more difficult to infer from this material but is at least a plausible option. But there is no sign of durable inequalities. Increases in complexity and status differentiation appear to have been temporary in nature. Egalitarianism need not be a stable category: social behavior could vary depending on changing circumstances or even recurring seasonal pressures. And although earliest coastal adaptations, cradles of social evolution in which access to maritime food resources such as shellfish encouraged territoriality and more effective leadership, may reach back as far as 100,000 years, there is—at least as yet—no related evidence of emergent hierarchy and consumption disparities. For all we can tell, social or economic inequality in the Paleolithic remained sporadic and transient.[12]

---

[11] Vanhaeren and d'Errico 2005; Pettitt, Richards, Maggi, and Formicola 2003; d'Errico and Vanhaeren 2016: 54–55.

[12] See esp. Shultziner et al. 2010: 333–334; Anghelinu 2012: 37–38; Wengrow and Graeber 2015. Marean 2014 argues for the antiquity and significance of coastal adaptations.

THE GREAT DISEQUALIZATION

Inequality took off only after the last Ice Age had come to an end and climatic conditions entered a period of unusual stability. The Holocene, the first interglacial warm period for more than 100,000 years, created an environment that was more favorable to economic and social development. As these improvements allowed humans to extract more energy and grow in numbers, they also laid the ground for an increasingly unequal distribution of power and material resources. This led to what I call the "Great Disequalization," a transition to new modes of subsistence and new forms of social organization that eroded forager egalitarianism and replaced it with durable hierarchies and disparities in income and wealth. For these developments to occur, there had to be productive assets that could be defended against encroachment and from which owners could draw a surplus in a predictable manner. Food production by means of farming and herding fulfills both requirements and came to be the principal driver of economic, social, and political change.

However, domestication of plants and animals was not an indispensable prerequisite. Under certain conditions, foragers were also able to exploit undomesticated natural resources in an analogous fashion. Territoriality, hierarchy, and inequality could arise where fishing was feasible or particularly productive only in certain locations. This phenomenon, which is known as maritime or riverine adaptation, is well documented in the ethnographic record. From about 500 CE, pressure on fish stocks as a result of population growth along the West Coast of North America from Alaska to California encouraged foraging populations to establish control over highly localized salmon streams. This was sometimes accompanied by a shift from mostly uniform dwellings to stratified societies that featured large houses for chiefly families, clients, and slaves.[13]

Detailed case studies have drawn attention to the close connection between resource scarcity and the emergence of inequality. From about 400 to 900 CE, the site of Keatley Creek in British Columbia housed a community of a few hundred members near the Fraser River that capitalized on the local salmon runs. Judging from the archaeological remains, salmon consumption declined around 800, and mammalian meat took its place. At this time, signs of inequality appear in the record. A large share of the fish bone recovered from the pits

---

[13] For the West Coast in general, see now briefly Boix 2015: 98–101; Morris 2015: 37. In practice, causation could be more complex: e.g., Sassaman 2004: 240–243, 264–265. Kelly 2013: 252–266, esp. 251 fig. 9.3, offers a general model. Aquatic foragers: Johnson and Earle 2000: 204–217, esp. 211–216.

of the largest houses comes from mature chinook and sockeye salmon, a prize catch rich in fat and calories. Prestige items such as rare types of stone are found there. Two of the smallest houses, by contrast, contained bones of only younger and less nutritious fish. As in many other societies at this level of complexity, inequality was both celebrated and mitigated by ceremonial redistribution: roasting pits that were large enough to prepare food for sizable crowds suggest that the rich and powerful organized feasts for the community. A thousand years later, potlatch rituals in which leaders competed among themselves through displays of generosity were a common feature across the Pacific Northwest. Similar changes took place at the Bridge River site in the same area: from about 800, as the owners of large buildings began to accumulate prestige goods and abandoned communal food preparation outdoors, poorer residents attached themselves to these households, and inequality became institutionalized.[14]

On other occasions, it was technological progress that precipitated disequalizing social and economic change. For thousands of years, the Chumash on the Californian coast, in what is now Santa Barbara and Ventura counties, had lived as egalitarian foragers who used simple boats and gathered acorns. Around 500 to 700, the introduction of large oceangoing plank canoes that could carry a dozen men and venture more than sixty miles out to sea allowed the Chumash to catch larger fish and to establish themselves as middlemen in the shell trade along the coast. They sold flint obtained from the Channel Islands to inland groups in exchange for acorns, nuts, and edible grasses. This generated a hierarchical order in which polygamous chiefs controlled canoes and access to territory, led their men in war, and presided over ritual ceremonies. In return, they received payments of food and shells from their followers. In such environments, foraging societies could attain relatively high levels of complexity. As reliance on concentrated local resources grew, mobility declined, and occupational specialization, strictly defined ownership of assets, perimeter defense, and intense competition between neighboring groups that commonly involved the enslavement of captives fostered hierarchy and inequality.[15]

Among foragers, adaptations of this kind were possible only in specific ecological niches and did not normally spread beyond them. Only the domestication of food resources had the potential to transform economic activity and social relations on a global scale: in its absence, stark inequalities might have

[14] Prentiss et al. 2007; Speller, Yang, and Hayden 2005: 1387 (Keatley Creek); Prentiss et al. 2012, esp. 321 (Bridge River).
[15] Flannery and Marcus 2012: 67–71 (Chumash). Complexity: Kelly 2013: 241–268, esp. 242 table 9.

remained confined to small pockets along coasts and rivers, surrounded by a whole world of more egalitarian foragers. But this was not to be. A variety of edible plants began to be domesticated on different continents, first in Southwest Asia about 11,500 years ago, then in China and South America 10,000 years ago, in Mexico 9,000 years ago, in New Guinea more than 7,000 years ago, and in South Asia, Africa, and North America some 5,000 years ago. The domestication of animals, when it did occur, sometimes preceded and sometimes followed these innovations. The shift from foraging to farming could be a drawn-out process that did not always follow a linear trajectory.[16]

This was especially true of the Natufian culture and its prepottery Neolithic successors in the Levant, the first to witness this transition. From about 14,500 years ago, warmer and wetter weather allowed regional forager groups to grow in size and to operate from more permanent settlements, hunting abundant game and collecting wild cereal grains in sufficient quantities to require at least small storage facilities. The material evidence is very limited but shows signs of what leading experts have called an "incipient social hierarchy." Archaeologists have discovered one larger building that might have served communal uses and a few special basalt mortars that would have taken great effort to manufacture. According to one count, about 8 percent of the recovered skeletons from the Early Natufian period, about 14,500 to 12,800 years ago, wore seashells, sometimes brought in from hundreds of miles away, and decorations made of bone or teeth. At one site, three males were buried with shell headdresses, one of them fringed with shells four rows deep. Only a few graves contained stone tools and figurines. The presence of large roasting pits and hearths may point to redistributive feasts of the type held much later in the American Northwest.[17]

Yet whatever degree of social stratification and inequality had developed under these benign environmental conditions faded during a cold phase from about 12,800 to 11,700 years ago known as the Younger Dryas, when the remaining foragers returned to a more mobile lifestyle as local resources dwindled or became less predictable. The return to climatic stability around 11,700 years ago coincided with the earliest evidence for the cultivation of wild crops such

---

[16] Chronology of domestication: Price and Bar-Yosef 2011: S171 table 1. On the question of the origins of agriculture, see esp. Barker 2006 and the contributions to the special issue of *Current Anthropology* 52, S4 (2011), S161–S512. Diamond 1997 remains the most accessible account of global variation in the scope and pace of domestication. Nonlinearity: Finlayson and Warren 2010.

[17] Natufians: Barker 2006: 126; Price and Bar-Yosef 2010: 149–152; Pringle 2014: 823; and cf. also Bowles and Choi 2013: 8833–8834; Bowles 2015: 3–5.

as einkorn, emmer, wheat, and barley. During what is known as the early Pre-Pottery Neolithic (about 11,500 to 10,500 years ago), settlements expanded and food eventually came to be stored in individual households, a practice that points to changing concepts of ownership. That some exotic materials such as obsidian appeared for the first time may reflect a desire to express and shore up elevated status. The later Pre-Pottery Neolithic (about 10,500 to 8,300 years ago) has yielded more specific information. About 9,000 years ago, the village of Cayönü in southeastern Turkey comprised different zones whose buildings and finds differed in size and quality. Larger and better-built structures feature unusual and exotic artifacts and tend to be located in close proximity to a plaza and a temple. Whereas only a small share of graves include obsidian, beads, or tools, three of the four richest in-house burials in Cayönü took place in houses next to the plaza. All of this may be regarded as markers of elite standing.[18]

There can be no doubt that most of the inequality we observe in the following millennia was made possible by farming. But other paths existed. I have already mentioned aquatic adaptations that allowed substantial political and economic disparities to arise in the absence of food domestication. In other cases, the introduction of the domesticated horse as a conveyance could have disequalizing effects even in the absence of food production. In the eighteenth and nineteenth centuries, the Comanche in the borderlands of the American Southwest formed a warrior culture that relied on horses of European origin to conduct warfare and raids over long distances. Buffalo and other wild mammals were their principal food source, complemented by gathered wild plants and maize obtained via trade or plunder. These arrangements supported high levels of inequality: captive boys were employed to tend to the horses of the rich, and the number of horses owned divided Comanche households rather sharply into the "rich" (*tsaanaakatu*), the "poor" (*tahkapu*), and the "very poor" (*tubitsi tahkapu*). More generally, foraging, horticultural, and agricultural societies were not always systematically associated with different levels of inequality: some foraging groups could be more unequal than some farming communities. A survey of 258 Native American societies in North America suggests that the size of the surplus, not domestication as such, was the key determinant of levels of material inequality: whereas two-thirds of societies that had no or hardly any surplus did not manifest resource inequality, four in five of those that generated

---

[18] Impact of Younger Dryas: Mithen 2003: 50; Shultziner et al. 2010: 335. Pre-Pottery Neolithic: Price and Bar-Yosef 2010: 152–158.

moderate or large surpluses did. This correlation is much stronger than between different modes of subsistence on the one hand and inequality on the other.[19]

A collaborative study of twenty-one small-scale societies at different levels of development—hunter-gatherers, horticulturalists, herders, and farmers—and in different parts of the world identifies two crucial determinants of inequality: ownership rights in land and livestock and the ability to transmit wealth from one generation to the next. Researchers looked at three different types of wealth: embodied (mostly body strength and reproductive success), relational (exemplified by partners in labor), and material (household goods, land, and livestock). In their sample, embodied endowments were the most important wealth category among foragers and horticulturalists, and material wealth was the least important one, whereas the opposite was true of herders and farmers. The relative weight of different wealth classes is an important factor mediating the overall degree of inequality. Physical constraints on embodied wealth are relatively stringent, especially for body size and somewhat less so for strength, hunting returns, and reproductive success. Relational wealth, though more flexible, was also more unevenly distributed among farmers and pastoralists, and measures of inequality in land and livestock in these two groups reached higher levels than those for utensils or boat shares among foragers and horticulturalists. The combination of diverse inequality constraints that apply to different types of wealth and the relative significance of particular types of wealth accounts for observed differences by mode of subsistence. Average composite wealth Gini coefficients were as low as 0.25 to 0.27 for hunter-gatherers and horticulturalists but were much higher for herders (0.42) and agriculturalists (0.48). For material wealth alone, the main divide appears to lie between foragers (0.36) and all others (0.51 to 0.57).[20]

Transmissibility of wealth is another crucial variable. The degree of intergenerational wealth transmission was about twice as high for farmers and herders as for the others, and the material possessions available to them were much more suitable for transmission than were the assets of foragers and horticulturalists. These systematic differences exercise a strong influence on the inequality

---

[19] Rivaya-Martínez 2012: 49 (Comanche); Haas 1993, esp. 308–309 tables 1–2 (North American societies).
[20] Borgerhoff Mulder et al. 2009: 683 fig. 1 (sample), 684 table 1 (43 wealth measures for these societies), S34 table S4 (inequality for different wealth types), 685 table 2, S35 table S5 (Ginis). High land inequality among the circumscribed horticulturalists of Dominica drives up mean material equality for this subsistence mode relative to foragers, which means that these two groups may have more in common than this small sample suggests. For the horticulturalist data, see Gurven et al. 2010.

of life chances, measured in terms of the likelihood that a child of parents in the top composite wealth decile ends up in the same decile compared to that of a child of parents in the poorest decile. Defined in this way, intergenerational mobility was generally moderate: even among foragers and horticulturalists, offspring of the top decile were at least three times as likely to reproduce this standing as those of the bottom decile were to ascend to it. For farmers, however, the odds were much better (about eleven times), and they were better still for herders (about twenty times). These discrepancies can be attributed to two factors. About half of this effect is explained by technology, which determines the relative importance and characteristics of different wealth types. Institutions governing the mode of wealth transmission account for the other half, as agrarian and pastoralist norms favor vertical transmission to kin.[21]

According to this analysis, inequality and its persistence over time has been the result of a combination of three factors: the relative importance of different classes of assets, how suitable they are for passing on to others, and actual rates of transmission. Thus groups in which material wealth plays a minor role and does not readily lend itself to transmission and in which inheritance is discouraged are bound to experience lower levels of overall inequality than groups in which material wealth is the dominant asset class, is highly transmissible, and is permitted to be left to the next generation. In the long run, transmissibility is critical: if wealth is passed on between generations, random shocks related to health, parity, and returns on capital and labor that create inequality will be preserved and accumulate over time instead of allowing distributional outcomes to regress to the mean.[22]

In keeping with the observations made in the aforementioned survey of Native American societies, the empirical findings derived from this sample of twenty-one small-scale societies likewise suggest that domestication is not a sufficient precondition for significant disequalization. Reliance on defensible natural resources appears to be a more critical factor, because these can generally be bequeathed to the next generation. The same is true of investments such as plowing, terracing, and irrigation. The heritability of such productive assets and their improvements fosters inequality in two ways: by enabling it to increase over

---

[21] Borgerhoff Mulder et al. 2009: 686, with S37 table S7; Smith et al. 2010a: 89 fig. 3.

[22] Model: Borgerhoff Mulder et al. 2009: 682. Correlation: Smith et al. 2010a: 91 fig. 5. Shennan 2011 also puts great weight on the shift from intangible to material property resources and its potential for creating inequality.

time and by reducing intergenerational variance and mobility. A much broader survey of more than a thousand societies at different levels of development confirms the central role of transmission. According to this global data set, about a third of simple forager societies have inheritance rules for movable property, but only one in twelve recognizes the transmission of real estate. By contrast, almost all societies that practice intensive forms of agriculture are equipped with rules that cover both. Complex foragers and horticulturalists occupy an intermediate position. Inheritance presupposes the existence of property rights. We can only conjecture the circumstances of their creation: Samuel Bowles has argued that farming favored rights in property that were impractical or unfeasible for foragers because farm resources such as crops, buildings, and animals could easily be delimited and defended, prerequisites not shared by the dispersed natural resources on which foragers tend to rely. Exceptions such as aquatic adaptations and horse cultures are fully consistent with this explanation.[23]

Historically, inequality was sometimes slow to take off. Catal Höyük, a Neolithic proto-urban settlement in southwestern Anatolia that reaches back to the eighth millennium BCE, is a striking example. Its several thousand residents relied on a mixture of horticultural hoe-farming and herding. Land was abundant, and there are no clear signs of governmental structures or social stratification. Residents inhabited family households where they stored grain, fruit, and nuts. Large numbers of stone artifacts have been recovered from this site. A comprehensive survey of 2,429 objects from twenty buildings and nine courtyards dating from 7400 to 6000 BCE reveals differences in the distribution of particular types of artifacts. Intact millstones and querns are very unevenly distributed across dwellings, whereas households generally enjoyed broad access to cooking features and stone tools. Intact querns are predominantly found in more elaborate buildings, but we cannot tell whether these represent higher-status households or whether they merely hosted cooperative tasks related to food processing. The observation that most millstones and querns had deliberately been broken long before they would have worn out may speak against the first of these interpretations. This custom may even reflect a widespread though not universal injunction against the intergenerational transmission of these valuable assets: in later Mesopotamian societies, querns featured prominently among

---

[23] Smith et al. 2010a: 92 (defensibility); Boix 2015: 38 table 1.1.B (global survey); Bowles and Choi 2013 (property rights). The latter develop a formal model in which climate amelioration renders farming more productive and predictable and leads to an expansion of agriculture and private property rights (8834 fig. 2).

heritable wealth. It is possible that leveling measures were actively applied so as to curb wealth imbalances among households.[24]

Yet over time, inequality increasingly became the norm. Archaeological evidence from Mesopotamia shows strong signs of stratification well before the first states were established in that region. In the village of Tell es-Sawwan on the Tigris north of modern Baghdad, for example, a mud wall with a ditch that contained many sling missiles, all made of clay, points to violent conflict some 7,000 years ago, conditions that were conducive to the creation of centralized leadership and hierarchy. Some of the richest burials at this site are for children, reflecting status distinction based on family wealth rather than personal achievement. At Tell Arpachiyah near Mosul, a site that was occupied at roughly the same time, what appears to be the residence of an elite family consisted of a large number of rooms with finds of fancy pottery, alabaster vessels, obsidian, and various types of ornaments and craft tools. In this settlement, leaders controlled trade by sealing shipments with blobs of clay that had simple seals carved into them before they dried—early precursors of complex sealing in later Mesopotamian history. It is telling that at Yarim Tepe, a cremated youngster had been buried not just with obsidian beads but also with a seal drill, marking him out as the offspring and perhaps intended heir of such an official.[25]

By that time, between 6000 and 4000 BCE, all the basic ingredients of structural inequality were already in place: numerous defensive structures that invoke competition for scarce resources and a need for effective leadership; secular public buildings that may be associated with governmental functions; house shrines and temples that speak to the importance of ritual power; signs of hereditary rank, exemplified by lavish child burials; and evidence of craft exchange between elite families in different settlements. Political, military, and economic development differentiated the population, and prominent position, control over economic exchange, and personal wealth went hand in hand.

In other contexts, political leadership came to be associated with high levels of material inequality. A cemetery at Varna by the Black Sea in what is now Bulgaria has yielded more than 200 occupied graves from the fifth millennium BCE. One burial stands out, a middle-aged man laid to rest with no fewer than 990

---

[24] Wright 2014.

[25] Mesopotamia: Flannery and Marcus 2012: 261–282, esp. 264–266, 268, 272, 274, 281. See also 451 for a cemetery with more than 1,000 burials in Susiana (Khuzestan), ranging from graves rich in copper and fancy painted pottery to poor ones with cooking pots, and see Price and Bar-Yosef 2010: 159 for inequality among more than 100 graves in Tell Halula on the Euphrates.

gold objects weighing more than three pounds total: he was covered in gold ornaments that were probably attached to his original clothing, carried heavy gold rings around his arms, and wielded an ax scepter; even his penis was sheathed in gold. This man's grave accounts for a third of all gold objects found at this site and a quarter of their total weight. Grave goods are very unevenly distributed overall: more than half of the occupied graves contain some goods, but fewer than one in ten is rich in deposits, and only a handful contain a wide range of materials, including lots of gold. The Gini coefficient for the number of goods per grave varies from 0.61 and 0.77, depending on the period, but would be much higher if we could adjust the distribution for value. Although we can only guess at the organization of this society, its hierarchical character is hardly in doubt. The gold-covered man and some of his lesser peers may well have been paramount chiefs.[26]

These finds point to a complementary source of inequality. The combination of surplus extraction from defensible resources and personal or familial property claims to these resources that included the right to transfer them to descendants or other kin laid the foundation for growing socioeconomic stratification. New forms of political and military power contributed to and amplified the resultant inequalities in income and wealth. Much like the shift to food domestication, the evolution of political hierarchies was a slow and gradual process and was highly contingent on ecological conditions, technological progress, and demographic growth. In the long run, the overall direction of change was from the small family-level groups of a few dozen people that were typical of simple forager economies to local groups and collectivities whose members typically numbered in the hundreds and on to larger chiefdoms or protostates that controlled thousands or tens of thousands. This was not always a linear progression, and not all environments supported more complex forms of social organization. As a result, complex state-level societies based on agriculture eventually came to share the planet with bands, tribes, and chiefdoms of herders, horticulturalists, and what remained of the ancestral population of hunter-gatherers. This diversity has been vital to our understanding of the driving forces behind the emergence of inequality, allowing us to compare the characteristics of different modes of subsistence and their consequences for the accumulation, transmission, and concentration of wealth as already summarized.[27]

[26] Biehl and Marciniak 2000, esp. 186, 189–191; Higham et al. 2007, esp. 639–641, 643–647, 649; Windler, Thiele, and Müller 2013, esp. 207 table 2 (also on another site in the area).
[27] Johnson and Earle 2000 provide an excellent survey of social evolution. For typical group size, see 246 table 8.

The documented range of variation in sociopolitical organization around the world has been similarly broad, making it possible to relate inequalities of power and status to inequalities in wealth. From a global perspective, agriculture is closely correlated with social and political stratification. In a sample of more than a thousand communities, more than three-quarters of simple foraging communities do not display signs of social stratification, as opposed to fewer than a third of those practicing intensive forms of farming. Political hierarchies are even more strongly dependent on sedentary agriculture: elites and class structure are virtually unknown among simple foragers but are attested for the majority of agrarian societies. Once again, however, it was the scale of the economic surplus rather than the mode of subsistence as such that served as the critical variable. In the survey of 258 Native American societies already mentioned, 86 percent of those groups without significant surplus production also lacked signs of political inequality, whereas the same proportion of those that generated moderate or large surpluses had developed at least some degree of political hierarchy. Among 186 societies from across the world that are documented in more detail, known as the Standard Cross-Cultural Sample, four in five hunter-gatherer communities had no leaders, whereas three-quarters of farming societies were organized as chiefdoms or states.[28]

But not all agricultural societies followed the same trajectory. A new global survey suggests that the cultivation of cereals played a critical role in the development of more complex social hierarchies. Unlike perennial roots, which are continuously available but rot quickly, grain crops are gathered en masse only at specific harvest times and are suitable for longer-term storage. Both of these features made it easier for elites to appropriate and hold on to surplus food resources. States first arose in those parts of the world that had first developed agriculture: once plants—and above all cereals—and animals had been domesticated, sooner or later humans shared their fate, and inequality escalated to previously unimaginable heights.[29]

---

[28] Global sample: Boix 2015: 38 table 1.1.C. North America: Haas 1993: 310 table 3. SCCS: Boix 2015: 103 table 3.1.D.

[29] Cereals: Mayshar, Moav, Neeman, and Pascali 2015, esp. 43–45, 47. Agriculture and state formation: Boix 2015: 119–121, esp. 120 fig. 3.3. See Petersen and Skaaning 2010 for variance in the timing of state formation, driven by geographical and climatic features that affected domestication, which supports Diamond 1997. Cf. also Haber 2012 for the role of crop storage in later phases of state formation.

THE ORIGINAL "1 PERCENT"

Unequal access to income and wealth preceded the formation of the state and contributed to its development. Yet once established, governmental institutions in turn exacerbated existing inequalities and created new ones. Premodern states generated unprecedented opportunities for the accumulation and concentration of material resources in the hands of the few, both by providing a measure of protection for commercial activity and by opening up new sources of personal gain for those most closely associated with the exercise of political power. In the long run, political and material inequality evolved in tandem in what has been called "an upward spiral of interactive effects, where each increment on one variable makes a corresponding increment on the other more likely." Modern scholars have come up with a wide variety of definitions that seek to capture the quintessential features of statehood. Borrowing elements of several of them, the state can be said to represent a political organization that claims authority over a territory and its population and resources and that is endowed with a set of institutions and personnel that perform governmental functions by issuing binding orders and rules and backing them up with the threat or exercise of legitimized coercive measures, including physical violence. There is no shortage of theories to explain the emergence of the earliest states. The putative driving forces are all in some way predicated on economic development and its social and demographic consequences: gains that the well-positioned reaped from the control of trade flows, the need to empower leaders to manage the problems arising from growing population densities and more complex relations of production and exchange, class conflict over access to the means of production, and the pressures created by military conflict over scarce resources that favored scaling up, hierarchy, and centralized command structures.[30]

From the perspective of the study of inequality, it may not, strictly speaking, be particularly important which of these factors mattered most: to the extent that state formation introduced steep and stable hierarchies into societies with significant surpluses, inequalities of power, status, and material wealth were bound to grow. Even so, a growing consensus now holds that

---

[30] Quote: Haas 1993: 312. Scheidel 2013: 5–9 presents and discusses various definitions of the state, several of which contribute to the summary given in the text. For the nature of premodern states, see herein, pp. 46–48. Maisels 1990: 199–220, Sanderson 1999: 53–95, and Scheidel 2013: 9–14 offer surveys of modern theories of state formation.

organized violence was central to this process. Robert Carneiro's influential theory of circumscription holds that the interaction between population growth and warfare under conditions of territorial boundedness explains why previously more autonomous and egalitarian households, reliant on scarce domesticated food resources and unable to exit stressful environments, were prepared to submit to authoritarian leadership and endure inequality to become more effective in competing with other groups. The most recent theories and simulation models of state formation likewise emphasize the crucial importance of intergroup conflict. The critical role of violence also goes a long way toward accounting for the specific characteristics of most premodern states, most notably despotic leadership and an often overwhelmingly strong focus on warmaking.[31]

Not all early states were alike, and centralized polities coexisted with more "heterarchical" or corporate forms of political organization. Even so, centralized authoritarian states commonly outcompeted differently structured rivals. They appeared independently around the world wherever ecological preconditions allowed, in the Old World as well as in the Americas and across a wide range of environments from the alluvial floodplains of Egypt and Mesopotamia to the highlands of the Andes. Defying this considerable diversity of context, the best-known among them developed into strikingly similar entities. All of them witnessed the expansion of hierarchies in different domains, from the political sphere to the family and religious belief systems—an autocatalytic process whereby "the hierarchical structure itself feeds back on all societal factors to make them more closely into an overall system that supports the authority structure." Pressures in favor of increasing stratification had an enormous effect on moral values, for the residue of ancestral egalitarianism was replaced by belief in the merits of inequality and acceptance of hierarchy as an integral element of the natural and cosmic order.[32]

In quantitative terms, agrarian states proved extremely successful. Although these numbers cannot be more than controlled conjecture, we can guess that 3,500 years ago, when state-level polities covered perhaps not more than 1 percent of the earth's terrestrial surface (excluding Antarctica), they already laid claim to up to half of our species. We are on more solid ground in estimating that by the beginning of the Common Era, states—mostly large empires such

---

[31] Circumscription theory: Carneiro 1970; 1988. For simulation models of state formation driven by warfare, see Turchin and Gavrilets 2009; Turchin, Currie, Turner, and Gavrilets 2013. Boix 2015: 127–170, 252–253 also stresses the role of warfare.

[32] Decentralized polities: e.g., Ehrenreich, Crumley, and Levy 1995; Blanton 1998. Quote: Cohen 1978: 70; see also Trigger 2003: 668–670 for pervasive hierarchization. Values: Morris 2015: 71–92, esp. 73–75, 92.

as Rome and Han China—comprised about a tenth of the earth's land mass but between two-thirds and three-quarters of all people alive at the time. Shaky as they may be, these figures convey a sense of the competitive advantage of a particular type of state: far-flung imperial structures held together by powerful extractive elites. Once again, this was not the only outcome: independent city-states might flourish at the interstices between these empires but only rarely succeeded in holding off their outsized neighbors as the ancient Greeks managed to do in the fifth century BCE. More often than not, they were absorbed into larger entities; on occasion, they built up their own empires, such as Rome, Venice, and the Mexica Triple Alliance of Tenochtitlan, Texcoco, and Tlacopan. Moreover, empires failed from time to time, giving way to more fragmented political ecologies. Medieval Europe is a particularly extreme example of this shift.[33]

More commonly, however, empire begat empire as new conquest regimes reconsolidated earlier power networks. In the very long run, this created a pattern of periodic unraveling and restoration, from the increasingly regular "dynastic cycles" of China to longer swings in Southeast Asia, India, the Middle East and the Levant, central Mexico, and the Andean region. The Eurasian steppe also spawned numerous imperial regimes that embarked on predatory raids and conquests, spurred on by the riches generated by sedentary societies to the south. States grew over time. Prior to the sixth century BCE, the largest empires on earth covered a few hundred thousand square miles. During the following 1,700 years, their mightiest successors routinely exceeded this limit by an entire order of magnitude, and in the thirteenth century, the Mongols' reach extended from Central Europe to the Pacific. And territory is only one metric: if we account for secular growth in population density, we see that the effective expansion of imperial rule was even more dramatic. To an even greater extent than today, our species used to be concentrated in the temperate zone of Eurasia as well as in parts of Central America and the South American Northwest. This is where empire thrived: for thousands of years, most of humanity lived in the shadow of these behemoths, with a few coming to tower far above ordinary mortals. This was the environment that created what I call the "original 1

---

[33] Estimates: Scheidel 2013, conjectured from McEvedy and Jones 1978 and Cohen 1995: 400. On the nature of the early state, see herein. For the structure and world history of empires, see esp. Doyle 1986; Eisenstadt 1993; Motyl 2001; Burbank and Cooper 2010; Leitner 2011; Bang, Bayly, and Scheidel forthcoming; and the précis in Scheidel 2013: 27–30. For city-states, see esp. Hansen 2000 and, very briefly, Scheidel 2013: 30–32.

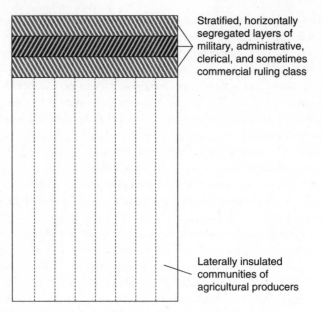

Stratified, horizontally
segregated layers of
military, administrative,
clerical, and sometimes
commercial ruling class

Laterally insulated
communities of
agricultural producers

Figure 1.1   General form of the social structure of agrarian societies

percent," made up of competing but often closely intertwined elite groups that
did their utmost to capture the political rents and commercial gains mobilized
by state-building and imperial integration.[34]

Premodern state formation separated a small ruling class from the mass
of primary producers. Though often internally stratified, this elite both transcended and collectively controlled the individual local communities that
formed the basic building blocks of the state. Ernest Gellner's famous image
captures these structures with unrivaled clarity (Fig. 1.1).[35]

Some members of the ruling class, such as local notables who had ascended
to state office or related honors, would have originated in or even remained

[34] For the evolution of steppe empires—which are absent from the present study mainly for want of relevant data—see Barfield 1989; Cioffi-Revilla, Rogers, Wilcox, and Alterman 2011; http://nomadicempires
.modhist.ox.ac.uk/. Cf. also Turchin 2009 for their role in large-scale state formation. Growing size: Taagepera 1978: 120.
[35] Fig. 1.1 from Gellner 1983: 9 fig. 1 as reproduced in Morris 2015: 66 fig. 3.6.

rooted in these communities, whereas others, such as foreign conquerors, might have been sufficiently detached to form what was in effect a separate society. Centralized governance was very limited by modern standards: states commonly amounted to little more than what Patricia Crone called "protective shells" for the general population, trying to keep it out of the reach of domestic and foreign challengers to the established regime. But rulers and their agents also provided protection in the sense that mafia organizations do in modern societies, capitalizing on the profits from their preeminence in the use of organized violence. They frequently exercised a large amount of despotic power, for civil society institutions were too weak to constrain elite action, including exercise of the power over life and death and the allocation of property. At the same time, many of these states were lacking in infrastructural power, the capacity to penetrate society and implement policies widely. Communities were largely self-governing, loosely held in check by a relatively small and often distant centralized dominant authority.

Governments were semiprivate in nature and relied on the co-optation and cooperation of diverse holders of political, military, economic, and ideological power to control subordinate populations and mobilize resources for rulers. The latter tended to employ a mixture of rewards and threats of violence to preserve balance between competing elites, for government was often primarily focused on managing conflicts among the rich and powerful. Rulers, their agents, and large landowners, categories that commonly intersected, were locked in conflict over the control of the surplus that could be siphoned off through state taxes and private rents. Whereas the employment of established elite members as state officials curtailed the autonomy of rulers, recourse to subordinate agents of lower status created new elite aspirants eager to divert state income and privatize gains from office in order to join existing elite circles. Rulers strove to make power and privilege a contingent and revocable function of state service, whereas their agents sought private benefits for themselves and their descendants; in the long run, the latter often proved more successful. Corruption and other forms of predation were common. As members of the ruling class competed for position and advantage, turnover among individuals could be high, yet elite rule as such tended to be stable as long as state structures were successfully maintained. The upper classes separated themselves from commoners by their lifestyle and worldview, which were frequently martial in nature and defined leaders as the exploiters of inferior agrarian producers. Conspicuous consumption served as an important means of manifesting and reinforcing power relations.[36]

These basic conditions profoundly shaped the distribution of income and wealth. Reduced to essentials, history has known only two ideal-typical modes of wealth acquisition: making and taking. The advent of surplus production, domestication, and hereditary property rights paved the way for the creation and preservation of personal fortunes. In the long run, institutional adaptations that were conducive to this process, technological progress, and the growing scale and scope of economic activity raised the ceiling on individual or familial wealth accumulation, thereby increasing at least the potential range of the dispersion of income and productive assets. In principle, the cumulative effect of random shocks would have been sufficient to make some households richer than others: differences in the return on capital such as land, livestock, buildings, and resources invested in loans and trade would have made sure of that. When their fortunes changed, others would take their place.

What may well be the earliest quantifiable evidence indicative of growing wealth inequality in subelite circles that appears to have resulted from economic development comes from ancient Mesopotamia several thousand years ago. Comparison of a sample of inheritance shares for sons in the Old Babylonian period (in the first half of the second millennium BCE) with documented dowries for daughters in the Neo-Babylonian era (in the late seventh and much of the sixth century BCE, roughly a thousand years later) reveals two notable differences. Converted into wheat wages, the latter are about twice as substantial as the former. As both data sets appear to refer to the same stratum—propertied urban residents, maybe the top decile or so of the urban population—this points to greater affluence overall, especially considering that we would expect sons to be favored over daughters. Moreover, the real values of the dowries are also much more unequally distributed. Because the Neo-Babylonian period was a time of unusually dynamic economic development, this contrast is perhaps best explained by the disequalizing effect of growth and commercialization.[37]

---

[36] On the nature of premodern states in general, see esp. Claessen and Skalník 1978b; Gellner 1983: 8–18; Tilly 1985; Giddens 1987: 35–80; Kautsky 1982, esp. 341–348; Haldon 1993; Sanderson 1999: 99–133; Crone 2003: 35–80 (quote: 51); North, Wallis, and Weingast 2009: 30–109 and a cross-disciplinary meta-survey in Scheidel 2013: 16–26.

[37] Makers and takers: Balch 2014. Babylonia: Jursa 2015 and personal communication. The median and mean real value of the dowries are about 70 percent and 130 percent higher, and the Ginis are 0.43 ($n = 82$) and 0.55 ($n = 84$) for the two periods, or 0.41 and 0.49 when the highest outlier is removed from each data set. For Neo-Babylonian economic dynamism, see Jursa 2010.

But this may be only part of the story, not just in this case but more generally. It is easy to appreciate how the defining features of premodern state formation just outlined would have influenced economic activity in peculiar ways. Political integration not only helped expand markets and lowered at least some transaction and information costs: the pervasive power asymmetries that commonly characterized premodern polities all but ensured an uneven playing field for economic actors. Fragile property rights, inadequate rule enforcement, arbitrary exercise of justice, the venality of state agents, and the paramount importance of personal relationships and proximity to sources of coercive power were among the factors likely to skew outcomes in favor of those in the upper reaches of the status pyramid and those profitably connected to them. This would have been true in even greater measure of various forms of "taking" that were available to members of the ruling class and their associates. Participation in governance opened up access to income from formal compensation, benefactions of rulers and other superiors, and the solicitation of bribes, embezzlement, and extortion, and it often also provided shelter from taxation and other obligations. Senior military positions might be rewarded with a share of war booty. What is more, direct service for the state was not even a necessary prerequisite. Ties of kinship, intermarriage, and other alliances with officeholders could yield commensurate benefits. Moreover, considering the often rather limited infrastructural power of the state, personal wealth and local influence made it easier to shield not only one's own assets from state or community demands but also those of friends and clients—in exchange for other benefits. If necessary, tax quotas could be met by shifting additional burdens onto the powerless.

Under these conditions, political power could hardly fail to exert a major influence on the distribution of material resources. In smaller and less hierarchical polities such as tribes or Big Man collectivities, the status of leaders depended in no small measure on their ability and willingness to share their bounty with the entire community. The ruling classes of agrarian states and empires generally enjoyed greater autonomy. Notwithstanding occasional and well-publicized displays of largess, the flow of redistribution tended to be reversed, further enriching the few at the expense of the many. The elite's collective capacity to extract surplus from primary producers determined the proportion of overall resources that was available for appropriation, and the balance of power between state rulers and various elite groups decided how these gains were apportioned among state coffers, the private accounts of state agents, and the estates of the landed and commercial wealth elite.[38]

The same features of premodern states that funneled resources toward the powerful also served as a powerful check on the concentration of income and wealth. Predation, disregard for private property rights, and the arbitrary exercise of authority not only helped create fortunes but also could just as easily destroy them in the blink of an eye. Just as state office, proximity to power, and the favor of rulers raised the well-connected to great wealth, the machinations of rivals and rulers' desire to curb the influence of their associates and to absorb their ill-gotten gains could just as easily rob them of their riches if not their lives. In addition to the vagaries of familial demography that help account for the survival or dispersal of private estates, violent redistribution limited the degree to which resources came to be concentrated within elite circles.

In practice, outcomes varied widely across historical societies. Mamluk Egypt in the Middle Ages occupied one end of the spectrum. A foreign and nonhereditary conquest elite collectively claimed control of the land, which was allocated to members of the state class contingent on their position within the power structure, which was subject to frequent adjustments. This made access to resources fluid and unpredictable, for violent factionalism ensured high turnover. At the other end of the spectrum, feudal societies having weak rulers, such as Spring and Autumn China or medieval Europe, allowed lords to enjoy relatively secure control of their assets. The same was true of the Roman Republic prior to its terminal crises, when aristocrats collectively ruled the polity for their own benefit and were appropriately keen to uphold private property rights. Most premodern societies, and more than a few contemporary developing countries, fall in between these ideal-typical extremes, combining sometimes violent political intervention in private property relations with a measure of respect for personal wealth. I explore this relationship in greater detail in the following pages.[39]

---

[38] For regressive distribution in despotic regimes, see, e.g., Trigger 2003: 389 and Boix 2015: 259. Winters 2011 tracks oligarchic power across world history, with its frequent focus on wealth defense (esp. 20–26). Notions of reciprocity mainly survived in the ideational domain. Elegantly defined by Claessen and Skalník 1978a: 640, "The early state is a centralized socio-political organization for the regulation of social relations in a complex, stratified society divided into at least two basic strata, or emergent social classes—viz., the rulers and the ruled—whose relations are characterized by political dominance of the former and tributary obligations of the latter, legitimized by a common ideology of which reciprocity is the basic principle."

[39] For Mamluk Egypt, see herein, p. 82; for the Roman Republic, herein, pp. 71–74 and chapter 6, p. 187.

Rents from access to political power are not exclusive to low levels of development. A recent study of dozens of super-rich entrepreneurs in Western countries shows how they benefited from political connections, exploited loopholes in regulation, and took advantage of market imperfections. In this respect, the difference between advanced democratic market economies and other types of states is a matter of degree. In some cases, it may well be possible to estimate how much elite fortunes owed to income from sources other than economic activity: if we are able to tell that Roman aristocrats of the second and first centuries BCE were simply too rich to have built up their wealth by farming and commerce alone, then more specific breakdowns ought to be feasible for more recent historical societies. *Ancien régime* France, which I briefly discuss later in this section, is merely one example. In the most general terms, there can be little doubt that personalized political connections and favors made a much larger contribution to elite wealth than they do in developed countries today. Rent-seeking elites in Latin America or Africa may come somewhat closer to what in global historical terms must count as traditional and indeed "normal" strategies of wealth appropriation and concentration. So do contemporary Russian "oligarchs," who resemble some premodern elite groups in the extent to which both the creation and the preservation of their fortunes have depended on personalized political power relations. Even allowing for considerable diversity of context, Russian credit card tycoon Oleg Tinkov's description of his peers— "temporary managers of their assets—they are not real owners"—applies in equal measure to the precarious standing of many of their predecessors from ancient Rome and China to the monarchies of early modern Europe.[40]

Piketty has sought to explain the very high levels of wealth inequality that were typical of eighteenth- and nineteenth-century Europe with reference to the large gap between the rates of economic growth and return on capital ("$r > g$"). In dynamic models featuring multiplicative and additive shocks—to the rate of return on capital, linked to investment strategies or luck; to demographic parameters, arising from mortality and parity; to preferences concerning consumption and saving; or to productivity, when external income is added in—this condition tends to amplify initial wealth disparities and leads to a high

---

[40] Entrepreneurs: Villette and Vullermot 2009. For the Roman Republic, see herein, p. 73; for France, pp. 83–84. I refer to "personalized" political favors to distinguish these factors from the role of tax reductions in the recent rise of top income shares in the United States and some other Anglo-Saxon countries that have benefited the affluent in the aggregate: see herein, chapter 15, pp. 415–417. Quote: "Lunch with the FT: Oleg Tinkov," *Financial Times*, December 30, 2015.

degree of wealth concentration. Unlike in the first half of the twentieth century, when negative shocks to the stock of capital and its rate of return in the form of wartime destruction, inflation, taxation, and expropriation greatly reduced wealth and, even more so, net income from wealth, the more stable conditions that had preceded this period of considerable leveling had favored holders of wealth. As a result, income from capital accounted for a larger share of total income than it has done since.

Was this situation representative of premodern societies more generally? Considering that the gap between the rate of economic growth and nominal returns on capital (as proxied by interest rates or fixed incomes from estates or endowments) had always been extremely large, it is plausible to assume that on the whole, capital owners enjoyed a perennial advantage. At the same time, we would expect the intensity of shocks to capital to have varied considerably, dependent on the likelihood of violent asset redistribution. In times of stability, the arbitrary exercise of autocratic rule could generate powerful shocks, especially to elites' fortunes, that might cause those fortunes to balloon just about as often as it destroyed them. As long as these interventions merely redistributed assets that had already been claimed by the top tier of society, the overall effect on the distribution of wealth may well have been neutral. By contrast, shocks resulting from war, conquest, or state failure yielded less predictable consequences: whereas military success was likely to raise inequality on the victorious side by enriching its ruling class, generalized leveling commonly ensued from the disintegration of governmental structures. I present historical evidence for these developments in this and later chapters.

In the long run, levels of wealth inequality must have been shaped by the frequency with which these more destabilizing violent ruptures occurred. Insofar as earlier mechanisms of income distribution and wealth accumulation differed from those observed in eighteenth- and especially nineteenth-century Europe, they may have done so with respect to the relative importance of elite income from sources other than labor. The more that personal fortunes depended on access to political rents, the more income from labor—at least if we can define corruption, embezzlement, extortion, military plunder, vying for benefactions, and taking over the assets of rivals as forms of labor—would have mattered than it did for entrepreneurial or rentier investors of capital in more orderly and pacified societies. As I argue in the remainder of this section, income of this nature could be a major, and at times perhaps even the principal, determinant of elite standing. This was true in particular of early, archaic states whose upper classes relied more on state-sponsored claims to rents in goods and labor services than on returns on private assets. These entitlements qualify the conventional distinction between income from capital and income from labor and once again underline the critical importance of political power relations in creating the original "1 percent." [41]

*

Fairly egalitarian modes of land ownership were once common in many of the regions that later came to host large empires. Among the Sumerians in southern Mesopotamia, one of the earliest civilizations known from written sources that date back more than 5,000 years, much farmland used to be controlled by extended patrilineal families of commoners who worked it as communal holdings. This type of ownership was also typical in early China, in the Shang and Western Zhou periods in the second millennium BCE, at a time when private land sales were supposedly inadmissible. In the Valley of Mexico in the Aztec period, most land was held and cultivated by *calpotin*, corporate groups whose holdings combined family fields with common land. The former were sometimes periodically reconfigured to take account of changes in family size. The same was true of the *ayllukuna* in the Peruvian highlands of the Inca period, endogamous groups that assigned parcels at different altitudes to individual member families and regularly adjusted them to ensure an equitable distribution. Arrangements such as these imposed a powerful constraint on the concentration and commercial exploitation of land.

Over time, however, inequality grew as capitalholders acquired land and political leaders superimposed tributary structures on existing holdings. By the time Sumerian documentation expanded in the course of the third millennium BCE, we already encounter temples that held large amounts of land and worked it with their own institutional labor force, and we see nobles who had somehow amassed larger holdings as well. Privatization of lineage land was possible as long as other group members agreed to it. Debt served as a potent instrument of converting surplus income into additional land: high annual interest rates of up to a third frequently compelled customary owners who had taken out loans to

---

[41] For the role of returns on capital and of shocks on these returns, see esp. the concise expositions in Piketty and Saez 2014: 841–842; Piketty 2015b: 73–78, and more generally Piketty 2014: 164–208. For the debate, see herein, chapter 15, pp. 411–423.

cede their holdings to creditors and might even condemn them to servitude if they had pledged themselves as collateral. This process created both large estates and a landless workforce to cultivate them. While creditors may have derived some of the disposable resources that they lent to others from the management of their own economic assets, political rents could also play an important role in providing them with the means to pursue this strategy. Privatization, in turn, reduced traditional social obligations to clients and supporters: the fewer costly social responsibilities were attached to private property, the more attractive it would have become to investors. A variety of social statuses developed to cater to the labor needs of capital owners, such as sharecroppers and debt bondsmen, with slavery, a more primordial type of subordination, added to the mix. Analogous processes could be observed 4,000 years later, but at a comparable level of socioeconomic development, among the Aztecs, where rural debt and recourse to landless serfs and slaves sustained growing inequality.[42]

The practices of state rulers provided both a model for, and often also the means of, encroachment. Sumerian kings sought to obtain land for themselves and their associates and insinuated themselves into the operation of temple estates to gain control over their assets. Temple administrators intermingled management of institutional assets with their own. Graft, corruption, and force were already well-established means of appropriation. Sumerian cuneiform records from the city of Lagash in the twenty-fourth century BCE show that the local kings and queens took over temple land and the workers attached to it; that aristocrats acquired land by foreclosing on high-interest loans; that officials misused state assets such as boats and fishing grounds, overcharged for basic services such as funerals and sheep shearing, withheld wages from workers, and generally filled their pockets through corruption; and that the wealthy stole fish from poor men's ponds. Whatever the merits of some of these allegations, the overall impression is that of a particular type of governance that encouraged encroachment and enrichment aided by the exercise of power for personal benefit. From early on, the ongoing acquisition and concentration of private wealth in elite circles caused concerns for rulers who needed to protect primary producers, who were expected to pay taxes and perform labor services for the state, from predatory lenders and domineering landlords. From the mid-third

---

[42] Hudson 1996b: 34–35, 46–49; 1996c: 299, 303; Trigger 2003: 316–321, 333; Flannery and Marcus 2012: 500–501, 515–516. The Sumerian experience is given pride of place here because it represents the earliest surviving example of these processes.

to the mid-second millennium BCE, Mesopotamian kings periodically decreed cancellation of debts in an attempt to slow the advance of private capital. For all we know, this was bound to be a losing battle.[43]

A telling illustration of these tensions can be found in the "Song of Release," a Hurrian myth translated into Hittite in the fifteenth century BCE. It features the Hurrian weather god Tessub, who appears in the city council of Ebla (in northwestern Syria) in the guise of a debtor, visibly in dire need and "dried out." King Megi has clashed with the city's powerful notables over the release of debt slaves, a measure deemed required by divine command but successfully opposed by Zazalla, a gifted orator who sways opinion in the elite council. Under his influence, the councilors offer Tessub gifts of gold and silver if he is in debt, oil if he is dried out, and fuel if he is cold but refuse to free the enslaved debtors in accordance with Megi's wishes:

> But we will make no release [of slaves]. There will be [no] rejoicing in your soul, O Megi.

They invoke the necessity of keeping debtors in bondage, for

> If we were to release them, who would give us to eat? On the one hand, they are our cupbearers; on the other, they serve (food) to us. They are our cooks, and they wash up for us.

Megi is reduced to tears by their obstreperousness and renounces any claim to his own bondsmen. Right before the surviving text breaks off, Tessub promises divine rewards if the other debts are remitted and threatens severe punishment if they are not.[44]

Accounts such as these reveal the limits of royal power in the face of elite privilege and appropriation. Ancient Near Eastern city-kings also had to tread carefully in expanding their own holdings in competition with local temples and other influential constituencies. Up to a point, balancing and the relatively modest scale of many of these polities served as a check on the degree of disequalizing intervention. Large-scale conquest, however, dramatically changed

---

[43] Hudson 1996a: 12–13, 16; Flannery and Marcus 2012: 474–502, esp. 489–491 on Lagash. For debt relief, see herein, chapter 12, pp. 359–360.

[44] Ebla: Hoffner 1998: 65–80, esp. 73–77. Quotes: 75 paragraphs 46, 48. The Hurrians were located in northern Mesopotamia, the Hittites in Anatolia.

this equation. The violent takeover of rival polities and territories opened the door to more overt predation and the accumulation of riches unfettered by customary local constraints. The agglomeration of existing polities into larger structures created new tiers of hierarchy and gave those at the top access to surplus from a broader resource base, developments that could hardly fail to intensify overall inequality by boosting top income and wealth shares.

The disequalizing effects of state formation by extensive conquest are clearly visible in the case of the Akkadian kingdom in the twenty-fourth to twenty-second centuries BCE. Considered the first "true" empire in history if we define empire in terms not merely of size but also of multiethnic heterogeneity, asymmetric core-periphery relations, and abiding local traditions of distinction and hierarchy, it exercised power over diverse societies from northern Syria into western Iran. This unprecedented expansion encouraged Akkad's rulers not only to assume divine rank—surviving texts report that Rimush, the son and successor of the empire's founder, Sargon, "accounted himself among the gods" and that his nephew Naram-Sin declared that "the people of his city asked of him that he be god of their city Agade . . . and they built his temple in Agade"—but also to seize and redistribute assets on a vast scale. Local city-state kings were replaced by Akkadian governors, and large amounts of land ended up in the hands of the new rulers and their senior agents. Because much of the most productive farmland was held by temples, rulers either had it confiscated or appointed relatives and officials as priests to assume control of these resources. A new imperial ruling class that transcended the internal divisions of this far-flung realm accumulated large estates. Appropriated land, handed over to officials, was used to support them and to reward their own clients and subordinates, some of whom were known as "the select." Later tradition expressed loathing for "the scribes who parceled out farmland in the steppe." The beneficiaries of state grants further added to their holdings by purchasing private land.

Some Akkadian records offer detailed insight into the growth of elite wealth. Yetib-Mer, the majordomo of god-king Naram-Sin, held almost 2,500 acres of land in different parts of the empire. Mesag, a notable in the late twenty-third century BCE, controlled more than 3,000 acres: he had been granted a third of it for his own subsistence and bought use rights to the remainder. His domain was parceled out to lesser administrators, craftsmen, and other clients, only a few of whom received large allotments in excess of ninety acres; indeed, most had to make do with much smaller plots. Access to material resources was thus sharply graduated across the state class. Coupled with the ability to reassign assets with little regard for established patterns of ownership, imperial amalgamation of productive resources created a "winner-takes-all" environment that disproportionately benefited a small power elite. In the judgment of a leading expert, "the Akkadian governing elite enjoyed resources far in excess of what Sumerian notables before them had known." [45]

Empire building had the potential to influence the distribution of income and wealth in ways that were unrelated to returns on economic activity and turned material inequality into a by-product of the underlying restructuring of power relations. Political unification on a large scale could improve overall conditions for commercial activity by lowering transaction costs, by boosting demand for high-end goods and services, and by enabling entrepreneurs to capitalize on networks of exchange established for extractive purposes, thereby widening the gap between capital holders and others. It spurred urban growth, especially in metropolitan centers, that exacerbated material imbalances. It also protected from popular demands and expectations wealthy elites who were allied to the central authorities, giving them freer rein in the pursuit of personal gain. All these factors, among others, were conducive to the concentration of income and wealth.

But empire also shaped inequality in a much more straightforward manner. State-directed allocation of material resources to members of the political elite and administrative personnel converted political inequality into income and wealth inequality. It directly and immediately reproduced power asymmetries in the economic sphere. The delegational nature of rule in premodern states required rulers to share gains with their agents and supporters as well as with preexisting elites. In this context, assigned claims to surplus could be more important than formal property rights in productive assets. This was particularly true in societies in which labor services represented a major component of state and elite revenue. Corvée arrangements in the Inca empire were among the most extensive recorded in history, but use of coerced labor was also widespread in Egypt, the Near East, China, and Mesoamerica, to name but a few places. Land grants were an almost universal means of rewarding key associates, being handed out by the chiefs of Hawai'i and the god-kings of Akkad and Cuzco, by Egyptian Pharaohs and Zhou emperors, by the kings

---

[45] Foster 2016: 40, 43, 56, 62, 72, 90, 92; also Hudson 1996c: 300. Quotes: Foster 2016: 8 (Rimush), 13 (Naram-Sin), 40 (scribes), 43 (elite). For the collapse of the Akkadian empire, see herein, chapter 9, p. 280. In subsequent imperial formations, elites and state personnel in the capital cities benefited disproportionately: e.g., Yoffee 1988: 49–52.

of medieval Europe and by Charles V in the New World. Attempts to make these prebendal estates hereditary within the families of the initial beneficiaries and eventually turn them into private property were an almost inevitable consequence. But even when successfully accomplished, these transformations merely perpetuated and cemented material inequality that had originated in the political domain.

In addition to grants of land and labor, participation in the collection of state revenue was another important pathway to power-based elite enrichment. This process is so well attested that a long book could, and indeed should, be devoted to it. To name just one lesser-known example, in the Oyo empire, a large Yoruba state in West Africa in the early modern period, petty kings and subordinate chiefs gathered at local tribute-taking centers before they converged on an annual festival at the capital. Tribute in the form of cowrie shells, livestock, meat, flour, and construction materials was presented to the king through the intermediation of officials who had been appointed to act as patrons for particular groups of tribute-bearers and who were entitled to a share of the proceeds in exchange for their troubles. Needless to say, formal entitlements frequently accounted for only a modest portion of the personal income that fiscal agents derived from their service.[46]

By the Middle Babylonian period, more than 3,000 years ago, centuries of exposure to a succession of imperial regimes had taught the inhabitants of Mesopotamia an important lesson—that "the king is the one at whose side wealth walks." What they could not know but would hardly have been surprised to learn was that this was to be true for thousands of years more and around the world. Violent predation and political preference greatly complemented and amplified the inequalities in income and wealth that had arisen from surplus production and hereditary transmissible assets. It was the interplay between these economic and political developments that spawned the original "1 percent." I am unable to improve on Bruce Trigger's pithy description of the Aztec *pipiltin*, who

> wore cotton clothes, sandals, feather work, and jade ornaments, lived in two-storey stone houses, ate the flesh of human sacrifices, drank

---

[46] Trigger 2003: 375–394 surveys these features across several early civilizations. For the Oyo, see 393. The contributions in Yun-Casalilla and O'Brien 2012 and Monson and Scheidel 2015 add up to a broad overview of fiscal regimes in world history.

chocolate and fermented beverages (in moderation) in public, kept concubines, entered the royal palace at will, could eat in the palace dining hall, and performed special dances at public rituals. They did not pay taxes.[47]

This, in a nutshell, was the public face of premodern inequality. It was only through their cannibalistic bent that this particular elite elevated the metaphorical consumption of human sweat and toil that was typical of their class to an unusually literal level. For much of human history, the very rich were indeed "different from you and me"—or, rather, our more ordinary ancestors. Material inequality may even have molded the human body. In the eighteenth and nineteenth century, when advances in medical knowledge had finally made it possible for the wealthy to purchase longer lives and limbs, the English upper classes famously towered over the stunted masses. If data sets that tend to be (much) less than perfect are to be trusted, such disparities may stretch much farther back in time. Egyptian pharaohs and members of the Mycenaean elite of Bronze Age Greece appear to have been visibly taller than commoners. The skeletal record of some heavily stratified societies shows greater dispersion in body height than in less strongly layered ones. Finally, and from a Darwinian perspective most important, material inequality routinely translated into reproductive inequality on an extravagant scale as elites accumulated harems and sired offspring by the dozen.[48]

To be sure, the degree of income and wealth inequality in premodern societies was not solely determined by the rapacity of their well-connected elites. The ancient Babylonian evidence for the dispersion of inheritances and dowries in subelite circles, already cited, allows us to catch a faint glimpse of what appear to have been growing disparities in response to economic growth and commercialization. In the next chapter and in chapter 9, I present archaeological data on house sizes before, during, and after the period of Roman rule in different parts of Europe and North Africa that reveal considerable variation in consumption inequality among urban commoners. Even so, although additional material could no doubt be adduced, especially from funerary contexts, for most of the

---

[47] The first quote is taken from the so-called "Babylonian Theodicy," a text composed in the Middle Babylonian language: Oshima 2014: 167, line 282, and the second one is from Trigger 2003: 150–151.

[48] Quote: Fitzgerald 1926. For stature inequality, see Boix and Rosenbluth 2014: 11–14, reprised in Boix 2015: 188–194; and see also Payne 2016: 519–520. Scheidel 2009b surveys reproductive inequality across world history.

premodern period it is hard, if not impossible, to gather meaningful information about the distribution of income and wealth in the general population.[49]

But it is not primarily for pragmatic reasons that I focus on the affluent. As we will see in chapter 3 and the appendix, in a number of cases social tables or census records make it possible to track, at least in very rough outlines, the distribution of material resources in particular societies from antiquity to the modern colonial period. Most of the Lorenz curves we could plot on the basis of these guesstimates would resemble hockey sticks rather than crescents, pointing to sharp disparities between a select few and a large majority at or not far from basic subsistence. With few exceptions, such as the ancient Greeks and the settlers of colonial North America, groups to which I return in chapters 3 and 6, agrarian populations that were organized in state-level polities generally lacked robust middle classes whose resources could have counterbalanced elite wealth. For this reason alone, variation in inequality was in large measure mediated by the share of resources commanded by the affluent.[50]

Finally, the introduction of large numbers of very poor individuals also raised overall inequality. In many premodern societies, the enslavement or deportation of outsiders was a powerful means to this end. The Neo-Assyrian empire in the Fertile Crescent was notorious for engaging in forcible resettlement on a huge scale, mostly from subjugated peripheries into the imperial heartland in northeastern Mesopotamia. Large-scale transfers commenced under the reign of Tiglath-Pileser III (745–727 BCE) when imperial expansion and consolidation gained momentum. One survey of the ancient records counts forty-three events involving 1,210,928 deportees alongside more than a hundred other deportations for which no or only partial tallies are known. Even though the advertised numbers are of dubious reliability, and although claims about the uprooting of entire populations need to be treated with caution—"the people of his land, male and female, small and great, without exception, I led them forth, I counted them as spoil"—the cumulative effect of this practice was massive.

Over the following century or so, the continuing inflow of deportees allowed Assyrian kings to build, populate, and provision several capital cities. The stone reliefs that glorify royal exploits convey the impression that deportees arrived with only minimal personal belongings, such as a bag or sack. Shorn of their former assets,

---

[49] See herein, p. 48 (Babylonians), pp. 76–77, and chapter 9, pp. 267–269 (housing).

[50] See herein, appendix, pp. 447–449 (distributions), chapter 6, pp. 188–199 (Greeks), chapter 3, p. 108 (America). The Lorenz curve is a graph used to plot the distribution of assets within a given population. Strong concentration among a few members causes the right-hand end of the curve to rise sharply.

they could typically expect nothing better than an existence at the margins of bare subsistence. Their position may even have deteriorated as the empire reached the peak of its power. For a long time, there had been no sign in the record that resettled subjects had been formally differentiated from the indigenous population: they were "counted together with the Assyrians." This phrase disappeared in the final phase of Assyrian conquests, from about 705 to 627 BCE, when great victories and ongoing expansion fostered a heightened sense of superiority. Deportees were downgraded to the status of forced laborers and employed in large public works projects.

Forced migration not only augmented the ranks of the poor but also added to the wealth and income of the upper class. Multiple texts mention the distribution of war captives at the court and to temples. When the last of the great conquerors, King Ashurbanipal (668–627 BCE), dragged in large numbers of deportees from Elam (now Khuzestan in southwestern Iran), he declared that "the choicest I presented unto my gods; . . . the soldiers . . . I added to my royal army; . . . the rest I divided like sheep among the capital cities, the abodes of the great gods, my officials, my nobles, the whole of my camp." Allocated captives were put to work on fields and orchards that had also been granted to officials, whereas others were settled on crown land. Practiced on a large scale, these arrangements simultaneously increased the share of workers in the population who had low income and no wealth and boosted the income of those near the top, a combination that could not fail to exacerbate inequality overall.[51]

Slavery produced similar results. The enslavement of outsiders was one of the few mechanisms capable of creating significant levels of inequality in foraging societies of small size and low or moderate complexity, not only among the aquatic foragers of the Pacific Northwest but across a wide range of tribal groups. Yet once again, it took domestication and state formation to boost the use of slave labor to new heights. Under the Roman Republic, several million slaves entered the Italian peninsula, where many of them were bought up by the wealthy to toil in their mansions, workshops, and agricultural estates. Two thousand years later, in the nineteenth century, in what is now Nigeria, the jihadist Sokoto Caliphate allocated enormous numbers of war captives to members of its political and military elite at exactly the same time when the "peculiar institution" was driving up material inequality in the Old South.[52]

[51] Oded 1979: 19, 21–22, 28, 35, 60, 78–79, 81–91, 112–113. See also herein, chapter 6, p. 200.

[52] Regarding slavery, see esp. Patterson 1982: 105–171 on the different modes of creating and acquiring slaves, Miller 2012 for slavery in global history, and Zeuske 2013 for the global history of slavery. For Rome, see Scheidel 2005a; for Sokoto, Lovejoy 2011; and for the United States, herein, p. 108.

Chapter 2

EMPIRES OF INEQUALITY

Disequalization had many fathers. The nature of productive assets and the way they were passed on to future generations, the size of the surplus beyond bare subsistence and the relative importance of commercial activity, and the supply of and demand for labor all interacted in complex and ever-changing ways to determine the distribution of material resources. The institutions that mediated this interplay were highly sensitive to the exercise of political and military power, to pressures and shocks that were ultimately rooted in the capacity to mobilize and employ violence. Characterized by stable and steep hierarchies and—at least by preindustrial standards—scoring high on key indices of social development such as energy capture, urbanization, information processing, and military capabilities, agrarian empires that were very large in size and that also endured for many generations provide the best insights into the dynamics of inequality in environments that were relatively well sheltered from significant violent disruptions. In this final respect, they represent the closest analogues to the Western world of the comparatively peaceful nineteenth century, a period of unprecedented economic and cultural transformation. As we will see, ancient empires and industrializing societies experienced very similar outcomes in terms of inequality in income and wealth. Civilizations that were separated by one and a half millennia or more and that had little in common beyond a shared experience of order, stability, and protected development sustained dramatic disparities in the distribution of material resources. Across time and different stages of economic development, the absence of major violent ruptures has been a vital precondition of high inequality.[1]

---

[1] Morris 2010 and 2013 observes relatively high levels of social development in agrarian empires. For the equivalence of preindustrial and early industrial inequality in both nominal and real terms, see herein, p. 101 and appendix, pp. 454–455.

I present two case studies to illustrate these premises: the Han and Roman empires, each of which, at the height of its power, claimed about a quarter of all people on earth. Ancient Rome has been labeled an empire of property in which wealth was created, above all, by acquiring land, whereas Chinese fortunes were made from officeholding rather than private investments. This contrast seems overblown: in both environments, political power was a critical source of income and wealth, inextricably intertwined with economic activity, and a powerful determinant of material inequality.[2]

EARLY CHINA

Following in the footsteps of the short-lived empire of Qin that had been the first to unite the earlier "Warring States," more than four centuries of Han rule (from 206 BCE to 220 CE) produced abundant evidence for the dynamics of the concentration of income and wealth in a fairly stable world empire: the conflict between rulers and elites over who controlled the land, its surplus and the rural labor force, and the economic and political forces that created and unmade large fortunes. Commercialization of farming was one factor: according to one account from the reign of the fifth Han emperor Wendi (180–157 BCE), smallholders who were forced to borrow money at high rates of interest lost their land (and sometimes even their own children, sold into slavery) to merchants and usurers who built up large estates they cultivated with the help of tenants, hired labor, or slaves.[3]

State rulers, who sought to preserve small-scale farmer-proprietors as the foundation of the fiscal and military conscription system, struggled to contain these pressures. On eleven occasions between 140 BCE and 2 CE, government land was distributed to the peasantry. Members of regional elites were compelled to relocate to the capital region not only as a way of ensuring their political loyalty but also to limit their power at the local level. When this practice fell into abeyance, it became even easier for the rich and well-positioned to accumulate assets by purchasing or occupying land and by dominating the poor. In 7 BCE, after generations of elite encroachment, top advisors at the court finally suggested legal restrictions to combat the concentration of landownership. However, measures

[2] Wood 2003: 26–32 proposes this ideal-typical contrast. For convergent developments and similarities between them, see Scheidel 2009a; Bang and Turner 2015. I provide a much more detailed discussion of inequality in these two empires in Scheidel 2016.
[3] For the Warring States reforms and their culture of mass mobilization, see herein, chapter 6, pp. 182–186.

that would have imposed an overall ceiling on elite land and slave holdings and envisioned confiscation of excess assets were swiftly derailed by powerful interests. Soon after, the usurper Wang Mang (9–23 CE) envisioned more energetic interventions. Later hostile sources attribute to him various grandiose schemes, from the nationalization of land to an end to the trade in slaves. Households were supposed to give up all land above a given limit to relatives and neighbors. Harking back to putative archaic traditions of periodic redistribution (known as the "well-field" system), regular adjustments of landownership were meant to ensure equitable conditions, and the sale of land, houses, and slaves was banned under penalty of death. Unsurprisingly, these regulations—inasmuch as they were indeed attempted and not merely invented or embellished by later Han propaganda—proved unenforceable and were soon abandoned. The new regime failed in short order as the Han, backed by landlords, successfully staged a comeback.[4]

Han sources preferentially attribute wealth acquisition through what we might call market activities to merchants, a class despised by the politically well-connected literati who generated the texts we now rely on. The historian Sima Qian described wealthy merchants as a class "commanding the services of the poor," and the largest fortunes attributed to them rivaled those of the most senior imperial officials. The imperial authorities consequently identified private commercial wealth as a target. Merchants were subject to higher taxes than were members of other professions. Fiscal intervention became much more aggressive under Emperor Wudi in the 130s BCE, when he embarked on costly military mobilization programs to confront the steppe empire of the Xiongnu to the north. Wudi established state monopolies on salt and iron. In so doing he not only captured profits previously pocketed by private entrepreneurs but also protected smallholders, who were needed as conscripts and taxpayers, from displacement by owners of merchant capital, who sought to invest in real estate. His government raised annual taxes on commercial property. Many large fortunes were supposedly wiped out. In keeping with the central thesis of this book, these equalizing measures were closely tied to mass mobilization warfare but petered out as the latter subsided.[5]

---

[4] Ch'ü 1972: 196–199; Hsu 1980: 31; Loewe 1986a: 205; Sadao 1986: 555–558. Wang Mang: Hsu 1980: 558; Sadao 1986: 558; Li 2013: 277.

[5] Merchants: Swann 1950: 405–464 (biographies); Ch'ü 1972: 115–116, 176; Sadao 1986: 576, 578 (activities). Sima Qian: Ch'ü 1972: 182–183. For Wudi's measures, see Hsu 1980: 40–41; Sadao 1986: 584, 599, 602, 604. On the scale of his military efforts, Barfield 1989: 54, 56–57; for his modernist policies in general, Loewe 1986a: 152–179. A second round of interventions was likewise rooted in violent turnover—namely, the usurpation of Wang Mang: Loewe 1986a: 232; Sadao 1986: 580, 606.

Measures against the concentration of commercial capital and its disequalizing social consequences ultimately remained unsuccessful not only because of discontinuities in policymaking but, above all, because merchants made sure to invest their gains in land to shield them from state demands. According to Sima Qian's *Shiji*, their strategy was

> to make riches through secondary occupations [e.g., trade] and preserve them by the fundamental occupation [i.e., farming].

Prohibitions could not prevent this: just as merchants could not effectively be barred from purchasing land, so they also managed to circumvent bans on joining the ranks of officialdom, and some rich entrepreneurs or their relatives even ascended to the titled nobility.[6]

Alongside economic activity, state service and, more generally, close proximity to the center of political power were the other principal sources of great wealth. High-ranking officials profited from imperial gifts and fiefs. Fiefholders were allowed to withhold a share of the poll taxes paid by the households that had been assigned to them. Great wealth accrued from favoritism and corruption: several imperial chancellors and other very senior officials were said to have accumulated wealth on a par with the largest recorded fortunes overall. In the later stages of the Eastern Han dynasty, the lucrative nature of top offices came to be reflected in the prices at which they could be purchased. Legal privilege shielded corrupt officials with growing generosity. Officials above a certain pay grade were not to be arrested without prior approval by the emperor, and similar protections extended to sentencing and punishment.[7]

Beyond investing their newfound wealth in legitimate ways, the well-connected also found it easy to bully and exploit commoners. Officials abused their powers by occupying public land or seizing it from others. The sources convey the default expectation that political power translated to durable material wealth in land, whether granted by the state or obtained through influence and coercion. Over time, these processes created an elite layer of titled nobles, officials, and favorites who formed coalitions and intermarried. The wealthy either held office

---

[6] Quote: Sadao 1986: 578 (*Shiji* 129); also 584 for manufacturers. Prohibition: Hsu 1980: 41–42; Sadao 1986: 577. Overlap with landlords and officials: Ch'ü 1972: 119–121, 181.

[7] Nominal salaries were relatively modest: Scheidel 2015c: 165–174. Favoritism: Hsu 1980: 46–53. Size of fortunes: Swann 1950: 463–464. Sale: Mansvelt Beck 1986: 332 (for 178 CE). Protection: Ch'ü 1972: 96–97.

themselves or were linked to those who did, and state service and connections to those who performed it in turn generated more personal wealth.[8]

These dynamics both favored and constrained familial continuity in wealth holding. On the one hand, the sons of high officials were more likely to follow in their footsteps. They and other junior relatives were automatically entitled to enter officialdom and benefited disproportionately from the recommendation system employed to fill governmental positions. We hear of officials among whose brothers and sons six or seven—in one case, no fewer than thirteen sons—also came to serve as imperial administrators. On the other hand, the same predatory and capricious exercise of political power that turned civil servants into plutocrats also undermined their success. Guan Fu, a highly placed government official, had accumulated a large fortune and owned so much land in his native region that widespread loathing of this preeminence inspired a local children's song:

> While the Ying River is clear the Guan family will be secure; when the Ying River is muddy the Guan family will be exterminated!

This ditty captured the precarious fortunes of the politically wealthy: more often than not, families that had risen high fell far. Risk extended to the very top of the status pyramid, to the families of the Han emperors' consorts.[9]

More systematic purges occurred across different elite strata. The founder of the Han dynasty had ennobled 165 followers to reward them with titles and income from fiefdoms, a group whose families came to monopolize high state office and amassed land. Under Wudi most of them were so thoroughly stripped of their titles and domains that by the time of the reign of his great-grandson Xuandi, it could be claimed that

> the descendants of the most celebrated meritorious generals were working as hired hands and in other servile statuses.

The top tier of the early Han elite thus did not last for much more than a century and was removed alongside the remnants of the ruling houses of the Warring

---

[8] Ch'ü 1972: 160–161, 175; Hsu 1980: 49, 54; Lewis 2007: 70.

[9] Ch'ü 1972: 94, 176–178 (continuities), and also 173–174 for specific families; Hsu 1980: 49 (principle of rise and fall).

States period. New favorites took their place. A century later, the usurper Wang Mang was keen to bring down and dispossess their descendants, and his own supporters were in turn supplanted by the followers of the Eastern Han dynasty. As a result of these multiple turnovers, only a few Western Han noble families were still visible later in the first century CE.[10]

The state class was rife with violent death and expropriation. Numerous holders of high offices were executed or forced to commit suicide. The biographies in the *Shiji* and *Hanshu* histories feature special sections on "harsh officials" who persecuted members of the ruling elite at the behest of their emperors. Many of those who were targeted lost their lives, and sometimes entire families were exterminated. Infighting between different segments of the state class likewise resulted in massive turnover and asset transfers. Within elite circles, this constant churn turned the pursuit of power and wealth into a zero-sum game: for some to gain, others had to lose. The dynamics of violent fortune-building and redistribution served as a constraint on the concentration of elite wealth: whenever a particular family or grouping pulled too far away from the rest, it was cut down as rivals took their turn.[11]

Yet although this prevented the emergence of a very few super-rich houses that might have preserved and expanded their positions and fortunes over the long term, it appears that the wealth and power elite as a whole kept gaining ground at the expense of the general population. Invasive state intervention abated over time, and the ascent of the Eastern Han prepared the ground for ever-higher inequality. The number of households held as fiefs by the twenty subkings of the Han, close relatives of the rulers, rose from 1.35 million in 2 CE to 1.9 million in 140 CE, equivalent to 11 percent and 20 percent of all households registered in imperial censuses. Although violent factionalism continued to claim lives and family fortunes as entire clans were slaughtered or driven into exile, the wealth class as a whole benefited from the new order. Instrumental in returning the Han to power, the great landowning families brought more and more land under their control and subordinated its cultivators through debt. Sources of the period refer to the elite practice of falsifying census accounts in order to conceal taxable assets. The decline in the number of registered households from more than 12 million in 2 CE to fewer than 10 million in 140

---

[10] On Wudi's purges, see Hsu 1980: 44–46 (quote from *Hanshu* 16:2b–3b); Ch'ü 1972: 164–165; Lewis 2007: 69, 120. Eastern Han: Loewe 1986b: 275.

[11] Ch'ü 1972: 97, 184, 200–202, 212–213, 218, 226, 228, 237–243; Loewe 1986b: 276–277, 289; Mansvelt Beck 1986: 328–329.

CE—at a time of expanding settlement in the southern reaches of the empire—thus reflects at least in part worsening noncompliance as landlords converted freeholders into landless tenants and shielded them from state agents.[12]

Under the Eastern Han, a more stable imperial elite appears to have formed, for social ascent into high ranks had come to be considered extraordinary. This closing of the ruling class is consistent with a growing number of cases of prolonged family prominence in producing senior officials over as many as six or seven generations, which left a few families overrepresented in the long run. Despite ongoing infighting and recirculation, we observe an underlying trend toward a more persistent concentration of both power and wealth. This process was accompanied by the formation of a more cohesive elite that was less dependent on officeholding. Privatization of wealth had finally reached levels that afforded more protection against predatory intervention even as dwindling state power rendered access to governmental positions less crucial. At the same time, polarization between landlords and tenants appears to have increased, with the latter entering arrangements of subordination beyond mere contractual obligations. As the imperial state unraveled, tenants morphed into retainers of powerful local (land-)lords. Dependent tenancy led to clientelism that supported private armies. In the third century CE, magnates became largely unchallengeable.[13]

The Han empire sustained an elite class made up of government officials, landlords, and commercial investors, groups whose membership showed considerable overlap and that competed for resources both among themselves and with others. Over the long term, the overarching theme is one of increasing concentration of landownership as the state's grip on subsistence producers weakened and rent crowded out tax. Prominent families became more powerful over time. The relationship of rulers and elites changed from centralized militaristic leadership under the Qin to a policy of accommodation under the Han that was sporadically interrupted only by aggressive ruler intervention. The restoration of the Han shifted the balance of power farther in favor of the wealth elite. The evolution of inequality was shaped by two factors: an extended period of peace that allowed the concentration of wealth at the expense of smallholders and

---

[12] State intervention: Lewis 2007: 67 (on conscription). Fiefdoms: Loewe 1986b: 257, 259. Landlords and Han line: Li 2013: 295; Lewis 2007: 69–70. For failed reform attempts, see Ch'ü 1972: 204; Hsu 1980: 55; Ebrey 1986: 619–621. Census: Li 2013: 297.

[13] Ebrey 1986: 635–637, 646 (social closure, elite autonomy); Hsu 1980: 56 (retainers); Lewis 2007: 263 (clientelism); Lewis 2009a: 135 (magnates).

ultimately even state rulers and ongoing predatory recirculation of the gains made by members of the elite class. The former pushed up inequality, whereas the latter slowed its rise. Yet by the second half of the Eastern Han period and the post-Han kingdoms of the third century CE, wealth concentration had won out.

The Han experience was merely the first iteration of what was to become a defining feature of the history of inequality in China. The violent dislocations that separated the main dynasties were bound to reduce some of the existing economic disparities. Land redistributions undertaken by new regimes would have contributed to this leveling but commonly gave way to recurring concentration of landownership, as under the dynasties of the Sui (from 581), Tang (from 618), Song (from 960), and Ming (from 1368). With each new dynasty, new elites of supporters were put in place that combined political influence and personal wealth. The aristocracy that was brought down at the end of the Tang period, a development I describe in chapter 9, had deep roots. A small number of prominent families were able to hold on to power for two or three centuries, enjoying privileged access to high office and amassing huge fortunes. Nobles, officials, and holders of official rank were generally exempt from taxation and labor services, which further precipitated the concentration of resources in their hands. Once again private land expanded at the expense of state holdings; once again landlords made peasant households under their control vanish from tax registers.

After the dramatic destruction of this class, an entirely new elite arose under the Song. Gifts by rulers created large estates and later efforts to provide farmers with cheap government loans soon faltered. Land concentration and clientelism expanded under the Southern Song; a belated attempt to cap estate sizes was met with elite hostility. The Mongol invaders rewarded leaders with generous land grants and operated a pension system for their rank and file. After Mongol landlords and officials had been expelled by the Ming, the new dynasty's founder, the Hongwu emperor, doled out large estates to his followers, who formed a new nobility; later attempts by him and his successors to reduce their endowments failed. On the contrary, elite holdings grew thanks to imperial largess, purchases, forcible encroachment, and commendation (whereby peasants ceded land to the rich to escape imperial taxation). In the pithy summary of a sixteenth-century source,

> South of the Yangzi, the poor and the rich rely on each other, the weak all commending their land.

Census falsification concealed the true extent of elite holdings. And once again, officeholding served as a pathway to wealth: the *Commentary to the Ming Code* bluntly stated that

> It is to be feared that many meritorious officials will use their power to obtain fields and mansions on a wide scale, and take possession of the population.

What we see is in some ways a rerun of processes that can be traced back to the Eastern Han period 1,500 years earlier:

> At the end of the Ming period the gentry had acquired numerous serfs, whom they held in hereditary subjection. There were almost no free commoners on the county. However, if a master's power ever grew weak they would kick over the traces and leave. Sometimes they would even rebelliously take possession of their masters' fields, seize their masters' possessions, and transfer their allegiance to some other person who had newly acquired rank. The original powerful family would enter a lawsuit over this, but the authorities would treat it solely on the basis of who was the strongest.[14]

The final dynasty, the Manchu Qing, which had confiscated and reallocated vast Ming estates to the imperial clan and others, was beset by a wide array of tax corruption schemes. Officials concealed embezzlement by fabricating arrears; exaggerated the scale of natural disasters that required tax exemptions; falsely declared barren status for their own land; borrowed tax advances from the rich, stole the money, and then applied the liabilities as arrears to commoners; reclassified land but collected taxes at the usual rate, pocketing the difference; and withheld or falsified receipts. Gentry and retired officials often paid no tax at all, with active officials and clerks passing the burden on to commoners in exchange for a cut of the profit. Finally, land was registered under as many as hundreds of false names, which made it too cumbersome to track down small arrears. Corruption by high officials was a standard mechanism of wealth accumulation,

---

[14] Land redistributions: Powelson 1988: 164, 166, 168, 171. (Similar attempts, modeled on China, were made in Vietnam: 290–292.) For the Tang, see herein, chapter 9, pp. 260–261. Song: Powelson 1988: 166–167. Ming: Elvin 1973: 235 (first quote), 236 (second quote), 240 (third quote, from a text from around 1800 regarding Shanghai county).

the more so the higher the rank. According to one estimate, average incomes of officials amounted to a dozen times their official, legal incomes in the form of salaries, rewards, and allowances, but well more than a hundred times for a governor-general and as much as 400,000 times in the case of He Shen, Grand Secretary of the Qing court in the second half of the eighteenth century. Executions and confiscations were employed as equally timeless countermeasures.[15]

Present-day China demonstrates the remarkable resilience of such practices. As a member of the Standing Committee of the Politburo, Zhou Yongkang was able to acquire 326 properties all over China worth $1.76 billion in addition to $6 billion deposited in hundreds of bank accounts that belonged to him and family members and securities worth another $8.24 billion. When he was arrested in December 2014, domestic and foreign banknotes worth $300 million were found in his various residences alongside stashes of gold. Thanks to his exalted rank, his exploits dwarf those of his rivals—his total wealth would have put him in the fifty-fifth spot in the Forbes World's Billionaires ranking for 2015—even though they tried hard: an entire ton of neatly boxed-up cash was discovered in one general's mansion and even a mid-level water-supply official in a resort town popular with party leaders managed to accumulate real estate and cash worth more than $180 million.[16]

THE ROMAN EMPIRE

But let us return one more time to the original "1 percent" of the ancient world. The evolution of Roman inequality in many ways resembles that of its Chinese counterpart, but the depth and richness of the evidence, from texts to archaeological remains, allows us to track the concentration of income and wealth in greater detail and relate it more closely to the rise and consolidation of imperial power. Quantitative information begins to flow from the second century BCE onward once Rome projected power well beyond the Italian peninsula and increasingly tapped into the resources of the Hellenistic kingdoms of the eastern Mediterranean. The size of aristocratic fortunes grew enormously as the empire expanded (Table 2.1).[17]

---

[15] Schemes: Zelin 1984: 241–246. Income multiples and countermeasures: Deng 1999: 217–219.

[16] Jacobs 2015; www.forbes.com/billionaires/.

[17] Shatzman 1975: 237–439 offers an exhaustive "economic prosopography" of the senatorial class from 200 to 30 BCE. For the early empire, see Duncan-Jones 1982: 343–344 and 1994: 39; for the fifth century CE, see herein, p. 78. The relevant individual fortunes are listed and discussed in Scheidel 2016. I standardize monetary valuations according to later denominations: 1,000 sesterces roughly equals the mean annual income for a family of four (for per capita GDP, see Scheidel and Friesen 2009: 91).

Table 2.1 The development of the largest reported fortunes in Roman society and the population under Roman control, second century BCE to fifth century CE

(a)

Period	Fortunes*	Multiple
Mid/late second century BCE	4–5 million	1
Early first century BCE	25 million	5
60s BCE	100 million	20
60s/50s BCE	200 million	40
First century CE	300–400 million	80
Early fifth century CE	350 million	70

(b)

Period	Population	Multiple
Early second century BCE	7–8 million	1
Mid-first century BCE	25 million	3
First/early fifth century CE	60–70 million	9

* Expressed in imperial-era sesterces

These numbers show that over the course of about five generations, the private wealth ceiling had risen by a factor of forty. On the most conservative assumptions, the aggregate wealth controlled by the senatorial class that governed the state increased by an order of magnitude between the second and the first centuries BCE. Inflation had been modest, and there is no sign that average per capita output or personal wealth among ordinary citizens had grown by more than a trivial fraction of the expansion experienced by upper-class fortunes. The Roman power set had therefore become vastly richer, not only in absolute but also in relative terms: the rate of growth of senatorial wealth considerably outpaced the concurrent increase in the number of people under Roman rule across the Mediterranean basin and its hinterlands. And elite enrichment extended farther into Roman society. By the first century BCE, at least 10,000 citizens and perhaps twice as many, most of them in Italy proper, cleared the census threshold of 400,000 sesterces for membership in the equestrian order, the next-highest rank after those of the senatorial class. Considering that personal fortunes of a few million had been exceptional just a few generations earlier, this shows that the lower reaches of the Roman ruling class also enjoyed considerable gains. Trends among common citizens remain obscure but would have been shaped by two disequalizing forces: strong urbanization, which generally tends to exacerbate inequality, and the creation of a slave population probably in excess of 1 million in Italy alone, which, being legally bereft of any private property and often, though not invariably, kept at subsistence incomes, can be expected to have widened economic disparities across society as a whole.[18]

Where did all the additional resources come from? Economic development grounded in market relations certainly picked up in the later stages of the Republican period. The use of slaves in cash crop production and manufacturing, as well as rich archaeological evidence for the export of wine and olive oil, points to the success of Roman capital owners. Yet this was only part of the story. Simple estimates of the likely scale of supply and demand suggest that landownership and related commercial activities could not have generated nearly enough income to make the Roman elite as rich as we know it became. And indeed, our sources emphasize the paramount significance of coercion as a source of top incomes and fortunes. Great wealth accrued from state administration outside Italy, and Roman-style governance was highly conducive to exploitation. Provincial administration was highly lucrative, and rent-seeking behavior was only weakly constrained by laws and courts set up to prosecute extortion; alliance-building and rent-sharing among the powerful provided insurance against indictment. Moreover, at a time when annual interest rates of 6 percent were common in Rome itself, wealthy Romans imposed rates of up to 48 percent on provincial cities, which were in desperate need of money to satisfy the demands of their governors. Members of the equestrian order benefited from the widespread practice of tax farming, as the right to collect certain taxes in a particular province were auctioned off to consortia that then proceeded to do what they could to turn a profit. Warfare was a similarly, if not more, important source of elite income. Roman commanders enjoyed complete authority over war booty and decided how to divide it among their soldiers, their officers and aides who had been drawn from the elite class, the state treasury, and themselves. Based on the number of military theaters and wars, it has been estimated that in the years between 200 and 30 BCE, at least a third

---

[18] For limited real income growth among commoners, see Scheidel 2007. The population figures are rough guesstimates. Equestrians: Scheidel 2006: 50. For the effects of urbanization, see herein, p. 93. Slaves: Scheidel 2005a.

of the 3,000-odd senators who lived in this period had a chance to enrich themselves in this fashion.[19]

When in the 80s BCE the Republican system entered a half-century of terminal instability, violent internal conflict created new fortunes by forcibly redistributing existing elite wealth. At the time, more than 1,600 members of the Roman ruling class—senators and equestrians—fell victim to proscription, a form of politically motivated outlawing that cost them their assets and often their lives as well. Supporters of the victorious faction profited from snapping up devalued confiscated assets at auction. Violent redistribution accelerated during the more sustained civil wars of the 40s and 30s BCE. In 42 BCE, another round of proscriptions wiped out more than 2,000 elite households. As a result of these dislocations and the ascent of newcomers who rode the warlords' coattails, Roman high society experienced its first great turnover since the beginning of the Republic. Families who had dominated the scene for centuries finally fell from power as others took their place. As the Roman Republic unraveled, it began to display features typical of monarchical regimes such as we just observed at some length in the case of Han China, including elite gains and losses from bloody internal power struggles and politically induced discontinuity in elite fortunes.[20]

The fall of the Republic led to the establishment of a permanent military dictatorship that preserved the outward trappings of Republican institutions. Great wealth now flowed from proximity to the new rulers—the emperors—and their court. Six personal fortunes of between 300 million and 400 million sesterces are reported for the first century CE, in excess of anything known from the Republican period: built up by top courtiers, most of them were eventually absorbed by the treasury. Recirculation of elite wealth took many forms. Aristocratic allies and favorites were often expected to include rulers in their wills. The first emperor Augustus claimed to have received 1.4 billion sesterces in legacies from his friends over the course of twenty years. Under his successors, the annals of Rome record a never-ending string of executions for treasonous acts

---

[19] For economic development, see, most recently, Kay 2014. Estimates of income sources: Rosenstein 2008, preceded by Shatzman 1975: 107, who observed, "It is obvious that income from agriculture was negligible in comparison with profits accruing from a senatorial career." Income of governors, lenders, and tax farmers: Shatzman 1975: 53–63, 296–297, 372, 409, 413, 429–437. Warfare: 63–67, 278–281, 378–381. Tan forthcoming analyzes the structure of elite incomes and the fiscal system of this period.

[20] Shatzman 1975: 37–44, 107, 268–272; Scheidel 2007: 332. For large estates created by the first round of proscriptions, see Roselaar 2010: 285–286.

and schemes, real or imagined, and confiscations of elite fortunes. The recorded or implied scale of confiscations at the top of Roman society, on the order of several percent of total elite wealth during some emperors' reigns, speaks to the ferocity of violent redistribution among the very rich. In the final analysis, largess and retrieval were simply two sides of the same process whereby rulers made and unmade elite fortunes in accordance with political calculations.[21]

More traditional varieties of political enrichment persisted under autocracy. Provincial governors were now paid up to 1 million sesterces a year for their good services but continued to extract great wealth on the side: one governor entered the province of Syria as a *pauper* and left it *dives* (rich) two years later. A century on, a governor of southern Spain unwisely bragged in his correspondence that he had extorted 4 million sesterces from his provincials and had even sold some of them into slavery. Much farther down the food chain, an imperial slave overseeing the imperial treasury in Gaul commanded the services of sixteen underslaves, two of whom were in charge of his apparently extensive set of silverware.[22]

Imperial unification and connectivity facilitated the expansion and concentration of personal wealth. Under Nero, six men were said to have owned "half" of the province of Africa (centered on modern Tunisia), albeit only until he seized their properties. While clearly hyperbolic, this claim need not have been dramatically far from the truth in a region where large estates could be described as rivaling city territories in size. The richest provincials joined the central imperial ruling class, eager to claim rank and attendant privilege and capitalize on the opportunities for further enrichment they offered. A survey of Roman literature has found that epithets of wealth were almost exclusively applied to senators of consular rank, who enjoyed the most favor and the best access to additional riches. Formal status ordering was grounded in financial capacity, and membership in the three orders of the state class—senators, knights, and decurions—was tied to staggered census thresholds.[23]

---

[21] Fortunes of supporters: Shatzman 1975: 400, 437–439; Mratschek-Halfmann 1993: 78, 97, 111, 160–161. For the emperors' assets, see Millar 1977: 133–201. Mratschek-Halfmann 1993: 44 (Augustus). Scale of confiscations: 52–54; Burgers 1993. Hopkins 2002: 208 aptly writes that by seizing and handing out wealth, emperors created "replacement aristocrats." Total national wealth and elite wealth conjectured from Scheidel and Friesen 2009: 74, 76 and Piketty 2014: 116–117 figs. 3.1–2, using 1700 France and England as analogs for national wealth as a multiple of annual GDP.

[22] Mratschek-Halfmann 1993: 106–107, 113–114, 214; *Inscriptiones Latinae Selectae* 1514.

[23] Mratschek-Halfmann 1993: 53, 58, 138–139; Hopkins 2002: 205.

This intimate association of personal wealth and political power was faithfully replicated at the local level. The mature Roman empire consisted of some 2,000 largely self-governing urban or differently organized communities that were loosely overseen—and opportunistically fleeced—by itinerant governors and small cadres of elite officials and imperial freedmen and slaves who were mostly concerned with fiscal matters. Each city was normally run by a council that represented the local wealth elite. These bodies, whose members were formally constituted as decurions, were in charge not only of local taxation and expenditure but also of assessing their communities' wealth for Roman state taxation, and they were responsible for raising funds that were to be handed over to collectors and tax farmers. If the rich archaeological and epigraphical evidence of generous civic spending in this period is anything to go by, these elites knew how to protect their own assets from the distant imperial center and retain much of the surplus at home, whether in their own pockets or to sustain public amenities.[24]

The gradual concentration of local wealth is well reflected in the remains of one of the best-known of all Roman cities, Pompeii, which was buried by the ashes of Mount Vesuvius in 79 CE. In addition to numerous inscriptions mentioning officeholders and the owners of produce assets, much of the housing stock at the time of destruction has survived, and on occasion we have even been able to identify the residents of particular buildings. The Pompeian elite consisted of an inner core of wealthy citizens who enjoyed privileged access to local offices. Stratification is also visible in the urban structure. The city contained around fifty grand mansions equipped with spacious atriums, colonnaded courtyards, and multiple dining rooms, as well as at least a hundred lesser upscale residences down to the threshold set by the smallest known residence of a member of the city council. This meshes well with the presence of around a hundred elite families known from the textual record, perhaps only part of whom belonged to the governing council at any given time. Broadly speaking, in a community of 30,000 or 40,000 (including the city's territory), 100 to 150 elite families and fancy urban residences would have represented the top 1 percent or 2 percent of local society. These families combined agricultural estates in the city's territory with urban manufacturing and trade; elite mansions regularly contained shops and other commercial premises.

The trend toward concentrating urban real estate in ever fewer hands is particularly striking. Archaeological investigation has revealed that all of the grand

<hr>

[24] Scheidel 2015a: 234–242, 250–251.

houses and many of the second-tier structures had been created by absorbing several smaller previous dwellings. Over time, a fairly egalitarian distribution of housing (and thus perhaps also wealth), arguably associated with the forcible settlement of Roman veterans in 80 BCE, gradually gave way to growing inequality, mostly at the expense of middling households, who got squeezed out of the urban fabric. As a culture of military mass mobilization and top-down redistribution was replaced by stable autocracy, polarization followed. High mortality and partible inheritance failed to disperse assets and flatten the social pyramid but merely served to recirculate wealth within elite circles.[25]

Archaeological evidence for Roman housing more generally indicates that stratification intensified under Roman rule. As I discuss in more detail in chapter 9, the distribution of residential house sizes in Britain and North Africa was more unequal in the Roman period than it had been before, and depending on our choice of data set the same may also have been true in Italy itself. This is not surprising: although the empire brought disproportionate benefits to those at or near the levers of power, it also favored the accumulation and concentration of wealth among wider elite circles. During the first 250 years of the monarchy, disruptive wars and other conflicts were extremely rare by historical standards. Imperial peace provided a protective shell for capital investment. Except for those at the very top, the wealthy were relatively secure in the possession and transmission of their properties.[26]

The net result was an intensely stratified society in which the richest 1 percent or 2 percent absorbed much of the available surplus beyond bare subsistence. It is possible to quantify Roman imperial inequality at least in rough outlines. At the peak of its development in the mid-second century CE, an empire of some 70 million people generated an annual GDP of close to the equivalent of 50 million tons of wheat, or approaching 20 billion sesterces. The corresponding mean per capita GDP of $800 in 1990 International Dollars appears plausible in relation to other premodern economies. According to my own reconstruction, the households of some 600 senators, 20,000 or more

---

[25] Mouritsen 2015 provides a succinct summary. See also Jongman 1988, esp. 108–112 (population), 207–273 (social inequality). A large share of the population of the neighboring city of Herculaneum appears to have consisted of slaves and ex-slaves: De Ligt and Garnsey 2012.

[26] House sizes: see herein, chapter 9, pp. 267–269, and, more specifically, Stephan 2013: 82, 86 (Britain), 127, 135 (Italy, with conflicting results for two different data sets), 171, 182 (North Africa). Skeletal remains still await fine-grained analysis to determine whether inequality in human body height also increased under the Romans. For the income sources of senators and knights, see Mratschek-Halfmann 1993: 95–127, 140–206; cf. also Andermahr 1998 for senatorial landownership in Italy.

knights, 130,000 decurions, and another 65,000 to 130,000 unranked wealthy families added up to a total of a quarter of a million households having an aggregate income of 3 billion to 5 billion sesterces. In this scenario, about 1.5 percent of all households captured between a sixth and close to a third of total output. These numbers may well underestimate their actual share, because they derive income from putative return on estimated wealth; political rents would drive up elite income even higher.

Although the distribution of income below elite circles is even more difficult to assess, a conservative range of assumptions points to an overall Gini coefficient of income in the low 0.4s for the empire as a whole. This value is much higher than it might seem. Because average per capita GDP amounted to only about twice minimum subsistence net of tax and investment, the projected level of Roman income inequality was not far below the maximum that was actually feasible at that level of economic development, a feature shared by many other premodern societies. Measured against the share of GDP that was available for extraction from primary producers, Roman inequality was therefore extremely severe. At most a tenth of the population beyond the wealth elite would have been able to enjoy incomes well above bare subsistence levels.[27]

Top incomes were so large that portions of them must have been reinvested, thereby further increasing the concentration of wealth. Power asymmetries may have compelled provincials to sell some of their land to pay taxes, a practice that we cannot even begin to quantify but that would help explain the emergence of transregional networks of aristocratic landownership in later centuries. This raises the question of whether or when Roman inequality reached a ceiling. Much depends on how much weight we are prepared to put on a clearly hyperbolic account from the 420s CE. Olympiodorus, a historian from Egypt, ascribes fantastical wealth to the leading families of Rome's aristocracy, "many" of whom supposedly took in 4,000 pounds of gold per year from their estates and a third as much again in kind, whereas those in the second tier could count on 1,000 or 1,500 pounds of gold per year. Converted into the currency of the earlier monarchy, the top income of 5,333 pounds of gold equals about 350 million sesterces in the first century CE, on a par with the very largest fortunes reported at that time. It appears that at the very top, a wealth plateau had first

[27] Scheidel and Friesen 2009: 63–74, 75–84 (income distribution and state share), 86–87 (Gini and extraction rate), 91 (GDP). Cf. also Milanovic, Lindert, and Williamson 2011: 263 table 2 for a Roman income Gini coefficient in the high 0.3s and an extraction rate of 75 percent. For other societies, see ibid. and herein, p. 100. For economically middling Romans, see Scheidel 2006; Mayer 2012.

been reached with the creation of the monarchy around the beginning of the Common Era and then persisted, with some fluctuations, until Roman power in the West finally unraveled in the course of the fifth century CE.[28]

At the same time, there are indications that inequality may have further intensified at the local and regional level as traditional urban elites came under growing pressure. Local wealth elites consequently came to be polarized between a minority that benefited from membership in supracommunal bodies and a large majority that did not. Some of the best evidence for this process comes from late Roman Egypt. Extant papyrus documents show how the established urban ruling class that had persisted into the fourth century CE was undermined as some of its members pulled away by holding state offices that brought exemptions from local fiscal obligations and enhanced opportunities for personal enrichment. By the sixth century CE, this kind of upward mobility appears to have put in place a new provincial aristocracy in Egypt that controlled large parts of the arable land and key positions in regional governance. A classic example is the house of the Apiones, a family that originated in the decurional order but that saw some of its members occupy some of the highest state offices and that eventually controlled more than 15,000 acres of highly productive land, much of which was concentrated in a single district of Egypt. And this need not have been an isolated phenomenon: one man may have controlled more than 23,000 acres of land in a single town in Italy in 323 CE. The tentacular holdings of the super-rich that extended across much of the empire were thus complemented by growing concentration of landownership at the communal and regional level.[29]

Another process, also well known from Chinese history, contributed to rising inequality. In different parts of the later Roman empire, we hear of farmers who sought protection by powerful landlords (as well as officials) who assumed responsibility for their dealings with the outside world, most notably imperial

---

[28] Investment and land acquisition: Jongman 2006: 249–250. Olympiodorus: Wickham 2005: 162; Brown 2012: 16–17; Harper 2015a: 56–58, 61 (plateau). If the later empire was poorer, the reported fortunes would indeed have been larger in relative terms: yet although this cannot be ruled out, there is little to support the notion of a precipitous decline in average per capita GDP as conjectured by Milanovic 2010: 8 and 2016: 67–68, esp. 68 fig. 2.9; cf. herein, p. 88. For the collapse of the western Roman aristocracy, see herein, chapter 9, pp. 264–266.

[29] Egypt: Palme 2015, with Harper 2015a: 51. For earlier land concentration in Roman Egypt, see herein, chapter 11, p. 325. Italy: Champlin 1980, with Harper 2015a: 54. More detailed land registers from the fourth-century CE Aegean document smaller holdings of not more than 1,000 acres: Harper 2015a: 52 table 3.6. Super-rich: Wickham 2005: 163–165.

tax collectors. In practice, this interfered with the gathering of state revenue and strengthened landlords' grip on the agrarian surplus. This in turn not only weakened the central authorities but also shifted fiscal burdens to less powerful parties, much to the detriment of middling property owners. Once again, further polarization between rich and poor was an almost inevitable outcome, and just as in late Han China, private armies and incipient warlordism were not always far behind. Over time, stratification and material inequality appear to have become even more extreme overall. What middle ground there may have been earlier was squeezed by the concentration of income and wealth within a politically powerful elite. After Rome and the western half of the empire were taken over by Germanic leaders, inequality may even have continued to rise in what remained of the empire in the eastern Mediterranean, up to the extraordinary levels estimated for the Byzantine empire around 1000 CE. The longer it lasted, the more tributary empire, with its characteristic intertwining of political and economic power and the polarizing outcomes it fostered, proved to be a relentless engine of disequalization.[30]

PATTERNS OF EMPIRE

Underneath their institutional and cultural differences, the empires of China and Rome shared a logic of surplus appropriation and concentration that generated high levels of inequality. Imperial rule mobilized flows of resources that were capable of enriching those at the levers of power on a scale that would have been unimaginable in smaller settings. The degree of inequality was therefore at least in part a function of the sheer scale of imperial state formation. Building on mechanisms of capital investment and exploitation that had first been developed thousands of years earlier, these empires raised the stakes ever higher. Greater profits were to be had from state office; lowered transaction costs for trade and investment over long distances benefited those who had income to spare. In the end, imperial income inequality and wealth polarization could be terminated and reversed only by dismemberment through conquest, state failure, or wholesale systems collapse, all of them intrinsically violent upheavals. The premodern historical record is silent on peaceful ways of combating entrenched imperial inequalities, and it is hard to see how any such strategies could have arisen within these specific political ecologies. Yet even imperial

---

[30] Byzantine inequality: Milanovic 2006.

collapse was more often than not merely a reset, paving the way for another wave of scaling up and polarization.

Inasmuch as inequality could be contained within intact imperial polities, it was by means of violent recirculation of assets within the elite. I have already mentioned the case of Mamluk Egypt (1250–1571), in which this principle played out in maybe its purest historically documented form. The sultan, his amirs, and their slave soldiers shared the proceeds of conquest: they formed an ethnically separate and spatially detached ruling class bent on extracting rents from the subordinate indigenous population, which was brutalized if revenue flows failed to meet expectations. Incessant jockeying for power within this class determined individual incomes, and violent conflict frequently altered these allocations. Local property owners sought refuge in extortion rackets that had them cede responsibility for their assets to strongmen from the Mamluk caste and pay fees in exchange for protection from taxation, a practice backed by elites, who took their cut. Rulers responded by increasingly resorting to out-right confiscation of elite wealth.[31]

The mature Ottoman empire had perfected more sophisticated strategies of forcible redistribution. For four centuries, sultans executed and expropriated thousands of state officials and contractors without judicial proceedings. During the early days of conquest in the fourteenth and fifteenth centuries, a nobility had formed as an alliance of warrior families with the house of Osman, which later incorporated warrior elites from elsewhere. Increasingly absolutist rule from the fifteenth century onward curtailed aristocratic power as the sultan asserted authority. Lowborn patrimonial personnel drawn from slaves replaced scions of noble families as officials. Even though these families continued to compete for office and power, eventually all state officials, regardless of their social background, came to be regarded as bereft of personal rights vis-à-vis the ruler. Officeholding was to be nonhereditary, and officials' assets were considered prebendal, in effect appurtenances of service rather than private property. When they died, gains made during office were to be deducted from their estates and absorbed by the treasury. In practice, all their possessions might be seized for the simple reason that officeholding and wealth were deemed indistinguishable. Confiscations at the time of death were complemented by the liquidation and expropriation of current officials who had attracted the sultan's attention. Elite members sought to resist this encroachment as best they could, and by

---

[31] Borsch 2005: 24–34 for the Mamluk system; Meloy 2004 for the rackets.

the seventeenth century some families had been able to preserve their fortunes for generations. In the eighteenth century, local elites became more powerful as offices and functions were increasingly leased out, which led to widespread privatization of the state administration and allowed officials to consolidate their wealth and standing. The center was no longer able to seize assets the same way as it had done before, and property rights stabilized to some extent. Confiscations returned one more time in the late eighteenth and early nineteenth centuries under the pressures of war, triggering resistance and avoidance strategies. In 1839 the Ottoman elite finally decided this contest in its favor when the sultan guaranteed life and property. As in other empires, Rome and Han China among them, the central state's ability to reshuffle the wealth of the ruling class had gradually eroded over time.[32]

In other cases, rulers were too weak or remote to interfere with wealth concentration in elite circles. The Spanish takeover of established imperial polities in Mesoamerica and the Andes is a particularly instructive example. In the course of the Reconquista in Spain, land was granted to nobles and knights who then enjoyed jurisdiction over its residents. Spanish conquerors subsequently extended this system to their New World territories, where similar practices were already in place: as we saw above, the Aztecs had set up coercive and extractive institutions that included land grants to elites, serfdom, and slavery. In Mexico, the conquistadores and later nobles quickly seized huge tracts of land, which were often confirmed as royal grants only after they had already been occupied. Hernán Cortés's lands in Oaxaca were put in entail in 1535 and remained in his family for 300 years, eventually encompassing 15 villas, 157 pueblos, 89 haciendas, 119 ranchos, 5 estancias, and 150,000 residents. Notwithstanding royal decrees that sought to limit the duration of such grants (known as encomiendas), they effectively turned into permanent and indeed hereditary holdings that sustained a small class of super-rich landlords. Encomenderos countered bans on forced labor by maneuvering locals into debt servitude in order to control their labor. Over time, this allowed them to carve more durable haciendas out of the original sprawling and diverse encomiendas, coherent estates that were worked by peons who divided their time between household plots and domain land and that de facto formed miniature states under the despotic control of landlords. Later changes were limited to the top,

---

[32] Yaycioglu 2012; and see also Ze'evi and Buke 2015 for the banishment, dismissal, and confiscation of the possessions of the highest officials (pashas).

most notably when Mexican independence in 1821 resulted in the ejection of Spanish hacendados and their replacement by local elites who largely preserved existing institutions. Landownership became even more concentrated during the nineteenth century, leading up to the revolution described in chapter 8.[33]

Much the same happened in Peru, where the Inca empire had likewise granted land and revenue to elite families and high officials. Francisco Pizarro and his officers were given the first encomiendas, and he himself claimed the right to assign land and control over its cultivators. Large tracts of land were awarded in this peremptory manner, and local residents were moved to the mines, both in contravention of royal injunctions. Some redistribution occurred only when Pizarro's resistance to imposing caps of land grants goaded him into an unsuccessful rebellion. Even so, land and wealth concentration became even more extreme than in Mexico, with around 500 encomiendas taking up much of the soil. Some of the rich silver lodes of Potosí were also awarded to favorites and worked by tributary Indians. Local tribal leaders cooperated by delivering their own villagers for work service and were appointed managers in return, sometimes even receiving their own estates. In characteristic imperial fashion, collusion between foreign and local elites ensured economic polarization and exploitation of the general population. Over time, illegal engrossment became legalized, just as it had been in Mexico. Bolivarian land redistribution after independence from Spain failed, and in the nineteenth century, even the communal lands of the indigenous people were absorbed into larger estates.[34]

It was not only in colonial contexts that power elites were able to hold on to fortunes they had acquired through political office or connections. To name just one example, in early modern France, those closest to the throne managed to leverage their influence into huge personal wealth that they retained after death and even dismissal. As the top minister of King Henri IV and his superintendent of finances for eleven years until the king's death in 1611, Maximilien de Béthune, Duke of Sully, survived his subsequent dismissal by thirty years and left more than 5 million livres, equivalent to the annual income of 27,000 unskilled laborers in Paris at the time. Cardinal Richelieu, who occupied a comparable position from 1624 to 1642, amassed four times as much wealth. Yet both were put in the shade by his handpicked successor, Cardinal Mazarin, who served from 1642 to 1661 and survived two years of exile during the Fronde risings of

---

[33] Powelson 1988: 84–85, 220–229; herein, chapter 8, pp. 241–242.
[34] Powelson 1988: 234–239.

1648 to 1653 but nevertheless left behind 37 million livres or 164,000 years' worth of unskilled wages. Comrade Zhou Yongkang of the Communist Party of China's politburo would have approved. Less powerful ministers also made out like bandits: Richelieu's ally Claude de Bullion obtained 7.8 million livres during eight years as finance minister, and Nicolas Fouquet, who held the same position for the same length of time, was assessed at 15.4 million when arrested in 1661, albeit with debts equaling assets. Such figures compare well with the largest aristocratic fortunes: in this period, the Princes de Conti, a branch of the ruling Bourbon family, were worth 8 million to 12 million livres. Even the aggressive Sun King Louis XIV enjoyed only moderate success in reining in later ministers: it took Jean-Baptiste Colbert eighteen years in charge of France's treasury to make a comparatively meager 5 million, and François Michel Le Tellier, Marquis de Louvois, had to labor for twenty-five years as minister of war to put aside 8 million. It seems that the best that could be achieved was to reduce a minister's takings from 1 million or 2 million per year to something closer to a few hundred thousand.[35]

Many more cases from around the world could easily be added but the basic point is clear. In premodern societies, very large fortunes regularly owed more to political power than to economic prowess. They differed mostly in terms of their durability, which was critically mediated by state rulers' ability and willingness to engage in despotic intervention. Intense resource concentration at the very top and high inequality were a given, and although wealth mobility varied, this was of little concern to those outside plutocratic circles. Sketched out in the opening chapter, the structural properties of almost all premodern states strongly favored a particular coercion-rich mode of income and wealth concentration that tended to maximize inequality over time. As a result, these entities were often about as unequal as they could be. As I set out in more detail in the appendix at the end of this book, rough estimates for twenty-eight preindustrial societies from Roman times to the 1940s yield an average extraction rate of 77 percent, a rate that measures the actualized proportion of the maximum amount of income inequality that was theoretically possible at a given level of per capita GDP. Exceptions were rare: the only reasonably well documented case is that of classical Athens in the fifth and fourth centuries BCE, where direct democracy and a culture of military mass mobilization (described in chapter 6) helped contain economic inequality. If modern estimates based

---

[35] Turchin and Nefedov 2009: 172–173; with http://gpih.ucdavis.edu/files/Paris_1380–1870.xls (wages).

on scant ancient evidence can be trusted, Athenian per capita GDP in the 330s BCE was relatively high for a premodern economy—maybe four to five times minimum physiological subsistence, similar to fifteenth-century Holland and sixteenth-century England—and the market income Gini coefficient reached around 0.38. By premodern standards, the implied extraction rate of about 49 percent was exceptionally modest.[36]

But the Athenian anomaly was not to last. In the heyday of the Roman empire, the richest man in Athens was the appropriately expansively named Lucius Vibullius Hipparchus Tiberius Claudius Atticus Herodes, who claimed descent from famous politicians of the fifth century BCE and indeed from the god Zeus himself. His more recent family was one of Athenian aristocrats who had acquired Roman citizenship, risen to high public office, and acquired a large fortune, perhaps not much smaller than those of the wealthiest individuals in Rome itself. His name points to a connection to the patrician Claudian clan of Rome that had ultimately produced several emperors. Herodes's family had even shared a typical experience of the Roman upper class when his grandfather Hipparchus's fortune—once casually put at 100 million sesterces—was confiscated by the emperor Domitian but (somewhat mysteriously) recovered later. Herodes showered Greek cities with benefactions and sponsored public buildings, most famously the Odeon theater in Athens. If he indeed owned 100 million—equivalent to two dozen times the largest private fortune known from the classical period—his annual capital income alone would have been enough to cover a third of Athens's total state expenditure back in the 330s BCE out of his own pocket—warships, government, festivals, welfare, public construction, and all—but he may well have been worth even more. Having become close to the emperor Antoninus Pius as a tutor of his adopted sons and successors, Herodes was the first Greek known to have held the highest traditional Roman state office, that of ordinary consul, in 143 CE. Imperial patronage and inequality had carried the day.

---

[36] 28 societies: Milanovic, Lindert, and Williamson 2011: 263 table 2, and herein, Appendix, pp. 447–448. Athens in the 330s BCE: using conversions of 1 drachma = 7.37 kg of wheat = $8.67 in 1990 International Dollars, per capita GDP and the income Gini were $1,647 and 0.38 according to Ober 2016: 8, 22; and see 9 for the extraction rate. Cf. Ober 2015a: 91–93; 2015b: 502–504 for values of $1,118/0.45 ("pessimistic" scenario) and $1,415/0.4 ("optimistic"). Comparanda from Milanovic, Lindert, and Williamson 2011: 263 table 2; Maddison project. Although the Milanovic, Lindert, and Williamson data set casts doubt on the notion of discrepant inequality experiences for monarchies and republics as conjectured by Boix 2015: 258–259, the case of classical Athens may lend some support to his model as long as we focus on the contrast between direct democracies and other forms of government.

Chapter 3

UP AND DOWN

TWIN PEAKS

How did economic inequality change in the long run? So far I have covered the early stages of this process. Power inequality and hierarchy emerged with the African Apes many millions of years ago and was gradually attenuated during the evolution of *Homo* over the last 2 million years or so. Holocene domestication produced an upswing in inequality of both power and wealth that peaked with the formation of the large predatory states already described. It is now time to zoom in on specific parts of the globe to see whether the evolution of income and wealth inequality has more generally followed a pattern that can be explained by particular disequalizing and leveling forces. My goal is to substantiate key arguments of this book: that increases in inequality were driven by the interaction of technological and economic development and state formation, as well as that effective leveling required violent shocks that at least temporarily curtailed and reversed the disequalizing consequences of capital investment, commercialization, and the exercise of political, military, and ideological power by predatory elites and their associates.

In my survey, which will take us all the way to the early twentieth century, I focus on Europe for the entirely pragmatic reason that in the aggregate and in the long run, European societies have produced the richest—or at least the most thoroughly researched—evidence for the evolution of material inequality up to the modern period. It is this evidence that makes it possible to reconstruct, at least in broad outlines, the repeated shifts between rising or stable inequality and equalizing shocks over the course of millennia (Fig. 3.1).

Farming appeared in Europe from 7000 BCE and spread widely within the following three millennia. Very broadly speaking, this fundamental economic

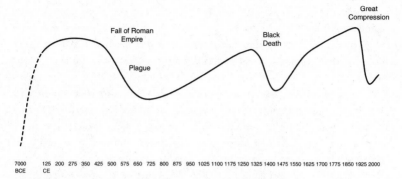

Figure 3.1   Inequality trends in Europe in the long run

transformation was bound to be accompanied by a gradual increase in inequality, even if we cannot expect to be able to trace this process in detail. It would be unwise to envision a straightforward linear trajectory: archaeological finds such as those at Varna indicate that short-term variation could be quite considerable. But if we take not one but three steps back to expand our survey from hundreds to thousands of years, we may safely posit an overarching upward trend as population densities increased, governance strengthened, and surpluses grew.

From this lofty vantage point, we are able to locate the first secular peak in material inequality in the period of the mature Roman empire in the first few centuries CE. In most of Europe, no comparable levels of population, urbanism, private wealth, and coercive capacity had before been reached. Greece is the only exception: thanks to its geographical proximity to the ancestral Near Eastern civilizational core, state-level development reached back farther in time than elsewhere in Europe. High levels of inequality had already been attained in the Mycenaean Late Bronze Age and probably peaked in the thirteenth century BCE. State collapse greatly reduced these disparities in the following centuries as palaces gave way to hamlets, a violent unraveling I discuss in chapter 9. Although the Greek city-state culture of the archaic and classical periods (about 800–300 BCE) achieved much higher levels of economic development (in some cases higher even than in most of the Roman world), institutions rooted in military mass mobilization restrained inequality. Yet just as elsewhere in Europe, the Roman period was a time of greatly increased inequality in this region as well.[1] Leaving aside for the moment the southern Balkans, which remained under the (sometimes shaky) control of the Byzantine continuation of the Roman empire, all other parts of Europe that had been subject to Roman rule underwent a severe compression in income and wealth inequality that commenced as Roman power disintegrated in the second half of the fifth century CE. As I show in chapter 9, this economic equalization was in large measure the direct result of state failure, a massive violent shock further reinforced by western Eurasia's first pandemic of bubonic plague from the sixth to the eighth centuries, which raised the value of labor relative to land. We have to allow for considerable variation in time and space: leveling may have been at its most thorough in post-Roman Britain, where earlier institutions and infrastructure were largely swept away, whereas inequalities may have proven more resilient in more sheltered regions such as the Iberian peninsula under Visigothic rule. Even so, the unraveling of far-flung elite exchange networks, urbanism, fiscal structures, and transregional wealth holdings was a ubiquitous process.[2]

It seems unwise even to try to put numbers on this great compression: difficult as it is to estimate Gini coefficients for the Roman empire, it would seem much harder still to devise them for the sub-Roman societies of the sixth, seventh, or eighth centuries. Suffice it to note that two downward pressures coincided: the shrinkage of per capita surpluses that reduced the scope for inequality and the dwindling of the extractive capacities of states and elites. Even Byzantine Greece was heavily affected by violent dislocations that were likely to mitigate existing disparities. For a while, Constantinople, the easternmost outpost of European urbanism at the time, may have been the last remaining bastion of imperial-style inequality, and even this well-defended center suffered a period of serious decline.[3]

European economies and polities began to recover at different times. The Carolingian expansion in the eighth century may be viewed as a period

---

[1] For Varna, see herein, pp. 40–41. For the Mycenaean collapse, see herein, chapter 9, pp. 270–273. For classical Greece, see herein, chapter 6, pp. 188–199. We must also allow for variation within the Roman world: the western part of the empire in the fourth and early fifth centuries arguably may have represented the pinnacle of inequality at the time: see herein, p. 78.

[2] State collapse: herein, chapter 9, pp. 264–269. Plague: herein, chapter 11, pp. 319–326.

[3] For what seems to me an overly imaginative attempt to track the late and post-Roman decline in income inequality, see Milanovic 2010: 8 and 2016: 67–68. For conditions in Constantinople in this period, see Mango 1985: 51–62; Haldon 1997: 115–117.

of resurgent inequality, as may the Muslim conquest of Spain. In Britain, the post-Roman nadir gave way to state formation under Essex leadership and the formation of a powerful and wealthy nobility. Byzantium, a society dominated by magnates, reasserted control over the Balkans in the ninth and tenth centuries. Aristocracies that had generally weakened after the fall of Rome once again gathered strength. Allowing for considerable geographical variation, feudalism's prominence from the ninth century onward gave elites greater control over the agrarian labor force and its surplus, a process that coincided with ongoing concentration of land among secular and church leaders. Europe subsequently experienced a phase of sustained economic and demographic growth from about 1000 to 1300. The presence of more people, more and bigger cities, more commerce, and more powerful elites all drove up economic inequality.

English inequality rose throughout this period. Whereas the Domesday Book survey of 1086 shows that most peasant households held enough land to achieve income above subsistence from their own plots alone, the Hundred Rolls survey of 1279 to 1280 suggests that most of their descendants could hope to break even only by supplementing their farm production with wage income from harvest work for others. A model simulation indicates that demographic growth by itself was insufficient to produce this outcome: rising inequality was driven by the interaction of rising population numbers; an easing of land transfers that encouraged smallholders to sell to the better-off in times of crisis to pay for food, seed, and livestock, or service debt; and the effects of partible inheritance that broke up holdings and prompted more distress sales. Some peasants became entirely landless, which raised asset inequality even further. Moreover, English land rents for commoners rose greatly between 1000 and the early fourteenth century even as the size of their holdings shrank. In France, meanwhile, typical plot size fell from around ten hectares to often fewer than three hectares between the ninth and the early fourteenth centuries.[4]

Growing inequality was also driven by income and wealth concentration at the top. England in 1200 was home to 160 magnates (barons) with average

---

[4] Bekar and Reed 2013, on England. In their model, these factors are capable of quintupling land Ginis from 0.14 to 0.68 (308), whereas land sales or population growth by themselves yield much smaller effects; see 302–311 for the simulation. See also Turchin and Nefedov 2009: 51–53 for a model of a peasant holding of fifteen acres that barely allowed tenants to make ends meet. Rents and plots: Grigg 1980: 68; Turchin and Nefedov 2009: 50–51.

incomes of 200 pounds, but by 1300 this group had expanded to around 200 peers having average incomes of 670 pounds, or twice as much in real terms. As is typical of periods of intensifying inequality, the largest fortunes grew the most: in 1200, the richest baron, Roger de Lacy of Chester, disposed of 800 pounds (or four times the average annual income for all peers), whereas by 1300, Edmund, Earl of Cornwall, took in 3,800 pounds, or almost three times as much in real terms—equivalent to five and a half times the average for all peers at the time. The middle ranks of the English elite swelled even more conspicuously as the number of belted knights rose from about 1,000 in 1200 to about 3,000 by 1300, at roughly equal income thresholds. Inequality in military compensation can be tracked via the pay ratio of knights relative to foot soldiers, which rose from 8:1 in 1165 to 12:1 in 1215 and 12–24:1 in 1300. Not coincidentally, French wine imports also peaked in the early fourteenth century. Elite incomes rose in real terms at the same time as those of commoners declined. Interaction effects between population growth and commercialization are likely to have produced similar outcomes in other parts of Europe.[5]

On the eve of the Black Death in 1347, Europe as a whole was more developed and more unequal than it had been since the days of the Roman empire. We can only guess how these two peaks compared. I suspect that even by the early fourteenth century, overall inequality may have fallen somewhat short of the levels attained almost a millennium earlier. There was no high medieval equivalent to a late Roman aristocracy that had held assets across the western Mediterranean and its hinterlands and that had siphoned off resources from an imperial fiscal behemoth without par in medieval Europe. Only the Byzantine empire may have suffered from an even higher extraction rate than the mature Roman empire, but it was chiefly located outside Europe proper. For what it is worth, an isolated estimate of the income Gini coefficient for England and Wales around 1290 puts inequality at a comparable level of per capita output at a slightly lower level than in the Roman empire of the second century. At the end of the day, more meaningful comparisons between Roman and high medieval inequality may remain beyond our reach. What matters here is the overall disequalization of income and wealth during the High Middle Ages, a trend we have no reason to doubt. Tax records that point to high levels of wealth concentration in Paris and London in the

---

[5] Turchin and Nefedov 2009: 55–58.

1310s (with Gini coefficients of up to 0.79 or probably more) merely document conditions near the endpoint of the prolonged commercial revolution of that period.[6]

All this changed when the plague struck Europe and the Middle East in 1347. Returning in wave after wave for several generations, it killed tens of millions. More than a quarter of the European population is thought to have perished by 1400—maybe a third in Italy and close to half in England. Labor became scarce: across the region, by the middle of the fifteenth century, real wages for unskilled urban workers had roughly doubled but had risen a little less among skilled craftsmen. English farm wages also doubled in real terms even as land rents fell and elite fortunes contracted. Commoners from England to Egypt enjoyed a better diet and grew taller bodies. As I show in chapter 10, tax records from Italian cities show a dramatic drop in wealth inequality as local or regional Gini coefficients fell by more than 10 points and top wealth shares by a third or more. Hundreds of years of disequalization had been undone by one of the most severe shocks humanity had ever experienced.[7]

SCALING NEW HEIGHTS

Once the plague abated in the late fifteenth century, European population began to recover. Economic development reached new heights, as did inequality. The formation of fiscal-military states in Europe, the creation of overseas colonial empire, and an unprecedented expansion of global trade fostered institutional change and new networks of exchange. Although commercial and tributary exchanges had always existed side by side, the former gradually became dominant as commercialization transformed tributary states and increased their dependence on commercial revenue. The growth of a more integrated world system supported by bullion extraction in the New World and intercontinental trade mobilized wealth and widened the gap between rich and poor on a global scale. As Europe became the hub of a worldwide exchange network, development gave more power to mercantile elites and drew rural majorities

---

[6] Byzantine inequality: Milanovic 2006. England and Wales: Milanovic, Lindert, and Williamson 2011: 263 table 2 (c.0.36), based on Campbell 2008. The next-oldest estimate, for Tuscany in 1427, postdates the Black Death but is higher (0.46), which is what we would expect from a heavily urbanized environment. Wealth concentration in Paris and London: Sussman 2006, esp. 20 table 9, for wealth Ginis (inferred from tax payments) of 0.79 in Paris in 1313 and 0.76 in London in 1319. The Parisian Gini would be higher still if the very poor had not been omitted from the underlying tax rolls (cf. 4).
[7] See herein, chapter 10, esp. pp. 300–311.

into market activities that put pressure on their attachment to the land. Tribute-taking elites morphed into commercial and entrepreneurial landowners, and merchants established closer ties to governments. Peasants were gradually separated from the land via enclosure, tax, debt, and the commodification of land-holding. Traditional means of enrichment rooted in the predatory exercise of political power persisted alongside these modernizing market-based processes: stronger states offered attractive pathways to riches. All this put upward pressure on wealth inequality.[8]

Late medieval and especially early modern Europe occupies a special place in the historical study of material inequality. For the first time, quantitative evidence for the distribution of wealth (though not yet income) becomes available that allows us solidly to track change over time and compare developments in different areas. These data are primarily derived from local registers of taxable property and complemented by information about land rents and the incomes of workers. In the following, I use information about the distribution of wealth and income side by side. Systematic disaggregation of these two indices is not normally possible for this period: students of premodern inequality generally need to be more eclectic in their choices than modern economists might prefer they be. This is not a major problem: in preindustrial societies, trends in wealth and income inequality could hardly have moved in different directions.[9]

Even though these data sets do not add up to genuine national statistics of inequality, they put our understanding of the structure and evolution of wealth concentration on a much more solid footing than for earlier periods. Thanks to their internal cohesiveness and their consistency over time, some of these late medieval and early modern data series may be a more reliable guide to the overall contours of change than modern attempts to reconstruct countrywide trends from disparate sources, even for the nineteenth century. Taken together, this evidence from several western and southern European societies shows that

---

[8] Scholarship on this transformation is vast. For a very high-flying bird's-eye view, appropriate in this context, see Christian 2004: 364–405. The contributors to Neal and Williamson 2014 survey the many-faceted rise of capitalism, and Goetzmann 2016 emphasizes the role of finance in the global evolution of civilization. Needless to say, "taking" remains a successful strategy of enrichment and disequalization in much of the world today: see herein, p. 71, for contemporary China, or Piketty's 2014: 446 reference to "theft" as a mechanism of accumulation, exemplified by the despotic rulers of Equatorial Guinea.

[9] For this last point, see most recently Alfani 2016: 7, with references. In the following, a narrative format that highlights particularly noteworthy figures and trends seems best suited to the limits and idiosyncrasies of diverse local data sets and avoids specious impressions of precision that might otherwise be conveyed by consolidated tabulations.

resources were more unequally distributed in large cities than in smaller towns or in the countryside, that inequality was generally going up after the end of the Black Death, and that this rise occurred under a wide variety of economic conditions.

Greater division of labor, differentiation in skills and incomes, spatial concentration of elite households and mercantile capital, and the inflow of poorer migrants had always driven up urban inequality. According to the Florentine census (*catasto*) of 1427, wealth inequality was positively correlated with the scale of urbanism. The capital city, Florence, boasted a Gini coefficient of wealth distribution of 0.79—probably closer to 0.85 if the unrecorded propertyless poor are included. Gini values were lower in smaller cities (0.71–0.75), lower still in the agricultural plains (0.63), and lowest in the poorest areas, the hills and mountains (0.52–0.53). Top income shares likewise varied accordingly, from 67 percent for the top 5 percent in Florence to 36 percent for their peers up in the mountains. Much the same picture emerges from other Italian tax registers. From the fifteenth to the eighteenth centuries, reported wealth concentration in the Tuscan cities of Arezzo, Prato, and San Gimignano was consistently higher than in the surrounding rural areas. The same pattern can be observed, albeit to a lesser extent, in Piedmont.[10]

High wealth inequality of at least 0.75 was a standard feature in the major cities of late medieval and early modern western Europe. Augsburg, one of Germany's leading economic centers in this period, provides a particularly extreme example: recovery from plague-related leveling witnessed an increase in the urban wealth Gini from 0.66 in 1498 to a stratospheric 0.89 by 1604. It is hard to imagine a more polarized community: a few percent of residents owned almost all assets, whereas between a third and two-thirds had nothing worth reporting at all. I return to this case in detail at the end of chapter 11. In the Netherlands, large cities experienced similarly high levels of wealth concentration (with Ginis of 0.8 to 0.9), whereas smaller towns lagged far behind (0.5–0.65). Urban income inequality was also very high in Amsterdam, where the relevant Gini coefficient reached 0.69 in 1742. English tax records from 1524 to 1525 reveal urban wealth Ginis that were generally above 0.6 and that

---

[10] Florentine *catasto*: van Zanden 1995: 645 table 1. (The distribution of capital among 522 merchant families in Florence in 1427 shows a Gini coefficient of 0.782: Preiser-Kapeller 2016: 5, based on http://home.uchicago.edu/~jpadgett/data.html.) Tuscany: Alfani and Ammannati 2014: 19 fig. 2. Piedmont: Alfani 2015: 1084 fig. 7.

could be as high as 0.82 to 0.85, well in excess of rural values of 0.54 to 0.62. The distribution of assets in probate inventories of personal estates was likewise correlated with settlement size. Urbanization rates held steady between 1500 and 1800 in some of these regions, most notably in Italy as well as in the Iberian peninsula, but grew considerably in England and the Netherlands, thereby raising overall levels of inequality.[11]

Beginning in the fifteenth century, the low point of the leveling brought about by the Black Death, inequality increased in virtually all parts of Europe for which we have data. The Netherlands provide some of the most detailed information. A precociously advanced economy with what was almost certainly the highest per capita GDP in the world at the time, it documents the disequalizing effects of commercial and urban development. By the late seventeenth century, the urban share of the population reached 40 percent, and only a third of the population worked in agriculture. Large cities manufactured and processed for export markets. A weak nobility had been eclipsed by a commercial elite that enjoyed freedom from despotic predation. Cities were highly unequal thanks to the urban concentration of capital and the urban residence of many landowners. In Amsterdam in 1742, almost two-thirds of all income was derived from capital investment and entrepreneurship. In response to a shift from labor-intensive to capital-intensive production techniques and the steady inflow of foreign labor that depressed real wages, the share of capital income in Holland rose from 44 percent in 1500 to 59 percent in 1650.[12]

Economic development and urban growth raised inequality over time as a small fraction of the Dutch citizenry captured a disproportionately large part of the newly created wealth even as the ranks of the urban poor kept expanding. In the longest available time series for reported wealth, from the city of Leiden, the wealth share of the top 1 percent grew from 21 percent in 1498 to 33 percent in 1623, 42 percent in 1675, and 59 percent in 1722. During the same period, the proportion of households whose assets did not reach the minimum taxation threshold increased from 76 percent to 92 percent. Most relevant information

[11] Germany: van Zanden 1995: 645–647, esp. 647 fig. 1 on Augsburg, and herein, chapter 11, pp. 336–337. Netherlands: van Zanden 1995: 647–649; Soltow and van Zanden 1998: 46 table 3.10. England: Postles 2011: 3, 6–9; 2014: 25–27. Soltow 1979: 132 table 3 calculates a wealth Gini of 0.89 for Copenhagen in 1789. Urbanization rates: De Vries 1984: 39 table 3.7.

[12] De Vries and Van der Woude 1997: 61 (urbanization); Soltow and van Zanden 1998: 23–25 (general conditions), 42, 46, 53–54 (capital and labor).

is derived from tax registers that record the annual rental value of houses in different parts of Holland, a more indirect and imperfect proxy of overall asset inequality that is likely to underestimate the latter considering that the wealthy spend a progressively smaller share of their income on housing the richer they become. A weighted value for much of Holland shows a sustained increase, from 0.5 in 1514 to 0.56 in 1561, 0.61 or 0.63 in the 1740s, and 0.63 in 1801. Between 1561 and 1732, the Gini coefficients of rental values went up everywhere, from 0.52 to 0.59 in the cities and from 0.35 to 0.38 in the countryside. The most recent standardized survey of material from fifteen Dutch towns finds a general upward trend from the sixteenth all the way into the late nineteenth century.[13]

Economic progress provides only a partial explanation for this phenomenon. Sometimes wealth concentration kept rising even once economic growth had stalled. Only in the northern Low Countries did the upward trend in inequality coincide with economic growth, whereas in the southern Low Countries there was no systematic relationship between these two variables at all. Divergent paths of economic development did not affect a shared tendency for inequality to increase. Nor did different tax regimes: whereas a strong emphasis on regressive consumption taxation in the south would have had disequalizing consequences, taxes in the Dutch Republic to the north were in fact uniquely progressive, focusing as they did on luxuries and real estate. And yet inequality tended to widen across the entire region.

This is not surprising: in the more dynamic north, the disequalizing forces of global trade and urbanization were complemented by growing wage dispersion that was at least in part rooted in sociopolitical power relations. In Amsterdam between 1580 and 1789, the wages of senior administrative officials, clerks, schoolmasters, and barber-surgeons rose more quickly—by a factor of five to ten—than did those of carpenters, which merely doubled. For some professions, such as surgeons, this may reflect the attachment of greater importance to their skills, even though skill premiums for workers did not generally increase during this period. However, generous raises for government officials

---

[13] Soltow and van Zanden 1998: 38 table 3.6, 39 (Leiden); van Zanden 1995: 652–653; Soltow and van Zanden 1998: 35 table 3.4 (rental values); cf. 139 for a Gini of 0.65 in 1808. Fifteen towns: Ryckbosch 2014: 13 fig. 1; cf. also 13 fig. 2 and 14 fig. 3 for time trends by city, which show somewhat more variation over time. The Gini for house rents in Nijvel rose from 0.35 in 1525 to 0.47 in 1800: Ryckbosch 2010: 46 table 4. In 's-Hertogenbosch, flat nominal house rent inequality between 1500 and 1550 masks a rise in real inequality adjusted for household size and price: Hanus 2013.

and cognate knowledge workers such as schoolmasters may well have been driven in the first instance by a desire to keep up with those in the same bourgeois stratum who benefited from growing capital income. Thus commercial capital income seems to have had a striking knock-on effect on wages for certain socially privileged groups. Rent-seeking by elites had a polarizing effect on the income distribution.[14]

In the territory (*contado*) of Florence, wealth inequality documented by property registers grew from a low of 0.5 in the mid-fifteenth century to 0.74 around 1700. In the city of Arezzo, it rose from 0.48 in 1390 to 0.83 in 1792, and it grew from 0.58 to 0.83 in Prato between 1546 and 1763. This concentration was very much driven by the growth of top wealth shares: between the late fifteenth or early sixteenth century and the early eighteenth century, the share of reported assets owned by the richest 1 percent of households rose from 6.8 percent to 17.5 percent in the *contado* of Florence, from 8.9 percent to 26.4 percent in Arezzo, and from 8.1 percent to 23.3 percent in Prato. Comparable trends are visible in registers from Piedmont, where wealth Ginis increased by up to 27 points in a number of cities and on a similar scale in some rural communities. In Apulia in the Kingdom of Naples, the wealth share of the richest 5 percent rose from 48 percent around 1600 to 61 percent around 1750. In Piemont and the Florentine state, the proportion of households whose wealth reached at least ten times the local median value grew from 3–5 percent in the late fifteenth century to 10–14 percent three centuries later: polarization intensified as more households pulled away from the median.[15]

Unlike in the Netherlands, much of this change took place in the context of seventeenth-century economic stagnation and an even more prolonged lack of net advances in urbanization. Three major disequalizing forces have been held responsible: demographic recovery from the attrition of the Black Death, the gradual expropriation and proletarianization of rural producers, and the formation of the fiscal-military state. As elsewhere in Europe, a growing supply of labor

---

[14] Soltow and van Zanden 1988: 40 (stalled growth); Ryckbosch 2014: 17–18, esp. 18 fig. 5, 22 (north/south), who concludes that Dutch and Flemish inequality was low in phases of skill-intensive export production of luxury goods and services and high in periods of large-scale standardized export production with low wages (23); Alfani and Ryckbosch 2015: 28 (taxes); van Zanden 1995: 660 table 8; Soltow and van Zanden 1998: 43–44, 47 (wages).

[15] Alfani and Ammannati 2014: 16 table 3 (Tuscany), 29 table 4 (wealth shares); Alfani 2015: 1069 table 2 (Piedmont); Alfani 2016: 28 table 2 (Apulia); 12 fig. 2, 13 (multiple of median value). Two Sicilian data sets also point to rising wealth inequality: Alfani and Sardone 2015: 22 fig. 5.

depressed its value relative to that of land and other capital. More and more land was acquired by the elite, a process we witness in the Netherlands and France as well. In addition, city-states endowed with autonomous communal traditions and powerful notions of citizenship and republicanism were subsumed within larger and more coercive states that levied heavier taxes. In Piedmont as well as in the southern Low Countries, public debt channeled resources from workers to wealthy creditors.[16]

These case studies highlight the long-term continuity of mechanisms of disequalization. Reaching back at least to the ancient Babylonians, intensive economic growth, commercialization, and urbanization had boosted inequality. The same was true of the Roman period and the High Middle Ages. As we have seen, appropriation of land by affluent capital owners and elite enrichment sustained by fiscal extraction and other state activities have an even longer pedigree, going back to the Sumerians. Early modern income and wealth concentration merely differed in terms of style and scale: alongside more conventional strategies of rent-seeking, elites might now benefit from purchasing public debt instead of stealing or extorting resources outright, global trade networks opened up unprecedented investment opportunities, and urbanization began to exceed any earlier levels. Yet deep down, the principal means of disequalization had remained fundamentally unchanged and once again powerfully reasserted themselves after a temporary hiatus that had been induced by a violent shock.

The effective complementarity of these well-established disequalizers goes a long way in accounting for similar outcomes across a wide range of economic and institutional conditions (Fig. 3.2). In the Dutch Republic, inequality rose thanks to global trade, economic growth, and urbanization, whereas fiscal pressures appear to have been the most crucial factor in Piedmont and rural proletarianization in Tuscany, and both of these mechanisms operated in the southern Low Countries. In England, the most dynamic economy of this period after the northern Low Countries, commercialization and urban expansion boosted material disparities: wealth Ginis in Nottingham rose from 0.64 in 1473 to 0.78 in 1524, and in one survey of probate inventories of personal estates increased from 0.48–0.52 in the first half of the sixteenth century to 0.53–0.66 over the following eighty years. Across nine samples of such records, the richest 5 percent had held 13 percent

---

[16] Alfani 2014: 1084–1090; Alfani and Ryckbosch 2015: 25–30.

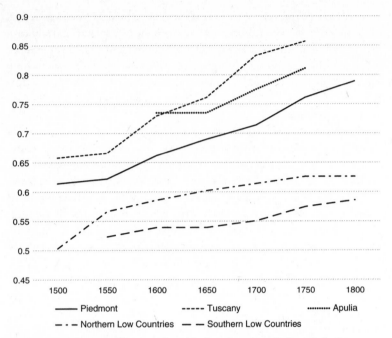

Figure 3.2 Gini coefficients of wealth distribution in Italy and the Low Countries, 1500–1800

to 25 percent of all assets at the beginning of this period and 24 percent to 35 percent later on.[17]

Economic conditions were strikingly different in Spain, which experienced ruralization, a shift from husbandry to farming, and low wages. In this context of stagnation or even retrenchment, the ratio of nominal per capita GDP to nominal wages climbed fairly steadily from the 1420s to the end of the eighteenth century, reflecting an ongoing disequalizing devaluation of labor as real wages fell, a phenomenon we also observe in many other European countries. The ratio of land rents to wages, another indicator of inequality,

<hr/>

[17] Fig. 3.2 from Alfani and Ryckbosch 2015: 16 fig. 2b and Alfani and Sardone 2015: 28 fig. 9. Cf. also Alfani 2016: 26 fig. 4 and 30 fig. 6 for similar trends for top wealth shares and a "richness index." Alfani and Ryckbosch 2015: 30 offer a comparative assessment of the different causes of rising inequality in the Netherlands and Italy. For England, see Postles 2011: 3, 6–9; 2014: 27.

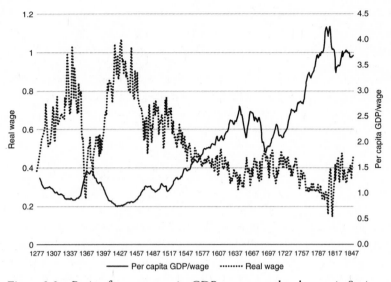

Figure 3.3 Ratio of mean per capita GDP to wages and real wages in Spain, 1277–1850

fluctuated more across this period but was likewise much higher in 1800 than it had been 400 years earlier (Fig. 3.3). These findings comport well with the observation that in the province of Madrid, wealth inequality as reconstructed from tax records increased between 1500 and 1840, albeit in a discontinuous fashion.[18]

In the French countryside, beginning in the sixteenth century, the twin pressures of demographic recovery and growing estates hollowed out the middle and polarized local communities between larger landowners and smallholders whose farms were too small to feed them, forcing them into tenancy and wage labor. For the time being, Portugal remains the only documented outlier.

---

[18] Spain: Alvarez-Nogal and Prados de la Escosura 2013. Fig. 3.3 from tables S2 and S4 (http://onlinelibrary .wiley.com/doi/10.1111/j.1468–0289.2012.00656.x/suppinfo). Madrid: Fernandez and Santiago-Caballero 2013. In Catalonia, the top 1 percent and 5 percent wealth shares either rose or remained fairly flat between 1400 and 1800, and the overall wealth Gini coefficient shows no clear trend: García-Montero 2015: 13 fig. 1, 16 fig. 3. Santiago-Caballero 2011 documents fairly stable inequality in the province of Guadalajara in the eighteenth-century, except for a modest dip late in this period associated with land reform (see herein, chapter 12, p. 355). For falling European real wages, see herein, chapter 10, pp. 301–302.

According to tax rolls, overall income inequality declined somewhat between 1565 and 1700 in an environment defined by stagnating economic development and urbanization and a weakening of overseas empire. Skills premiums largely held steady in this period, whereas the ratio of land rents to wages fell throughout the seventeenth century before only partly recovering by the 1770s. Yet, looked at more closely, the moderate reduction in income inequality was mostly a phenomenon of small towns and rural communities, whereas urban inequality changed little, if at all, in the long term.[19]

In the absence of violent compressions, inequality might rise for a variety of different reasons that were determined by local economic and institutional conditions, but rise it (almost) always did. For what they are worth, the results of modern attempts to devise national Gini income coefficients for this period are largely consistent with the trends revealed by more localized empirical data sets. Overall income inequality in the Netherlands is thought to have increased from 0.56 in 1561 to 0.61 in 1732 before falling back to 0.57 by 1808, the period of the Napoleonic Wars. Considering the shaky foundations of the underlying schematic computations, these numbers are probably best seen as an indication of fairly high and stable inequality. The corresponding Gini values for England and Wales increased from 0.45 in 1688—well above the putative medieval peak of 0.37—to 0.46 in 1739 and 0.52 in 1801. At around 0.56, it was also high in France in 1788. All of these values are higher than those for the Roman and Byzantine empires, as was per capita output: roughly four to six times minimum subsistence in the Netherlands, five to seven times in England and Wales, and four times in France, compared to something like twice the base minimum in Rome, Byzantium, and medieval England. However, as already noted, economic development as such was not the only pathway to higher inequality: at two and a half times minimum subsistence, Old Castile in 1752 did not boast per capita surpluses much larger than ancient Rome's but experienced high income inequality (0.53), which reflects the effects of strong social and political forces of disequalization.[20]

---

[19] France: The classic study is Le Roy Ladurie 1966, esp. 239–259, and also 263–276 for falling real wages. Portugal: Reis, Santos Pereira, and Andrade Martins n.d., esp. 27 fig. 2, 30–32, 36–37 figs. 5–6. In 1770, inequality was lower in Porto than it had been in 1700 and also lower than in 1565 Lisbon, lower in small towns and rural areas than in 1565 but higher in large towns than it had been in both 1565 and 1700 (27 fig. 2). Their work is based on income tax data, improving on the survey of material from 1309 to 1789 by Johnson 2001, which suggests a similar trend. Little is known about Central Europe: see Hegyi, Néda, and Santos 2005 for the distribution of elite wealth proxied by the number of serfs in Hungary in 1550.

[20] Milanovic, Lindert, and Williamson 2011: 263 table 2. Naples in 1811 supposedly exhibited a very low income Gini of 0.28, which seems doubtful.

In all cases in which they can be roughly estimated, effective extraction rates—the actualized proportion of maximum feasible inequality at a given level of per capita GDP—either remained flat or rose between the sixteenth and the beginning of the nineteenth century. Three centuries after the abatement of the Black Death, income inequality in the better-documented parts of western and southern Europe had reached levels that in nominal terms—expressed in gross Gini coefficients—for the first time surpassed those of the Roman period. When adjusted for effective subsistence requirements that were sensitive to per capita GDP, they roughly approximated those experienced in classical antiquity and the High Middle Ages. Without exception, by 1800 real wages of urban workers were lower than they had been in the late fifteenth century, and although "real" inequality adjusted for divergent cost-of-living indices for high and low income groups was somewhat more volatile than nominal measures, the overall trend was likewise upward.[21]

BEYOND EUROPE

What about the rest of the world? Ottoman probate inventories from four cities in Asia Minor that record complete estates, including all real and personal property as well as cash, credits, and debts, shed some light on the evolution of wealth inequality between 1500 and 1840. As in Europe, mean wealth and levels of inequality were positively associated with city size. In three cities with extensive data series, Gini coefficients of asset concentration in 1820 and 1840 were higher than they had been when these series began, varying from the early sixteenth to the early eighteenth century. The same broadly applies to the top decile of wealth shares. Aggregate Ginis for rural probates rose from 0.54 in the 1500s and 1510s to 0.66 in the 1820s and 1830s, an increase that may be linked to the commercialization of agriculture and changing property relations

---

[21] Extraction rates: for the concept, see herein, appendix, p. 447. Extraction rates rose in Piedmont, Tuscany, and the southern Low Countries as per capita GDP stagnated or even shrank: Alfani and Ryckbosch 2015: 24 fig. 5b, with 18 table 2. In the Dutch Republic and in England, unadjusted extraction rates (relative to bare subsistence) declined in the former and fluctuated in the latter case in the context of intensive economic growth, whereas extraction rates adjusted for rising social minima remained flat: Milanovic, Lindert, and Williamson 2011: 263 table 2; Milanovic 2013: 9 fig. 3. For real wages, see herein, chapter 10, pp. 301–302. "Real" inequality was higher in England, France, and the Netherlands in 1800 than it had been in 1450 or 1500: Hoffman, Jacks, Levin, and Lindert 2005: 161–164, esp. 163 fig. 6.3(a–c). I note in passing that economic inequality could also translate to significant disparities in terms of body height: Komlos, Hau, and Bourguinat 2003: 177–178, 184–185, on France.

characterized by diminishing state control over land and expanding privatization. The observed rise in wealth inequality is also consistent with evidence for falling real wages elsewhere in the Ottoman empire. Thus trends in inequality east of the Aegean quite closely resembled those in western and southern Europe.[22]

Before moving on to the "long nineteenth century" up to the Great War, it is worth asking whether multimillennial reconstructions of the contours of inequality similar to that in Figure 1.1 are feasible for other parts of the globe. For now, the answer must be largely negative. We may surmise, but cannot properly document, that swings in the concentration of income and wealth in China mapped on to what is known as its "dynastic cycles." As I have tried to show in the previous chapter, there is reason to believe that inequality increased under the long rule of the Han dynasty, culminating perhaps in the later stages of the Eastern Han period in the second and early third centuries CE, just as Roman inequality may have peaked in the final stages of the full-sized empire in the fourth and early fifth centuries CE. The prolonged "Period of Disunion" from the early fourth to the late sixth century may well have witnessed some degree of compression, especially in the northern half of the region, which was first fiercely contested between numerous ephemeral foreign conquest regimes and that later experienced a resurgence of mass mobilization warfare and ambitious land distribution schemes.[23]

Income and wealth are bound to have both grown and become more concentrated under the Tang dynasty of the seventh through ninth centuries until its elites were largely wiped out in its final phase of disintegration, as described in chapter 9. Unprecedented economic growth, commercialization, and urbanization under the Song dynasty likely generated disequalizing outcomes similar to those observed in parts of early modern Europe, and large landlords were powerful in the later Southern Song state. Trends in the Mongol period are more difficult to pin down, as economic decline, plague, invasion, and predatory rule all interacted in complex ways. Inequality once again grew under the Ming, although it is instructive to see that by international standards, its overall levels were not particularly high in the terminal phase of the Qing or even

---

[22] Canbakal and Filiztekin 2013: 2, 4, 6–7, 8 fig. 7 (urban Ginis), 19 fig. 9 (top decile), 20 fig. 10 (rural Ginis), 22. For a more detailed study of one of these cities, Bursa, see also Canbakal 2012. Pamuk forthcoming surveys developments after 1820.

[23] For Han inequality, see herein, pp. 63–69. Developments in the Period of Disunion are summarized by Lewis 2009a.

before the Maoist revolution. Even less can be said here about South Asia except that high inequality both in the Mughal empire in the eighteenth century and under British control 200 years later provides further confirmation of the disequalizing effects of large-scale predatory imperial or colonial rule.[24]

For much of the past 600 years, inequality trends in the New World can only be sketched out in a highly impressionistic way. It is likely that the formation of the Aztec and Inca empires in the fifteenth centuries raised economic disparities to new levels as tributary flows extended over longer distances and powerful elites accumulated increasingly hereditary assets. Countervailing forces operated during the following two centuries: even as the Spanish expansion and predatory colonial rule by a small conquest elite would have sustained or arguably even increased existing levels of wealth concentration, the catastrophic demographic attrition caused by the arrival of novel Old World infections I describe in chapter 11 made labor scarce and even drove up real wages, at least for a while. Even so, after these epidemics had abated, the population recovered, land/labor ratios fell, urbanization increased, and colonial rule was fully consolidated; by the eighteenth century, Latin American inequality was probably as high as it had ever been. Revolutions and independence in the early nineteenth century may have had an equalizing effect until the commodities boom of the second half of that century pushed inequality to ever higher levels, a process of income concentration that with only intermittent pauses continued well into the late twentieth century (Fig. 3.4).[25]

THE LONG NINETEENTH CENTURY

This brings us to the onset of modern economic growth in the nineteenth century. The concurrent shift from local data sets to national estimates of income

---

[24] For the Tang, see herein, chapter 9, pp. 260–264. For later dynasties, see very briefly herein, pp. 69–71. China in 1880, India in 1750 and 1947: Milanovic, Lindert, and Williamson 2011: 263 table 2. Prerevolutionary China: herein, chapter 7, pp. 223, 227. Formal studies of Asian inequality remain in short supply. Broadberry and Gupta 2006: 14 table 5, 18 table 7 find that real wages of unskilled workers in the Yangzi Delta were lower in the mid-Qing period (1739–1850) than they had been under the late Ming (1573–1614), that in northern and western India there were lower in 1874 than they had been under the Mughals, and that in southern India they were lower in 1790 than they had been in 1610. Although all this points to rising inequality, these findings would need to be more fully contextualized to provide more certainty. For Japan, see herein, chapter 4, p. 118.
[25] See herein, pp. 58–59 (pre-Columbian inequality), and herein, chapter 11, pp. 317–319 (epidemics) and chapter 13, pp. 378–382. Fig. 3.4 is based on Williamson 2015: 35 table 3 and Prados de la Escosura 2007: 296–297 table 12.1, adjusting Williamson's inequality levels to bring them in line with the latter's lower income Ginis and account for the presence of the Aztec and Inca empires and the effects of epidemic mortality.

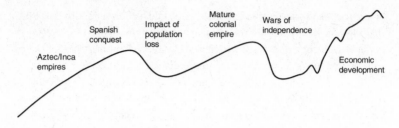

Figure 3.4   Inequality trends in Latin America in the long run

and wealth distribution introduces considerable uncertainties. For this reason alone, the question whether industrialization exacerbated British inequality has proven surprisingly difficult to address. The only thing we can be sure of is that the concentration of private wealth steadily intensified from 1700 until the early 1910s, a period during which real per capita GDP more than trebled: thus, the wealth share of the richest 1 percent rose from 39 percent in 1700 to 69 percent in the early 1910s. By 1873, the concentration coefficient of landownership had risen to 0.94, effectively making it impossible for this type of inequality to grow much further. The picture is less clear regarding the distribution of income. Evidence from tax returns and social tables as well as the land rent/wage ratio fairly conclusively points to an increase in income inequality between the middle of the eighteenth century and the beginning of the nineteenth. However, although information on housing inequality derived from house-tax data and reported wages has been marshaled to show that incomes continued to become more unequal during the first half of the nineteenth century as well, it remains controversial how much weight this particular material can bear.[26]

This is even more true of an earlier notion that various indicators of inequality rose during the first half or two-thirds of the nineteenth century and subsequently declined until the 1910s, producing a gently inverted U-curve that would be compatible with the economist Simon Kuznets's idea that economic modernization might first increase and then lower inequality within a society in transition. The observation that wage dispersal grew between 1815 and 1851, peaked in the 1850s

---

[26] Wealth: Lindert 2000b: 181 table 2. Income concentration at the very top was so extreme that the share of the next most affluent 4 percent declined from 43 percent to 18 percent as the overall share of the top 5 percent rose from 82 percent to 87 percent. Landownership: Soltow 1968: 28 table 3. Income inequality up to the first decade of the nineteenth century: Lindert 2000b: 18–19, 24.

and 1860s, and subsequently declined until 1911 may be an artifact of the under-lying data for different professions, which exhibit contradictory trends. Similarly, measures of housing inequality constructed from house duties that suggest Ginis of 0.61 in 1830 and 0.67 in 1871 for all inhabited houses and a decline from 0.63 in 1874 to 0.55 in 1911 for private residences likewise cannot readily be taken at face value. Schedules of income shares are also of little use. Revised social tables suggest a fair degree of stability over time, with national income Ginis of 0.52 in 1801/1803 and 0.48 in 1867 for England and Wales and of 0.48 for the United Kingdom in 1913. It is important to be precise: although we cannot be sure whether English or British income inequality remained largely unchanged in the course of the nineteenth century, we are simply unable to confirm that it did not.[27]

Outcomes in Italy are similarly uncertain. The most recent study of Ital-ian income inequality presents a number of different indices that all point to basic stability between 1871 and World War I (and beyond), in contrast to an earlier survey of aggregated household budgets that suggested a gradual decline in inequality between 1881 and the war at a time when the putatively disequal-izing effects of industrialization were being offset by massive emigration to the western hemisphere. National income data are unavailable for France. In Paris, wealth concentration, as measured by the share of the top 1 percent of estates in

---

[27] For the notion of a "Kuznets curve" (for which see herein, chapter 13, pp. 369–372) during British industrialization, see Williamson 1985 and 1991, esp. 64 table 2.5, forcefully and to my mind compellingly challenged by Feinstein 1988. Wage dispersion: Williamson 1991: 61–62 table 2.2, based on six unskilled and twelve skilled occupations, cf. also 63 table 2.3. Feinstein 1988: 705–706 shows that the curve for the twelve skilled occupations is made up of seven that show a gradual rise in nominal annual earnings and five that exhibit erratic swings. He concludes, "The structure of pay by skill displayed a high degree of stability over the century: there was no surge of inequality in the first half, no egalitarian leveling in the second." (710; and see also Jackson 1987). For a critique of house dues, see 717–718. Top income shares: William-son 1991: 63 table 2.4, with Feinstein 1988: 718–720. Social tables: Feinstein 1988: 723 table 6, and see also Jackson 1994: 509 table 1: 0.47–0.54 in 1688 (without and with paupers), 0.52–0.58 in 1901 and 1903, and 0.48 in both 1867 and 1913. Jackson 1994: 511 deems it unlikely that inequality peaked in the mid-nineteenth century, and Soltow 1968: 22 table 1 had already arrived at a similar conclusion of broad stability in this period. Lindert 2000b: 21–24 shows that trends in English real inequality across the nine-teenth century depend on which measure we select. This holds true regardless of evidence for stagnant real wages of English workers in the first half of the nineteenth century and rising ones in the second half: see Allen 2009 for an explanation of this phenomenon. The observation that "real"—i.e., class-specific—ine-quality declined throughout the nineteenth century (Hoffman, Jacks, Levin, and Lindert 2005: 162 fig. 6.3(a)) is likewise inconsistent with a scenario of rising followed by falling inequality. The evidentiary weak-ness of any claim that inequality in industrializing Britain followed a Kuznets curve makes it difficult to account for its continuing popularity of this notion in post-1988 scholarship: see, e.g., Williamson 1991; Justman and Gradstein 1999: 109–110; Acemoglu and Robinson 2000: 1192–1193; 2002: 187 table 1; and, most recently, Milanovic 2016: 73 fig. 2.11, 74–75, who references Feinstein's critique in an endnote (248–249 n.25).

all personal wealth, rose from a 50 percent to 55 percent range between 1807 and 1867 to 72 percent by 1913, whereas the top 0.1 percent's share increased more strongly, from 15–23 percent to 33 percent. Across the whole country, elite wealth shares grew more steadily from 43 percent (for the top 1 percent) and 16 percent (for the top 0.1 percent) in 1807 to 55 percent and 26 percent, respectively, in 1913. Spanish income inequality rose from the 1860s to the time of World War I.[28]

There are no national German data for this period. In Prussia, the top 1 percent income share grew from around 13 percent or 15 percent in 1874 to 17 percent or 18 percent in 1891. The net trend was flat between 1891 and 1913, as top income shares were virtually identical in both of these years and had fluctuated only little in between. Inasmuch as top incomes changed, they moved in a procyclical fashion, going up with economic growth. The most detailed survey of Prussian income Gini coefficients tracks a continuous rise from 1822 to a peak in 1906 that was followed by a modest fall until 1912 and a partial recovery by 1914. Since the outbreak of World War I truncated the "peaceful" evolution of inequality at that point, we cannot tell whether this brief reduction was merely a blip or might have turned into a secular inflection point. In the Netherlands, the nineteenth century was a period of consolidation after centuries of rising inequality, already described. Disequalization had not yet fully run its course: between 1808 and 1875, the Gini coefficient for the distribution of rentable housing values rose in eight out of ten provinces, and inequality among high earners increased from 1742 to 1880 to the early 1910s. Yet at the same time, real wages recovered and skill premiums declined. The Gini coefficient of national income distribution appears to have been similar in 1800 and 1914, which suggests that inequality had largely stabilized at a (high) plateau.[29]

Scandinavian countries provide relatively rich but sometimes puzzling information for this period. A one-off assessment in Denmark in 1870 put

---

[28] Italy: Rossi, Toniolo, and Vecchi 2001: 916 table 6 show a gradual decline in Ginis and top decile income shares between 1881 and 1969, whereas Brandolini and Vecchi 2011: 39 table 8 present various metrics that strongly indicate stability between 1871 and 1931. France: Piketty, Postel-Vinay, and Rosenthal 2006: 243 fig. 3, 246 fig. 7; Piketty 2014: 340 fig. 10.1. Spain: Prados de la Escosura 2008: 298 fig. 3; see herein, chapter 13, pp. 372–373.
[29] Prussia: Dell 2007: 367 fig. 9.1, 371, 420 table 9I.6 (income shares). There was hardly any decline in the top 1 percent income share, about 0.8 percent between 1900 and 1913, less than previously assumed: earlier studies reckoned with a decline of the order of 1 percent to 2 percent between 1896/1900 or 1901/1910 and 1913: Morrison 2000: 234, and see 233, 257, also for Saxony. Dumke 1991: 128 fig. 5.1a finds rising inequality and capital shares from 1850 to 1914. Prussian Gini: Grant 2002: 25 fig. 1, with 27–28. Netherlands: Soltow and van Zanden 1998: 145–174, esp. 152, 163–165, 171. They note the absence of any Kuznetian wage dispersion during industrialization as skills premiums fell: 161–162, 174.

the top 1 percent income share for married couples and single adults at 19.4 percent. When reports resumed in 1903, this share stood at 16.2 percent and reached 16.5 percent in 1908, followed by a short-lived surge induced by profiteering in World War I that can also be observed in other neutral countries. Although the implied attenuation of inequality between 1870 and 1903 is not dramatic, we must nevertheless wonder about the reliability of the earlier measurement.[30]

Similar reservations apply to records concerning a one-time tax in 1789 that have been taken to suggest an income Gini coefficient of 0.6 to 0.7, values that would have put inequality close to or even right at the theoretically possible maximum for that economy. These concerns make it difficult to conceive of an ongoing attenuation of income inequality between the late eighteenth and the early twentieth centuries. By contrast, reports of the dominance of big landowners in the late eighteenth century lend credence to calculations that point to significant wealth deconcentration among the most affluent tenth of Danish society between 1789 and 1908.[31]

Developments in Norway and Sweden likewise raise questions about the quality of the record. In Norway, the top 1 percent wealth share remained stable at between 36 percent and 38 percent from 1868 to 1930 after it had declined from a higher level calculated for 1789. The top 1 percent income share also moved very little within a narrow band from 18 percent to 21 percent between 1875 and 1906 but suddenly collapsed to around 11 percent by 1910/13. This is hard to explain, and it is far from clear whether a recession in 1908 and 1909 is sufficient to account for this divergence. If this drop is real and not merely an artifact of the evidence, it points to some sort of shock-driven leveling event. Trends

---

[30] The implied Gini coefficient of income distribution for 1870 is high, anywhere between notional extremes of 0.53 and 0.73. Given a Danish per capita GDP of $2,000 in 1990 International Dollars at the time, an intermediate value of 0.63 would imply an extraction rate of three-quarters, not impossible but akin to that in very unequal premodern societies. Only a value at the lower bound of the Gini estimate would put it on a par with England and Wales in 1801, which was very unequal to begin with. However, a plausibly lower 1870 Gini in the mid-0.5s would be located within the confidence intervals for the 1903 and 1910 estimates, thereby making it impossible to rule out the null hypothesis of no significant change in inequality between 1870 and 1910. See Atkinson and Søgaard 2016: 274, euphemistically noting the "limited data coverage" for the period from 1870 to 1903. Implied Gini for 1870: 277 fig. 5. For 1789: Soltow 1979: 136 table 6, from which Atkinson and Søgaard 2016: 275 infer an extravagantly high top 1 percent income share of 30 percent. Danish per capita GDP was around $1,200 in 1990 International Dollars about 1820, which would have accommodated an income Gini of up to 0.75, and was presumably lower still in 1789.

[31] Wealth inequality: Soltow 1979: 130 table 2, 134, with Roine and Waldenstrom 2015: 572 table 7.A2 (for a drop in the top 1 percent share from 56 percent in 1789 to 46 percent in 1908; but cf. 579 table 7.A4 for unchanged top deciles across this period).

in Sweden resemble those in Norway, with a drop in the top 1 percent's income share from 27 percent in 1903 to 20–21 percent from 1907 to 1912. However, wage inequality rose from 1870 to 1914, and unlike in Denmark and Norway, the concentration of wealth increased slightly between 1800 and 1910.[32]

Inequality grew, with only brief pauses, for maybe as long as a quarter of a millennium in what became the United States of America (Fig. 3.4). Trends during the colonial period are poorly documented: even so, it is likely that the expansion of slavery raised income and wealth inequality in the late seventeenth and for much of the eighteenth century. The War of Independence and its immediate aftermath led to a temporary compression as hostilities destroyed capital, military service and casualties and runaway slaves diminished the labor supply, overseas trade suffered disruptions, and urban elites were disproportionately hard hit by these dislocations. Wealthy loyalists departed, others ended up impoverished, and the gaps between urban and rural wages and between white-collar and unskilled urban earnings shrank. Between 1800 and 1860, the rapid growth of the labor force, technological progress that favored industry and cities, and improved financial institutions drove up inequality to unprecedented levels. By 1860, the income Gini coefficient for the entire country reached 0.51, up from 0.44 in 1774 and 0.49 in 1850, and the "1 percent" received a tenth of total income, up from 8.5 percent in 1774 and 9.2 percent in 1850. The slave states generally registered even higher levels of inequality. Greatly increased concentration of property in the hands of the most affluent Americans and a massive rise in earnings disparities among workers both contributed to this development: the wealth share of the richest 1 percent of households more than doubled from about 14 percent in 1774 to 32 percent in 1860, whereas the Gini coefficients of earnings soared from 0.39 to 0.47.[33]

---

[32] Norway: Aaberge and Atkinson 2010: 458–459 (who note that the early data are poor: 456); Roine and Waldenström 2015: 572 table 7.A2 (but cf. 579 table 7.A4 for a top 10 percent wealth share in 1930 that was higher than it had been in 1789). Cf. also Morrison 2000: 223–224 for gradual leveling in two Norwegian counties between 1855 and 1920, based on much earlier work by Soltow. Sweden: WWID; Soltow 1985: 17; Söderberg 1991; Piketty 2014: 345 fig. 10.4.

[33] For the colonial period, see Lindert and Williamson 2014: 4, 28–29. For 1774: Lindert and Williamson 2016: 36–41, esp. 38 table 2–4 for an income Gini of 0.44 and top 1 percent income shares of 8.5 percent for all households and of 0.41 and 7.6 percent for free households. At 0.37 and 4.1 percent, New England was exceptionally egalitarian. Revolutionary period: 82–90. The urban/rural wage premium for unskilled male earnings fell from 26 percent to 5 percent and from 179 percent to 35 percent for average urban/rural earnings. The premium for urban white-collar workers relative to urban male unskilled earnings collapsed from 593 percent to 100 percent. Rising inequality up to 1860: 114–139. Disparities grew both between free and slaves and among the free population. For Ginis and income shares, see 115–116 tables 5–6 and 5–7. Property and earnings inequality: 122 tables 5–8 and 5–9.

As I show in more detail in chapter 6, the Civil War leveled fortunes in the South but further boosted inequality in the North, two countervailing regional trends that left national metrics largely unchanged. Disequalization subsequently continued up to the early twentieth century: the top 1 percent income share almost doubled from approximately 10 percent in 1870 to about 18 percent in 1913, and skill premiums increased. Urbanization, industrialization, and massive immigration by low-skilled workers were responsible for this trend. A whole series of indices for top wealth shares likewise shows a sustained rise from 1640 to 1890 or even 1930. By one measure, between 1810 and 1910, the share of all assets held by the richest 1 percent of U.S. households almost doubled, from 25 percent to 46 percent. Wealth concentration was most pronounced at the very top: whereas in 1790 the largest reported fortune in the country had equaled 25,000 times the average annual working wage, in 1912 John D. Rockefeller was worth 2.6 million times the equivalent wage, a relative increase by two orders of magnitude.[34]

I have already mentioned the long secular increase in inequality in Latin American economies leading up to the time of the world wars. As commodity exports enriched regional elites, income concentration soared: one estimate for the southern cone of South America—Argentina, Brazil, Chile, and Uruguay—posits an overall income Gini increase from 0.575 in 1870 to 0.653 in 1920, whereas an alternative analysis reckons with a more dramatic rise from 0.296 in 1870 to 0.475 in 1929, albeit in population-weighted terms. Although the numbers are highly uncertain, the general direction of the trend seems clear enough. Japan is a more idiosyncratic case. Skill premiums appear to have declined during the Tokugawa period, and levels of inequality were fairly low when the country's isolation ended in the 1850s. Mercantile elites' prior inability to secure gains from international trade may have been one reason for this. Moreover, as agricultural productivity improved and the nonagricultural sector expanded during isolation, the fact that taxes were set based on fixed assumptions about output

---

[34] For the period 1860 to 1870, see herein, chapter 6, pp. 174–179. For 1870–1910: Lindert and Williamson 2016: 171–193, esp. 172 (top income shares about 1910, with WWID), 192–193. Smolensky and Plotnick 1993: 6 fig. 2 (not referenced by Lindert and Williamson 2016 but used by Milanovic 2016: 49 fig. 2.1, 72 fig. 2.10) extrapolate a national income Gini of about 0.46 in 1913 from the relationship between known income Ginis, the top 5 percent income share, and the unemployment rate between 1948 and 1989 (9, 43–44), which if correct would suggest a significant fall in overall income inequality between 1870 and 1913. However, the validity of this procedure and the comparability of the estimates for these dates remain uncertain, and, more crucially, this idea seems incompatible with the strong increase in top income shares during this period. Wealth shares: Lindert 1991: 216 fig. 9.1; Piketty 2014: 348; Roine and Waldenström 2015: 572 table 7.A2. Largest fortunes: Turchin 2016a: 81 table 4.2.

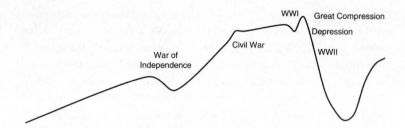

Figure 3.5   Inequality trends in the United States in the long run

prevented the "300 lords" who held large domains from capturing the expanding agricultural surplus, causing their share in overall revenues to fall. It took Japan's opening to the global economy and its subsequent industrialization to push inequality to ever higher levels.[35]

All in all, national trends during the century leading up to the period of the world wars are about as clear as we can expect them to be for a period that produced what by current standards must count as relatively modest amounts of data of often limited quality and consistency. For an extended period of time up to 1914, ranging from several decades to more than a century depending on the available evidence for individual countries, inequality mostly either increased or remained flat. In England, income inequality was already so high in the early nineteenth century that it probably could not have risen much more, although the concentration of wealth, likewise considerable, did in fact continue to soar to unprecedented heights. While the Netherlands, another precociously unequal country—and, perhaps, Italy—experienced stability, disparities in wealth or income rose in France, Spain, and, for the most part, in Germany, as well as in the United States, in those Latin American countries that are adequately documented, and in Japan. On a conservative reading of the record, Nordic countries likewise appear to have experienced fairly stable

---

[35] Latin American Gini estimates: Bértola and Ocampo 2012: 120 table 3.15; Prados de la Escosura 2007: 296–297 table 12.1. Rodríguez Weber 2015: 9–19 offers a more nuanced account for Chile. Using (land) rent/(urban) wage ratios, Arroyo Abad 2013: 40 fig. 1 finds net increases in inequality in Argentina and Uruguay between 1820 and 1900 but not in Mexico and Venezuela. Japan: Bassino, Fukao, and Takashima 2014; Bassino, Fukao, Settsu, and Takashima 2014; Hayami 2004: 16–17, 29–31; Miyamoto 2004: 38, 43, 46–47, 55; Nishikawa and Amano 2004: 247–248. For growing inequality during modernization, see herein, chapter 4, p. 118.

inequality for most of this period, except for some degree of wealth deconcentration among the affluent in the nineteenth century and a couple of sudden and poorly explained drops in top income shares just a few years before the outbreak of World War I. Between the late eighteenth or early nineteenth century and World War I, top 1 percent wealth shares rose in six of the eight countries for which we have data: Britain, France, the Netherlands, Sweden, Finland, and the United States.

At the same time, properly documented compressions of inequality were rare: after the moderately equalizing shocks of the American, French, and Latin American revolutions in the late eighteenth and early nineteenth centuries, the American Civil War is the only event known to have made a dent in one region's concentration of wealth. Aside from such sporadic instances of invariably violent leveling, inequality was mostly either maintained at high levels or grew even further. Broadly speaking, this was true regardless of whether countries industrialized earlier or later or not yet at all, whether land was scarce or abundant, and how political systems were configured. Technological progress, economic development, the widening globalization of the flows of goods and capital, and the ongoing strengthening of states, coupled with a century of unusually peaceful conditions, created an environment that protected private property and benefited capital investors. In Europe, this allowed the long secular upswing in inequality that had commenced with the abatement of the Black Death near the end of the Middle Ages to continue for more than four centuries. Other parts of the globe may have witnessed less prolonged phases of disequalization but were steadily catching up.[36]

At the end of chapter 14, I explore possible answers to the question of whether the world was about to enter an age of even more extreme maldistribution of income and wealth. But of course this is not what happened. Shortly before eleven o'clock in the morning on June 28, 1914, a nineteen-year-old Bosnian Serb shot and killed the Austrian Archduke Franz Ferdinand and his wife Sophie as they were riding in an open-topped car through the streets of Sarajevo. Asked how badly he had been wounded, the dying crown prince ever more faintly responded *"es ist nichts"*—"it is nothing." He was mistaken.

---

[36] My survey confirms Alfani's observation, based on a much more limited data set, that the process of nineteenth-century wealth concentration described by Piketty "was in fact only the final part of a much longer process" (Alfani 2016: 34).

Thirty-six years and more than 100 million violent deaths later, much of Europe and East Asia had repeatedly been wrecked, and mass-murdering communists ruled a third of the world's population. Between 1914 and 1945 (or the closest years on record), the income shares of the "1 percent" shrank by two-thirds in Japan; by more than half in France, Denmark, Sweden, and probably also the United Kingdom; by half in Finland; and by more than a third in Germany, the Netherlands, and the United States. Inequality also collapsed in Russia and its imperial possessions, as well as in China, Korea, and Taiwan. The concentration of wealth in elite hands, although more resilient outside revolutionary settings and therefore slower to recede, generally followed the same pattern. In western Europe, the ratio of the stock of capital to annual GDP plummeted by about two-thirds between 1910 and 1950 and perhaps by close to half worldwide, a rebalancing that greatly diminished the economic preeminence of wealthy investors. Two of the four horsemen of violent leveling—mass mobilization warfare and transformative revolution— had been unleashed with devastating consequences. For the first time since the Black Death, and on a scale perhaps unrivaled since the fall of the western Roman empire, access to material resources came to be distributed much more equally—and, uniquely, across large parts of the globe. By the time this "Great Compression" had run its course, commonly in the 1970s or 1980s, effective inequality both in the developed world and in the most populous developing countries of Asia had plunged to depths that had been unknown since the transition to sedentism and food domestication thousands of years earlier. The following chapters tell us why.[37]

---

[37] Communist regimes controlled roughly 860 million out of 2,560 million people in 1950. Income shares: WWID, summarized by Roine and Waldenström 2015: 493 fig. 7; and see herein, chapter 5, pp. 130–137 for more detailed analysis. (We have only sporadic data for top 1 percent income shares in the United Kingdom, which experienced a comparable compression, reflected in a drop of a third between 1937 and 1949 alone. The ratio between the loss rates for the 0.1 percent and the 1 percent from 1913 or 1918 to 1949 allows us to infer a top 1 percent income share of about 25 percent in 1913 and an overall decline by a little more than half by 1949.) For Russia and East Asia, see herein, chapter 7, pp. 221, 227. Wealth shares: Roine and Waldenström 2015: 572–581 and esp. 539 fig. 7.19, reproduced herein, chapter 5, p. 139. Capital/income ratios: Piketty 2014: 26 fig. 1.2 (reproduced herein, chapter 5, p. 140), 196 fig. 5.8; data appendix table TS12.4. (For criticism of the highly conjectural global estimate, see Magness and Murphy 2015: 23–32; but the overall trend is quite clear.) For the completion of the leveling process, see herein, chapter 15, p. 405; for the challenge of defining effective inequality levels, see herein, in the appendix. By some multidimensional inequality measures, contemporary Scandinavian countries have become as egalitarian as forager societies: Fochesato and Bowles 2015. For a very brief summary of the evolution of inequality up to the twentieth century, see herein, chapter 14, pp. 389–391.

Part II

WAR

Chapter 4

TOTAL WAR

"THE WAR SITUATION HAS DEVELOPED NOT NECESSARILY TO JAPAN'S ADVANTAGE": TOTAL WAR AS TOTAL LEVELER

Japan was once one of the most unequal countries on earth. In 1938, the country's "1 percent" received 19.9 percent of all reported income before taxes and transfers. Within the next seven years, their share dropped by two-thirds, all the way down to 6.4 percent. More than half of this loss was incurred by the richest tenth of that top bracket: their income share collapsed from 9.2 percent to 1.9 percent in the same period, a decline by almost four-fifths (Fig. 4.1).

However rapid and massive these shifts in the distribution of income, they pale in comparison to the even more dramatic destruction of the elite's wealth. The declared real value of the largest 1 percent of estates in Japan fell by 90 percent between 1936 and 1945 and by almost 97 percent between 1936 and 1949. The top 0.1 percent of all estates lost even more—93 percent and more than 98 percent, respectively. In real terms, the amount of wealth required to count a household among the richest 0.01 percent (or one in 10,000) in 1949 would have put it in only the top 5 percent back in 1936. Fortunes had shrunk so much that what used to count as mere affluence was now out of reach for all but a very few. Discontinuous data series make the overall reduction in Japanese inequality more difficult to trace with precision: yet, suggesting as they do a drop in the national income Gini from anywhere between 0.45 and 0.65 in the late 1930s to around 0.3 in the mid-1950s, the downward trend is unmistakable and reinforces the impression of massive leveling conveyed by the contraction of top income and wealth shares.[1]

As far as elites' incomes are concerned, Japan morphed from a society whose income distribution was as unequal as that of the United States on the eve of

---

[1] Moriguchi and Saez 2010: 133–136 table 3A.2 (income shares); 148 table 3B.1 (estates); 81 fig. 3.2 (Ginis), with Milanovic 2016: 85 fig. 2.18.

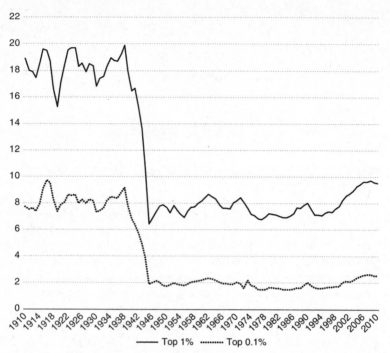

Figure 4.1 Top income shares in Japan, 1910–2010 (in percent)

the stock market crash of 1929—a high-water mark of the "1 percent"—to one akin to Denmark today, the most equal developed country in the world today in terms of top income shares. And elites' wealth had been largely wiped out: only Lenin, Mao, or Pol Pot could have done a more thorough job (see chapter 7). But Japan had not achieved the ideal of "getting to Denmark," nor had it been taken over by raving communists. What it had done instead was enter—or, depending on one's definition, start—World War II, first by trying to establish control over China and then by setting up a colonial empire that reached from Burma in the west to the atolls of Micronesia in the east and from the Aleutians north of the Arctic Circle to the Solomon Islands south of the equator. At the height of its power, it laid claim to roughly as many souls as the British Empire did at the time—close to half a billion people, or a fifth of the world population.[2]

---

[2] "Getting to Denmark" is academic shorthand for establishing political and economic institutions that are highly conducive to human welfare, a concept that goes back to Pritchett and Woolcock 2002: 4 and that has since been popularized especially by Fukuyama 2011: 14.

To sustain this extravagant venture, Japan's military had grown more than twentyfold in size, from a quarter of a million troops in the mid-1930s to more than 5 million by the summer of 1945, or one in seven Japanese males of any age. Armament production surged on the same scale. By war's end, around 2.5 million Japanese soldiers had perished. During the last nine months of the conflict, American bombers rained death and destruction on Japan, killing almost 700,000 civilians. For all their horrors, the two atomic bombs were merely a coda to years of inordinate exertion, suffering, and devastation. As total war ended in total defeat, Japan was occupied by hundreds of thousands of American troops and subjected to invasive institutional reforms designed to snuff out future imperialist ambitions.

These dramatic developments did not simply provide the context in which an exceptional degree of leveling took place: they were the sole cause of this process. Total war compressed inequality on an unprecedented scale. And as recent scholarship has made abundantly clear, this outcome was by no means limited to Japan. Other major parties to World War II, and to World War I before it, experienced similar transformations, though not always quite as extreme. The same was true of several close bystanders. Mass mobilization war served as one of the two principal means of leveling in the twentieth century. Transformative—communist—revolution was the other: but inasmuch as these revolutions were driven by the world wars, total war was the single ultimate cause. Returning to my simile of the Four Horsemen, war and revolution were as twins, charging side by side.

Japan provides us with a textbook case of war-driven leveling. In the following, I accordingly go into some detail in describing that country's experience during wartime and under occupation as I seek to identify the numerous and varied factors that conspired to destroy wealth and that severely compressed the spread of incomes. I then offer a more systematic global assessment of the leveling associated with the two world wars in both the short and the medium terms, briefly considering the experiences of individual countries, the war's influence on subsequent policymaking, and major secondary effects such as unionization and democratization. In later chapters, I explore how far back we can trace leveling outcomes brought about by mass mobilization warfare, the effects of other types of warfare that have been much more common historically, and finally the effects of civil war. We will see that over the course of human history, the violence of war has affected inequality in very different ways: only the most broadly based forms of military activity have been capable of narrowing the gap between rich and poor.

Inequality had been rising in Japan since the country had opened itself to the world in the late 1850s. This was a striking departure from earlier conditions. Provincial data from the end of the Shogunate suggest that personal income inequality and poverty levels had been relatively low by contemporary international standards. There is no indication that wage inequality had widened during the Tokugawa period: instead, there is some evidence for a gradual decline of skill premiums from the mid-sixteenth to the mid-nineteenth centuries, measured in urban rice wages. If true, this would point to falling income inequality among workers. The gap between elite and commoners may also have been narrowing. In the later stages of this period, local lords found themselves at a disadvantage in the struggle over who got to control the growing surplus: constrained by static agrarian tax rates, they were losing out to merchants and farmers. As the volume of international trade greatly diminished in the eighteenth and early nineteenth centuries, elites more generally were unable to capture gains from commercial activities, which likewise helped contain inequality.[3]

All this changed as Japan joined the world economy and underwent rapid industrialization. Although reliable numbers remain in short supply, both the national income Gini coefficient and top income shares are thought to have risen from the mid-nineteenth century onward. Industrialization accelerated in the wake of the Russo–Japanese war of 1904 to 1905. Increasing trade with Europe sustained export-led growth even as price inflation depressed real wages. Profit shares for big business rose in response to World War I, and income growth began to outpace wage growth. Inequality increased accordingly during the interwar period. By the 1930s, the wealth elite was riding high: landlords, shareholders, and corporate executives reaped large gains from economic development. Ownership of equities was highly concentrated and lucrative thanks to generous dividends. Executives were often also major shareholders and received large salaries and bonuses. Low taxes protected their incomes and facilitated ongoing wealth accumulation.[4]

---

[3] Saito 2015: 410; Bassino, Fukao, and Takashima 2014: 13; Hayami 2004: 16–17, 29–30.

[4] According to the most recent reconstruction, the Gini rose from 0.35 in 1850 (admittedly a guess) to 0.43 in 1909, 0.5 in 1925, 0.52 in 1935, and 0.55 in 1940: Bassino, Fukao, and Takashima 2014: 20 table 5. See 19 table 1 for top 1 percent income shares. They note a lack of consensus regarding trends in inequality between 1880s and 1930s, when inequality was either continuously rising or first falling and then rising (9). See also Saito 2015: 413–414 for the likelihood of a post-Shogunate rise in inequality over time. Short-term fluctuations notwithstanding, the WWID shows fairly stable top 1 percent income shares in the first third of the twentieth century. Economic development and disequalization: Nakamura and Odaka 2003b: 9, 12–13, 24–42; Hashimoto 2003: 193–194; Saito 2015: 413 n. 57; Moriguchi and Saez 2010: 100.

Japan's attack on China in July 1937 put a sudden end to these cozy arrangements. As the initial campaign broadened into an open-ended invasion of the most populous country on earth, Japan was forced to commit increasingly large resources to its military. After its gradual occupation of French Indochina from September 1940, Japan's all-out attack on the United States, the United Kingdom, the Dutch East Indies, Australia, and New Zealand in December 1941 raised the stakes even higher. In the first six months of the Pacific War, Japanese forces operated across a vast area from the Hawaiian islands and Alaska to Sri Lanka and Australia. By 1945, well more than 8 million Japanese men, almost a quarter of the entire male population of the country, had ended up serving in the military. Arms production increased twenty-one times in real terms between 1936 and 1944, and government spending more than doubled between 1937 and 1941, then tripled over the course of the next four years.[5]

This extraordinary mobilization effort had a significant effect on the economy. During the war years, government regulation, inflation, and physical destruction flattened the distribution of income and wealth. The first of these three mechanisms was the most important. State intervention gradually created a planned economy that preserved only a façade of free market capitalism. What started out as emergency measures expanded and became institutionalized over time. The command economy of Manchuria, which had been under Japanese military occupation since 1932, provided a model. In spring 1938, the National General Mobilization Law gave the government wide-ranging powers to press the Japanese economy into service for the war effort (which soon escalated to total war, *kokka sōryokusen*): the ability to hire and fire, determine working conditions, produce, distribute, move and price goods, and settle labor disputes. In 1939, the Ordinance to Control Corporate Dividends and Capital Circulation restricted dividend increases. Farm rents and certain prices were frozen, and wages and land prices began to be regulated. Executive bonuses were capped in 1940, and the following year rental income was fixed by the authorities. Income taxes for individuals and corporations rose almost every year—in 1937, 1938, 1940, 1942, 1944, and 1945. The top marginal income tax rate doubled between 1935 and 1943. The government intervened in stock and bond markets to boost war bonds at the expense of corporate shares and bonds, which then yielded lower returns. Substantial price inflation, alongside fixed urban and land rents and land prices, depressed the value of bonds, deposits, and real estate.

---

[5] Nakamura 2003: 70 table 2.5, 82.

With the start of the Pacific War, the state requisitioned all private ships exceeding 100 tons' displacement, few of which would return: four of every five merchant ships were lost in the war. Under the Munitions Corporations Law of 1943, businesses that were officially designated as munitions companies were forced to appoint production supervisors who took orders directly from the government, which determined investment in equipment, work management, and capital allocation; profits and dividends were set by the state. From 1943 the government enforced an all-encompassing shift into armaments production: ill-founded promises of future compensation were the only inducement. In 1944 the state assumed further powers, and some businesses were nationalized. One survey lists about seventy different economic controls that were created between 1937 and 1945—a wide range of measures that included rationing, capital controls, wage control, price control, and land rent control.[6]

The *zaibatsu* system of business conglomerates that were tightly controlled by a few wealthy families began to weaken. As corporate savings and investment by the rich proved insufficient to raise the necessary capital for wartime industrial expansion, funds had to be borrowed from outside these formerly closed circles, and the Industrial Bank of Japan reduced the market share of private financial institutions. Whereas major shareholders used to hold senior executive positions, the growth in capitalization and outside loans began to sever the intimate ties between ownership and management, with adverse consequences for wealth accumulation. More generally, war pressures gave rise to the novel idea that a firm should not be the sole possession of stockholders but rather a communal organization that involved each of its members. This doctrine encouraged separation of ownership and management and gave more rights to workers, including profit sharing.[7]

A series of wartime interventions foreshadowed the comprehensive land reform later undertaken under U.S. occupation. Before the war, landlords— most of them of modest wealth—owned half of all farmland, and a third of all farmers worked as their tenants. Rural poverty had triggered disputes and unrest during the interwar period, but reform attempts had remained feeble at best. This changed with the Farmland Adjustment Law of 1938, which pushed owners to sell tenanted land and allowed for compulsory purchase of uncultivated

---

[6] See Moriguchi and Saez 2010: 100–102 for this trio. For the various state interventions, see esp. Hara 2003 and Nakamura 2003; and cf. Moriguchi and Saez 2010: 101 for a very brief overview. Controls: Nakamura 2003: 63–66 table 2.2.

[7] Nakamura 2003: 85; Okazaki 1993: 187–189, 195.

land. In 1939 the Land Rent Control Order froze rents at current levels and gave the government the right to order rent reductions. The Land Price Control Order of 1941 fixed land prices at 1939 values, and the Land Control Order of the same year gave the government the power to decide which crops were to be planted. With the Food Control Law of 1942, the authorities began to determine the price of staples. All rice beyond that required for personal consumption was to be sold to the state, and all land rents beyond personal needs were to be transferred to the treasury. Growing subsidies were handed to rice farmers to encourage production in the absence of price incentives. This allowed the income of primary producers to keep pace with inflation, whereas landlords' incomes were eroded, a divergence that produced considerable leveling in the countryside. Real farm rents fell by four-fifths between 1941 and 1945, and from 4.4 percent of national income in the mid-1930s to 0.3 percent in 1946. Outcomes for landlords could have been even worse, as various proposals for confiscation were circulated but never implemented.[8]

Workers benefited not only from rent controls, state subsidies, and increasing government intervention in business management but also from an expansion of welfare provisions that were created out of concern for the physical condition of recruits and workers and for the express purpose of reducing anxiety among the citizenry. A Welfare Ministry was set up in 1938 and immediately became a major driving force behind social policy. Its officials initiated partially state-funded health insurance schemes, which were greatly expanded from 1941 onward, as was poor relief. Various public pension schemes aimed to curb consumption, and the country's first-ever public housing projects were launched in 1941.[9]

The second leveling force, inflation, accelerated during the war. Consumer prices rose 235 percent between 1937 and 1944 and jumped another 360 percent from 1944 to 1945 alone. This sharply lowered the value of bonds and deposits even as rent controls ate into the real incomes of landlords.[10]

Unlike in European theaters, the third factor, the physical destruction of capital in Japan proper, became operative only in the final stages of the war, although commercial shipping had already begun to be hit much earlier. By September 1945, a quarter of the country's physical capital stock had been wiped

[8] Takigawa 1972: 291–304; Yuen 1982: 159–173; Dore 1984: 112–114; Kawagoe 1999: 11–26.
[9] Kasza 2002: 422–428; Nakamura 2003: 85. Kasza 2002: 429 concludes that "[w]ar outweighed all other factors in causing Japan's welfare transformation from 1937 to 1945."
[10] Moriguchi and Saez 2010: 101; 129–130 table 3A.1.

out. Japan lost 80 percent of its merchant ships, 25 percent of all buildings, 21 percent of household furnishings and personal effects, 34 percent of factory equipment, and 24 percent of finished products. The number of factories in operation and the size of the workforce they employed nearly halved during the final year of the war. Damage varied greatly by industry: although losses in iron and steel works were minimal, 10 percent of the textile industry, 25 percent of machinery production, and 30 percent to 50 percent of the chemical industry were put out of business. The large majority of these losses were directly caused by air raids. According to the U.S. Strategic Bombing Survey of 1946, the allies had dropped 160,800 tons of bombs on Japan, less than an eighth of the volume of the bombing of Germany but with greater success against less well defended targets. The firebombing of Tokyo during the nights of March 9–10, 1945, which even by conservative estimates killed close to 100,000 residents and destroyed more than a quarter-million buildings and homes across an area of sixteen square miles, was only one outstanding episode; so were the annihilation of Hiroshima and Nagasaki five months later. The compilers of the survey estimated that some 40 percent of the built-up area of sixty-six cities that had been bombed was destroyed and that some 30 percent of the entire urban population of the country had lost their homes. Yet despite the losses this caused to owners of real estate and investors, the overall effect must not be overestimated. Thanks to the aggressive wartime expansion of heavy and chemical industry, the volume of production equipment that survived in 1945 exceeded that available in 1937. And with the exception of shipping, physical destruction was largely compressed into the last nine months of the war, well after top income and wealth shares had entered freefall (see earlier, Fig. 4.1). Allied bombing merely accelerated an ongoing trend.[11]

Gains from capital almost disappeared during the war years: the share of rent and interest income in total national income fell from a sixth in the mid-1930s to only 3 percent in 1946. In 1938, dividends, interest, and rental income together had accounted for about a third of the income of the top "1 percent," with the remainder divided between business and employment income. By 1945, the share of capital income had dropped to less than an eighth and that of wages to a tenth; business income was the only significant revenue source left to the (formerly) wealthy. In both absolute and relative terms, dividends and

[11] Capital stock: Minami 1998: 52; Yoshikawa and Okazaki 1993: 86; Moriguchi and Saez 2010: 102. Losses: Nakamura 2003: 84; Yoshikawa and Okazaki 1993: 86. Bombing: *United States strategic bombing survey* 1946: 17.

wages, which had been subjected to increasingly severe government controls, had taken the heaviest hits. Rentiers and highly paid executives had been all but ruined as a class. This decline was disproportionately severe among the uppermost tiers of the "1 percent."

At the same time, it was not accompanied by any comparable compression among the next most affluent income groups. The income share of households between the ninety-fifth and ninety-ninth percentiles (the highest 4 percent of incomes below the top 1 percent) hardly fell at all during the war and thereafter stabilized for a long time at around the same level as in the early twentieth century, or about 12 percent to 14 percent of national income. Although most had suffered income losses, only the richest Japanese also lost out in relative terms: whereas before World War II the top "1 percent" had consistently captured about half as much again income as the next 4 percent combined, after 1945 they never again made more than half as much as that group. Thus the entire loss of income share among the top "1 percent" translated to a gain in the share of the subelite 95 percent of the population, whose portion of national income rose by a fifth from 68.2 percent in 1938 to 81.5 percent in 1947. This represented a truly spectacular shift, which lifted the income share of the 95 percent from one comparable to the United States in 2009 to one equivalent to Sweden today—in the course of less than a decade.[12]

"NO LONGER IS THE FUTURE TO BE SETTLED BY A FEW": LEVELING REINFORCED AND CONSOLIDATED

Yet what happened during the war itself was only part of the leveling process. Japan may have been unique among the major belligerents in that *all* the observed net income compression since the late 1930s took place during World War II rather than mostly during and to a lesser degree after the war, as it commonly did elsewhere (see herein, Table 5.2). Yet just as in those other countries, the deconcentration of income and wealth in the longer term was shaped by the equalizing character of postwar policies. In the Japanese case, all these policies can be shown to have been a direct outcome of the war. By the time Emperor Hirohito had acknowledged, on August 15, 1945, that "the war situation has

---

[12] Capital income share: Yoshikawa and Okazaki 1993: 91 table 4.4; Moriguchi and Saez 2010: 139 table 3A.3, and see also 91 fig. 3.7. During the period from 1886 to 1937, capital income had averaged about half of the top 1 percent income share (92). Income shares: Moriguchi and Saez 2010: 88 fig. 3.4; 134–135 table 3A.2; WWID.

not developed necessarily to Japan's advantage" and the time had come for "bearing the unbearable"—unconditional surrender and occupation by Allied forces—Japan's economy was in shambles. The lack of raw materials and fuel had caused production to collapse. In 1946, real GNP was 45 percent lower than it had been in 1937, and the volume of imports amounted to an eighth of those in 1935 in real terms. As the economy recovered, a whole bundle of policies and war-related effects served to maintain the income compression that had occurred during the war and to flatten the wealth distribution even further.[13]

Hyperinflation commenced as the war ended. After rising fourteenfold between 1937 and 1945, the consumer price index surged much more rapidly between 1945 and 1948. Although reported indices vary, by one measure consumer prices in 1948 were 18,000 percent higher than they had been at the time Japan invaded China. What little was left of fixed capital income evaporated.[14]

Both corporations and landlords became the targets of aggressive restructuring. The three main goals of the U.S. occupation government were the dissolution of the *zaibatsu*, democratization of labor, and land reform, measures that were to be implemented in conjunction with punitively progressive taxation. The ultimate objective was to eliminate not only the material capacity for war but also the perceived sources of imperialist aggression. Economic reforms formed part of a broader range of fundamental democratizing changes designed to reshape Japanese institutions: a new constitution, female suffrage, and a thorough revision of the court and police system, to name just a few. All of this was implemented as a direct consequence of the war, which had resulted in foreign occupation.[15]

Interventions in the economy explicitly pursued leveling as a means to achieve the desired outcomes. The "Basic Directive" for the American occupation authorities entitled "Democratization of Japanese Economic Institutions" urged the promotion of a "wide distribution of income and of the ownership of the means of production and trade." Aiming for the creation of a social welfare state, occupation policy goals were closely associated with those of the New Deal. In 1943 and 1945, American researchers assessed that the low distribution of wealth to Japanese industrial workers and farmers had stunted domestic

---

[13] GNP and exports: Yoshikawa and Okazaki 1993: 87–88.
[14] Moriguchi and Saez 2010: 129–30 table 3A.1; cf. Nakamura 2003: 90–92. For large variation in rates according to different indices, see Kuroda 1993: 33–34; and cf. also Teranishi 1993a: 68–69; Yoshikawa and Okazaki 1993: 89.
[15] Nakamura 2003: 87; Miwa 2003: 335–336.

consumption and driven overseas economic expansionism. This was now to be addressed by labor reorganization with higher wages that would promote domestic consumption and facilitate demilitarization. Economic democratization and leveling were not ends in themselves: the underlying policy goal was to combat militarism by restructuring features of the economy that might be conducive to overseas aggression. Once again, in the final analysis, war and its consequences were responsible for these changes.[16]

The occupiers wielded the weapon of taxation with a heavy hand. Between 1946 and 1951, a massive and progressive property tax was levied on the net value of assets, with a low exemption level and a top marginal rate of 90 percent. Applied to assets rather than income or just estates, it was overtly confiscatory in nature. From the American perspective, the tax was meant to redistribute private property and to transfer the proceeds to the lower classes to shore up their purchasing power. In the beginning, it covered one in eight households, and it eventually transferred 70 percent of the property of the richest 5,000 households to the state, as well as a third of the assets of all those liable to pay. This levy specifically targeted the affluent at a time when the overall tax burden was fairly low. Redistribution rather than revenue maximization was the governing principle. Also in 1946, many bank deposits were frozen and subsequently eroded by inflation, and those above a certain threshold were eliminated two years later.[17]

The occupation authorities held a dim view of the *zaibatsu*, family-owned business conglomerates, regarding them as close partners of the militaristic leadership of the war years and more generally as a force that perpetuated semifeudalistic relations between management and labor, which depressed workers' wages and helped capitalists amass huge profits. The biggest *zaibatsu* were dissolved, breaking their hold on the country's economy. (More ambitious plans for the reorganization of hundreds of businesses fell victim to Cold War policy changes.) *Zaibatsu* families were forced to sell 42 percent of total stock holdings, which resulted in a huge decline in the proportion of shares held by corporations. In a national purge of senior management in 1947, some 2,200 executives at 632 corporations were dismissed or chose to retire in anticipation of being removed. The previous system of close corporate control by capitalists

---

[16] Miwa 2003: 339–341. Real GNP indeed grew by 40 percent between 1946 and 1950, mostly for consumption rather than investment: Yoshikawa and Okazaki 1993: 87.

[17] Miwa 2003: 347; Minami 1998: 52; Moriguchi and Saez 2010: 102; Nakamura 2003: 98 table 2.14; Teranishi 1993b: 171–172; Yoshikawa and Okazaki 1993: 90.

had thus been dismantled. General MacArthur's New Year's Day message of 1948 declared that

> Allied policy has required the breaking up of that system which in the past has permitted the major part of the commerce and industry and natural resources of your country to be owned and controlled by a minority of feudal families and exploited to their exclusive benefit.[18]

Initial plans for intervention had been very harsh. In 1945 and 1946, the occupation government considered plans to remove manufacturing and energy-generating equipment to keep living standards at late 1920s or early 1930s levels and absorb everything above that threshold as war reparation. Although policy quickly changed in response to the new realities of the Cold War, plenty of invasive measures were in fact implemented. Armaments factories and related businesses were confiscated as reparation. In July 1946, arguing that "war is not a business for profit," the Americans ordered the cessation of war compensation payments that had been promised for wartime losses; outstanding claims were canceled. This added further pressure to the balance sheets of firms and banks. Many companies faced liquidation over the next few years. Others used up reserve funds, capital, and equity and even shifted the burden to creditors in order to survive.[19]

Defeat brought other losses as well. The 1930s had witnessed considerable outflow of capital for investment in Japan's colonies in Taiwan, Korea, and Manchuria. During the war years, Japanese companies operated more aggressively in the colonies and occupied territories, including in China. Under the San Francisco Peace Treaty of 1951, Japan forfeited all its foreign assets worldwide—most of which had already been seized by various countries.[20]

The financial sector was devastated. By 1948 banking losses had grown to such an enormous extent that they could be addressed only by erasing all capital gains and retained earnings and cutting banks' capital by 90 percent, in addition to writing off deposits above a certain threshold. Stockholders not only

---

[18] Nakamura 2003: 87; Minami 1998: 52; Estevez-Abe 2008: 103; Miwa 2003: 345; Miyazaki and Itô 2003: 315–316; Yonekura 1993: 213–222. Quote: Miwa 2003: 349.

[19] Miwa 2003: 336–337, 341–345; Nakamura 2003: 86–87, 91 (quote). The stated objective of this and related measures was the "elimination of wartime gains" (Miwa 2003: 346)—which, judging from the observed income compression, may at that point have been more imaginary than real.

[20] Yamamoto 2003: 240; Miyazaki and Itô 2003: 309–312.

incurred huge losses but were even prohibited from purchasing new issues for the next three years. As a result, capital income effectively disappeared. In 1948, dividends, interest, and rental incomes together accounted for no more than 0.3 percent of the top 1 percent of incomes, compared to 45.9 percent in 1937 and 11.8 percent in 1945.[21]

Unionization became a key concern. Union membership had been less than 10 percent before the war, and existing unions had been disbanded in 1940 and replaced by patriotic industrial associations of workers. This form of worker organization was employed to motivate the labor force for the war effort and provided a basis for the creation of enterprise-based unions under occupation. The Labor Union Law was drafted immediately after the arrival of U.S. forces, in the fall of 1945, based on prewar plans that had failed. Passed at the very end of that year, it gave workers the right to organize, strike, and engage in collective bargaining. Membership soared: in 1946, 40 percent of workers were unionized, and almost 60 percent were by 1949. Benefits on top of wages increased, and the health insurance and pension systems created during the war were expanded. Unions proved instrumental in establishing cooperative industrial relations, with their emphasis on seniority wages, job security—and, most important from a leveling perspective, by fostering consensus regarding a new wage structure that determined pay based on age, need, living standards, prices, and inflation. A minimal living wage was set for entry-level workers and raised with age, seniority, and family size. Frequent living wage adjustments to keep pace with inflation reduced the initially wide income gaps between white- and blue-collar workers.[22]

Finally, land reform was another major goal of the occupation authorities: in rare agreement with the Maoists who were taking over China at the time, they regarded landlordism as a great evil that was to be eradicated. A government memo held that land redistribution was essential in moving Japan in a peaceful direction, noting that the Japanese army had persuaded poor farmers that overseas aggression was their only way out of poverty: in the absence of land reform, the countryside might remain a hotbed of militarism. Once again, the underlying rationale for intervention was closely related to the war. A land reform bill designed by the Japanese Ministry of Agriculture and passed at the very end of

---

[21] Teranishi 1993b, esp. 172; Moriguchi and Saez 2010: 138 table 3A.3.

[22] Unionization: Hara 2003: 261; Nakamura 2003: 88; Miwa 2003: 347; Yonekura 1993: 223–230, esp. 225 table 9.3; Nakamura 2003: 88; cf. Minami 1998: 52. Benefits: Hara 2003: 285; Yonekura 1993: 227–228; Estevez-Abe 2008: 103–111.

1945 was rejected by the United States as too moderate, and a revised scheme became law in October 1946. All land owned by absentee landlords (defined as those not residing in the same village where that land was located) was subject to compulsory purchase, as was all tenanted land in excess of one hectare held by resident landlords. Owner-cultivated land in excess of three hectares could also be included if it was deemed inefficiently cultivated. Compensation levels, once set, were rapidly eroded by rampant inflation. The same was true of rents, which were to be paid in cash amounts frozen at late 1945 levels and consequently gradually eliminated by inflation. The concurrent decline in real land values was nothing short of dramatic: between 1939 and 1949, the real price of paddy land relative to that of rice fell by a factor of 500, and by about half as much relative to the price of cigarettes. A third of all farmland in Japan was covered by the reform and was thus transferred to half of the country's rural households. Tenanted land, which had accounted for almost half of the land before the war, fell to 13 percent in 1949 and 9 percent in 1955, whereas the owner–cultivators' share in the rural population more than doubled, from 31 percent to 70 percent, and landless tenants almost disappeared. The income Gini in rural towns dropped from 0.5 before the war to 0.35 after. Even though this reform was grounded in Japanese wartime measures and ideas, implementation on this drastic scale was a direct result of occupation. With characteristic modesty, General MacArthur called the scheme "possibly the most successful land reform program in history."[23]

The years of total war and subsequent occupation, from the invasion of China in 1937 to the Peace Treaty of 1951, completely restructured the sources and distribution of income and wealth in Japan. The sharp drop in top income shares and the dramatic collapse of the size of large fortunes observed at the beginning of this chapter were caused above all by a decline in the return on capital, which affected the population well beyond the very rich. The composition of the largest 9 percent of estates changed considerably. Whereas in 1935 shares, bonds, and deposits had accounted for almost half of all assets in this category, by 1950 their share had dropped to a sixth, and farmland had declined from close to a quarter to less than an eighth. Most of these changes occurred during

---

[23] Memo: Miwa 2003: 341; and see also Dore 1984: 115–125 on the relationship between tenancy, rural poverty, and aggression. Land reform: Kawagoe 1999: 1–2, 8–9, 27–34; Takigawa 1972: 290–291; Yoshikawa and Okazaki 1993: 90; Ward 1990: 103–104; and see also Dore 1984: 129–198 and Kawagoe 1993. MacArthur: in a letter to Prime Minister Yoshida Shigeru from October 21, 1949, quoted by Ward 1990: 98; Kawagoe 1999: 1.

the war itself: all of the decline in top income shares and, in absolute terms, almost all (about 93 percent) of the drop in the real value of the top 1 percent of estates between 1936 and 1949 had already been completed by 1945.[24]

Nevertheless, the occupation period, as a direct outgrowth of the war, was of critical importance in making wartime measures permanent and putting them on a more solid footing. As General MacArthur put it in his first New Year's Day message to the people of Japan, no longer was the future to be "settled by a few." U.S. intervention in the Japanese economy focused on taxation, corporate governance, and labor organization, all areas in which the war leadership had already inflicted huge financial pain on the established wealth elite. The war and immediate postwar years thus prompted a secular shift from a rich and powerful class of shareholders who had controlled management and demanded high dividends to a more egalitarian corporate system of lifetime employment, seniority-based wages, and company unions. Alongside the restructuring of businesses and labor relations as well as land reform, progressive taxation was a key mechanism for sustaining wartime leveling. Formalized from the 1950s onward, the Japanese tax system imposed a marginal rate of 60 percent to 75 percent on top incomes and an estate tax in excess of 70 percent on the largest fortunes. This helped contain income inequality and wealth accumulation well into the 1990s, just as strong protections for tenants depressed housing rental income and collective bargaining ensured ongoing wage compression.[25]

The war and its consequences made leveling sudden, massive, and sustainable. The bloodiest years in Japanese history, a war that cost millions of lives and visited enormous destruction on the homeland, had produced a uniquely equalizing outcome. This outcome was made possible by a novel type of warfare that required full demographic and economic mobilization. Extreme violence had flattened extreme income and wealth inequalities within Japanese society. In its grim progression from popular mobilization to destruction and occupation, total war had leveled totally.

---

[24] Moriguchi and Saez 2010: 94 table 3.3.
[25] Okazaki 1993: 180; Moriguchi and Saez 2010: 104–105. For the MacArthur quote also used in the section heading, see Department of State 1946: 135.

Chapter 5

THE GREAT COMPRESSION

"THE DRAMA OF THE THIRTY YEARS WAR": THE GREAT LEVELING OF INEQUALITY FROM 1914 TO 1945

How typical was the Japanese experience? Did World War II, or the two world wars more generally, produce similar outcomes in other countries as well? The very short answer is yes. Although each case is defined by a specific configuration of circumstances, what Charles de Gaulle called "the drama of the thirty years war," from 1914 to 1945, resulted in a significant and often dramatic deconcentration of income and wealth across the developed world. Notwithstanding alternative or complementary factors, which I review in chapters 12 and 13, there can be no doubt that modern mass mobilization warfare and its economic, political, social, and fiscal elements and consequences served as a uniquely powerful means of leveling.[1]

As we have seen in the previous chapter, inequality plummeted in Japan during World War II and remained low thereafter. Several other countries that participated in that conflict and for which comparable data sets are available show a strikingly similar pattern, such as the United States, France, and Canada (Fig. 5.1).[2]

For some of the other main belligerents, the time resolution of the relevant evidence for top income shares is of lesser quality, a problem that tends to obscure the sudden nature of wartime compression. Even so, the underlying trend is the same, as in the case of the top 0.1 percent income shares in Germany and the United Kingdom (Fig. 5.2).

---

[1] Quote: "le drame de la guerre de trente ans, que nous venons de gagner . . . ": Charles de Gaulle's speech at Bar-le-Duc, July 28, 1946, quoted from http://mjp.univ-perp.fr/textes/degaulle28071946.htm. For succinct statements of this thesis, see most recently Piketty 2014: 146–150; Piketty and Saez 2014: 840; Roine and Waldenström 2015: 555–556, 566–567.

[2] Here and in the following, all information regarding top income shares is drawn from the WWID. For the sake of consistency, I use identical time frames for each country, from 1937 to 1967.

Figure 5.1 Top 1 percent income shares in four countries, 1935–1975 (in percent)

Two related issues are at stake: the direct effect of war on inequality while the war was being fought (and in its immediate aftermath whenever no precisely matching data are available, as in the case of Germany, shown in Fig. 5.2) and its longer-term effect over the course of the following decades. I proceed in several stages. First, I analyze the wartime evolution of top income shares in those countries for which relevant evidence has been published, noting how it varied depending on these countries' degree of involvement in the conflict. Second, I compare the extent of wartime leveling to subsequent developments so as to demonstrate the exceptional nature of the direct effects of war on inequality. Third, I review—in much less detail than for Japan—the factors that accounted for the wartime compression of income and wealth distribution. Finally, I address the question of how the world wars, and especially World War II, were responsible for the persistence and often continued strengthening of more egalitarian access to material resources after 1945.

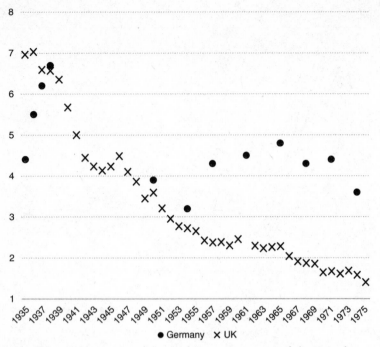

Figure 5.2   Top 0.1 percent income shares in Germany and the United Kingdom (in percent)

Table 5.1 summarizes the currently published information regarding the development of top income shares—generally the top 1 percent except for a few cases in which the necessary time depth or resolution can be achieved only by focusing on smaller tiers within that bracket, such as the top 0.1 or even 0.01 percent of incomes. The benchmark dates are 1913 and 1918 for World War I and 1938 and 1945 for World War II, although in some cases slightly different dates were used and these ranges do not always precisely match the years in which individual countries participated in these wars. A word of caution: all these figures ought to be taken with a grain of salt. But ultimately these top income share statistics are the best data at our disposal. They reach back much farther in time than standardized Gini coefficients and give us a good sense of how strongly change was concentrated at the very top of the income distribution. That said, even though the manner in which I use these data may create the impression of quantitative precision, this format should not mislead us into

Table 5.1   The development of top income shares during the world wars

| Country | Change (in percent) | | | |
| | World War I | | World War II | |
Country	Absolute	Relative	Absolute	Relative
Argentina	–		+2.92	+14[d]
Australia	–		-1.95	-19[a]
Canada	–		-8.28	-45[a]
Denmark	+9.63	+59[c]	-1.96	-15[a]
Finland	–		-5.47	-42[a]
France	-1.05	-6[a]	-6.73	-47[a]
Germany	+4.43 (-6.47)	+25 (-36)[a]	-4.7	-29[a]
India	–		-6.41	-36[b]
Ireland (0.1%)	–		-1.39	-23[c]
Japan	-0.83	-5[b]	-13.49	-68[a]
Mauritius (0.1%)	–		-5.46	-55[b]
Netherlands	+0.99	+5[c]	-2.82	-18[a]
New Zealand	–		-0.44	-6[a]
Norway	–		-3.62	-28[a]
Portugal (0.1%)	–		-1.36	-28[c]
South Africa	-0.93	-4[b]	+3.35	+20[b]
Spain (0.01%)	–		-0.19/-0.41	-15/-27[c]
Sweden	-4.59	-22[c]	-2.55	-21[c]
Switzerland	–		-1.29	-11[c]
United Kingdom	–		-5.51	-32[a]
(0.1%)	-2.56	-23[a]	-2.34	-36[a]
United States	-2.08	-12[a]	-3.66	-25[a]

Key: Top 1 percent shares unless stated otherwise. [a]principal belligerent; [b]secondary/colonial belligerent; [c]bystander; [d]remote neutral

taking specific details at face value. All this evidence can do is convey a sense of the direction and magnitude of change, which is the best we can hope for.[3]

---

[3] Argentina 1938/1945, Australia 1938/1945, Canada 1938/1945, Denmark 1908/1918, 1938/1945, Finland 1938/1945, France 1905/1918, 1938/1945, Germany 1913/1918(1925), 1938/1950, India 1938/1945, Ireland 1938/1945, Japan 1913/1918, 1938/1945, Mauritius 1938/1945, Netherlands 1914/1918, 1938/1946, New Zealand 1938/1945, Norway 1938/1948, Portugal 1938/1945, South Africa 1914/1918, 1938/1945, Spain 1935/1940/1945, Sweden 1912/1919, 1935/1945, Switzerland 1939/1945, United Kingdom 1937/1949 (1%), 1913/1918, 1938/1945 (0.1%), United States 1913/1918, 1938/1945.

This tabulation reflects the superior quality of the data for World War II and shows a clear trend associated with this event. The average percentage drop of top income shares in countries that actively fought in the war as frontline states (and that sometimes suffered occupation) is 31 percent of the prewar level, a robust finding considering that this sample consists of a dozen countries. (Exclusion of the somewhat marginal case of New Zealand would raise the mean farther, to 33 percent.) The median drop is 28 percent to 29 percent, and every single case registers a net decline. There are far fewer less developed or more remote colonial participants (India, Mauritius, and South Africa), and no consistent trend can be observed; the mean drop amounted to 24 percent. The sample of neutral neighbors (Ireland, Portugal, Sweden, and Switzerland) is likewise small but at least shows a consistent negative trend, for a mean drop also of 24 percent. Argentina, neutral almost until the end and geographically extremely distant from the main theaters, is a clear outlier: its "1 percent" gained 14 percent on its prewar income share.

The evidence for World War I is both scarcer and more complex, a complexity that reflects genuine differences from World War II in the timing of the war's effects on inequality. As we will see hereafter, in Germany and to some extent also in France, these effects were deferred until after 1918 for political and fiscal reasons. The overall outcome for the main belligerents thus depends on whether we use German data for 1918 or for 1925: only in the latter case do we observe an average drop of 19 percent for top income shares. Two marginal participants register a mean drop of 5 percent, whereas three neutral neighbors experienced a 14 percent increase but saw no consistent trend. For now, we may conclude that World War II had an extremely powerful and direct effect on elite incomes that also extended to neighboring nonbelligerents. The only two countries that experienced growing inequality at the time were the ones farthest removed from the hostilities.

We must now relate these wartime changes to developments in the generation or so after the end of World War II. In almost all countries that had been actively involved in that conflict, top income shares continued to fall during this period, either continually or after a temporary recovery after the war. This trend generally continued for several decades but eventually began to be reversed at various points ranging from 1978 to 1999, when top market income shares once again began to rise. Table 5.2 compares the average annual rate of contraction of top income shares (the top 1 percent unless otherwise noted), expressed in percentage points, during the war years, the postwar period, and, in a few cases

Table 5.2 Variation in the rate of reduction of top 1 percent income shares, by period

			Annual decline	
Country	Period	Years	In percentage points	As multiple of postwar rate of decline (rounded)
Japan	World War II	1938–1945	1.927	n/a
	Postwar	1945–1994	−0.013	
Canada	World War II	1938–1945	1.183	15 ½
	Postwar	1945–1978	0.076	
France	World War II	1938–1945	0.961	68 ⅔ (net), 7 (cont.)
	Postwar (net)	1945–1983	0.014	
	Postwar (cont.)	1961–1983	0.136	
Netherlands	World War II	1941–1946	0.956	6
	Postwar	1946–1993	0.162	
India	World War II	1938–1945	0.916	4 ⅔ (net), 2 ½ (cont.)
	Postwar (net)	1945–1981	0.195	
	Postwar (cont.)	1955–1981	0.385	
Germany	World War I	1914–1918	−0.312	n/a
	Hyperinflation	1918–1925	1.557	25 ½
	"World War I+"	1914–1925	0.589	9 ⅔
	World War II	1938–1950*	0.392	6 ½
	Postwar	1950–1995	0.061	
USA	World War I	1916–1918	1.345	11
	Depression	1928–1931	1.443	12
	World War II	1940–1945	0.932	8
	Postwar	1945–1973	0.119	
UK	World War II	1937–1949	0.459	3
	Postwar	1949–1978	0.147	
for 0.1%	World War I	1913–1918	0.512	5 ½
	World War II	1939–1945	0.353	4
	Postwar	1945–1978	0.091	

(Continued)

Table 5.2 (*Continued*)

Country	Period	Years	Annual decline In percentage points	Annual decline As multiple of postwar rate of decline (rounded)
Finland	World War II	1938–1947	0.781	11 (net), 2 ⅓ (cont.)
	Postwar (net)	1947–1983	0.07	
	Postwar (cont.)	1963–1983	0.334	
Australia	Depression	1928–1932	0.645	6 (net), 4 ⅓ (cont.)
	World War II	1941–1945	0.585	5 ½ (net), 4 (cont.)
	Postwar (net)	1945–1981	0.106	
	Postwar (cont.)	1951–1981	0.149	
Denmark	World War II	1940–1945	0.49	4
	Postwar	1945–1994	0.13	
Norway	World War II	1938–1948	0.362	3
	Postwar	1948–1989	0.121	

(whenever change was rapid), also during the Great Depression. When applicable, the postwar rates of loss are computed in two ways: (1) as the net rate of decline between the end of World War II and the year with the lowest subsequently recorded top income share, regardless of intervening fluctuations, and (2) as the rate of continuous decline from the highest to the lowest postwar value, a procedure that takes into account variation over time. The "multiple of postwar rate of decline" in Table 5.2 roughly measures how many times larger the annual decrease during wartime was than in the postwar period of decline, as defined in the two ways described.

These data reveal a uniform pattern. The annual rate of decline of the top income shares in wartime was invariably several times, and indeed often a great many times, higher than in the postwar period, regardless of how the postwar rates are calculated. For many of the main belligerents, the difference in scale is huge. In France, the top income share declined sixty-eight times as quickly during the war as it did during the following thirty-eight years: 92 percent of the country's total reduction in the top income share since 1938 had occurred by 1945. This proportion is almost as high in Canada, where 77 percent of the overall compression since 1938 took place during the war. Japan leads the pack: wartime leveling was so severe that 1945 was the year with the smallest top income share on record, a record low that has never since been reattained. In the United Kingdom, almost half of the total fall in the top 0.1 percent's income share between before the Great War and the late 1970s happened during the two world wars proper. In the United States, the annual rate of decline was an order of magnitude higher in both world wars than in the postwar period, and the same is true of Finland in World War II. It is telling that in countries that were less severely affected by the war, such as Denmark, Norway, Australia, and India, the average wartime compression rates were merely three to five times as high as afterward. (Although the British rate of decline during World War II was also relatively modest, much compression had already occurred in World War I.)

Only the German evidence is more complicated. If we take into account deferred leveling by measuring the World War I rate up to 1925, the first year after 1919 for which there is tangible information, then Germany's "wartime" compression rate was an order of magnitude higher than in the post–World War II period. Another problem arises from the lack of data between 1938 and 1950, which makes it impossible to tell how much of the overall drop in this interval occurred between 1938 and 1945. Especially among industrialized nations, World War II generated a very powerful leveling effect that greatly exceeded anything that has happened since. There is no better way to highlight the fundamental discontinuity in the evolution of income inequality in war and peace. The information for World War I, by contrast, is not only less rich but also more challenging to interpret. I consider the reasons for the observed differences in the timing of war-related leveling hereafter in my survey by country.

Less widely available than information on top income shares, Gini coefficients of national income distributions likewise point to sharp discontinuities in wartime. Thus the entire net decline in market income inequality in the United States that occurred during the twentieth century took place during the 1930s and 1940s: on one measure, after gently declining by about 3 points between 1931 and 1939, the Gini coefficient plunged fully 10 points during the following six years and then stabilized within a very narrow range that lasted until 1980; on another, it fell about 5 points between 1929 and 1941 and another 7 points during the war itself. British after-tax income inequality declined by

7 points between 1938 and 1949—and perhaps by up to twice as much between 1913 and 1949—and subsequently remained flat into the 1970s. The Japanese evidence is poor but indicates an even steeper drop, by at least 15 points, between the late 1930s and the mid-1950s, followed by stability up to around 1980 or beyond.[4]

Changes in the concentration of wealth further underline the critical importance of the world wars. In eight out of ten countries for which relevant evidence is available, the highest recorded degree of wealth concentration occurred right before the outbreak of World War I. The period between 1914 and 1945 witnessed a severe contraction of top wealth shares (Fig. 5.3).[5]

In seven countries with usable data that were involved in one or both of the two world wars, the top 1 percent wealth shares fell by an average of 17.1 percentage points (equivalent to a sixth of total recorded private national wealth), a drop of about a third from the mean pre–World War I peak of 48.5 percent. By comparison, the average difference between the earliest reported postwar value and the lowest recorded value overall (dating variously from the 1960s to the 2000s) is 13.5 percentage points. While this may make the postwar compression seem comparable in scale to that of the war period, we must bear in mind that the latter includes the interwar years and often several years after 1945 as well, which impedes meaningful year-on-year comparison. Moreover, considering that wealth deconcentration was sustained by progressive inheritance taxes that were in place for a long time after the wars themselves had ended, it is not surprising that this process should have been more drawn out. What matters here is that this form of taxation was itself a direct outcome of the war effort, as I show hereafter. Moreover, in five of these countries, the drop in the war and interwar years accounts for between 61 percent and 70 percent of the total decline in top wealth shares. In a sixth case, the United Kingdom, the decline in this period was in fact very large (representing more than a fifth of private

---

[4] Smolensky and Plotnick 1993: 6 fig. 2, with 43–44, for extrapolated Ginis of about 0.54 in 1931, about 0.51 in 1939, and about 0.41 in 1945 and for documented Ginis of 0.41 ± 0.025 between 1948 and 1980. Atkinson and Morelli 2014: 63 report gross family income Ginis of 0.5 for 1929, 0.447 for 1941, and 0.377 for 1945, likewise followed by stability. For Britain, see Atkinson and Morelli 2014: 61 for a drop from 0.426 in 1938 to 0.355 in 1949, with Milanovic 2016: 73 fig. 2.11 for an estimated market income Gini of 0.5 in 1913. For Japan, see herein, p. 115 n. 1. Among the national data sets collected by Milanovic 2016, only the Netherlands shows a decline in income Ginis between 1962 and 1982 that is comparable in scale to that between 1914 and 1962 (81 fig. 2.15).

[5] Fig. 5.3 from Roine and Waldenström 2015: 539 fig. 7.19 (http://www.uueconomics.se/danielw /Handbook.htm). For the early Scandinavian data points, see herein, chapter 3, pp. 106–108.

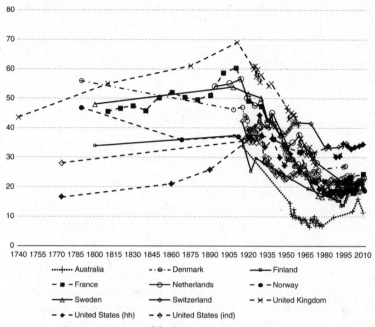

Figure 5.3 Top 1 percent wealth shares in ten countries, 1740–2011 (in percent)

national wealth). Considering that the country's pre-1914 degree of wealth concentration had been so extreme, the postwar decline had to be even stronger simply to bring top wealth shares into convergence with the new common standard of around 20 percent.

It is worth noting that wealth compression at the very top could be much more pronounced than among the richest "1 percent" overall. To pick a particularly striking example, the value of the largest 0.01 percent of estates in France fell by more than three-quarters between the beginning of World War I and the mid-1920s and by another two-thirds during World War II. This represents an overall drop of close to 90 percent during the war period, whereas the wealth share of the top percentile declined by less than half of its prewar high. The key point in all of this is of course the timing of the inflection point right at the beginning of the period of the world wars, when a widespread earlier trend toward ever greater wealth inequality was arrested and forcefully reversed. We

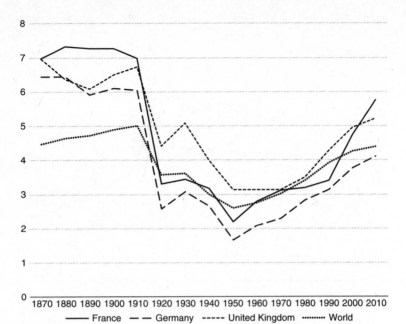

Figure 5.4 Ratios of private wealth to national income in France, Germany, the United Kingdom, and the world, 1870–2010

must also bear in mind that short of radical expropriation and redistribution, there is no mechanism that could have reconfigured wealth shares anywhere near as rapidly as income shares.[6]

That much elite wealth was not merely redistributed but effectively wiped out in the war period becomes clear from changes in the ratio of private wealth to national income in three major belligerent countries (Fig. 5.4). The strongest decline took place in World War I, followed by another compression during and around World War II. Mirroring these changes, the share of capital incomes in the earnings of the highest-earning households plummeted (Fig. 5.5). These observations underscore the fact that elite losses were in the first instance a

---

[6] The only true outlier is thus Norway, where almost all deconcentration occurred after the 1940s. All data from Roine and Waldenström 2015: 572–575 table 7.A2. France: Piketty 2007: 60 fig. 3.5.

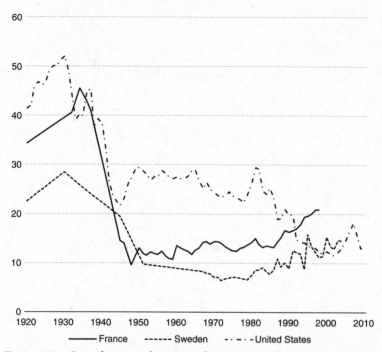

Figure 5.5 Capital income share in total gross income for top 1 percent of incomes in France, Sweden, and the United States, 1920–2010 (in percent)

phenomenon of capital and capital income. Why were these wars so detrimental to owners of capital?[7]

The world wars were unlike any other conflicts the world had ever seen. The mobilization of manpower and industrial production soared to previously unimaginable heights. Almost 70 million soldiers were mobilized in World War I, a figure unprecedented in the annals of warfare. Around 9 million or 10 million of them were killed, alongside some 7 million civilian casualties from war or war-related miseries. France and Germany mobilized about 40 percent of their entire male population, the Austro-Hungarian and Ottoman empires 30 percent, the United Kingdom 25 percent, Russia 15 percent, and the United States 10 percent. Enormous financial resources were required to fund operations.

---

[7] Fig. 5.4 from Piketty 2014: 26 fig. 1.2 and 196 fig. 5.8; see also 118 fig. 5.5 from Roine and Waldenström 2015: 499 fig. 7.5 (http://www.uueconomics.se/danielw/Handbook.htm).

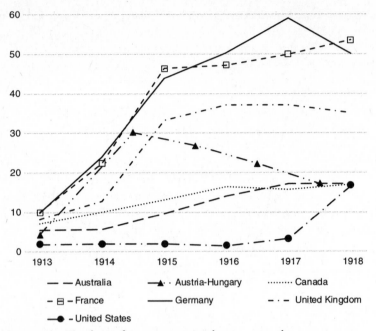

Figure 5.6 The share of government spending in national income in seven countries, 1913–1918 (in percent of GDP)

Among the principal belligerents for which we have information, the share of GDP commandeered by the state increased anywhere from four to eight times (Fig. 5.6).[8]

France and Germany both lost about 55 percent of their national wealth and the United Kingdom 15 percent. And World War II was even worse. Well more than 100 million soldiers were mobilized, and more than 20 million of them died, as did 50 million or more civilians. The main belligerents manufactured 286,000 tanks, 557,000 combat aircraft, 11,000 major naval vessels, and more than 40 million rifles, among many other armaments. Total war costs and losses (including loss of life) have been estimated at $4 trillion in 1938 prices, an order of magnitude greater than annual global GDP at the

<hr />

[8] Fig. 5.6 from Broadberry and Harrison 2005b: 15 table 1.5; Schulze 2005: 84 table 3.9 (Austria-Hungary: military expenditure only).

outbreak of the war. Conquest pushed state shares to astounding levels. In 1943 Germany secured the equivalent of 73 percent of GNP for the state, almost all of it for war and some of it squeezed out of subjugated populations. The following year, by one account, the Japanese state is thought to have spent as much as 87 percent of GDP, likewise drawing on the resources of its doomed empire.[9]

These gargantuan struggles were for the most part funded by borrowing, printing money, and collecting taxes. Borrowing variously translated to future taxation to service public debt, inflation to erode it, or default. Only the leading Western powers successfully managed inflation. In the United States and United Kingdom, prices rose only threefold between 1913 and 1950. Other belligerents were not as lucky: prices rose 100 times in France and 300 times in Germany during the same period and increased 200 times in Japan between 1929 and 1950 alone. Bondholders and rentiers fell by the wayside.[10]

Up to 1914, marginal tax rates on income even in the most developed countries were very low, if income taxes existed at all. High taxes and steep progressivity were born of the war effort. Top rates surged in World War I and its immediate aftermath before falling back later in the 1920s, although never all the way down to prewar levels. They were raised again in the 1930s, often to cope with the fallout of the Great Depression, and reached new heights in World War II, from which they have been very gradually sliding down more or less ever since (Fig. 5.7).[11]

Averaging these developments across different countries clarifies the underlying trend and highlights how the two world wars were the critical junctures of fiscal evolution (Fig. 5.8).[12]

Fig. 5.8 neatly illustrates the critical importance of war. We can see that Japan, uniquely among all these nations, introduced a higher top income tax rate in response to the demands of the Russo–Japanese War of 1904 to 1905, which was in some ways a dress rehearsal for World War I. Sweden, a nonbelligerent, largely missed out on the World War I surge in top taxation

[9] National wealth: Broadberry and Harrison 2005b: 28 table 1.10. Cost: Harrison 1998a: 15–16 table 1.6; Broadberry and Harrison 2005b: 35 table 1.13. To put this in perspective, the same multiple of global GDP today would translate to about $1 quadrillion. GNP/GDP: Germany: Abelshauser 1998: 158 table 4.16. This share falls to 64 percent if foreign contributions are excluded. Japan: Hara 1998: 257 table 6.11.
[10] Piketty 2014: 107; Moriguchi and Saez 2010: 157 table 3C.1.
[11] Taxes: Piketty 2014: 498–499. See also Scheve and Stasavage 2010: 538 for initially low rates. Fig. 5.7 from Roine and Waldenström 2015: 556 fig. 7.23 (http://www.uueconomics.se/danielw/Handbook.htm).
[12] Fig. 5.8 from Scheve and Stasavage 2016: 10 fig. 1.1.

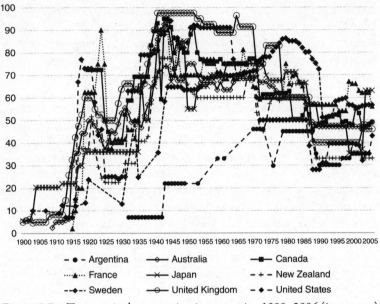

- ● - Argentina	─◇─ Australia	─■─ Canada
····▲···· France	─✕─ Japan	- + - New Zealand
--◆-- Sweden	─⊖─ United Kingdom	- ◆ - United States

Figure 5.7 Top marginal tax rates in nine countries, 1900–2006 (in percent)

and continued to lag behind until the next war. Most strikingly, Argentina, which remained shielded from both world wars, shows a completely different pattern. Kenneth Scheve and David Stasavage find a strong fiscal war effect among belligerents and a much weaker response among other countries in their sample (Fig. 5.9).[13]

Military mass mobilization, progressive graduation of tax rates, and the targeting of elite wealth on top of income constituted the three main ingredients of fiscal leveling. Scheve and Stasavage argue that mass mobilization wars are different in terms of taxation strategies not simply because they are very expensive but also, more specifically, because they increase the need for societal consensus that translates to political pressure for disproportionately heavy extraction of resources from the rich. Mass conscription was not by itself an

---

[13] Fig. 5.9 from Scheve and Stasavage 2016: 81 fig. 3.9 (for ten mobilization and seven nonmobilization countries in World War I); see also Scheve and Stasavage 2012: 83.

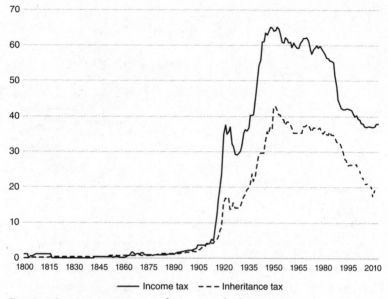

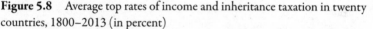

Income tax - - - Inheritance tax

Figure 5.8 Average top rates of income and inheritance taxation in twenty countries, 1800–2013 (in percent)

equalizing force, considering that wealth elites were less likely to serve due to age or privilege and stood to profit from commercial involvement in the war industry. Fairness concerns required military conscription, as a tax in kind, to be accompanied by what the British Labour Party Manifesto of 1918 called the "conscription of wealth." Particular emphasis was placed on the taxing of war profits: in World War I top rates of tax on what were deemed "excess" profits reached 63 percent in the United Kingdom and 80 percent in France, Canada, and the United States. In 1940, President Roosevelt called for similar measures "so that a few do not gain from the sacrifices of the many." Wartime preoccupation with fairness also justified heavier burdens on unearned incomes: although progressive income taxes were a potent means of compressing inequality, it was estate taxes that had a disproportionately strong effect on the rich.[14]

---

[14] Political pressure: Scheve and Stasavage 2010: 530, 534–535; 2012: 82, 84, 100. Pigou 1918: 145 is a classic statement, quoted in Scheve and Stasavage 2012: 84. See also Scheve and Stasavage 2016: 202 fig. 8.1 on the Google Ngram surge of the relative frequency of "equal sacrifice" during the world wars. For public attitudes in the United States, see Sparrow 2011. Manifesto: Scheve and Stasavage 2010: 531, 535. Quote

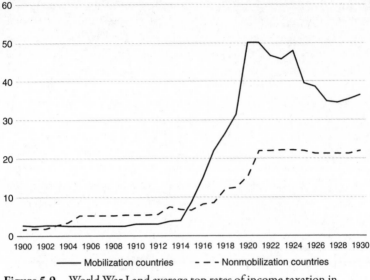

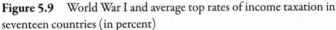

Figure 5.9 World War I and average top rates of income taxation in seventeen countries (in percent)

The leveling effects of fairness concerns were significantly mediated by regime type. In World War I, the democracies of the United Kingdom, the United States, and Canada were prepared to "soak the rich," whereas more autocratic systems such as Germany, Austria-Hungary, and Russia preferred to borrow or print money to sustain their war effort. The latter, however, later paid a high price through hyperinflation and revolution, shocks that likewise compressed inequality. Especially during World War I, before a common template for funding mass mobilization warfare had been established, the mechanisms of leveling therefore varied considerably between countries.[15]

France was among the countries hardest hit by both world wars, having endured fighting on its soil throughout World War I, as well as two invasions

---

from 529: "Those who have made fortunes out of the war must pay for the war; and Labour will insist upon heavily graduated taxation with a raising of the exception limit. That is what Labour means by the Conscription of Wealth." Cf. also 551 for the notion of "conscription if current income above that what is absolutely necessary" in a paper from 1917. For the notion of equal sacrifice in political debates, see 541. Excess profits: Scheve and Stasavage 2010: 541–542. Roosevelt quote from Bank, Stark, and Thorndike 2008: 88. Estate taxes: Piketty 2014: 508; Scheve and Stasavage 2010: 548–549.

[15] Scheve and Stasavage 2016: 83 fig. 3.10.

and occupation during World War II. During the first war and in its immediate aftermath, a third of the French capital stock was destroyed, the share of capital income in national household income fell by a third, and GDP contracted by the same proportion. Taxation was slow to take off: at the beginning of the conflict, the top inheritance tax rate stood at a paltry 5 percent, and although an income tax was first introduced in 1915, effective top rates remained low for the remainder of the war and rose significantly only in 1919. A war profit tax created in 1916 likewise began to yield large revenue only once the war was over, as did increased estate taxes. This lag effect, together with rampant postwar inflation, accounts for the fact the compression of top income shares was primarily a phenomenon of the 1920s instead of the actual war years, whereas war profits briefly had the opposite effect. By the middle of that decade, the average value of the largest 0.01 percent of estates had dropped by more than three-quarters compared to the prewar level.[16]

The destruction of elite wealth continued in World War II as France suffered four years of predatory German occupation and major damage from allied bombing and liberation. This time, two-thirds of the capital stock was wiped out, twice the rate of attrition of the first war. Foreign assets, which had accounted for a quarter of the largest French fortunes, evaporated. Top income shares fell precipitously in this period, and postwar inflation subsequently eroded the value of bonds and war debt within just a few years. As Piketty has argued, the entire reduction of the top 1 percent income share between 1914 and 1945 was due to losses in nonwage income, as capital was buffeted by combat, bankruptcies, rent control, nationalization, and inflation. Cumulative leveling across the two wars was massive: 10,000 percent inflation expropriated bondholders, real rents fell by 90 percent between 1913 and 1950, and a nationalization program in 1945 and a one-off tax on capital holdings of up to 20 percent for large fortunes and of 100 percent for those that had grown much during the war helped reset capital accumulation to close to zero. The value of the top 0.01 percent estates consequently declined by well more than 90 percent between 1914 and 1945.[17]

In the United Kingdom, top income tax rates rose from 6 percent to 30 percent during World War I, and a new war profits tax levied on companies—raised

---

[16] Piketty 2007: 56, 58 fig. 3.4; Hautcoeur 2005: 171 table 6.1. Effects of WW1: Hautcoeur 2005: 185; Piketty 2007: 60 fig. 3.5.
[17] Piketty 2014: 121, 369–370; Piketty 2014: 273 fig. 8.2; 275 (capital losses); Piketty 2007: 55–57, 60 fig. 3.5 (top estates).

to 80 percent by 1917—became the single most important tax in terms of revenue. On this occasion, the country lost 14.9 percent of its national wealth, and it lost another 18.6 percent in World War II. The threshold for the top 0.1 percent of incomes fell from forty to thirty times mean income in World War I and from thirty to twenty times in World War II. The drop in after-tax top income shares (reported only from 1937) was even more pronounced—almost half for the top 1 percent and two-thirds for the top 0.1 percent between 1937 and 1949. The share of the largest 1 percent of fortunes in all private wealth contracted from 70 percent to 50 percent—less dramatic than the concurrent collapse from 60 percent to 30 percent in France, but nonetheless significant.[18]

Across the Atlantic, the experience of the United States demonstrates that considerable war-induced leveling could occur in the absence of physical destruction and serious inflation. The country's top 1 percent income share fell on three separate occasions, by almost a quarter during World War I, by the same proportion during the Great Depression, and by about 30 percent of what remained during World War II. Overall, this top bracket lost some 40 percent of its share in total income between 1916 and 1945. As in other countries, this trend was more extreme in the uppermost tiers: thus the share of the top 0.01 percent of incomes declined by 80 percent during the same period. Decomposition of income shares shows that much of this attrition was driven by a dwindling of gains from capital. Top wealth shares suffered more during the Great Depression than in World War II but cumulatively fell by a third from their pre-Depression peak. In the United States, the Great Depression played a greater role in equalizing income and wealth disparities relative to the wars themselves than among the other main belligerents: I return to this in chapter 12.[19]

Even so, wartime leveling was considerable, and steeply progressive taxation to fund the war effort was instrumental in this process. The War Revenue Act of 1917 raised surtax top rates from 13 percent to 50 percent and taxed profits above 9 percent of invested capital at 20 percent to 60 percent. As war expenses continued to rise, the Revenue Act of 1918, passed only after the end of the war, imposed even higher rates on the largest incomes and on excess profits. Effective tax rates went from 1.5 percent in 1913 and 1915 to 22 percent

---

[18] Broadberry and Howlett 2005: 217, 227; Atkinson 2007: 96–97, 104 table 4.3; Ohlsson, Roine, and Waldenström 2006: 26–27 figs. 1, 3.

[19] Piketty and Saez 2007, esp. 149–156. However, the overall income Gini coefficient may have peaked in 1933 due to very high unemployment: Smolensky and Plotnick 1993: 6 fig. 2, with Milanovic 2016: 71. For the Great Depression, see herein, chapter 12, p. 363.

in 1918 for incomes of $50,000 and rose from 2.5 percent to 35 percent for those of $100,000. The top rate for the estate tax, newly created in 1916, rose from 10 percent to 25 percent in the following year. War was the sole cause of these aggressive interventions: "the highly contingent politics of mobilizing for World War I drove the creation of a democratic-statist tax regime." Although the Revenue Acts of 1921 and 1924 repealed the excess profits tax and greatly lowered surtax rates, remaining top rates were still far above the prewar level, and, most important, the estate tax remained in place. We thus observe both a degree of postwar fiscal relaxation, which coincided with a renewed surge in top incomes, and a ratchet effect in terms of the share of income and wealth claimed by the government, even as growing loopholes were hollowing out the progressive tax regime.[20]

Subsequent equalization was driven in part by very high marginal tax rates on income and inherited wealth. This process commenced with the New Deal and culminated in further turns of the screw during the war years. In "this time of grave national danger, when all excess income should go to win the war," as Roosevelt put it, the top tax rates for income and estates peaked at 94 percent in 1944 and 77 percent in 1941, respectively, and the thresholds for the highest rates were greatly lowered, thereby ensnaring wider high-income circles. Excess profit taxation also made a comeback. At the same time, the administration and the labor unions resisted a federal sales tax that would have been regressive in nature—remarkable restraint considering such a tax existed at the time even in Sweden. Wage income was compressed more broadly across the economy as the result of wage controls managed by the National War Labor Board. Responsible for approving all wages pursuant to the Wage Stabilization Act of October 1942, this body was prepared to raise wages at the lower end but not for higher earners, whose share in total wage income fell accordingly. The highest wages lost out the most relative to lower ones: between 1940 and 1945, earners in the top 90 percent to 95 percent of the wage distribution lost a sixth of their share, those in the top 1 percent a quarter, and the top 0.01 percent 40 percent. Businesses responded by offering benefits instead of higher wages, by itself an increase in the real income of workers. State intervention and its knock-on

---

[20] For taxation in World War I, see esp. Brownlee 2004: 59–72; Bank, Stark, and Thorndike 2008: 49–81. Tax rates: Bank, Stark, and Thorndike 2008: 65, 69–70, 78; Rockoff 2005: 321 table 10.5. Quote: Brownlee 2004: 58. Mehrotra 2013 also considers the World War I shock crucial for the creation of radical laws and as a basis for further fiscal elaboration in World War II. Relaxation: Brownlee 2004: 59; Bank, Stark, and Thorndike 2008: 81.

effects served to compress the overall wage income structure, which represented a clear break with prior trends owing to "factors unique to the World War II period." Other factors amplified this trend. Executive compensation, which had been flat in real terms during the Depression, declined relative to lower-level wages from 1940 onward, a process driven not so much by government intervention as by growing union power and falling returns to firm size. As a consequence of all these congruent developments, income Gini coefficients declined rapidly during the war, by between 7 and 10 points, and several indices for the distribution of non-elite incomes and wages show a sudden drop in the same years that was often followed by several decades without further change.[21]

Canada followed a somewhat different trajectory, with no discernible effect of the Great Depression on top income shares but dramatic deconcentration during World War II. Massive increases in top income tax rates contributed to this shift, as the top rate hit 95 percent in 1943 and effective rates for the top 1 percent of earners rose from only 3 percent in 1938 to 48 percent five years later.[22]

The evolution of top income shares in Germany is somewhat anomalous in that they registered an increase during World War I, a period of extremely high military mobilization rates and state spending (Fig. 5.10).[23]

The absence of wartime destruction is insufficient to account for this phenomenon. Inequality temporarily soared as an authoritarian government protected wartime profits, especially those of the wealthy elite in the industrial sector that was closely allied to the political and military leadership. Organized labor had been brought to heel, and although new taxes on capital were introduced, they remained rather modest in scale. In this respect, German conditions resembled those in France, where a combination of profiteering and low taxes pushed up top incomes in 1916 and 1917. Instead of relying on

---

[21] Tax rates: Piketty and Saez 2007: 157; Piketty 2014: 507; Brownlee 2004: 108–119 (quote from 109); Bank, Stark, and Thorndike 2008: 83–108. Interventions and inequality: Goldin and Margo 1992: 16 (quote), 23–24; Piketty and Saez 2007: 215 table 5B.2; and herein, p. 137 (Ginis). Executive pay: Frydman and Molloy 2012. The Gini coefficient for wages fell from 0.44 in 1938 to 0.36 in 1953: Kopczuk, Saez, and Song 2010: 104. The Goldsmith-OBE series, the ratio of top decile to average wages, and the wage gap between the ninetieth and fiftieth percentiles all point to a single episode of equalization in the 1940s; only the ratio of wages at the fiftieth to those at the tenth percentile shows a secondary decline in the 1960s after an initial stronger drop in the 1940s: Lindert and Williamson 2016: 199 fig. 8–2.

[22] Saez and Veall 2007: 301 table 6F.1 and 264 figs. 6A.2–3 for visualization. See 232 for the effect of the war. Earnings at the ninetieth percentile as a multiple of the national median fell from 254 percent in 1941 to 168 percent in 1950 and have changed little since: Atkinson and Morelli 2014: 15. The state share of GDP grew from 18.8 percent in 1935 to 26.7 percent in 1945: Smith 1995: 1059 table 2.

[23] Dumke 1991: 125–135; Dell 2007. Fig. 5.10 from WWID. For mobilization rates and state share of GDP, see herein, pp. 141–142 and Fig. 5.9.

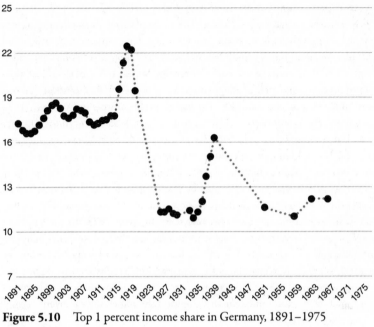

Figure 5.10 Top 1 percent income share in Germany, 1891–1975 (in percent)

massive and progressive taxation, Germany's government funded war expenditure in the first instance by issuing debt. Monetary expansion covered about 15 percent of outlays, but inflation was suppressed by severe price controls: although the money base increased fivefold during the war, wholesale inflation and food price inflation reached only a more manageable 43 percent and 129 percent, respectively. This stands in marked contrast to outcomes among Germany's allies—Austria-Hungary experienced consumer price inflation of 1,500 percent, and consumer prices in Istanbul rose 2,100 percent in the same period.[24]

Yet war-induced leveling could only be deferred, not avoided. A combination of political turmoil and hyperinflation in the immediate postwar years

---

[24] Top incomes: Dell 2007: 372; Dumke 1991: 131; Dell 2005: 416. The evidence of top incomes does not support the revisionist argument by Baten and Schulz 2005 that German inequality did not rise during World War I. Funding and inflation: Ritschl 2005: 64 table 2.16; Schulze 2005: 100 table 3.19; Pamuk 2005: 129 table 4.4.

greatly depressed top incomes, with a 40 percent fall in the top 1 percent and a collapse by three-quarters for the top 0.01 percent. This was an elite experience not shared by those between the ninetieth and ninety-ninth percentiles, and middle class households gained income share. The money stock had expanded first to fund the war and then to pay for reparations as well as social and employment programs, the latter a direct consequence of the 1918 revolution that had been unleashed by the war itself. The end of price controls in 1919 and 1920 caused previously contained inflation to burst into the open. The Consumer Price Index for a family of four in Berlin rose from 1 to 7.7 between the summer of 1914 and January 1920 but to 5 trillion by October 1923. Rentiers lost the most: their share of national income plummeted from 15 percent to 3 percent even as entrepreneurs were able to maintain their share. The destruction of monetary wealth through inflation at a time of shrinking wealth overall—real national income was a quarter to a third lower in 1923 than it had been in 1913—amplified leveling because monetary assets were more unequally distributed. Policy changes also contributed to this process of equalization. In the postwar years, wage adjustments for low-paid workers resulted in wage compression, and the share of transfer payments in national income tripled between 1913 and 1925. Not coincidentally, the top inheritance tax rate went from 0 percent to 35 percent in 1919.[25]

National Socialist rule subsequently caused top income shares to recover thanks to curbs on consumption and wage growth, profits from the burgeoning arms industry, and expropriation of Jewish property. During World War II, Germany extracted 30 percent to 40 percent of the national products of France, the Netherlands, and Norway, mitigating the need for domestic levies. Inequality measures from the war years are lacking, but by the time the dust had settled, top income shares had dropped back to post-hyperinflation levels. This was the result less of capital losses than of a combination of declining output, fiscal reform, and inflation. Physical destruction of industrial assets was quite limited, for Allied bombing had focused on the transportation infrastructure and civilian housing, and gross industrial capital actually grew by a fifth between 1936 and 1945. However, net industrial output declined by almost three-quarters between 1944 and 1950. The country also underwent severe inflation for three years after the war's end, and in 1946 the top inheritance tax rate quadrupled,

[25] Dell 2005: 416; 2007: 373; Holtfrerich 1980: 190–191, 76–92, 327, 39–40 table 8, 266, 273, 221 table 40, 274, 232–233, 268; Piketty 2014: 503 fig. 14.2, 504–505.

increasing from 15 percent to 60 percent. The loss of wartime forced labor contributed to labor scarcity, unions were reestablished, and the occupation authorities imposed wage controls. Just as in the case of World War I, much of the observed leveling may have occurred in the immediate aftermath of the conflict.[26]

In the Netherlands, war profits pushed up top income shares in the early stages of World War I, a short-lived boost that turned into a steep decline that continued throughout the postwar depression of 1920 to 1923 and reduced the capital share in national income from 75 percent to 45 percent and greatly compressed net income inequality. Top income shares once again fell during the Great Depression and, to a similar extent, under German occupation. The highest earners were particularly hard hit by World War II, when the top 0.01 percent income share dropped by 40 percent. The German authorities introduced wage controls that were maintained after liberation and favored the lowest income brackets; rents were frozen at 1939 levels. Tax rates, which had previously been kept rather low, soared after the war to compensate for the damage.[27]

Finland, which was heavily engaged in World War II, experienced a dramatic decline in the top 1 percent income share by more than half between 1938 and 1947, and the Gini coefficient for taxable income fell from 0.46 to 0.3 during the same period. In Denmark, income shares dropped by a sixth for the top 1 percent and by a quarter for the top 0.1 percent between 1939 to 1945, and the top 1 percent wealth share declined by a quarter between the late 1930s and the late 1940s. Under German occupation, the Danish government introduced substantial tax increases and adjusted wages. This, together with other war-related effects, produced the opposite outcome of what had happened during World War I, when inequality had risen in the absence of redistributive policies, although top wealth shares had already contracted at the time. Finally, in Norway, another Scandinavian country under German occupation, top income shares likewise dropped substantially and much faster than after the war. Between 1938 and 1948, the top 0.5

---

[26] Dell 2005: 416–417; 2007: 374–375; Harrison 1998a: 22; Abelshauser 2011: 45 fig. 4, 68–69; Piketty 2014: 503 fig. 14.2, 504–505; Klausen 1998: 176–177, 189–190.

[27] Top incomes: see herein, p. 133. Soltow and van Zanden 1998: 176–177, 184 (between 1939 and 1950, the real wages of administrative personnel and skilled industry workers fell by 23.5 percent and 8 percent, respectively, but rose 6.4 percent for unskilled laborers); Salverda and Atkinson 2007: 454–458; Soltow and van Zanden 1998: 183–185.

percent lost almost a third of their share in overall income, and top wealth shares also started to fall at that time.[28]

This quick survey shows that although the precise means of leveling differed between countries, overall outcomes were similar. Low savings rates and depressed asset prices, physical destruction and the loss of foreign assets, inflation and progressive taxation, rent and price controls, and nationalization all contributed to varying degrees. Depending on their particular configuration, these factors accounted for the scale and timing of the compression of income and wealth inequality. They all flowed from the same source, the stresses of total war. Piketty has boldly generalized from the experience of his native France:

> To a large extent, it was the chaos of war, with its attendant economic and political shocks, that reduced inequality in the twentieth century. There was no gradual, consensual, conflict-free evolution toward greater equality. In the twentieth century it was war, and nor harmonious democratic or economic rationality, that erased the past and enabled society to begin anew with a clean slate.[29]

*

This sweeping claim raises the question whether this was true across the board. We may test his conclusion in two ways: by determining whether any of the belligerents experienced different outcomes and by comparing their experience with that of countries not directly involved in these conflicts. The first of these tests is more difficult to perform than one might expect. As we have already seen (Tables 5.1 and 5.2), the proposition that the violent dislocations of the world war period were of critical importance is fully supported by the evidence of top income shares for all belligerent countries for which the relevant evidence has been published. Unfortunately, major parties are missing from this survey: Austria-Hungary and Russia in World War I and Italy in both wars. The same is true of Belgium, a country hard hit by both conflicts, to say

---

[28] Finland: Jäntti et al. 2010: 412 table 8A.1. Denmark: Ohlsson, Roine, and Waldenström 2006: 28 fig. 5; Atkinson and Søgaard 2016: 283–284, 287 fig. 10. Norway: Aaberge and Atkinson 2010: 458–459, and see herein, Tables 5.1–2.

[29] Piketty 2014: 146–150, who notes that "the budgetary and political shocks of two wars proved far more destructive to capital than combat itself" (148). Quote: Piketty 2014: 275.

nothing of the various central and eastern European states in what have been called the "bloodlands" of this period, or of China in World War II. All we can say for now is that there is no conflicting evidence in the form of a conspicuous absence of leveling in this period. According to a single reconstruction of the Gini coefficient of incomes that does not indicate any major war-related changes, Italy is currently the only possible exception. It is hard to be sure how much weight this can bear.[30]

As for the second test, several neutral countries registered upticks in inequality during World War I. The Dutch top 1 percent income share surged by a third, from 21 percent to 28 percent, between 1914 and 1916 before falling back to 22 percent by 1918. High monopoly profits and dividends early in the war were responsible but were soon contained by shortages of raw materials. As the war dragged on, the Netherlands was unable to escape the need for mobilization and elevated public spending: state expenditure more than doubled in constant prices, the military expanded from 200,000 to 450,000 troops, and schemes for managing food production and distribution had to be implemented. New taxes were eventually required to fund these efforts, including highly progressive defense taxes and a special tax of 30 percent of estimated war profits levied on persons as well as businesses. These measures soon helped check the initial rise in inequality. Sweden likewise witnessed a sudden rise in top income shares during World War I, followed by a sharp decline by 1920, and so did Denmark. In both countries, the top 1 percent income share briefly exploded to an exceptional 28 percent in 1916 or 1917. The Danish state was slow to impose price and rent controls, and a collective bargaining agreement that did not expire until 1916 depressed real wages for workers at a time of rapid economic growth. Taxation rose only feebly. (There are no usable income share data for Norway for these years.[31])

By contrast, World War II coincided with opposite trends in several of the few European countries that escaped the conflict. Top income shares in Ireland declined significantly between 1938 and 1945, but data resolution is poor. Price and wage controls and shortages of raw materials during the war years are thought to have contributed to this process. In Portugal, the

---

[30] Bloodlands: Snyder 2010. For Italy, see Brandolini and Vecchi 2011: 39 fig. 8; but cf. Rossi, Toniolo, and Vecchi 2001: 921–922 for possible short-term equalization during both world wars. For Italy's war economy, see Galassi and Harrison 2005; Zamagni 2005.
[31] Netherlands: Salverda and Atkinson 2007: 441; Dumke 1991: 131; De Jong 2005. Sweden: WWID; Atkinson and Søgaard 2016: 282–283, 287 fig.10.

highest income shares dropped even more in that period: the top 0.1 percent lost 40 percent of their share between 1941 and 1946, but the reasons remain to be explained. Spain also underwent significant leveling in the 1930s and 1940s. I discuss this in the next chapter, as an example of the effects of civil war.[32]

Leaving aside for the moment Switzerland and Sweden, which receive more detailed attention hereafter, additional evidence for nonbelligerent countries at the time of World War II is scarce. Most of the non-Western world was still ruled by colonial powers, and independent countries were mostly confined to Latin America, where the evidence is often poor. Even so, Latin American data offer two valuable insights. One concerns the radically different evolution of income inequality in Argentina, which in the early twentieth century had been one of the richest countries in the world. During World War II, the country's top 1 percent income share was higher than before or after. This outcome was comparable to that observed in several European neutral nations in World War I, where war profits had driven up elite incomes. In the early 1940s, Argentina experienced economic growth driven by foreign demand: the country provided 40 percent of the grain and meat consumed in Britain. Top income shares and the volume of exports were closely positively correlated as the Argentinian elite disproportionately captured gains from trade. Not only did the distant war fail to necessitate mobilization and supporting fiscal measures or depress returns of capital, but it also gave a temporary boost to inequality in ways that were unfeasible in Europe and other parts of the globe embroiled in the conflict. The second insight derives from the more general observation that in all Latin American countries for which relevant information exists, income inequality was very high in the 1960s, the earliest period that allows systematic comparison. For fifteen countries that computed standardized market income Gini coefficients from that decade, values range from 0.40 to 0.76, with a high mean of 0.51 and a median of 0.49. Qualitative evidence is likewise inconsistent with the notion of an earlier wartime decline in inequality. What appears to have been a significant compression in Chile at the time of World War II has been explained with reference to specific domestic economic and political factors. Wage inequality in a number of Latin American countries began to

---

[32] Nolan 2007: 516 (Ireland); Alvaredo 2010b: 567–568 (Portugal). For Spain, see herein, chapter 6, pp. 204–206.

increase after World War II, in marked contrast to Europe, North America, and Japan.[33]

A survey of top income shares in former British colonies at the time of independence also shows them to be relatively high compared to Western levels that had recently been reduced by World War II. A few exceptions merely serve to underline the importance of war effects. In India, the top 1 percent income share contracted by more than a third during the war years. As revenue from regressive indirect taxes declined with shrinking imports, the Indian government prioritized progressive direct taxes on personal and corporate income. A super-tax on the highest earners and a surtax on excess corporate profits both reached 66 percent. As a result, the share of income tax in total tax revenue tripled from 23 percent in 1938 and 1939 to 68 percent in 1944 and 1945: considering the small tax base of just a few hundred thousand individuals, this shift occurred at the expense at the upper class. At the same time, labor union membership almost doubled, and work stoppages motivated by disputes over compensation became more frequent.[34]

In Mauritius, which saw the introduction of an income tax in 1932, the top 0.1 percent share of incomes fell by almost two-thirds between 1938 and 1946. Tax increases during the war coincided with a massive shift between gross and net income shares in that elite group. Whereas in 1933 the 0.1 percent biggest earners accounted for 8.1 percent of gross income and 7.6 percent of net income—a negligible difference—by 1947 those values had dropped to 4.4 percent and 2.9 percent, respectively, documenting not only a general decline in elite incomes but also the leveling consequences of fiscal transfers. Top income shares in Malaysia and Singapore, which had been under predatory Japanese occupation, were also quite low right after 1945, at levels similar to Mauritius's, which in turn were comparable to those in the United Kingdom and the United States at that time.[35]

---

[33] Argentina: Alvaredo 2010a: 267–269, 272 fig. 6.6. For the rapid leveling that occurred between 1948 and 1953, see herein, chapter 13, p. 380. Latin American Ginis from SWIID: Argentina 39.5 (1961), Bolivia 42.3 (1968), Brazil 48.8 (Brazil), Chile 44.0 (1968), Colombia 49.8 (1962), Costa Rica 47.8 (1961), Ecuador 46.3 (1968), El Salvador 62.1 (1961), Honduras 54.1 (1968), Jamaica 69.1 (1968), Mexico 49.8 (1963), Panama 76.0 (1960), Peru 53.3 (1961), Uruguay 43.0 (1967), Venezuela 45.1 (1962). For wartime developments, see herein, chapter 13, p. 379. Rodríguez Weber 2015: 8 fig. 2, 19–24 (Chile); Frankema 2012: 48–49 (wage inequality).
[34] Colonies: Atkinson 2014b. India: Raghavan 2016: 331, 341–344. However, this pressure on the rich was offset by war-driven price inflation that benefited industrialists and large landowners and hurt middling and lower-income groups (348–350). For longer-term trends, see Banerjee and Piketty 2010: 11–13.
[35] Atkinson n.d. 22, 28 fig. 5.

I now turn to Switzerland and Sweden, nonbelligerents in both world wars. They are of particular interest because they show how the interaction between close proximity to mass mobilization warfare and nationally specific political and economic conditions shaped the development of inequality in societies that were neutral bystanders. In 1914, Switzerland, then a country of fewer than 4 million, mobilized 220,000 soldiers. In the absence of effective compensation or employment protection, this caused considerable hardship, which, together with war profiteering, radicalized labor and eventually culminated in strikes and domestic military deployments in November 1918. Aggregate revenues of the federal government, cantons, and communities doubled during the war years, sustained by war taxes on income, wealth, and war profits, all of which were, however, kept at fairly moderate rates. After the war, proposals for a direct federal income tax and a one-time levy on wealth to retire war debt (with a top rate of 60 percent) were both rejected. Instead, a new and more progressive war tax was instituted in 1920 to service the war debt. Because we lack information on top income shares before 1933, we cannot ascertain how the income distribution was affected by this experience. Data on top wealth shares partly fill this gap: the share of the largest 0.5 percent of estates fell by almost a quarter during World War I.[36]

In 1939, the Swiss mobilized 430,000 troops, fully a tenth of their national population but a figure that was reduced to 120,000 after the fall of France. Drawing on the lessons of the previous war, those serving in the military received compensation to forestall a recurrence of social tensions. In this period, state revenue rose by an even smaller margin than it had after 1914, by about 70 percent. A series of emergency taxes was introduced to help fund this expansion: a war profit tax with rates of up to 70 percent of relevant gains, a wealth tax of 3 percent to 4.5 percent on individuals and of 1.5 percent on legal entities, a war tax on income with an eventual top rate of 9.75 percent, and a dividend tax of up to 15 percent. This shows that with the exception of the war profit tax, these levies were modest and not particularly progressive compared to those enacted by several of the main belligerents at the time. Most of the additional federal expenditure was financed by debt, which quintupled during the war. As in World War I, top wealth shares decreased: this time the top 0.5 percent of estates lost 18 percent of their share. At the same time, elite income shares were not much affected by the war. The top 1 percent income share fell by a tiny

[36] Zala 2014: 495–498, 502; Oechslin 1967: 75–97, 112; Dell, Piketty, and Saez 2007: 486 table 11.3.

amount—about 1 percentage point, or about a tenth of the total—and only the highest income tier (the top 0.01 percent) registered a substantial drop, by about one quarter, between 1938 and 1945—and even this merely returned it to the mid-1930s level. Swiss top income shares generally showed very little movement between 1933 and 1973, fluctuating mildly within a narrow—and low—range of 9.7 percent to 11.8 percent.[37]

Overall, the war mobilization effect on inequality remained rather muted. As elsewhere, the world wars prompted an expansion of direct taxation, even if this was always billed as a temporary measure. In a peculiarly Swiss context of broad-based resistance to such increases, such policies might well not have been feasible in the absence of foreign threats. As in developed countries elsewhere, mobilization for World War II in particular created demand for social services after the war, which promoted development of a welfare state. Swiss society was thus exposed to war-related experiences that were conducive to the reduction of income and wealth disparities. To some extent, the development of top wealth shares conformed to this expectation. Yet from a comparative perspective, the absence of strong war-induced shocks and the associated avoidance of highly progressive taxation are consistent with the observed lack of significant income compression in this period or thereafter. Once we factor in the unusually decentralized nature of Swiss political and fiscal institutions and the fact that top income shares were already low by international standards, it is not surprising that the relative weakness of wartime pressures failed to bring about more substantial leveling.[38]

Swedish inequality developed in a somewhat different manner from the 1910s to the 1940s (Fig. 5.11). But just as in many other developed countries at the time, external shocks, in the form of the two world wars and the Great Depression, acted as critical catalysts for redistributive fiscal reform and the eventual expansion of the welfare state.[39]

I already noted the short-lived peak in top income shares in World War I, comparable to what happened in Denmark and the Netherlands. Swedish elites sided with Germany and raked in large profits while food shortages caused by the Entente naval blockade and labor unrest rocked the country. Hunger marches near the end of the war triggered heavy-handed police responses.

---

[37] Zala 2014: 524–525; Oechslin 1967: 150 table 43, 152–160; Grütter 1968: 16, 22; Dell, Piketty, and Saez 2007: 486 table 11.3.
[38] Oechslin 1967: 236, 239; Grütter 1968: 23; Zala 2014: 534–535; Dell, Piketty, and Saez 2007: 494.
[39] Fig. 5.11 from WWID.

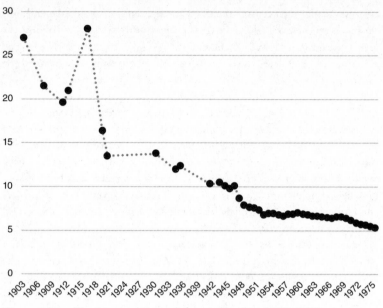

Figure 5.11   Top 1 percent income share in Sweden, 1903–1975 (in percent)

Popular discontent paved the way for the country's first Liberal-Social Democrat coalition government, which started to take tentative steps in a more progressive direction under the growing shadow of the Russian Revolution not far from Sweden's shores. Once the war had ended, overseas markets collapsed and industrial overcapacity ushered in financial crisis and unemployment. Fig. 5.11 indicates that the wealthy suffered disproportionately, and all the more so as the ratio of inherited wealth to national income temporarily crashed at that time. Significant tax progressivity first appeared during these years, even though rates even for high-income earners remained very low (Fig. 5.12). All this underlines how the beginnings of Sweden's trajectory toward one of the most egalitarian income distributions in the world were firmly grounded in the experience of World War I and its attendant dislocations.[40]

---

[40] Gilmour 2010: 8–10; Hamilton 1989: 158–162; Roine and Waldenström 2010: 310; Ohlsson, Roine, and Waldenström 2014: 28 fig. 1. Wage differentials also fell in those years, as agricultural incomes were strong and administrative wages lost ground: Söderberg 1991: 86–87. Fig. 5.12 from Stenkula, Johansson, and Du Rietz 2014: 174 fig. 2 (adapted here using data kindly provided by Mikael Stenkula); and cf. 177 fig. 4

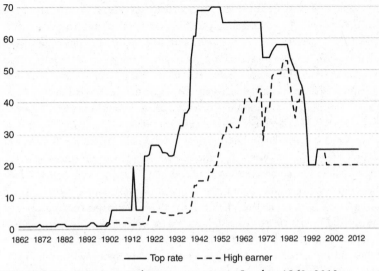

Figure 5.12 State marginal income tax rates in Sweden, 1862–2013 (in percent)

Further war effects made themselves felt once the Nazi war machine had shifted into high gear. In the words of a leading Social Democratic politician in 1940, Swedes soon found themselves "living in front of the muzzle of a loaded cannon." The country was exposed to both German and Allied pressure. At one point Germany threatened to bomb Swedish cities unless granted transit concessions. Later in the war, Germany drew up a contingency plan for an invasion in the event of an Allied incursion into Sweden. Sweden took account of its precarious security situation by greatly expanding its military. Military spending increased eightfold in the course of the war. Whereas fiscal responses to the Great Depression had remained modest, the tax reform of 1939 greatly raised top rates and created a temporary defense tax that became highly progressive only for the highest earners and that was further sharpened in 1940 and 1942. In addition, the statutory corporate tax rate rose to 40 percent. The strengthening

including local income taxes, for a similar picture overall. Cf. also Roine and Waldenström 2008: 381. It simply will not do to claim, along the lines of Ohlsson, Roine, and Waldenström 2006: 20 or Henrekson and Waldenström 2014: 12, that Sweden did not experience serious shocks because it did not actively participate in the world wars: close proximity to the conflicts and exposure to assorted foreign threats or other war-related impositions precipitated a significant mobilization effect—merely on a lesser scale than among belligerents.

of military capacity was the official rationale for all these measures. Thanks to the threat of war, in a telling departure from the fractious politics of the 1920s and 1930s, these reforms were passed with little debate or controversy as an almost unanimous political decision.[41]

Yet even more so than in Switzerland, pretax top income shares remained insensitive to wartime pressures, regardless of whether we consider the top 1 percent or more elite tiers within that bracket. Earlier decline in the 1930s appears to have been driven in the first instance by the effects of the Great Depression, an explanation that would be consistent with the concurrent development of wealth shares. World War II, by contrast, did not witness a further fall in top income shares or an acceleration in the secular decline of top wealth shares. However, earlier studies found that substantial equalization across income groups took place in the late 1930s and the 1940s. More specifically, it was the war period proper that produced the strongest leveling, as both interindustry wage differentials and the ratio of urban to rural wages both collapsed between 1940 and 1945, thereby narrowing income inequality among workers. Information on top income shares fails to capture this compression.[42]

Moreover, mass mobilization generated social effects well beyond the fiscal sphere. It transformed what had been a right-wing military force into a people's army based on mass conscription and volunteerism. Some 400,000 men served out of a population of 6.3 million. Shared military and civilian service helped overcome existing distrust and fostered teamwork and mutual dependency.

---

[41] Gilmour 2010: 49 (quote), 47–48, 229–230, 241–242; Hamilton 1989: 179; Fig. 5.12; Roine and Waldenström 2010: 323 fig. 7.9; Stenkula, Johansson, and Du Rietz 2014: 178; Du Rietz, Johansson, and Stenkula 2014: 5–6. Consensus: Du Rietz, Johansson, and Stenkula 2013: 16–17. (This information was omitted from the final version in Stenkula, Johansson, and Du Rietz 2014). A wartime coalition government brought stability after turbulence in the previous two decades: Gilmour 2010: 238–239; cf. also Hamilton 1989: 172–177.

[42] Roine and Waldenström 2010: 320 fig. 7.8; Ohlsson, Roine, and Waldenström 2014: 28 fig. 1. The top 1 percent wealth share in Sweden, as computed from wealth taxation, slid down at fairly steady rates for about four decades starting in 1930: Ohlsson, Roine, and Waldenström 2006: fig. 7. Waldenström 2015: 11–12, 34–35 figs. 6–7 identifies two structural breaks: in the 1930s for the national wealth/income ratio (following a smaller one at the time of World War I) and in the early 1950s for the private wealth/income ratio—concluding that these "break points highlight that political institutional changes associated with the World Wars were probably as important as the actual wars in shaping aggregate wealth-income ratios, especially over the long run" (12). Gustafsson and Johansson 2003: 205 argue that income inequality in Goteborg declined steadily from the 1920s to the 1940s, a process mainly driven by the fall and deconcentration of capital income from 1925 to 1936 and mainly by income taxes from 1936 to 1947. Equalization: Bentzel 1952; Spånt 1981. For substantial equalization across income groups, see Bergh 2011: fig. 3 as reproduced from Bentzel 1952. Wages: Gärtner and Prado 2012: 13, 24 graph 4, 15, 26 graph 7. Agricultural wages rose because they were exempted from wage stabilization: Klausen 1998: 100. The share of capital income in top incomes collapsed between 1935 and 1951: see herein, Fig. 2.6.

Sacrifice went beyond service as such: some 50,000 soldiers were invalided as the result of injuries, accidents, and harsh service conditions. Rationing likewise served as a crucial means of leveling class differences. The war thus promoted homogeneity and civic engagement. As John Gilmour puts it in his landmark study of wartime Sweden, the country

> experienced significant social, political and economic disruption as a result of wartime conditions and emerged in 1945 as an altered society in attitude and aspiration. . . . [T]he wartime conscription experience . . . provided a model proving ground for many of Per Albin's *Folkhem* ideals of social levelling. . . . Sweden gained societal benefits from war without suffering the same loss of lives and property as the belligerents and occupied nations.[43]

In this sense, Sweden did experience a major war mobilization effect that was conducive to the subsequent expansion of the welfare state. In the longer term, the experience of the war years is thought to have had a more general ideational effect as well: the vision of Sweden as a small country that had been saved by a coalition government and consensus contributed to the formation of the ideal of a solidaristic society sustained by a redistributive welfare state.[44]

Postwar policy was grounded in the war footing of the tax system and the shared war experience of the general population. In 1944, as the war was drawing to a close, the Social Democrats together with the Trade Union Confederation developed a policy program meant to equalize income and wealth by means of progressive taxation. This was part of the Social Democrats' commitment to ensure that

> the majority is liberated from dependence upon a few owners of capital, and the social order based on economic classes is replaced by a community of citizens cooperating on the basis of freedom and equality.[45]

The budget proposal for 1947 to 1948 provided for spending at more than twice the level a return to prewar levels would have entailed. Although some of

---

[43] Gilmour 2010: 234–235, 245–249, 267. See also Klausen 1998: 95–107. Quotes: Gilmour 2010: 238, 250, 267. Grimnes 2013 describes similar developments in occupied Norway.
[44] Östling 2013: 191.
[45] Du Rietz, Henrekson, and Waldenström 2012: 12. Quote from the "Post-War Program" of 1944, in Hamilton 1989: 180. Cf. also Klausen 1998: 132.

it was earmarked for the war debt, it also allowed welfare to be stepped up. Tax rates came down a bit from their wartime peaks, but reductions in income tax were to be offset by higher taxes on wealth and estates, shifting more of the burden onto the wealthy. The Social Democratic finance minister Ernst Wigforss conceded that the estate tax would hurt the largest fortunes, citing America and Britain as models: the new top rate on inheritances was 47.5 percent, a 150 percent increase. The bill was discussed almost exclusively from a redistribution perspective, and debate was intense. The Social Democrats, empowered by the will of the voters that had been shaped by the war experience, carried the day, and Sweden embarked on an ambitious social experiment. In 1948, wartime reforms were effectively made permanent, and leveling resumed.[46]

Just as in belligerent countries that kept taxes and spending high after the fighting had ceased, this process was intimately connected to the war. Redistributive policies and leveling of social and economic inequalities had long been advocated by certain political parties and labor unions. Mass mobilization war served as a catalyst that helped turn these ideals into realities. The case of Sweden is instructive in demonstrating that even a comparatively limited war mobilization effect could be sufficient to create the fiscal infrastructure as well as the political will and electoral support that were required for progressive policy preferences to carry the day.[47]

"A REVOLUTIONARY MOMENT IN THE WORLD'S HISTORY IS A TIME FOR REVOLUTIONS, NOT FOR PATCHING": FROM VIOLENT SHOCKS TO EQUALIZING REFORM

This was even more true of those countries that fought in the world wars. A common chain of events served to lower inequality and subsequently maintain or in many cases further reinforce wartime leveling: loss of capital to destruction,

---

[46] Lodin 2011: 29–30, 32; Du Rietz, Henrekson, and Waldenström 2012: 33 fig. 6; Du Rietz, Johansson, and Stenkula 2013: 17. The wartime 40 percent corporate tax had already been made permanent in 1947: Du Rietz, Johansson, and Stenkula 2014: 6.

[47] "This development gives support to an idea that the acceptable burden of taxation increases in crises and the acceptance of the higher tax level remains after the crises, giving rise to a stepwise increasing function of tax rates and public expenditures" (Stenkula, Johansson, and Du Rietz 2014: 180). By contrast, Henrekson and Waldenström 2014, esp. 14–16, seek to deny a war effect and explain policy changes with reference to ideology—but this does not explain *why* the Socialist Democrats were able to implement their ambitious policies. Roine and Waldenström 2008: 380–382 posit a strong impact of taxation on the postwar decline in top income shares.

expropriation, or inflation; decline of returns to capital due to policy intervention such as tax policy and rent, price, wage, and dividend controls; and postwar commitment to continuing high and progressive taxation. Depending on political, military, and economic circumstances specific to individual countries, leveling could be sudden or more gradual, concentrated during the war years or deferred to postwar crises, or spread out across longer periods. Yet the outcome was always the same, regardless of whether countries lost or won, suffered occupation during or after the war, and were democracies or run by autocratic regimes. Mass mobilization for the purpose of mass violence was the engine of a transnational transformation of the distribution of income and wealth.

We can thank Piketty for an answer to the question of why inequality did not quickly recover after 1945 that is elegant in its simplicity. Capital accumulation is a process that takes time, and the nineteenth century, largely peaceful in much of the West, had offered favorable conditions. Once capital had been destroyed on a large scale in the period of the world wars, it proved much more difficult to rebuild as long as wartime measures such as progressive taxes on income and estates remained in place. And they were kept in place as the hugely inflated warfare state morphed into the postwar social state, harnessing for the provision of welfare the fiscal instruments originally created for the mass mobilization of people and industrial resources.[48]

War mobilization was also instrumental in promoting labor unionization. This is important because high rates of union membership, which sustain collective bargaining and protect workers' rights, are commonly regarded as a leveling force and are indeed negatively correlated with income inequality in the long run. Even so, inasmuch as the expansion of unions was largely a function of mass mobilization warfare, there is no compelling reason to regard the former as an independent agent of income compression. The significance of the war mobilization effect is clearly visible in the case of the United Kingdom, where union membership almost quadrupled during and right after World War I before

---

[48] Piketty 2014: 368–375. Estate taxes in particular had a major effect on the transmission of wealth. In France, inheritance flows as a share of national income dropped dramatically in the war period, from 20–25 percent to less than 5 percent (380 fig. 11.1). Dell 2005 compares the experience of France (where severe war shocks and postwar tax progressivity sharply reduced wealth concentration and prevented a recovery), Germany (which also experienced shocks but opted for less progressivity and hence witnessed some reconcentration of wealth), and Switzerland (which was spared major shocks and imposed little progressivity, and where wealth inequality remained high); see also Piketty 2014: 419–421. In terms of top income shares, the only exception to postwar leveling among the former belligerents was Finland: after sustained and considerable leveling between 1938 and 1947, the country experienced a substantial recovery of top income shares in

it kept sliding back down for about fifteen years and returned to its previous peak only during World War II. In the United States, unionization rates, which briefly rose and then fell back at the time of World War I, soared in response to two shocks. The first was the Great Depression, which prompted the New Deal and the National Labor Relations Act of July 1935 guaranteeing workers' rights to organize in unions and engage in collective bargaining. Once the initial surge had stalled a few years later, war provided another powerful impulse that caused union membership to reach its all-time high in 1945, followed by fairly steady decline thereafter. Key elements of this pattern were replicated across developed countries: very low rates of unionization prior to World War I, large increases in the later stages and immediate aftermath of that war, a partial decline and a strong recovery, and new peaks during World War II. Significant variation is limited to the postwar period, as membership soon began to decline in some countries but held steady for longer in others where it fell only more recently. Only a very few countries in this survey, most notably Denmark and Sweden, experienced substantial and sustained growth beyond World War II levels. The OECD average in Fig. 5.13 nicely clarifies the overall trend.[49]

Once it had greatly expanded during the world wars, union membership acted as a brake on the recovery of inequality, in conjunction with progressive fiscal measures and other forms of government regulation. As we will see in chapter 12, democracy, unlike unionization, is not consistently correlated with inequality. Even so, it is worth noting that the world wars were closely associated with the expansion of the franchise. Max Weber had already identified the underlying dynamics:

---

the 1950s and 1960s alongside a strong rise in the income Gini coefficient. It was only during the 1970s that the top 1 percent income share fell to levels lower than in the late 1940s, whereas the Gini coefficient never returned to that low level (WWID; Jäntti et al. 2010: 412–413 table 8A.1). Taxation greatly increased in World War II but was relaxed for the general population as thresholds rose and the proportion of population taxed declined thereafter: Jäntti et al. 2010: 384 fig. 8.3(b); and see also Virén 2000: 8 fig. 6 for a decline in the gross tax rate in the 1950s and early 1960s. It is unclear how this would have bolstered top incomes. Fiscal instruments: Piketty 2014: 474–479. See 475 fig. 13.1 on the state's share in GDP: in France, the UK, and the United States, the share of taxes in national income tripled between 1910 and 1950, followed by different trends ranging from stagnation (in the United States) to growth by another half (in France). This established a new equilibrium, with much of states' budgets eventually committed to health and education and replacement incomes and transfers (477). Roine and Waldenström 2015: 555–556, 567 likewise consider high marginal tax rates to be a crucial determinant of low postwar inequality. It is not much of an exaggeration for Piketty 2011: 10 to say that "the 1914–1945 political and military shocks generated an unprecedented wave of anti-capital policies, which had a much larger impact on private wealth than the wars themselves."

[49] Scheve and Stasavage 2009: 218, 235; but cf. 218–219, 235 on the question of causation. See also Salverda and Checchi 2015: 1618–1619. UK: Lindsay 2003. Fig. 5.13 from http://www.waelde.com/UnionDensity (slight discontinuities around 1960 are a function of shift between datasets). For detailed statistics see esp. Visser 1989.

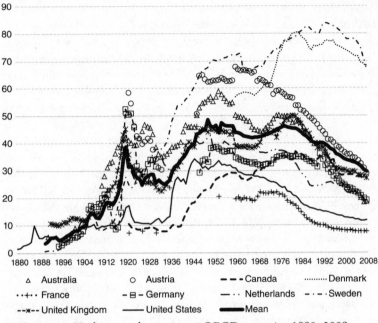

Figure 5.13 Trade union density in ten OECD countries, 1880–2008 (in percent)

> The basis of democratization is everywhere purely military in character
> . . . . Military discipline meant the triumph of democracy because the
> community wished and was compelled to secure the cooperation of
> the nonaristocratic masses and hence put arms, and along with arms
> political power, into their hands.[50]

Since then modern scholarship has repeatedly linked mass warfare and the
extension of political rights. Insofar as raising mass armies requires societal
consent, extensions of the franchise may be regarded as a logical corollary of
intense military mobilization. As I argue in the next chapter, this principle
already applied as far back as ancient Greece. In the more recent past, all French
men aged twenty-five or older were entitled to elect assembly members in

---

[50] Weber 1950: 325–326. Andreski 1968: 20–74, esp. 73, argues that levels of stratification are inversely correlated with the degree of military participation in a given population.

revolutionary France. Universal male suffrage was granted in Switzerland in 1848 after a civil war between cantons the year before, in the United States in 1868 (and in 1870 for blacks) in the wake of the Civil War, in Germany in 1871 after its war with France, and in Finland in 1906 in the wake of reforms prompted by the Russo–Japanese War. More limited suffrage extensions in the nineteenth and early twentieth centuries have been interpreted as responses to concerns about unrest and possible revolution. By contrast, early instances that are not related to war or threats of violence are rare. Broadly speaking, European peacefulness after 1815 had retarded political reform. This changed dramatically with the unprecedentedly massive mobilizations of the world wars. Full male suffrage was introduced in 1917 in the Netherlands and in 1918 in Belgium, Ireland, Italy, and the United Kingdom. Universal suffrage became the law in Denmark in 1915; in Austria, Estonia, Hungary, Latvia, Poland, and (technically) Russia in 1918; in Germany, Luxembourg, the Netherlands, and Sweden in 1919; in Anglophone Canada, the United States, and Czechoslovakia in 1920; and in Ireland and Lithuania in 1921. In the United Kingdom women thirty or older also received the vote in 1918, an age restriction removed ten years later. World War II resulted in the next big push, as universal suffrage was introduced in Quebec in 1940, in France in 1944, in Italy in 1945, in Japan in 1946, in the Republic of China (soon limited to Taiwan) and Malta in 1947, and in Belgium and South Korea in 1948. The connection between mass war and mass franchise is not merely implicit in this chronology but was expressly made. To give just two examples, Woodrow Wilson sought to sell women's suffrage "as a war measure":

> essential to the successful prosecution of the war of humanity in which we are engaged . . . . We have made partners of the women in this war. Shall we admit them only to a partnership of sacrifice and suffering and toll and not to a partnership of privilege and of right?

The judicial ban of white-only primaries in the United States in 1944 could be said to have been prompted by a turn in public opinion against the exclusion of minorities who shared in the "common sacrifices of wartime."[51]

---

[51] Link: Ticchi and Vindigni 2008: 4 provide references. For a scheme, never implemented, to create a new constitution with universal suffrage that coincided with the Levée en Masse in France in 1793, see 23 and n. 46. Responses: e.g., Acemoglu and Robinson 2000: 1182–1186; Aidt and Jensen 2011, esp. 31. Other instances: universal suffrage was enacted in New Zealand, Australia, and Norway prior to World War I. Peace:

The observed pattern chimes well with the abatement of franchise reform in the interwar period, when universal suffrage was introduced in Turkey (1930), Portugal (in stages from 1931 to 1936), and Spain (1931), leaving aside the lifting of age restrictions in Ireland and the United Kingdom in 1928. The generally slow pace of democratization in countries that were remote from the great wars and free from the need to offer concessions or rewards in return for mass mobilization has also been noted. Exposure to total war created a uniquely important impetus for formal democratization.[52]

The massive violent shocks of modern mass mobilization warfare depressed inequality by a wide variety of means. Postwar attitudes were shaped by the experience of these unique shocks. Conscription and rationing have been identified as ubiquitous and potent stimulus for change, and in many of the affected countries evacuations and exposure to bombing and other military activity directed against civilians further reinforced the social effects of conflict, most notably in the first half of the 1940s. Widely diffused across national populations, these dislocations eroded class distinctions and raised expectations of fairness, participation, inclusion, and the acknowledgment of universal social rights, expectations that were fundamentally at odds with the highly skewed distribution of material resources that had characterized the prewar period. Wartime state planning gave a boost to collectivist thinking. A large body of scholarship concurs that the experience of the world wars was a crucial catalyst for the creation of the modern welfare state.[53]

Ticchi and Vindigni 2008: 23–24. Quotes in Ticchi and Vindigni 2008: 29 n. 27, 30 n. 38. For the world wars and waves of democratization, see, e.g., Markoff 1996b: 73–79; Alesina and Glaeser 2004: 220. Mansfield and Snyder 2010's finding that war has no more than scattered effects on democratization stems in no small part from their failure to distinguish between mass mobilization warfare and other types of conflict.
[52] Ticchi and Vindigni 2008: 30, with references, especially concerning Latin America.
[53] This connection has been attributed to a variety of factors, from war-related social solidarity, ideals of equality, and political consensus building to the assertiveness of the working class due to full employment and unionization, the huge increase in state expenditure and capabilities, and the morale-building function of promises of postwar reform. Titmuss 1958 is a classic statement (for a brief survey of the debate on his position, see Laybourn 1995: 209–210). Among recent studies, Klausen 1998 provides the most forceful argument in support of the critical importance of World War II in postwar welfare state creation in different countries, whereas Fraser 2009: 246–248 makes a strong case specifically for the United Kingdom, as does Kasza 2002: 422–428 for Japan; the latter also concisely theorizes the relationship between mass war and welfare, emphasizing the demand for healthy soldiers and workers, the effects of the absence of male breadwinners, calls for social justice and equality of sacrifice even for elites, and war-induced urgency that induced rapid change (429–431). See, furthermore, Briggs 1961; Wilensky 1975: 71–74; Janowitz 1976: 36–40; Marwick 1988: 123; Hamilton 1989: 85–87; Lowe 1990; Porter 1994: 179–192, 288–289; Goodin and Dryzek 1995; Laybourn 1995: 209–226; Sullivan 1996: 48–49; Dutton 2002: 208–219; Kasza 2002: 428–433; Cowen 2008: 45–59; Estevez-Abe 2008: 103–111; Fraser 2009: 209–218, 245–286; Jabbari 2012: 108–109; Michelmore 2012: 17–19; Wimmer 2014: 188–189; and cf. more generally Addison 1994.

The cataclysmic nature of World War II greatly accelerated the course of social policy, as the need for postwar reform and redistributive welfare provisions came to be appreciated across the political spectrum, not least as a vital means of shoring up morale. It was hardly by coincidence that the *Times*—not exactly a champion of progressivism—published the following editorial just days after France's surrender and Churchill's famous prediction that "the Battle of Britain is about to begin":

> If we speak of democracy we do not mean a democracy which maintains the right to vote but forgets the right to work and the right to live. If we speak of freedom we do not mean a rugged individualism which excludes social organization and economic planning. If we speak of equality we do not mean a political equality nullified by social and economic privilege. If we speak of economic reconstruction we think less of maximum (though this job too will be required) than of equitable distribution.[54]

Highly progressive taxation, unionization, and democratization were among the most important means to this end. To say, as the Swedish economists Jesper Roine and Daniel Waldenström do in their authoritative survey of the development of top income shares over the last century, that

> macroshocks explain most of drop, but there is also a role for a shift in policy and probably also in an economy-wide shift in the balance between returns to capital and labor[55]

detracts from the unique significance of modern mass mobilization warfare for modern leveling. To the extent that shifts in policy and economic change were themselves an outgrowth of the world wars, they should not be treated as

---

This effect could even spill over into colonies: see Lewis 2000 for Kenya. For the role of state expansion see also Berkowitz and McQuaid 1988: 147–164, esp. 147; Cronin 1991; and cf. Fussell 1989; Sparrow 2011 on the cultural impact of World War II; likewise Kage 2010, who observes that World War II mobilization produced greater civic engagement in the generation that came of age around that time. Bauer et al. 2016, esp. 42–43 table 2 and fig. 1, survey studies that find that exposure to war violence tends to increase prosocial behavior and community participation. Ritter 2010: 147–162 provides a general survey of postwar welfare reforms in various countries.

[54] *The Times*, July 1, 1940, quoted by Fraser 2009: 358.

[55] Roine and Waldenström 2015: 555.

separate factors. Policies that resulted in the compression of material inequalities were very much the product of the exigencies of war. It does not matter whether this outcome was deliberate or inadvertent—only that it was ubiquitous. Sir William Beveridge's bold wartime appeal

> that any proposals for the future, while they should use to the full the experience gathered in the past, should not be restricted by consideration of sectional interests established in the obtaining of that experience. Now, when the war is abolishing landmarks of every kind, is the opportunity for using experience in a clear field. A revolutionary moment in the world's history is a time for revolutions, not for patching,

did not fall on deaf ears, neither in Britain nor elsewhere.[56]

And while economic change was no doubt determined in complex ways, much of it was likewise deeply rooted in the effects of global mass mobilization warfare. Consider Peter Lindert and Jeffrey Williamson's

> appeal to fundamental factor-market changes that occurred over the Great Leveling after 1910: not only those military and political shocks, but also the great slowdown in labor supply growth, a rapid advance of education, the slowdown in technological bias against the unskilled, a much more antitrade world economy that deflected labor-intensive imports from American shores and suppressed American skill- and capital-intensive exports, and a retreating financial sector.

Three of the last five of these developments were intimately connected to the military and political shocks of the first half of the twentieth century: the severe abatement of immigration, the hiatus in global economic integration, and falling relative incomes in the financial sector are all better understood as consequences and manifestations of these shocks than as meaningfully separate factors. Of the two remaining elements, ongoing improvements in the supply of education might be expected to act on inequality in a gradual fashion, whereas most of the available evidence points to short and discontinuous reductions in skill premiums and returns to higher education right at the time of the two world wars.

---

[56] Beveridge 1942: 6.

The final component, productivity growth in unskilled labor-intensive sectors of the American economy, was incapable of generating the observed episodes of rapid and substantial compression across a variety of indices of inequality, from top income shares and the distribution of incomes and wages to relative financial sector wages and returns on education. Moreover, the "Great Compression" was a process that unfolded all over the industrialized world and sometimes even beyond. Some of the affected countries had been sources and other destinations of migrants; the finance sector played a much greater role in some of these economies than in others, and they differed in the extent to which their citizens enjoyed access to education. The one thing they all had in common was the shared experience of violent shocks and their impact on capital holdings, on fiscal, economic, and welfare policies, and on global exchange. From this perspective, the violence of war and revolution was not merely one equalizing influence among many but rather a singularly overwhelming force that defined political, social, and economic outcomes.[57]

Nor did ideology act as an autonomous agent: while the redistributive agenda of progressive political organizations provided an intellectual and ideological infrastructure on which wartime and postwar policymaking could draw, governments' willingness and ability to both fund and implement much more ambitious social policies owed much to the global eruptions of violence to which they struggled to respond.[58] Mass leveling was born of mass violence—as well as the fear of future mass violence on an even vaster scale. The postwar

---

[57] Lindert and Williamson 2015: 218 (quote), with 206 for another list of these six factors. Milanovic 2016: 56 table 2.1 argues in a similar vein by differentiating "malign" equalizing forces such as wars, state collapse, and epidemics from "benign" factors, identified as social pressures through politics (exemplified by socialism and trade unions), education, aging, and technological change in favor of the low-skilled. Therborn 2013: 155–156 contrives to separate "far-reaching peaceful social reform" from 1945 to about 1980 from the preceding violent shocks. For the curtailment of immigration, see Turchin 2016a: 61–64. As Lindert and Williamson 2015: 201 fig. 8–3 illustrate, relative salaries in the U.S. financial sector plummeted precisely during World War II after having grown somewhat during the 1930s. For discontinuous changes in U.S. skill premiums, see herein, chapter 13, pp. 375–376; for unionization rates, see herein, pp. 165–167; for the potentially disequalizing consequences of population aging, see herein, chapter 16, pp. 426–427.

[58] See the literature cited herein, at n. 53. Economic policy in particular was sensitive to war effects: to give just one example, Soltow and van Zanden 1998: 195 note that 1918 and 1945 were focal points of public debate about how the Dutch economy should be organized in the Netherlands. Even if Durevall and Henrekson 2011 are right to maintain that in the long run, the growth of the state's share in GDP was primarily a function of economic growth rather than driven by a ratchet effect of war-related jumps, economic growth by itself cannot account for the emergence of war-driven progressive taxation and regulation that was conducive to sustained leveling. Lindert 2004, who tracks the rise of the welfare state in the long term and in relation to economic development, calls the 1930s and 1940s a "crucial watershed" when war and fear boosted social democracy (176), even if it took until the 1970s for the expansion of western welfare systems to have run its course.

expansion of the welfare state on both sides of the Iron Curtain may have been influenced by competition between the West and the Soviet bloc. More specifically, the development of income inequality in eighteen Western countries from 1960 to 2010 was constrained by the Cold War: controlling for other factors such as top marginal tax rates, union density, and globalization, the Soviet Union's relative military power was negatively and very significantly correlated with national top income shares. It appears that the Soviet threat served as a disciplining device to inequality that helped foster social cohesion. This constraint promptly disappeared after the collapse of the Soviet Union in 1991. Almost half a century after the end of the last one, world war was finally no longer a realistic prospect.[59]

---

[59] Obinger and Schmitt 2011 (welfare state); Albuquerque Sant'Anna 2015 (Cold War). The nature of the proximate factors (other than marginal tax rates) through which Soviet military power could have affected top income shares is a matter in need of investigation. For the future of war, cf. herein, chapter 16, pp. 436–439.

Chapter 6

PREINDUSTRIAL WARFARE
AND CIVIL WAR

"NOTHING NOW IMPEDED THE VIGOR WITH WHICH WAR COULD BE WAGED": THE (RE)EMERGENCE OF MASS MOBILIZATION WARFARE IN THE WEST

In their recent study of taxation and warfare, Kenneth Scheve and David Stasavage demonstrate just how much modern mass mobilization warfare represented a break with the past. Military mobilization rates for a panel of thirteen major powers since the end of the Thirty Year's War indicate that military strength rose as populations grew over time while mobilization rates remained quite stable, averaging around 1 percent or 1.5 percent of the total population. The two world wars temporarily displaced the mean rate for the half-century from 1900 to 1950 to 4–4.5 percent, more than three times the average level of the preceding 250 years (Fig. 6.1). This meshes well with the notion that modern mass mobilization warfare served as a leveling force that was both powerful and rare: as I showed in chapter 3, in its absence, material inequality, with but few apparent exceptions, had been either growing or stable at high levels throughout these previous centuries.[1]

Mass mobilization wars—in which a significant proportion of the total population (say, at least 2 percent, as in Scheve and Stasavage's taxonomy) served in the military—are only sporadically attested in the generations before 1914. Duration is likewise important, as very short-lived surges cannot be expected to have had a major effect of the distribution of private resources. The Franco–Prussian War of 1870 to 1871 certainly involved high mobilization levels but lasted fewer than ten months and had effectively been decided after only a month and a half. In the previous decade, the American Civil War was a more promising candidate as a potential leveling force. Although conventionally defined as a civil war, it had

---

[1] Fig. 6.1 from Scheve and Stasavage 2016: 177 fig. 7.1.

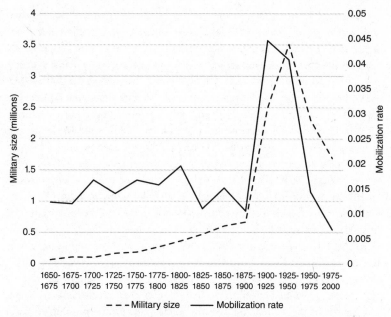

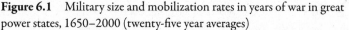
- - - Military size ——— Mobilization rate

Figure 6.1 Military size and mobilization rates in years of war in great power states, 1650–2000 (twenty-five year averages)

many of the characteristics of large-scale interstate warfare and involved massive mobilization of manpower on both sides. Between 1861 and 1865, the Union mobilized a little more than 2 million soldiers, roughly a tenth of its population, and the Confederacy raised perhaps up to 1 million troops out of a nonslave population of 5.6 million, maybe a seventh or even a sixth of that group and about a ninth of the overall southern population—a less meaningful ratio. Leaving aside differences in age structure, these mobilization rates were impressive even by later world war standards. The Confederate effort did not fall far short of the very high French and German rates of a fifth in World War I, a war of equal duration, and the Union rate was not much lower than the U.S. rate of an eighth in World War II and was much higher than in World War I, when it only reached 4 percent. The Civil War therefore clearly qualifies as a mass mobilization war.[2]

---

[2] The presence of large armies alone does not necessarily meet that criterion: in China in 1850, for instance, close to 9 million people would have had to serve in the military in order to clear a 2 percent threshold. For all we can tell, that did not happen even during the Taiping Rebellion: see herein, chapter 8, pp. 238–240.

In principle, key characteristics of this conflict—expansive conscription, multiyear duration, huge costs, and massive casualties—might have been conducive to policy measures that resulted in leveling. Yet this did not happen. It is true that the Civil War changed fiscal regimes more thoroughly than had earlier wars on American soil. In 1862 the Union created an income tax, followed by the Confederacy the following year. However, the Union income tax as originally introduced was both very low and only very mildly progressive, featuring a 3 percent rate on most taxable incomes and one of 5 percent for the highest earners. In 1864 Congress created tax brackets with somewhat higher rates of up to 10 percent, an upgrade undertaken in response to draft riots and rudimentary arguments about fairness. Even so, the tax failed to bring in much income. Initially retained to service the war debt, it was allowed to lapse in 1872. Consumption taxes, which are inherently regressive, remained the main source of revenue, and the only direct tax that produced notable income, a tithe tax on agricultural products that was essentially a formalization of impressment, was also effectively regressive. Meanwhile, the Confederacy largely relied on printing money, unleashing runaway inflation of more than 9,000 percent by war's end.[3]

The war's eventual effect on inequality differed massively between North and South. In the Union, the wealthy made huge profits by supplying the military and underwriting war debt. The number of millionaires dramatically increased in the 1860s. Famous tycoons such as John P. Morgan, John D. Rockefeller, and Andrew Carnegie started out as civil war profiteers. Perhaps inevitably, concentration of this kind at the very top is not reflected in studies of census samples that point to substantially similar levels of wealth inequality in 1860 and 1870, and income from property in general became only slightly more concentrated. By contrast, overall income disparities greatly expanded during this decade: in New England, the income Gini coefficient rose by more than 6 percentage points and the top 1 percent income share rose by half of its previous level; other regions registered similar, albeit often more moderate, changes. There can be no doubt that the Civil War raised inequality in the North.[4]

[3] Bank, Stark, and Thorndike 2008: 23–47 on Civil War, esp. 31–34, 41–42.
[4] Turchin 2016a: 83 table 4.4, 139, 161. For the evidence of the census data, see herein, n. 7, and also Soltow 1975: 103. Between 1860 and 1870, the estimated Gini coefficient of property income rose from 0.757 to 0.767, and the top 1 percent share from 25 percent to 26.5 percent—changes that are well within likely margins of error: Lindert and Williamson 2016: 122 table 5–8. Income Ginis went up 6.1 points in New England, 3.1 points in the Middle Atlantic states, 6.7 points in the Eastern Northern Central states, and 5.9 points in the Western Northern Central states, whereas the corresponding top 1 percent income shares grew from 7 percent, 9.1 percent, 7 percent, and 6.9 percent to 10.4 percent, 9.2 percent, 9.1 percent, and 9.7 percent: 116 table 5–7A, 154 table 6–4A.

The opposite was true of the defeated South, where the abolition of slavery eliminated a huge share of the wealth of the plantation-owning elite. In 1860, slaves accounted for a staggering 48.3 percent of all private wealth in the Southern states, significantly more than the total value of all farmland and associated buildings. Slaveownership had driven up inequality in the South to higher levels than elsewhere in the country: by 1860 the Gini coefficient of household income reached 0.61 in the Southern Atlantic states, 0.55 in the Eastern Southern Central region, and 0.57 in the Western Southern Central region, compared to 0.51 for the country as a whole and up from 0.46 in the South in 1774. Although slaveownership was fairly widespread, with a quarter of southern households owning slaves, about a quarter of all slaves were concentrated in the richest half-percent of households. Wholesale emancipation without compensation in conjunction with wartime dislocations and the widespread physical destruction inflicted on some of the Southern states greatly reduced regional assets, losses that were disproportionately borne by the upper tiers of the planter class.[5]

The most detailed evidence comes from a sample of census data from 1860 and 1870 that allows us to track changes during the Civil War and its immediate aftermath. For the Southern states, these data document wealth destruction on an enormous scale: mean per capita wealth fell by 62 percent within this one decade. These losses were unevenly distributed across wealth brackets and asset classes (Table 6.1).[6]

The wealthiest 10 percent lost ground relative to the remainder of the population: their share in all personal property fell from 73 percent to 59.4 percent even as their share of real property went up slightly, from 68.4 percent to 71.4 percent, causing their share in total wealth to decline from 71 percent to 67.6 percent. Except for the top 1 percent, the degree of loss of personal property increased with wealth, whereas the less affluent were more heavily affected by loss of real property. The former development was driven in the first instance by the abolition of slavery, which destroyed much of the personal property holdings of the upper tiers of southern society, whereas those

---

[5] Slaves as wealth: Wright 2006: 60 table 2.4, with 59 table 2.3 (farmland and buildings accounting for 36.7 percent of southern private wealth). Cf. also Piketty 2014: 160–161 figs. 4.10–11 for earlier decades. Ginis: Lindert and Williamson 2016: 38 table 2–4, 116 table 5–7; and cf. also 115 table 5–6 for 1850. Slaveownership: Gray 1933: 530 with Soltow 1975: 134 table 5.3.

[6] I am greatly indebted to Joshua Rosenbloom and Brandon Dupont, who very generously computed these results for me from IPUMS-USA, https://usa.ipums.org/usa/. For the nature of these data, see Rosenbloom and Stutes 2008: 147–148.

Table 6.1 Property in 1870 relative to 1860 (1860 = 100), for Southern whites

Property type	Wealth shares				
	0–55	55–90	90–95	95–99	99–100
Real	46.4	66.0	68.0	77.3	74.3
Personal	72.3	32.1	18.8	18.0	22.8
Total	61.9	48.2	38.4	40.8	46.0

who had not owned slaves had far less to lose. This process would have had a much more massive leveling effect on Southern society had it not been partly offset by stronger devaluation or diminution of real estate holdings among the less affluent. This is also well brought out by the Gini coefficients of wealth distribution for Southern whites in 1860 and 1870. Although the Ginis for real property registered only a small decrease (from 0.72 to 0.7), personal property inequality fell dramatically from 0.82 to 0.68. Total wealth inequality consequently steered a middle course as the Gini for all assets dropped from 0.79 to 0.72. Considering the short time frame, this amounts to a substantial compression of overall inequality. Even the inclusion of freed slaves in the 1870 sample does little to change this overall trend.

Changes in the distribution of income echoed this transformation (Table 6.2). Across the entire Southern population, the Gini coefficient of property income fell from 0.9 in 1860 to 0.86 in 1870. Overall, the southern "1 percent" saw their share in total income dwindle by more than a third, and regional income Gini coefficients sharply contracted by between 7 and 9 points.[7]

---

[7] The overall wealth Ginis for all Southerners in the IPUMS-USA data were 0.8 in 1860 and 0.74 in 1870. Earlier studies calculated more moderate leveling during that decade. Soltow 1975: 103 estimates wealth Ginis of 0.845 for free Southerners in 1860 and 0.818 for Southern whites in 1870. Jaworski 2009: 3, 30 table 3, 31, drawing on 6,818 individuals from the entire United States studied in both 1860 and 1870, computes a decline of the wealth Gini from 0.81 to 0.75 in the Atlantic South caused by losses at the top and a rise from 0.79 to 0.82 in the South Central region caused by rapid wealth accumulation by white-collar workers. Rosenbloom and Dupont 2015 analyze wealth mobility in that decade and find considerable turnover at the top of the wealth distribution. Property income: Lindert and Williamson 2016: 122 table 5–8. Table 2.4: 116 table 5–7, 154 table 6–4A (all Ginis rounded to two digits behind the decimal point). For a comparison of free households in 1860 and white households in 1870, see 116 table 5–7, 155 table 6–4B, for top income share reductions by 32 percent, 23 percent, and 49 percent of 1860 levels and Gini reductions by 4, 3, and 8 points.

Table 6.2 Inequality of Southern household incomes

Region	Gini coefficient		Top 1 percent share	
	1860	1870	1860	1870
South Atlantic	0.61	0.53	13.7	8.5
East South Central	0.56	0.49	12.5	8.5
West South Central	0.57	0.48	16.0	7.5

Yet Southern leveling was not a function of mass mobilization warfare as such but simply a consequence of military defeat. For all its trappings as one of the first "modern" wars of mass mobilization, its harnessing of industrial resources, and its strategic targeting of civilian infrastructure, the Civil War, in terms of its consequences for material inequality, was still a very traditional conflict in which victorious elites gained and defeated elites lost—and did so disproportionately relative to the general population. I discuss this historically widespread outcome later in this chapter. In the 1860s, only the methods differed from those commonly applied in more archaic conflicts, such as outright plunder. In this particular case, the main result was a shift of wealth and power from Southern planters to Northern capitalists. Aided by the absence of redistributive mechanisms—itself a function of the relative weakness of the federal government and of democratic institutions more generally—the wealthy elite on the victorious side gained by profiting from war and war-related economic development instead of enriching themselves by capturing Southern assets. In a war fought in earlier centuries, they might have taken over Southern plantations or transferred Southern slaves to their own holdings. The wealthy elite on the losing side forfeited assets, in this case not to outright seizure by the winners but to expropriation without transfer. This mitigated the scale of their losses, as slaves were freed without depriving planters of their labor.

At the same time, the totalizing character of the conflict and the consequent pervasiveness of the loss of human property made defeat more costly and intrusive than it would have been in a more traditional premodern war fought with more limited ambitions and capabilities. The Civil War was a hybrid, located at a particular juncture of social evolution, with one foot in modernity (represented by mass engagement and nationwide impact) and one in the past (represented by unconstrained profiteering among victorious elites and heavy depletion of elite assets only among the losers). Perhaps for the last time in history, inequality outcomes differed greatly between the winning and losing sides.

By contrast, judging from the evidence of top income shares, elites generally lost out in both world wars regardless of whether their countries had won or had been defeated.[8]

The only other early modern series of conflicts that qualify as mass mobilization events on a large scale are the wars of the French Revolution and the Napoleonic era. In 1793 France was under exceptional strain as it found itself at war with many of Europe's major powers, including Austria, England, Prussia, and Spain. On August 23 of that year, the French National Convention launched the "levée en masse," seeking to draft all unmarried able-bodied men aged eighteen to twenty-five. The rhetoric of the moment—and increasingly also the practice that followed—was that of mass mobilization warfare:

> From this moment until such time as its enemies shall have been driven from the soil of the Republic, all Frenchmen are in permanent requisition for the services of the armies. The young men shall fight; the married men shall forge arms and transport provisions; the women shall make tents and clothes and shall serve in the hospitals; the children shall turn old lint into linen; the old men shall betake themselves to the public squares in order to arouse the courage of the warriors and preach hatred of kings and the unity of the Republic.[9]

History would show that this was a momentous step. Carl von Clausewitz, whose distinguished military career began that year when he first fought the French at the tender age of thirteen, later marveled at this innovation in the final book of his treatise *On War*:

> In 1793, a force appeared that beggared all imagination. Suddenly war again became the business of the people—a people of thirty million, all of whom considered themselves citizens. . . . The full weight of the nation was thrown into the balance. The resources and efforts now available for use surpassed all conventional limits; nothing now impeded the vigor with which war could be waged.[10]

---

[8] The swift recovery of top income shares in the United States and Japan in the 1920s appear to be only partial exceptions.

[9] Quoted from Schütte 2015: 72.

[10] Clausewitz 1976: 592.

Under Napoleon's leadership, military forces of unprecedented size campaigned all over Europe. Between the 1790s and 1815, about 3 million Frenchmen served in the military, or a ninth of the country's total population—a level of mobilization comparable to that of the United States in the Civil War and World War II. As we will see in chapter 8, the distribution of income is thought to have become somewhat more equitable between the onset of the French Revolution and the post-Napoleonic period. We cannot tell, however, whether this change owed more to domestic revolutionary expropriations and redistributions than to the costs and consequences of France's external wars. Mass mobilization warfare and revolution have repeatedly come in tandem: Germany and Russia after World War I and China after World War II are the best-known examples. The French case is unusual in that revolution preceded rather than followed mass war. This makes it hard, perhaps impossible, to disentangle their equalizing effects but gives priority to the revolution, inviting us to treat the consequences of war as an outgrowth of the revolution. For this reason I consider the French experience in chapter 8, which is devoted to leveling by revolutionary means.[11]

"MEN OF SERVICE IN FARMING AND WARFARE": PREMODERN MASS MOBILIZATION WARFARE

Military mass mobilization has largely been a modern phenomenon, at least in the narrow sense in which this concept has been defined in the previous pages: in most cases, at least a tenth of the entire population had served in the military. A lower threshold would allow us to include more belligerents in the Napoleonic Wars or the world wars without changing the overall picture. Scheve and Stasavage's minimal requirement of 2 percent of a country's population serving in the military at a given time translates to a higher overall proportion for longer conflicts, as soldiers died or were replaced for other reasons. Considering the prominent role of infectious disease as a source of attrition in premodern armies, prolonged mobilization even at this threshold level would gradually have claimed a very large share of the total effectively eligible population of able-bodied men. For that reason alone—not to mention economic, fiscal, and organizational constraints—traditional agrarian

---

[11] See herein, chapter 8, pp. 232–238.

societies were unlikely to sustain this kind of effort for any significant amount of time.[12]

That some imperial polities were capable of fielding very large armies was simply a function of their size and not a sign of mass mobilization. For instance, in the eleventh century CE, the Northern Song Dynasty maintained huge military forces to contain the threat posed by the Jin to the north. Reported troop totals of up to 1.25 million may reflect disbursement of stipends, some of which were pocketed by corrupt officers, rather than actual strength, but even an army of 1 million would not have exceeded 1 percent of a population of at least 100 million at the time. The mature Mughal Empire controlled well more than 100 million subjects and never mobilized even 1 percent of them. The mature Roman Empire kept maybe 400,000 men under arms out of a population of 60 million to 70 million, a rate of well less than 1 percent. Ottoman mobilization levels were even lower.[13]

We have to venture farther back all the way into the pre-Christian era to identify more promising cases. The Warring States of China deserve pride of place. The Warring States period, from the fifth to the third centuries BCE, was characterized by the consolidation of seven major kingdoms that engaged in intense military competition. Ongoing inconclusive conflict turned these polities into increasingly centralized territorial states that strove to mobilize their demographic and other resources to the fullest extent possible. Reorganization of administration likely affected the concentration of elite power and material wealth. Whereas territory and population had formerly been controlled as fiefs by locally entrenched elite families, Warring States rulers imposed a system based on districts (*xian*) that brought them under their direct control and allowed them to collect taxes and conduct military levies. To break the power of hereditary nobles, kings had officials transferred, dismissed, or even executed. Senior officials, who used to be drawn from the ruling families, came to be recruited from lower elite circles, serving thenceforth as waged personnel whose standing depended entirely on their service to the state. Eventually the

---

[12] In keeping with the overall focus of this book, I refer here to state-level sedentary societies, leaving aside different types such as small-scale groups that engage in sporadic or seasonal warfare with high participation rates or pastoral steppe populations such as the hordes of Genghis Khan and his successors that drew in much of the adult male population.

[13] Kuhn 2009: 50 (Song); Roy 2016: ch. 3 (Mughals); Rankov 2007: 37–58 (higher figures for late antiquity are not credible: Elton 2007: 284–285); Murphey 1999: 35–49 (Ottomans).

majority of officials known from the sources were of obscure origin, as older families had been displaced.[14]

Administrative restructuring may have involved the reorganization of land: beginning in the sixth century BCE, states reordered fields into grid systems and grouped households into units of five. In the process, the state shored up private landownership, cutting out elite intermediaries who might extract rent or labor in competition with the central state as they had done before. These interventions involved redistribution of land. The most detailed reforms known, associated with Shang Yang in the state of Qin (from 359 BCE onward), envisioned the imposition of a rectangular grid across the countryside. That roads and footpaths found in that region form a rectilinear pattern indicates that these ambitious changes were in fact implemented. Reformers sought to create equal-sized blocks of land, allocated to individual households depending on the number of adult males. To the extent that this actually happened, it would have equalized assets among the rural commoner population. However, military rewards reintroduced disparities: in late Warring States Qin, each head cut off by a soldier bought him an upgrade in rank and a fixed amount of land equivalent to subsistence for a family of five. Moreover, fiefs still existed, although merely as units of income rather than areas of actual control. In Qin, for example, members of the highest nine of the seventeen ranks were entitled to income from this source. Although fiefs were not meant to be hereditary, elites sought to privatize them through purchase or moneylending that plunged farmers into debt.[15]

The ultimate purpose of this restructuring was to raise larger armies and more revenue for the war effort. The farming population was regarded as a reservoir of military manpower: the idea that farmers and soldiers were the same was expressed in the concept of *geng zhan zhi shi*, "men of service in farming and warfare." Divisions between urban and rural were likewise to be broken down, merging the entire population into a cohesive whole. This allowed the extension of previously aristocratic valorization of legitimate violence—that had focused on ceremonial combat involving chariots, and hunting—to the commoner population, which was conscripted for massed infantry warfare.[16]

---

[14] Hsu 1965: 39 table 4, 89; Li 2013: 167–175, 196. Political discourse of the period showed greater attention to the people, noting their poverty and distress, which the state was meant to alleviate: claims of "benefiting the people" or "loving the people" made an appearance: Pines 2009: 199–203.

[15] Li 2013: 191–194; Lewis 1990: 61–64; Lewis 1999: 607–608, 612.

[16] Li 2013: 197; Lewis 1990: 15–96, esp. 64 (quote).

The whole period was replete with military conflict: one modern count tallies up 358 wars between 535 and 286 BCE, or more than one per year. Multi-year campaigns appeared, and operations spread across larger geographical areas. Military mobilization levels were high, although we cannot be sure how much trust to put in often extravagant reported figures. Thus the main states of Qi, Qin, and Chu could each supposedly draw on up to 1 million soldiers, perhaps a rough representation of overall available manpower. Battles involving 100,000 or more combatants are frequently mentioned, with an upward trend. The most infamous instance is the battle of Changping in 260 BCE, wherein a Zhao army of 400,000 was said to have been massacred by Qin troops. Total fatality numbers for the losers of twenty-six major battles in the fourth and third centuries BCE add up to 1.8 million, and another survey yields close to 1.5 million killed by Qin armies in fifteen battles during the same period. Although such figures are almost certainly considerably inflated, the widespread occurrence of mass mobilization and heavy attrition is not in doubt. It is striking to be told that the entire male population aged fifteen or older in Henei commandery was mobilized for the nearby battle of Changping.[17]

Whether all this promoted leveling of income and wealth remains an open question. The state's struggle against hereditary nobles and its reliance on salaried officials and lifetime fiefs increased social mobility and ought to have impeded transgenerational wealth concentration. Block grants of land to commoners would have reduced disparities within the general population. Yet private landownership was a double-edged sword. Whereas previously farmers had been dependents and Gini coefficients of effective control over land would have been very high, the alienability of private land facilitated its reconcentration, a feature that was indeed noted in criticisms of Qin governance that were made in the early Han period. Later observers plausibly claimed that peasants lost their land owing to the pressures of taxation and unpredictable service obligations to the state, which forced them to take out usurious loans extended by the rich who at first kept them afloat but eventually took over their land. Ongoing warfare had not only spurred equalizing land reform and privatization but also came to undermine the resultant system of private smallholdings. More generally, this period was defined by growing commerce, monetization, and urbanization, as

---

[17] Campaigns: Li 2013: 187–188; Lewis 1999: 628–629; Lewis 1999: 625–628 (army sizes); Li 2013: 199; Bodde 1986: 99–100 (fatalities); Li 2013: 194 (Henei). Mobilization of 100,000 soldiers in a kingdom of 5 million people would have cleared the 2 percent threshold already mentioned.

towns were transformed from fortresses of the nobility into larger cities. All of these trends are predictors of increasing inequality. They also mesh well with reports of farmers losing their land to become landless workers or tenants while capital-holders such as merchants and entrepreneurs bought up their holdings. In this context it made sense for the state to consider surplus resources a source of evil, something to be soaked up by perpetual warfare.[18]

Yet growing private output could not all have been siphoned off for the war effort. Archaeology has produced ambiguous findings. One study notes a merging of lower elites and commoners in burials in the state of Chu in this period. A previous expression of stratification based on who was entitled to place certain objects in their graves faded as the same kinds of goods appeared across the board. Disparities were now expressed in quantitative terms, such as the opulence of the grave goods or tomb size. Wealth rather than ritual rank emerged as the key marker of status and differentiation. Bronze weaponry was now deposited in graves of all statuses, a sign of popular militarization but not necessarily of wider-ranging egalitarianism.[19]

All in all, the Warring States period was an arena for countervailing forces that were just as likely to compress as to boost inequality. These forces need not have operated synchronously: initial gains in leveling when established nobilities were displaced, and land reassigned to farmers may well have been eroded and reversed over time as the wealthy employed strategies of reconcentration that were grounded in market transactions rather than feudal entitlements. Ongoing expansion of military efforts coincided with the growth of private wealth and may also have been accompanied by its concentration. State capture of private resources was unlikely to contain a rise of private wealth inequality in the face of intensifying military mass mobilization. The system may even have been effectively quite regressive, considering that it imposed a very heavy double tax—military labor and agricultural products—on those least able to afford it, the farmers, whereas other forms of wealth may have been easier to shield from state demands. Infantry warfare as practiced at the time was relatively low-cost, relying as it did above all on conscription, mass-produced weapons (presumably involving forced labor by convicts and other state workers, as in later centuries), and the food that the farmers themselves produced. Qin farm taxes were

---

[18] Lewis 2007: 44–45; Hsu 1965: 112–116; Sadao 1986: 556; Lewis 2007: 49–50. Quote from Lewis 2007: 50.
[19] Falkenhausen 2006: 370–399, esp. 391, and 412, invoking egalitarianism as well as militarization. This contrasts rather awkwardly with the disappearance of such weaponry from Qin graves, possibly for utilitarian reasons (413).

reputedly much higher than later on under the Han dynasty. There was no need to pay for expensive equipment such as warships that might have required more sophisticated and perhaps more invasive and progressive forms of taxation. We thus have no compelling reason to interpret mass mobilization and protracted mass warfare among the Warring States period as a successful driver of net redistribution. Inasmuch as mass mobilization warfare in this period was associated with equalization, redistributive measures were a means of launching the warfare state but not its outcome. The modern experience of the world wars did not apply.[20]

Much the same is true of the Roman Republic, which likewise maintained high levels of military mobilization for many generations. Military participation ratios are hard to pin down with precision. Although we have access to a large amount of reasonably credible information on army strength for the later stages of the Republic from the late third into the first centuries BCE, the size of the underlying Roman citizen population remains a matter of controversy that focuses on the meaning of periodically recorded census tallies. Our estimates of military mobilization rates vary depending on whether we believe that some of these counts covered all Roman citizens regardless of age and gender or that they tracked adult males only. The evidence tends to support a conservative assessment of Roman citizen numbers that translates to military participation ratios that were generally high and that could on occasion reach fairly extreme levels. Thus at the height of the Second Punic War against Carthage, Rome may have drafted between 8 percent and 12 percent of its entire population, equivalent to 50 percent to 75 percent of all men aged seventeen to forty-five. Later crises in the 80s and 40s BCE would also have caused up to 8 percent or 9 percent of the population to serve in the military, even if only in the short term. In the longer term, for much of the second and first centuries BCE, somewhere around half of all male Roman citizens would have had to average about seven years of service to maintain military forces on the scale attested in our sources. Even if we allow for a substantially larger citizen population, participation rates could have been correspondingly lower—perhaps by as much as half—but would nevertheless remain high by premodern standards.[21]

---

[20] As for higher Qin taxes, we cannot be sure whether this was true or merely hostile propaganda: Scheidel 2015b: 178 n. 106.

[21] Scheidel 2008 surveys the debate about the number of Roman citizens. For mobilization rates, see esp. Hopkins 1978: 31–35; Scheidel 2008: 38–41. Lo Cascio 2001 argues for a larger base population and lower participation.

But once again, there are good reasons to doubt that this form of military engagement constrained inequalities of income or wealth. Although the oligarchy in charge of state operations shied away from seizing elites' wealth, impressments and periods of absence from farms necessitated by military service adversely affected the general population. One telling episode from the Second Punic War against Carthage illustrates the state's reluctance to target the rich even under extreme circumstances. In 214 BCE, when Rome was at the verge of insolvency and perhaps even collapse during Hannibal's invasion of Italy, and with mobilization rates standing at a historic high, the senate ordered citizens to hand over some of their slaves to serve as rowers in the navy. Contributions were graduated according to census class, albeit in a half-hearted and inconsistently progressive fashion. Those assessed at 50,000 asses (the Roman currency denomination at the time), equivalent to the threshold for the fourth of seven Roman census brackets and thus denoting a middling status, were to provide one slave; those who cleared 100,000 asses in assets owed three, those with more than 300,000 asses five, and those with a million or more eight. It is striking that the wealthiest members of the citizenry were not taxed proportionate to the size of their fortunes, let alone in a straightforwardly progressive manner. The scheme placed the heaviest burden on the upper reaches of the commoner population instead of on the wealth elite. Even in an acute emergency, Rome's oligarchic ruling class made as few concessions as it could get away with, in marked contrast to a democratic political system such as that of classical Athens, which, as we shall see, heavily taxed the rich to cover war expenditures.[22]

Rome preferred to rely on revenue from its expanding empire: in 167 BCE, the only direct war tax on the household wealth of citizens was abolished. The last two centuries of the Roman Republic witnessed massive accumulation of wealth among its ruling class, a development I have already sketched out in chapter 2. Several million slaves were imported into Italy during this period, which further widened wealth and income disparities, as it would do again much later in the Old South. Effectively controlled by a narrow oligarchy and increasingly funded by imperial tribute, the mature Roman Republic was capable of sustaining military mass mobilization at a time of growing inequality. I flag what was, at best, a possible short-lived exception to this process at the very end of this chapter.

---

[22] Livy 24.11.7–8, with Rosenstein 2008: 5–6. For Athens, see hereafter.

This leaves us with what is by far the most promising candidate of egalitarianism and curbs on wealth and income inequality associated with broadly based popular military participation: the case of ancient Greece. After larger and more centralized Bronze Age polities had collapsed in the late second millennium BCE, a process that flattened hierarchies and economic disparities on a vast scale (described in chapter 9), Greece came to be characterized by intense political fragmentation. What emerged from the wreckage developed into the largest city-state culture in history, which eventually comprised more than 1,000 separate *poleis* or city-states having a total population of 7 million or more. Most of them were small: territories of twenty to forty square miles were common among 672 *poleis* for which some information is available. Although the largest and most powerful *poleis*, above all Athens, enjoy disproportionate prominence in the historical record, general sociopolitical structures are reasonably well known across a wide range of these entities.[23]

For many generations, the emergence and consolidation of this pluralistic system has been the subject of scholarly debate: owing to the paucity of evidence dating from the early formative stages of this process, much remains uncertain. In the most general terms, development appears to have followed the trajectory sketched out in Josiah Ober's recent model of *polis* evolution, which addresses three key questions: why postcollapse rulers were unable to re-create more centralized social orders, why so many small polities appeared, and why authority came to be so diffused. Ober argues that a combination of geographical conditions unfavorable to imperial amalgamation, the exceptional severity of the Bronze Age collapse, and the concurrent spread of iron technology that helped democratize weapons use all "conspired to blaze a distinctive variant on a relatively familiar city-state path to state formation, a strongly *citizen-centered* path" that shaped long-term outcomes. Postcollapse Early Iron Age communities were poor and relatively undifferentiated, and although later elites sought to restore hierarchies in the wake of renewed demographic and economic growth, some communities retained egalitarian norms that helped them outcompete others.

Ober maintains that thanks to the widespread availability of iron weaponry and the prevailing simple infantry mode of warfare, "it was a social choice rather than economic constraint that determined how many of a community's men could be mobilized" and assumes that "under these conditions, higher

<hr>

[23] Hansen 2006b: 28–29, 32 (population); Ober 2015a: 34 fig. 2.3 (territories); Hansen and Nielsen 2004; Hansen 2006a (nature of the *polis*).

mobilization rates and superior morale were positively correlated with citizen-centered institutions and negatively correlated with the rule of small and exclusive bodies of elites." In other words, this particular environment selected in favor of inclusive forms of social and political organization. At the same time, the growth of individual *poleis* through the absorption of less competitive ones was contained by the same citizenship norms that enhanced their competitiveness. Although ongoing economic expansion and especially commercial development and trade threatened to undermine egalitarianism, the ability to mobilize as many men as possible for war remained the most crucial determinant of state success. This became all the more true as combat styles converged upon the model of the phalanx, in its mature form a rectilinear military formation that drew much of its impact from relative size. Phalanx warfare provided a strong incentive for the mobilization of men beyond elite circles, and all the more so as basic equipment such as shield and spear proved sufficient for effective participation.[24]

Although there is no consensus on exactly how the evolution of military tactics and sociopolitical institutions were connected, it is clear that by the sixth century BCE, much of the Greek world had developed a culture of citizenship associated with mass participation in infantry warfare. Widely shared military contributions coincided with the formation of extensive bodies of citizens who treated each other as equals within specified domains. Reinforced by a strong element of amateurism in governance, the resultant tradition of civic rights afforded citizens protection against powerful individuals and held governmental power in check. Rule egalitarianism was a hallmark of this system, even as political practice varied along a broad spectrum from authoritarian or oligarchic to democratic institutions.[25]

To what extent did this culture equalize the distribution of material resources? On a literal reading of the ancient literary evidence, the seemingly most straightforward example is provided by the most warlike of all Greek *poleis*, Sparta. According to the canonical tradition, at an early stage Sparta underwent extensive reforms associated with a (probably mythical) lawgiver named Lycurgus. One of the most famous features of the resultant system was the aggressively egalitarian institution of shared mess halls that required all men, including the

[24] Ober 2015a: 128–137, esp. 128–130 (quote: 130), 131 (quotes), 131–132, 135–136.
[25] Some scholars posit a close (causal) link, whereas others doubt it. Van Wees 2004: 79 and Pritchard 2010: 56 are among the most critical voices. See van Wees 2004: 166–197 for the mixed character of the early phalanx. Rights: Ober 2015a: 153.

top leadership, to dine together daily in small groups that were provisioned by equal-sized contributions of various kinds of food made by each group member. The same lawgiver was credited with equalization of land ownership:

> he persuaded the citizens to pool all the land and then redistribute it afresh: then they would all live on equal terms with one another, with the same amount of property to support each.[26]

All farmland in Laconia, the Spartan core region, was supposedly divided into 30,000 equal plots, 9,000 of which were allocated to the male citizens of Sparta and cultivated by helots, communally held slaves who operated in serf-like conditions and were attached to the land. This was to ensure both equality among the citizenry and freedom from the need to engage in nonmilitary pursuits. Moveable possessions were also subject to redistribution, precious metal money was suppressed, and sumptuary laws restricted investment in private residences. The citizenry experienced intense military mobilization: from ages seven to twenty-nine, virtually all Spartan males were expected to undergo a communal and militaristic education and training regimen that put strong emphasis on endurance and deprivation. Albeit highly agonistic in character, pitting individuals against each other in competition for honor and status, this institution was once again highly egalitarian, and—unusually for a traditional society—even accompanied by public education for girls that also prioritized physical prowess. The intended outcome was a citizenry of equals (*homoioi*) conditioned to maximize their military capabilities. These norms reportedly sustained the ongoing expansion of Spartan power, most notably the conquest and reduction to helot status of the neighboring Messenians in the seventh century BCE, which led to further distribution of land shares to the citizenry and the creation of a Spartan-led alliance system in the Peloponnese in the following century. The ancient historical record conveys the impression of a permanent state of military mass mobilization that shaped society and daily life to an extreme degree and that was intimately connected to egalitarian norms that also governed access to material resources.

Unfortunately for modern students of war-related leveling, this tradition, much of which derives from stylized narratives composed by admiring outsiders in later centuries, is problematic for two reasons. We cannot tell to what extent

---

[26] Plutarch, *Lycurgus* 8.1 (transl. by Richard J. A. Talbert).

this idealized system actually operated in practice, and we do know that growing resource inequality became a pressing concern from the fifth and especially the fourth centuries BCE onward. These are two distinct issues, considering that the latter does not rule out the former: in the apparent absence of mechanisms for the periodic adjustment of renewed inequalities, it is perfectly possible that an initially equalized distribution of wealth gradually gave way to more uneven outcomes. But the question remains whether these later conditions were entirely new or merely represented a worsening of earlier economic differentiation. The most thorough study of this problem has come to the conclusion that Spartan property had always been unequally distributed and private in character, yet constrained by a communal ideology that sought to impose an egalitarian lifestyle. There is no doubt that land allotments could be passed on across generations, a mechanism that even under egalitarian starting conditions promotes inequality in the longer term. The specifics of Spartan inheritance practices facilitated a growing concentration of land and other property within the citizenry. As Spartans whose holdings were no longer sufficient to provide the required standardized mess contributions forfeited full citizen status, wealth concentration caused citizen numbers to contract over time, from around 8,000 in 480 BCE to maybe 4,000 by 418 BCE and then to 1,200 by 371 BCE. By the 240s BCE the total was down to 700, only about a hundred of whom counted as affluent. Those whose assets had fallen below the mess contribution threshold were classed as the "inferiors" (*hypomeiones*): wealth inequality was eroding citizen egalitarianism.[27]

The uncertainties surrounding the historical evidence call for a conservative assessment of the leveling effect of Spartan military mass mobilization. The sources offer us a glimpse of a self-styled warrior society that cherished egalitarian norms, even if they were perhaps never fully implemented in real life and although they certainly waned over time as intergenerational wealth transmission produced increasingly unequal outcomes. Military mass mobilization as such was not greatly affected by this trend, as lower-status Spartans and the citizens of subjugated cities in Laconia fought in the Spartan phalanx and even helots performed military support functions. A combination of imposed egalitarianism in daily life and rent extraction from a large subordinate working population sustained mass mobilization of the core citizenry for a long period of

---

[27] Hodkinson 2000. Concentration: 399–445, esp. 399, 437. For the disequalizing effect of hereditary resources, see herein, chapter 1, pp. 37–38.

time—indeed, for several centuries. This fact alone allows us to posit an intimate connection between mass mobilization and equality—primarily equality of consumption and lifestyles, but at least initially also a considerable degree of resource equality overall, especially at a time when conquered land and its helotized inhabitants had been parceled out to Spartan citizens. Yet in the absence of any kind of progressive taxation—mess contributions were effectively regressive, for they imposed fixed levies regardless of personal wealth—and periodic redistribution of land, mass mobilization and egalitarian norms were incapable of containing rising wealth and income inequality in the long run. This problem began to be addressed only in the third century BCE, after wealth concentration had reached very high levels—and then, in a manner typical of historical leveling schemes, with recourse to violence (see herein, chapters 8 and 12).

Persistent military mass mobilization appears to have been more successful in curtailing resource inequality in the best-documented *polis*, Athens in the classical period of the fifth and fourth centuries BCE. The evidence is sufficient to allow us to pinpoint a close and arguably self-reinforcing connection between an expansion of military participation, a strengthening of citizen rights, and redistributive measures that favored commoners over the wealth elite. We can trace these developments over the course of almost three centuries. Around 600 BCE Athens suffered from growing inequality fueled by population growth and abundant labor. The poor were said to be indebted to the rich and suffered enslavement for nonpayment. One of Athens's main local rivals, the neighboring *polis* of Megara, introduced what one source scathingly labels "unbridled democracy"—a very early instance of popular government—that introduced retroactive debt relief requiring creditors to repay interest on loans, a measure meant to support the poor at the expense of the wealthy. Political reform encouraged popular military mobilization that enhanced Megara's naval power—Greek warships were propelled by oars, making the number of rowers a critical determinant of sea power—leading to victories over Athens and control of the contested island of Salamis in between the two polities. This setback was quickly followed by a whole series of reforms in Athens that included some form of debt cancellation and the prohibition of debt bondage alongside other enhancements of civic rights. The fortunes of war turned soon thereafter: Athenian success may well have been rooted in improved consensus and collaboration.

Almost a century later, in 508 BCE, Sparta invaded and temporarily seized Athens during an intervention in a domestic leadership struggle. Popular mobilization soon put an end to this incursion, with the massed citizen militia—"seventeen ranks deep"—forcing the Spartans to withdraw. This conflict closely coincided with a radical restructuring of the entire Athenian population and territory into a series of voting and conscription districts, a reform designed to foster cohesion and allowing the creation of a unified citizen army. Unprecedented military successes against several major regional powers were the immediate payoff. Once a basic framework of military and political institutions that depended on popular participation had been put in place, a self-reinforcing feedback loop between military and political mobilization gradually developed over time. In the words of the Greek historian Herodotus,

> while they were oppressed under tyrants, they had no better success in war than any of their neighbors, yet, once the yoke was flung off, they proved the finest fighters in the world.

In practice, there was not just one big yoke but many small ones: multiple constraints on political participation weakened over time as military commitments rose.[28]

Momentous changes occurred over the next generation. Athens expanded its navy multiple times until it was the largest in Greece. In 490 BCE a Persian invasion of Athens was repelled by a citizen army of 8,000, which represented about 40 percent of the entire male citizen population of fighting age. Military commanders and other top officials now came to be directly elected by the citizen assembly, and unpopular politicians could be temporarily expelled ("ostracized") by popular vote. In 480 BCE, faced with another Persian assault, an Athenian decree envisaged the full mobilization of its entire adult male citizenry, maybe 20,000 men in all, alongside its resident aliens, to man its 200 warships. Capitalizing on Persia's defeat, Athens quickly established an extensive alliance system whose financial contributions helped fund its navy and gradually turned it into the center of a naval empire. The 460s BCE witnessed Athenian military operations of unprecedented geographical scope, both in Greece and in the Levant. These military efforts once again fed back into constitutional change, disempowering elite bodies and strengthening democratic governance grounded in the assembly, a representative council, and large people's courts.

---

[28] See Scheidel 2005b: 4–9 for a fuller account of this whole sequence of developments. Pritchard 2010: 56–59 urges restraint. Quote: Herodotus 5.78.

Benefits for the general population soared: state pay for jury duty was introduced; by 440 BCE some 20,000 Athenians received some form of state pay for their services; and many thousands more were allotted land in conquered territories. Naval power and democracy thrived together, considering that the former critically relied on popular mass mobilization (augmented by the use of private slaves).

Military mobilization and attrition reached new heights during the Peloponnesian War with Sparta and its allies (431–404 BCE). Yet although Athens's finances were increasingly under strain, state payments to the lower classes actually expanded in the later stages of that conflict. Naval power was essential throughout the war. As a hostile oligarchic source put it,

> This is why the poor and the common people there rightly have more than the noble and rich: because it is the common people who row the ships and who add to the power of the city.

The exceptional scale of Athenian mobilization is reflected in the final body count: 24,000 out of 60,000 adult male citizens were killed in combat, alongside perhaps another 20,000 who perished in a plague that had been exacerbated by siege conditions. By any standard, this certainly qualifies as a form of total war. Yet after demographic recovery was underway, the Athenians renewed its imperialist policies by creating a new navy. Its strength peaked at 283 warships in 357 BCE. Once again, mass mobilization went hand in hand with domestic bargaining that boosted state subsidies: pay for assembly attendance rose six- to ninefold, and jurors were more fully employed than before. A special fund was created to subsidize attendance of state festivals. In a final all-out effort, a war against Macedonian dominance after the death of Alexander the Great in 323 BCE, Athens mobilized all male citizens up to age forty and launched a fleet of 240 warships; maybe a third out of the entire adult male citizenry was dispatched overseas or served in the navy.[29]

How did this affect the distribution of income and wealth? Unlike in much of the fifth century BCE, when proceeds from empire had subsidized

---

[29] Quote: Old Oligarch 1.2, quoted from van Wees 2004: 82–83. Cf. also Aristotle, *Politics* 1304a: "When the naval mob was responsible for the victory at Salamis and thereby for the hegemony of Athens, which was based on its sea-power, they made the democracy stronger." Note that the undeniably polemical character of this and similar statements does not necessarily make them untrue, as implied by Pritchard 2010: 57. Hansen 1988: 27 (Athenian casualties); Hansen 1985: 43 (Lamian War).

the Athenian war machine, fourth-century military operations heavily relied on domestic taxation of the rich—and thanks to the naval focus of military mobilization, warmaking involved redistribution to poorer citizens who crewed and rowed ships. After the loss of its empire, the Athenian treasury drew on a combination of indirect taxes such as tolls and harbor dues, profits from minting, and lease income from public land, including mines. Direct taxes were fewer: a poll tax levied on resident aliens, a property tax for special military expenses collected from affluent Athenians, and contributions known as liturgies that were imposed only on the richest members of the citizenry. Although some of these liturgies were used to stage public religious festivals and theatrical performances, the most important and most onerous liturgy provided for the outfitting of warships. Those selected in any given year were responsible for one vessel, hiring the crew (for which they were compensated with a fixed amount of state funding, which need not have been sufficient), undertaking repairs, and purchasing equipment; they might even have been liable to cover a ship's loss at sea. In elite circles, these obligations, and the competitive spending they encouraged, were commonly regarded as a money pit. The system changed over time: while in the fifth century BCE naval liturgists—who also used to serve as their ships' captains—were drawn from among the 400 wealthiest citizens, in the fourth century BCE 1,200 (or later, just possibly, only 300) estates were asked to contribute. Depending on the period and the scheme in operation, anywhere from 1 percent to 4 percent of Athenian households were thus encumbered. This liturgy, called trierarchy, rotated among them and did not have to be held twice in a row.[30]

The average cost of a naval liturgy equaled approximately eight times the annual minimal subsistence income of an Athenian household of five and a substantial fraction of typical elite incomes. Even the rich were obliged to borrow or mortgage to raise the cash required. In the mid-fourth century BCE, each year each member of a (maximal-sized) liturgical class of 1,200 would have had to spend on average the equivalent of three annual subsistence household incomes to support a fleet of 300 warships, sponsor public festivals, and pay the property tax. Based on what we know about the wealth threshold for inclusion in the liturgical class, the average annual return on a fortune that just cleared that threshold might have been completely absorbed by these obligations,

---

[30] Ober 2015b: 508–512; van Wees 2004: 209–210, 216–217.

especially after taking living expenses into account. One recent study conjectures that the wealthiest 400 households in Athens enjoyed a mean income equivalent to twelve subsistence household incomes. For this group, liturgies would have translated to an average annual tax burden of about a quarter of their total income. Notwithstanding serious shortcomings of the evidence, it is fairly safe to conclude that classical Athens imposed a significant amount of income taxation on its wealthy elite.[31]

Unless we are missing details about an unequal allocation of expenses within the liturgical class—its richest members were merely expected to advance expenses that they then recouped from the others—this system was not consistently progressive, for it extracted fixed amounts regardless of actual incomes beyond a given cutoff point. Even so, it was highly progressive in that other citizens paid no direct taxes at all. Two key points are to be made. One is that this practice was primarily grounded in the huge fiscal demands of (naval) mass mobilization. An electorate that both regularly served in the military and was politically empowered made sure that the richest carried a large share of the financial burden. The other more specifically concerns leveling: liturgies were bound to reduce—or, in extreme cases, perhaps even prevent—wealth accumulation in the Athenian elite.

This matters because in this period Athens experienced rapid economic growth, especially in the nonagrarian sector. Liturgies thus served as a brake on inequality in an environment that was otherwise conducive to increasing disparities. The contemporary comic complaint,

When will we get a break from liturgies and trierarchies wiping us out?

was therefore not just hyperbole. For what it is worth, the notion that fiscal interventions checked inequality is consistent with what we can say about the distribution of wealth in classical Athens at the time. Two independent modern estimates project a fairly equitable distribution of land, with 7.5 percent to 9

---

[31] Burden: see Pyzyk forthcoming, with Ober 2015b: 502. In this scenario, the richest (roughly) 1 percent of Athenians would have received as little as 5 percent to 8 percent of all private income. A revised model that doubles mean incomes for this group would lower the tax burden to an eighth (and double the top 1 percent's income share to about 13 percent) but still implies a higher tax burden for the 800 next most affluent households: Ober 2015b: 502–503; 2016: 10 (doubled elite income). For the nature of Athenian wealth, see Davies 1971; 1981. Income taxation: this disregards the additional effect of occasional emergency property tax levies well beyond the mean assumed in my calculations: see Thucydides 3.19.1 for a charge in 428 BCE that was equivalent to the annual cost of outfitting 300 warships.

percent of Athenians owning 30 percent to 40 percent and perhaps as few as 20 percent to 30 percent owning no land at all. A middling group representing the "hoplite" population—those having enough resources to afford a full panoply for phalanx warfare—would have held 35 percent to 45 percent. The implied Gini coefficient of landownership of 0.38 or 0.39 is low from a comparative historical perspective but congruent with the absence of evidence for very large estates. This does not, however, rule out a more uneven distribution of non-agrarian assets.[32]

A few bold historians have gone farther, variously guesstimating an income Gini coefficient of 0.38 for all of Athens or a wealth Gini of 0.7 for citizens only, with 1 percent and 10 percent top wealth shares of about 30 percent and 60 percent—but none of this rises above controlled conjecture. We are on firmer ground in assessing Athenian real wages for certain occupations, which were high by preindustrial standards: as a multiple of minimum subsistence they were on a par with those in the early modern Netherlands. This observation, together with the lack of evidence for high levels of land concentration or very large fortunes more generally, points to a fairly egalitarian distribution of material resources within the Athenian citizenry. Finally, unless our guesstimates regarding the size of the Athenian economy in the fifth and fourth centuries BCE are very wide of the mark, in both the 430s and 330s BCE public spending amounted to somewhere around 15 percent of GDP.[33]

Moreover, even though the fiscal expansion had in the first instance been propelled by mass warfare, it had come to include a very substantial share for civilian spending: in years without major wars, a little more than half of all public expenditure covered nonmilitary activities such as subsidized participation in the political and juridical system, festivals, welfare provisions, and public construction, all of which benefited substantial elements of the general population. This is remarkable for three reasons: the state share in GDP is high for a

---

[32] Quote: Theophrastus, *Characters* 26.6, quoted from van Wees 2004: 210. Land Ginis: Scheidel 2006: 45–46, summarizing Osborne 1992: 23–24; Foxhall 1992: 157–158; Morris 1994: 362 n. 53; 2000: 141–142. See now also Ober 2015a: 91.

[33] Income and wealth Ginis: Ober 2016: 8 (and cf. 2015a: 91–93); Kron 2011; 2014: 131. Wealth inequality would have been much higher when resident aliens and especially slaves are included, as noted by Ober 2015a: 343 n. 45. Real wages: Scheidel 2010: 441–442, 453, 455–456; Ober 2015a: 96 table 4.7. Foxhall 2002 emphasizes the gap between radical political egalitarianism and more limited resource egalitarianism. Public spending: Ober 2015b: 499 table 16.1, 504.

premodern society; the share of civilian outlays in all expenditure is likewise comparatively high; and after revenue from empire had dried up, progressive taxation of the Athenian elite had replaced tributary predation as a source of public spending. The convergence of military mass mobilization, democracy, progressive taxation, a sizeable state share in GDP, substantial civilian spending, and limited inequality lends fourth-century BCE Athens, in particular, a curiously and precociously "modern" appearance.

What was true of Athens need not have been true in equal measure of the other more than 1,000 *poleis* that made up the mature ancient Greek city-state culture, and there is no obvious way of finding out. Although Athens and Sparta may well have been extreme in terms of their commitment to military mass mobilization, other *poleis* are also credited with fielding military forces that were bound to strain their demographic resources. We find that democratic governance became more common over time and that warmaking intensified: the century from the 430s to the 330s BCE was a period of almost permanent war, involving large field armies and navies, and although mercenaries gradually gained in importance, citizen levies often remained crucial. Archaeology provides what may well be the most broadly based proxy of material inequality available to us. The size of houses—private residences—in this period strongly clusters around the median: by 300 BCE, houses at the seventy-fifth percentile were only about a quarter larger than those at the twenty-fifth percentile. In fourth-century BCE Olynthus, admittedly a planned city, the Gini coefficient of house size was a trifling 0.14.[34]

Much in the historical record therefore supports the conclusion that the sprawling city-state civilization of ancient Greece enjoyed relatively moderate levels of wealth and income inequality that were sustained by a pervasive culture of mass mobilization warfare and mediated by strong citizenship institutions and, increasingly, democratization. By retarding territorial consolidation, the same culture also obstructed the accumulation of property beyond the confines of one's own *polis*. Early on, in the archaic period of the seventh and sixth centuries BCE, political and social barriers to economic integration and thus rising wealth concentration had been high, which set the scene for the classical period as political fragmentation and interstate hostility persisted: in this respect, imperial Athens was the exception that proved the rule. In later centuries,

---

[34] Morris 2004: 722; Kron 2014: 129 table 2.

domination by and incorporation into larger imperial structures undermined Greek egalitarianism and provided novel opportunities for the concentration of wealth.[35]

"THAT FOE STRIPPED ME OF MY ROBE, CLOTHED HIS WIFE IN IT": TRADITIONAL PREMODERN WARS

The overwhelming majority of wars in history were not conflicts of military mass mobilization across society. They were often fought by what Charles Tilly called "specialists in violence" and, reduced to bare essentials, were primarily competitions between ruling elites for the control of people, land, and other resources—"the sport of kings," in Arnold Toynbee's words. In wars in which only one side suffered major destruction, plundering or conquest were likely to increase inequality among the victors and depress it among the ravaged or defeated: the leaders of the winning side could expect to gain (more so than their followers, let alone the general population), whereas those on the losing side were exposed to losses or ruin. The more "archaic" the nature of the conflict, the more strongly this principle would have applied. Despoliation of the vanquished can be traced back as far as the earliest written records, as in this Sumerian lament from the third millennium BCE:

> Alas! That day of mine, on which I was destroyed!
> The foe trampled with his booted feet into my chamber!
> That foe reached out his dirty hands toward me!
> . . . That foe stripped me of my robe, clothed his wife in it,
> That foe cut my string of gems, hung it on his child,
> I was to tread the walks of his abode.[36]

But although many suffered in war, the rich simply had more to lose—and their peers on the winning side stood more to gain. To stay in Mesopotamia for a moment, consider the case of the Neo-Assyrian empire, a couple of millennia

---

[35] Just as in the modern period, there is no compelling evidence that democracy by itself curtailed inequality: see herein, chapter 12, pp. 365–366. Judging from the brief survey of Athenian history already given, military mass mobilization and democratization may have been linked in a similar manner as in the period of the world wars (see herein, pp. 192–194). Lack of consolidation: Foxhall 2002: 215. Note also Aristotle's unhelpfully vague allusion to ancient laws in "many places" that had capped land acquisition (*Politics* 1319a).

[36] Tilly 2003: 34–41; Toynbee 1946: 287. Gat 2006 and Morris 2014 survey the changing nature of warfare across history. Lament quoted by Morris 2014: 86.

after the glory days of Sumerian culture. Assyrian royal inscriptions boast with tiresome frequency about the exploits of rulers as they went about sacking and looting cities and slaughtering and deporting their inhabitants. More often than not references to the plunder are generic, so we cannot, strictly speaking, be sure whose belongings were taken. But whenever the texts are more specific, enemy elites are singled out as the main target. When in the ninth century BCE the Assyrian ruler Shalmaneser III defeated Marduk-mudammiq, king of Namri, he

> plundered his palaces, took [the statues of] the gods, his property, goods, palace women, his horses broken to the yoke without number.

The seizure of palace property is repeatedly singled out in other inscriptions of his, one of which even tells us about "doors of gold" being ripped out and carried away. Deportations ensnared rival rulers alongside their families as well as high-ranked individuals more generally, such as palace personnel and palace women. Other Assyrian kings were said to have distributed war booty to elite beneficiaries. What one state's ruling class lost another one's gained. If one side was consistently more successful in war than others, the victorious conquest elite would have accumulated more and more assets over time while leaving their vanquished peers behind, a process that would have raised the overall Gini coefficient by lengthening the tail at the very apex of the income and wealth distribution. As I argued in the first two chapters, the growth of very large tributary empires thus facilitated a disproportionate concentration of material resources in the top tier of their ruling classes.[37]

The zero-sum character of traditional warfare is well illustrated by the Norman conquest of England in 1066. In terms of landed wealth, the existing English aristocracy had been divided into a handful of extremely wealthy earls and several thousand minor thanes and other landlords. After initially seeking to co-opt this group, when confronted with years of rebellion after his initial victory at Hastings, William the Conqueror switched to a policy of systematic expropriation. The ensuing massive transfers greatly increased the crown's share of all land and placed fully half of all land in the hands of some 200 nobles, half of it held by ten close associates of the new king. Despite their privileged

---

[37] Yamada 2000: 226–236, esp. 227 (quote), 234, 260; Oded 1979: 78–79, and herein, chapter 1, p. 61 (distribution).

position, the latter ended up somewhat less extravagantly rich than the previous earls had been, whereas the other barons were on average much better off than most of the previous thanes had been. This violent redistribution reached deep into the ranks of the English elite: by the time of the Domesday Book survey of 1086, landowners who can unambiguously be identified as English held only 6 percent of the land by surface or 4 percent by value, and although their actual share may well have been greater, there is no doubt that Norman nobles had largely taken over. Many dispossessed thanes left the country to make a living as warriors overseas. Over time, this initial process of concentration was effectively reversed as crown land dwindled and nobles gave much of their lands to subordinate knights, thereby re-creating a much larger but individually less wealthy elite stratum. At this stage, however, feudal relations complicate any observations about the distribution of landed property. Changes in the income distribution are even harder to pin down, but in the most general terms, it appears that the Norman conquest initially resulted in greater concentration of income from land within a substantially smaller ruling class that was subsequently gradually undone.[38]

In traditional wars or conquests of this kind, leveling would have largely focused on the leaders of the losing side, such as the various Near Eastern potentates brought down by the wrath of Ashur or King Harold's thanes. A more recent example is provided by the city of Prato in Tuscany, where the Gini coefficient of wealth—inferred from wealth tax records—fell from 0.624 in 1487 to 0.575 in 1546, at a time when the plague had abated and nearby communities generally recorded growing inequality. In 1512 Prato suffered a bloody sack by Spanish troops that was said to have caused thousands of fatalities and have involved three weeks of relentless pillaging. In such situations, the affluent were primary targets as sources of both bounty and ransom. At the end of chapter 11, I discuss in more detail the case of the German city of Augsburg, which was hit hard by both hostilities and plague during the Thirty Years War and which consequently experienced a quite dramatic compression of wealth disparities. Although plague played a significant role in this process, war-related destruction

---

[38] Nobility: Thomas 2008: 67–71, esp. 68; Morris 2012: 320–321. New distribution: Thomas 2008: 48–49, based on Thomas 2003; Thomas 2008: 69. Changes in the spatial distribution of landownership (scattered English holdings being replaced by more compact Norman estates) would not have affected this process, and the subsequent rise of primogeniture merely helped preserve existing holdings: Thomas 2008: 69–70, 102.

of capital value and extraordinary levies on the rich were paramount in forcing down inequality.[39]

It would be easy but pointless to multiply such accounts from the annals of warfare, for the general principle is clear even if reliable measurement commonly remains out of reach. In traditional warfare, the scale of leveling depended on a variety of factors such as the volume of extraction and destruction, the objectives of victors or conquerors, and, not least, how we define our units of analysis. If invaders and invaded, looters and looted, victors and vanquished are viewed as discrete entities, we would expect leveling to have occurred among the latter. If war resulted in outright conquest and members of the victorious party settled in their newly gained territories, the partial or sweeping substitution of one elite for another need not have had major consequences for overall inequality, whereas the incorporation of existing elites and their possessions into imperial structures would create larger polities with greater scope for inequality overall. Yet crude taxonomies of this kind are bound to oversimplify more complex realities. On either side, military and civilian elites might have experienced different outcomes. Wars that did not have clear winners or losers are particularly problematic. Two examples will suffice. The Peninsular War of 1807 to 1814, fought between France and Spain and its allies on Spanish soil, caused widespread destruction and coincided with increased volatility in Spanish real wages and a temporary surge in overall income inequality. By contrast, the years immediately following this conflict witnessed rising real wages, rising nominal wages in relation to land rent, and lower income inequality in general. Destructive warfare and protracted domestic turbulence in Venezuela in the 1820s and 1830s likewise appears to have led to a sharp drop in the ratio of land rents to wages.[40]

"WE NO LONGER COUNTED UP WHAT WE HAD KILLED BUT WHAT IT WOULD BRING US": CIVIL WAR

This leaves us with a final question: how does civil war affect inequality? Modern scholarship has generally focused on the reverse—whether inequality contributes to the outbreak of internal conflicts. There is no straightforward answer to that second question. Overall (or "vertical") income inequality—between

---

[39] Prato: Guasti 1880; Alfani and Ammannati 2014: 19–20. Augsburg: herein, chapter 11, pp. 335–341.

[40] Alvarez-Nogal and Prados de la Escosura 2013: 6 fig. 3, 9 fig. 3, 21 fig. 8, and herein, chapter 3, p. 99 fig. 3.3 (Spain); Arroyo Abad 2013: 48–49 (Venezuela).

people or households within a given country—is not positively correlated with the likelihood of civil war, although the poor quality of data from many developing countries raises doubts about the reliability of any specific finding. Intergroup inequality, on the other hand, can be shown to promote internal conflict. Some recent work has complicated the picture. A wide-ranging survey of human body height inequality, used as a proxy of resource inequality, claims a positive correlation with civil war in a large global dataset that reaches back to the early nineteenth century. And according to another study, the probability of civil war increases with land inequality unless the latter is extremely high, in which case the former declines as small elites are better able to repress resistance. For now, all we can say is that the considerable complexities of this question are only beginning to be understood.[41]

By contrast, the impact of civil war on inequality has attracted very little attention. A pioneering study of 128 countries from 1960 to 2004 found that civil war increased inequality, particularly during the first five years after a conflict. On average, the income Gini coefficient rose 1.6 percentage points in countries during civil war and 2.1 percentage points during the recovery phase of the following ten years, peaking about five years after the end of the war if peace was maintained. There are several reasons for this trend. Inasmuch as civil war reduces physical and human capital, its value goes up while that of unskilled labor declines. More specifically, in developing countries with extensive agricultural populations, farmers may lose access to markets and suffer income losses through exclusion from commercial exchange, losses that provide an incentive to downshift to subsistence practices. At the same time, war profiteers reap great profits by exploiting diminished security and the weakening or absence of state power. Profiteering tends to benefit a small minority, allowing it to accumulate resources at a time when the state's capacity to collect taxes has abated. This retrenchment, in conjunction with increased military expenditure, also curtails social spending, which in turn harms the poor. Redistributive measures, schooling, and health care suffer, with negative effects that are the stronger the longer the conflict lasts.[42]

---

[41] Overall inequality: Fearon and Laitin 2003; Collier and Hoeffler 2004. Intergroup inequality: Ostby 2008, Cederman, Weidmann, and Skrede 2011. Height inequality: Baten and Mumme 2013. Land inequality: Thomson 2015.

[42] Bircan, Brück, and Vothknecht 2010, esp. 4–7, 14, 27. The section title quotes a Hutu killer reminiscing about the genocide near the end of the Rwandan civil war of 1990–1994: Hatzfeld 2005: 82. Perpetrators' narratives reference some of the observations made in the study: "we can't say we missed the fields. . . . Many suddenly grew rich. . . . We were not taxed by the commissioners" (63, 82–83).

These problems persist beyond the war proper, accounting for the even higher Gini coefficients observed in the immediate aftermath of civil wars. In that period, winners may reap disproportionate rewards from their victory as "personal and patrimonial links determine the distribution of assets and access to economic gains." Civil war shares this feature with traditional premodern wars in which the leadership on the winning side stands to gain and inequality grows. The same could be observed in the nineteenth century, when civil war confiscations of land in Spain and Portugal in the 1830s boosted large estates and exacerbated inequality.[43]

Almost all of the relevant observations come from traditional societies or developing countries. Full-blown civil wars have been exceedingly rare in more developed economies. Moreover, in some cases in which civil war was associated with major leveling, as in Russia after 1917 or in China from the 1930s and 1940s, revolutionary reforms rather than civil war as such were the main driver of this process. For the purposes of this study, the American Civil War has been treated as the equivalent of interstate war, with the results described earlier in this chapter. This leaves us with only a single major case—that of the Spanish Civil War from 1936 to 1939. Unlike in Russia or China, the victorious party did not pursue a redistributive agenda, and the outcome of the war was not revolutionary in any meaningful sense of the term. Collectivization in areas under anarchist control during the conflict were short-lived. In the years after 1939, the Francoist regime implemented a policy of economic autarky which caused economic stagnation. A succession of civil war shocks and subsequent economic mismanagement accounted for the decline of top income shares. For this period only the uppermost income shares (for the richest 0.01 percent) have been computed, a category that experienced a drop by 60 percent between 1935 and 1951. This trend conflicts with the development of the Gini coefficient of overall income, which was fairly stable during the civil war and the World War II period but which shows wild fluctuations between 1947 and 1958 (Fig. 6.2).[44]

To complicate matters further, the Gini coefficient of wage income dropped considerably, by about a third, between 1935 and 1945. To the best of my knowledge, there is currently no compelling explanation for these outcomes. Leandro Prados de la Escosura has offered hypotheses regarding the competing

---

[43] Quote: Bircan, Bruck, and Vothknecht 2010: 7. 1830s: Powelson 1988: 109.
[44] On civil war and development, see, e.g., Holtermann 2012. Spain: Alvaredo and Saez 2010, esp. 493–494; WWID. Fig. 6.2 reproduced from Prados de la Escosura 2008: 302 fig. 6.

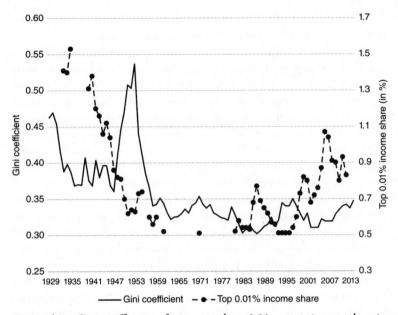

Figure 6.2 Gini coefficients of income and top 0.01 percent income share in Spain, 1929–2014

effects of declining returns to capital (which depressed top income shares), wage compression from reruralization under Franco (with reduced overall wage inequality), and rising returns to property, especially land, under autarky (which offset these effects to produce the overall Gini coefficient of income inequality). All this took place in the context of zero net real per capita GDP growth from 1930 to 1952, with the proportion of the population living in poverty more than doubling during roughly the same period. Despite superficial similarities in terms of the fall of top income shares and the compression of wages, inequality developed rather differently in Spain than in other European countries of the time. Unlike among the parties to World War II and some of the bystanders, there was no progressive taxation and overall income inequality did not diminish. I agree with Prados de la Escosura that "the distinction between Spain, where the Civil War had a divisive effect in society, and most western countries, where the World Wars tended to increase social cohesion, may be relevant to understanding the post-war era." Even so, in both cases, the underlying driving forces that shaped the distribution of income and wealth were the same: violent shocks that were mediated by government policies.[45]

I conclude my survey by going once again far back into the past to consider a hybrid case, the civil wars that brought down the Roman Republic from the 80s to the 30s BCE. They are hybrid in that they were internal conflicts within Roman society, triggered by runaway elite competition, but unfolded in the context of the aforementioned culture of military mass mobilization and thus displayed key features of interstate mass mobilization warfare. Some of Rome's highest military participation rates on record were achieved in this period of domestic upheaval. This specific combination of elite infighting and popular mobilization offered novel opportunities for the redistribution of income and wealth.

The most violent of these conflicts—fought in the 80s and in the 40s and 30s BCE—devastated the Roman ruling class. Political opponents were proscribed—publicly declared to be fair game for anyone wishing to kill them for a reward—and their estates confiscated by the victorious faction. In the civil war of 83 to 81 BCE, 105 senators were said to have been killed, at a time when senate membership stood at around 300, and in 43 BCE, 300 senators (out of 600) and 2,000 knights, the next highest tier of the Roman elite, supposedly lost their lives in this manner, although we can only name about 120 of them. These two episodes affected inequality in different ways. The first round of expropriations, undertaken by proponents of oligarchic reaction, allowed well-placed supporters to profit by snapping up seized assets at auction. This may very well have increased wealth concentration, especially in the wake of massive attrition prior to the civil war: in the decade from 90 to 80 BCE, no fewer than 291 senators are said to have died of violent causes. A shortage of heirs is likely to have led to consolidation rather than dispersal of elite property. Land confiscated from local communities was given to veterans but often eventually ended up on the market, resulting in transactions that may also have fostered concentration. By contrast, the expropriations of 43 and 42 BCE were motivated by exceptional fiscal demand in preparation for military campaigning against domestic opponents outside Italy rather than by a desire to settle scores. In this case the proceeds were less likely to benefit cronies and were primarily used to meet exorbitant promises of compensation to a huge citizen army. Close associates of that faction's leader were rewarded only after the conclusion of the

---

[45] Prados de la Escosura 2008: 294 fig. 2 (wage Gini); 288 table 1 (GDP 1930–1952), 309 fig. 9 (poverty 1935–1950); 301 (quote).

conflict in 30 BCE via disbursements that enriched "new men" at the expense of the established nobility.[46]

Levels of troop compensation in this final round of civil wars probably had significant redistributive consequences. Prior to the onset of civil wars, Roman soldiers had been rather modestly compensated. Incipient warlordism pushed up bonuses in military campaigns against foreign enemies: they rose from very low levels to the equivalent of seven times annual base pay in 69 BCE and to thirteen times in 61 BCE. Civil war in the 40s BCE triggered a further and more dramatic surge to twenty-two times the newly increased base stipend (or forty-two times the previous one) in 46 BCE. This outlay was soon exceeded by the promise of the same reward to a much larger number of servicemen four years later. All in all, we can estimate that an amount of money equivalent to at least ten times regular annual state income, or perhaps half a year's worth of the GDP of the Roman empire at the time, was transferred to soldiers between 69 and 29 BCE—and almost all of that between 46 and 29 BCE—to buy and reward loyalty in civil wars. The total number of recipients may have reached 400,000 men, who together with their families would have accounted for up to a third of the entire Roman citizenry. In the absence of evidence for price inflation, this was likely to boost non-elite incomes in real terms. The distributional effect within Roman society, in the Italian heartland, is more opaque. Much of this money was obtained by extorting resources from overseas provinces. But there were exceptions: in 43 BCE, a levy of one year's worth of income from real estate and a 2 percent wealth tax were imposed on the rich, alongside the massive confiscations that have already been mentioned. Several later levies also specifically targeted the wealthy. For the only time in Roman history, fiscal extraction became effectively progressive and the revenue thus generated was used in a redistributive manner.[47]

This, however, was to remain a one-off anomaly. Reliance on provincial revenue again became the norm once peace was restored and stable autocracy introduced after 30 BCE. It was only for a few years, in the late 40s BCE, that the disposable income distribution would have temporarily shifted in favor of the general citizen population. In the longer run, the following centuries of political and economic stability were undoubtedly conducive to high levels of wealth concentration, as we saw in chapter 2.

---

[46] Shatzman 1975: 37–44.
[47] Scheidel 2007: 329–333.

"WHATEVER THE COST MAY BE": WAR AND INEQUALITY

This part of the book has taken us through thousands of years of warfare. Military conflict has long been a pervasive feature of human history, but only certain kinds of war attenuated another equally pervasive phenomenon—the unequal distribution of income and wealth. For winners and losers alike, modern mass mobilization warfare proved to be a potent means of leveling. Whenever the war effort permeated all of society, capital assets lost value, and the rich were made to pay a fair share, war did not merely "kill people and break things" but also narrowed the gap between rich and poor. In World War II, this effect was at work both during the war itself as well as in its aftermath, sustained by the persistence of war-driven policies. The citizens of developed countries owed a generation or more of declining inequality to the unprecedented violence of this global conflict. A similar compression of material disparities had occurred in or after World War I. Earlier instances of this particular style of warfare are rare and are not normally associated with leveling. In the American Civil War, it was not mobilization as such but defeat and occupation that destroyed fortunes in the South. Evidence for ancient precursors of mass warfare yields ambiguous or negative findings, as in China and the Roman Republic. In the warrior state of ancient Sparta, resource imbalances gradually grew out of arguably more equalized earlier conditions. Classical Athens may be the best premodern example of the leveling influence of widespread popular military participation. Just as in part of the twentieth century, Athenian democracy appears to have been reinforced by the shared experience of war mobilization and to have in turn favored policies that constrained the rise of inequality. Considering the dramatic differences in overall development and the limitations of the ancient evidence, we should be wary of putting too much weight on this analogy. Even so, the experience of ancient Athens suggests that with the right combination of institutional arrangements in place, a culture of military mass mobilization could serve as a leveling mechanism even in a thoroughly premodern environment.[48]

Wars that were more limited in scope were ubiquitous throughout history but failed to deliver consistent outcomes. Traditional wars of plunder and conquest commonly benefited victorious elites, boosting inequality. This would have been especially true whenever defeated polities were incorporated into larger ones, a process that would add additional layers of wealth and power at

---

[48] Quote in the text: I owe this apt characterization of military activity to former Arkansas Governor Mike Huckabee, offered in the first Republican presidential primary debate on August 6, 2015.

the top of the hierarchy. Civil war rarely functioned as a source of leveling—and if so only partially (as, in different ways, in the 1860s United States and in 1930s and 1940s Spain) or very briefly (as, perhaps, in ancient Rome). The only civil wars that truly transformed the distribution of income and wealth were those that swept to power radical regimes that were bent on comprehensive expropriation and redistribution and that did not shy away from whatever amount of bloodshed was required to make this happen. It is to this process, the Second Horseman of violent leveling, that we now turn.

Part III

REVOLUTION

Chapter 7

COMMUNISM

"FOR THE POWER OF THE PROLETARIAT": REVOLUTIONARY LEVELING IN THE TWENTIETH CENTURY

If conflict between states sometimes reduces inequality, then what are the consequences of conflict within states? We have already seen that in recent history, civil wars have had no unambiguous effect and, if anything, tend to exacerbate existing disparities. Is this also true of internal conflicts that do not merely pit one faction against another but that strive for a more comprehensive restructuring of society? Such ambitious endeavors have been rare. The overwhelming majority of violent popular uprisings in history sought redress for specific grievances and were, equally overwhelmingly, unsuccessful. More ambitious movements that succeeded both in seizing power and in flattening the income and wealth distribution appeared only in the relatively recent past. Much as in the case of war, intensity of effort was a critical variable. Whereas most wars did not produce equalizing outcomes, military mass mobilization was capable of upsetting the established order. Among revolts, only similarly pervasive mobilization of resources in every single town and village resulted in radical leveling. Returning to our initial metaphor, mass mobilization warfare and transformative revolution acted as equally powerful apocalyptic horsemen as they swept away entrenched interests and reshaped access to material resources. It was the sheer amount of violence that mattered most: just as the two world wars were the bloodiest wars in human history, so the most equalizing revolutions were among the bloodiest of all internal upheavals on record. My comparative survey of revolts and revolutions confirms the central importance of large-scale violence as a means of leveling.

I adopt the same approach as before, moving back in time. The most relevant evidence once again comes from the twentieth century, when the major communist revolutions caused dramatic deconcentration of income and wealth, covered in this chapter. In the next chapter, I turn to possible antecedents, most notably the French Revolution, and consider the effects of premodern attempts to change internal conditions by force, such as peasant uprisings. Much as in the case of war, we encounter a divide between modern or industrial and premodern or preindustrial: for the most part, only recent revolutions have proved sufficiently powerful to affect the distribution of wealth and income of large populations.

"WAR TO THE DEATH AGAINST THE RICH": THE RUSSIAN REVOLUTION AND THE SOVIET REGIME

As we have seen in chapter 5, the catastrophe of World War I, through its unprecedented mobilization of people and resources for mass slaughter, compressed income and wealth inequality in the main belligerent nations. The scale and timing of this effect varied considerably between countries. In Germany, top income shares grew during the war and collapsed after defeat; in France, they declined only fairly gently in the aftermath of the war; in the UK, they dropped by a fair amount during and right after the war before temporarily recovering in the mid-1920s; and in the United States, wartime decline was also soon followed by a strong resurgence. It is particularly unfortunate that comparable data from some of the most heavily affected countries—Austro-Hungary, Italy, and Belgium—have yet to be published. Unlike for World War II, which almost invariably produced both stronger and clearer leveling outcomes, the record for the "Great War" is thus somewhat mixed and even partly unknown.[1]

It was in Russia that World War I was followed by the most dramatic reduction in inequality. Yet in contrast to the other cases, leveling was brought about not by wartime interventions and dislocations or postwar financial collapse but rather by radical revolutionary upheavals born of the wreckage of the war. The empire of Czar Nicholas II had been one of the biggest players in this conflict: it had mobilized some 12 million soldiers, close to 2 million of whom had perished. Another 5 million more had been wounded, and 2.5 million had been captured or were reported missing. Moreover, 1 million civilians are thought to have died as well. For all we can tell, no major compression need have occurred

---

[1] For Germany, France, the UK, and the United States, see herein, chapter 5, p. 133. Most of the indices for Italy in Brandolini and Vecchi 2011: 39 fig. 8 show moderately declining inequality between 1911 and 1921, but the resolution is insufficient to disentangle developments during the war and its immediate aftermath, which might have witnessed a recovery.

in the war years from 1914 to 1917: taxation was highly regressive, heavily relying on indirect taxes; taxes on income and war profits did not get off the ground until the very end; domestic bond programs were only moderately successful; and much of the state's deficit was covered by issuing currency. Accelerating inflation, especially under the provisional government of 1917, did not harm only the rich.[2]

Whatever the direct consequences of the war itself, they were bound to pale next to what happened once the Bolsheviks struck in November 1917 and hostilities against the Central Powers ceased the following month. A massive economic downturn that year had already triggered widespread peasant uprisings that had resulted in the takeover of estates, and striking workers had established control over many factories. These revolts culminated in the armed takeover of the capital by the Bolsheviks on November 6 and 7, 1917. On November 8, the very next day after the storming of the Winter Palace in St. Petersburg, the newly created Council of the People's Commissars passed a "Land Decree" written by Lenin himself. Forcible redistribution was very much at the top of the agenda.

This decree was sweeping in the extreme. Its immediate political goal was to secure the support of the peasantry by legalizing, after the fact, peasants' seizure and distribution of landholdings owned by nobles and the state, a process that had been unfolding since the summer of that year. Yet in formal terms, it aimed much higher, seeking nothing less than the destruction of private ownership of land:

> The landowners' right of property in land is herewith abolished without compensation. . . . The right of private property in land is to be abolished for all time. The land shall not be bought, sold, leased or otherwise alienated. . . . The right to use the land shall be given to all citizens, regardless of sex, of the Russian state, who desire to work it by their own hands. . . . Hired labor is not permissible. . . . The lands shall be distributed among those who use them on the principle of equalization, that is, on the basis . . . of the normal units of labor or food.[3]

For the time being, these measures were effectively limited to elite holdings—those of large landowners, the imperial family, and the Church. The land of regular peasants (and Cossacks) was not targeted for confiscation. Expropriation

---

[2] Gatrell 2005: 132–153.
[3] Leonard 2011: 63. Quote: Tuma 1965: 92–93.

and distribution were to be handled by local committees. Subsequent decrees nationalized all banks, placed factories under the control of workers' councils (soviets), and confiscated private bank accounts. In economic terms, the land-owning class—about half a million people, including families—was wiped out, as were the top tiers of the bourgeoisie, another 125,000 persons or so. Many of the "former people," as the members of the elite came to be known, were killed; even more emigrated. Dramatic deurbanization also contributed to leveling, for the combined population of Moscow and St. Petersburg—former centers of wealth and income concentration—fell by more than half between 1917 and 1920. As the communist party mouthpiece *Pravda* gloated in an editorial on January 1, 1919,

> Where are the wealthy, the fashionable ladies, the expensive restaurants and private mansions, the beautiful entrances, the lying newspapers, all the corrupted "golden life"? All swept away.

Lenin's "war to the death against the rich" had been won.[4]

In a society in which the majority of the population still worked the land, the Bolsheviks' initial land decree alone was a major propellant of leveling, further reinforced by the other confiscatory measures. By 1919, almost 97 percent of cultivable land had come to be held by peasants. But from the beginning the new regime considered these transfers insufficient, worried that equal distribution would merely "create petite bourgeois farmers and would neither guarantee equality nor prevent differentiation." Indeed, only the abolition of private holding as well as ownership of land could hope to accomplish complete and permanent leveling. The next major land decree in February 1918 already pushed for collectivization:

> In determining the mode and order of granting use of lands, preference is to be given to working agricultural cooperatives against individuals.[5]

Expression of this ambition was merely a faint harbinger of the horrors to come. For the time being, the communists were focused on surviving a civil war

---

[4] Tuma 1965: 92–93 (first decree); Davies 1998: 21 (further decrees); Figes 1997: 523 ("former people"). Deurbanization: Davies 1998: 22; for Petersburg, see Figes 1997: 603; see 603–612 on hunger and depopulation in urban centers for want of food. Figes 1997: 522 (Pravda); Lenin, "How to organize competition," December 1917, quoted in Figes 1997: 524.

[5] Powelson 1988: 119 (land); Tuma 1965: 91, 94 (quotes).

and asserting control over the entire country. The years from 1918 to 1921 were a period of "war communism" in which the state relied to an unusual degree on open coercion. Private manufacture was banned, production was organized by state allocation, private trade was prohibited, and peasant food surpluses were seized; money became marginalized. Food was requisitioned by armed brigades that assaulted villages and distributed to the urban population and the army through a graduated rationing system. All large firms and many smaller ones were nationalized. In the countryside, as the state was unable to compensate producers for their food, outright confiscation became the method of choice, once again under the banner of leveling: "together with the poor peasantry . . . for the power of the proletariat," poorer peasants were expected to coerce their better-off neighbors into handing over their surplus food. Initially, "Committees of Rural Poor" were set up to control the distribution of grain, farm equipment, and household supplies, and they received free grain in return for their efforts. The central leadership thought that ample incentive existed to seize crops from those who produced more. Even so, committee members often had to be brought in from the outside, for villagers proved reluctant to turn on members of their own communities, contrary to the communists' expectation that they would eagerly embrace class warfare. Niall Ferguson quotes from a letter Lenin wrote to a provincial commissar in August 1918:

> Comrade! . . . Hang (and I mean hang so that the *people can see*) *not less than 100* known kulaks, rich men, bloodsuckers . . . . Do this so that for hundreds of miles around the people can see, tremble, know and cry: they are killing and will go on killing the bloodsucking kulaks . . . . Yours, Lenin. P.S. Find tougher people.

The experiment was soon abandoned. Although Lenin called for "ruthless war on the kulaks! Death to all of them!" in reality most of these "kulaks" (literally "fists," as in "tight-fisted") or *relatively* well-off farmers were not much more affluent than their fellow villagers.[6]

These heavy-handed interventions ensured leveling, but their economic consequences were disastrous: peasants curbed production and destroyed

---

[6] Leonard 2011: 64; Davies 1998: 18–19 (war communism); Tuma 1965: 95 (quote); Powelson 1988: 120 (committees); Figes 1997: 620 (outsiders); Ferguson 1999: 394 (first Lenin quote); Figes 1997: 618 (second Lenin quote).

livestock and tools to avoid requisition, and both the amount of land under cultivation and yields dropped considerably from prerevolutionary levels. The regime promoted voluntary collectivization as a response to these production shortages, but that arrangement was successfully resisted by farmers: by 1921, less than 1 percent of the Russian population worked on collective farms. Thorough leveling had been achieved at a high price: between 1912 and 1922, the proportion of rural peasant households having no horses or only one horse rose from 64 percent to 86 percent, whereas that of households having three or more fell from 14 percent to 3 percent. Villagers were now poorer overall—but more equally so. Rampant inflation contributed: by 1921 prices were almost 17,000 times as high as they had been back in 1914. Barter increasingly replaced money, and the black market boomed.[7]

The dramatic downturn in output, together with the deaths of many millions in the civil war, prompted a temporary reversal in 1921 in favor of the New Economic Policy. Markets were again permitted to operate, and peasants were able to pay taxes in kind and sell or consume their surplus. Tenancy and hired labor were once more allowed to be practiced. Liberalization was rewarded with economic recovery, as the area under cultivation grew by half between 1922 and 1927. At the same time, these policies facilitated renewed differentiation among producers by favoring those who produced surplus food for commercial exchange. This led to a very modest expansion of the kulak population, whose share in the peasantry rose from 5 percent to 7 percent. Yet they were far from rich, averaging two horses and two cows and some tradable food. Overall, the earlier loss of kulak assets and the distribution of land to landless laborers had flattened the income distribution, resulting in *oserednyachenie*, or "middle-peasantization." Industrial entrepreneurs were far fewer in number and far less wealthy than they had been before the Revolution. Private capital played virtually no role in industry: in 1926 and 1927 only 4 percent of industrial investment came from the private sector, whereas the opposite was true of the agrarian sector.[8]

Hints of renewed differentiation among peasants, and especially their pervasive resistance to collectivization, drew Stalin's ire. Beginning in 1928, the state once again resorted to coercion to obtain the grain that was needed to support industrialization—effectively a transfer of resources from the privatized

---

[7] Tuma 1965: 96 (consequences); Powelson 1988: 120 (collectives); Leonard 2011: 67 (households); Davies 1998: 19 (inflation).

[8] NEP: Leonard 2011: 65; Tuma 1965: 96. Recovery: Leonard 2011: 66; Tuma 1965: 97. Differentiation: Tuma 1965: 97; Leonard 2011: 67. Capital: Davies 1998: 25–26.

countryside to the socialized industrial sector. By 1929, despite drives that promoted collectives and tangible support in the form of better credit, only 3.5 percent of grain land was farmed in collectives, as opposed to 1.5 percent in state farms and 95 percent on individual holdings. Stalin, fixated on kulak obstruction and ignoring the poor performance of the collectives, characteristically opted for force to alter this situation.[9]

On January 30, 1930, the resolution "On measures for the elimination of kulak households in districts of comprehensive collectivization" provided for the elimination of kulaks as a class by means of execution, deportation, or imprisonment in local labor colonies. Better-off peasants were taxed multiple times and then expelled from their land; poorer ones were more readily induced to join collectives. The party stepped up its antikulak rhetoric and encouraged peasants to grab their land. So as to find enough targets, the definition of kulak expanded to cover those who hired labor, who owned productive installations (such as a mill), or who traded. Arrests and forcible seizures were commonplace. However, considering that previously affluent peasants had already been impoverished by discriminatory taxation, most of those to be targeted were merely middle-income peasants who ended up being expropriated based on the evidence of outdated tax records and the need to meet the government's dekulakization quotas. Leveling consequently extended much farther down the social spectrum than communist rhetoric would have us believe.[10]

Coercion carried the day: by 1937, fully 93 percent of Soviet agriculture had been forcibly collectivized, individual farms had been crushed, and the private sector had been reduced to small garden plots. This transformation had come at enormous cost: more than half of the value of livestock was lost, as was a seventh of the total capital stock. The cost in human lives was even more staggering. Violence spread explosively. After 60,000 "first-category" kulaks had been arrested in a matter of days in February 1930, the tally rose to 700,000 by the end of that year and to 1.8 million by the end of the following year. An estimated 300,000 deportees died during the process owing to the horrific conditions they experienced during transport and at their destination. Maybe 6 million peasants starved to death. Kulak household heads were deported en masse, although those considered particularly dangerous were summarily executed instead.[11]

---

[9] Davies 1998: 34 (grain); Tuma 1965: 99 (land); Powelson 1988: 123 (Stalin). Allen 2003: 87 notes the potential for rising rural inequality in the 1920s in the absence of communal organization.

[10] Tuma 1965: 99; Powelson 1988: 123; Werth 1999: 147–148.

[11] Leonard 2011: 69 (collectivization); Werth 1999: 146, 150–151, 155; Davies 1998: 51 (violence).

Violent equalization through collectivization and dekulakization in the countryside went hand in hand with the persecution of "bourgeois specialists," "aristocrats," entrepreneurs, shopkeepers, and craftsmen in the cities. This trend continued with the "Great Terror" of 1937 and 1938 when Stalin's NKVD arrested more than 1.5 million citizens, close to half of whom were liquidated. The educated elite was specifically targeted, and people who had undergone higher education were overrepresented among the victims. No fewer than 7 million people entered the gulag complex between 1934 and 1941. This system helped sustain leveling by obviating the state's need to pay high wages to workers in marginal locations that featured terrible work conditions. Although these savings were in part offset by the cost of coercion and low productivity, they should not be underestimated: in later years, elevated wages offered to workers in undesirable locales significantly contributed to overall Soviet income inequality. Collectivization created a quarter of a million collective farms (*kolkhozy*) that encompassed most of the peasant population. Yet even as peasants suffered greatly, so did urban workers: real wages outside farming may have dropped by almost half between 1928 and 1940, and personal consumption fell in both city and countryside.[12]

The human suffering caused by these policies is too well known to require detailed recounting. What matters most in the context of this survey is that their overall result was rapid leveling on what in global historical terms may well have been truly unprecedented in scale, considering that not only the elite but also much larger middling groups experienced expropriation and redistribution. Yet as soon as economic performance improved, even under continuing severe repression from about 1933 onward, income inequality immediately began to creep back up. As per capita output and consumption strongly grew in the mid-1930s, pay differentials for workers widened as well: the policies of "Stakhanovism" called for and rewarded greater productivity, and the living standards of elite and mass living standards began to diverge more. Even the blood of millions was not enough to drown differentiation forever.[13]

Owing to the uneven quality of Russian, and especially Soviet-era, data, it is difficult to measure the evolution of income inequality with precision. Income concentration near the end of the Czarist period was considerable but

---

[12] Werth 1999: 169, 190, 206–207, 191–192, 207; Davies 1998: 46, 48–50. Plant food consumption by peasants held steady while animal food consumption fell: Allen 2003: 81 table 4.7.
[13] Davies 1998: 54.

not exceptionally high by the standards of the time. Around 1904 or 1905, Russia's "1 percent" received about 13.5 percent to 15 percent of all income, compared to 18 percent or 19 percent in France and Germany at the time or in the United States a decade later. Abundance of land helped prop up the value of rural labor. The market income Gini for this period has been put at 0.362. We cannot tell how far this value fell between 1917 and 1941. A low P90/P10 ratio of 3.5 for industrial sector wages in 1928 has been reported from Soviet sources. In general, Soviet-era Gini coefficients were much lower than in the Czarist period. This is clear from an estimate of a market Gini of 0.229 for nonfarm households in the Soviet Union in 1967, which meshes well with corresponding values of 0.27 to 0.28 for the entire country between 1968 and 1991. P90/P10 ratios also point to a fair degree of stability from the 1950s to the 1980s. The P90/P10 ratio in the 1980s was roughly 3, compared to 5.5 in the United States in 1984.[14]

Driven entirely by political intervention, further leveling occurred in the decades after World War II. Farm incomes, which had been extremely low, were allowed to rise more quickly than urban wages were, and the latter were leveled up by raising lower wages, narrowing wage differentials, and increasing pensions and other benefits. Policy inspired by communist ideology particularly favored manual workers: the wage premium for all nonmanual workers fell from 98 percent in 1945 to 6 percent in 1985, and technical-engineering personnel experienced a similar drop. White-collar wages declined to well below the mean for manual workers. Even at times of substantial economic growth, despotism was capable of greatly flattening and reshaping the income distribution.[15]

The end of the Soviet system ushered in a rapid and dramatic reversal. In 1988, more than 96 percent of the workforce was employed by the state. Wages accounted for almost three-quarters of all income but self-employment for less than a tenth of that amount—and there was no income from property. As Branko Milanovic puts it, observed income distributions "were logical extensions of the ideological premises of Communism," with their emphasis

---

[14] Income share and Gini: Nafziger and Lindert 2013: 38, 26, 39; cf. Gregory 1982. Nafziger and Lindert 2013: 34 (ratio). Ginis: Nafziger and Lindert 2013: 34; SWIID. Ratios: Nafziger and Lindert 2013: 34. Flakierski 1992: 173 documents variation from 2.83 to 3.69 between 1964 and 1981. For a slight increase in this ratio in the 1980s, see Flakierski 1992: 183. United States: http://stats.oecd.org/index.aspx?queryid=46189.
[15] Davies 1998: 70; Flakierski 1992: 178. Of course, party elites' access to luxury imports raised effective consumption inequality.

on state-disbursed incomes, collective consumption, wage compression, and minimization of wealth accumulation. All this suddenly gave way once those premises were no longer forcibly upheld. In the Russian Federation, where market income Ginis had hovered around 0.26 to 0.27 for much of the 1980s, inequality exploded after the fall of the Soviet Union. Market income Ginis almost doubled, from 0.28 in 1990 to 0.51 five years later, and have ranged from 0.44 to 0.52 ever since. In Ukraine, where Ginis similar to Russia's were observed in the 1980s, they leaped from 0.25 in 1992 to 0.45 the very next year, although they have since gradually declined to closer to 0.30. Between 1988/1989 and 1993/1995, the average Gini increase for all former socialist countries was 9 points. Top incomes rose alongside overall inequality: with very few exceptions, formerly socialist economies experienced substantial shifts into the top 20 percent at the expense of other income brackets. The Russian top quintile's share rose from 34 percent to 54 percent of national income in this period. To put this in perspective, in the United States, at a time of conspicuously growing income inequality, the top quintile share grew from 44 percent to 51 percent between 1980 and 2013, an increase a third as large over a period five or six times as long. Private wealth also returned with a vengeance. In Russia, the richest 10 percent currently control 85 percent of national wealth. By 2014, the country's 111 billionaires had come to hold a fifth of its total wealth.[16]

Following the dissolution of the Communist Party of the Soviet Union and then of the Soviet Union itself in late 1991, exploding poverty drove the surge in income inequality: within three years, the proportion of people living in poverty had tripled to more than a third of Russia's population. By the time of the financial crisis of 1998, their share had grown to almost 60 percent. Yet over the longer term, rising inequality has been boosted by the decompression of wage incomes, much of it resulting from growing regional variation. Strongly disproportionate income growth in Moscow and in oil- and gas-rich parts of the country point to the successful capture of rents by those in the highest income-brackets. Wealth concentration at the very top had been made possible by the transfer of state assets to private owners.[17]

The dynamics of leveling and reconcentration of income and wealth in Russia were very much a function of organized violence. Inequality, which was

---

[16] Milanovic 1997: 12–13, 21–22, 40–41, 43–45; Credit Suisse 2014: 53.
[17] Treisman 2012.

fairly substantial at the end of the prerevolutionary period, fell dramatically in the two decades following the Bolshevik takeover of 1917. This compression was driven by state coercion and the mobilization of the poor to harass the often only moderately less poor on an enormous scale, a process that was directly responsible for the death or deportation of many millions of people. Causation is as clear as it can be: no violence, no leveling. As long as the system that was created in this transformation was kept in place by party cadres and the KGB, inequality remained low. As soon as political constraints were removed and replaced by a mixture of price-setting markets and crony capitalism, income and wealth disparities surged, most strikingly in the Russian and Ukrainian heartland of the former Soviet Union.

"THE MOST HIDEOUS CLASS WAR": MAO'S CHINA

With a time lag of about a generation, this story repeated itself on an even grander scale in China under communist rule. The biggest turnover occurred in the countryside, where most of the population lived. Forcible equalization was cast in terms of class struggle, a somewhat problematic notion in a rural society that was not always as unequal as party doctrine required. Communist claims that the richest 10 percent controlled 70 percent to 80 percent of all land were exaggerated. The most comprehensive data set, based on samples comprising 1.75 million households in sixteen provinces from the 1920s and 1930s, suggests that the top decile owned approximately half of all farmland. In some areas, the most affluent 10 percent or 15 percent owned not more than between a third and half of the land, a far cry from intense concentration. Indeed, in the northern village of Zhangzhuangcun, made famous by William Hinton's classic study of land reform in the late 1940s, middling and poor peasants had already owned 70 percent of the land prior to the communist takeover.[18]

Yet just as in the Soviet Union, where middling farmers had been branded and exterminated as kulaks, the Chinese communist leadership was loath to let inconvenient facts get in the way of its mission. Radical leveling was already part of party policies in the early 1930s in the communist-held "Jiangxi base

---

[18] Moise 1983: 27 (claims); Brandt and Sands 1992: 182 (half); this was not extreme by standards of the period (184). Walder 2015: 49–50 cites an estimate that 2.5 percent of the population owned almost 40 percent of all land in the late 1930s. Moise 1983: 28; Hinton 1966: 209.

area": landlords were expropriated and often condemned to forced labor, and rich peasants were allowed to retain only some inferior land. Debates within the party pitted a radical position—equalization, an objective favored by Mao at the time—against a more radical option—the expropriation of the rich and their subsequent consignment to an inferior status. The "Long March" of 1934 and 1935 took the communists to Shaanxi province, a poorer area where tenancy was much less common: even so, notwithstanding the scarcity of tangible inequality, redistributions were swiftly carried out.[19]

Whereas the "United Front" policy against the Japanese invaders had called for moderation, the party openly embraced class struggle from 1945 onward. Collaborators in occupied areas served as the initial targets, and their properties were seized. The following year, 1946, witnessed a shift to a more general antilandlord campaign. Rent and interest reductions were retroactively applied to the Japanese period, to be paid as dues that could exceed the total wealth of those affected and thereby result in expropriation. Mao's directive in Manchuria was simply to confiscate the land of traitors, tyrants, bandits, and landlords and hand it over to poor peasants.[20]

Before long, programmatic goals founded upon preconceived notions of inequality clashed with conditions on the ground. Because the rural rich had already sold much of their land to middling peasants, this led to a shortage of suitable class enemies and also widened the gap between middling farmers and the poor. This, in turn, created pressure among cadres to completely expropriate the "rich" and to target middling farmers as well despite policy injunctions against such an expansion. Violence was still kept at bay, as most "landlords" continued to live in their villages. The next step up was taken in October 1947 with the "Outline Land Law" that abolished all landownership of "landlords" and institutions and voided all existing rural debt. All land—no longer merely confiscated properties—in each village was to be evenly divided among the population, with each person (including "landlords") receiving the same share in real terms, which then became their private property. "Landlords'" animals, houses, and implements were to be seized and redistributed as well.[21]

Although the wholesale reallocation of property was unfeasible in practice and equalization was instead pursued by making adjustments to existing landholding patterns, beatings and killings became more frequent as a means

[19] Moise 1983: 33–34, 37–38.
[20] Moise 1983: 44–45; Dikötter 2013: 65.
[21] Moise 1983: 48, 51, 55–56.

of enforcing these measures. After the communists' victory in the civil war, the land reform program of 1950 focused on "landlords," a class defined by economic criteria: their land and cognate assets were to be seized and redistributed, and fines levied on top of these expropriations ate into their commercial assets, which were formally exempt from confiscation. "Landlords" were forbidden from selling their properties before they could be seized. Their land was to be given to landless laborers and poor peasants. Persecution was carefully calibrated: those classified as "rich peasants" suffered only moderately, and lower-income groups were fully protected. Violence was an integral part of this process: because repossession was meant to be implemented from within each village, the local peasants had to be convinced that they were able (and willing) to take matters into their own hands. Mobilization was accomplished with the help of staged public denouncements and humiliations of landlords in village gatherings known as "bitterness meetings." Beatings, not officially encouraged yet not prohibited either, frequently occurred. These meetings often led to confiscations and even death sentences for the "landlords." After each session the material possessions of the victims were divided among the crowd, which had earlier voted on whom to target. The condemned were buried alive, dismembered, shot, or strangled. This was what the leadership had wanted: as Mao reminded party leaders in June 1950,

> Land reform in a population of over 300 million people is a vicious war. . . . This is the most hideous class war between peasants and landlords. It is a battle to the death.[22]

The party had determined *a priori* that 10 percent of the rural population consisted of "landlords" or "rich peasants," even though in some places as many as 20 percent or 30 percent of villagers came to be persecuted; at least one person was expected to die in each village. Between half a million and a million were killed or driven to suicide. By the end of 1951, more than 10 million landlords had been expropriated and more than 40 percent of the land had been redistributed. Some 1.5 million to 2 million perished between 1947 and 1952, and millions more were stigmatized as exploiters and class enemies. The rural economy suffered accordingly, for fear of appearing to be well-off dissuaded peasants from working

---

[22] Moise 1983: 56, 67–68, 102–112. On land reform in general, see now Walder 2015: 40–60. Consequences: Margolin 1999b: 478–479; Dikötter 2013: 73–74, 76 (quote).

more than the minimum necessary for survival: villagers felt it was "glorious to be poor"—an altogether sensible strategy in the face of violent leveling.[23]

The eventual transfer of close to half of all land mostly affected those at the top and the bottom of the wealth spectrum. In some cases, "landlords" ended up with average holdings smaller than the village mean, having been eclipsed by better-protected "rich peasants." Even so, the overall extent of leveling had been dramatic: the new top 5 percent to 7 percent—"rich peasants"—owned no more than 7 percent to 10 percent of the land. Local outcomes could be even more extreme. In Zhangzhuangcun, in the more thoroughly reformed north of the country, most "landlords" and "rich peasants" had lost all their land and often also their lives or had fled. All formerly landless workers had received land, which eliminated this category altogether. As a result, "middling peasants," who now accounted for 90 percent of the village population, owned 90.8 percent of the land, as close to perfect equality as one could possibly hope for.[24]

China's cities did not escape these purges. In the early stages of revolutionary reform, private businesses were hit by inflated wage increases and punitive taxes, and most foreign businessmen were hounded out of the country. In January 1952, when land reform had been largely completed, the party launched its campaign against the urban "bourgeoisie." Employing the techniques first developed in the villages, it used denunciation meetings that pitted workers against managers, who were subjected to verbal and physical abuse. Even though outright killings remained relatively rare, beatings and sleep deprivation were common, and hundreds of thousands were driven to suicide. Once again the state set quotas: the most reactionary 5 percent of the "bourgeoisie" was to be targeted, and maybe 1 percent executed. Around 1 million people were killed and another 2.5 million sent to camps. The remainder got away with paying fines, levied to fund the war in Korea. Almost half of all small businesses came under investigation, and a third of owners and managers were found guilty of fraud. At the end of 1953, industrialists, who had already been subject to very high taxes, were finally compelled to hand over their entire capital to the state. Once again, many of them ended up taking their own lives.[25]

---

[23] Dikötter 2013: 74, 82–83. For higher numbers, cf. Margolin 1999b: 479 (2 million to 5 million dead, plus 4 million to 6 million sent to camps).

[24] Moise 1983: 138–139; Hinton 1966: 592. See also Walder 2015: 49–50: the share landownership of the richest 2.5 percent had fallen from close to 40 percent in the 1930s to 2 percent twenty years later, and from 18 percent to 6.4 percent for the next most affluent 3.5 percent of the population, while the share of poor and middling peasants rose from 24 percent to 47 percent.

[25] Margolin 1999b: 482–484; Dikötter 2013: 166–172; Walder 2015: 76–77.

The subsequent collectivization of farms in 1955 and 1956 further erased economic differentiation: the share of rural families who belonged to cooperatives rose from 14 percent to more than 90 percent, and private plots were limited to 5 percent of total land. By 1956 most industry had been nationalized. The latter was ostensibly accomplished by convincing more than 800,000 big or small business owners to "voluntarily" surrender their assets to the state. From 1955 onward, an extensive rationing system for food, clothing, and assorted consumer durables helped preserve the equalization that had been achieved by violent means.[26]

All these violent interventions soon paled in comparison with the horrors of the "Great Leap Forward" from 1959 to 1961, during which mass starvation induced by failed government policies claimed anywhere from 20 million to 40 million lives. Direct state action lagged not far behind: by the end of the Maoist period, between 6 million and 10 million Chinese had been killed or driven to suicide by the state, and about 50 million others had passed through the *laogai* camp system, where 20 million of them died.[27]

The brutality that accompanied land reform and the expropriation of urban industry and commerce thus belonged to an even bigger wave of violence unleashed by the communist leadership. A considerable flattening of previous disparities in income and wealth was the reward. The market income Gini coefficient for all of China prior to the revolution is empirically unknown but need not have been much above 0.4 in the 1930s. Whereas its evolution in the early years of communist rule remains obscure, in 1976, the year of Mao's death, it stood at 0.31; by 1984, it had fallen to 0.23. The urban income Gini around 1980 was as low as 0.16. Economic liberalization radically reversed this trend: within the next twenty years, the national market income Gini more than doubled, from 0.23 to 0.51. Today it may even be a little higher, around 0.55. Moreover, the Gini for family net wealth rose from about 0.45 to 0.73 between about 1990 and 2012. Much of this decompression has been driven by urban–rural divergence and regional variation, heavily influenced by government policies. What is particularly striking is that Chinese income inequality has progressed far beyond the level that is typical of a country of China's per capita GDP, defying the hopeful Kuznetian expectation that intensive

---

[26] Dikötter 2013: 237–238, 241; Walder 2015: 95–97. Work units became providers of welfare such as health care, pensions, and housing (ibid. 91–94).
[27] Margolin 1999b: 498.

economic growth would eventually depress inequality that had grown during the earlier stages of economic development. Considering that China accounts for close to a fifth of the present world population, this represents a weighty exception that underlines the significance of factors other than economic growth per se in shaping the distribution of income. Both the flattening and widening of income and wealth disparities in China over the last eighty years were ultimately determined by political power and, for the first half of that period, by violent force.[28]

"NEW PEOPLE": OTHER COMMUNIST REVOLUTIONS

Similar leveling was achieved by communist governments that were set up under Soviet occupation or through revolutionary action. A few examples will suffice. In North Vietnam, the process followed the Chinese playbook, albeit with far less brutality. Land inequality had been considerable: in 1945 some 3 percent owned a quarter of all land. Early communist policy measures between 1945 and 1953 were largely nonviolent: the preferred methods were transfer by sale, rent reductions, and punitively progressive taxation of landlords rather than confiscation and requisition. Taxation in particular discouraged landownership, as tax rates of nominally 30 percent to 50 percent could effectively approach 100 percent once surcharges were included. This prompted many landlords to sell or cede their land to their tenants. The landlord share consequently declined from 3 percent owning a quarter to 2 percent owning 10–17 percent. Beginning in 1953, however, the party leadership more stridently embraced the Chinese model. Peasant mobilization became the order of the day, and denunciation meetings were organized at the village level. For each district the politburo set quotas of "despot landlords" to be punished. Land reform legislation called for the expropriation of the most "despotic" of the rich and for forced sale in exchange for token compensation for the others. Although "rich peasants" were supposed to remain unharmed, in areas where "landlords" were in inconveniently short supply, members of the former category were also targeted if they "exploited land

---

[28] Brandt and Sands 1992: 205 (1930s); see also Walder 2015: 331 table 14.2. Ginis: SWIID; Xie and Zhou 2014: 6930, 6932; Walder 2015: 331. Level: Xie and Zhou 2014: 6931 fig. 2 for visualization; for Kuznets, see herein, chapter 13, pp. 369–374. For similar wealth statistics (0.45 in 1995, 0.55 in 1995, and 0.76 in 2010), see Bourguignon 2015: 59–60, based on Zhong et al. 2010 (misattributed by Bourguignon) and Li 2014. Large gaps between urban and rural incomes go back to the Mao years: Walder 2015: 331–332.

by feudal means" (i.e., through leases), in which case they could also be compelled to sell their land.

After the French defeat in 1954, some 800,000 people left the north to move south, the affluent overrepresented among them. Most of the land thus acquired was given to the poor. State-sponsored violence gradually increased in stages from 1953 to 1956. As in China, many "landlords"—5 percent of the population had been placed in that category—were left with smaller-than-average landholdings and survived as village pariahs. Unlike in China, however, not more than a few thousand of them were executed. Reallocation was guided by the subsistence needs of households, resulting in a fairly equal distribution of land in real terms (except for "landlords," who retained less); the poor benefited the most from these schemes. Just as in the Soviet Union and China, equalization was soon followed by a collectivization drive, as a result of which increasingly large cooperatives came to cover 90 percent of the cultivated area. After 1975 these policies were extended to the South as well. "Landlords" and the Church were expropriated and private businesses nationalized without compensation.[29]

The North Korean regime was more aggressive from the start, first seizing land from landlords in 1946 and then enforcing collectivization in the 1950s until almost all peasants were organized in larger units. In Fidel Castro's Cuba, land expropriation unfolded in stages, beginning with American holdings and followed by all estates larger than sixty-seven hectares. By 1964 three-quarters of all farmland had been seized and organized as cooperatives of resident workers that were soon converted into state farms. By the late 1960s, all other private businesses had been nationalized as well. In Nicaragua in 1979, the victorious Sandinista rebels—Marxist socialists rather than hard-core communists—initiated land reform by seizing the estates of the Somoza family, which covered a fifth of all farmland. Expropriation expanded in the early 1980s to include other large estates. As a result, by 1986 half of all farmland and half of the rural population had been involved in reform, mostly by creating cooperatives or setting up smallholdings. Even so, by the time the Sandinistas were voted out of power in 1990, Nicaragua's market income Gini was still very high, in the low to mid-0.50s—similar to those of Guatemala and Honduras and higher than in El

---

[29] Inequality: Moise 1983: 150–151; cf. Nguyen 1987: 113–114 for the 1930s. Reform and outcomes: Moise 1983: 159–160, 162–165, 167, 178–179, 191–214, 222; Nguyen 1987: 274, 288, 345–347, 385–451, 469–470.

Salvador at the time, all of them countries characterized by severe maldistribution of income and wealth. In this environment, the revolutionary government's abstention from violent coercion and commitment to democratic pluralism appear to have been decisive factors in constraining effective leveling.[30]

Whereas the redistributive measures in Central America and even Vietnam were relatively nonviolent by the horrific standards set by Lenin, Stalin, and Mao, the opposite was true of Cambodia under the Khmer Rouge. Even in the absence of conventional metrics there can be no doubt that violent government intervention led to massive leveling across the country. The hasty evacuation of the cities within a week of the communists' victory in 1975 displaced up to half of the Cambodian population, including all residents of the capital Phnom Penh. Considering that urban–rural income variation tends to be an important element of national inequality, this was bound to have a significant compression effect. Urban residents were counted among the "New People," who were treated as class enemies and deported, often several times. The regime sought to "proletarianize" them by seizing their possessions: they lost their assets in stages, first during evacuation and then when stripped by peasants and cadres at their destinations. After they settled in the countryside, the state tried to keep them from consuming the crops they struggled to grow.

Loss of life was enormous—probably close to 2 million people, or a quarter of Cambodia's entire population. Attrition was disproportionately concentrated among city dwellers: some 40 percent of Phnom Penh's inhabitants were dead four years later. Former officials and high-ranking soldiers were singled out for particularly harsh treatment. At the same time, the emergence of a new elite was curtailed by ever-expanding purges of party cadres. For example, 16,000 members of the Communist Party of Kampuchea were killed at the infamous Tuol Sleng prison alone, a tally all the more remarkable when considering that party membership had reached no more than 14,000 in 1975. Among the general population, the causes of excess deaths were fairly evenly split among ruralization, executions, imprisonment, and hunger and disease. Hundreds of thousands were murdered hidden from public view, most often beaten to death with blows to the head by iron bars, ax handles, or farm tools. Some of the corpses of the killed were used as fertilizer.[31]

---

[30] North Korea: Lipton 2009: 193. Rigoulot 1999 summarizes the nature of communist terror in that country. Cuba: Barraclough 1999: 18–19. Nicaragua: Kaimowitz 1989: 385–387; Barraclough 1999: 31–32.
[31] Margolin 1999a.

"ALL SWEPT AWAY": TRANSFORMATIVE REVOLUTION AS VIOLENT LEVELER

The Cambodian experience, in all its surreal and rapidly self-destructive violence, is merely an extreme instance of a much broader pattern. Over the course of about sixty years, from 1917 into the late 1970s (and continuing into the 1980s in Ethiopia), communist revolutionary regimes successfully forced down inequality through expropriation, redistribution, collectivization, and price-setting. The actual amount of violence expended in the implementation of these measures varied hugely between cases, with Russia, China, and Cambodia on one end of the spectrum and Cuba and Nicaragua on the other. Yet it would go too far to consider violence merely incidental to forcible leveling: even though it would in principle have been possible for Lenin, Stalin, and Mao to achieve their goals with much more limited loss of life, sweeping expropriations crucially depended on the application of at least some violence and a credible threat of escalation.

The underlying project was always the same: to restructure society by suppressing private property and market forces, leveling class differences in the process. These interventions were political in nature, representing violent shocks that rivaled those caused by the modern world wars discussed in earlier chapters. In this respect, leveling by mass mobilization warfare and by transformative revolution have much in common. Both of them critically relied on large-scale violence—whether latent or applied—to produce the observed outcome. The overall human cost of this process is well known: just as the world wars directly or indirectly claimed up to 100 million lives, communism has been held responsible for a comparable number of fatalities, mostly in China and the Soviet Union. In its tragic brutality, transformative communist revolution is mass mobilization warfare's equal—the second of our Four Horsemen of apocalyptic leveling.[32]

---

[32] Courtois 1999: 4 (body count).

Chapter 8

BEFORE LENIN

"WE SHOULD DO OUR UTMOST TO CUT OFF THE HEADS OF RICH MEN": THE FRENCH REVOLUTION

Had anything like that ever happened before? Did earlier periods witness revolutionary action that resulted in substantial leveling of income or wealth inequality? We will see that the twentieth century was—once again—anomalous in this regard. Although premodern societies certainly did not suffer from a shortage of popular uprisings in city and countryside, they did not normally appear to have altered the distribution of material resources. In much the same way as mass mobilization warfare, revolution as a leveling device had few antecedents in the preindustrial age.

Among earlier challenges to traditional authority, the French Revolution holds pride of place in the popular imagination and would seem a particularly promising candidate among potentially equalizing conflicts. France near the end of the *ancien régime* was characterized by high levels of wealth and income disparities. The best estimate we have puts the country's income Gini coefficient at around 0.59, close to England's at the time, although the margin of error (from 0.55 to 0.66) is wide. Gross inequities in the tax system helped shaped the disposable income distribution. The nobility owned a quarter of the land but was exempt from the main direct tax, the *taille*, and successfully resisted payment of newer taxes such as the capitation tax of 1695 and the *vingtième* of 1749. Much the same was true of the clergy, which held another tenth of the land and also received the *dime*, no longer a tithe but variable and generally substantial. Direct taxes were thus in effect almost entirely borne by the urban bourgeoisie and the peasantry. Moreover, inasmuch as richer bourgeois were able to escape taxation by purchasing titles and offices, the actual burden fell largely on smaller farmers and workers. Among indirect taxes, the salt tax (*gabelle*) was one of the most onerous, levied by imposing compulsory purchases of salt on individual households, which again hit the poorer harder than the rich. The overall fiscal extraction system was therefore highly regressive.

In addition, peasants owed seigneurial contributions to nobles and clergy, such as corvée labor and other obligations in time and money. Only a minority of farmers held enough land to get by—although even those arrangements technically counted merely as tenancies—whereas the majority of the rural population worked as sharecroppers and landless laborers. In the decades leading up to the Revolution, conditions worsened further owing to population pressure and the creeping reintroduction of feudal rights as well as the curtailment of pasture on common lands that excluded poor farmers who owned only a few animals and struggled to support them. This led to pauperization in the countryside and the growth of an urban proletariat. Land rents doubled between 1730 and 1780, and the price of agricultural goods rose faster than agricultural wages; urban workers were also adversely affected.[1]

The dismantling of the *ancien régime* and its institutions, which unfolded in stages between 1789 and 1795, entailed several measures that benefited the poor over the rich. In August 1789 the National Constituent Assembly declared "personal" feudal rights abolished, even though formal implementation dragged on into the following year. Although rents were still due, tenants increasingly resisted payment, and riots spread in late 1789 and early 1790. Peasants raided seigneurial chateaux and burned records. This unrest was accompanied by widespread violent agitation against (indirect) taxes, causing tax collection to stall. In June 1790, all personal feudal dues (such as corvée) were finally abolished without compensation, and common lands were ordered to be distributed among local residents. Consecutive Parisian assemblies repeatedly responded to rural unrest by abolishing the most unpopular levies, the onerous *dime* among them. However, the addition of new taxes to replace them did not generally reduce the burden on the peasantry and caused renewed resentment. Although "real" feudal rights (such as annual dues) nominally remained in force unless peasants bought them out by indemnifying landlords at twenty to twenty-five times the annual rate, this compromise arrangement was rejected by peasants, who withheld payments or rebelled. In 1792, a major flare-up of rural violence

---

[1] Inequality: Morrisson and Snyder 2000: 69–70 and 61–70 on prerevolutionary inequality in general. See also Komlos, Hau, and Bourguinat 2003: 177–178 for French eighteenth-century body height differences according to class. Tax system: Aftalion 1990: 12–15; Tuma 1965: 59–60. Access to land: Hoffman 1996: 36–37; Sutherland 2003: 44–45. Aftalion 1990: 32–33 (peasants, worsening); Marzagalli 2015: 9 (rents and prices).

resulted in antifeudal attacks in large parts of the country that became known as the "guerre aux châteaux."

After Parisians stormed the Tuileries in August 1792, the Legislative Assembly felt empowered to address rural violence with more sweeping reform: all landholders now became proprietors unless landlords were able to produce actual title deeds, which were rare in arrangements governed by customary rights. Even this final provision was done away with by the Jacobins in July 1793. At least on paper, this amounted to a major redistribution of wealth, for the millions of peasants who had paid fixed rents had technically been tenants even if they de facto operated as smallholders. By this reckoning, as much as 40 percent of all land in France—land that had already been held but not legally owned by peasants—was formally privatized in 1792. What mattered more in terms of income was the abolition of any feudal dues linked to these lands. It is important to note that from the very beginning, the antifeudal measures of August 1789, rural reform had been driven by the assemblies' concerns about the "threat from below"—that is, crowd action. Peasant activism, which became increasingly violent, and metropolitan reform legislation were intertwined in "a dialectic process that led, not to compromise, but to a mutual radicalization."[2]

The confiscation and redistribution of land more forcefully promoted leveling. In November 1789, the National Assembly expropriated all Church property in France for use by the nation, primarily to address budget shortfalls without having to institute new taxes. These lands, known as *biens nationaux*, were sold off in large tracts of land, a practice that benefited the urban bourgeoisie and wealthier farmers. Even so, the peasantry is estimated to have acquired some 30 percent of these properties. Starting in August 1792, the land of nobles who had emigrated was likewise seized and sold, this time in smaller lots and expressly to benefit the poor, a move that reflected the more egalitarian aspirations of the Legislative Assembly. Peasants consequently ended up with some 40 percent of those lands as well. That confiscated land could be purchased by paying in installments spread out over twelve years helped those of more modest means but ultimately worked to the advantage of all buyers once rapid inflation greatly eroded interest on the installments. Overall, however, redistribution was quite limited in scale: merely 3 percent of all farmland in France was acquired

---

[2] Tuma 1965: 56–57, 60–62; Plack 2015: 347–352; Aftalion 1990: 32, 108. Quote: Plack 2015: 347, from Markoff 1996a. See also Horn 2015: 609.

by peasants in this way, and even nobles and émigrés were able secretly to participate in purchases via middlemen. The leveling effects of land confiscation, though real, should thus not be overrated.[3]

Inflation was fueled by assignats, paper money issued in ever larger quantities from 1790 onward. Initially backed by confiscated Church assets, assignats came to be churned out in such huge quantities that five years later they had lost more than 99 percent of their value. The effect on inequality was mixed. Inflation imposed an indiscriminate tax on the population that was effectively regressive, for the rich would hold proportionately less of their wealth in cash than others. At the same time, it also benefited the less wealthy in several ways. As already mentioned, it reduced the real price of farmland and livestock paid for in installments. Fixed money rents, which increasingly replaced sharecropping, worked to the advantage of tenants. Inflation also wiped out rural debt, favoring the poor. At the other end of the spectrum, creditors of the *ancien régime* were partly repaid in devalued assignats, unless debts were voided outright. Those who had bought offices lost out by being recompensed in depreciated currency, a practice that strongly disfavored the elite. Top offices, which were usually purchased by nobles, represented most of the capital tied up in and lost in the venality business.[4]

The established wealth elite was hit hard, not merely by the abolition of feudal obligations they used to be owed but also, and especially, by the nationalization of Church property and the subsequent confiscation of the estates of émigrés and political opponents. Mass mobilization for war in 1793 prompted extraordinary levies: in Paris and various *departments*, forced loans were imposed on the rich in order to raise the necessary funds. Local revolutionary committees drew up lists of suitable payers, and dues were payable within a month. Additional locally created taxes were employed as an illegal yet effective way of soaking the rich. During the "Terror," thousands were imprisoned under suspicion of hoarding or violating price controls. The Revolutionary Tribunal in Paris alone handed down 181 death sentences for such transgressions. That the assets of the condemned fell to the state provided a powerful incentive for singling out rich targets. The quote in the section heading is taken from a speech by the delegate Joseph Le Bon, who urged that "among those charged with crimes

---

[3] Tuma 1965: 62–63; Aftalion 1990: 99–100, 187; Plack 2015: 354–355.
[4] Aftalion 1990: 100, 185–186; Morrisson and Snyder 2000: 71–72; Postel-Vinay 1989: 1042; Doyle 2009: 297.

against the Republic we should do our utmost to cut off the heads of rich men who are generally known to be guilty."[5]

Nobles left France in growing numbers. In the end, 16,000 of them, more than one in ten, had departed for safer shores. Outright persecution commenced in 1792. The following year, the government ordered the public burning of patents of nobility and of feudal entitlement documents. Only a relatively small number of nobles lost their lives: 1,158 of the 16,594 individuals sentenced to death by extraordinary courts belonged to the nobility, representing less than 1 percent of that order. However, their share in the condemned went up over time, culminating in the "Great Terror." Of the 1,300 decapitated corpses buried over the course of just six weeks in June and July 1794 in two pits in a former monastic garden, the Garden of Picpus, off Paris's eastern gate, more than a third were the remains of nobles, including princes, princesses, dukes and assorted ministers, generals, and high officials, whereas many of the others had been commoners in noble employ.[6]

Those who stayed in France and survived counted not only their blessings but also their losses. In Count Dufourt de Cheverny's account,

> I had lost in the first three years of the Revolution, twenty-three thousand livres of income in seigneurial dues . . . my pension from the royal treasury granted by Louis XV, and several other items . . . . I had had to suffer incursions by national guards, enormous taxes imposed by the Jacobins, all sorts of requisitions, seizure, under the name of patriotic donation, of what was left of my silverware . . . . My four months imprisonment had involved excessive expenditure . . . . My best trees were taken for the navy, and not a week went by when I did not have to take my requisitioned grain to military stores in Blois . . . . I make no mention of . . . the burning of all feudal title-deeds . . .[7]

Insofar as the Revolution hurt the rich and benefited the poor, some leveling can be expected to have occurred. But although the overall direction of this trend is clear, its scale is difficult to determine. Regarding the income distribution, the abolition of feudal encumbrances ought to have had a positive effect

---

[5] Aftalion 1990: 130–131, 159–160.
[6] Doyle 2009: 249–310, esp. 287–289, 291–293.
[7] Quoted from Doyle 2009: 297–298.

Table 8.1 Income shares in France, 1780–1866

Income share	1780	1831	1866
Top 10 percent	51–53	45	49
Bottom 40 percent	10–11	18	16

on workers and a negative one on landlords. Mass mobilization in warfare also tended to raise real wages. By one measure, real wages of adult male rural laborers rose by a third between 1789 and 1795. In one western French department, the share of harvesters in the crops increased from a sixth to a fifth. There are also indications of rising real incomes of urban workers: between the 1780s and the 1800s, wages rose more quickly than grain prices did.[8]

Regarding the distribution of wealth, changes in the distribution of landholding likewise point to an attenuation of inequality. In one new *department* where clergy and nobles had held 42 percent of the land in 1788, their share dropped to 12 percent by 1802 even as the share of peasants grew from 30 percent to 42 percent—yet this also suggests that intermediate groups benefited the most. In a sample from the southwest of France, the share of farmers whose holdings were insufficient to support them without recourse to outside employment or charity fell from 46 percent to 38 percent, and that of those who had sustainable holdings increased from 20 percent to 32 percent. In the longer term, these transfers consolidated small farms and smallholdings and ensured their survival despite enduring conditions of poverty. Reform fell far short of a radical redistribution of landed wealth. In many departments, the greatest landowners under Napoleon belonged to the same families as before the Revolution, and between a fifth and a quarter of land lost to confiscations was eventually repurchased by family members. Only a tenth of all land of the nobility was permanently lost to that group.[9]

Christian Morrisson and Wayne Snyder's somewhat heroic attempt to estimate changes in the French income distribution points to a decrease at the top and growth at the bottom of the income distribution (Table 8.1).[10]

One problem is that this comparison is limited to income distribution within the French labor force and thus excludes the shares of elite rentiers.

---

[8] Leveling: see esp. Morrisson and Snyder 2000: 70–72 and Aftalion 1990: 185–187. Real wages: Postel-Vinay 1989: 1025–1026, 1030; Morrisson and Snyder 2000: 71.

[9] Morrisson and Snyder 2000: 71; Aftalion 1990: 193; Doyle 2009: 294.

[10] Table 8.1 from Morrisson and Snyder 2000: 74 table 8. But cf. ibid. 71: "There are no viable indicators that can be used to approximate how the distribution of income changed between 1790 and the 1830s."

Moreover, and perhaps more important, these estimates do not allow us to distinguish between the distributive consequences of the revolutionary period (1789–1799) and the subsequent Napoleonic monarchy and Bourbon restoration periods. This makes it impossible to ascertain whether or to what extent initial leveling—in the period of intense reform activity in the first half of the 1790s—had been more pronounced than these figures suggest. For example, followers of Napoleon bought up land that might otherwise have been available to the poor, and under the Bourbons 25,000 families, many of them nobles, were indemnified for revolutionary expropriations. It is very well possible that the income distribution had temporarily become more compressed in the 1790s than it was a generation later.[11]

That said, there is no indication that the French Revolution resulted in anything even remotely comparable to the leveling brought about by the major twentieth-century revolutions. Changes in landownership, wealth concentration, and income distribution occurred at the margins. This was by no means trivial to those affected: if correct, a 70 percent relative increase in the income share of the bottom 40 percent was bound to represent a significant improvement for the poorest elements of French society. But this process was far from transformative overall. This finding meshes well with the comparatively moderate degree of violence directed against the propertied classes: however much it may have scandalized conservative contemporary observers, a revolution that by later standards turned out to be quite restrained in its means and ambitions yielded correspondingly less leveling.

"GIVE ALL THINGS TO GOD FOR ALL TO USE IN COMMON": THE TAIPING REBELLION

In the context of this survey, one particular nineteenth-century revolutionary movement merits special attention for two reasons: its ostensibly communitarian aspirations and the immensity of violence it generated. From 1850 to 1864, large parts of eastern and southern China were engulfed by the Taiping Rebellion. The bloodiest conflict in history up to that point, it is thought to have claimed some 20 million lives. An uprising against the Qing state, it was fueled

---

[11] Morrisson and Snyder 2000: 69 table 6 put the prerevolutionary top decile income share at 47 percent to 52 percent. Postrevolutionary developments: Tuma 1965: 66; Doyle 2009: 295. For private wealth shares, cf. Piketty 2014: 341.

by millenarian expectations of a "Heavenly Kingdom." Launched by the failed aspiring bureaucrat Hong Xiuquan, whose visions and program combined Chinese traditions of popular protest with Christian elements, it drew on a wide range of popular resentments from resistance to Manchu rule and hatred of state officials to ethnic tensions. Starting out in southwest China in 1850 and 1851 as an uprising mostly of peasants but also of charcoal-burners and miners, it quickly snowballed into a massive armed insurrection of 500,000 by 1852 and perhaps as many as 2 million the next year. What has been called a "vast army of the poor" wended its way through the economic heartland of China and soon seized Nanjing, which was chosen as the new capital of the Heavenly Kingdom on earth. Establishing control over tens of millions of people, the Taiping leadership promoted the worship of God and, more mundanely, the liberation of the Han from foreign domination. This was joined by a social agenda: Because only God was considered to be capable of owning anything at all, the notion of private property was at least notionally rejected. Celebration of universal brotherhood was meant to gather all as if into a single family. These lofty sentiments found their purest expression in a document first published in early 1854, "The Land System of the Heavenly Dynasty." It was based on the premise that

> all people on this earth are as the family of the Lord their God on High, and when people of this earth keep nothing for their private use but give all things to God for all to use in common, then in the whole land every place shall have equal shares, and everyone be clothed and fed. This was why the Lord God expressly sent the Taiping Heavenly Lord to come down and save the world.[12]

Ideally, all land was to be divided into equal shares for all adult men and women and half shares for children and was to be "cultivated in common." Land was to be graded according to its productivity and shared out evenly so as to achieve perfect equality. If there was not enough land for all to receive standardized shares, people were to be moved to locations where it was available. Each family was expected to rear five chickens and two sows. Every twenty-five families would set up a central treasury to pool and store their surpluses beyond subsistence. This earthly paradise of strict egalitarianism had distant historical roots

---

[12] Kuhn 1978: 273–279 (quote: 278); Platt 2012: 18; Bernhardt 1992: 101; Spence 1996: 173 (quote).

in earlier notions of "equal-fields" systems but, oddly, failed to provide for periodic redistribution to preserve equality over time.

Yet this oversight, if so it was, scarcely mattered—for the simple reason that there is no sign that this program was ever implemented or indeed even widely known at the time. Although some homes and estates of the wealthy were raided in the early stages of the Taiping advance and some of the loot shared with local villagers, most of it went to the rebel organization. These activities never developed into a broader redistributive scheme, let alone systematic land reform or real-life agrarian communism. Faced with stiffening Qing resistance and eventual counterattacks, the Taiping were primarily concerned with maintaining revenue flows to fund their own operations. As a result, traditional landlord–tenant relations remained largely intact. At most, some change occurred at the margins. In Jiangnan, where numerous Qing land and tax records had been destroyed and many landlords had either fled or were no longer able to collect rents, the new regime briefly experimented with having peasants pay taxes directly to state agents. This arrangement proved short-lived. Taxes might have been lower than before, and it had become easier for tenants to resist demands for high rents. In both gross and net terms, some income deconcentration is likely to have occurred as the Taiping withheld Qing-style privileges from the wealthy. Faced with stiffened tenant resistance, and for once expected to pay their full share of taxes topped up by special levies, landlords saw their incomes come under downward pressure.

But all this fell far short of any systematic leveling as envisioned in the utopian schemes that were never put into practice—or may not even have been intended to be. The latter might be signaled by the fact that on top of generally maintaining traditional land tenure arrangements, the Taiping leadership eagerly embraced hierarchical stratification by claiming a lavish lifestyle replete with harems and palaces. The Qing's violent destruction of the Taiping in the 1860s, which cost millions of lives from combat and famine, did not suppress an egalitarian experiment, for there was none. Neither communitarian doctrine nor extensive military mobilization of the peasantry appear to have produced significant leveling, nor could it have been sustained had it indeed been attempted. Prior to 1917, the gap between ideological goals and preindustrial realities was too wide to be bridged by force.[13]

---

[13] See Bernhardt 1992: 102 for the lack of evidence of its ever even being mentioned in records from Jiangnan. Relations: Kuhn 1978: 279–280; 293–294; Bernhardt 1992: 103–105, 116.

"FOR THE RUSTICS SOUGHT TO BETTER THEMSELVES BY FORCE": RURAL REVOLT

Much the same is true of most popular uprisings in history. Most people for most of recorded history were agriculturalists, and the distribution of wealth and income in any given premodern society was in large part determined by the configuration of landownership and control over agricultural products. Any survey of leveling by revolutionary means must thus pay particular attention to the effects of rural revolts. Such events were generally very common: apparent variation across space and time may well have more to do with the nature of the evidence than with actual conditions. Yet despite their frequency, it is rare to encounter rural revolts that turned into genuine revolutionary movements that then achieved a noticeable degree of leveling.[14]

The most promising cases are, once again, of relatively recent origin. Land reform in Mexico in the wake of the revolution of 1910 is one of them. Mexico had always experienced a great deal of resource inequality, going back to the Aztec period. In the sixteenth century, Spanish conquerors received huge grants of land and forced labor. The war of independence from 1810 to 1821 merely replaced rich peninsulares with Creole and Mestizo elites, and concentration of landownership kept growing in the later stages of the nineteenth century. The wealthy colluded with the state to acquire more land and profited from increasing commercialization. Disparities on the eve of the revolution were thus quite extreme. Altogether, 6,000 estates, controlled by 1,000 families and corporations, comprised more than half of all land in a country of 16 million, two-thirds of whom worked in the agricultural sector. Most rural residents were almost or completely landless, half of them smallholders who had precarious rights to land and the other half employed on large estates where they owed heavy rents and labor services. Debt tied peons to the land. In the central state of Mexico, only 0.5 percent of household heads owned property, only 856 people owned land, and sixty-four *hacendados* among them held more than half of all private land. Both economic wealth and political power were concentrated within a tiny ruling class.[15]

The revolution, which began as a struggle among competing elite factions and did not originally feature plans for land reform, prompted the mobilization

---

[14] The quote in the section caption is from Thomas Walsingham's account of the English peasant revolt of 1381, quoted from Dobson 1983: 132.

[15] Tuma 1965: 111; Powelson 1988: 218–229; Barraclough 1999: 10–11.

of rural forces that pursued their own redistributive agenda. Armed groups took over haciendas. Most notably, in the south, the peasant armies led by Emilio Zapata occupied large estates and redistributed land. Violent rural revolt created conditions on the ground that had to be addressed by central authorities whose influence had waned. In acknowledging the supremacy of public over private interests, the new constitution of 1917 legitimized expropriations. These were officially accepted only when peasant armies needed to be pacified: local violence rather than top-down legislation was the key driver of redistribution. Even so, formal allocations of land to the poor proceeded only slowly in the 1920s, and landlords obtained concessions such as caps on expropriation claims. Most of the land redistributed between 1915 and 1933 was of poor quality. Up to 1933, less than 1 percent of all land was reallocated per year, and less than a quarter of that land was actual cropland. Landlords were able to seek injunctions, and fear of foreign intervention prevented more sweeping seizure of large estates.

The fallout of the Great Depression—unemployment and declining incomes—finally ramped up the pressure, and the rate of redistribution increased under the more radical government of Lázaro Cárdenas, who also nationalized the oil industry in 1938. Forty percent of arable land was expropriated between 1934 and 1940, and peons now also qualified for assignments. Land was handed over to tenants, workers, and land-poor peasants, organized in collectives (*ejidos*), but was farmed in parcels. Once again peasant mobilization on the ground provided the necessary impetus for these measures. As a result, by 1940, half of all land had been covered by land reform, and half of the rural poor had benefited. Ten years later, the share of landowners had increased to more than half of the population, up from 3 percent in 1910, and by 1968, two-thirds of all farmland had been transferred. This drawn-out process illustrates the obstacles to large-scale redistribution and leveling in an electoral democracy and the importance of shocks—rural violence and later also the Great Depression—in jump-starting or accelerating redistributive action. Although Mexico did not undergo anything like the radical restructuring that was typical of communist revolutions or takeovers, peasant mobilization created and sustained momentum for redistribution in the face of establishment resistance. Even Cárdenas's more activist government critically relied on this input.[16]

---

[16] Tuma 1965: 121–123; Barraclough 1999: 12; Lipton 2009: 277.

Similar developments can be observed in 1950s Bolivia. A revolution in 1951 and 1952 was directed against oligarchic power that had severely oppressed both the indigenous peasantry and Spanish speakers. Most Indians worked as serfs on large estates or lived in communities that had forfeited their best arable land to estates. In the course of the uprising, organized peasants occupied large estates and burned hacienda buildings, prompting absentee owners to abandon their holdings. Subsequent agrarian reform in 1953 that provided for the expropriation of poorly managed large estates and the scaling back of others was de facto often just a recognition of processes that were already well under way. Large estates that had covered more than half of all farmland were taken over by tenants and nearby peasants, and more than half of the poor consequently enjoyed improved access to land. But violent resistance does not always succeed. The communist-led Salvadoran peasant uprising in January 1932 failed in a matter of days and provoked the army into massacring large numbers of peasants, an event known as the *matanza* or "slaughter," and subsequent palliative reform measures remained feeble at best. In fact, successful peasantry-based revolutions have been rare even in the recent past. I discuss the critical role played by violence, or the threat of violence, in encouraging land reform and the failure of most peaceful attempts in chapter 12.[17]

Moving back from the recent history of developing countries into the premodern period, we find that Chinese history has been particularly rich in recorded peasant revolts. Kent Gang Deng has surveyed no fewer than 269 instances of what he defines as major peasant rebellions that occurred over 2,106 years of Chinese history, from the fall of the Qin to the end of the Qing dynasties. "Equality" was repeatedly promoted as a goal, especially concerning land ownership, and the redistribution of wealth and land featured among the measures taken by rebel groups. Even if most rebellions were unsuccessful, they could serve as a catalyst for change by encouraging tax reform or land redistribution. In those cases when they managed to overthrow an established regime, they acted as what Deng calls "the terminator of the corrupt state apparatus" and a redistributor of wealth. I return to this issue in the next chapter in the context of state collapse and its leveling effects.[18]

---

[17] Bolivia: Tuma 1965: 118, 120–123, 127–128; Barraclough 1999: 12, 14–16; Lipton 2009: 277. El Salvador: Anderson 1971; and see also at the end of this chapter. On land reform more generally, see herein, chapter 12, pp. 346–359.

[18] Deng 1999: 363–376, 247 table 4.4, 251 (quote). Although most recorded rebellions failed, no fewer than forty-eight new regimes were installed by rebels in that period (223–224 table 4.1). Most rebellions were launched by rural unrest.

At the same time, it merits attention that even though leveling agenda were explicitly advanced by rebels, concrete change could be minimal or absent even in cases of success. The movement led by Li Zicheng is a good example. A rebel leader supposedly of shepherd origin, he came to command large armies drawn largely from the peasantry and helped bring down the Ming dynasty. He briefly held Beijing as a self-styled emperor in 1644 before being destroyed by the advancing Manchus. Although he was said to disdain wealth and planned to seize and redistribute the fortunes of the wealthy and even equalize landowner-ship, nothing came of this. As we have seen, much the same was true of the more massive and longer-lasting Taiping rebellion two centuries later.[19]

China stands out for the unique time-depth of its historical record of rural revolt. Evidence from other ancient societies is much sparser. Perhaps not by accident, in the slave-owning societies of ancient Greece and Rome, slave upris-ings and cognate events rather than peasant revolts appear in the sources. In principle, the freeing of slaves on a large scale would have served as a very potent leveling mechanism: in slave-rich environments, slaves embodied a large amount of the capital owned by the elite, and the sudden loss of that capital would have flattened the overall distribution of wealth. Equalization in the Old South in the wake of the American Civil War, described in chapter 6, offers powerful tes-timony to this effect. Yet this did not normally happen. The reported escape of more than 20,000 Athenian slaves after a Spartan invasion in 413 BCE certainly resulted in substantial losses for the wealthy but was an opportunistic response to interstate warfare and not a revolt in a narrow sense. Some leveling must have occurred when the Messenian helots—communal slaves held in serflike condi-tions by the Spartan warrior-citizen class—were set free in 370 BCE by foreign intervention: yet once again, this was not the result of autonomous helot action. In fact, a previous helot uprising in 462 BCE had failed. Two large uprisings of slaves in Roman Sicily (about 136–132 and 104–101 BCE) had some potential for leveling as the attempted creation of independent slave "kingdoms" would have deprived large owners of their estates and incomes. But neither of them succeeded, nor did the famous Spartacus rebellion in Italy in 73 to 71 BCE.

Violent action by certain groups in the later Roman empire have some-times been read as signs of rural unrest or revolt with equalizing aspirations. However, modern identifications of the *circumcelliones* of Roman North Africa in the late fourth and early fifth centuries CE as some sort of "Jacquerie" lack

---

[19] Mousnier 1970: 290.

an empirical basis beyond hostile contemporary rhetoric that cast them as a menace to society—claims that "rural rebels are roused up against their land-owners" and "notes of credit were extorted from creditors and given back to the debtors" represent the two principal surviving allegations of class warfare. All we can be sure of is that this group consisted of violent itinerant harvesters who were embroiled in Christian sectarian conflict at the time of St. Augustine. The Bagaudae (or Bacaudae) of Roman Gaul are only a marginally more promising case: they first appear as rebels in sources of the third century CE and reemerge in the fifth, clearly associated with crisis and the weakening of Roman rule. They may simply have sought to fill power vacuums by asserting or trying to assert local control: there is not much to support notions of peasant revolt or class conflict, even if the scant sources have at times been made to look that way.[20]

In Europe, reports of peasant uprisings begin to flow freely in the late Middle Ages. Complemented by numerous urban revolts, they continued well into the early modern period. One study counts no fewer than around sixty peasant rebellions and some 200 urban risings in late medieval Germany alone, and a broader survey of medieval Italy, Flanders, and France gathers a much larger number of instances. The Flemish peasant revolt of 1323 to 1328 was the biggest rural movement prior to the German Peasants' War of 1524 and 1525 and stands out for the unusual scale of its initial success. Peasant armies, at first allied to urban constituencies, drove off nobles and knights; they also exiled aristocrats and officials. By the time the rebellious citizen of Bruges captured the Flemish ruler, Count Louis, in 1323 and had him locked up for five months, the rebels were in control of much of Flanders. Conflicting interests of the urban and rural elements of the movement and the threat of French military intervention subsequently led to a peace in 1326 that would have severely limited peasant autonomy and imposed fines and payment of arrears. Because peasant leaders, chosen by popular assemblies, were excluded from the negotiations, these terms were immediately rejected by rural rebels, who proceeded to re-establish authority over most of the country until they were defeated in battle by the French in 1328. Just how much leveling occurred under peasant control remains an open question. They seized and redistributed some of the land of the exiles and set up their own governance with taxation and courts.

---

[20] *Circumcelliones*: Shaw 2011: 630–720 (quotes from Augustine on 695–696), and 828–839 for a dissection of modern historiographical constructs. Bagaudae: e.g., Thompson 1952, rejected by Drinkwater 1992.

And the commoners rebelled against the councilors, aldermen, and lords . . . . They elected captains for their fortresses and against the law formed squadrons. They marched out and captured all the councilors, aldermen, lords, and tax collectors. Once the lords had fled, they destroyed their homes. . . . All who rebelled were commoners and rustics. . . . They burnt all the mansions of the nobility . . . and plundered all their possessions in Western Flanders.[21]

Later compensation claims did document the orderly expropriation of movable goods and crops that belonged to wealthy landowners. What is less clear is whether allegations of extremism and violence were hostile propaganda or based in fact: occasional references to atrocities that involved killings of the rich are of dubious quality. By contrast, the savagery of reprisal upon the rebels' defeat at Cassel, which cost more than 3,000 peasants' lives, is well documented. The victorious French cavalry immediately started massacring civilians, and rebel leaders were apprehended and executed:

> After the victory the glorious monarch of France did not look on these matters favorably; rather because of God's omnipotence by which kings rule . . . he burnt villages and massacred the rebels' wives and children to leave a lasting memory of his vengeance against their crimes and rebellions.

Rapid pacification followed, accompanied by crushing demands for arrears and indemnities. In a sense the rebellion had failed due to its own success: a badly shaken elite organized an international crusade with papal blessing to crush this movement before it could entice peasants in other regions to follow the Flemish example. This offers an early but powerful example of the forces of repression mobilized by armed resistance of primary producers. Under these circumstances, sustainable leveling was not a viable outcome.[22]

---

[21] See Fourquin 1978 on popular rebellion in the Middle Ages; Cohn 2006 on social revolt in the late Middle Ages, with the collection of sources in Cohn 2004; Mollat and Wolff 1973 specifically on the later fourteenth century; Neveux 1997 on the fourteenth through seventeenth centuries; and also Blickle 1988. For the early modern period, see Mousnier 1970 on seventeenth-century France, Russia, and China, and see Bercé 1987 on peasant wars in the sixteenth to eighteenth centuries. For the Nordic countries in the medieval and early modern periods, see Katajala 2004. Numbers: Blickle 1988: 8, 13 (Germany). Cohn 2006 covers more than a thousand events, about a hundred of which are documented in Cohn 2004. Flanders: TeBrake 1993; see also Cohn 2004: 36–39 for sources. *Chronicon comitum Flandrensium*, quoted from Cohn 2004: 36–37.
[22] TeBrake 1993: 113–119, 123, 132–133; *Chronicon comitum Flandrensium*, quoted from Cohn 2004: 37.

The same was true of the "Jacquerie" of 1358 in northern France. It differed greatly from the Flemish uprising in its short duration of just two weeks and ostensible lack of organizational structure. Peasants attacked and destroyed castles and big houses of the nobility until they were put down by mounted knights in the battle of Mello. Elite sources revel in the atrocities allegedly perpetrated by the rural mob, topped by Jean de Bel's notorious account of how a knight was roasted on a spit in front of his wife and children.

> Going forth with their arms and standards, they overran the countryside. They killed, slaughtered, and massacred without mercy all the nobles whom they could find, even their own lords. . . . They levelled the houses and fortresses of the nobles to the ground and . . . they delivered the noble ladies and their little children upon whom they came to an atrocious death.

Yet although we cannot be sure how the peasants actually comported themselves, there are no doubts about the response of the ruling class:

> For the knights and nobles recovered their strength and, eager to avenge themselves, united in force. Overrunning many country villages, they set most of them on fire and slew miserably all the peasants, not merely those whom they believed to have done them harm, but all they found.[23]

However violent they may have been in practice, local risings of this sort stood no chance of addressing entrenched inequalities. Even partial exceptions were relatively few in number. The English Peasants' Revolt of 1381, for instance, was ostensibly a failure. Triggered by the imposition of new taxes to fund the war in France, at a more fundamental level it was driven by the people's desire to protect gains from the rising cost of labor triggered by the Black Death—gains the elite sought to contain with the help of labor statutes and feudal constrictions. The movement was quickly put down, although not before rebels had taken the Tower of London, ransacked palaces and mansions in the capital, personally confronted King Richard II, and executed the Archbishop

---

[23] Cohn 2004: 143–200 on the rebellion, and 152 for the roasted knight. Quotes: *Chronique* of Jean de Venette, in Cohn 2004: 171–172.

of Canterbury and the Lord Chief Justice, among other luminaries—and not before risings had occurred across much of the country, though mostly in the east. Whether or not the rebels really

> planned much more radical and merciless evils: they determined not to give way until all the nobles and magnates of the realm had been completely destroyed,

as Henry Knighton tendentiously averred, nothing of the sort came to pass. It was all over in a few weeks: rebel leaders were caught and executed, and well more than a thousand malcontents lost their lives. Yet although Wat Tyler's alleged demand that "all men should be free and of one condition" had been met with lethal force, and although labor statutes were upheld and serfdom was not abolished, actual living conditions of workers nevertheless continued to improve. This had little to do with the fact that the loathed poll taxes had been dropped. A much more potent violent force than rebel arms ensured further leveling: the recurrent waves of plague that raised the value of labor. As we will see in chapters 10 and 11, bacteria combated inequality much more effectively than any human uprising could hope to do. Both peasant violence and elite counterviolence were dwarfed by the lethality of pandemic disease.[24]

Only rarely did violence directly lead to improvements, however temporary. When more than 200 mountain villages in Florence's territory rebelled in 1401 to 1404, their determination—according to Pagolo Morelli's *Ricordi*, "there was not a peasant who would not have gone happily to Florence to burn it down"—was sufficient to extract material concessions from the ruling city, most notably tax exemptions and debt forgiveness. Nevertheless, no substantial degree of leveling was likely to have been sustained by such provisions. Likewise, little came of the Rebellion of the *Remences* in Catalonia in 1462 to 1472 that reacted to growing seigneurial pressures motivated by the labor scarcities caused by the Black Death. Other Spanish revolts in 1450 and in 1484 and 1485 also failed. In 1514, peasants rose in Hungary after they had been mobilized by their overlords for a crusade against the Ottomans. Under the leadership of György Dózsa, they attacked manors and killed landlords; yet military defeat exposed

---

[24] 1381: Hilton 1973; Hilton and Aston, eds. 1984; Dunn 2004. Dobson 1983 collects sources. Quotes: *Chronicon Henrici Knighton*, in Dobson 1983: 136, and Tyler as paraphrased by the *Anonimalle Chronicle*, in Dobson 1983: 165.

them to the usual wave of terror. The largest of all rural uprisings in western Europe, the German Peasants' War of 1524 and 1525, which engulfed much of southern Germany, sought to preserve income gains achieved in the wake of the plague and resist seigneurial rights and encroachment on common lands, goals that were reinforced by the spread of antiauthoritarian ideas. Although peasant armies stormed castles and secured supplies from monasteries, their aspirations fell far short of generalized leveling. Key demands focused on tax reductions and the restriction or cessation of seigneurial obligations and serfdom. Radical utopian visions remained marginalized, such as Michael Gaismair's call for the abolition of all status distinctions and the nationalization of estates and mines. Failure was pervasive and bloody: defeated in a series of battles, as many as 100,000 peasants are believed to have lost their lives in the war and the repression that followed. As so often occurred, elite reaction proved vastly more violent than peasant action itself.[25]

And so it went. In 1278 Bulgaria may have found itself under the short-lived rule of a "peasant emperor," the erstwhile swineherd Ivajlo, who had mobilized peasants against Tatar incursions and then removed the sitting ruler. But contrary to hopeful Marxist readings of his revolt as a social movement, modern scholarship has found "no sign that he or his followers protested against social injustices or sought any social reforms"—and in any case, he lasted only a single year. In 1670 and 1671, backed by Cossacks, Stepan Razin, the leader of a massive peasant uprising in southern Russia, disseminated subversive declarations, one of which urged the punishment of the titled elite, the abolition of ranks and privileges, and the promotion of Cossack equality. The movement ended in bloody failure. The same was true of, among many others, Kett's Rebellion in England in 1549, directed against enclosures that constricted peasants' livelihood; the Russian Cossack rebellion of 1773 to 1775, largely aimed against intensification of serfdom; the Saxon peasants' revolt of 1790, born of outrage about noble hunting rights that despoiled fields; the Galician peasant uprising of 1846, directed against feudal obligations; and the Malabar rebellion in India in 1921, likewise launched in resistance to the tightening of landlords' rights.[26]

Modern attempts to impose a measure of order on often chaotic events have identified specific popular concerns and engines of revolt. In Italy, France,

---

[25] Florence: Cohn 2006: 49–50, with sources in Cohn 2004: 367–370. Spain: Powelson 1988: 87. Germany: Blickle 1988: 30; 1983: 24–25. Gaismair: ibid., 224–225, and cf. 223–236 for other radicals. Failure: 246; 1988: 31.
[26] For Bulgaria, see Fine 1987: 195–198 (quote: 196). Cossacks: Mousnier 1970: 226.

and Flanders in the late Middle Ages, direct confrontations with landlords remained rare, whereas politically flavored revolts were more common, often provoked by fiscal abuse. The dislocations of the Black Death prompted a surge in uprisings in the second half of the fourteenth century. Sixteenth-century revolts responded to the revival of serfdom. In the seventeenth century, peasants sought to resist states' fiscal expansion via direct taxes that hit the countryside harder than the cities. Finally, in the late eighteenth century, rural revolt owed much to a growing sense that the removal of surviving servitudes had become overdue. Peasant revolts frequently started out as tax revolts, including the peasant revolt in Flanders in 1323 to 1328, the English peasant uprising of 1381, the "Harelle" in Rouen in 1382, the Transylvanian peasant revolt of 1437, the "Poor Conrad" rebellion in Württemberg in 1514, the Slovenian peasant rebellion of 1515, the Swedish Dacke war in 1542 and 1543, the Finnish Club War of 1595 and 1596, the four French Croquant risings between 1594 and 1707, the Swiss peasant war of 1653, the White Lotus rebellion in China from 1794 to 1804, the Palestinian Peasants' Revolt of 1834, the Imsul peasant revolt in Korea in 1862, the opening stages of the Romanian peasant revolt of 1906 and 1907, and also the Tambov rebellion against the Soviets in 1920 and 1921. It was an element in the German Peasants' War of 1524 and 1525 and the Donghak peasant revolution in Korea in 1894, and the same is true of the major French, Russian, and Chinese risings in the seventeenth century. This list is as incomplete as it is representative.[27]

Just like their late medieval antecedents, early modern peasant revolts rarely had any discernible effect on the distribution of income and wealth. The German Peasants' War bought the south German peasantry concessions that proved beneficial in the long run by constraining the spread of what is known as the "second serfdom"—protections that were to set them apart from rural populations to the north and east which had not joined the risings. The Swiss peasant war of 1653 more immediately resulted in lower taxes and debt relief. Although examples such as these suggest that violent resistance could on occasion make a difference, the general picture is nonetheless clear: more significant leveling was beyond the scope of premodern rural revolts. This was a function of both aspirations and capabilities. As Yves-Marie Bercé has observed, "[v]ery few revolts were successful in seizing the totality of power; in truth, they did not

---

[27] Middle Ages: Cohn 2006: 27–35, 47. Black Death: esp. Mollat and Wolff 1973, with Cohn 2006: 228–242. Later phases: Bercé 1987: 220.

even conceive of doing so." Indeed, the closer they came to this outcome, as the Flemish peasant movement of the 1320s may arguably have done, the stronger the countervailing forces they were bound to unleash.[28]

"LONG LIVE THE PEOPLE AND DEATH TO THE WOLVES": REVOLT IN CITIES AND CITY-STATES

What was true of rural revolts applied even more to urban risings. In most historical settings, cities were embedded in vast rural landscapes, their populations greatly outnumbered by the peasantry. Rulers and nobles could draw on soldiers, arms, and resources from surrounding areas to bring rebellious towns to heel. The bloody crushing of the Paris commune in 1871 is merely one relatively recent example. If urban revolts had any prospect of success, it would have been in self-governing city-states whose local elites could not readily fall back on external resources of repression.

In chapter 6, ancient Greece served as an early example of military mass mobilization and concurrent egalitarianism. This raises the question whether this environment also produced revolutionary movements that aimed for or even achieved overall leveling. Radical visions certainly emerge in plays and utopian texts. In Aristophanes's comedy "Ekklesiazusai," staged in Athens in 392 BCE, the Athenian women abolish private property and the family, decreeing equality for all. Four years later, in his "Ploutos," undeserved wealth is taken away from its owners. Plato, in the "Republic," was vexed by the idea that there were "not one, but two states, the one of the poor, and the other of rich men," and his later "Laws" consequently envisages a maximum ratio of nonlanded wealth of 4 to 1 for the richest and poorest citizens. More radical utopians went farther: Euhemeros, writing in the early third century BCE, imagined the island of Panchaia, whose inhabitants owned no private property beyond houses and gardens and mostly received equal supplies, and Iamboulos, later that century, wrote of an Island of the Sun that was completely bereft of private property or family life and characterized by universal equality—and thus happiness.[29]

In practice, however, nothing of this kind ever seems to have happened among the ancient Greeks. Just as in later periods of history, significant leveling would have required significant force. The most extreme case on record may be

---

[28] Bercé 1987: 157, 179, 218 (quote).
[29] Fuks 1984: 19, 21, 25–26.

a civil war in the major Peloponnesian polis of Argos in 370 BCE, during which 1,200 wealthy citizens were sentenced to death in mock trials and beaten to death with clubs; their assets were confiscated and given to the masses. Yet such gory scenes, with more than a whiff of Mao's China, were not the norm. As we will see in chapter 12, the record is dominated by land reforms associated with coups but without the large-scale violence we observe in modern revolutionary settings.[30]

Genuinely radical urban revolts were generally rare in history. One notable case concerns the "zealots" in Thessalonica from 1342 to 1350: popular elements seized control of the city, killed and expropriated aristocrats, and redistributed their wealth. But although hostile sources paint them as extremists, there is no evidence for a program of systematic confiscation or redistribution. Alongside the ancient Greek polis culture, medieval and early modern Italy, with its clusters of often independent city-states, is another leading candidate for more ambitious urban movements. Urban risings were indeed often recorded in this environment. Yet once again, just as rural revolts infrequently confronted landlords directly, urban violence, even if sometimes motivated by economic concerns, rarely targeted capitalists and employers. Riots in response to corruption or professional exclusion were much more common, as were tax revolts. And much like rural risings, even urban revolts with their relatively modest agenda tended to fail. As good an example as any is provided by the well-known Ciompi revolt in Florence in 1378, which was led by textile workers who found themselves excluded from a guild that shaped the labor market in a highly unequal way. Although they managed to take over the city, their demands were modest: incorporation via newly created guilds and a tax on wealth. Even so, the movement was crushed with reactionary bloodshed.[31]

"THUS THEY WERE ENTIRELY DESTROYED": OUTCOMES

This is what the *Chronique des quatre premiers Valois* had to say about the rebellious peasants of the short-lived Jacquerie of 1358—and what proved to be a common theme throughout history. During the 1932 uprising in El Salvador,

---

[30] Argos: Fuks 1984: 30, mostly based on Diodorus 15.57–58.
[31] Thessalonica: Barker 2004: 16–21, esp. 19. Italy: Cohn 2006: 53–75. The section heading is taken from Niccola della Turcia's *Cronache di Viterbo*, reporting the motto of rebels in Viterbo in 1282 when local nobles were chased out of the city, quoted from Cohn 2004: 48. Causes: Cohn 2006: 74, 97. Ciompi: Cohn 2004: 201–260 for sources.

communist rebels killed at most three dozen people, whereas the military slaughtered thousands during the repression that followed, including women and children: estimates range from 8,000 to 40,000. This outcome should not have been entirely unexpected: right before the start of the revolt one of the rebel leaders, Alfonso Luna, told war minister Joaquin Valdés that "the peasants will win with their machetes the rights you are denying them," to which the latter replied, "You have machetes; we have machine guns." Short of capturing what Yves-Marie Bercé called the "totality of power," no uprising could hope to flatten income and wealth inequality as such, even had this indeed been a goal—which it rarely was. The means of violent expropriation and control required for the great upheavals witnessed in the twentieth century were simply not available to premodern societies. Nor were there firm ideological commitments to this end. Even the much-maligned Jacobins of the French revolutionary "Terror" shied away from wholesale expropriation and equalization. They had no idea what real terror on a national scale would eventually come to look like.[32]

Deliberate systematic leveling through violent revolt was therefore beyond preindustrial means. Only in the twentieth century do we encounter revolutionaries who wielded both machine guns and radical programs. It was only then that the conclusion of the *Chronique des quatre premiers Valois* could finally be applied to other side, to lords and landlords—the original 1 percent. Only then could power be exercised pervasively enough, to transformative enough ends, and for long enough for truly substantial leveling to occur. Although the premodern world was no stranger to violent popular dissent, social evolution required a step-up in the capacity for violence and the scope of its application in order to pursue radically equalizing policies, whatever the cost to ruled and rulers alike. But there is a final twist to this story. Even when society was deeply penetrated by ruthless revolutionaries, enforced equality lasted only as long as these regimes were in power and stayed the course. The moment they fell, as in the Soviet Union and its satellites or in Cambodia, or changed track, as in China or Vietnam, inequality of income and wealth rapidly returned. This principle applied even under dramatically different circumstances, as the experience of Russia and China shows: economic collapse and explosive inequality in the former, massive economic growth and a gradual rise of inequality in the latter.[33]

---

[32] Jacquerie: Anonymous, about 1397–1399, quoted from Cohn 2004: 162. El Salvador: Anderson 1971: 135–136, 92 (quotes). Quote: herein, p. 250. Jacobins: Gross 1997.
[33] See Milanovic 2013: 14 fig. 6.

The kind of leveling brought about by "modern" and often blood-drenched transformative revolution could be maintained only as long as repression— latently or overtly violent in nature—constrained market forces. As soon as this repression is relaxed or removed, equalization is reversed. In the previous chapter, I mentioned the increase of Russia's market income Gini coefficient from 0.26–0.27 in the 1980s to 0.51 in 2011 and the Chinese rise from 0.23 in 1984 to 0.55 in 2014. Vietnam's market income Gini may have reached 0.45 by 2010, although lower values are also being cited, and Cambodia's was estimated as 0.51 in 2009. Development in Cuba has followed the same pattern: after the market income Gini dropped from 0.55 or 0.57 in 1959, the year of the communist revolution, to 0.22 in 1986, it appears to have risen to 0.41 in 1999 and 0.42 in 2004, although one estimate put it already as high as 0.55 by 1995. In the majority of these cases, nominally communist regimes remain in power, but economic liberalization has rapidly driven up inequality. The same has been true of the postcommunist societies of Central Europe. Whether communism's sacrifice of a hundred million lives bought anything of value is well beyond the scope of this study to contemplate. But one thing is certain—that whatever it so bloodily bought in terms of greater material equality is now well and truly gone.[34]

---

[34] Ranis and Kosack 2004: 5; Farber 2011: 86; Henken, Celaya, and Castellanos 2013: 214; but cf. also Bertelsmann Stiftung 2012: 6 for caution and Veltmeyer and Rushton 2012: 304 for a lower Cuban estimate for 2000 (0.38). SWIID registers a decline from 0.44 in 1962 to 0.35 in 1973 and 0.34 in 1978. In view of this, the question whether communism's effect on social policy in Western nations (see herein, chapter 5, pp. 172–173) has been its most durable contribution to economic equalization is worth considering.

Part IV

COLLAPSE

Chapter 9

STATE FAILURE AND SYSTEMS COLLAPSE

"AND SNEER OF COLD COMMAND": STATE FAILURE AND SYSTEMS COLLAPSE AS LEVELERS

The more violence that wars and revolutions unleashed and the more deeply they penetrated society, the more they were capable of lowering inequality. But what if these dislocations destroyed entire states and the existing social and economic order? Based on the evidence presented so far, we might expect ever greater upheaval to result in ever stronger leveling. This grim prediction receives ample support from historical evidence that ranges across thousands of years of recorded history. State failure and systems collapse upended hierarchies and compressed material inequalities on a sometimes dramatic scale. Complementing the predominantly more recent processes discussed in some of the previous chapters, most of these cataclysmic events took place in the premodern age.

I begin by defining terms. Large social structures may unravel with different degrees of intensity and severity. At one end of the spectrum we find processes that are primarily related to the exercise of political power, conventionally known as state failure. From a contemporary perspective, states are considered to be failing if they are unable to supply public goods to their members: corruption, lack of security, breakdown of public services and infrastructure, and loss of legitimacy serve as markers of state failure. Yet this definition holds states to standards that need not have applied in the more distant past. The notion that states are supposed to provide varied public goods beyond basic security and that failure or collapse can be inferred from their inability to meet this expectation seems anachronistic for most of history. For the purposes of this global survey, we are better served by a bare-bones characterization of essential state functions. Inasmuch as premodern polities focused in the first instance on checking internal and external challengers, protecting the key allies and associates of rulers, and extracting the revenues required to perform these tasks and enrich the power elite, state failure is best understood as the loss of the capacity to accomplish even these basic objectives. The erosion of control over subjects and territory and the replacement of state officials by nonstate actors such as warlords are typical outcomes, and in extreme cases political power could even devolve to the community level.[1]

At the opposite end the spectrum is bounded by a more expansive concept—that of systems collapse, a phenomenon that goes well beyond the failure of political institutions of governance. A more comprehensive and at times all-encompassing process of unraveling, systems collapse has been defined as "rapid, significant loss of an established level of social complexity." Extending across different domains of human activity, from the economic to the intellectual sphere, it typically results in diminished stratification, social differentiation and division of labor, the abatement of flows of information and goods, and a decline in investment in civilizational features such as monumental architecture, art, literature, and literacy. These developments accompany and interact with political disintegration that weakens or altogether removes centralized control functions. In severe instances, population as a whole contracts, settlements shrink or are abandoned, and economic practices regress to less sophisticated levels.[2]

Breakdowns of states or entire civilizations are of vital importance to our understanding of the forces that are capable of leveling disparities of income and wealth. As we have seen in the discussion of the effects of civil war, state failure may create new opportunities of enrichment for the few. Yet existing elites are likely to suffer, and insofar as larger states splinter into smaller entities, the potential for resource concentration at the top will shrink. Systems collapse is bound to be even more detrimental to the rich and powerful. The dismantling of centralized bodies of governance undermines formal hierarchies and the elite class as such and prevents the latter's immediate replacement by rivals who might hope to operate on a comparable scale. Premodern societies frequently left only inadequate written evidence and sometimes literacy disappeared in the wake of collapse. In such cases, we are able to infer elite decline from proxies

---

[1] Rotberg 2003: 5–10 lists features of state failure from a modern perspective. For the nature and limitations of premodern states, see Scheidel 2013: 16–26. Tilly 1992: 96–99 identifies essential state functions with model clarity.

[2] Tainter 1988: 4 (quote), 19–20. For historical examples, several of which are covered in this chapter, see 5–18.

that include, in the words of the eminent archaeologist and theorist of systems collapse Colin Renfrew, "cessation of rich, traditional burials . . . abandonment of rich residences, or their reuse in impoverished style by 'squatters' . . . cessation in the use of costly assemblages of luxury goods."[3]

State failure was a powerful means of leveling because of the multiple ways it interfered with the enrichment of the ruling class. As we have seen in the opening chapters, in premodern societies, elite wealth was primarily derived from two sources—the accumulation of resources through investment in productive assets or activities such as land, trade, and finance and predatory accumulation via state service, graft, and plunder. Both income streams critically depended on the stability of the state: the former because state power provided a measure of protection for economic activity and the latter even more so for the simple reason that state institutions served as a vehicle for generating and allocating gains. State failure might lower returns on capital and completely erase profits derived from the exercise of or from proximity to political power.

As a result, established elites stood to lose on a grand scale. Political turmoil not only deprived them of opportunities for continuing enrichment but also threatened their existing property holdings. Significant reductions in elite income and wealth were likely to curtail inequality: although everybody's assets and livelihoods were at risk in times of state failure or systems collapse, the rich simply had vastly more to lose than the poor did. A subsistence peasant household could afford to lose only a relatively modest fraction of its income and still get by. Greater shortfalls might threaten its members' survival, but those who perished or fled no longer belonged to a given population and thus no longer played a role in that population's distribution of resources. The wealthy, on the other hand, were able to survive even after having lost most of their income or property. Those among the formerly rich and powerful who weathered the storm, and those who replaced them in whatever diminished positions of leadership remained, were likely to end up far less wealthy not only in absolute but also in relative terms.

The compression of material disparities in the wake of state failure or systems collapse was a function of different scales of impoverishment: even if these events left most or all people worse off than before, the rich had farther to fall. Moreover, we have to allow for the possibility that to the extent that political unraveling interfered with predatory surplus extraction, commoners may even

---

[3] Renfrew 1979: 483.

on occasion have experienced an improvement in their living standards. In that case, leveling would not merely have been the result of a race to the bottom conducted at different speeds but might also have been reinforced by gains among the working population. However, owing to the nature of the evidence, it is generally easier—or at least somewhat less desperately difficult—to document the decline of elites than to identify concurrent improvements among poorer groups. For this reason alone, I focus primarily on changes in the fortunes of the rich and powerful and their implications for the distribution of income and wealth. My discussion begins with some of the best-documented premodern case studies. After moving on to less clear-cut evidence that probes the limits of our knowledge, I conclude with a modern example of state failure, Somalia, to see whether its equalizing properties can still be observed in the world today.

"FOXES AND HARES CROSS WHERE THE GRANDEES OF STATE RESIDED BUT RECENTLY": THE DESTRUCTION OF THE TANG ELITE

The terminal phase of the Tang dynasty in China shows with exceptional clarity how state disintegration led to the destruction of elite wealth. Established in 618 CE, the Tang emperors built on the successes of the short-lived Sui dynasty in reimposing political unity on the far-flung territories that had once been held by the Han and Western Jin dynasties. Under the Tang, initial land allocation programs meant to equalize access to resources gradually gave way to growing concentration of both wealth and power within the highest tiers of the imperial ruling class. A small number of eminent families came to form an entrenched aristocracy, and although individual families were unable to hold on to top positions for more than a few generations, as a group they monopolized political power for several centuries. Privilege derived from holding high state office fueled personal enrichment, a process that was tempered only by interfamilial rivalries and eventually more violent factionalist struggles that checked or reversed the rise of individual families but that failed to undermine their collective grip on the most lucrative positions of public service. Wealth accumulation was greatly aided by the fact that even distant relatives of the imperial family, as well as all families endowed with noble titles and all officials and holders of official rank, were exempt from taxation and labor services, an eminently regressive system that openly favored the powerful and well-connected. Members of the same group engaged in private purchase of public land, a practice repeatedly but unsuccessfully prohibited by their rulers.

As a result, elite landownership expanded at the expense of the state, and attempts to implement land equalization schemes ceased after political instability commenced in the mid-eighth century CE. The growth of large estates sheltered peasants from state taxation, allowing landlords to convert the agricultural surplus into private rent. Linked to long-distance trade, these commercialized estates helped sustain an increasingly rich elite. Those who disposed of sufficient capital to run mills diverted water from peasants, a practice that prompted complaints but only sporadic state intervention. An eighth-century observer who claimed that

> the nobles, officials, and powerful local families set up their estates one next to the other, swallowing up peasants' land as they please without fear of the regulations. . . . They illegally buy the peasants' equal-field land. . . . They thus leave the peasants no place to live

may have relied on stereotypes and hyperbole but nonetheless put the finger on a pressing problem—the ongoing concentration of landed wealth. The most extravagant disparities were created at the very top, by families that back in the sixth and seventh centuries had closely attached themselves to the imperial court by abandoning their local bases and relocating to the capital cities of Chang'an and Luoyang, where close proximity to the throne ensured the most immediate access to political power and attendant lucre. This spatial clustering helped them secure access to senior government positions and provincial offices. Distinct from a provincial upper class that rarely ascended to state offices, these families formed a closed central elite that was increasingly interconnected by marriage. The most detailed study of this group and the numerous tomb epitaphs it left behind finds that by the ninth century CE, at least three-fifths of all known members of the resident imperial elite of Chang'an were linked by ties of kinship and marriage, including the majority of senior officials such as ministers and most top-tier officials in charge of provincial administration. What has been called a "highly restricted marriage and kin network" had thus come to control the Tang state, in no small part for the personal benefit of its members.[4]

Yet metropolitan residence came with a price: extremely profitable in times of order and stability, it exposed the top tier of the Tang elite to violent action

---

[4] Tang land schemes: Lewis 2009b: 48–50, 56, 67, 123–125; cf. also Lewis 2009a: 138–140 for earlier equal-field schemes. Quote: Lewis 2009b: 123. Aristocracy: Tackett 2014: 236–238 (quote: 238).

when the central authorities were no longer able to fend off challenges by usurpers. In 881 CE, Huang Chao, a rebel warlord, took the main capital city of Chang'an. Just a few days into the occupation, resistance by high officials triggered violent reprisals that resulted in the killing or suicide of four current or former chief ministers and claimed hundreds of other lives. Huang Chao soon lost control over his troops, who went on a looting rampage in a city filled with staggering elite wealth that been built up over centuries. The power elite became a favorite target: according to one source, the soldiers "especially detested bureaucrats, killing all those they got their hands on." Three thousand literati were supposedly massacred in response to the publication of a mocking poem. And that was only the beginning: although Huang Chao's rebellion failed, Chang'an was sacked several times by rival warlords in the years to come, events that devastated the city and impoverished its residents. In Zheng Gu's words,

> At sunset, foxes and hares cross
> Where the grandees of state resided but recently.
> How doleful to hear jade flutes,
> But not see the fragrant carriages go by.

The properties of the wealthy in the city's vicinity also suffered gravely. Wei Zhuang, a scion of one of the greatest capital families, describes the desolation of his family estate:

> On a sea of a thousand mulberry trees, there is nobody in sight.
> Hearing a lone note played from a flute, I shed a tear in the emptiness.

Mulberry trees were understood to be a symbol of wealth. Zheng Gu also bemoaned the fate of the estate of his cousin Wang Bin:

> Desolate and forsaken were the old fields . . . . Inquiring in turn about each of the neighbors, [my cousin] pointed over and over again toward the tombs . . . . After prolonged shortages, the servants had all dispersed.[5]

Over the course of these recurrent crises, nobles who lost their lives probably numbered in the thousands, and those who survived were deprived of their

---

[5] Huang Chao: Tackett 2014: 189–206. Quotes: 201–203.

urban residences and suburban estates. Purges continued until little was left of the old elite. In 886, after a failed coup, hundreds of officials who had backed the contender were executed. In the year 900, the court eunuchs killed almost everyone close to the emperor in response to a plot to eradicate them, and in retaliation they and their allies were all eliminated the following year. In a single incident in 905, seven of the most influential ministers still alive were killed and tossed into the Yellow River. Perpetrated in rapid succession, these serial atrocities effectively wiped out the metropolitan elite.

Violence quickly spread beyond the capital proper. Luoyang was sacked and destroyed in 885, and from the 880s to the 920s, provincial centers all over the country came to be engulfed in fighting and purges that caused huge loss of life among the regional elites:

Household after household has been emptied of valuables;
Everywhere, refined mansions with elaborate eaves have been burned
to the ground.[6]

In the end, few were spared. The central ruling class quickly disappeared and by the late tenth century had almost completely vanished from the historical record. In the capital region, excavated tomb epitaphs, associated with those able to afford elaborate burial sites, became exceedingly scarce after the outbreak of violence in 881. Local branches of the elite did not escape the carnage. Some survivors are known, often from their mournful writings, but normally had lost their possessions. With their ancestral wealth gone and their networks dismantled, there was no way for them to regain elite status. From 960 onward, the advent of a new empire under the Song dynasty ushered in entirely different families who often hailed from the provinces and who seized the levers of power as central institutions were being rebuilt.[7]

The violent and comprehensive demise of the Tang aristocracy may be a particularly extreme example of how state failure obliterates wealth at the top of the social pyramid and levels the distribution of assets by impoverishing and even exterminating the rich. Even so, violence that did not directly target state elites could result in a comparable degree of leveling. State failure deprived them of income derived from political office and connections as well as from

---

[6] Tackett 2014: 208–215 (quote: 209–210).
[7] Epitaphs: Tackett 2014: 236; 225 fig. 5.3: their frequency fell from about 150–200 per decade in the period from 800 to 880 to 9 per decade during the following four decades. Changeover: 231–234.

economic activity, and it diminished their wealth as territories were lost to the state they helped control and domestic or foreign challengers took over elite holdings. In all these cases, the overall outcome would be similar, even if it is hard to measure in any meaningful sense of the term: a reduction in inequality achieved by cutting off the uppermost end of the tail of the income distribution (on the Lorenz curve) and by greatly compressing the share of the top fraction of a percent of the population in total income and wealth. For the simple reason that the rich stood to lose so much more than the poor, equalization was likely to occur regardless of whether state failure caused general impoverishment or primarily wrought havoc on elite groups.[8]

"FRAUGHT WITH SO MANY MISERIES AND DIVERSE AFFLICTIONS": THE DISINTEGRATION OF THE WESTERN ROMAN EMPIRE

The fall of the western half of the Roman Empire and the resultant ruin of its wealth elite is a less bloody but no less revealing case of leveling through state collapse. By the early fifth century CE, enormous material resources had ended up in the hands of a small ruling class with intimate ties to political power. Very large fortunes are documented in the western half of the Mediterranean basin, which comprised the empire's original Italian core and its extensive Iberian, Gallic (now French), and North African territories. The senate in Rome, according to long-standing tradition populated by the richest and politically best-connected Romans, had come to be dominated by a very few grand and closely interconnected families that were based in the city of Rome itself. Those super-rich aristocrats were said to have "possessed estates scattered across almost the whole Roman world." One concrete example mentions holdings in Italy, Sicily, North Africa, Spain, and Britain owned by a single couple. The result of marriage and inheritance as well as officeholding, transregional landed wealth was sustained not only by the basic security provided by a unified imperial state but also by the state-sponsored movement of goods for fiscal purposes that allowed estate owners to benefit from reliable trade networks. As in Tang China, senators' immunity from surtaxes and service obligations that weighed heavily on lower elite strata further boosted their fortunes. In the end, the very

---

[8] In societies in which elite income was to a significant extent a function of gains directly derived from the exercise of political power, state failure would affect elites more disproportionately than wars that only interfered with economic activity. The effect of the U.S. Civil War on the Southern states provides an example of moderate leveling in the latter scenario: see herein, chapter 6, pp. 174–180.

richest families supposedly commanded annual incomes comparable to the revenue the state expected to draw from entire provinces and maintained palatial dwellings in the city of Rome and elsewhere. The wealthiest provincials, though unable to compete with the central elite, likewise benefited from imperial connectivity: two landowners from Gaul are known to have owned estates in Italy and Spain and in the southern Balkans, respectively.[9]

The ability to amass and profitably maintain supraregional wealth was critical in creating a top echelon of the propertied class that towered over lesser notables. So was privileged access to high political office in an empire of tens of millions of subjects where graft and corruption were routine elements of governance and the richest and most privileged officials were in the best position to shield their assets from state demands. Their preeminence and the extreme disparities it generated thus depended in their entirety on the solidity of imperial power. Internal conflicts and external challenges mounted as the fifth century progressed. Between the 430s and 470s CE, the Roman state lost control first over North Africa and then over Gaul, Spain, Sicily, and finally even Italy itself as Germanic kings took over. The eastern Roman Empire's attempt to regain Italy in the second quarter of the sixth century caused major turmoil and soon failed due to renewed Germanic incursions. This dramatic breakdown of Mediterranean unity dismantled the extensive networks of estates owned by a Rome-based top elite that was no longer capable of holding on to possessions outside Italy and eventually in large parts of Italy itself.

Intensifying political decentralization effectively wiped out the uppermost tier of western Roman high society. A process that had begun in the hinterlands of the Mediterranean basin in the fifth century reached the Italian peninsula in the sixth and seventh. Holdings of landlords residing in the city of Rome largely came to be confined to the surrounding region of Latium, and even the popes were deprived of Church estates in southern Italy and Sicily. This meltdown helps us understand why, according to the "Dialogues" composed by Pope Gregory in 593 CE, an elite Roman such as the bishop Redemptus would believe that "the end of all flesh was come" as men joined monasteries to find refuge from a world "fraught with so many miseries and diverse afflictions." Aristocracies became much more localized in scope and far less wealthy than they had once been. Decline manifested itself in various ways, from the

---

[9] Wickham 2005: 155–168 is the best analysis; see herein, chapter 2, pp. 78–79. Ammianus 27.11.1 (quote). Holdings: *Life of Melania* 11, 19, 20.

downgrading or abandonment of fancy country villas to the unceremonious disappearance of the venerable senate from the record and the fact that no senatorial families can be traced beyond the early seventh century. The writings of Pope Gregory offer what is perhaps the most striking illustration of the depths to which formerly wealthy families had fallen. The Church's leader repeatedly mentions destitute aristocrats whom he helped keep afloat with small acts of charity. A former governor of Samnium, an Italian region, was given four gold coins and some wine; widows and orphans of noble houses whose members had in previous generations held the highest ranks of office likewise received modest donations.[10]

The demise of Rome's super-rich could hardly have been more spectacular, and it foreshadowed the fall of the Tang aristocracy: the main difference was that murderous endings, albeit not unknown, appear to have been far less common in the Roman case. Violence had nonetheless been central to this process, generously applied in the carving up of the empire. The eradication of the top sliver of western Roman society was bound to have dampened inequality. Moreover, and crucially, devolution extended far into the lower tiers of the propertied class as "even regional and sub-regional elites disappeared" in most parts of the former western Roman Empire. And although new military elites rose through these upheavals, in the absence of large-scale imperial reunification anything even remotely resembling late Roman levels of wealth concentration remained far beyond their reach. Increased peasant autonomy at least in some areas further impeded resource extraction at even the local level.[11]

This last development raises the question whether leveling was driven not merely by attrition at the top but also by gains at the bottom. One type of evidence that might be considered a proxy of material welfare, human skeletal remains, is compatible with this notion but is too ambiguous to firmly substantiate it. Indicators of physical well-being such as body height and the incidence of dental and bone lesions did indeed improve with the fall of the western Roman Empire. This suggests that ordinary people were in better shape than they had been under imperial rule. Unfortunately, we cannot safely identify the principal cause of these changes: although population loss and deurbanization in the wake of political disintegration may well have reduced parasitic loads,

[10] Breakdown: Wickham 2005: 203–209 .Quotes: Gregory the Great, *Dialogues* 3.38. Papal charity: Brown 1984: 31–32; cf. Wickham 2005: 205.

[11] Brown 1984: 32 (violence); Wickham 2005: 255–257 (quote: 255), 535–550, 828.

increased real incomes, and improved diets, a concurrent but causally unrelated pandemic of bubonic plague (discussed in the next chapter) was likely to produce similar effects.[12]

A different category of archaeological material holds considerably greater promise because it allows us to measure resource inequality in a more straightforward manner. In a recent Stanford dissertation, Robert Stephan studied changes in house sizes in different parts of the Roman world before, during, and after Roman rule. House size represents an acceptable proxy for per capita economic well-being: household income and residential house size are strongly correlated across cultures, and housing generally serves as a marker of status. Measurements from ancient and early medieval Britain are particularly useful for our purposes. The relevant data are broadly distributed in space and time, the quality of modern scholarship is high, and, perhaps most important, Roman state collapse was exceptionally severe in this region. Once Roman rule had ceased in the early fifth century CE, no centralized state claimed Britain for several centuries, and small polities predominated. Socioeconomic complexity was greatly reduced as villas were abandoned, urban economies faded, and all ceramic production ceased except for its most basic variety: manual fashioning unaided even by the potter's wheel. Settlement remains reflect no real signs of hierarchy in terms of spatial differentiation or the nature of small finds, and burials with rich grave goods are rarely documented in most parts of Britain. In short, local elites, insofar as they existed, failed to leave much of a mark on the historical record of the late fifth and sixth centuries CE. Roman-era structures were more thoroughly erased than in most other parts of the former empire: the island experienced pervasive systems collapse rather than mere state failure.[13]

This process profoundly affected the median size of residential structures as well as the degree to which houses varied in size, both of which decreased dramatically compared to the imperial period. This compression reversed the preceding increase in both metrics associated with the Roman conquest in the first century CE, which had raised economic output and stratification (Figs. 9.1–3).[14]

---

[12] Koepke and Baten 2005: 76–77; Giannecchini and Moggi-Cecchi 2008: 290; Barbiera and Dalla Zuanna 2009: 375. For the varied challenges of interpreting body height, see Steckel 2009: 8. For height inequality, see Boix and Rosenbluth 2014, and cf. herein, chapter 1, p. 59.

[13] House sizes: Stephan 2013. Cf. Abul-Magd 2002 on the distribution of house sizes in Amarna (New Kingdom Egypt), and Smith et al. 2014 and Olson and Smith 2016 for inequality in pre-Columbian Mesoamerican house sizes and furnishings. Britain: Esmonde Cleary 1989; Wickham 2005: 306–333, esp. 306–314.

[14] Reproduced from Stephan 2013: 86–87, 90.

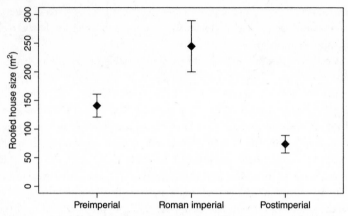

Figure 9.1 Median house sizes in Britain from the Iron Age to the Early Middle Ages

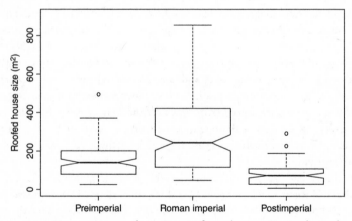

Figure 9.2 House size quartiles in Britain from the Iron Age to the Early Middle Ages

These findings make it all the more unfortunate that data samples from other parts of the Roman world that have been studied in the same way suffer from various shortcomings, such as reliance on a small number of sites or the lack of representative data for particular periods, and thus do not properly

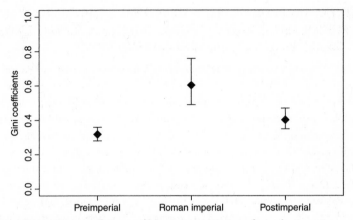

Figure 9.3 Gini coefficients of house sizes in Britain from the Iron Age to the Early Middle Ages

support further assessments of changes in housing inequality. Even so, archaeology offers us a glimpse of the correlations between imperial rule on the one hand and economic growth and inequality on the other.

Despite their geographical limitations, these data show that postimperial wealth deconcentration was a fairly comprehensive process that was not narrowly confined to those at the very top. Although we are unable to measure the overall degree of post-Roman leveling, the impact of state failure in an environment where the rich had ruled for centuries must have been very considerable indeed. The consequences of collapse differed greatly from those of conquest that preserved the scale and characteristics of earlier state structures: whereas the Norman conquest of England preserved or even briefly increased wealth inequality, the fragmentation of a previously very large sphere that had been exploited by a small central ruling class had very much the opposite effect.[15]

---

[15] See Stephan 2013: 131 (Italy), 176 (North Africa); but note that the Gini coefficient for residential structures in North Africa is also lower for the post-Roman than for the Roman period: 182. It is worth noting that this case study provides an instructive counterpoint to developments in ancient Greece, where economic growth and expanding house sizes did not coincide with greater variation, arguably thanks to a different set of sociopolitical structures and norms: see herein, chapter 6, p. 198. For post-Roman leveling, see herein, chapter 3, p. 88; for the Norman conquest, herein, chapter 6, pp. 200–201.

"MANY OF THE TOWNS OF THAT PERIOD DO NOT SEEM TO US TODAY TO BE PARTICULARLY IMPOSING": SYSTEMS COLLAPSE IN THE LATE BRONZE AGE MEDITERRANEAN AND THE PRE-COLUMBIAN AMERICAS

By the thirteenth century BCE, the eastern Mediterranean had turned into a system of powerful states interconnected by diplomacy, war, and trade: Ramesside Egypt and the Hittite empire in Anatolia were vying for supremacy, the Middle Assyrian empire expanded in Mesopotamia, city-states flourished in the Levant, and the Aegean was dominated by large palaces that managed economic production and distribution. Nobody would have predicted the rapid collapse of this state system in the decades after 1200 BCE. All over the region cities suffered damage or wholesale destruction—in Greece, Anatolia, Syria, and Palestine. Just after 1200 BCE, the Hittite empire failed, and its capital city Hattuša was partly destroyed and abandoned. The important city of Ugarit on the Syrian coast was wiped out a few years later, as were other sites farther inland. Cities such as Megiddo (in the plain of the biblical "Armageddon") followed suit. In Greece, the mighty palaces were destroyed one by one. What rebuilding took place in some of them was undone near the end of the century. Farther south, the Egyptian state lost control of Palestine and from about 1100 began to unravel, torn between the priestly elite of Thebes in the south and assorted dynasts in the Nile Delta. Assyria did not escape unscathed, either. To various degrees, institutions of rule and extraction fell apart, cities disappeared or survived much diminished, the use of writing retreated, and empires splintered into statelets and city-states. Output and exchange declined, and social complexity was diminished.[16]

The reasons for this great unraveling are still much debated, and many factors appear to have had a hand in it. The so-called "Sea Peoples," groups of raiders who "live on ships" and appear in records from Egypt, Syria, and Anatolia, have traditionally borne at least some of the blame. After their attack on Egypt was thwarted in 1207 BCE, thirty years later they renewed their efforts as a coalition. As Ramses III claimed,

> all at once the lands were removed and scattered in the fray. No land could stand before their arms . . . . They laid their hands upon the lands as far as the circuit of the earth.

---

[16] Cline 2014: 102–138 provides the most recent survey of the evidence for this collapse.

Although the pharaoh's forces managed to defeat them, other societies were not as fortunate. The settlement of the Philistines in Palestine may have been a result of these movements, as was at least some of the destruction visible in archaeological remains. Several sites also show damage that is consistent with seismic activity, repeated tremors that may have serially struck the region as an "earthquake storm" in the late thirteenth and early twelfth centuries BCE. In addition there is evidence of drought around 1200 BCE and a general shift to greater aridity. Whatever the precise configuration of malign forces operating at the time, it appears that different factors coincided, probably not by chance but in an interrelated fashion: the net result was a multiplier effect that shattered the world-system of the late Bronze Age.[17]

This collapse was particularly severe in the Aegean. Around the middle of the second millennium BCE, settlements grew in southern mainland Greece as warrior elites accumulated wealth and set up fortified centers. Increasing stratification is visible in the appearance of monumental tombs and socially differentiated grave goods. Palace complexes were soon erected at those sites. Clay tablets written in what is called Linear B script and in an early form of Greek document a redistributive economy that was centered on these palaces, lorded over by kings and their senior officials. Superiors claimed goods and services from those beneath them. This system owed much to earlier palace economies that had grown up on the southern island of Crete (known as the Minoan culture) but shows more signs of violence and fortification and less diffusion of affluence. Sizeable kingdoms were established around the major palace centers on the mainland, creating a network of polities now known as the Mycenaean culture.[18]

Even though we know much less about the nature of political control and the distribution of income than we would like, the existence of elite-focused redistributive centers seems hard to reconcile with notions of egalitarianism. For all we can tell, Mycenaean palace societies were very hierarchical. Patronymics recorded on the Linear B tablets reflect intermarriage among a small number of elite families: specific personal names, social position, and wealth all appear to have been controlled by the same privileged families. The tablets offer little evidence that finished prestige goods were allocated to the working population.

---

[17] Cline 2014: 139–170 and Knapp and Manning 2015 review various factors. See esp. Cline 2014: 2–3 (quote), 1–11, 154–160 (destruction), 140–142 (earthquakes), 143–147 (drought), 165, 173; and Morris 2010: 215–225 (collapse).

[18] On the early phase of Mycenaean culture, see Wright 2008, esp. 238–239, 243–244, 246.

As two eminent experts of the period aptly put it, "much of what goes up, stays up." Luxury items made of gold, silver, ivory, and amber are almost exclusively found in elite tombs. In at least one case, the archaeological material suggests that wealth circulation became more restricted over time, an observation consistent with rising inequality driven by the concentration of power and resources in the hands of a small ruling class. Circulation may have taken the form of gift exchange within palatial elites, supplemented by exports and imports meant to furnish them with foreign goods that signaled elevated status.[19]

The dismantling of Mycenaean civilization was a drawn-out process. Signs of destruction, possibly related to earthquakes, first appear at some major sites in the mid-thirteenth century BCE. Further damage is recorded later that century, followed by the construction of new fortifications—a telling indicator of military threats. A wave of destruction events followed around 1200 BCE, laying waste to the palaces of Mycenae, Tiryns, Thebes, and Orchomenos and, a little later, to all of Pylos. Here as elsewhere, the causes remain a matter of conjecture: seismic activity, droughts, and epidemics have been invoked alongside invasions, rebellions, and shifts in the pattern of trade and the movement of people. The final result was systems collapse, rooted in the palace system's inability to respond to the disasters that had struck.[20]

At many sites, Mycenaean civilization continued into the early eleventh century BCE. Although destroyed palaces were never rebuilt, reuse and new construction did at times occur, and in some places, elites flourished for a while. Refuge sites that could more easily be defended came to play a greater role. However, a new series of destruction events around 1100 BCE finished off much of what remained. After the palaces had disappeared, only villages survived, except in those areas where the former had been so dominant that little survived their downfall and widespread abandonment ensued, as in Pylos. Most regions, less severely disrupted, "returned to small-scale, tribal existence." High-quality building styles were gone, and writing disappeared entirely. The tenth century BCE was a nadir of overall development and complexity. The biggest settlements in Greece at the time may have housed 1,000 or 2,000 people, but most of the population resided in small villages and hamlets and adopted a more itinerant lifestyle. Many sites were given up for good. International trade

[19] Galaty and Parkinson 2007: 7–13; Cherry and Davis 2007: 122 (quote); Schepartz, Miller-Antonio, and Murphy 2009: 161–163. In one center, Pylos, skeletons recovered from wealthier graves even display better dental health: 170 (Pylos).

[20] Galaty and Parkinson 2007: 14–15; Deger-Jalkotzy 2008: 387–388, 390–392.

ties had been severed, housing was for the most part very basic—featuring one-room dwellings—and graves were poor. Individual burials became the norm, a marked change from the previous Mycenaean emphasis on lineage.[21]

The elite of the palace period were gone. We have no information on what happened to them. Maybe some of them left for the East to join raiders active at the time—not unlike English thanes escaping from the Norman conquest 2,000 years later. At first some may have decamped to remote sites for protection, on islands or near the coast. This need not concern us here: what matters is that this group vanished as a whole. The extractive superstructure the palace system had placed on the rural population had been shorn and was not replaced. By the tenth century BCE, only the biggest—or rather least small—settlements may have maintained something like a recognizable elite stratum. The character of grave goods from this period suggests that only few individuals had access to imported goods. In fact, signs of stratification and elite wealth had become so sparse that modern archaeologists have lavished their attention on a single structure, a house in Lefkandi on the island of Euboea that dates from about 1000 BCE: 150 feet long and thirty feet wide, made of mud bricks and surrounded by wooden posts, it contained two burials with some gold jewelry. What would barely have merited notice a couple of centuries earlier counts as a standout and remains unique among the sites discovered in this period.[22]

The conspicuous scarcity of large structures, prestige goods, and other markers of wealth and status in Early Iron Age Greece stands in dramatic contrast to the conditions of the Mycenaean period. Not only had polities crumbled, but social and economic activity had also both declined, becoming much more fragmented. Under these circumstances, substantial extraction and concentration of surplus would have been a serious challenge even if sufficiently powerful institutions had still existed. Although the general population undoubtedly suffered great hardship, the rich and powerful faced a much steeper fall. Systems collapse on this scale could not fail to massively reduce earlier disparities in income and wealth. What is more, even as new elites began to form from the tenth century onward and economic growth took off in the eighth, the miserable equality of near-universal impoverishment of the postpalatial period may arguably have

[21] Final phase of Mycenaean civilization: Deger-Jalkotzy 2008: 394–397. Temporary elite survival: Middleton 2010: 97, 101. For conditions in the post-Mycenaean period, see Morris 2000: 195–256; Galaty and Parkinson 2007: 15; Middleton 2010.

[22] Fate of the elite: Galaty and Parkinson 2007: 15; Middleton 2010: 74. Imports: Murray 2013: 462–464. Lefkandi: Morris 2000: 218–228.

prepared the ground for the resilient egalitarianism of later centuries of Greek history, a rare constraint on inequality that I discussed in chapter 6.

Two thousand years after the great unraveling of the Mycenaean palace system, the Classic Maya civilization in southern Yucatan collapsed in similarly spectacular fashion. By the Late Classic period (about 600–800 CE), state formation had advanced beyond individual city-states: cities such as Tikal and Calakmul became the centers of larger polities that claimed suzerainty over the rulers of other city-states, drawing them in through a system of visits, gift exchange, shared rituals, and intermarriage. Monumental construction flourished in the urban centers, where massive investments in temples and palaces were undertaken. Elite material culture rose to new heights of splendor: luxury objects including imported jade and marble abound in finds from this period. Conditions changed in the late eighth and early ninth centuries as regional powers faded and were supplanted by intense military rivalry among lesser polities. Growing interpolity conflict seems to have gone hand in hand with increasing exploitation and a growing gap between social classes. The proliferation of palaces within some cities, elite consolidation that is reflected in changing burial practices and greater emphasis on lineage, and cultural elite integration across political boundaries all point to heightened stratification and, in all likelihood, material inequality.[23]

In the course of the ninth century CE, new construction ceased at some of the main centers, and wholesale collapse followed, though not all at once: archaeologists have uncovered considerable geographical and temporal variation within Yucatan, as transition events in different areas were spread out over several centuries. Yet in the end, loss of social complexity was widespread and severe. In Tikal, one of the biggest cities, building activity ended by 830 CE, and maybe 90 percent of the population is thought to have left or have been lost eighty years later. Other major sites were likewise abandoned: the largest cities were most heavily affected while smaller settlements experienced greater continuity. Once again, the causes behind this downfall are contested. Modern explanations suggest that collapse may have been an overdetermined outcome as multiple factors interacted in undermining Mayan societies—most notably endemic warfare, population pressure, and environmental degradation and drought.[24]

[23] Willey and Shimkin 1973: 459, and cf. 484–487; Culbert 1988: 73, 76; Coe 2005: 238–239. Coe 2005: 111–160 gives a general survey of this period.

[24] Maya collapse, see Culbert 1973, 1988; Tainter 1988: 152–178; Blanton et al. 1993: 187; Demarest, Rice, and Rice 2004b; Coe 2005: 161–176; Demarest 2006: 145–166. Variation: Demarest, Rice, and Rice 2004a. Causes: Willey and Shimkin 1973: 490–491; Culbert 1988: 75–76; Coe 2005: 162–163; Diamond 2005: 157–177; Kennett et al. 2012; cf also Middleton 2010: 28.

Whatever the precise configuration of circumstances, it is clear that violence played a major part in this process. Its sheer scale is also well documented. Similar to what had happened in Mycenaean Greece, urban centers endowed with palaces devolved into warring centers and eventually declined to small villages. In the southern interior heartland, elaborate administrative and residential structures, temples, and the practice of erecting stelas were all lost, as were writing and the famous Mayan calendrical system. Production of luxury goods came to an end. Elite institutions and attendant cultural activities such as the stela cult devoted to noble lineages simply disappeared. In the pithy assessment of one leading modern authority, the entire ruling class had "gone with the wind."[25]

The main difference to Early Iron Age Greece lies in the survival and indeed flourishing of elite culture at major northern sites, most notably Chichen Itza in the Terminal Classic Period of the ninth and tenth centuries and then Mayapan and Tulum. Chichen Itza's elite weathered their polity's catastrophic decline in the eleventh century, which was linked to extended drought, long enough to ensure cultural and institutional continuity into the period of the Mayapan state from the twelfth and thirteenth centuries onward. In the south, however, and just as in Early Iron Age Greece, the preceding massive unraveling had not been confined to urban centers or the ruling class but rather had engulfed the general population: demographic contraction of up to 85 percent has been conjectured in modern scholarship. The basic economy of millions of people had been dismantled.

This raises the question how Mayan systems collapse acted on the distribution of resources. The wholesale elimination of state hierarchies and the material trappings of elite culture created an environment that would have been incapable of sustaining earlier levels of stratification and inequality. Even as the lives of commoners were harmed by growing dislocations, at least in the short term they may well have benefited from the end of customary burdens imposed by state elites. More specifically, one study has found a sharp decline in radiocarbon dates from elite contexts after the mid-eighth century as opposed to greater continuity in commoner contexts, which might suggest disproportionate attrition among the privileged, though the matter remains open to debate. Perhaps the best concrete data have been supplied by careful investigation of human remains from various sites in the southern lowlands of Yucatan. In the Late Classic period, distinctions between elite and subordinate burials

---

[25] Coe 2005: 162–163 (quote: 162); also Tainter 1988: 167: "The elite class . . . ceased to exist."

correlated with systematic dietary privileges: higher-status individuals ate better. That both of these features faded after 800 CE, at a time when elite products such as hieroglyphic texts with calendar dates became far less frequent, points to an attenuation of status difference as well as material inequality.[26]

Other early New World states experienced similar processes of decomposition and attendant leveling. Two telling examples will have to suffice. In the first half of the first millennium CE, Teotihuacan in central Mexico (northeast of present-day Mexico City) was one of the world's largest cities. In the sixth or early seventh century CE, after a period during which burials show increasing status stratification, carefully targeted fires destroyed the monumental architecture in the city's center. Huge stones were laboriously removed, statues shattered, and fragments hurled down. The floors and walls of the northern and southern palaces were burned, and great effort was put into reducing public buildings to rubble. Even some buried skeletons were dismembered, one of them endowed with rich adornments that denote elite standing. The presence of a political agenda seems clear, but less so the identity of the perpetrators who sought to eliminate Teotihuacan as a power center: local unrest may have preceded outside aggression. The implications for inequality of this targeting of elite and state assets are fairly straightforward: it is hard to imagine that the systematic physical dismantling of the ruling power was not accompanied by a dismantling of the polity's institutions of control and exploitation. Even in the absence of textual evidence, the idea that the existing elite might have managed to survive more or less intact is incompatible with the archaeological data, although though some of its members may have migrated and even maintained privileged positions elsewhere.[27]

The same is true of the fall of the Tiwanaku civilization in the Andean highlands, an even more dramatic case of systems collapse. Located at an altitude of almost 13,000 feet close to Lake Titicaca in the Andean altiplano, the city of Tiwanaku became the center of an empire that expanded from about 400 CE onward and lasted into the tenth century CE. In its mature imperial form, the capital had been carefully designed as an imposing ceremonial core,

---

[26] Decline of Chichen Itza: Hoggarth et al. 2016. Mayapan: Masson and Peraza Lope 2014. Commoners: Tainter 1988: 167; Blanton et al. 1993: 189. Relief: Tainter 1988: 175–176. Dates: Sidrys and Berger 1979, with criticism in Culbert 1988: 87–88; Tainter 1988: 167–168. Burials and diet: Wright 2006: 203–206. Calendar dates: Kennett et al. 2012.

[27] Millon 1988: 151–156. Cowgill 2015: 233–239 speculates about the role of intermediate elites who may have weakened the state by taking over resources that had previously been available to the authorities (236–237). Elite émigrés may have been involved in the rise of regional centers following the fall of Teotihuacan.

spatially aligned according to cosmological principles and surrounded by a huge moat that restricted access and that was meant to give the center the appearance of a sacred island. This enclosed area not only contained the state's principal main ceremonial edifices but also accommodated numerous residences for rulers and the associated elite, and even grave sites. The elite residential areas, which were opulently laid out and furnished, benefited from an elaborate water supply system. Local burials were rich in grave goods. Housing outside the moat was generally less lavish. Even so, consistently executed spatial orientations with carefully planned alignments, good-quality construction, and the presence of a wide range of diverse artifacts suggest that it housed a class of people that was of lower status than the sequestered elite yet much better-off than rural commoners. If analogies to later Inca culture are anything to go by, these more peripheral urban residents may have belonged to junior lineages of the ruling families or may have been tied to the latter through collateral of fictive kinship. Imperial Tiwanaku was thus expressly built and rebuilt as a center that served as a focal point of political and religious power and that serviced the ruling class and its associates. This purpose constrained the capital's size to a few tens of thousands of residents in a densely settled area that could readily have supported a larger urban population. For all we can tell, rural commoners were excluded from the city. Just as in Bronze Age Greece, artisans appeared to have been attached to the center in order to produce goods destined for circulation within privileged circles. Socioeconomic stratification was thus reinforced by spatial segregation that detached the wealthy and powerful few from the general population.[28]

There are signs that the power of rulers and elites further increased in the late phase of the empire and social inequality grew. Decline, after setting in, was rapid and terminal. Climate change in the form of severe drought is thought to have undermined Tiwanaku's complex structures of control. Its state collapsed, taking rulers, nobles, and their ceremonial center with it. The capital city itself was abandoned in stages and had completely emptied by 1000 CE. Archaeologists have unearthed tell-tale signs of extensive violence: the East and West Palaces in the center were both destroyed—the former, indeed, was completely razed to the ground. Just as in Teotihuacan, there is also evidence for the deliberate destruction of monumental ritual structures: sculptures, symbols of elite power, were defaced and buried, a task that must sometimes have required considerable effort. Whether factionalist conflict or other sources of violence

---

[28] Kolata 1993: 104, 117–118, 152–159, 165–169, 172–176, 200–205.

were responsible for these upheavals remains debated and may never be known: what is clear is that the political hierarchy did not survive these convulsions. The downfall of the center was accompanied by agricultural collapse in its hinterland. Cities disappeared from the Lake Titicaca basin for several centuries, as political fragmentation and localized economic activity became the norm. Population shrank and retreated into defensible areas, where extensive fortification of settlements speak to violent and unsettled conditions. As key sources of wealth, such as surplus extraction, specialized craft production, and long-distance trade, were lost, the old elite simply vanished.[29]

In other cases, we know hardly anything about the exercise of state power and how its collapse affected elite power and wealth. The Harappan culture in the Indus valley, with its numerous cities that flourished in the second half of the third millennium BCE, is a famous example. This whole system unraveled between 1900 and 1700 BCE, and many sites shrank or were abandoned. Once again, whatever system of hierarchy and differentiation had previously been in place could hardly have survived this process.[30]

For later generations, the physical dimension of systems collapse was often the most conspicuous. More than 2,400 years ago, the Athenian historian Thucydides noted that the cities celebrated in Homer's epics did not look particularly imposing in his own day. When the Spanish conquistador Hernán Cortés passed close to the Mayan sites of Tikal and Palenque, he did not even notice them, because they were covered by jungle and the area was largely depopulated. Imperial Angkorian sites in South East Asia shared a similar fate: the clearing of the main sites did not start until the early twentieth century, and Preah Khan Kompong Svay, an enormous city that covers ten square miles and that was sporadically used as a residence by Khmer rulers of the eleventh and twelfth centuries CE, is located in what is now the middle of nowhere. When I visited it with a companion in a helicopter in 2008, we were the only ones there except for a few guards from an isolated nearby village and a long snake.[31]

By obliterating much of the historical record beyond archaeological remains, all-encompassing systems collapse almost inevitably makes it impossible to

---

[29] Inequality: Janusek 2004: 225–226. For the collapse, see Kolata 1993: 282–302; Janusek 2004: 249–273. Specifics: Kolata 1993: 269, 299; Janusek 2004: 251, 253–257.

[30] Wright 2010, esp. 308–338 for decline and transformation; and see 117 for size variation among urban houses.

[31] Thucydides 1.10; Diamond 2005: 175 (Cortés); Coe 2003: 195–224 (collapse of the civilization of Angkor).

measure attendant changes in income and wealth inequality. At the same time, these cataclysmic events strongly imply compression on a grand scale. Whatever disparities and forms of exploitation survived into postcollapse periods were bound to be a far cry from what had been feasible and often typical in highly stratified imperial polities. Moreover, general impoverishment well beyond former elite circles by itself reduced the potential for surplus extraction and lowered the upper ceiling for resource inequality. Considering the exceptional nature of equalizing mass mobilization warfare, transformative revolution, and catastrophic epidemics, Ozymandian collapse may well have been the single most potent and reliable leveler in all of history. Though more common than one might think—many lesser-known cases could have been added—it was nonetheless relatively rare and mercifully so, considering the sheer amount of violence and suffering that accompanied such dramatic changes. By contrast, swift regeneration of state structures, often as the result of outside takeovers, has been a common outcome. The smoother the transition, the more readily inequalities would have been maintained or restored.

"MAY DEPRESSION DESCEND UPON YOUR PALACE, BUILT FOR JOY": STATE FAILURE AND ELITE DECLINE IN THE ANCIENT NEAR EAST

States have failed for as long as they have existed. During the so-called Old Kingdom period, Egypt's rulers kept the country united from the twenty-seventh to the twenty-third centuries BCE and created a powerful court in Memphis. The famous Great Pyramids of Giza are the most visible manifestation of centralized state power. Decentralization occurred in the twenty-second and early twenty-first centuries BCE as local governors gained autonomy and two rival courts emerged in the northern and southern halves of the country. Its effect on inequality may have been mixed: provincial rulers and notables likely gained as they diverted resources that had previously accrued to the center, while the wealth and power of the pharaoh and his inner circle declined: the latter is well illustrated by the comparatively poor quality of courtiers' tombs in the terminal phase of state integrity. Although the absence of more tangible evidence makes it hard even to advance conjectures, a weakening at the very top should at least in principle have shortened the outermost end of the tail of the income and wealth distribution.[32]

---

[32] As Adams 1988: 30 notes with respect to ancient Mesopotamian polities, among the oldest known states in history, "whether initially defensive or predatory in their orientation, neither cities nor larger, territorially organized states could permanently overcome the vulnerability that their physical and social environments imposed on them." Egypt: Kemp 1983: 112.

The spectacular collapse of the Akkadian empire in Mesopotamia and Syria might be expected to have had similar consequences, perhaps on a larger scale. From the twenty-fourth to the twenty-second centuries BCE, relentless campaigning brought in plunder that was handed over to temples, members of the royal family, and elite associates. Land across the southern Mesopotamian region of Sumer came to be owned by Akkad's rulers and their relatives, as well as by senior court officials. By allowing the accumulation of assets in different regions, empire precipitated much greater concentration of wealth than had previously been possible—a trend already explored in the opening chapter— and its eventual failure was bound to reverse this process. Later centuries imagined the fall of Akkad in an overly dramatized fashion, invoking a divine "curse" provoked by imperial overreach (the quote in the section heading is taken from the key account). Reality was more mundane: when power struggles within Akkadian high society, coupled with foreign pressure and drought, destabilized the empire, local polities in Sumer and elsewhere re-established independence, and the city's territorial sway shrank dramatically. Elite income and wealth at the top must have dwindled accordingly.[33]

More often than not, such contractions would have been short-lived, for new imperial powers picked up the pieces until they in turn succumbed to decentralization or conquest. In pharaonic Egypt, "intermediate periods" of fragmentation were invariably followed by renewed unification. From the twenty-second to the sixth centuries BCE, Mesopotamia came to be dominated by the successive kingdoms of Ur (known among scholars as "Ur III"), Babylon (under Hammurabi and later the Kassites), and Mitanni as well as by several iterations of the Assyrian empire and by the Neo-Babylonian empire. To give just one more concrete example, when Mari, a middling power on the Euphrates near the present Syrian–Iraqi border, was destroyed by Babylon's king Hammurabi around 1759 BCE, it took only a single generation for one of its former secondary centers, Terqa, to establish a new kingdom (Hana) that was effectively coextensive with the former realm of Mari and that had gained independence from Babylon.[34]

By contrast, wholesale collapse of the kind discussed in the previous section was relatively rare, especially in areas where new powers could rapidly arise and

---

[33] "Empire": Scheidel 2013: 27, summarizing existing definitions. Curse and quote: *The Cursing of Agade*, Old Babylonian version 245–255 ("The electronic corpus of Sumerian literature," http://etcsl.orinst.ox.ac .uk/section2/tr215.htm). Kuhrt 1995: 44–55, esp. 52, 55, offers a précis of Akkadian history and its ending. See also herein, chapter 1, pp. 56–57.

[34] Kuhrt 1995: 115.

take over. The fissure of large imperial states into several smaller political units would have put some downward pressure on income and wealth concentration at the very top, even if it fell short by far of the extensive leveling associated with more comprehensive forms of collapse. This presents us with a vexing challenge: premodern societies did not normally leave behind adequate evidence that would allow us firmly to document or measure the resultant attenuation of economic disparities. Yet we cannot afford to give up and turn our back on them—for the simple reason that these early societies were much more likely to experience intermittent state failure and deconcentration than much better documented recent or modern states. By disregarding the potential for equalization that was inherent in state failure, we risk neglecting a potent leveling force. In this situation, the best we can do is to search for proxy data that signal, however vaguely, change in this direction.

I limit myself to just one example meant to illustrate the complexities and limitations of this approach. After about 1069 BCE, in the wake of the Late Bronze Age crisis already described, Egypt came to be effectively divided between Upper Egypt in the south, which was under the control of the high priests of the god Amen in Thebes, and Lower Egypt in the north, with Tanis at the center. The inflow of Libyan military elements precipitated further decentralization in the north. Several autonomous regional power bases vied for control for part of the tenth century and then, especially, from the late ninth century BCE onward (a period conventionally associated with the Twenty-First to Twenty-Third Dynasties). This devolutionary process may have squeezed local elite purchasing power insofar as the latter depended on access to state revenues, other income streams associated with state service, and income from private assets or economic activity that was sensitive to state integrity. A cache of burials from Saqqara, the main burial site for the old capital city of Memphis, arguably reflects relative elite impoverishment in this context. The finds were made in a subsidiary shaft of the tomb of Tia, a brother-in-law of the famous pharaoh Ramses II of the Nineteenth Dynasty, at the height of Egypt's imperial glory in the thirteenth century BCE; this side shaft belonged to Tia's secretary Iurudef. A long time after, probably during the tenth century BCE, this shaft and associated chambers were filled up with coffins and burials. A total of seventy-four individuals were interred in this way, some in coffins, others wrapped in mats, and others still uncoffined. The generally poor quality of the coffins catches the eye. Although there are signs that the site was briefly entered by grave robbers in antiquity, they appear to have quickly given up, perhaps discouraged by the unpromising appearance of this assemblage. Workmanship was markedly poor compared to coffins of the same period from sites in the south of Egypt: they were put together from smaller pieces of wood and decoration was confined to key parts of these containers. Writing appears on only a few of them and in most cases is either fake, made up of meaningless pseudohieroglyphs, or corrupt and illegible.[35]

And this is not an isolated find: burials with similarly crude coffins with pseudolettering and only vestigial mummification have been unearthed at several other sites in Middle Egypt and tentatively dated to the same period. Yet even in their impoverished state, these burials reflect elite practice, as only the privileged would have had access to any anthropoid wooden coffins, however poorly executed. This can be interpreted as circumstantial evidence for the decline of upper-class spending power and demand in the Memphis area relative to the more stable southern region. Even royal tombs at Tanis, at that time the biggest center in the north, reveal widespread reuse of older objects, including ritual vessels, jewelry, and sarcophagi.[36]

It is true that coffin reuse had by then also become common among the southern elite in Thebes. In that case, however, the underlying cause is to be sought not so much in the elite's inability to pay for new ones as in the scarcity of raw materials created by separation from the north and, above all, in security concerns about rampant tomb robbery. The latter prompted a move away from expensive coffin elements that could be stripped off, such as gilding, and greater emphasis on the preparation of the bodies through more elaborate embalming, an investment that was not at risk from predators. The concurrent shift away from conspicuous tomb chapels and toward secret group tombs also fits this rationale. It is not surprising that we find no prima facie evidence for elite impoverishment in Thebes, considering that this group, led by the priests of Amen, not only maintained control over a large portion of Egypt but also took to looting the riches stored in earlier royal tombs and thus did not want for sources of income. In this regard, they differed from their status peers in the north, where more intense fragmentation and dislocations depressed elite income and expenditure and eroded specialized craft skills that critically depended on that elite's spending power.[37]

---

[35] Saqqara: Raven 1991: 13, 15–16, 23, and the catalog 23–31 with Plates 13–36; see now also Raven forthcoming. For the date, see Raven 1991: 17–23; Raven et al. 1998.

[36] Middle Egypt: Raven 1991: 23. Tanis: Raven et al. 1998: 12.

[37] Thebes: Cooney 2011, esp. 20, 28, 32, 37.

I have chosen this example to illustrate the difficulties of identifying signs of leveling in circumstances of more limited state failure. Comprehensive systems collapse generally produces archaeological evidence that leaves little doubt about the erosion of wealth and income disparities. Less dramatic dislocations, by contrast, cannot be expected to have left a similarly solid footprint in the often sporadic and ambiguous proxy data that is all we have at our disposal. In these contexts, any attempt to detect a dip in elite fortunes, let alone a general attenuation of inequality, is necessarily fraught with great uncertainties and will often fail to rise above the level of conjecture. Serious problems of interpretation add to this conundrum, most notably the much-discussed hazards of relating changes in burial practices or other depository patterns to socioeconomic conditions and the obvious question of whether it is legitimate to generalize from particular finds. Consideration of material such as the burials from Egypt's Third Intermediate Period takes us to—and perhaps beyond—the limits of how far we can push the study of inequality. Most leveling that was driven by political fragmentation took place in the premodern past, a potentially widespread phenomenon that will for the most part forever remain obscured from the modern observer. It forms a kind of "dark matter" in the history of inequality, almost certainly present but hard to pin down.

"THE COUNTRY IS SO BROKEN": CONTEMPORARY STATE FAILURE IN SOMALIA

However severe the limitations of much of the historical evidence, it lends support to the thesis that the violent unraveling of predatory states of the premodern era curtailed inequality by depriving established elites of wealth and power. This raises the question whether this type of leveling can still be observed in recent history or, indeed, in the world today. At first blush, the answer might seem to be negative: as we have seen near the end of chapter 6, civil wars in developing countries are more likely to raise than to lower inequality. Then again, although these conflicts tend to weaken state institutions, they are rarely accompanied by collapse of governance or reductions in overall socioeconomic complexity on the scale witnessed in some of the more dramatic premodern cases I have just discussed.

Yet some contemporary cases may at least come close. The eastern African country of Somalia is generally regarded as the most serious instance of state collapse in the recent past. Following the overthrow of the regime of Mohamed

Siad Barre in 1991, the country splintered into rival factions and territories and has since lacked overarching governmental institutions. While quasistates such as Somaliland and Puntland emerged in the northern half of the country, the remainder has been variously controlled by warlords, by militias—including the jihadist al-Shabaab—and, intermittently, by foreign troops from neighboring countries. Only in the last few years has the nominal federal government begun to exercise control in and beyond Mogadishu. Between 1991 and the Ethiopian intervention in 2006, Somalia was effectively a failed state.

Levels of human welfare are generally very low. One study that measures deprivation in Arab countries (broadly defined), based on factors such as child mortality, nutrition, schooling, and access to basic services, puts Somalia in last place. Data are so scarce that the most recent issue of the Human Development Index refrains from including the country in its global rankings but assigns Somalia the sixth-worst score on the multidimensional poverty index among all developing countries. The country was also found to have the sixth-largest proportion of the population living in severe poverty. There is no doubt that in many ways Somalia is "so broken," as its most famous export, the author and activist Ayaan Hirsi Ali, once put it in an interview.[38]

What concerns us here is a more specific question: whether and how the fall of the central government and subsequent fragmentation of the country affected income and wealth inequality. Owing to the shortcomings of the evidence, any answer to this question inevitably involves a great deal of uncertainty and needs to be taken with more than just a grain of salt. That said, there are various indications that when viewed in a broader regional context, stateless Somalia has been doing reasonably well not just in terms of economic development but also in terms of inequality.

The reason for this seemingly counterintuitive finding lies in the fact that conditions up to 1991 were extremely unfavorable for much of the country's inhabitants. Under the rule of Siad Barre from 1969 to 1991, the extraction of resources for the benefit of the dictator and his allies was the single most important purpose of government. Despite his initial avowed policy of clanlessness, Barre came to favor his own clan and others that supported him while treating others with brutality and targeting them for expropriation. Violence on an increasingly large scale was meted out to opposing groups. Land reform

---

[38] Nawar 2013: 11–12; *Human development report* 2014: 180–181 (and cf. 163 for the lack of an overall index score); http://www.theguardian.com/world/2010/may/08/ayaan-hirsi-ali-interview.

benefited politicians and well-connected urban businessmen. State officials and cronies stripped nationalized businesses of their assets and siphoned off much of public spending, 90 percent of which eventually went to administration and the military. Foreign aid, driven up by Cold War rivalries and the manipulation of refugee numbers, was diverted to the regime.

Corruption was extreme even by the unenviable standards of the region. Senior officials and the Barre family robbed the reserves of the largest banks, ultimately driving them into bankruptcy. A single nationalized bank catered to a politically connected elite, and the deliberate overvaluation of the Somali currency benefited affluent consumers of imports at the expense of exports by the poor, such as meat. Operating a "gatekeeper state," the Barre regime controlled the flow of wealth in and out of the country. In the aggregate, these nefarious interventions created inequality both within Mogadishu and between the capital and the rest of the country. Spending on social services was minimal. Thus even though a centralized government was in place, public goods were mostly provided by the informal sector and local bodies or groups, such as clan networks. Pastoralists, the majority of the labor force, were at best ignored and at worst exploited by the regime; they received hardly any public funds.[39]

Under these circumstances, the loss of state structures had no major effect on the provision of public goods. Fission even reduced violence, especially in the period between the withdrawal of foreign forces in 1995 and the Ethiopian invasion of 2006: violent conflict was concentrated in the years when the state actually fell apart, from 1990 to 1995, and when efforts to rebuild it first gathered momentum, from 2006 to 2009. Although warlords and militias extracted rents from civilians, constrained by scale and competition they did so to a lesser degree than the previous dictatorship, and taxation and obstacles to trade and business activity were much lower than before. As a result, Somalia has repeatedly outperformed or tied both its immediate neighbors as well as a comparison set of West African countries on various measures of living standards. Most development indicators improved after the collapse of the state, and the only main exceptions, school enrollment and adult literacy, were more affected by the decline in foreign aid than by any changes in state services. A comparison between Somalia and forty-one other sub-Saharan countries for thirteen measures of development shows that although Somalia ranked poorly

---

[39] Clarke and Gosende 2003: 135–139; Leeson 2007: 692–694; Adam 2008: 62; Powell et al. 2008: 658–659; Kapteijns 2013: 77–79, 93. Hashim 1997: 75–122; Adam 2008: 7–79; Kapteijns 2013: 75–130 offer general accounts of Barre's rule.

on all documented indicators in the final years of statehood, it has since made progress not only in absolute terms but also, and more remarkably, relative to many of these other states. This is true in comparison both with countries that had been at peace and those that experienced wars at approximately the same time as Somalia.[40]

Two factors can be expected to have depressed Somali inequality after state collapse: (1) the disappearance of a relatively unified national wealth and power elite that had greatly benefited from rent extraction and (2) the cessation of systematic policies of discrimination against the rural majority in favor of urban businesses and state officials. For what it is worth, the tiny amount of empirical information that exists is consistent with this prediction. Somalia's Gini coefficient of income for 1997 of 0.4 was lower than in neighboring countries (0.47) and in West Africa (0.45) at the time. The Standardized World Income Inequality Database registers a drop in Somalia's income inequality in the early 2000s, even though the margins of uncertainty are very considerable. It is hard to know how much weight to give the observation that the income Gini coefficient of 0.43 to 0.46 currently estimated for Somaliland, which is somewhat less bereft of central governance than Somalia was in 1997, is higher as well. Considering the nature of the evidence, we are on firmer ground in relating improvements in other welfare indicators to the demise of a kleptocratic and brutal state: in Barre's Somalia, government was indeed the problem and not the solution. Leveling through state collapse remains a more elusive issue. Even so, the case of Somalia lends at least a measure of support to the overall argument developed in this chapter.[41]

PREDATORY STATES ARE ALL ALIKE: EACH COLLAPSE LEVELS IN ITS OWN WAY . . .

The experience of a country such as Somalia under Barre's rule is of wider interest simply because predatory or "vampire" states in the developing world have more in common with premodern traditions of state rule that combined high levels of elite predation with low levels of public goods provision than they do

---

[40] Nenova and Harford 2005; Leeson 2007: 695–701; Powell et al. 2008: 661–665. Cf. already Mubarak 1997 for Somalia's postcollapse economic resilience.

[41] Inequality: Nenova and Harford 2005: 1; SWIID; Economist Intelligence Unit 2014. I paraphrase from President Ronald Reagan's First Inaugural Address of January 20, 1981, "government is not the solution to our problem, government is the problem."

with modern western societies. To be sure, multiple caveats apply. Premodern states generally lacked the intrusiveness of Somalia's "scientific socialism," which would have limited the amount of the damage they could inflict on their subjects. It is also necessary to qualify my Tolstoyan definition of predatory states, for premodern states are known to have varied substantially with respect to the quality and quantity of public goods they generated. There can be no one-size-fits-all template. Nevertheless, it is easy to see how the termination of states of the more rapacious kind could have yielded benefits for human welfare in general and inequality in particular—regardless of how many of their residents might have preferred odious governance to none at all. One economic model suggests that an unbridled predatory state might be more detrimental to welfare than anarchy.[42]

In some cases, collapse acted on inequality by making everyone worse off—but the rich more so. Substantial reductions in overall complexity, as in Early Iron Age Greece or Late Classic Yucatan or the post-Tiwanaku Titicaca basin, were most likely to produce this outcome. In other contexts in which disruptions were more narrowly confined to the political sphere, as most recently in Somalia, leveling need not necessarily have involved widespread worsening of living conditions but could have been achieved by affecting mostly those at the top. The security environment was bound to be a significant variable: the distributional consequences of state failure may vary a lot depending on whether it exposes the general population to invasive predation by outsiders (for example, intruders from the steppe preying on agricultural communities) or affects it less severely. Yet although the degree of leveling would have varied accordingly, overall outcomes were likely to be the same: a reduction in disparities of income and wealth brought about by the violent termination of state hierarchies and extractive institutions. The collapse of states and civilizations represents the third and most ancient and most widely traveled horseman of the apocalypse in the global history of leveling: one who trampled down inequalities just as he wrecked lives all over.

---

[42] Public goods: Blanton and Fargher 2008, a pioneering global cross-cultural survey. Model: Moselle and Polak 2001.

Part V

PLAGUE

Chapter 10

THE BLACK DEATH

THE FOURTH HORSEMAN: MICROBES, MALTHUS, AND MARKETS

So far we have focused on human-on-human violence and its effect on inequality: mass mobilization wars that encouraged bargaining in favor of the masses and that soaked the rich; blood-drenched revolutions that destroyed "land-lords," "kulaks," and the "bourgeoisie" alongside genuine "one-percenters"; and the collapse of entire states that wiped out wealthy elites who had extracted and hoarded as much of the available surplus as they could. We now have to consider yet another leveler—the Fourth Horseman, epidemic disease. It differs from the other three in that it involves other species but not in violent terms: yet some bacterial and viral assaults on human societies were much more lethal than almost any human-caused disaster.

How do epidemics reduce inequality? They do so by acting as what the Reverend Thomas Malthus in his 1798 *An Essay on the Principle of Population* called "positive checks." In its barest outlines, Malthusian thinking is rooted in the premise that in the long run, population tends to grow more quickly than resources. This in turn triggers checks on further population growth: "preventive checks" that depress fertility through "moral restraint"—that is, delayed marriage and reproduction—and "positive checks" that raise mortality. These latter checks, in Malthus's own words,

> include every cause . . . which in any degree contributes to shorten the natural duration of human life: . . . all unwholesome occupations, severe labour and exposure to the seasons, extreme poverty, bad nursing of children, great towns, excesses of all kinds, the whole train of common diseases and epidemics, wars, pestilence, plague, and famine.[1]

---

[1] Quoted from Malthus 1992: 23 (book I, chapter II) using the 1803 edition.

Phrased in this sweeping fashion, this inventory of "positive checks" conflates direct consequences of population pressure with events such as epidemics that need not be caused or even exacerbated by demographic conditions but that might be exogenous in nature. Modern research has emphasized the importance of responses to population growth and resource stress that increase productivity and thereby help ward off Malthusian crises. The most sophisticated neo-Malthusian models thus envision a ratchet effect in which population and production develop through tradeoffs between scarcity pressures and technological or institutional progress. Moreover, the Demographic Transition of the last 150 years is thought to have mitigated Malthusian constraints through a combination of runaway innovation coupled with declining fertility in the face of rising real incomes, a novel feature of modernity that cannot be observed in the same way in earlier periods of history. For this reason, Malthusian mechanisms are primarily relevant for our understanding of premodern societies, which are also the subject matter of this chapter. The best available evidence, for late medieval and early modern England, strongly suggests that severe manifestations of fatal disease in the form of epidemics represented at least primarily—though not necessarily exclusively—exogenous inputs that curbed population growth regardless of prevailing living conditions, even if they coincided with periods of resource stress that may have amplified their consequences.[2]

In premodern, agrarian societies, plagues leveled by changing the ratio of land to labor, lowering the value of the former (as documented by land prices and rents and the price of agricultural products) and raising that of the latter (in the form of higher real wages and lower tenancy rents). This served to make landowners and employers less rich, and workers better off, than before, lowering inequality in both income and wealth. At the same time, demographic change interacted with institutions in determining actual shifts in prices and incomes. Depending on workers' ability to bargain with employers, epidemics produced different outcomes: the existence of price-setting markets for land and especially labor was a fundamental precondition for successful leveling. Microbes and markets had to operate in tandem to compress inequality.

---

[2] Responses: the work of Ester Boserup is a classic (Boserup 1965; 1981). See esp. Boserup 1965: 65–69; Grigg 1980: 144; Wood 1998: 108, 111. Models: Wood 1998, esp. 113 fig. 9, with Lee 1986a: 101 fig. 1. Malthusian constraints: e.g., Grigg 1980: 49–144; Clark 2007a: 19–111; Crafts and Mills 2009. Inputs: see Lee 1986b, esp. 100 for the exogeneity of the Black Death and its seventeenth-century resurgence in England.

Finally, as we shall see, any leveling that did occur tended not to last and, except in rare circumstances, was ultimately undone by demographic recovery that resulted in renewed population pressure.

"ALL BELIEVED IT WAS THE END OF THE WORLD": THE LATE MEDIEVAL PANDEMIC

Sometime during the late 1320s, plague erupted in the Gobi Desert and began to spread across much of the Old World. Plague is caused by the bacterial strain *Yersinia pestis*, which resides in the digestive tracts of fleas. Rat fleas are the most popular hosts, but dozens of rodent species are known to carry plague-infected fleas. Those fleas generally prefer clinging to rodents and seek out new victims only when the original host population is depleted: this is what causes plague among humans. Plague occurs in three varieties, among which bubonic plague has been the most common. It is best known for the conspicuous enlargement of lymph nodes in the groin, armpits, or neck—common locations of flea bites—but is named for the blood-filled buboes that are caused by subcutaneous hemorrhaging. Cell necrosis and intoxication of the nervous system are the consequences, killing within a few days some 50 percent or 60 percent of those infected. A second and even more pernicious version, pneumonic plague, is transmitted directly between persons via airborne droplets emanating from infected lungs. Fatality rates approach 100 percent. Very rarely, the pathogen travels in insects, causing what is known as septicemic plague, which unfolds very rapidly and is invariably fatal.[3]

In the second quarter of the fourteenth century, rodents bore infected fleas east to China, south to India, and west to the Middle East, the Mediterranean, and Europe. The caravan routes of central Asia served as conduits of dissemination. In 1345 the epidemic reached the Crimean Peninsula, where it was picked up by Italian merchant shipping and introduced to the Mediterranean. Contemporary sources trace this process to the siege of the Genoese settlement of Caffa on the Crimea: when the plague broke out among Tartars besieging the town, their leader, Janibeg, supposedly ordered the corpses of plague victims to be catapulted across the city walls, thereby infecting the Genoese within. Yet

---

[3] I mainly follow Gottfried 1983, still the most systematic study, and Dols 1977 for the basic narrative and Horrox 1994 and Byrne 2006 for primary sources.

this was hardly necessary and would not even have been effective, for bubonic plague relied on rodents and pneumonic plague on human hosts who were actually alive. Existing commercial connections were sufficient to ensure the transfer of the requisite rodents and fleas.[4]

Plague struck Constantinople late in 1347, and it is to the retired Byzantine emperor John VI Cantacuzenos that we owe a particularly precise account of its symptoms:

> No physician's art was sufficient; neither did the disease take the same course in all persons, but the others, unable to resist, died the same day, a few within a few hours. Those who could resist for two or three days had a very violent fever at first, the disease in such cases attacking the head. . . . In others the evil attacked not the head, but the lung, and forthwith there was inflammation inside which produced very sharp pains in the chest. Sputum suffused with blood was brought up and disgusting and stinking breadth from within. The throat and tongue, parched from the heat, were black and congested with blood. . . . Abscesses formed on the upper and lower arms, in a few also in the jaw, and in others on other parts of the body. . . . Black blisters appeared. Some people broke out with black spots all over their bodies; in some they were few and very manifest; in others they were obscure and dense. Great abscesses were formed on the legs or the arms, from which, when cut, a large quantity of foul-smelling pus flowed. . . . Whenever people felt sick there was no hope left for recovery, but by turning to despair, adding to their prostration and severely aggravating their sickness, they died at once.[5]

After the deadly cargo had passed through the Bosporus and the Dardanelles, the plague hit the great Arab cities of Alexandria, Cairo, and Tunis in 1348. By the following year, the entire Islamic world had been engulfed by the pandemic, with huge losses being reported, especially in urban centers.

Farther west, the Genoese ships that had left the Crimea introduced plague to Sicily in the fall of 1347. Within the next few months, it spread to much of southern Europe. The populations of Pisa, Genoa, Siena, Florence, and

---

[4] Gottfried 1983: 36–37.
[5] Byrne 2006: 79.

Venice were decimated alongside those of many lesser towns. The epidemic reached Marseille in January 1348 and quickly ravaged southern France and Spain. The northward march of the plague remained unchecked: it struck Paris in spring 1348, then Flanders and the Low Countries. From Scandinavia, where it appeared in 1349, it made its way even to the remote outposts of Iceland and Greenland. In the fall of 1348, the plague entered England through its southern ports and made landfall in Ireland the following year. Germany was also affected, though less severely than many other parts of Europe.[6]

Contemporary observers told anguished tales of sickness, suffering, and death—of the neglect of funerary customs and of general disorder and despair. The experiences of the major cities were given pride of place by urban writers. Agnolo di Tura left a striking account of the plague in Siena, made all the more painful by his own tribulations:

> The mortality in Siena began in May. It was a cruel and horrible thing; and I do not know where to begin to tell of the cruelty and the pitiless ways. It seemed that almost everyone became stupefied by seeing the pain. And it is impossible for the human tongue to recount the awful truth. Indeed, one who did not see such horribleness can be called blessed. And the victims died almost immediately. They would swell beneath the armpits and in their groins, and fall over while talking. Father abandoned child, wife husband, one brother another; for this illness seemed to strike through breadth and sight. And so they died. And none could be found to bury the dead for money or friendship. Members of a household brought their dead to a ditch as best they could, without priest, without divine offices. Nor did the death bell sound. And in many places in Siena great pits were dug and piled deep with the multitude of dead. And they died by the hundreds, both day and night, and all were thrown in those ditches and covered with earth. And as soon as those ditches were filled, more were dug. And I, Agnolo di Tura . . . buried my five children with my own hands . . . . And so many died that all believed it was the end of the world.[7]

---

[6] Gottfried 1983: 33–76.
[7] Gottfried 1983: 45.

The mass graves mentioned by Agnolo recur in many other narratives, conveying a sense of the vast scale of loss of life. In Giovanni Boccaccio's classic description of the plague in Florence,

> such was the multitude of corpses . . . that there was not sufficient consecrated ground for them to be buried in . . . . So when all graves were full, huge trenches were excavated in the churchyards, into which new arrivals were placed in their hundreds, stowed tier upon tier like ships' cargo, each layer of corpses being covered with a thin layer of soil till the trench was filled to the top.

These accounts have since been corroborated by the discovery of mass graves in different parts of Europe, sometimes containing DNA evidence of plague.[8]

The devastation of the countryside, home to the great majority of the medieval population, attracted much less attention. Boccaccio had to remind his readers that

> in the scattered hamlets and the countryside proper, the poor unfortunate peasants and their families had no physicians or servants whatever to assist them, and collapsed by the wayside, in their fields, and in their cottages at all hours of the day and night, dying more like animals than human beings.[9]

By 1350 the plague had run its course in the Mediterranean, and by the following year it abated all over Europe—if only for the time being. Little would be gained by recounting the casualty numbers proffered by medieval witnesses who struggled to measure the immeasurable and often fell back on rounded or stereotypical figures. Even so, the 23,840,000 plague deaths calculated for Pope Clement VI in 1351 need not be wide of the mark. Modern estimates of overall losses range from 25 percent to 45 percent. According to the latest reconstruction by Paolo Malanima, Europe's population fell from 94 million in 1300 to 68 million in 1400, a drop of more than a quarter. Attrition was most severe in England and Wales, which may have lost almost half of their preplague population of close to 6 million and which did not reach preplague levels until

---

[8] Horrox 1994: 33. Mass graves: the Black Death Network, http://bldeathnet.hypotheses.org. Cf. also herein, chapter 11, p. 231.
[9] Horrox 1994: 33.

the early eighteenth century, and in Italy, where at least a third of the people perished. Reliable estimates for the Middle East are hard to come by, but mortality in Egypt or Syria is commonly put at comparable levels, especially after taking into account aggregate losses up to the early fifteenth century.[10]

Specifics aside, there is no doubting the vast impact of the Black Death. As Ibn Khaldun wrote in his universal history,

> Civilization both in the East and the West was visited by a destructive plague which devastated nations and caused populations to vanish. . . . The entire inhabited world changed.

Indeed it did. In the years during and immediately after the pandemic, human activity declined. In the longer run, the disease and the dislocations it had wrought left their mark on a wide range of attitudes and institutions: the authority of the Church weakened, hedonism and asceticism flourished side by side, and charity increased, boosted both by fear and by the demise of the heirless; even artistic styles were affected, and practitioners of medicine were forced to reconsider long-cherished principles.[11]

The most fundamental changes occurred in the economic sphere, especially in labor markets. The Black Death arrived in Europe at a time when the population had grown massively—by a factor of two or even three—over the course of three centuries. From about 1000 CE onward, a combination of technological innovation, improved agricultural methods and crops, and the abatement of political instability allowed settlement, production, and population to expand. Cities grew in size and number. Yet by the late thirteenth century, this prolonged efflorescence had run its course. As the Medieval Climate Optimum came to an end, an abundance of hungry mouths drove up the price of food just as productivity declined and demand began to outstrip supply. The advance of arable land stalled and pasturage shrank, reducing the supply of protein even as basic grains became an ever-more dominant staple of an increasingly meager diet. Population pressure diminished the value of labor and hence real incomes. At best, living standards stagnated. The early fourteenth century witnessed further deterioration when unstable weather conditions caused inferior harvests

---

[10] Gottfried 1983: 77; cf. also 53 (35–40 percent in the Mediterranean); unpublished work cited by Pamuk 2007: 294; Dols 1977: 193–223.

[11] Quoted by Dols 1977: 67. Gottfried 1983: 77–128 discusses the plague's manifold consequences.

that resulted in catastrophic famines. Although population levels declined during the first quarter of the century, subsistence crises continued for another generation, and epizootics depleted livestock.[12]

It appears that much of Europe was caught in some sort of modified Malthusian trap, in which endogenous problems such as an unfavorable land/labor ratio driven by prior demographic growth and exogenous shocks in the form of climate change that lowered output made life precarious for the laboring masses and favored elites who controlled the means of production—above all, land. The Black Death led to a dramatic downturn in population numbers that left the physical infrastructure untouched. Thanks to productivity gains, production declined less than population did, causing average per capita output and incomes to rise. Regardless of whether the plague actually killed more people of working age than it did those younger or older, as is sometimes maintained, land became more abundant relative to labor. Land rents and interest rates dropped both in absolute terms and relative to wages. Landowners stood to lose, and workers could hope to gain. Yet how this process played out in real life very much depended on the institutions and power structures that mediated the effective bargaining power of medieval laborers.

Contemporary observers in western Europe were quick to note the boost that mass mortality gave to wage demands. The Carmelite friar Jean de Venette reported in his chronicle around 1360 that in the wake of the epidemic,

> in spite of there being plenty of everything, it was all twice as expensive: household equipment and foodstuffs, as well as merchandise, hired labour, farm workers and servants. The only exception was property and houses, of which there is a glut to this day.

According to the Chronicle of the Priory of Rochester, attributed to William Dene,

> such a shortage of labourers ensued that the humble turned up their noses at employment, and could scarcely be persuaded to serve the eminent for triple wages.[13]

---

[12] E.g., Gottfried 1983: 16–32; Pamuk 2007: 293. See herein, pp. 331–332, for the crises of the early fourteenth century.

[13] Horrox 1994: 57, 70.

Employers lost no time pressuring the authorities to curb the rising cost of labor. Less than a year after the arrival of the Black Death in England, in June 1349, the crown passed the Ordinance of Laborers:

> Since a great part of the population, and especially workers and employees ("servants"), has now died in this pestilence many people, observing the needs of masters and the shortage of employees, are refusing to work unless they are paid an excessive salary. . . . We have ordained that every man or woman in our realm of England, whether free or unfree, who is physically fit and below the age of sixty, not living by trade and exercising a particular craft, and not having private means of land of their own upon which they need to work, and not working for someone else, shall, if offered employment consonant with their status, be obliged to accept the employment offered, and they should be paid only the fees, liveries, payments or salaries which were usually paid in the part of the country where they are working in the twentieth year of our reign [1346] or in some other appropriate year five or six years ago. . . . No one should pay or promise wages, liveries, payments or salaries greater than those defined above under pain of paying twice whatever he paid or promised to anyone who feels himself harmed by it. . . . Artisans and labourers ought not to receive for their labour and craft more money than they could have expected to receive in the said twentieth year or other appropriate year, in the place where they happen to be working; and if anyone takes more, let him be committed to gaol.[14]

The actual effect of these ordinances appears to have been modest. Just two years later, another decree, the Statute of Labourers of 1351, complained that

> said employees, having no regard to the said ordinance but rather to their own ease and exceptional greed, withdraw themselves to work for great men and others, unless they are paid livery and wages double or treble what they were accustomed to receive in the said twentieth year and earlier, to the great damage of the great men and the impoverishing of all the Commons

---

[14] Horrox 1994: 287–289.

and sought to remedy this failure with ever more detailed restrictions and penalties. Within a generation, however, these measures had failed. In the early 1390s, Henry Knighton, the Augustinian canon of Leicester, noted in his chronicle that

> the workers were so above themselves and so bloody-minded that they took no notice of the king's command. If anyone wished to hire them he had to submit to their demands, for either his fruit and standing corn would be lost or he had to pander to the arrogance and greed of the workers.[15]

To rephrase this in less prejudicial terms, market forces asserted themselves over attempts to contain wage growth through government fiat and coercion, as the individual interests of employers, especially landowners, trumped their unenforceable collective interest in presenting a united front to workers. And as in England so elsewhere. In 1349, France likewise tried to limit wages to preplague levels but admitted defeat even sooner: in 1351, a revised law was already permitting wage raises by a third. Before long, the going rate had to be paid whenever employers wished to hire.[16]

Thanks to the efforts of the economic historian Robert Allen and his collaborators, we now enjoy access to a number of extended time-series of real wages for skilled and unskilled urban workers that sometimes reach back into the Middle Ages and that have been standardized to facilitate systematic comparison across time and space. Long-term trends in unskilled wages documented for eleven European and Levantine cities show a clear picture. In those few cases in which preplague wages are available—in London, Amsterdam, Vienna, and Istanbul—they were low before to the initial outbreak and rose rapidly afterward. Real incomes peaked in the early or mid-fifteenth century, at a time when corresponding data appear in other cities as well and show similarly elevated levels. From about 1500 onward, real wages in most of these cities tended to slide, returning to preplague levels by around 1600 and then either stagnating or dropping even farther for the following two centuries. London, Amsterdam, and Antwerp were the only exceptions in maintaining more generous levels of compensation throughout

---

[15] Horrox 1994: 313, 79.
[16] Gottfried 1983: 95.

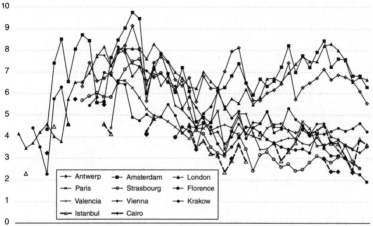

◆ Antwerp	■ Amsterdam	▲ London
✳ Paris	◦ Strasbourg	● Florence
✚ Valencia	✕ Vienna	◆ Krakow
△ Istanbul	✛ Cairo	

1300 1330 1360 1390 1420 1450 1480 1510 1540 1570 1600 1630 1660 1690 1720 1750 1780

Figure 10.1   Real wages of urban unskilled workers in Europe and the Levant, 1300–1800

the early modern period, even though in the latter two cities, real wages temporarily declined sharply in the late fifteenth century before they recovered again. Both the plague-related rise and the subsequent drop were considerable across the board—on the orders of 100 percent and 50 percent, respectively (Fig. 10.1).[17]

Much the same picture emerges for skilled wages in fourteen cities, again with a rough doubling between the immediate preplague period and the mid-fifteenth century wherever data are available, a widespread slide between 1500 and 1600, and stagnation or further decline until 1800, with the same three northwestern European exceptions as in the other dataset (Fig. 10.2).[18]

The linkage between demographic change and real incomes is striking: in all the cities under review, real wages peaked a little after population numbers had reached their low point. Demographic recovery reversed wage growth, and in many places, real wages continued to decline after 1600 as population kept expanding. Although rural wages are less well documented,

---

[17] See esp. Allen 2001; Pamuk 2007; Allen et al. 2011. Fig. 10.1 from Pamuk 2007: 297 fig. 2.
[18] Fig. 10.2 from Pamuk 2007: 297 fig. 3.

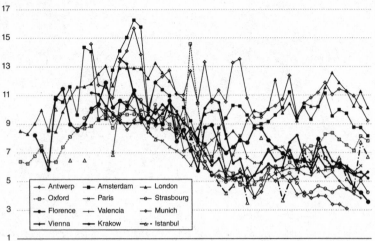

Figure 10.2 Real wages of urban skilled workers in Europe and the Levant, 1300–1800

a strong plague-induced increase is visible in the material from England (Fig. 10.3).[19]

Similar outcomes can be observed in the eastern Mediterranean. The cost of labor rose rapidly in the wake of the Black Death, albeit only for a period of time shorter than in Europe. As the historian al-Maqrizi remarked,

> artisans, wage workers, porters, servants, grooms, weavers, laborers, and their like—their wages multiplied many times over; however, not many remain, since most of them died. A worker of this type is not found except after strenuous searching.

Religious, educational, and philanthropic endowments proliferated, fueled by bequests from plague victims and gifts from survivors who had inherited wealth. This encouraged construction work in a context of labor scarcity, and artisans prospered alongside unskilled urban labor. The temporary increase in living standards boosted demand for meat: according to one breakdown of income

---

[19] Population and income: Pamuk 2007: 298–299. Fig. 10.3 compiled from Clark 2007b: 130–134 table A2; see also 104 fig. 2.

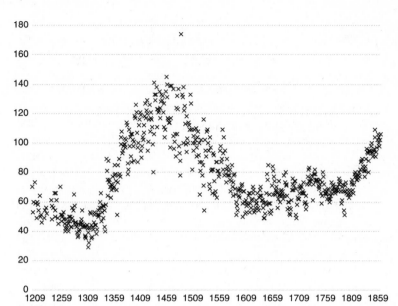

Figure 10.3   Rural real wages measured in terms of grain in England, 1200–1869

and prices, in the early fourteenth century, the average Cairene might consume a modest 1,154 calories per day, including 45.6 grams of protein and 20 grams of fat, but by the mid-fifteenth century was able to dispose of 1,930 calories, including 82 grams of protein and 45 grams of fat.[20]

Byzantine and Ottoman data are of uneven quality but broadly support a picture comparable to that for much of Europe. By 1400, Byzantine urban real wages had risen well above preplague levels, a surge that was mirrored by a doubling of slave prices. Ottoman records show that real incomes of construction workers in Istanbul remained high until the mid-sixteenth century and were not consistently exceeded until the end of the nineteenth century, which underlines the unusual character of the plague-related upswing.[21]

---

[20] Rapid rise: Dols 1977: 268–269, and cf. 255–280 on the regional economic consequences of the plague in general. Europe: Pamuk 2007: 299–300, and see herein, Fig. 5.9. Quote from Dols 1977: 270. Endowments: 269–270. Diet: Gottfried 1983: 138, derived from work by Eliyahu Ashtor.
[21] Byzantium: Morrison and Cheynet 2002: 866–867 (wages), 847–850 (slaves). Istanbul: Özmucur and Pamuk 2002: 306.

For all its severity, the initial wave of the Black Death alone would not have been sufficient to cause urban real wages to double and to sustain this increase for several generations. Repeated recurrences were required to prevent a swift demographic recovery. A whole series of subsequent plague visitations is well documented in the late medieval record. The plague reappeared in 1361, raging from the spring of that year to the following spring. Known as the "children's plague" (*pestis puerorum*) because of the large number of young people it killed, it seems to have targeted, above all, those who had not yet been alive at the time of the initial outbreak. It led to enormous mortality, second only to that caused by the Black Death itself: modern guesses posit losses of 10 percent to 20 percent of the European population and of fully a fifth in England. A relatively less devastating third plague occurred in 1369. This set the tone for the following century or more. To count only national epidemics in England alone, they are reported for 1375, 1390, 1399–1400, 1405–1406, 1411–1412, 1420, 1423, 1428–1429, 1433–1435, 1438–1439, 1463–1465, 1467, 1471, and 1479–1480. The final decades of this period witnessed particularly massive attrition, culminating in the 1479–1480 epidemic, reportedly the worst event since 1361. Whenever systematic counts are available, we can see that other countries fared equally poorly: we know of fifteen epidemics in the Netherlands between 1360 and 1494 and of fourteen in Spain between 1391 and 1457. Across Europe, the plague struck two or three times per generation, keeping population numbers down. As a result, by the 1430s, Europe's population may have been half or less than what it had been near the end of the thirteenth century. Varying by region, demographic recovery finally resumed in the 1450s, the 1480s, or as late as the sixteenth century. The observed improvement in the living standards of the laboring population was rooted in the suffering and premature death of tens of millions over the course of several generations.[22]

What do we know about the plague's effects on inequality? The underlying logic is clear. A reduction in the price of land and food and a rise in the price of labor were bound to favor the poor over the rich and thus were likely to attenuate both wealth and income inequality. For a long time, historians have relied on proxies that are suggestive of changes along these lines. Demand for wheat fell, but prices for meat, cheese, and barley (this last used for brewing beer) held up, pointing to improvements in diet that gave workers access to foodstuffs that used to be the preserve of the better-off. Demand for luxury

---

[22] Gottfried 1983: 129–134 gives a succinct summary.

goods grew more generally. In addition to higher wages, English workers could demand and obtain meat pies and ale as part of their compensation. For harvesters in Norfolk, the share of bread in the cost of diet declined from close to half in the late thirteenth century to 15–20 percent by the late fourteenth and early fifteenth centuries, whereas the share of meat rose from 4 percent to 25–30 percent within the same period.

A strong signal of leveling is provided by two sumptuary laws from the same country. In 1337, Parliament decreed that only nobles and clerics with the lavish annual income of at least 1,000 pounds were entitled to wear furs, considered a marker of status. But within fifteen years of the arrival of the Black Death, a new law of 1363 permitted everyone except the lowliest manual laborers to wear furs. The authorities merely sought to ordain which animal skins could be worn by members of which social group, from rabbit and cat at the bottom end of the social order to white muscalid furs at the top. It was a sign of growing mass affluence and eroding status barriers that even these more modest restrictions came to be disregarded.[23]

And whereas ordinary mortals were now in a position to afford what used to be elite prerogatives, the nobility faced crisis as the value of the agricultural products of their estates dropped and the wages of those who made them rose. As tenants were carried off by disease, landowners had to hire more wage laborers to farm, in return for better pay. Those still employed as tenants enjoyed longer terms of contract and lower rents. Society experienced a wholesale reversal of the earlier trend that had made the landlord class stronger and richer and most people poorer: now it was the other way around as the elite captured less of the surplus and others received more for about a century and a half. Land incomes for English rentiers fell by 20 percent to 30 percent in the first half of the fifteenth century alone. Members of the gentry suffered downward mobility, whereas great lords managed to maintain their standing on reduced income. The plague contributed to a dramatic contraction of the nobility: over two generations, three quarters of noble families were left without heirs, causing old families to disappear even as new ones emerged. Elite ranks shrank in size and fortune: the number of belted knights, which had tripled to some 3,000 during the thirteenth century, dropped to 2,400 by 1400 and to 1,300 by 1500, at comparable real income thresholds. At the top, the number of peers fell from 200 in

[23] Pamuk 2007: 294–295 (luxury goods); Dyer 1998 (changes in living standards); Gottfried 1983: 94 (ale and pies); Turchin and Nefedov 2009: 40 (Norfolk); Gottfried 1983: 95–96 (laws).

1300 to sixty in 1500, often thanks to downward mobility and mergers designed to compensate for declining family fortunes. The highest recorded aristocratic incomes also fell dramatically between 1300 and the fifteenth century.[24]

General developments such as these are strongly indicative of a degree of leveling. But only in the last few years has solid quantitative evidence finally emerged to support this. In a pioneering initiative, Guido Alfani has gathered and analyzed data from urban archives in Piemont in northern Italy. Information about the distribution of assets has been preserved in local property registers. Many of them record only real estate, and only in some cases do they include other types of assets, such as capital, credit, and movables, comparable to the detailed coverage in the famous Florentine *catasto* of 1427. These limitations leave us with inequality in landownership as the only variable that is susceptible to systematic comparative analysis. Alfani's survey is based on data from thirteen Piemontese communities. Although the oldest data set reaches back to 1366, in most cases records begin to be available from the late fifteenth century onward. Throughout that latter period, we observe a persistent trend of rising inequality. In most cases, eighteenth-century entries from each town yield higher Gini coefficients than the corresponding records from the end of the medieval period. This holds true for urban as well as rural communities—and regardless of whether inequality is measured through Gini coefficients or the wealth shares of the richest decile, both of which are used in Fig. 10.4. This general trend toward property concentration is emblematic of the ascending phase of a "super-curve" generated by the economic expansion of the early modern period, which I discussed in the third chapter.[25]

The most striking finding concerns the years before and during the plague. In the three towns for which data from that period are available, Chieri, Cherasco, and Moncalieri (which jointly account for the pre-1450 urban data in Fig. 10.4), inequality fell during the fourteenth and early fifteenth centuries, when the plague kept returning in wave after wave. In several Piemontese and Tuscan communities, the percentage of households that owned at least ten times median local household wealth declined during the same period. This leveling

---

[24] Gottfried 1983: 94, 97, 103. Tenant contracts: Britnell 2004: 437–444. Land incomes: Turchin and Nefedov 2009: 65. Heirs: Gottfried 1983: 96. Elite numbers and fortunes: Turchin and Nefedov 2009: 56, 71–72, 78.

[25] Alfani 2015. Fig. 10.4 from 1084 fig. 7, using the data at http://didattica.unibocconi.it/mypage/dwload. php?nomefile= Database_Alfani_Piedmont20160113114128.xlsx. For breakdowns by cities and villages, see 1071 figs. 2a–b and 1072 fig. 3.

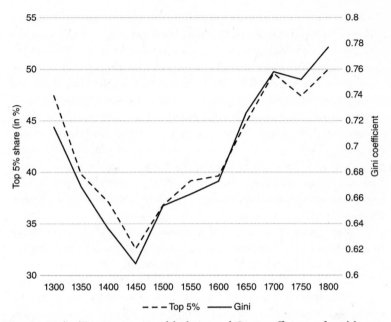

Figure 10.4 Top 5 percent wealth shares and Gini coefficients of wealth distribution in the cities of Piedmont, 1300–1800 (smoothed reference years)

effect is perfectly consistent with the data on real wages already reviewed: in nearby Florence, the real wages of unskilled workers approximately doubled in the same period (see herein, Fig. 10.1). Higher disposable incomes made it easier for workers to acquire property even as plague-related shocks caused devolution among the elite. The shape of the distribution is also significant, considering that the turnaround from dropping to rising inequality coincides with the demographic inflection point, when population numbers bottomed out and began their gradual recovery.[26]

Just as in the case of most real wage series, this compression of inequality was not to last. Not only did the concentration of landholdings intensify after the mid-fifteenth century and generally rise from then on, but also, more remarkably, the plague recurrence of 1630, which was the worst regional mortality

---

[26] Decline in share of wealthy households: Alfani 2016: 14 fig. 2 [*recte* fig. 3]. For this measure, see herein, chapter 3, 92.

crisis since the Black Death itself and which is thought to have killed as much as a third of the population of northern Italy, failed to have any comparable effect on inequality: Gini coefficients and top wealth shares in 1650 or 1700 were consistently higher than they had been in 1600, even after the preceding 150 years of recovery. This suggests that after the initial shock of the Black Death and its immediate recurrences, which hit landowners who were ill-prepared to deal with the economic consequences, the propertied classes eventually developed strategies for protecting their estates in times of demographic shocks: institutional adaptations such as the use of *fideicommissum* (which allowed property to be retained within the family even in the absence of suitable heirs) may have been instrumental in keeping elite holdings intact. It seems that even the most violent of epidemics could be tamed by cultural learning, blunting the leveling effect of Malthusian relaxation.[27]

A very similar picture can be drawn from archival data for wealth taxes from different parts of Tuscany. To give a particularly striking example, the distribution of wealth in the rural town of Poggibonsi is well documented from 1338 to 1779 and shows leveling in the wake of the Black Death and ongoing concentration thereafter (Fig. 10.5). Comparable evidence from ten other rural communities in the territory of Florence as well as the cities of Arezzo, Prato, and Sam Gimignano does not always produce similarly clear-cut results but mostly converges in revealing the same overall trends (Fig. 10.6). The only observed period of significant decline is associated with the plague; in rural areas, inequality generally grew from about 1450 onward; after around 1600, observed Gini coefficients were almost always higher than they had been in previous centuries, invariably peaking during the eighteenth century. Moreover, in several communities, the Lorenz curves flattened right after the Black Death, suggesting that leveling was driven primarily by losses among the wealthy.[28]

Further corroboration of these dynamics comes from the territory of Luca, where inequality underwent both a sharp drop and a swift recovery during and after the plague (Fig. 10.7). There is now also evidence of growing wealth

---

[27] See esp. Alfani 2015: 1078, 1080, and see also Alfani 2010 for a case study of the plague effects in the city of Ivrea in Piedmont, where postplague immigration of the poor immediately raised urban wealth inequality. Figs. 10.1–2 show that the seventeenth-century plague did not have a consistent effect on urban real wages. These differences between the late medieval and seventeenth-century plague phases underline the need for more systematic comparative study.

[28] Alfani and Ammannati 2014: 11–25, esp. 19 graphs 2a–b, 25 fig. 2. They also demonstrate why David Herlihy's earlier claims of rising Tuscan inequality after the Black Death are incorrect (21–23). Figs. 10.5–6 are from 15 table 2 and 29 table 4.

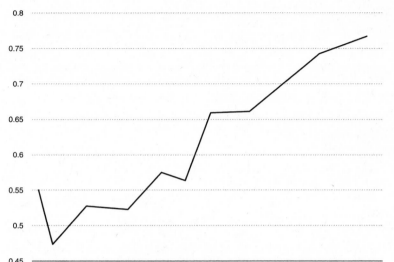

Figure 10.5 Gini coefficients of wealth in Poggibonsi, 1338–1779

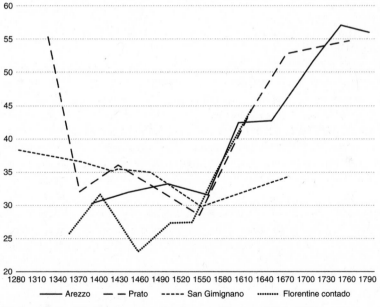

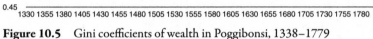

Figure 10.6 Top 5 percent wealth shares in Tuscany, 1283–1792

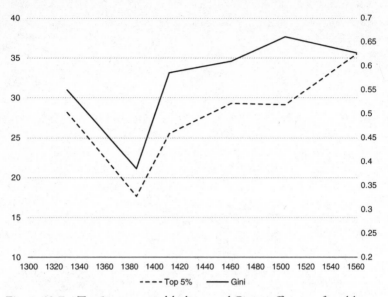

Figure 10.7 Top 5 percent wealth shares and Gini coefficients of wealth distribution in Lucca, 1331–1561

concentration in Lombardy and Veneto from around 1500 to 1600, but as yet preplague data are lacking.[29]

The Italian experience of the seventeenth century highlights the significance of factors other than demographic change as such. Abortive attempts to stabilize wages at preplague levels have already been mentioned. Elites had a powerful incentive to contain the leveling effects of the Black Death and its recurrences. The success of such measures varied widely between different societies depending on their power structure and even their ecology. In western Europe, workers benefited because gains from labor scarcity were usually passed on to them. Not only did restrictions on wages and mobility fail, but the demographic shock of the plague also largely killed off the earlier medieval institution of serfdom. Peasants asserted their mobility, moving to other manors if they offered better work conditions. This drove down rents and led to the commutation and eventual elimination of labor services that had been a standard feature

---

[29] Fig. 10.7 from Ammannati 2015: 19 table 2 (Ginis), 22 table 3 (top quintiles). Lombardy and Veneto: Alfani and di Tullio 2015.

of the manorial economy. Tenants ended up paying only rent and had the opportunity to work as much land as they could manage. This fostered upward mobility and led to the creation of a yeoman class of prosperous peasants. In Redgrave Manor in England, to give just one example, holdings averaged twelve acres in 1300, twenty acres in 1400, and more than thirty acres by 1450. All over western Europe similar adjustments occurred. By 1500, what is known as copyhold had become the dominant tenancy arrangement in Western, Southern, and Central Europe: contracts stipulated fixed annual rent payments based on the best deal that tenant-farmers could obtain through bargaining.[30]

On occasion workers resorted to violence in resisting elite attempts to deny them their newfound gains. As we saw in chapter 8, popular rebellions in the form of peasant uprisings such as the Jacquerie in France (1358) and the Peasants' Revolt of 1381 in England were the result. The latter was triggered by the imposition of poll taxes designed to offset diminished state revenue but was effectively motivated by the desire to preserve gains from higher incomes that had accrued to workers against lords who wanted to maintain their own privileged economic position: one rebel demand was for the right to freely negotiate wage labor contracts. In the short term, the uprising was put down by force, but although new restrictive statutes were passed and Richard II famously promised the peasants that "you will remain in bondage, not as before but incomparably harsher," the movement did deliver concessions to peasants: poll taxes were abandoned, and peasant bargaining expanded over time. Conservative poets of the period bemoaned "vagabond laborers" who "see the world in need of their services and labor, and . . . are arrogant because there are so few of them": "for the very little they do they demand the highest pay." By and large workers managed to benefit from labor scarcity, at least while it lasted.[31]

Yet in other regions landlords were more successful in suppressing worker bargaining. In eastern European countries—Poland, Prussia, Hungary—serfdom was introduced after the Black Death. The classic description of this process goes back to Jerome Blum, who observed in 1957 that central and eastern Europe faced the same problems of depopulation, abandoned land, and falling land and grain prices as were experienced farther west. The landed nobility resorted to legal measures to stem a decline in revenue, imposing ceilings on

---

[30] Gottfried 1983: 136–139.
[31] Gottfried 1983: 97–103; Bower 2001: 44. See also Hilton and Aston, eds. 1984, also for France and Florence.

wages and the price of urban goods. Unlike in western Europe, the powerful strove mightily to increase labor obligations instead of reducing them, especially labor dues, cash payments, and restrictions on freedom of movement. In various countries, such as Prussia, Silesia, Bohemia, Moravia, Silesia, Russia, Lithuania, Poland, and Livonia, tenants were prohibited from leaving without permission or without paying a large fee or all arrears, or except at a certain time, or in some cases at all. Poaching of workers was forbidden by law or lordly agreement; cities could be ordered to reject migrants, and rulers entered treaties for their return to their native countries. Tenant debt was a powerful instrument of retention. Obligations and restrictions continued to expand in the sixteenth century. A number of factors conspired to constrain workers, perhaps most important the growing political power of the nobility who held increasing jurisdictional sway over the peasants on their manors, alongside unfavorable developments in commercialization and urbanism. As nobles expanded their powers at the expense of the state and cities failed to provide a counterweight, workers were trapped in increasingly coercive arrangements. Although revisionist scholarship on this issue has come a long way in casting doubt on this classic reconstruction, the fact remains that outcomes for workers differed much from those in western Europe.[32]

A different set of constraints applied to Mamluk Egypt. As already noted, the country had been hard hit by the Black Death, and urban real wages and consumption levels had indeed risen as they did elsewhere, at least at first. However, an unusual configuration of political and economic power enabled the elite to resist worker demands. As a foreign conquest class, the Mamluks controlled land and commanded other resources in a centralized and collectivist fashion. Members of the Mamluk ruling class drew income from their individual *iqta'*, revenue assignments from land and other sources. When profits fell as a result of labor scarcity and disruptions in farming, the state's default response was to raise entitlements by squeezing a shrinking number of taxpayers harder. In urban settings, this led not only to higher taxes but also to confiscations, forced purchases, and the establishment of monopolies. These coercive responses help explain the short-lived nature of wage gains documented in late medieval Cairo.[33]

---

[32] Blum 1957: 819–835. Revisionism has now culminated in Cerman 2012.

[33] Dols 1977: 275–276. See herein, Fig. 11.2. However, Borsch's argument that certain urban real wages had fallen precipitously between 1300/1350 and 1440/1490 seems hard to sustain: see Borsch 2005: 91–112, with Scheidel 2012: 285 n. 94 and, more generally, Pamuk and Shatzmiller 2014.

Repression was even more severe in the countryside. The Mamluks were absentee rentiers disconnected from their estates, unable and unwilling to act as responsible landowners prepared to bargain in order to address changing circumstances. Maintaining rent flows was the responsibility of a centralized bureaucracy that formed an intermediate layer separating Mamluks from agrarian producers. These managers readily put pressure on peasants, resorting to violence if expedient. Peasants responded with migration to the cities and even revolts. Bedouins infiltrated abandoned land, a process that further reduced the revenue base. Moreover, owing to the peculiarities of the Egyptian environment, manpower losses caused by plague and flight were bound to disrupt an elaborate irrigation system that relied on ongoing maintenance. This rendered agricultural assets more vulnerable than they were in Europe. The shift in the land/labor ratio may thus not have been as great as in Europe if the amount of arable decreased apace. The combination of these features—the overwhelming collective bargaining power of Mamluks who relied on collectivist exploitation and controlled the state, their detachment from the land by intermediate management, the lack of technological upgrading to substitute capital for labor, producers' evasion of raised demands, and the consequent deterioration of the overall resource base—depressed production and incomes in rural areas. The contrast to the rise of contractualism in western Europe that delivered both higher real incomes to workers and significant leveling effects could hardly have been more pronounced.[34]

The different welfare outcomes of the Black Death and the persistence of inequality during the Italian plague resurgence of the seventeenth century show that even the most devastating epidemics cannot by themselves equalize the distribution of wealth or income. Institutional arrangements were capable of blunting the force of demographic shocks, manipulating labor markets by coercive means. One form of violence could be offset by another: if microbial assaults were met with sufficient human force to suppress bargaining, elites were able to maintain or quickly restore high levels of inequality. This means that the leveling effects of plagues were constrained in two ways: in time, inasmuch as they were almost invariably gradually unmade as population numbers recovered, and by the social and political environment in which they unfolded. It was thus only in some cases and for some time that epidemic disease substantially reduced inequality.

---

[34] Dols 1977: 232; see 154–169 for rural depopulation, and see 276–277 for revolts in the late fourteenth century. Combination: Borsch 2005: 25–34, 40–54. Contrast: Dols 1977: 271, 283.

Chapter 11

PANDEMICS, FAMINE, AND WAR

"WE WERE BORN TO DIE": THE NEW WORLD PANDEMICS

The Black Death of the mid-fourteenth century, together with its periodic recurrences that lasted until the seventeenth century in Europe and well into the nineteenth century in the Middle East, may be the best known of history's big pandemics but was by no means the only one. By the time it had finally begun to abate in Europe, the Spanish crossings of the Atlantic unleashed a similarly massive, and arguably even more catastrophic, series of pandemics in the New World.

Ever since rising sea levels had severed the Beringian connection between Alaska and Siberia at the end of the last Ice Age, the populations and disease environments of the Old and New Worlds had developed independently. Interacting with a wider range of pathogen-infested animals than their American counterparts, the inhabitants of Afroeurasia had increasingly been exposed to often fatal infectious diseases such as smallpox, measles, influenza, plague, malaria, yellow fever, and typhus. By the end of the medieval period, the gradual merging of the Old World's regional disease pools in the wake of commercial and eventually military contacts had ensured maximum coverage, causing many of these killer diseases to become endemic. By contrast, indigenous Americans enjoyed a less severe disease environment and lacked any prior exposure to these Old World scourges. Exploration and conquest opened up what Alfred Crosby called the "Columbian exchange," transatlantic contacts that swiftly introduced a plethora of lethal infections to the Americas. And although the New World returned the favor by sending syphilis the other way, the European pathogen contribution to the Americas was much more diverse and vastly more catastrophic.[1]

---

[1] See Diamond 1997: 195–214 for the differences between the pre-Columbian Old and New World disease pools. Crosby 1972 and 2004 are classic accounts of the Columbian exchange. For a very brief summary, see Nunn and Qian 2010: 165–167.

Smallpox and measles were the most devastating of the diseases introduced by Europeans: long endemic as early childhood diseases in the Old World, they struck the Americas in epidemic outbreaks. Although most sailors would have been exposed to these diseases in childhood and enjoyed protection as adults, occasional active carriers joined expeditions across the Atlantic. Influenza, the third big killer, provided no adult immunity at all. Those three were the most communicable of the novel infections thus introduced, transmitted as they were by droplets or bodily contact. Others such as malaria, typhus, and plague required suitable vectors to be introduced as well—mosquitoes, lice, and fleas, respectively. But this was only a matter of time.

Within a year of Christopher Columbus's first voyage, infections began to ravage the first European foothold, the island of Hispaniola. Its indigenous population dwindled from possibly hundreds of thousands to 60,000 by 1508, 33,000 by 1510, 18,000 by 1519, and fewer than 2,000 by 1542. Multiple epidemics swept through the Caribbean and soon reached the mainland. The first pandemic of smallpox struck in 1518, devastating the islands, and in 1519 caused enormous mortality among the Aztecs and Maya of Mesoamerica. Its impact was such that Aztec survivors would later count dates from its appearance, recognizing it a momentous event that ushered in a new era of terrors. Transmitted on contact and lacking remedies, it hit virgin populations with the utmost force. In the words of an Aztec observer,

> Sores erupted on our faces, our breasts, our bellies; we were covered with agonizing sores from head to foot. The illness was so dreadful that no one could walk or move. The sick were so utterly helpless that they could only lie on their beds like corpses, unable to move their limbs or even their heads. They could not lie face down or roll from one side to the other. If they did move their bodies, they screamed with pain.

In its unchecked ferocity, the epidemic paved the way for Spanish conquest: as Bernardino de Sahagún noted about the capture of the mighty Aztec capital of Tenochtitlan,

> the streets were so filled with dead and sick people that our men walked over nothing but bodies.[2]

---

[2] The following survey is based on Cook 1998. My section caption is a quote from the Mayan *Chilam Balam de Chuyamel* in Cook 1998: 216. Quotes: 202, 67.

Within a few years, in the 1520s, smallpox reached the Andean empire of the Inca, where it cut down vast numbers, probably including the ruler, Huayna Capac. The second great pandemic commenced in 1532, this time caused by measles. Once again, losses were enormous, and they extended from Mexico to the Andes. A particularly severe epidemic, probably typhus, devastated central Mesoamerica from 1545 to 1548. In later events, several diseases appeared side by side, as in the late 1550s and early 1560s, when influenza seems to have played a major role. More and more disasters were reported, culminating in the compound pandemic from 1576 to 1591, when a whole salvo of outbreaks decimated the remaining population, first typhus and later a combination of smallpox and measles (1585–1591), one of the most violent events to date. Epidemics continued throughout the first half of the seventeenth century, possibly with lessened force and great regional variation yet nonetheless highly disruptive. Even though mass mortality and attendant dislocation aided the Spanish advance, the new rulers soon sought to stem the tide and by the late sixteenth century deployed more physicians and imposed quarantines in the hope of preserving an indigenous labor force they could exploit. The effects of such measures would have been small at best: epidemics occurred in waves, about once a generation, and for the first 150-odd years, death tolls declined only moderately. Moreover, the violence of conquest itself, through the manifold economic, social, and political shocks it inflicted on indigenous populations, could hardly have failed to exacerbate the overall mortality crisis.

The cumulative demographic impact was undoubtedly catastrophic. The only real question concerns the scale of loss of life, a problem that has exercised generations of scholars but that is made hard to address by the absence of solid information on precontact population levels. For Mexico alone, cumulative attrition ranging from some 20 percent to some 90 percent has been proposed in the literature. Most estimates put total losses above half. It seems reasonable to conclude that the mortality levels associated with the Black Death should best be considered a mere minimum for the New World. Overall depletion by at least half seems likely for Mexico, and much higher levels of loss seem possible at least for more limited areas.[3]

---

[3] For the debate, see McCaa 2000; Newson 2006; Livi Bacci 2008 (who emphasizes the multiplicity of causal factors). Arroyo Abad, Davies, and van Zanden 2012: 158 note that the quadrupling of real wages in Mexico between the sixteenth and the mid-seventeenth century is logically consistent with a population loss of about 90 percent, a tantalizing if inconclusive bit of support for very high mortality estimates; see herein. I follow McCaa 2000: 258.

It has long been an open question whether this dramatic demographic contraction compressed resource inequality. The evolution of wealth would have been mediated by shifts in state power as the stratified empires of the Aztecs and Inca were replaced by similarly stratified Spanish dominions. Hard data are required to determine how demographic change played out in labor markets. Jeffrey Williamson, in a bold attempt to sketch out a "history without evidence" of Latin American inequality, merely observed that standard Malthusian logic predicted rising real wages in response to the huge population losses that had occurred in the sixteenth century but was unable to cite evidence in support of this conjecture. In 2014, a pioneering study of incomes in Latin America during three centuries starting in the 1530s finally changed this situation. Fig. 11.1 shows the rise and fall of real wages of workers in the Mexico City area.[4]

Figure 11.1   Real wages expressed in multiples of bare-bones consumption baskets in central Mexico, 1520–1820 (ten-year moving average)

---

[4] Williamson: 2009: 15; Arroyo Abad, Davies, and van Zanden 2012. Fig. 11.1 from 156 fig. 1, using the data at http://gpih.ucdavis.edu/Datafilelist.htm#Latam.

This inverted U-curve invites a Malthusian interpretation of changing wages in response to population decline and subsequent recovery, but the lack of progress in the sixteenth century, when epidemic mortality was particularly severe, is in need of explanation. The answer probably lies in Spanish reliance on coercion to secure labor in the face of demographic contraction, a practice rooted in pre-Columbian regimes of forced labor. Government intervention may consequently have suppressed wage bargaining for an extended period of time. This interpretation meshes well with the fact that coercion was at its most intense in the early stages of Spanish rule in Mexico. Thus, the "encomienda"— a grant to extract labor and tribute from the indigenous population that was assigned to individual beneficiaries—was the standard form of elite remuneration in the first generation after the conquest. This arrangement was abolished in 1601 except for mining, although it de facto persisted into the 1630s. Even so, the total number of encomiendas had already dropped from 537 in 1550 to 126 by 1560.

Initially, wages were also subject to severe constraints that were relaxed over time. In sixteenth-century Mexico, the viceroyalty set wages and coercion was ubiquitous. From the early seventeenth century, liberalization of labor markets allowed real wages to rise. The results were remarkable: whereas in 1590 workers were still remunerated at a minimal subsistence level, by 1700 real wages were not much behind northwestern European levels, thought to be the highest in the world at the time. If the observed sixteenth-century lag was caused by state intervention, subsequent liberalization permitted labor scarcity to be reflected in actual compensation levels. Unlike western European labor statutes at the time of the Black Death that generally had little effect, the more deeply entrenched mode of forced labor in Mexico bestowed greater powers of intervention on the authorities. And workers' gains did not persist for very long: real wages declined from the 1770s onward and by 1810 had returned to bare subsistence.[5]

By far the most striking feature of the increase of real wages in Mexico is its tremendous scale, by a factor of four as opposed to a "mere" doubling in the cities of western Europe after the Black Death. The Mexican surge is logically consistent with, and thus may well imply, much more massive loss of life. The later downturn in real incomes is reminiscent of analogous developments in much of early modern Europe—albeit once again more substantial than in the

[5] Arroyo Abad, Davies, and van Zanden 2012: 156–159.

latter case and indeed stronger than predicted by demographic recovery alone. Even though the observed scale of these changes may raise doubts about the reliability of the record, the overall picture seems clear. Several generations of workers benefited from labor scarcity after it had become so severe that market institutions could no longer be prevented from mediating compensation levels. This phase was followed by a return to the unhappy status quo ante as population grew and the bargaining power of workers declined.

Proxies of well-being such as general living standards and human stature are broadly compatible with the observed rise in real wages. However, as so often in premodern history, we lack the data needed to ascertain the impact of these developments on income inequality as such. In the most general terms it is hard to imagine that a quadrupling of real incomes of workers could have failed to have some leveling effect overall, but for now we are unable to advance beyond this basic intuition. At the risk of engaging in circular reasoning, it is fair to say that the emerging New World data, for all their limitations, are compatible both with the logic of plague-driven leveling and with empirical postplague data from Europe a few centuries earlier. Although Spanish conquest elites would have assumed the positions formerly occupied by the Aztec ruling class, thereby preserving asset concentration at the very top of society, a strong increase in the real income of at least some workers ought to have attenuated overall inequality to some degree, however temporary this may have turned out to be. It is likely that seventeenth-century Mexico shared this feature with fifteenth-century western Europe.[6]

"THE DEAD OUTNUMBERED THE LIVING": THE JUSTINIANIC PLAGUE

The search for further examples of leveling caused by pandemics takes us farther back in time. The Black Death of the fourteenth century was not the first plague pandemic of the Old World. Back 800 years earlier, the same disease had already struck and ravaged Europe and the Middle East in much the same way during a pandemic known as the Justinianic Plague, which lasted from 541 to about 750 CE. On that occasion, the plague first appeared in Pelusium on the coast between Egypt and Palestine in July 541, spreading to nearby Gaza by August and to the Egyptian metropolis of Alexandria by September. On March 1 of the

---

[6] Contra Williamson 2009: 14, it is not obvious *a priori* that Spanish conquest would have greatly raised inequality from pre-Columbian levels, at least not in the territory of the highly exploitative and stratified Aztec and Inca empires.

following year, the East Roman emperor Justinian claimed that "the incidence of death has traversed all places," although the imperial capital Constantinople itself was struck only about a month later, with devastating consequences:

> Now the disease in Byzantium ran a course of four months, and its greatest virulence lasted about three. And at first the deaths were a little more than the normal, then the mortality rose still higher, and afterwards the tale of dead reached five thousand each day, and again it even came to ten thousand and still more than that. Now in the beginning each man attended to the burial of the dead of his own house, and these they threw even into the tombs of others, either escaping detection or using violence; but afterwards confusion and disorder everywhere became complete.... And when it came about that all the tombs which had existed previously were filled with the dead, then they dug up all the places about the city one after the other, laid the dead there, each one as he could, and departed; but later on those who were making these trenches, no longer able to keep up with the number of the dying, mounted the towers of the fortifications in Sycae, and tearing off the roofs threw the bodies in there in complete disorder; and they piled them up just as each one happened to fall, and filled practically all the towers with corpses, and then covered them again with their roofs.

Just as it would eight centuries later, the epidemic proved unstoppable: Syria was hit in the summer of 542, North Africa later in the same year, and Italy, Spain, southern France, and the Balkans in 543. Numerous waves followed: one modern count identifies as many as eighteen separate iterations between 541 and 750, with outbreaks documented for Iran and Mesopotamia in the east; the Iberian peninsula in the west; Britain, Ireland, and Scandinavia in the north; Yemen in the south; and all the regions in between.[7]

The historical accounts are consistent with *Y. pestis*. Byzantine sources repeatedly emphasize swellings in the groin, the classic symptom of bubonic plague. Swellings were said to appear elsewhere as well—in armpits, behind the ears, or on thighs; likewise black carbuncles that were regarded as a harbinger

---

[7] The literature is fairly large: the most comprehensive recent survey is Stathakopoulos 2004: 110–154, to be used alongside the case studies in Little 2007. Specifically for the initial wave, see also the convenient discussion by Horden 2005. The quote in the section caption is from ancient sources referenced in Stathakopoulos 2004: 141, and the quote is from Procopius, *Persian War* 2.23.

of imminent death; and coma, delirium, vomiting of blood, and raging fevers. What is more, molecular biology has now confirmed the presence of *Y. pestis* at the time. Ten of twelve skeletons from a late Roman cemetery in Aschheim in Bavaria show elements of *Y. pestis* DNA, two of them in sufficient quantity to reconstruct the entire DNA sequence of the bacterium. Beads found on one of these skeletons date it roughly to the second quarter of the sixth century CE, the time of the initial outbreak of the Justinianic Plague.[8]

Reported mortality figures tend to be very high but generally seem unreliable. Observers imagined that the initial outbreak in Constantinople carried off thousands of—even as many as 10,000—people each day, reducing the city's population by more than half. Similarly extreme claims were occasionally made for later outbreaks in the same and other locations. What cannot be in doubt is the overwhelming impression of massive mortality, to which observers attached stereotypical numbers. Considering that the disease was the same as in the late Middle Ages and was active for a comparable amount of time, we may suspect that overall attrition was also similar, perhaps on the order of a quarter or a third of the population of western Eurasia and North Africa. Mass mortality on this scale was bound to have a powerful effect on the labor supply. In Constantinople, the senior church official John of Ephesus rather insensitively complained about the profits made by those who disposed of the bodies of plague victims and about the rising cost of laundry. A mere three years after the plague's first appearance, the emperor Justinian condemned rising demands by workers and sought to ban them by government fiat:

> We have ascertained that, in spite of the punishment inflicted by Our Lord God, persons engaged in trade and literary pursuits, as well as artisans and agriculturists of different kinds, and sailors, when they should lead better lives, have devoted themselves to the acquisition of gain, and demand double and triple wages and salaries, in violation of ancient customs. Hence it has seemed advisable to us, by means of this imperial edict, to forbid all persons to yield to the detestable passion of avarice; in order that no one who is the master of any art or trade, or any merchant of any description, or anyone engaged in agricultural pursuits, may, hereafter, demand as salary or wages more than ancient

---

[8] Symptoms: Stathakopoulos 2004: 135–137; DNA: Wagner et al. 2014; Michael McCormick, personal communication. Corroborating evidence from a second site is currently in the process of being published.

custom prescribes. We also decree that the measurers of buildings, tillable land, and other property, shall not charge more for their services than is just and that they shall observe the established practice in this respect. We order that these rules shall be observed by those who have control of the work, as well as by those who purchase the materials. We do not permit them to pay more than is authorized by common usage. They are hereby notified that anyone who demands more than this, and who is convicted of having accepted or given more than was agreed upon in the beginning, will be compelled to pay three times the amount to the treasury.[9]

This is the earliest known attempt to contain bargaining power in the face of an epidemic, a precursor to similar measures in medieval England and France and in early Spanish Mexico. But as the plague lingered and demand for labor grew, this decree's effect on wages would have been limited at best. We may legitimately assume real wage growth to have been widespread, as economists have readily surmised, even though empirical evidence is limited to the Middle East, especially Egypt, where documentary evidence has survived to an unparalleled extent. Egyptian records of real wages go back to the third century BCE. But this evidence is discontinuous: for the first thousand years, the documentation refers to unskilled rural wages; in the medieval period, to unskilled urban wages. Although these data cannot thus be put on the same footing, they do reflect the same trends and cohere into a single overarching narrative. Among rural wages, we mostly encounter daily wages of 3.5 to 5 liters of wheat equivalent, well within the core range of 3.5 to 6.5 liters that was typical of premodern societies and associated with living standards close to physiological subsistence. By contrast, much higher wheat wages, in excess of 10 liters, are attested for the late sixth, seventh, and eighth centuries CE (Fig. 11.2).[10]

This surge in real incomes is derived from papyrological evidence for the compensation of unskilled rural workers in the aftermath of the Justinianic Plague. In several records from the late sixth and seventh centuries CE, when the demographic impact of the plague ought to have peaked, irrigation workers are reported to have received cash wages equivalent to 13.1 to 13.4 liters of wheat

---

[9] Stathakopoulos 2004: 139–141 (numbers). McCormick 2015 surveys archaeological evidence for mass graves from this period. John of Ephesus: Patlagean 1977: 172. Quote: *Novella* 122 (April 544 CE).
[10] Economists: Findlay and Lundahl 2006: 173, 177. Egyptian evidence: Fig. 11.2 is constructed from Scheidel 2010: 448 and Pamuk and Shatzmiller 2014: 202 table 2.

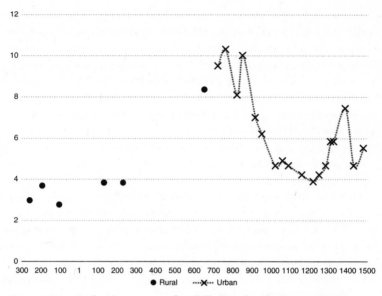

Figure 11.2   Daily wheat wages of unskilled rural and urban workers in Egypt, third century BCE to fifteenth century CE (in kilograms of wheat)

per day, or about three times as much as before. In other cases from the same period, we hear of combined cash wages and food allowances worth in excess of 7.7 to 10.9 liters of wheat per day, or roughly twice as much as before. These findings are supported by evidence for even higher wages for skilled workers, of up to 25 liters per day. Further corroboration is provided by the observation that from the first to the second half of the sixth century—that is, from right before the first plague outbreak to right after it—the proportion of extant land leases of infinite duration rose from about 17 percent to 39 percent, whereas those of one year's duration fell from 29 percent to 9 percent of the total. This suggests that tenants were quickly able to command more favorable terms. This, and especially the extraordinary surge in real incomes, is explicable only in the context of a huge increase in the bargaining power of workers across professions, both skilled and unskilled, in response to massive demographic attrition.[11]

---

[11] Scheidel 2010: 448–449; Sarris 2007: 130–131, reporting on Jairus Banaji's unpublished Oxford dissertation of 1992.

The second part of the story is provided by wheat wages for unskilled urban workers in Cairo. As shown in Fig. 11.2, these data become available only during the final stages of the plague period in the early eighth century but continue to the end of the Middle Ages. Real incomes were elevated until about 850, a century after the final attestation of plague in Egypt in the 740s, at historically high levels of mostly around 10 liters of wheat equivalent per day, or close to three times basic subsistence for a family of four. Over the following 350 years, as population recovered, Cairene wheat wages slid by more than half to the lowest physiologically sustainable levels until they temporarily recovered in the wake of the Black Death in the late fourteenth century. Lower-quality data from Baghdad also show a secular decline of real incomes between the eighth and thirteenth centuries, albeit on a somewhat lesser scale. A similar picture emerges from the reconstruction of consumption baskets that relate the nominal wages of unskilled urban workers in Cairo to the price of a basic range of consumer goods. This exercise also points to higher real incomes during and right after the plague, followed by decline and then another recovery at the time of the Black Death: although the scale of variation is somewhat less than for wheat wages alone, the overall pattern is the same.[12]

Just as in the late Middle Ages, serial recurrences of the Justinianic Plague depressed population numbers for a long time. In Egypt, we hear of ten episodes covering thirty-two years between 541 and 744, or during one of every six years. Southern Mesopotamia experienced fourteen episodes lasting thirty-eight years from 558 to 843, or during one out of every seven and a half years. There are even more attestations for Syria and Palestine, regions for which income data are lacking. Şevket Pamuk and Maya Shatzmiller trace what is often considered the "Golden Age of Islam" from the eighth to the eleventh centuries CE to the high-wage environment created by the plague, which in their view resembled in some ways the Black Death's effect on tastes and consumption in parts of late medieval Europe. A telling sign comes in the form of source references to widespread consumption of meat and dairy among the salaried middle classes, which was predicated on an expansion of animal husbandry. Other factors were urbanization and concurrent growing division of labor and demand for manufactured goods, as well as imported foodstuffs and clothing beyond a narrow elite.[13]

---

[12] For the Cairene data, see Pamuk and Shatzmiller 2014: 198–204, and see 205 for the calculation of wheat wages based on the assumption of 250 working days per year. Baghdad: 204 fig. 2. Consumption basket: 206–208, esp. 207 fig. 3.

[13] Pamuk and Shatzmiller 2014: 209 Table 3A (outbreaks), 216–218 (Golden Age).

Yet, once again, the effect of these processes on income or wealth inequality can only be surmised: in the absence of direct documentation, we may accept explosively increased real wages of rural workers as a credible proxy of a contraction of income inequality and an erosion of elite wealth. In an environment in which unskilled real wages had been about as low as they could be and documented levels of asset inequality were very high, a more generalized leveling effect seems eminently plausible. Just as the Black Death in medieval Europe, the Justinianic Plague had arrived at a time of considerable and well-established resource inequality. Egyptian land and tax lists throw some light on inequality in landownership from the third to the sixth centuries CE. What these records have in common is that by omitting both transregional wealth and the landless they—potentially greatly—understate overall land inequality. The data, which can thus only yield lower thresholds for actual property concentration, are nevertheless suggestive of high inequality: for samples of urban landowners, computed land Ginis range from 0.623 to 0.815, and for villagers, they range from 0.431 to 0.532. A reconstruction of the structure of landholding in a whole *nome* or major administrative district suggests a Gini of 0.56 just for landowners, who, at least in theory, need not have accounted for more than about a third of the total population. On the more relaxed assumption that merely half of the *nome* inhabitants were landless workers or tenants (or that somewhat fewer were landless but that some elite members also owned additional land in other *nomes*), the overall land Gini would have been close to 0.75. If true, this level of concentration would be similar to the high land Ginis of 0.611 (for all landowners) and 0.752 (for the entire population) for Egypt in 1950 right before land reform. The potential for plague-driven leveling in asset inequality was thus quite considerable.[14]

Late antique and early medieval income inequality in Egypt is completely unknown and forever unknowable. Even so, all these developments are logically consistent with gains for workers and, considering the shift from land to labor, losses for the traditional wealth elite, although economic differentiation and urbanization would simultaneously have created new mechanisms for generating inequality. What matters most is that unlike in the Mamluk period, when collectivist absenteeism suppressed worker bargaining, private landownership predominated and reasonably free labor markets created an environment that rendered asset valuations and wages sensitive to changes in land/labor ratios.

---

[14] Bowman 1985; Bagnall 1992.

Under these circumstances, a significantly diminished labor supply could hardly have failed to attenuate overall income inequality, just as diminishing land values were likely to reduce wealth inequality. The strikingly elevated real incomes of unskilled workers form the strongest element of this reconstruction, the best proxy of income compression for which we can hope. They show that state attempts to contain wage growth failed utterly, just as they eventually did in western Europe after the Black Death. What is equally important is the gradual erosion of wage gains in response to demographic recovery. The violent shock of what we might call the "First Black Death" was capable of delivering what look like considerable welfare benefits, but those wore off alongside the demographic shock itself. In this respect, the two great plague pandemics had much in common.

"NOTHING REMAINED BUT RUINS AND FORESTS": THE ANTONINE PLAGUE

Information about the leveling effects of pandemics inevitably thins as we go even farther back in time. The most promising case is an earlier event known as the Antonine Plague. This epidemic was first encountered by Roman military forces on a Mesopotamian campaign in 165 CE, reached the city of Rome the following year, and by 168 CE appears to have spread across large parts of the empire—in the words of the late Roman historian Ammianus, "from the frontiers of Persia all the way to the Rhine and to Gaul." Its medical cause remains unclear, but much speaks in favor of smallpox (*Variola major*). Transmitted between people by inhalation of the airborne *Variola* virus, the disease causes rashes that develop into skin pustules accompanied by high fevers. A more severe hemorrhagic version is also known. If the Antonine Plague was indeed smallpox attacking a virgin population, anywhere from 20 percent to 50 percent of those infected could have died, with infection rates reaching 60 percent to 80 percent of the total population. The only customized epidemiological model for this event predicts aggregate losses of around 25 percent, which is as good a guesstimate as we are ever likely to get.[15]

Thanks to the preservation of relevant papyrus documents, Egypt provides the only detailed information on the scope and consequences of this pandemic. According to these records, in the Fayyum village of Karanis the number of

---

[15] For this event, see esp. Duncan-Jones 1996; Lo Cascio 2012. The quote in the section caption is from Orosius, *History against the pagans* 7.15. Ammianus, *History* 23.6.24. Smallpox: Sallares 1991: 465 n. 367; Zelener 2012: 171–176 (model).

taxpayers fell by between a third and half between the 140s and the early 170s CE. In some small villages in the Nile Delta, losses were even higher, ranging from 70 percent to more than 90 percent between 160 and 170 CE. Although flight rather than death may have been in part responsible for these contractions, flight itself cannot be neatly separated from epidemic outbreaks considering that the latter often trigger the former. Moreover, specific mortality data reinforce the impression of mass mortality: in the village of Soknopaiou Nesos, seventy-eight of 244 registered males died in just two months, January and February of 179 CE.[16]

Land rents in kind are attested from several districts of Middle Egypt. In all documented areas, annual rents fell significantly between the pre-epidemic period and those postoutbreak years for which data are available. In the Fayyum Oasis, mean and median land rents were 62 percent and 53 percent lower during the period from 211 to 268 CE (for which nineteen cases are known) than they had been between 100 and 165 CE (thirty-four cases). In the territory of the city of Oxyrhynchus, the mean and medians dropped by 29 percent and 25 percent between the years from 103 to 165 CE (twelve cases) and the period from 205 to 262 CE (fifteen cases). Similar reductions are also discernible in a less robust data set from Hermopolis.[17]

Changes in prices and wages that were denominated in cash are more difficult to track, because overall price levels roughly doubled within a generation after the outbreak of the epidemic—arguably as a consequence of the dislocations caused by precisely that event, including a surge in coin debasement driven by concurrent and quite possibly related fiscal exigencies. This means that data from the pre- and postplague periods need to be adjusted to permit direct comparison. This exercise yields an overall picture that suggests a consistent shift in value from landed wealth to labor between the two periods from the beginning of the second century to the 160s CE and from the 190s to the 260s CE. The gap in between reflects the dearth of documentation from the actual plague years, itself a telling sign of the severity of this disaster. In this survey, all values are expressed relative to the price of wheat, which is standardized at 100 for both periods but which rose by about 125 percent in nominal terms. Thus values that rose by less than that in nominal terms fall short of 100 in the postplague period and vice versa (Fig. 11.3).[18]

---

[16] Duncan-Jones 1996: 120–121.

[17] Scheidel 2012: 282–283, updating Scheidel 2002: 101.

[18] Fig. 11.3 is taken from Scheidel 2012: 284 fig. 1, mostly building on Scheidel 2002: 101–107.

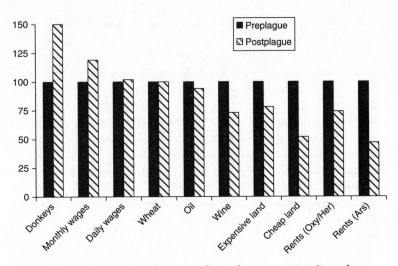

Figure 11.3 Changes in real prices and rents between 100–160s and 190s–260s CE in Roman Egypt

The value of rural labor as documented in contracts rose by between a few percent and close to a fifth depending on duration of employment, whereas the real price of donkeys, which also represents labor and which happens to be particularly well documented, went up by half. Conversely, the price of non-essential foodstuffs such as oil and, especially, wine dropped relative to that of wheat, enabling workers to purchase more higher-status goods. Expressed in terms of oil and wine, real wages rose considerably more than wheat wages did. The value of land is difficult to compare over time, because we are unable to hold land quality constant: even so, a rough survey produces results that are very similar to the much more securely attested drop in real land rents. What is most important here is that despite the uneven quality of the different datasets, all variables move in the directions that are consistent with a model of the relaxation of Malthusian constraints in the wake of demographic attrition: as labor gained, land lost. Moreover, the price of wheat—unlike that of local wine and oil, for which there was no comparable foreign demand—may well have been propped up by large-scale exports imposed by the Roman state: in its absence, if local demand had been the sole determinant, wheat prices would probably have dropped farther relative to wages or other staples. This complicates the picture and obscures the actual scale of the shift in real prices, which, according to the evidence for land values, appears to have been much more considerable.[19]

There is one snapshot of how cultivation patterns changed in the wake of the epidemic. In the village of Theadelphia in the Fayyum in 158 and 159 CE, a few years before the arrival of the disease, some 4,000 to 4,300 acres of land were sown with grain and some 350 acres planted with vines and fruit trees. By 216 CE, arable land had shrunk to 2,500 acres, or around 60 percent of the previous total, whereas arboricultural land had expanded to more than a thousand acres, or three times the previously planted area. Thus although less land was used overall than before the epidemic, much more of it was given over to higher-value crops. This resembles the pattern we see in the aftermath of the Black Death, when more wine was produced wherever the climate permitted and fruit trees spread, as did sugar cane in the Mediterranean. Demand for basic staples dropped as population levels fell and the abandonment of marginal land raised yields; more land and income were available for higher-end products. This may count as a strong signal of higher living standards for the masses.[20]

Considering the lack of equivalent evidence from Egypt, we cannot document this process more systematically, but it jibes well with the relative movement of agricultural prices. More generally, scholars have found signs of increased mobility of tenant-farmers and villagers, land flight of farmers, migration to cities, and an overall increase in urbanization levels, all of which are consistent with a postplague scenario of increased opportunity for workers and urban prosperity, just as after the Black Death. Once again there is no direct quantifiable information of the epidemic's effect on inequality as such. That is hardly surprising considering the more general lack of such information for any premodern pandemics, with the rare exception of the late medieval and early modern Italian registers discussed earlier. As a rule, the leveling effects of epidemic mortality need to be inferred from rising real incomes and improved consumption regimes, both of which are documented in this case. It is quite likely that mid-second-century CE Egypt had been subject to considerable demographic pressure: its population may have been as large as 7 million,

---

[19] This may also help explain the lack of difference in overall purchasing power for consumption baskets before and after the plague, calculated in Scheidel 2010: 427–436. Different levels of outside demand may also account for the lack of rising wheat wages after the Antonine Plague compared to the Justinianic Plague, as shown in Fig. 11.2 herein. Moreover, the death toll of the Antonine Plague may simply have been more modest owing to the difference in pathogens and especially in time duration (decades as opposed to centuries).

[20] Sharp 1999: 185–189, with Scheidel 2002: 110–111.

comparable to conditions around 1870, and the urbanization rate reached at least a quarter, although some have even argued for more than a third. In other parts of the Roman world, prolonged population growth promoted by two centuries of peace may also have tested the limits of the agrarian economy. In this environment, the potential for leveling was large. Crucially, labor arrangements in Roman Egypt were governed by market institutions, and landowners tended to be close to their properties, similar to conditions in western Europe at the time of the Black Death but unlike those of the Mamluk period in late medieval Egypt. There were no powerful institutional constraints that would have prevented labor scarcity and land devaluation from being expressed in a more equitable distribution of income and wealth.[21]

"THAT WOULD HARDLY BE ENOUGH TO DO ANY GOOD": FAMINE AS A LEVELER?

Before we conclude our review of epidemics as an equalizing force, we need to consider the contribution of another and not wholly dissimilar agent of mass mortality: famine. If very large numbers of people perished from lack of food, could this alter the distribution of material resources among the survivors just as a plague might? The answer is not quite certain but is unlikely to be positive. For one, famines have not normally been as lethal as major epidemics. So far as we can tell, food scarcity that at least doubled baseline mortality for two consecutive years—a conservative threshold for "famine"—has been uncommon in history, and much more serious events have been extremely rare. For this reason alone, famine has generally played a fairly modest role in regulating population size. It is also telling that the reported death toll of famines tends to be inversely correlated with the quality of the evidence: the less reliable the record, the more severe attrition is reputed to be. Moreover, mortality estimates are difficult, if not impossible, to separate from the effects of migration, as residents abandoned afflicted areas, and of epidemic disease, which has routinely accompanied famines. Even an extraordinarily catastrophic event such as the famine that ravaged northern China in 1877 and 1878 and that is thought to have claimed anywhere from 9 million to 13 million lives would have no more than tripled baseline mortality in the affected population of 108 million. We cannot

[21] Scenario: Scheidel 2002: 110, with references. Population: Scheidel 2001: 212, 237–242, 247–248 (Egypt); Frier 2001 (empire). Borsch 2005: 18–19 notes similarities to western Europe.

tell whether this disaster influenced inequality, and much the same is true of the Bengal famines of 1770 and 1943, the latter of which took place during a time of wartime compression.[22]

This observation introduces another qualification. Although some of the most dramatic famines ever recorded did indeed occur during periods of great leveling, they were not by themselves responsible for that process. It was not the Ukrainian famine of 1932 to 1933 that suppressed material disparities but rather the program of forcible collectivization that was undertaken at that time. China's devastating famine that had been prompted by the Great Leap Forward in 1959 to 1961 occurred after redistribution and subsequent collectivization culminating in the mid-1950s had already ensured massive leveling.[23]

Two historical famines merit closer attention owing to their scale and their potential to reshape the distribution of income and wealth. One is the "Great Famine" of 1315 to 1318, which preceded the Black Death by a generation. In those years, exceptionally cold and wet weather in northwestern Europe caused widespread crop failures and coincided with epizootics that decimated livestock. Mass mortality ensued on what appears have been an unprecedented scale. But did this calamity precipitate shifts in the price and labor akin to those of the plague? It did not. Although workers' wages went up a bit, consumer prices rose much more quickly in both town and country. Landlords came under pressure as lower output offset higher prices, but they weathered the storm much better than commoners, who often struggled for bare survival.[24]

Data are scarce, but what little information is available does not point to significant leveling. The Italian records of wealth distribution I have already used set in a little too late, or their resolution is too low, to reveal changes in the first half of the fourteenth century. Welfare ratios in London and Florence that relate skilled and unskilled urban wages to prices show no improvement in the period between 1300 or 1320 and 1340. Nor do rural real wages in England, which remained more or less stable from 1300 to 1349 and which experienced a secular rise only in the wake of the Black Death. In this respect, the contrast between the consequences of the two disasters is striking. The observed absence of famine-induced leveling is not hard to understand: mass mortality was limited to a few years and appears to have been considerably more modest than

---

[22] Watkins and Menken 1985, esp. 650–652, 665. For India, see herein, chapter 5, p. 157.

[23] See herein, chapter 7, pp. 219 and 224–227.

[24] Jordan 1996: 7–39 (famine), 43–60 (prices and wages), 61–86 (lords), 87–166 (commoners).

during the initial wave of the plague. Buffered by existing underemployment, attrition was neither prolonged nor severe enough to anticipate the economic effects of serial plague.[25]

The Irish potato famine of 1845 to 1848 is the second candidate. A (plant) epidemic as well as a food crisis, it was triggered by the spread of the *phytophthora infestans* water mold that in 1846 and 1848 caused near-total failures of the potato crop that had become an indispensable mainstay of the Irish diet. As many as a million Irish lost their lives. Coupled with emigration and a downturn in the birthrate, this event reduced the census population from 8.2 million in 1841 to 6.8 million ten years later. The number of agricultural laborers shrank even more quickly, from 1.2 million in 1845 to 900,000 in 1851. At first sight, this demographic contraction bears a close resemblance to that brought about by the initial wave of the Black Death from 1347 to 1350. And just as that wave might not on its own have been sufficiently devastating to usher in lasting changes, the Irish famine's death toll was infamously said by a contemporary English observer to "hardly be enough to do any good" in terms of ameliorating overall living conditions. The demographic consequences of serial recurrences of the plague in the late Middle Ages were to some extent mimicked by those of ongoing emigration that not only prevented a recovery but also kept Ireland's population shrinking: 4 million left the island between 1850 and 1914, eventually almost halving the population from its early 1840s peak. However, unlike the plague, departures were sensitive to age, primarily concentrated among those in their late teens or early twenties. Moreover, and again unlike the plague, the potato blight damaged the capital stock by reducing yields. This limits the value of functional analogies.[26]

In some ways, the massive demographic losses through famine and subsequent migration as well as declining fertility yielded economic benefits comparable to those of a major pandemic. In a departure from earlier trends, real wages and living standards rose steadily after the famine. Areas that had lower wages

---

[25] For wealth shares, see herein, Figs. 5.4–7; for welfare ratios, see herein, Figs. 5.1–2. Clark 2007b: 132–133 table A2 computes rural real wages. If the mean real wage from 1300 to 1309 is standardized at 100, it averaged 88 in 1310–1319, 99 in 1320–1329, and 114 in both 1330–1339 and 1340–1349 but 167 in 1350–1359, 164 in 1360–1369, and 187 in 1370–1379. A clear rupture occurred between 1349 (129) and 1350 (198). For the scale of famine mortality, see Jordan 1996: 145–148 (maybe 5–10 percent in urbanized Flanders in 1316).

[26] On the famine, see Ó Gráda 1994: 173–209, esp. 178–179, 205. "Hardly be enough": Nassau William Senior according to Benjamin Jowett, quoted from Gallagher 1982: 85. Ó Gráda 1994: 224, 227 (emigration), 207 (capital stock).

experienced higher rates of departure, which ought to have reduced interregional inequalities. At the same time, the poorest were less likely to leave than those who could more readily afford the journey. It is also unclear whether improvements in overall living conditions were accompanied by greater equality in the distribution of assets or income. Owing to desertion and evictions, the famine years had witnessed a dramatic reduction in the number of the very smallest landholdings, those of less than an acre—a process that widened inequality in access to land. Distributional change remained modest over the following sixty years: most of it took place in the bottom ranks as the share of small plots gradually rose again. Holdings of one to fifteen acres lost ground even as larger ones gained—a regressive trend overall. Even a demographic shock as powerful as the potato famine and the persistent outflows it spurred does not appear to have resulted in leveling on the scale observed for the Black Death. When it came to flattening inequality, plagues ruled supreme.[27]

"THE ENTIRE INHABITED WORLD CHANGED": PANDEMICS AS LEVELERS AND THE LIMITS OF OUR KNOWLEDGE

Much of our current knowledge of the role of pandemics in leveling inequality is fairly new. Whereas the socioeconomic consequences of the Black Death have long been well established, other demographic disasters have only recently been probed for their impact on income and wealth. Thus the Egyptian evidence for price changes associated with the Antonine and Justinianic plagues has begun to be analyzed only in the twenty-first century, and the first studies of real wages in early modern Mexico and of changing wealth inequality in northern Italy appeared in the 2010s. This ongoing expansion raises hope that further material exists, awaiting collection and interpretation. Archives from the Black Death period and its aftermath seem to be the most promising candidates. We are also in need of studies of the leveling effect of major plagues in China, where plague events are attested both for the time of the Antonine Plague and the Black Death.

In other cases, however, the surviving information may never be sufficient to shed light on questions of real incomes and inequality. A good example is

---

[27] For rising real wages and living standards, see Ó Gráda 1994: 232–233, 236–254; Geary and Stark 2004: 377 fig. 3, 378 table 4. Earlier trends: Mokyr and Ó Gráda 1988, esp. 211, 215, 230–231 (rising inequality); Ó Gráda 1994: 80–83 (no sign of a sharp fall in real wages); Geary and Stark 2004: 378 table 4, 383 (some increase followed by stagnation). Landholdings: Turner 1996, esp. 69 table 3.2, 70, 72, 75, 79 table 3.3.

what is known as the Plague of Cyprian, a major pandemic that tore through the Roman empire in the 250s and 260s CE. Its demographic fallout appears to have been nothing short of dramatic. One contemporary observer, Dionysios, the bishop of Alexandria—the second-largest city of the empire—wrote about "these continuous pestilences . . . this varied and vast destruction of mankind" that had so greatly shrunk the Alexandrian population that residents aged fourteen to eighty were now less numerous than those aged forty to seventy had been before the onset of the epidemic. Because this count was said to be derived from registers for the public corn dole, it need not be entirely fictitious, and the scale of mortality it implies is nothing short of staggering: according to model life tables, the reported shift corresponds to a loss of more than 60 percent of the metropolitan population. Contemporary data on real wages, let alone income and wealth inequality, are unavailable. Even so, a sudden and large jump in nominal wages for rural workers on two Egyptian estates in the 250s CE might possibly reflect labor shortages triggered by this epidemic.[28]

Once we move into the pre-Christian era, the light dims even further. What may conceivably be the earliest extant evidence for rising real wages induced by population losses comes from Babylonia in the sixth century BCE. In southern Babylonia during the reign of king Nebuchadnezzar in the 570s BCE, workers who were building the royal palace in Babylon were paid between 450 and 540 liters of barley, or roughly five shekels of silver per month, which translates to a daily wheat wage equivalent of 12 to 14.4 liters, similar to cash wages that imply a daily wheat wage of 11.3 to 12 liters. Comparably elevated wheat wages are attested from southern Babylonia in the reign of Nabonidus in the 540s BCE, ranging from 9.6 to 14.4 liters a day for a median of 12 liters. All these values are far above the core range of 3.5 to 6.5 liters per day that appears to have been the premodern norm and also higher than wheat wages reported a generation later under Dareios I, around 505 BCE, when workers received merely the equivalent of 7.3 liters or less. Later real wages from Babylon are lower still—as low as 4.8 liters by the early first century BCE.[29]

This temporary Neo-Babylonian surge is currently unexplained. An optimistic observer might be tempted to envision a temporary efflorescence driven by productivity gains in market-oriented farming, high labor specialization,

---

[28] Harper 2015b is the most comprehensive study. Parkin 1992: 63–64 (Dionysios); Freu 2015: 170–171 (wages).

[29] Jursa 2010: 811–816; see also Scheidel 2010: 440–441. For this period, see also herein, chapter 1, p. 48.

and growing monetization, all of which are attested for this period. However, fading gains from demographic losses incurred during the bloody collapse of the Assyrian empire near the end of the seventh century BCE are another option. The latter may have stimulated plague-scale population losses farther south in Babylonia, which was a key player in this cataclysmic conflict. That, however, must remain speculation, and the seemingly rapid deterioration in real wages in the late sixth century BCE would seem hard to explain purely in terms of a demographic recovery.

Yet despite such persistent gaps in our knowledge, plague-induced leveling processes that were once primarily or even exclusively associated with the Black Death can now be shown to have been a recurrent phenomenon of world history. All the findings presented in this chapter converge in supporting a Malthusian scenario of population-forced leveling mediated by institutional frameworks. What these leveling episodes also had in common was the extraordinary loss of life, running in the tens of millions in each of the major cases. The transience of leveling was yet another shared characteristic, as demographic recovery almost invariably absorbed these gains. Pandemics thus served as a mechanism for compressing inequalities of income and wealth that was at once exceedingly brutal and ultimately unsustainable. In both respects, it makes good company for the other effective leveling processes reviewed so far: the sacrifices of mass mobilization warfare, the atrocities of transformative revolution, and the ravages of wholesale state collapse. All these events flattened material inequality by inflicting enormous bloodshed and human suffering. Our quartet of horsemen is now complete.

"GOD HUMBLED WHAT HAD BEEN HIGH": AUGSBURG IN THE THIRTY YEARS WAR

Four parts for Four Horsemen: the neat separation of the principal levelers in history has helped structure the discussion but, inevitably, fails to do justice to the messier circumstances of real life in the past. More often than not, two or more of the horsemen would join forces as different leveling mechanisms operated and interacted side by side. The experience of the south German city of Augsburg in the seventeenth century provides an excellent illustration of the compound influence of different factors—in this case, war and plague.[30]

---

[30] This section is based on the monumental study by Roeck 1989. The quote in the section caption (790) is from the Augsburg chronicler Jacob Wagner.

Augsburg was one of the centers of the south German economy in the early modern period, an engine of the recovery from the Black Death of the late Middle Ages. Growing from 20,000 residents in 1500 to 48,000 in 1600, it became the second-largest German city at the time. Economic development and urbanization drove up resource inequality as wealth both expanded and became increasingly unevenly distributed. Detailed registers of wealth taxes that were based on periodic assessments of all urban households serve as a fairly accurate proxy of actual assets and their distribution. Several confounding variables need to be taken into account. Even those residents who were recorded as holding no taxable property would have owned some personal belongings whose inclusion might somewhat reduce measured inequality. At the same time, a general exemption for every household's first 500 gulden in cash applied—an amount that, taxed at 0.5 percent, was equivalent to a tax payment of 2.5 gulden, or more than anyone below the top fifth of the income distribution paid in 1618. Jewelry and silverware were likewise exempt from taxation. All these exceptions favored the affluent and must have more than compensated for the omission of the meager belongings of the untaxed poor. Overall, the observed trends thus seem fairly representative. The data document a striking degree of change over time. Thanks to the accumulation and concentration of capital, the Gini coefficient of inequality in wealth taxes rose from 0.66 in 1498 to 0.89 in 1604 (Fig. 11.4).[31]

Economic stratification in 1618 was intense: the richest 10 percent of households paid 91.9 percent of wealth taxes, for a Gini coefficient of 0.933. Even this privileged tier was heavily stratified: the top 1 percent, comprising patricians and the richest merchants, accounted for almost half of all wealth tax revenues. Two-thirds of registered weavers and construction workers did not owe any tax at all, nor did fully 89 percent of all day laborers. At the bottom of Augsburg's society, we encounter a large impoverished stratum of some 6,000 residents, including about 1,000 vagrant beggars, 1,700 people who mostly lived on alms, and another 3,500 who partly did so. With only 2 percent of the population counting as rich or well off, a third as middling, and two-thirds as poor (and at least half of those barely making ends meet at the very margins of subsistence), there is no sign of an emerging middle class sustained by economic

---

[31] For the registers, see Roeck 1989: 46–62. Fig. 11.4 is based on Hartung 1898: 191–192 tables IV-V; see also van Zanden 1995: 647 fig. 1.

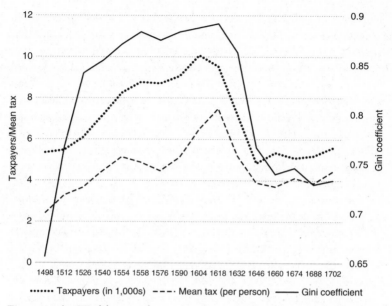

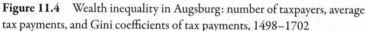

Figure 11.4 Wealth inequality in Augsburg: number of taxpayers, average tax payments, and Gini coefficients of tax payments, 1498–1702

growth. Instead, we observe falling real wages, just as in many of the other urban populations surveyed in the previous chapter.[32]

Such was the situation right at the beginning of the Thirty Years War, a complex and protracted series of military operations that caused a devastating conflagration without precedent in German history. Resulting in widespread destruction of housing and capital and enormous loss of life, hostilities coincided with and to a significant extent prompted recurrences of the plague and the spread of a relatively novel disease, typhus, which boosted mortality even further. During the earliest stages of the war, the city of Augsburg was not a direct target and was only indirectly affected, most notably by currency depreciation. The debasement of coin to pay for the war drove price inflation in the 1620s and 1630s, initially by up to an order of magnitude. The lower orders

---

[32] Roeck 1989: 400–401 (10 percent), 432 (1 percent), 407, 413–414 (workers), 512 (no middle class). Roeck's Gini estimate for 1618 is more precise than the lower one derived from Hartung 1898. For falling real wages elsewhere, see herein, Fig. 10.1–2.

appear to have suffered most, whereas net gains accrued to rich merchants who bought up real estate, mostly from middling owners in distress. A comparison of the tax contributions of 1625 with those of 1618 reveals that more merchants now paid even more than before and that their total contribution had gone up by three-quarters, a sign of rapid wealth concentration among the most successful members of this group. Among patricians, representatives of "old money," winners and losers were balanced. Nimble owners of merchant capital were best positioned to exploit war-related currency destabilization. The poor became poorer, whereas more gains are recorded among the more affluent middling residents: winners include goldsmiths and innkeepers, thanks to their direct access to scarce goods such as precious metal and food.[33]

But any such gains quickly evaporated when pestilence and war struck Augsburg. Plague delivered the first big blow, part of a larger wave that swept from Amsterdam across Germany and on to Italy. War helped introduce the epidemic to the city via billeted soldiers in October 1627. The plague proceeded to ravage the city for the remainder of that year and in 1628, carrying off some 9,000 residents out of 40,000 to 50,000. The spatial distributions of welfare disbursements and of the contraction of Augsburg's population between 1625 and 1635 match closely, which suggests that the plague disproportionately killed the poor. A second outbreak in 1632 and 1633 had the same effect. This imbalance contributed to the leveling effect experienced in the city overall. The resultant dislocations also reduced liquidity. In 1629 the city imposed a "haircut" on its creditors by reducing the high interest payments on loans taken out in previous years. Creditors who sought to bring lawsuits were deterred by suspension of any payments of interest or principal while such suits were being adjudicated.[34]

Swedish forces arrived in April 1632. A peaceful takeover nonetheless resulted in high costs of occupation that were to borne by residents, among whom Catholic households were singled out. Some 2,000 troops were billeted in the city, and massive fortification works had to be paid for. Special taxes were introduced, including a moderately progressive poll tax. Municipal interest payments ceased completely as the city faced bankruptcy. Capital owners were the main victims. During occupation, mortality surged again, this time owing to the return of the plague in 1632 that was followed by hunger brought on by a blockade by Catholic forces.[35]

[33] Roeck 1989: 553–554 (inflation), 555–561 (real estate), 562–564 (winners).
[34] Roeck 1989: 630–633, 743–744, 916.
[35] Roeck 1989: 575, 577 (debt service), 680–767 (Swedish occupation), esp. 720–722, 731–732, 742.

Conditions deteriorated further after the Swedish defeat in the Battle of Nördlingen in September 1634. Imperial troops lost little time in placing Augsburg under siege. The siege lasted for almost half a year, into March 1635, and caused tremendous hardships. The poor suffered most: the chronicler Jacob Wagner tells of people who were reduced to eating animal skins, cats and dogs, and human corpses. The latter need not have been mere cliché, as gravediggers reported missing flesh from breasts and other body parts, and some citizens were seen gnawing on the bones of dead horses lying in the streets. The stench of the dead and dying hung heavily over the city. Meanwhile the Swedish garrison put relentless pressure on the local governing council, which was compelled to raise huge extraordinary contributions: the first levy alone equaled tax obligations for an entire year. Only the wealthy could be expected to meet such demands.[36]

In March 1635 the garrison accepted terms of surrender that allowed it to depart under cover but that forced the city to host imperial troops and pay an indemnity. After Catholic households had borne the brunt of previous levies, now it was the propertied Protestants' turn to part with many of their remaining assets. A census taken in the same year sheds some light on the situation. The distribution of real estate holdings had changed little, but housing had lost much of its value, for rents had declined, houses for sale were in poor condition, and potential speculators were unable to acquire undervalued assets for lack of liquid funds. Four years later, Jacob Wagner claimed that house prices had dropped to a third of the pre-occupation level and that the workshops of the craftsmen stood half empty. The city's elite complained about the burden. A delegation sent to the Habsburg emperor at Nuremberg in 1636 claimed that Augsburg's remaining 1,600 Protestant families had become greatly impoverished because they had been forced to spend huge amounts on billeting and other expenses. In 1840, a year after the withdrawal of the garrison, another legation averred that over the previous five years, the Protestants of Augsburg had had to pay eightfold tax and had lost more than a million gulden, which, if true, would amount to a multiple of the city's annual revenues.[37]

The balance sheet of the cumulative impact of plague and war up to 1646 makes for grim reading. Augsburg's population fell by some 50 percent or 60 percent between 1616 and 1646, similar to what happened in other badly affected cities, such as Munich, Nuremberg, and Mainz. Yet its socioeconomic

---

[36] Siege: Roeck 1989: 15–21. Cannibalism: 18 and 438 n. 467.
[37] Roeck 1989: 765 (garrison and indemnity), 773 (Protestants), 790 (real estate), 870, 875 (legations).

Table 11.1 Share and number of taxable households in Augsburg by tax bracket, 1618 and 1646

Contribution	Share, in % (Number)		Change, in %	
Bracket	1618	1646	of share	of number
Nothing	48.5 (4,240)	37.2 (1,570)	−23.3	−63
1–15 kr.	13.2 (1,152)	4.2 (176)	−68.2	−84.7
16–30 kr.	7.0 (614)	22.0 (928)	+214.3	+51.1
31–60 kr.	6.7 (587)	12.4 (522)	+85.1	−11.1
1–10 fl.	16.5 (1,440)	18.0 (761)	+9.1	−47.2
10–100 fl.	6.6 (577)	5.7 (241)	−13.6	−58.2
100–500 fl.	1.35 (118)	0.5 (20)	−63.0	−83.1
500+ fl.	0.01 (10)	0 (0)	−100	−100
Total	100 (8,738)	100 (4,218)	−51.7	

Kr.: kreutzer; fl.: gulden

composition changed even more radically at both ends of the spectrum (Table 11.1). The number of poor residents fell disproportionately: four-fifths of the households of weavers disappeared, not just due to death or emigration but also because many had to give up their profession. As most of them had been poor, this loss, together with extreme attrition among the destitute, who had initially made up a sizeable share of the city's residents, induced leveling by significantly reducing the share of those living in poverty.[38]

Much had also changed at the top of urban society. Formerly super-rich households were now merely rich, whereas the number of those that were merely rich declined by five-sixths. The number of those comfortable or moderately well-off had been halved but roughly held steady as a proportion of the (much diminished) total population. The share of those in the income tiers right above bare subsistence ballooned even as the proportion of the poor and destitute fell. The overall leveling effect was massive.

These shifts were accompanied by a decline in taxable wealth that was even more severe than the drop in population size—about three-quarters compared to half. A breakdown of tax revenue by wealth deciles reveals that this sharp drop had been caused almost entirely by losses among the richest 10 percent.

---

[38] Roeck 1989: 880–949 (population losses: 881–882). Table 11.1 based on Roeck 1989: 398 table 28, 905 table 120.

Whereas in 1618 the top decile had contributed 91.9 percent of the wealth tax, in 1646 its share was 84.55 percent. In absolute terms, payments in this group had declined from 52,732 to 11,650 gulden, which represents more than 94 percent of the total drop in wealth tax revenue. "Old money," represented by patrician families, had been hit the hardest: their mean tax contribution declined by almost four-fifths.[39]

And it was not over yet: 1646 witnessed a second siege, by French and Swedish forces, that failed but that nevertheless doubled the annual death rate. A memorial composed by local merchants that year bemoaned the decline of commerce due to assaults, plunder, and new or higher tariffs, all of which were caused by war, as were blockades and the costs of billeting. Taken together, these factors were said to reduce opportunities for investment and credit, hurting the interests of capital owners. The final year of the war, 1648, brought another risk of siege, and 2,400 soldiers were stationed in the city until peace was finally negotiated.[40]

The city that survived was but a shadow of its former self. Reduced to less than half its prewar population, it saw thousands of its poorest residents carried off by plague and starvation while its capital-owning elite were bled dry. Very large fortunes had disappeared, and lesser ones had been much reduced in number. Real estate had lost value, loans had become worthless, and safe investment opportunities had dwindled: in short, capital had been greatly eroded. In the end, the severe population losses increased demand for labor among the survivors, improving the circumstances of the laboring classes beyond the abject poverty many of them had previously suffered. By the end of the war, the Gini coefficient of (proxied) taxable wealth had fallen from more than 0.9 to about 0.75, still high—and indeed much higher than it had been after the Black Death—but not nearly as extreme as before. This leveling effect, bought at a painfully high price, persisted for the remainder of the seventeenth century.[41]

*

The experience of Augsburg in what was one of the most horrific wars ever fought in western Europe, at a time of plague worse than any since the Black Death, might seem extraordinary. And yet the driving forces behind the observed

---

[39] Registration peculiarities suggest that intervening changes in how fortunes were assessed obscure even greater loss of actual wealth: Roeck 1989: 907–908. Shares: 909 table 121 (top decile), 945 (patricians).
[40] Roeck 1989: 957–960 (siege), 307, 965 (deaths), 966 (investment), 973–974 (1648).
[41] Roeck 1989: 975–981 for a final summary. Persistence: herein, Fig. 11.4.

flattening of income and wealth inequality were hardly unusual. Massive violence and human suffering were required to dispossess the rich and reduce the working population to an extent that left the survivors noticeably better off. Different forms of attrition at both the top and the bottom of the social spectrum converged in compressing the distribution of income and wealth. As we have seen in this and the previous three parts of this book, similar processes played out in very different environments and for a wide variety of reasons, from Bronze Age Greece to Japan in World War II, from England during the Black Death and Mexico in the throes of the Atlantic Exchange, to Mao's People's Republic. Spanning as they do much of recorded human history and several continents, what all these cases have in common is that substantial reductions in resource inequality depended on violent disasters. This raises two pressing questions: Has there been no other way to level inequality? And is there now? It is time to explore less bloody alternatives to our Four Horsemen.

Part VI

ALTERNATIVES

Chapter 12

REFORM, RECESSION, AND REPRESENTATION

"FATHER OF ALL AND KING OF ALL?" IN SEARCH OF PEACEFUL LEVELING

All the chapters so far have made for rather depressing reading. Time and again we have seen how substantial reductions of the gap between rich and poor were bought at a high price—high in human suffering. Yet not all violence serves this end. Most wars were just as likely to raise as to lower inequality, depending on which side one was. Civil wars have produced similarly inconsistent outcomes but for the most part have tended to widen rather than narrow inequality. Military mass mobilization has turned out to be the most promising mechanism, as exceptional violence has yielded exceptional outcomes. But although this was generally true of the worst wars in human history—the two world wars—this phenomenon and its equalizing consequences were rare in earlier periods: ancient Greece may be the only precursor. And if the most intense type of warfare was the most likely to compress income and wealth disparities, this was even truer of the most intense revolutions: the communist revolutions of the twentieth century, after all, leveled on a grand scale. By contrast, less ambitious ventures such as the French Revolution generated weaker effects, and most popular unrest in history failed to equalize at all.

State collapse served as a more reliable means of leveling, destroying disparities as hierarchies of wealth and power were swept away. Just as with mass mobilization wars and transformative revolutions, equalization was accompanied by great human misery and devastation, and the same applies to the most catastrophic epidemics: although the biggest pandemics leveled mightily, it is hard to think of a remedy to inequality that was dramatically worse than the disease. To a great extent, the scale of leveling used to be a function of the scale of violence: the more force was expended, the more leveling occurred. Even though this is not an iron law—not all communist revolutions were particularly violent, for example, and not all mass warfare leveled—it may be as close as we can hope to get to a general premise. This is, without any doubt, an exceedingly bleak conclusion. But has this been the only way? Has violence always been the source of leveling in the same way that war, according to Democritus, is the "father of all and king of all"? Are there peaceful alternatives that have produced similar results? In this and the next chapter, I review a wide variety of potential candidates, most notably land reform, economic crises, democratization, and economic development. I conclude by considering counterfactual alternatives: in the absence of massive violent shocks, how would inequality have developed over the course of the twentieth century?[1]

"UNTIL IT BECAME A TEMPEST UPROOTING EVERYTHING?" LAND REFORM

Land reform deserves pride of place for the simple reason that for most of the past, most people lived on the land, and cultivated land generally represented the bulk of private wealth. In France 300 years ago, land accounted for two-thirds of all capital; it represented about 60 percent in Britain. This would have been typical of hundreds if not thousands of years of history around the world. The distribution of land was thus a key determinant of inequality. Attempts to change landownership in favor of the poor were made throughout recorded history. Land reform is not inherently associated with violence: in theory, nothing keeps societies from peaceably adjusting ownership of land to benefit the poor. In practice, however, things usually worked out differently: as we will see, successful land reform almost invariably depended on the exercise or threat of violence.[2]

---

[1] What about the role of ideas—or, more specifically, of egalitarian ideology—in equalizing the distribution of income and wealth? It goes without saying that just like other elements of what we might broadly define as the stock of knowledge, ideologies that cover a broad spectrum from various religious doctrines, abolitionism, and social democracy to hypernationalism, fascism, and scientific socialism have long been deeply enmeshed in leveling processes. Ideologies have both precipitated violent shocks and helped maintain resultant equality gains (most recently in modern welfare states) and have in turn been molded and at times greatly boosted by such shocks (cf. herein, chapter 5, pp. 165–173). Moreover, normative ideas tend to be broadly related to specific levels of development: there are good reasons why egalitarian beliefs are more widespread in foraging and modern high-income societies than among agriculturalists (Morris 2015). However, what matters most for the purposes of this study is whether ideology can be shown to have acted as an autonomous and peaceful means of leveling: whether it has brought about substantial economic equalization outside the context of violent shocks. This has not normally been the case: I discuss a possible exception—recent developments in Latin America—hereafter. A second, related question—whether over the course of the last century or so ideology would have had a chance to do so in the absence of violent shocks—involves a counterfactual scenario that I consider at the end of chapter 14.

[2] France and Britain: Piketty 2014: 116–117 figs. 3.1–2.

The most striking examples have already been discussed in chapter 7. Neither the violent nature nor the leveling power of the Soviet and Chinese revolutions are in doubt, although in some cases—for instance, that of Cuba—violence was latent rather than widely expressed. Radical land reform along these lines faded with the end of the Cold War: Cambodia, Ethiopia, and Nicaragua in the 1970s and 1980s are among the most recent examples on record. Since then, Zimbabwe has been the only major case of coercive land redistribution. In that country, land reform had proceeded at a gentle pace in the 1980s and much of the 1990s, with about a tenth of farmland being transferred from white farmers to 70,000 mostly poor black families. Radicalization commenced in 1997 when veterans of the liberation war staged "land invasions" by occupying land owned by white large landowners. In response, another eighth of farmland was earmarked for compulsory acquisition. By now, some 90 percent of the land controlled by 6,000 white farmers back in 1980 has been given to a quarter-million families. The share of large white-owned farms in all land has collapsed from 39 percent to 0.4 percent. This represents a huge transfer of net wealth from a small elite to poor households. The more aggressive second phase of land reform from 1997 onward owed much to violent agitation by the veterans. When the Mugabe government failed to honor promises of welfare and financial support, the veterans and those they helped mobilize challenged not only white settlers but also the authorities, pressuring Mugabe into consenting to the forcible seizure of white-owned commercial farms. After initial attempts to rein in this movement, Mugabe joined it in 2000 by targeting such farms and enacting measures to protect occupiers. We see here echoes of the Mexican revolution of the early twentieth century, when local occupation of estates likewise drove government action. Local violence was a critical means of expanding the scope of land redistribution and thus wealth equalization.[3]

Many land reforms in history were the result of war. In the fourth chapter, I reviewed a particularly extreme case: land reform in Japan under American occupation that entailed effectively uncompensated confiscation and a wholesale restructuring of landownership across the country. This was a novel phenomenon of the post–World War II era: up to that point, foreign occupiers had never promoted a redistributive agenda. Soviet rule in Central Europe was the principal manifestation of equalization sponsored by conquering forces.

---

[3] Moyo and Chambati 2013a: 2; Moyo 2013: 33–34, 42, 43 table 2.2; Sadomba 2013: 79–80, 84–85, 88. For Mexico, cf. herein, chapter 8, pp. 241–242.

Historically, war had provided an impetus for land reform in other ways. One well-established mechanism was reform in response to the threat of war, employed as a means of shoring up a country's military capabilities.

By some accounts, the Taika ("Great Change") Reforms in Japan after 645 CE may be interpreted as an early example of this process. Modeled on land equalization schemes undertaken by Sui and Tang rulers in nearby China, farmland was to be surveyed and reorganized in a grid system of equal-sized plots, rice lands were to be assigned to individual households based on the number of their productive members, and periodic reallocations were planned to account for changing circumstances. The assigned plots, technically public, were meant to be inalienable. As so often is the case, we cannot be sure how widely or faithfully this ambitious program was actually implemented. What matters here is that it was undertaken in the context of ongoing reform under the threat of both internal and external war. Involvement in Korea in the 660s pitted Japan against Tang China, raising concerns about military invasion by the superpower next door. Militarization ensued, interrupted by the Jinshin war of succession in 672 and 673. The first-ever census was held in 689, and universal conscription for all adult males was introduced. The threat of war appears to have provided an impetus for domestic reforms designed to suppress local elites and foster cohesion among the general population, which was to be prepared for military mobilization.[4]

We are on safer ground with Czarist Russia. Within a month of defeat in the Crimean War of 1853–1856, Czar Alexander II promised "laws equally just for all." Reforms included the emancipation of serfs within five years, a measure meant to create a larger army supported by universal conscription. Peasants were now able to own the plots they cultivated. However, equalization was held back by the peasants' obligation to pay redemptions equal to 75 percent or 80 percent of the land's value. Financing was provided by government bonds that the peasants had to repay at 6 percent interest over forty-nine years, a drawn-out drain on their resources that often left them with smaller allotments than they had worked before. Differentiation increased as some received land but others did not, poorer peasants became proletarianized, and more affluent households pulled away from the rest. Unrest in the wake of defeat in the war against Japan in 1905 triggered another round of land reform. At the time, peasants still owned only 3.5 percent of all land. Refusing to make further redemption payments,

---

[4] Powelson 1988: 176 (reforms); for the context, see Batten 1986; Farris 1993: 34–57; Kuehn 2014: 10–17.

they went on strike and attacked estates, sacking more than a thousand manorial houses. In response to this violence, all outstanding redemption payments were canceled and peasants given the right to claim their land as hereditary property. As a result, by the time of World War I, more than half of all land had become the property of the peasantry. Even so, the persistent wealth gap between a few large estates and a great many smallholdings raised overall land inequality and workhorses came to be more unequally distributed than they had been earlier.[5]

This was not an isolated instance. War-driven land reforms that ended up exacerbating inequality have a long pedigree. The Napoleonic Wars had triggered land reform in a number of countries, with unpalatable outcomes in the longer term. In Prussia, the shock of defeat in 1806 prompted the abolition of serfdom the following year, and although tenants were allowed to purchase land from nobles and the crown, prices were high, and large landowners—the Junkers—strengthened their grip on the land and retained a dominant position until the communists expropriated all large estates without compensation in 1945. In Spain, the Napoleonic Wars likewise encouraged liberalization. Entails were abolished in 1812 and public land put up for sale, yet subsequent civil wars resulted in ever greater concentration of landownership—likewise in Portugal. In Austria, it was the revolution of 1848 that persuaded the government to make sure that serfs were freed from feudal obligations: nominally introduced in the 1780s, laws to this end had not until then been properly enforced. Redemption prices for transferred land were set at twenty times annual revenue and equally shared between peasants, state, and landlords (who thus forfeited a third of their landed wealth)—an example of buying peace in response to popular unrest.[6]

Other reform attempts motivated by war were more radical but proved short-lived. Founded in 1901, the Bulgarian Agrarian National Union was unsuccessful in reaching the rural masses until the massive shock of defeat in World War I, which led to surrender, political chaos, and territorial losses, brought them to power in 1920. Its land reform program was ambitious: ownership was capped at thirty hectares, excess holdings were subject to compulsory sale on a sliding scale (with compensation levels shrinking with size) and transferred to the landless and smallholders, and Church land and property obtained by speculation and war profits were confiscated. This soon triggered a violent

---

[5] Leonard 2011: 2 (quote), 32–33; Tuma 1965: 74–81, 84–91; Leonard 2011: 52–58.
[6] Powelson 1988: 104–105, 109.

backlash by the establishment, which led to the overthrow of the government. War effects played out in a more indirect fashion in Guatemala during and after World War II. During the war years, the oppressive rule of large landowners was weakened by the loss of the German coffee market and the nationalization of many German-owned coffee plantations, undertaken under American pressure. This paved the way for agrarian reform by a democratically elected government in 1952: land from large estates was redistributed and owners compensated with state bonds priced in accordance with the generally greatly undervalued tax declarations they used to file. By 1954, in a peaceful and orderly process, 40 percent of the rural population had received land. Yet a coup that year installed a military regime that annulled the land reform and renewed repression. Fully 150,000 died in the long civil war that followed. By the 1990s, 3 percent of owners held two-thirds of all land, and 90 percent of the rural population was almost or entirely landless. Violence featured in this process in different ways: first remotely, by facilitating change, and then through its absence under a peaceful government that proved no match for violent intervention and repression.[7]

In other cases, concerns about potential violence, internal or external, precipitated land reform. Anti-communism was a particularly potent motivating factor. At the end of World War II, land inequality in South Korea was high: fewer than 3 percent of rural households owned two-thirds of all land, whereas 58 percent had none. Subsequent land reform was driven by the fear that North Korean communists, who had expropriated land in their own part of Korea as early as 1946, might mobilize the local peasantry in the south. American support and a commitment to land reform by all parties that contested the first election in 1948 resulted in expropriation and redistribution on a grand scale. First, all Japanese colonial holdings were seized. In the early 1950s, private property was capped at three hectares of good cropland, excess land was transferred to peasants by seizure or sale for minimal compensation (one and half times annual rent), and rents were fixed at low levels for those who continued to work others' land. A little more than half of all land changed hands. The redistributive effect was huge: landlords lost 80 percent of their income whereas the bottom 80 percent of rural households gained 20 percent to 30 percent. By 1956, the richest 6 percent of landowners held merely 18 percent of all land, and the share of tenants had fallen from 49 percent to 7 percent. The Gini coefficient of landownership, which had been as high as 0.72 or 0.73 in 1945, fell to the 0.30s

---

[7] Powelson 1988: 129–131 (Bulgaria); Barraclough 1999: 16–17 (Guatemala).

by the 1960s. The leveling effect of land reform was amplified by the consequences of the Korean War: as most industrial and commercial properties were destroyed and hyperinflation rendered compensation worthless, the landed elite disappeared completely and a highly egalitarian society emerged that was later sustained by broad access to education. In this case, concerns about war or revolution were overtaken by actual mass mobilization war, with equalizing consequences akin to those encountered in chapter 5.[8]

Anxiety about revolution and actual war likewise converged in South Vietnam, which instituted land reform in 1970 at the urging of the United States: all tenanted land was to be turned over to the cultivators, who were to receive a certain amount for free; owners were compensated. The reform was implemented within three years, and the tenancy rate subsequently dropped dramatically—from 60 percent to 15 percent in the Mekong Delta, for example. In Taiwan, by contrast, general concern about war rather than war itself served as the principal agent of leveling. Evicted from the mainland by the victorious communists, in 1949 the Kuomintang government embarked on land reform as a means of shoring up local support. Its American supporters likewise urged redistribution to counter communism. Motivation was strong and institutional obstacles weak: the leadership had no obligations to local landlords, and many blamed defeat on the failure of land reform on the mainland. As in South Korea, caps were placed on individual properties, and rents were reduced. After the sale of public land to tenants, in 1953 landlords were compelled to sell excess land in return for compensation well below market prices. As a result, farm incomes rose, the share of tenants declined from 38 percent in 1950 to 15 percent ten years later, and the Gini coefficient of landownership dropped from about 0.6 to between 0.39 and 0.46 during the same interval. The Gini for overall income fell dramatically from 0.57 in 1953 to 0.33 in 1964.[9]

Land reform in Romania in 1921 may have been an early example of this containment strategy: it benefited poorer peasants and smallholders who received expropriated land and is sometimes thought to have been motivated

---

[8] You n.d.: 13, 15–16; Barraclough 1999: 34–35; You n.d.: 43 table 3; Lipton 2009: 286 table 7.2; You n.d.: 23; and see esp. You 2015: 68–75. Estimates for the 1960s vary from 0.2 to 0.55 but center on the 0.30s: 0.34, 0.38, or 0.39. For the central importance of security concerns and American influence in driving policy, see You 2015: 85–86.

[9] South Vietnam: Powelson 1988: 303. Taiwan: Barraclough 1999: 35; You n.d.: 13–14, 16–17, 27; You 2015: 68–69, 75–78, 86–87; also Albertus 2015: 292–297. Chen Cheng, the architect of land reform, expressly defined land reform as a means of depriving communist agitators of "propagandistic weapons" (quoted by You 2015: 86).

by the fear that revolution might spread from the neighboring Soviet Union. Fear of communist agitation also spurred reform in Latin American countries. The "Alliance for Peace," established by the United States in 1960 in response to Castro's takeover of Cuba, promoted land reform and provided advice and financial support to this end. Chile was a candidate: after timid earlier steps, concerns about electoral defeat in 1964 led a right-wing and centrist coalition to embrace broader land reform with foreign support. By 1970 many large estates had been expropriated, but disbursements were moderate. Allende's leftist government made more progress until it was brought down by a coup in 1973. Although this halted the process, by then a third of land had come to be held by smallholders, compared to a tenth only a decade earlier.[10]

Against a background of high inequality and rural violence in Peru throughout the 1960s, the leaders of a military coup in 1968, opposed to the country's traditional oligarchy and trained in U.S. counterinsurgency principles, opted for land reform as a means of staving off all-out civil war. Within a few years, most large estates had been expropriated, a third of all farmland was transferred, and a fifth of the farm workforce had benefited. Breaking the power of the large landowners benefited mainly the military and middling peasants rather than the poor. Similarly motivated measures were taken in Ecuador, Colombia, Panama, and the Dominican Republic. In El Salvador, a junta launched land reform in 1980, one year after the outbreak of guerilla warfare, with American encouragement and financial support.[11]

A decade earlier, fear of revolution had also helped induce land reform in Egypt. Land had been rather (though not extremely) unevenly distributed, with the top 1 percent of landowners controlling a fifth and the richest 7 percent owning two-thirds. Tenancy rates were high and the position of tenants was poor, akin to that of laborers. In the decade leading up to Nasser's military coup of 1952, the country had been riven by instability, witnessing a rapid succession of seventeen governments, martial law, strikes, and riots. Members of the ruling class had been targeted for assassination. The new regime launched land reform

---

[10] Romania: see Eidelberg 1974: 233 n.4 for references to this position, not shared by Eidelberg himself (234). Chile: Barraclough 1999: 20–28. See also Jarvis 1989 on the later unraveling of the reform's redistributive effects, mostly via sales by smallholders.

[11] Peru: Barraclough 1999: 29–30; Albertus 2015: 190–224, who emphasizes the rift between the ruling military and the landed elite. Even so, considering that the Peruvian land Gini was inordinately high to begin with (in the mid-0.9s), even robustly redistributive outcomes left it high, in the mid-0.8s: Lipton 2009: 280. Other countries: Lipton 2009: 275; Diskin 1989: 433; Haney and Haney 1989; Stringer 1989: 358, 380. El Salvador: Strasma 1989, esp. 408–409, 414, 426.

the year it took power. Just as in East Asia at the same time, the United States provided advocacy and support in order to contain communist influence. The minister of agriculture, Sayed Marei, invoked those fears in justifying reform:

> We remember the days preceding the revolution of July 1952; we remember how the Egyptian village became restless as a result of dangerous agitation; we remember the events that led to bloodshed and destruction of property.... Would the large landowners have preferred to be left exposed to the wind blowing through this unrest, exploiting want and poverty, until it became a tempest uprooting everything...?

Caps were placed on private landownership, but owners received compensation, and land recipients were required to repay the state over decades in a scheme not unlike that devised in Czarist Russia after 1861. Because these payments were much lower than previous rents had been, this arrangement worked to the peasants' advantage. The distribution of wealth was less affected than that of income, with about a tenth of land changing hands. In Iraq, coups and Baathist rule had a greater effect, and collectivization greatly reduced inequality of landownership in the 1960s and 1970s. A failed communist uprising in Sri Lanka in 1971 that is thought to have cost thousands of lives prompted land reforms the very next year, providing for the expropriation of private, and later also corporate, land in excess of a given ceiling. Prompted once again by violence, this intervention represented a radical departure from the failure of all previous governments since independence to tackle land inequality.[12]

All these examples consistently point to the paramount importance of violence, whether applied or latent, in bringing about meaningful land reform. Yet results varied greatly. Indeed, land reform has a poor track record in alleviating inequality. A survey of twenty-seven reforms during the second half of the twentieth century shows that in a large majority of cases (twenty-one, or 78 percent), land inequality either remained largely unchanged or even grew over time. Cronyism might undermine peaceful land reform. In Venezuela in the 1960s, a democratically elected government redistributed a tenth of the country's farmland—half from expropriations and half from state land—to a quarter

---

[12] Quote from Al-Ahram on September 4, 1952, quoted by Tuma 1965: 152. Albertus 2015: 282–287 (Egypt); Lipton 2009: 294 (Iraq). Sri Lanka: Samaraweera 1982: 104–106. Since then, village expansion and regularization of encroachments have been the main mechanisms of adding land to smallholdings: World Bank 2008: 5–11.

of the landless poor. At the time, the country was transitioning from a largely agricultural economy to an urban economy based on oil exports. This allowed the government to pay generous compensation from oil revenue—indeed, so generous that landlords promoted strikes and demands for land by their workers so that they themselves could qualify for expropriation and receive compensation in excess of market levels. Reform along these lines would have done little to mitigate material inequality.[13]

Sometimes compensation was introduced through the back door. In the course of its expansion across the Italian peninsula, the ancient Roman Republic had confiscated large amounts of arable land from defeated enemies and converted it into public land that was either assigned to settlers or let out for rent. The latter benefited those who could afford to cultivate and invest in large tracts of land and caused public holdings to become concentrated in the hands of the wealthy. After an earlier effort to impose legal limits on access to this type of land, matters came to a head in 133 BCE when a populist reformer from within the oligarchic ruling class, Tiberius Gracchus, pushed through a redistribution program that limited each possessor to a little more than 300 acres of public land. Excess holdings were to be seized without compensation for prior investments and allocated to poor citizens. Assigned fields became inalienable to prevent the rich and powerful from buying out or otherwise displacing the newly created smallholders. Elite opposition to this reform proceeded in stages. Efforts to enhance this program by providing settlers with startup funds cost Gracchus his life at the hands of enraged oligarchs. The redistribution scheme survived its instigator by not more than four years, and in the 110s BCE, rents were abolished and all holders of public land—including those in possession of the maximum allowed amount—began to enjoy it as private property that could be sold. Thus although this program may have created a respectable number of new smallholders (equivalent to a few percent of the citizen population), its longer-term effect on the distribution of landed wealth was likely modest at best.[14]

In the modern Philippines, the lack of a credible threat of war or revolution allowed landlord elites to drag their feet: even as land reform remained a

---

[13] Lipton 2009: 285–286 table 7.2. Cf. also Thiesenheusen 1989a: 486–488. Albertus 2015: 137–140 offers a more optimistic assessment regarding Latin America, where more than half of all farmland was subject to reform-related transfers between 1930 and 2008 (8–9), but it is telling that some of the most successful redistributions occurred in Bolivia, Cuba, and Nicaragua alongside Chile, Mexico, and Peru (140). Venezuela: Barraclough 1999: 19–20.

[14] Roselaar 2010, esp. 221–289.

perennial campaign slogan, for decades, little changed. Even when a more serious attempt was made after 1988, results were modest, just as they had been in India, Pakistan, and Indonesia. In Iran in the 1970s, although most sharecroppers obtained some land through compulsory sales of excess landlord holdings, the process actually increased inequality among smallholders owing to seller favoritism coupled with compensation requirements and the lack of state support, all of which advantaged better-off peasants. The Hawaiian "Great Mahele" of 1848 is a particularly extreme example of peaceful land reform that created unfair outcomes. At that point land, which had been farmed collectively, was shared out among the king, the chiefs, and the general population. Because formal claims were necessary to establish private ownership—something many commoner households failed to make—and because the Alien Landownership Act soon permitted outsiders to acquire land, over time, most of the land not claimed by the crown fell under non-Hawaiian commercial ownership.[15]

Nonviolent land reform fully succeeded only in the rarest of circumstances. The distribution of common land in late eighteenth-century Spain is at best a partial example. Triggered by riots that forced King Charles III to flee Madrid in 1766—and thus not without violent impetus—it produced substantially varying results that were determined by local circumstances. Frequently only those who were able to afford farm equipment stood to gain. In some regions, the reform failed owing to a lack of funds among rural workers and to manipulative interventions by the elite. It was successful only when the upper class was either not particularly invested in landownership—as in Malaga, which was dominated by commercial elites—or when the relative scarcity of rural workers paired with abundant land limited the bargaining power of landlords, as in Guadalajara.[16]

In nineteenth-century Serbia, equalizing land reform was made possible by growing independence from imperial rule. The Ottomans had imposed a feudal regime that allocated land to well-connected Muslim beneficiaries. In addition, powerful Turks illicitly established quasi-private property claims by encroaching on Serbian peasants. The local rural population was compelled to pay high rents and render labor services. After uprisings from 1804 onward ushered in a transitional period of dual rule—Serbian autonomy under

---

[15] You 2015: 78–81 (Philippines); Lipton 2009: 284–294 (South Asia); Hooglund 1982: 72, 89–91 (Iran). Increased inequality in landownership is not an uncommon outcome of land reform: see, e.g., Assunção 2006: 23–24 for Brazil.
[16] Spain: Santiago-Caballero 2011: 92–93. In Guadalajara, its effect on inequality remained modest: 88–89.

Ottoman suzerainty—that lasted from 1815 to 1830, illegal property claims were rescinded and feudal landlords and land rents came under pressure. Settlements in the early 1830s ordered most Turks to leave Serbia within a few years after selling their land to locals. Feudalism was abolished, and Serbs acquired private rights in land. Some of the land ceded by departing Turks was distributed to smallholders. Remaining large landowners were required to sell the cultivators' houses and a certain amount of farmland to the peasants who worked their estates. As a result, large landholdings almost completely disappeared and landownership became extremely widespread: by 1900, 91.6 percent of Serbian households owned houses and other real estate. In this case, inequality was reduced at the expense of a "foreign" elite that was forced out of its traditional position of privilege. Land reforms that targeted former colonial or other captured elite holdings similarly occurred in a whole series of other countries.[17]

Genuinely peaceful reform often appears to have required some form of foreign control that checked the power of local elites. It worked in Puerto Rico in the late 1940s—and even there it was an outgrowth of equalizing reforms in the United States that had been driven by the Great Depression and World War II and coincided with top-down land reform in Japan under American occupation. Colonial rule was also instrumental in Irish land reform. In the late 1870s, the so-called "Land War," agitation for fair rents and tenant protection from eviction, involved organized resistance in the form of strikes and boycotts but only very little actual violence. The British Parliament addressed these grievances in a series of acts that regulated rents and provided for loans at fixed interest for tenants who wanted to purchase land from willing landlords. In 1903, the Wyndham Act finally bought peace as the government agreed to cover, out of state revenue, a 12 percent premium between compensation offered by tenants and the asking prices of landlords, thereby subsidizing the privatization of smallholdings. This allowed smallholders to take control of more than half of all Irish farmland by the time of independence in the early 1920s.[18]

The search for land reforms that were both peaceful and effective has not been particularly successful. The most redistributive interventions were made possible by—often violent—revolution and civil war, as in Revolutionary France, Mexico, Russia, China, Vietnam, Bolivia, Cuba, Cambodia, Nicaragua, and Ethiopia, as well as by other forms of violent agitation, as in Zimbabwe.

---

[17] Zébitch 1917: 19–21, 33; Kršljanin 2016, esp. 2–12. For other cases since 1900, see Albertus 2015: 271–273 table 8.1.

[18] Barraclough 1999: 17 (Puerto Rico); Tuma 1965: 103 (Ireland).

In other cases, equalizing land reform was the result of war that led to foreign occupation (in Japan, Central Europe, and, to some extent, in North and South Korea after World War II), the threat of war (in early medieval Japan, Prussia, and Taiwan), other war-related disturbances (in Guatemala), concerns of about revolution (in Chile, Peru, Egypt, and Sri Lanka), or a combination of such concerns and actual war (in South Korea and South Vietnam). According to the most recent survey, no fewer than 87 percent of all major land reforms undertaken outside Latin America between 1900 and 2010 took place in the wake of a world war, decolonization, communist takeover, or the threat of communist agitation.[19]

Peaceful reform might benefit the rich, as in Hawai'i and Venezuela, or be implemented at arm's length, as in Ireland and Puerto Rico. Evidence for autonomous land reform that unfolded peacefully and resulted in significant leveling is in short supply. This finding is not surprising: in societies at a level of development that made land reform a desideratum, elite resistance was always likely to block or water down redistributive policies unless violent shocks or the threat of violence encouraged more substantive concessions. This helps explain the apparent lack of nonviolent land reforms characterized by high "floors" (the size of new smallholdings) and low "ceilings" (the caps placed on landlord properties).[20]

This picture does not change if we look farther back into the more distant past. Nominally ambitious land redistribution schemes are repeatedly attested as a feature of state-building, as in the Warring States and Sui and Tang dynasties of China, and in the context of rulers' struggle to roll back elite wealth, as in Han China: I have already referred to them in earlier chapters. In ancient Greece, land reform and cognate measures, most notably debt relief, were

---

[19] Survey: Albertus 2015: 271–273 table 8.1 (twenty-seven of thirty-one "major" land reforms, defined as those in which at least 10 percent of cultivable land changed hands over a continuous period with at least one year in which more than 1 percent was expropriated). For two of the other four—Egypt and Sri Lanka—see herein. Of all fifty-four land reforms, thirty-four, or 63 percent, in Albertus's data set are associated with the aforementioned factors. Albertus himself stresses the critical importance of coalitional splits between landed and political elites that made land reform possible, often under conditions of autocracy (esp. 2015: 26–59). His findings are fully consistent with my own perspective.

[20] Lipton 2009: 130. For the reasons given herein, his examples—South Korea and Taiwan—do not qualify as genuinely nonviolent reforms. For problems with land reform implementation in general, see 127, 131–132, 145–146. Tuma 1965: 179 derives this conclusion from his global survey of land reform: "the more fundamental the crisis and the more widespread it is, the more imperative, radical, and likely the reform appears to be." He also distinguishes between reforms that unfold within a private property framework and are limited in scope, which preserve inequality or may even increase it, and those that eliminate private tenure through collectivization and do eliminate wealth concentration (222–230).

commonly associated with violent coups. Reports extend across several centuries, from the archaic to the Hellenistic periods. When in the seventh century BCE Kypselos, the first tyrant of Corinth, killed or expelled the members of a rival clan, he may have seized its land for redistribution. Around the same time or a little later, Theagenes in the neighboring polis of Megara slaughtered the herds of the rich, which had been put to pasture on the fields of the poor. During a subsequent spell of radical democracy, the wealthy were exiled and their assets seized; the poor were said to have entered the homes of the affluent to extort free meals or engage in violence. Lenders were ordered to repay interest on debt, although there is no sign of outright debt cancellation. In 280 BCE, one Apollodorus seized power in the city of Kassandreia with the help of slaves and manufacturing workers. He is said to have confiscated "the property of the rich and redivided it among the poor and raised the pay of soldiers," a state of affairs that lasted only four years. In a similar context, Klearchos became tyrant of Heraclea Pontica in 364 BCE touting a program of land redistribution and debt cancellation.[21]

Peaceful land reform also failed to make much headway in Sparta. As we have seen in chapter 6, landed wealth had come to be increasingly unevenly distributed, marginalizing an ever larger proportion of the citizenry. By the mid-fourth century BCE, the number of full citizens had declined to 700 (down from more than ten times that number a century and a half earlier), about 100 of whom were classed as wealthy, with the others their debtors. Another 2,000 or so Spartan men were categorized as second-class citizens in part because their income had dropped below the required threshold. Extreme inequality within the citizen body, to say nothing about other subordinate strata of Spartan society, paved the way for reform attempts.

The first intervention, meant to be accomplished without bloodshed by king Agis IV in the 240s BCE, aimed for debt cancellation and the redistribution of land in 4,500 equal allotments not only to citizens but also to suitable members of subject *poleis*. When these efforts were thwarted while he was away on a military campaign, Agis went into exile and the reform failed. The next round was already a little more violent, as King Cleomenes III in 227 BCE staged a coup with the help of mercenaries, killing four of Sparta's five senior magistrates

---

[21] For China, see herein, chapter 2, pp. 63–64, 69 and esp. chapter 6, pp. 182–183. For all we can tell, the Solonic reforms in Athens did not involve actual land redistribution, and the nature of debt relief remains obscure. Moreover, they may have been influenced by foreign policy incentives: see herein, chapter 6, p. 192. Link 1991: 56–57, 133, 139; Fuks 1984: 71, 19.

(the ephors) and about ten others and expelling eighty more. His program was similar to Agis's, and this time it was actually implemented, accompanied by military reform that was swiftly rewarded with military and diplomatic successes. Finally brought down by military defeat in 222 BCE, Cleomenes fled the country; there is no indication that his redistributions were tampered with. Massive loss of life in this defeat would, however, have greatly reduced the number of landowners. Further military disaster in 207 BCE prompted the third and most radical round of reform, led by Nabis, who freed and enfranchised thousands of "slaves," probably helots. He supposedly killed, tortured, or exiled wealthy Spartans and gave their land to the poor. Once he had been deposed through foreign intervention in 188 BCE, a reactionary settlement compelled the expulsion or sale of the recently enfranchised helots. This is yet another illustration that the successful implementation of land reform tends to require a measure of violence, and it also shows how this may unleash even greater counterviolence in return.[22]

"BREAKING THE TABLETS": DEBT RELIEF AND EMANCIPATION

For all we can tell, land reform that was not associated with violence one way or another has rarely, if ever, been a potent means of combating inequalities of income and wealth. Much the same might be said about debt relief. Debt has certainly been a driver of inequality, forcing farmers to sell their land and cutting into disposable incomes. At least in theory, the reduction or cancellation of debt might have helped to improve the position of poor borrowers at the expense of wealthy lenders. In practice, there is no good evidence that any such measures ever made a real difference. Debt relief programs are attested from the earliest literate societies on record: Michael Hudson has gathered more than two dozen references to the cancellation of interest or debt itself and the freeing of debt-bondsmen in Mesopotamia between 2400 and 1600 BCE, an ancient Near Eastern tradition that is reflected in the semicentennial Jubilee restitutions ordained in the Book of Leviticus of the Old Testament. The royal relief decrees of the Sumerians, Babylonians, and Assyrians are best understood as an element of the perennial struggle between state rulers and wealth elites over the control of the surplus and the ability to tax and raise troops that I already

---

[22] Hodkinson 2000: 399; Cartledge and Spawforth 1989: 42–43, 45–47, 54, 57–58, 70, 78. The Greek data also mesh well with Albertus's 2015 emphasis on the importance of autocracy in implementing land reform.

discussed in the opening chapter. If relief was both effective and recurrent, we would expect it to have been priced into the terms of loans (which might explain documented high interest rates); if it was effective but rare or frequent but ineffectual, it would have had little effect on inequality. Either way, it seems hard to interpret debt relief as a potent instrument of leveling.[23]

Abolition of slavery might seem like a promising leveling force. In those—relatively few—societies in which much of elite capital was tied up in slaves, emancipation had the potential to compress asset inequality. In practice, however, large-scale abolitionist processes were frequently entangled with violent disturbances. After a failed attempt in 1792, the British parliament passed a ban on the slave trade in 1806 as a measure that initially targeted only non-British colonies and that was meant to serve Britain's national and, more specifically, military interests vis-à-vis the French during the Napoleonic War. Abolition proper was precipitated by massive slave uprisings in Demerara in 1823 and especially in Jamaica in 1831 and 1832. The Emancipation Act promptly followed in 1833, compelling freed slaves to work without pay for their former owners for several years and offering compensation to slave owners. The required outlay of 20 million pounds was huge, equivalent to 40 percent of the country's annual public spending and worth $2.3 billion today (or indeed more than $100 billion in current dollars if expressed as a share of the British economy then and now). Although this was less than the market value of the freed slaves—estimates at the time mention 15 million, 24 million, and as much as 70 million pounds—in conjunction with four to six years of unpaid apprenticeship, the total value of the compensation package need not have resulted in a major shortfall. More than half of the payout went to absentee owners and creditors, most of them London-based merchants and rentiers. None of the large-scale rentiers is known to have declined compensation. Under these circumstances, leveling was bound to be very limited at best. Moreover, at a time when British state revenue heavily relied on indirect taxes such as customs and excise duties, the need to take on a large amount of debt to fund this scheme effectively redistributed income from the majority of the population to more affluent slave owners and purchasers of public debt.[24]

Other instances of emancipation were even more directly linked to violent conflict. France abolished slavery in 1794 at the height of the French Revolution

---

[23] Hudson 1993: 8–9, 15–30, 46–47 (Mesopotamia); *Leviticus* 25, with Hudson 1993: 32–40, 54–64. See also more generally Hudson and Van De Mieroop 2002. It is astonishing that Graeber 2011, in his global survey of debt, does not properly address this question.

[24] Draper 2010, esp. 94–95, 106–107, 164, 201.

as a tactical measure designed to draw the rebellious slaves of Saint-Domingue (now Haiti) back to its side and away from its enemies. This measure was subsequently reversed by Napoleon. In 1804, when Haiti declared independence, former slave owners were expelled and those who stayed behind were killed in the massacre of whites that year. Another violent shock was required to end slavery in the remaining French colonial possessions: the revolution of 1848, part of a Europe-wide wave of unrest, once again brought down the French monarchy and resulted in immediate emancipation. Owners received some compensation in cash and credit, albeit on less generous terms than they had in Britain. War was instrumental in abolition in most Spanish colonies in Latin America. After colonial rule succumbed to local risings triggered by Napoleon's invasion of Spain in 1808, the newly formed states soon passed emancipation laws. In chapter 6 I discussed the violent destruction of slavery in the American Civil War, in which the uncompensated expropriation of slave owners was partly offset by collateral damage to non-elite groups that reduced the overall extent of leveling. Meanwhile, the British suppression of the Atlantic slave trade, essentially an act of state violence, had contributed to the decline of what remained of Latin American slavery. Brazil and Cuba were the main holdouts. In the case of Cuba (and Puerto Rico), it was once again violent conflict that prompted policy change. Revolution in Cuba in 1868 led to emancipation in part of the island during a war that lasted a decade. Reforms curtailed slavery from 1870 until abolition was achieved in 1886. When Brazil continued to import African slaves in breach of diplomatic commitments to the contrary, the British navy attacked Brazilian ports in 1850 to destroy slave ships, forcing the country to prohibit the slave trade. Only the final phase of the process was not primarily driven by violence: slavery was gradually dismantled from 1871 onward, and final abolition in 1888 was not accompanied by compensation to owners.[25]

Broadly speaking, the more violence was involved, through war or revolution, the more effective leveling was likely to be (as in Haiti, much of Latin America, and the United States), whereas the more peaceful the process was, the more compensation was forthcoming and the better able owners were to negotiate this transition (as in the British and French colonies). Only Brazil represents a partial exception. Emancipations that reduced wealth inequality were thus commonly associated with the violent leveling forces covered in

---

[25] Schmidt-Nowara 2010; 2011: 90–155 provides recent overviews.

earlier chapters of this book. Conversely, emancipations that were both peaceful and significantly equalizing (in material terms) were rare, possibly even nonexistent. More generally, abolition events had an even weaker effect on income inequality, considering that owners regularly retained control of the land and were able to benefit from alternative exploitative labor arrangements, such as sharecropping in the postbellum South.

"ON A SOUND AND PROSPEROUS BASIS": ECONOMIC CRISES

As we have seen, economic contractions were capable of reducing inequality. Massive downturns caused by systems collapse, discussed in chapter 9, had leveling effects that we can discern from archaeological evidence. Severe economic dislocations in the wake of transformative revolutions could yield similar outcomes, albeit on a less dramatic scale. But what was the role of "peaceful" macroeconomic crises, downturns that were not rooted in violent shocks? For most of human history, the consequences of such crises for the development of inequality are impossible to investigate. An early example is a sustained depression in Spain during which real per capita output fell throughout the first half of the seventeenth century as wool exports, trade, and urban activity declined. Inequality outcomes differed depending on our choice of proxies: whereas the ratio of land rents to wages dropped during this period, suggesting higher returns to labor than to land and thus lower income inequality, the ratio of nominal per capita output to nominal wages remained fairly stable, implying the absence of major change in the distribution of income. This, which may be in part a function of the limitations of the available data, highlights the difficulties of exploring leveling induced by economic forces in premodern societies.[26]

Substantive evidence is available only for the more recent past. Major economic crises have not had a systematic negative effect on inequality. The most comprehensive survey to date looks at seventy-two systemic banking crises from 1911 to 2010 as well as 100 consumption declines of at least 10 percent from their peak and 101 GDP declines by the same margin between 1911 and 2006. These different types of events overlapped only moderately: for instance, only eighteen of the banking crises coincided with the recessions. Thirty-seven of seventy-two systemic banking crises in twenty-five countries

---

[26] Álvarez-Nogal and Prados de la Escosura 2013: 9, 18–21. See also herein, chapter 3, p. 99 fig. 3.3.

yield useable information. Outcomes were biased in favor of increasing disparities: whereas income inequality fell in only three cases, it rose in seven, a figure that grows to thirteen if one includes cases in which no precrisis data are available. Consumption declines were more likely to produce different outcomes: among thirty-six usable cases, inequality fell in seven and rose in only two. There is no discernible trend for GDP contractions. Among both types of macroeconomic crises, the majority of cases registered very little change in inequality. A separate study of sixty-seven instances of GDP collapse in developing countries identifies ten cases in which these events caused inequality to rise, which indicates that poorer countries may be more vulnerable to this kind of shock. We must conclude that macroeconomic crises do not serve as an important means of leveling and that banking crises even tend to have the opposite effect.[27]

A survey of sixteen countries between 1880 and 2000 confirms this last finding but adds a temporal dimension. Financial crises tended to raise inequality before World War I and after World War II by depressing lower-level incomes more quickly than they did those at the top. The main exception is the Great Depression, when real wages rose even as the incomes of the most affluent, who were heavily dependent on capital income, fell. The Great Depression was the only macroeconomic crisis that had a powerful impact on economic inequality in the United States: the wealth share of the richest 1 percent of Americans declined from 51.4 percent to 47 percent between 1928 and 1932, just as the top 1 percent income share dropped from 19.6 in 1928 to 15.3 percent three years later—and from 23.9 percent to 15.5 percent over the same period if capital gains are included. Losses among the top 0.01 percent were particularly pronounced: their income share including capital gains fell from 5 percent to 2 percent between 1928 and 1932. The ranks of the wealthy shrank accordingly: membership in the National Association of Manufacturers fell by more than two-thirds between the early 1920s and 1933, and the number of banks declined from about 25,000 to 14,000 between 1929 and 1933.[28]

<hr/>

[27] Atkinson and Morelli 2011: 9–11, 35–42; Alvaredo and Gasparini 2015: 753. Atkinson and Morelli 2011: 42–48; Morelli and Atkinson 2015 find that rising inequality has not been significantly correlated with the outbreak of economic crises.

[28] Bordo and Meissner 2011: 11–14, 18–19 (periodization); Saez and Zucman 2016: Online Appendix table B1 (wealth shares; cf. previously Wolff 1996: 436 table 1, with 440 fig. 1); WWID (income shares); Turchin 2016a: 78 fig. 4.1, 190.

The Great Depression's global effect on inequality was generally more modest. In Australia, the top 1 percent income share fell from 11.9 percent in 1928 to 9.3 percent in 1932 but averaged 10.6 percent from 1936 to 1939, not far below the precrisis level. In France, it dropped from 17.3 percent in 1928 to 14.6 percent in 1931 before recovering slightly, and it dropped from 18.6 percent to 14.4 percent in the Netherlands between 1928 and 1932, where this was likewise followed by a partial rebound. Corresponding declines were weak and brief in Japan and were weaker still in New Zealand. During these years, top income shares remained stable in Germany, Finland, and South Africa and actually rose in Canada and Denmark. The equalizing consequences of the Great Depression thus seem to have been largely confined to the United States. Yet even there it produced mixed outcomes: after a few years of leveling, income concentration held steady until the beginning of the war, whereas different measures of wealth inequality show conflicting trends.[29]

President Herbert Hoover famously erred in asserting, in a speech given four days before the stock market crash of October 29, 1929, that "the fundamental business of the country, that is the production and distribution of commodities, is on a sound and prosperous basis." But the basis of American inequality may have been sounder than it would soon appear to have been: signs of a rebound of elite income and wealth in the late 1930s should make us wonder how long this trend might have continued had it not been snuffed out by renewed world war. After all, resilience and rebounds of top income shares have also been typical of the more recent past. The stock market crash of 1987 failed to arrest the steady rise of top incomes at the time and the modest equalizing effect of the bursting of the dotcom bubble in 2000 and the 9/11 dislocations of the following year had fully worn off by 2004. The same was true of the Great Recession of 2008, whose negative effect on top income shares had also been fully undone four years later. This holds true regardless of whether we consider the top 1, 0.1, or 0.01 percent share of American incomes. Equalizing effects in other developed countries were heterogeneous but likewise modest. Economic crises may be serious shocks but in the absence of violent pressures are not normally capable of reducing inequality all by themselves.[30]

---

[29] The top 1 percent income share and the overall income Gini coefficient remained flat between 1932 and 1939: WWID; Smolensky and Plotnick 1993: 6 fig. 2. Wolff 1996: 436 table 1 observes a partial recovery in top wealth shares between 1933 and 1939 whereas Saez and Zucman 2016: Online Appendix table B1 document an ongoing reduction.

[30] For the Great Recession see Piketty and Saez 2013; Meyer and Sullivan 2013 (USA); Jenkins, Brandolini, Micklewright, and Nolan, eds. 2013, esp. 80 fig. 2.19, 234–238 (Western countries up to 2009). See also Piketty 2014: 296.

"BUT WE CAN'T HAVE BOTH": DEMOCRACY

At first sight, the expansion of democratic institutions may seem like a plausible candidate as a peaceful means of leveling. However, as we have seen in chapters 5 and 6, formal democratization cannot readily be treated as an autonomous development unrelated to violent action. Much as the evolution of ancient Athenian democracy appears to have been intertwined with mass mobilization warfare, the extension of the franchise in many Western countries at specific points during the first half of the twentieth century was very significantly linked to the shocks of the two world wars. For this reason alone, even if democratization could be shown to have had an equalizing effect on the distribution of material resources in those societies, any such process would at least in part have been driven by the pressures of war.[31]

Moreover, scholarship on the relationship between democracy and inequality has long produced contradictory results. This ambiguity of outcomes has now been confirmed by the most ambitious and comprehensive survey of this problem to date. Drawing on 538 observations from 184 different countries from independence or 1960 (whichever is later) until 2010, Daron Acemoglu and his associates find no consistent effect of democracy on market or even disposable income inequality. An observed negative effect on the Gini coefficient of disposable income distribution does not reach statistical significance. It is true that the lack of precision of many of the underlying inequality measures leaves room for doubt. Yet the lack of a significant relationship is made all the more striking because democracy does have a robust effect on tax revenue as a share of GDP. This suggests that democracy's role in shaping the net distribution of resources is complex and heterogeneous and that the often presumed association of democracy with equalizing redistributive policies is far from straightforward. Two reasons for this stand out: equalization can be impeded if democracy is "captured" by powerful constituencies, and democratization provides opportunities for economic development that may by itself increase income inequality.[32]

---

[31] See herein, chapter 5, pp. 167–169 and chapter 6, pp. 192–194.

[32] Acemoglu, Naidu, Restrepo, and Robinson 2015: 1902–1909 (literature review), 1913–1917 (data), 1918–1927 (effect on taxes), 1928–1935 (effect on inequality), 1954 (reasons for heterogeneity). The observed effect on disposable income Ginis is small—about 2 to 3 points (1928). Their findings expand on those of more limited earlier studies that likewise failed to identify a connection between democracy and redistributional and welfare policies, such as Mulligan, Gil, and Sala-i-Martin 2004, and represent a departure from some of their own earlier arguments (e.g., Acemoglu and Robinson 2000). For economic growth and inequality, see herein, chapter 13, pp. 368–374.

More specific studies by Kenneth Scheve and David Stasavage undermine the notion that democratization in the West constrained material inequality. They find that partisanship—whether governments were controlled by parties of the left or not—had no effect on overall income inequality in thirteen countries between 1916 and 2000 and only a small dampening effect on top 1 percent income shares. Centralized, national-level wage bargaining likewise failed to make much difference. They also explore the relationship between franchise extension and partisanship on the one hand and top income tax rates on the other. Because top rates tend to be negatively correlated with inequality and are often better documented than inequality as such, they may serve as a rough proxy for the period before reliable inequality measures became available. Scheve and Stasavage find that the introduction of universal male suffrage did not have a strong effect on top income tax rates: in fifteen countries, the mean top rate in the five years leading up to universal male suffrage was only minimally lower than in the following decade. Incremental extensions of the franchise, as in Britain between the Reform Act of 1832 and the introduction of universal male suffrage in 1918, also did not raise top tax rates. These rates were driven up by World War I, and electoral reforms followed rather than preceded this rapid surge. Finally, comparison of average top income tax rates before and after the transition to a left-wing government reveals only a small mean increase of 3 percentage points (from 48 percent to 51 percent) between the five year–year periods before and after such events.[33]

By contrast, the strength of trade unions is in fact negatively correlated with inequality. Yet as I have shown in chapter 5, unionization rates were highly sensitive to the shocks of the two world wars and thus cannot be considered a direct function or manifestation of democracy per se. U.S. Supreme Court Justice Louis Brandeis once opined, "We can either have democracy in this country or we can have great wealth concentrated in the hands of a few, but we can't have both." As it turns out, we can indeed have both, at least as long as we define democracy in formal terms rather than in the more expansive substantive sense undoubtedly intended by this eminent scholar. Conversely, even outside socialist countries, the absence of strong democratic government has by no means been incompatible with economic equality: South Korea and Taiwan had an excellent record preserving the equalization gains produced by earlier violent shocks long before democratization gathered steam in the late 1980s, and much the same used to be true of Singapore.[34]

---

[33] Partisanship and centralized bargaining: Scheve and Stasavage 2009: 218, 229–230, 233–239. Top income tax rates: Scheve and Stasavage 2016: 63–72, esp. figs. 3.5–7.
[34] Unionization: see herein, chapter 5, pp. 165–167. Asian countries: WWID.

Chapter 13

ECONOMIC DEVELOPMENT AND EDUCATION

"A LONG SWING": GROWTH, SKILLS, AND INEQUALITY

The processes I have reviewed so far have produced little tangible evidence of peaceful leveling: nonviolent land reform, economic downturns, and democratization may work on occasion but have no systematic negative effect on inequality. Significantly equalizing land reforms or emancipation of slaves were commonly associated with violent action, a connection that lends further support to the core thesis of this book. Large-scale emigration of low-income individuals has the potential to reduce inequality in a given population: for instance, it has been hypothesized that the migration to the New World of many millions of Italians during the generation leading up to World War I helped stabilize or perhaps even lower Italy's Gini coefficient of income and top income shares at a time of disequalizing industrialization. Transfers of this kind act as a demographic leveling mechanism akin to—but more benign than—the pandemics discussed in chapters 10 and 11. Yet although emigration may serve as a leveling device that is both peaceful and effective, it needs to occur on a large scale to have a palpable effect and—at least for all but the smallest populations—thus depends on very specific and historically rare circumstances, most notably the huge outflow of migrants to the United States between the mid-nineteenth century and World War I and, to a lesser extent, since the 1980s. Actual outcomes can be quite complex, depending on the composition of the migrating group relative to that of the source population and the role of remittances. Due to the resources required and the policies of many host countries, emigrants today are frequently drawn from better-off or better educated segments of society. Moreover, any assessment of migration's consequences for inequality would be incomplete without considering its disequalizing effects on receiving populations.[1]

This leaves us with what is sometimes regarded as one of the most powerful forces of compression: economic development. At first sight, the notion that greater national wealth reduces income disparities might seem plausible: after all, the world's richest economies today by and large enjoy lower levels of inequality than they did several generations ago, and they also tend to do well compared to many less developed economies. But matters are not nearly that simple. If we had more reliable data for oil-rich countries, such as those in the Persian Gulf, we would almost certainly encounter higher levels of inequality, especially if resident aliens were included. We would thus need to qualify any association between high per capita GDP and moderate inequality by excluding economic development that heavily relies on commodity exports. But this complication is dwarfed by the problems arising because the development of the relatively low-inequality rich Western economies, as well as Japan, South Korea, and Taiwan, had generally been shaped by the massively violent shocks of the first half of the twentieth century and the policies and economic consequences they helped produce. Simply put, this means that although these societies are now both wealthy and often not particularly unequal, the latter condition need not have arisen from the former. Considering the severity of these transformative shocks and the multifaceted nature of their effect on overall social, political, and economic development, the question of how much subsequent levels of inequality were determined by economic growth and per capita output as such would seem rather meaningless.[2]

---

[1] Ginis for Italy: Rossi, Toniolo, and Vecchi 2001: 916 table 6 (decline since 1881); Brandolini and Vecchi 2011: 39 fig. 8 (stability between 1871 and 1911). Italian emigration: Rossi, Toniolo, and Vecchi 2001: 918–919, 922. Positive selection among emigrants: Grogger and Hanson 2011. Mexico has been a partial exception: Campos-Vazquez and Sobarzo 2012: 3–7, and esp. McKenzie and Rapoport 2007 for the complexity of outcomes. Remittances tend to reduce inequality but only to a small extent: see, e.g., Acosta, Calderon, Fajnzylber, and Lopez 2008 for Latin America. Immigration lowered U.S. real wages between 1870 and 1914: Lindert and Williamson 2016: 180–181. Card 2009 estimates that immigration accounted for 5 percent of the increase in U.S. wage inequality between 1980 and 2000. Throughout history, migration occasionally created fairly egalitarian settler societies from scratch: examples range from ancient Greek colonists to American pioneers. However, the picture may change substantially once we take account of corresponding increases in intergroup inequality between indigenes and newcomers.

[2] Alvaredo and Piketty 2014: 2, 6–7 comment on the inadequacy of the current evidence for petro-states. Note Piketty's argument that strong economic growth in the decades after World War II was associated with falling inequality primarily because the violent shocks of 1914 to 1945 and their policy consequences had caused the rate of return on capital (after tax and wartime losses) to fall below the rate of growth: Piketty 2014: 356 fig. 10.10.

In the following, I explore the contribution of economic development to income inequality in two ways: by considering claims that per capita GDP per se is systematically correlated with inequality measures and by focusing on parts of the world that were not involved in the violent dislocations from 1914 to 1945—or up to the 1970s if we include communist revolutions in Asia—or, more precisely, that were not as directly involved in them as were most rich Western countries and large parts of Asia: Africa, the Middle East, and, above all, Latin America.

We owe the classic formulation of the idea that income inequality is linked to and driven by economic development to economics Nobel laureate Simon Kuznets. Back in the 1950s, Kuznets, a pioneer in the study of income disparities in the United States, proposed a deliberately simple model. Economic advances beyond the traditional agrarian mode initially raise inequality if mean incomes are higher—and perhaps also more unevenly distributed—in cities than in the countryside, and urbanization increases the urban share of the population and the weight of the urban sector in the national economy, thereby inflating income differentials and also overall inequality. Once the majority of the population has shifted into the nonagrarian sector, these disparities will diminish, a process reinforced by rising wages in the urban sector in response to more settled conditions and the growing political power of urban workers. This last factor, in turn, offsets the unequalizing effect of the higher savings rate of the wealthy by curtailing it through fiscal policies such as taxation, inflation, and controls of the return on capital. As a result, in Kuznets' own words,

> One might thus assume a long swing in the inequality characterizing the secular income structure: widening in the early phases of economic growth when the transition from the pre-industrial to the industrial civilization was most rapid; becoming stabilized for a while; and then narrowing in the later phases.

It is worth noting that he assigned considerable importance to political factors, especially with respect to the development of net income inequality after taxes and transfers: fiscal measures and welfare benefits,

> in narrowing income inequality . . . must have accentuated the downward phase of the long swing, contributing to the reversal of trend in the secular widening and narrowing of income inequality.

Yet in his model, even these factors were preceded by and logically predicated upon economic change; for this reason,

> the long swing in income inequality must be viewed as a part of a wider process of economic growth.

Although Kuznets himself self-effacingly characterized his contribution as

> perhaps 5 per cent empirical information and 95 per cent speculation, some of it possibly tainted by wishful thinking . . . a collection of hunches calling for further investigation,

this model eventually rose to great prominence. It became popular not merely, as Piketty somewhat caustically observes, because it was optimistic in outlook and offered capitalist economies "good news in the midst of the Cold War" but also because it appeared to square well with a growing amount of empirical data from around the world that had not yet been available to Kuznets himself.[3]

Across-country data aggregations that relate per capita GDP in different places to a measure of inequality, usually the Gini coefficient of the income distribution, ostensibly provide a striking illustration of Kuznets' prediction. When applied to global data sets and plotted in a chart, this procedure usually yields an inverted U-curve. Low-income countries tend to display lower income inequality than those with middle incomes, whereas inequality is, once again, lower among rich countries (Fig. 13.1).

This central trend across different countries has been employed as a proxy of change over time in support of the idea that income inequality first rises and then falls with intensive economic growth. Thus inequality in an ideal-typical economy undergoing economic development would be expected to track this inverted U-curve as it matures.[4]

Yet this approach suffers from multiple and very serious problems. Data quality is a concern: surveys that draw on large numbers of observations from different parts of the world are feasible only if they accommodate evidence of

---

[3] Kuznets 1955: 7–9, 12–18, with quotes from 18, 19, 20, 26. Piketty 2014: 11–15 (quote: 13).

[4] Fig. 13.1 reproduced from Alvaredo and Gasparini 2015: 718 fig. 9.4, the most recent and comprehensive compilation available to me. According to an apt characterization by two critics of this approach, "Observations drawn from different countries at different income levels are being used to approximate the evolution of income in a single country" (Deininger and Squire 1998: 276).

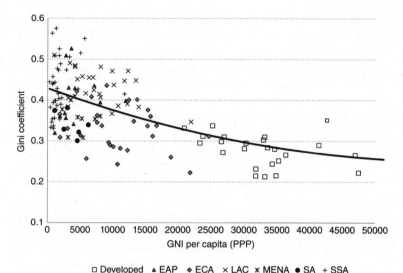

○ Developed ▲ EAP ◆ ECA × LAC ✳ MENA ● SA + SSA

Figure 13.1   Gross National Income and Gini coefficients in different countries, 2010

EAP: East Asia and Pacific, ECA: Eastern Europe and Central Asia, LAC: Latin America and Caribbean; MENA: Middle East and North Africa, SA: South Asia, SSA: Sub-Saharan Africa.

questionable precision and reliability. Robust findings require data to be fully compatible across countries, which is not always the case. Moreover, and even more damagingly, it has increasingly become clear that across-country panels are effectively invalidated by massive macroregional idiosyncrasies. Thus the appearance of an inverted U-curve in such panels is largely a function of exceptionally high levels of inequality in middle-income countries in two different parts of the globe, Latin America and southern Africa. According to a survey of income Gini coefficients in 135 countries in or close to the year 2005, Latin American countries are very heavily concentrated at the top of the inequality spectrum. At that time, the income share of the richest 10 percent averaged 41.8 percent in Latin America compared to a mean of 29.5 percent in the rest of the world. If Latin America and a few highly unequal countries in southern Africa (South Africa, Namibia, and Botswana) are excluded or replaced by regional dummy variables, the inverted U-shape simply disappears from across-country charts. This holds true regardless of whether Gini coefficients or top income deciles are used to measure inequality. In most of the world, countries having dramatically different per capita incomes, from low-income countries in Sub-Saharan Africa and South Asia to middle-income countries in Asia and Eastern Europe to high-income developed countries, now often cluster in an income Gini range of about 0.35 to 0.45. There is no systematic income-dependent inequality curve. Inequality outcomes relative to per capita GDP are fairly heterogeneous in general, and especially at the high end, which the high-inequality United States shares with low-inequality Japan and parts of Europe.[5]

Within-country analysis is therefore the only reliable way of documenting change over the course of per capita growth. A pioneering study of longitudinal data undertaken in 1998 found no support for the Kuznets thesis. In forty out of forty-nine countries under review, no significant inverted U-shaped relationship between per capita GDP and inequality emerged as these economies developed over time. In four of the nine remaining cases, the data supported the opposite scenario of a U-shaped distribution that seems to turn the model on its head. Only five of the forty-nine countries showed a significant inverted U-shaped pattern, although two of them suffered from data anomalies that cast doubt on this finding. This leaves us with all of three countries having a significant Kuznetian correlation between economic development and inequality— one of which, Trinidad and Tobago, is rather small. (Mexico and the Philippines are the other two.) Although it must be noted that the time frame of this survey may have been too short to produce more robust observations, these findings fail to inspire much confidence in the Kuznets thesis.[6]

Since then, longer-term within-country surveys have likewise produced little tangible support for the hypothesized correlation. The best example currently available appears to be Spain, where the Gini coefficient of income first rose and then fell between 1850 and 2000. If we are prepared to discount sharp

---

[5] Data quality: Bergh and Nilsson 2010: 492 and n. 9. Palma 2011: 90 fig. 1 (Gini distribution), 92 and fig. 3 (top deciles), 93–109, esp. 95 fig. 5, 96, 99 fig. 7 (inequality/per capita GDP relationship). The powerful pull effect of Latin America was already noted by Deininger and Squire 1998: 27–28. For Latin American "excess inequality," see, e.g., Gasparini and Lustig 2011: 693-694; Gasparini, Cruces, and Tornarolli 2011: 179–181. In addition, Frazer 2006: 1467 points out that the low-inequality left tail of the inverted U-curve in across-country panels may owe much to the relative scarcity of data for high inequality/low income countries in Sub-Saharan Africa that privileges low-inequality/low-income countries elsewhere, a group that contributes more observations and drives down inequality at the low end of the per capita GDP scale. Alvaredo and Gasparini 2015: 720 note further problems: the implied inflection point of $1,800 is very low, and the relationship between inequality and per capita GDP is much weaker if only developing countries are considered, considering that rich ones pull down the right tail of the curve. In almost half the countries in their sample, they "fail to find any significant correlation between the type of the inequality pattern and different measures of development and growth" (723).

[6] Deininger and Squire 1998: 261, 274–282, esp. 279.

short-term fluctuations in the 1940s and 1950s in the wake of the Spanish Civil War and the establishment of the Franco regime discussed in chapter 6, we can observe a secular increase in income inequality from a Gini value of around 0.3 in the 1860s, when per capita GDP was about $1,200 (expressed in 1990 International Dollars), to a peak in the low 0.5s in the late 1910s, when per capita GDP was about $2,000, and a subsequent overall decline to the mid-0.3s by 1960, when per capita GDP had reached $3,000—all of this, arguably, as the result of a gradual shift from farming into industry. Conversely, as we will see, long-term time series from Latin American countries generally fail to show an overall inverted U-curve pattern related to economic development. More importantly, early industrializers likewise fail to reach an inflection point in inequality trends associated with a per capita GDP of $2,000: Britain reached that level around 1800, the United States around 1850, and France and Germany twenty years later, and in none of these countries did income (or wealth) inequality begin to decline—nor had it visibly fallen to lower levels by the times these economies reached $3,000, as they did between 1865 and 1907.[7]

Another study more recently focused on the relationship between the relative share of the agricultural population and inequality in order to test Kuznets' original bisectorial model. Once again, the predicted correlation is not borne

[7] Here I diverge from the argument regarding the presence of what he calls "Kuznets waves" or "cycles" presented in Milanovic 2016: 50–59, 70–91. For countries affected by the shocks of 1914–1945, and for longer-term evidence for several countries, including Britain and the United States, see herein, chapter 3, pp. 103–111 and chapter 5, pp. 130–141. For Spain, see Prados de la Escosura 2008: 298 fig. 3, 300; see Maddison project for GDP figures. It is striking that the Gini closely tracks per capita GDP, which declined after the Civil War: 300 fig. 5. For civil war effects, see herein, chapter 6, pp. 204–206. See Roine and Waldenström 2015: 508 for work rejecting earlier findings concerning a Kuznets curve in Sweden since 1870. They also stress that because it was primarily a capital income phenomenon, the great leveling of 1914 to 1945 cannot be explained in Kuznetian terms (551). Milanovic 2016: 88 table 2.2 lists levels of per capita GDP ranging from $1,500 to $4,800 in 1990 International Dollars that are associated with national inequality peaks (expressed by Gini coefficients), but his survey remains problematic for several reasons. The suggested inequality peaks for the Netherlands in 1732, Italy in 1861, and the United Kingdom in 1867 may not be genuine or directly comparable to later values. As for the Netherlands, only if we are prepared to put the conjectural Ginis for 1561, 1732, and 1808 on the same footing as the somewhat lower value for 1914 is it possible to posit a pre-1914 decline, which was in any case followed by a much stronger and better documented subsequent reduction (81 fig. 2.15). The notion of an Italian inequality peak in 1861 depends on Brandolini and Vecchi 2011: 39 fig. 8, who show very similar Ginis of around 0.5 for both 1861 and 1901 and identical lower ones for 1871 and 1921; their estimates generally fluctuate between 0.45 and 0.5 for the whole period from 1861 to 1931, which makes it impossible to identify a meaningful turning point. For British inequality, see herein, chapter 3, pp. 104–105. Leveling that commenced after Gini maxima in the United States in 1933 and Japan in 1937 is causally related to World War II rather than economic development per se. This leaves only the case of Spain referenced in the main text. There is no sign of GDP-related equalization in Latin America: see herein, p. 383.

out by the evidence: it does not show up across countries and is not significant within individual countries. Finally, little support for a regular linkage of economic output and inequality emerges when we compare multiple within-country series via nonparametric regressions. This approach shows that developments in different countries vary a lot even at comparable levels of per capita GDP: both developing and developed countries betray considerable variation in the timing and direction of inequality trends relative to economic development. All in all, despite continuing efforts to identify inverted U-patterns and the existence of a few supporting cases, the preponderance of the evidence fails to support the idea of a systematic relationship between economic growth and income inequality as first envisioned by Kuznets sixty years ago.[8]

Is there a predictable connection between economic development and inequality? The answer depends on our frame of reference. We have to entertain the possibility that there may be multiple Kuznetian cycles, or at least swings whose presence interferes with tests designed to look for a single curve. In the broadest terms, there can be little doubt that economic transitions promote inequality—not only from agrarian to industrial systems but already from foraging to the agrarian mode and, in the present, from an industrial to a postindustrial service economy. But what about leveling? As I argue in the appendix, effective inequality—relative to the maximum theoretically possible degree of income concentration in a given society—need not always decline as economies grow richer. Conventional measures of nominal inequality do not offer much support to the notion that at certain stages of development, economic advances predict an attenuation of inequality. The main alternative—that in the absence of violent shocks, transitional increases in inequality are unlikely to be reversed—is far more consistent with evidence across the long run of history.

Another popular perspective centers on what is known as the "race between education and technology." Technological change shapes demand for particular skills: if supply lags behind demand, income differentials or "skill premiums"

<hr>

[8] Agricultural share: Angeles 2010: 473. While this does not disprove a systematic relationship between economic growth per se and inequality, it rejects the original formulation of the model and in so doing is consistent with other findings that undermine it. Deininger and Squire 1998: 275–276 already found that the effect of intersectoral movement is trivial to inequality outcomes, whereas interoccupational inequality matters most. Comparisons: Frazer 2006, esp. 1465 fig. 5, 1466 fig. 6, 1477–1478. Continuing efforts: the most noteworthy recent attempt is Mollick 2012, on top income shares in the United States 1919–2002 (see herein, p. 413). Abdullah, Doucouliagos, and Manning 2015 argue for a link between rising inequality and per capita GDP in Southeast Asia and maintain that the required inflection point has not yet been reached— which means that there is currently no evidence for a Kuznetian downturn. Like Angeles 2010, they also fail to find the predicted relationship between inequality and nonagricultural employment levels.

increase; if supply catches up with demand or overshoots, premiums decline. Yet important caveats apply. This relationship is primarily germane to labor income but is less likely to affect gains from capital. In societies having high levels of inequality of income from wealth, this is bound to mute the effects of the interplay between the demand and supply of specific types of labor on overall inequality. Moreover, in earlier periods, constraints on labor income other than skills could play an important role: slavery and other forms of coerced or semidependent labor might have distorted income differentials.[9]

Factors such as these may help explain why in premodern societies skill premiums and inequality were not systematically related. For parts of Europe, time trends have been traced back to the fourteenth century. Skill premiums collapsed in response to the Black Death as real wages of unskilled workers rose, a process I discussed in chapter 10. In Central and Southern Europe, they rose again once population recovered, whereas they remained low and quite stable in Western Europe until the end of the nineteenth century. The latter outcome is unusual and appears to have been made possible in part by flexible supply of skilled labor and in part by productivity growth in the agricultural sector that helped sustain unskilled wages, both of which benefited from improved labor market integration. However, although the late medieval fall in skill premiums went hand in hand with a general leveling of income inequality, the relationship between these two variables was far less straightforward later on: stable skill premiums in Western Europe from 1400 to 1900 did not translate to stable inequality.[10]

The more advanced an economy has become and the better its labor markets function, the more skill premiums can be expected to contribute to overall income inequality. We must ask to what extent mechanisms that regulate the supply of skills, foremost education, are themselves shaped by underlying factors. Mass schooling has been an outgrowth of modern Western state formation, a process associated with economic growth but also driven by interstate competition. More specifically, the interplay between demand for and supply of education was sensitive to one-time violent shocks. This is well illustrated by the evolution of skill premiums in the United States since the end of the nineteenth century. Skill ratios in the manual trades were much lower in 1929 than they had been in 1907. Yet most of this decline was concentrated in the late 1910s: in four of the five

---

[9] The concept of the "race" was coined by Tinbergen 1974.
[10] Premodern skill premiums: van Zanden 2009, esp. 126–131, 141–143. For rising inequality after about 1500, see herein, chapter 3, pp. 91–101.

occupations for which we have data, the entire net reduction within this twenty-two-year period took place between 1916 and 1920. At that time, World War I raised relative demand for unskilled workers and reshaped the distribution of manual labor wages. Wartime inflation and an abatement of immigration flows precipitated by the conflict also contributed to this sudden and powerful equalizing change. The ratio of white-collar to blue-collar earnings followed the same pattern: once again, the entire net decline between 1890 and 1940 occurred over the course of just a few years between 1915 and the early 1920s.[11]

A second compression of wage dispersion is documented for the 1940s. World War II created renewed strong demand for unskilled labor, inflation, and growing state intervention in labor markets. This led to a narrowing of the ratio of top to bottom wage shares for all male workers and reduced the earnings gap between workers with high school and college education. Returns to education experienced a dramatic fall between 1939 and 1949, both for workers with nine years of schooling compared to high school graduates and for high school graduates compared to those with a college education. Although the war-related GI Bill subsequently contributed to this equalizing pressure, even increased access to college could not prevent a partial recovery already under way in the 1950s. The sharp downturns of the late 1910s and the 1940s are the only such changes of this magnitude on record. Thus even though ongoing increases in the supply of educational opportunities were instrumental in constraining wage skill-based differentials until they finally surged in the 1980s, actual leveling was almost entirely limited to relatively short periods in which the country went through violent shocks caused by warfare.[12]

"IF YOU COMBINE INTELLECTUAL AND PROFESSIONAL CAPACITY WITH A SOCIAL CONSCIENCE, YOU CAN CHANGE THINGS": LEVELING WITHOUT SHOCKS?

I now turn to my second strategy of identifying equalizing economic forces by looking for examples of inequality attenuation in countries that had not directly

---

[11] Goldin and Katz 2008: 57–88 analyze the long run of American skill premiums since the 1890s. For the first decline, see esp. 60 fig. 2.7 (manual trades), 63 (immigration), 65 (World War I), 67 fig. 2.8 (white/blue collar earnings).

[12] Goldin and Margo 1992 is the foundational study of the "Great Compression" of wages related to World War II. Returns to education: Goldin and Katz 2008: 54 fig. 2.6, 84–85 table 2.7 and fig. 2.9; Kaboski 2005: fig. 1. GI Bill and recovery: Goldin and Margo 1992: 31–32; Goldin and Katz 2008: 83. Cf. Stanley 2003: 673 on the limited impact of the GI Bill.

been subjected to the violent shocks of 1914 to 1945 and their fallout during the following generation and that had also been spared revolutionary transformations. For most of the world, this approach yields little solid evidence for leveling by peaceful means. Since the 1980s, Western countries generally have not registered more than highly temporary declines in income inequality. Drops in the Gini coefficient of market income in Portugal and Switzerland in the 1990s conflict with information regarding top income shares. Post-Soviet countries have partly recovered from the post-1989 or post-1991 surge in inequality that had been caused by huge increases in poverty. Very large countries such as China and India have witnessed rising inequality, as have other populous countries, such as Pakistan and Vietnam. Those four countries alone account for about 40 percent of the world population. Offsets in that part of the world, such as in Thailand, have been few and far between. In the Middle East, Egypt reportedly experienced inequality declines in the 1980s and again in the 2000s, but the most recent studies stress the shortcomings of the data. Moderate fluctuation since reform-driven attenuation of inequality in the 1950s and 1960s (discussed herein, in the section on land reform in chapter 12) may be the most plausible scenario for this country. Other examples include Iran in the 1990s and especially the 2000s as well as Turkey in the 2000s. Israeli disposable income inequality has been rising even as market income inequality has remained fairly stable, a puzzling pattern indicative of regressive redistribution.[13]

Sub-Saharan Africa is sometimes regarded as a beneficiary of peaceful income equalization during the first decade of this century. Yet this impression rests on shaky foundations: for all but one of the twenty-eight countries for which standardized income Gini coefficients are available for that period, the underlying data are poor and margins of uncertainty generally very wide. In the one case that has produced high-quality information, South Africa, inequality remained fairly flat—at a very high level. No significant trend could be observed in thirteen of the twenty-seven other countries, and in five more, inequality actually grew. Only ten of the twenty-eight countries registered a decline, and they account for only a fifth of the population of the overall sample. What is more, confidence intervals for the relevant Gini coefficients tend to be

---

[13] See SWIID; WWID. Developments in Indonesia have been more complex. For Western countries, see herein, chapter 15, pp. 405–409; for postcommunist inequality, see herein, chapter 7, pp. 222, 227 and chapter 8, p. 254. For Egypt, see esp. Verme et al. 2014: 2–3, and cf. also Alvaredo and Piketty 2014. Seker and Jenkins 2015 conclude that rapid poverty decline in Turkey between 2003 and 2008 was driven by strong economic growth rather than equalizing distributional factors.

very wide: at the 95 percent confidence level, they average about 12 percentage points, clustering mainly between 9 and 13 points. (The mean is roughly the same for countries with declining inequality and for all others.) In many cases, these margins exceed the scale of the implied changes in inequality. Under these circumstances, it is difficult, if not impossible, to identify an overall trend. Yet even were we prepared to take these results at face value, they would not point to a consistent process of inequality attenuation. Although some countries in the region may well have enjoyed a measure of peaceful leveling in recent years, there is simply not enough reliable evidence on which to base more general conclusions about the nature, extent, and sustainability of such developments.[14]

This leaves us with the biggest and best-documented case—that of Latin America. Most of the countries in the region for which we have data have shown a significant reduction of income disparities since the beginning of this century. There is a good reason for considering developments in Latin America in greater detail. In terms of the violent leveling forces discussed in the previous chapters, the entire region provides the closest—albeit in many ways not particularly close—counterfactual to much of the Old World and North America that we can find on the planet. With only the rarest of exceptions untouched by intense violent shocks such as mass mobilization warfare and transformative revolutions, Latin America allows us to explore the evolution of inequality in a more sheltered environment.[15]

Some series of proxy data and creative modern reconstructions reach back several centuries. Reliable income Gini coefficients are often available only from the 1970s onward, when more states began to conduct surveys, and have greatly improved in quality since the 1990s. Findings for earlier periods thus need to be taken with a grain of salt. Even so, it has become possible to trace the long-tern

---

[14] Recent inequality decline: Tsounta and Osueke 2014: 6, 8. Twenty-eight countries: SWIID for Angola, Burkina Faso, Burundi, Cameroon, Central African Republic, Comoros, Cote d'Ivoire, Ethiopia, Ghana, Guinea, Kenya, Madagascar, Mali, Mozambique, Namibia, Niger, Nigeria, Rwanda, Senegal, Seychelles, Sierra Leone, South Africa, Swaziland, Tanzania, Uganda, Zambia, Zimbabwe. Alvaredo and Gasparini 2015: 735–736 also comment on the poor data quality. Ten countries with falls in inequality: Angola, Burkina Faso, Burundi, Cameroon, Cote d'Ivoire, Mali, Namibia, Niger, Sierra Leone, and Zimbabwe. This includes dubious cases—most notably that of a supposed decline in Angola, a notoriously unequal society. A strong drop observed in Zimbabwe may be related to political violence (see herein, chapter 12, p. 347).

[15] Exceptions include the extremely bloody Paraguayan War of 1864 to 1870 and the Cuban revolution up to 1959. Revolutions in Mexico in the 1910s and Nicaragua in 1978 and 1979 were much more limited in scope and ambition. Even partial state failure as in Haiti in 2010 has likewise remained rare. De facto participation in the two world wars was comparatively minimal at best. For the limits of Latin America's uses as a counterfactual, see herein, pp. 386–387 and chapter 14, p. 397.

evolution of Latin American income inequality, at least in broad outlines. The first age of globalization sustained export-led economic growth from the 1870s into the 1920s, driven by exports of organic and mineral commodities to the industrializing Western world. This process proved disproportionately beneficial to elites and raised inequality.[16]

Export-driven development first slowed in the wake of World War I, which dampened European demand, and it ground to a halt when the Great Depression hit the United States in 1929. World War II further curtailed at least some forms of trade. The years from 1914 to 1945 have been characterized as a period of transition and decelerating growth. In six documented countries, income inequality continued to rise during this period, from 0.377 in 1913 to 0.428 in 1938, weighted for population. Although spared direct involvement in the wars, Latin America was nonetheless very much exposed to the fallout from violent and macroeconomic shocks that occurred outside the region. Interruptions of trade and an inflow of changing ideas were among the most consequential consequences. These shocks ushered in the end of the first phase of globalization, a decline in economic liberalism, and a turn toward increasing state intervention.[17]

In the following decades, Latin American governments adapted to this global trend by more heavily promoting industrial capacity, primarily aimed at domestic markets, and by relying on protectionist measures to facilitate this development. This eventually revived economic growth and left its mark on the distribution of incomes. Outcomes varied greatly across the region. In the more developed economies, growth boosted the middle class, the urban sector, and the share of white-collar workers in the waged labor force. These changes were on occasion accompanied and reinforced by more welfare-oriented and redistributive policies. External influences played a significant role, as Britain's 1942 Beveridge Report on social insurance and other Western postwar programs inspired social security schemes in southern South America. Inequality

---

[16] Williamson 2009 (now also in Williamson 2015: 13–23) is the boldest attempt at long-term conjecture; see also Dobado González and García Montero 2010 (eighteenth and early nineteenth centuries); Arroyo Abad 2013 (nineteenth century); Prados le la Escosura 2007 (inequality since the mid-nineteenth century); Frankema 2012 (wage inequality across the twentieth century); and also Rodríguez Weber 2015 (Chile since the mid-nineteenth century). First globalization phase: Thorp 1998: 47–95; Bértola and Ocampo 2012: 81–137. Inequality rise: Bértola, Castelnuovo, Rodríguez, and Willebald 2009; Williamson 2015: 19–21.

[17] After 1914: Thorp 1998: 97–125, esp. 99–107 on international shocks; Bértola and Ocampo 2012: 138–147, 153–155. See Haber 2006: 562–569 for industrial development already in this period. Ginis: Prados de la Escosura 2007: 297 table 12.1.

was affected in different ways. Income disparities sometimes weakened, as in Argentina and possibly also in Chile; sometimes they grew, most notably in Brazil; and in other countries they increased at first and declined later, as in Mexico, Peru, Colombia, and Venezuela, where large reservoirs of unskilled surplus labor and high demand for skilled workers boosted inequality until these pressures subsided in the 1960s and 1970s.[18]

Although a widespread move toward somewhat greater income equality is commonly invoked in the literature, population-weighted Gini coefficients speak a different language, especially if we focus on net outcomes over longer periods of time. Among six countries for which we have data going back to 1938, inequality increased in all but one between that year and 1970, and the population-weighted overall income Gini coefficient consequently went from 0.464 to 0.548. In a larger sample of fifteen countries, income inequality rose in thirteen of them between 1950 and 1970, and more moderately from 0.506 to 0.535 overall—a very high level by international standards. Notably, in two of the three countries that experienced net reductions in inequality, these improvements were effectively confined to the 1950s: in Argentina, they coincided with Juan Perón's aggressively statist and redistributive government, and in Guatemala, they occurred during and after a bloody civil war. Venezuela is thus the main candidate for peaceful leveling through economic development, possibly joined by Chile if we accept an alternative set of inequality estimates that suggest leveling between 1930 and 1970, which would have been driven by economic and (peaceful) political change.[19]

Public borrowing to sustain protectionist policies and nationalized industries in the 1970s triggered debt crises in the 1980s, which came to be known as a "lost decade" during which economic growth stalled and poverty expanded. This, in turn, spurred on economic liberalization that opened up the region's economies and furthered their integration into global markets. Inequality

---

[18] Thorp 1998: 127–199; Bértola and Ocampo 2012: 138–197, esp. 193–197; Frankema 2012: 51, 53 on wage compression. Ginis: Prados de la Escosura 2007: 297 table 12.1; but for conflicting data on Chile, compare Rodríguez Weber 2015: 8 fig. 2.

[19] 1938–1970: Argentina, Brazil, Chile, Colombia, Mexico, and Uruguay, with a net drop in Argentina. 1950–1970: the same countries plus Costa Rica, the Dominican Republic, El Salvador, Guatemala, Honduras, Panama, Peru, and Venezuela, with net drops limited to Guatemala and Venezuela. See Prados de la Escosura 2007: 297 table 12.1. The Gini outcomes are consistent with the movement of top income shares in Argentina, according to WWID. For Perón's policies (such as price controls, minimum wages, transfers, unionization, labor rights, and pension system), see Alvaredo 2010a: 272–276, 284. For Chile, see the previous note.

outcomes varied considerably among different countries, whereas in the 1980s and 1990s, the region as a whole witnessed moderate increases in the population-weighted income Gini coefficient by a little less than 2 points per decade and saw a peak around 2002.[20]

What all this shows is that Latin American income inequality increased under a wide variety of economic conditions: export-led growth, state-led industrialization and protectionism, economic stagnation, and liberalization. In the four countries having the longest time series, population-weighted income Gini coefficients climbed from 0.348 in 1870 all the way to 0.552 in 1990; for six countries, from 0.377 in 1913 to 0.548 in 1990; and for fifteen, from 0.506 in 1950 to 0.537 in 1990. Although this conceals local variation and flattens temporary swings, and although the precise values often remain unknown, the long-term trend could not be clearer. Inasmuch as progress is to be found, it was limited to a mere deceleration in the rise of inequality in the second half of the twentieth century. As we can see in Fig. 13.2, occasional leveling was short-lived and limited to periods of economic downturn, triggered by foreign macroeconomic crises first in Britain and then the United States in the 1900s and 1930s and, finally, by deep recession arising from both domestic and international factors in the 1980s.[21]

The most recent phase in the evolution of Latin American income inequality began soon after 2000. Perhaps for the first time in recorded history, inequality fell across the region. In fourteen out of seventeen countries that have produced relevant data series, income Gini coefficients in 2010 were lower than they had been in 2000. Costa Rica, Honduras, and probably Guatemala are the only documented exceptions. For the other fourteen countries, the average Gini of market income fell from 0.51 to 0.457 and the average Gini of disposable income from 0.49 to 0.439, or more than 5 points by either measure. This compression is certainly impressive in terms of both scale and geographical scope but needs to be put in proper perspective. It lowered inequality for market income from a level typical of India, a highly unequal society, to one closer to that of the United States, whereas the fall in net inequality took Latin America from Chinese and Indian heights to a

---

[20] Thorp 1998: 201–273; Haber 2006: 582–583; Bértola and Ocampo 2012: 199–257. Rising inequality: 253 (growing wage gaps). Heterogeneity: Gasparini, Cruces, and Tornarolli 2011: 155–156, and see also Psacharopoulos et al. 1995 for the 1980s. Ginis: Prados de la Escosura 2007: 297 fig. 12.1 (1980/90); Gasparini, Cruces, and Tornarolli 2011: 152 table 2 (1990s/2000s); Gasparini and Lustig 2011: 696 fig. 27.4 (1980/2008).
[21] Fig. 13.2 from Prados de la Escosura 2007: 296–297 table 12.1.

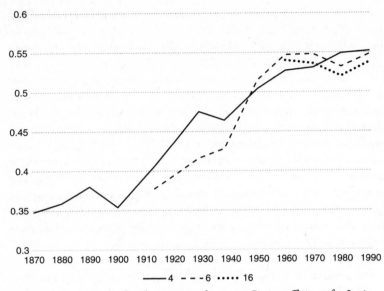

Figure 13.2 Estimated and conjectured income Gini coefficients for Latin America, 1870–1990 (population-weighted averages for four, six, and sixteen countries)

Gini still 7 points above that for the United States, the undisputed inequality champion among Western countries. The effect of these changes on the exceptionally skewed distribution of Latin American incomes should thus not be overrated.[22]

To make matters worse, since 2010 this downward trend has continued in fewer than half of the countries for which we have data (in Argentina, Bolivia, the Dominican Republic, Ecuador, El Salvador, Uruguay, and Venezuela). In those years, inequality has remained fairly stable in Brazil, Chile, Guatemala, Panama, and Peru and has begun to climb again in Mexico and Paraguay and possibly also in Honduras, where the evidence is poor. Costa Rica had always bucked the regional trend with gently rising inequality ever since the 1980s. All this raises serious questions about the causes and sustainability of the leveling

---

[22] Data from SWIID. For a similar statistic, see Cornia 2014c: 5 fig. 1.1 (a drop from 0.541 in 2002 to 0.486 in 2010). Palma 2011: 91 notes that between 1985 and 2005, Brazil's global income Gini ranking fell from being the fourth-highest (i.e., fourth-worst) in 1985 to being the sixth-highest in 2005, a very modest improvement in relative terms.

that occurred in the first decade of this century: could it have been a short-lived improvement that has run its course?

It is impossible to explain this leveling as the result of Kuznetian downward pressure on inequality once countries in the region had passed some sort of inflection point in development at which economies had become rich enough for incomes to be more equitably distributed. In 2000, per capita GDP in the fourteen countries with declining inequality varied by a factor of 7.6 between the richest and the poorest one (Argentina and Bolivia, respectively). Dispersion across this wide range was quite regular even if biased toward the lower end: mean annual per capita GDP fell between $1,000 and $2,000 in five countries, between $2,000 and $4,000 in another five, and between $5,000 and $8,000 in the other four. This alone rules out the possibility that the synchronized leveling observed in the following decade was connected to levels of economic development per se. Formal testing has confirmed that notwithstanding strong economic growth in those years, the Kuznets model cannot account for most of the observed decline.[23]

Recent studies have identified several reasons for this process: falling skill premiums and strong foreign demand that compressed market income inequality by reducing sectoral earnings gaps, recovery from earlier unequalizing macroeconomic crises that had exacerbated poverty, strong labor markets driven by more rapid economic growth, and the redistributive effect of certain government transfers on disposable income inequality. At least in theory, the first of these factors holds particular promise as a potential peaceful driver of equalization in the longer term. Market reforms in the 1990s tended to be accompanied by an expansion of the educational system, an expansion that has since continued and increased the supply of skilled workers, which in turn lowered returns on higher-level schooling and skill premiums and thus overall labor income inequality. There is no single answer to the question whether the reduction in skill premiums owed more to improved supply or diminishing demand. In some countries, premiums shrank in response to weaker demand, as in Argentina, which casts doubt on future prospects for economic development. In El Salvador and Nicaragua, inequality fell because real (rather than just relative) earnings of workers having secondary or tertiary education declined in the face of weaker demand. El Salvador is a particularly worrying case: real wages fell at all

[23] GDP: World Bank, GDP per capita (current US$), http://data.worldbank.org/indicator/NY.GDP .PCAP.CD. Test: Tsounta and Osueke 2014: 18.

levels of educational attainment but more so for more educated workers. This serves as a reminder that equalizing outcomes do not always arise from desirable economic developments.[24]

In some cases, the distributional benefits of falling skill premiums may have been bought at a high price. According to one striking finding, education is now valued so little in Bolivia that the wage premium for workers having tertiary education compared to those who underwent only primary schooling is zero. This points to an alternative or at least complementary cause of reduced skill premiums. The quality of education may have deteriorated with increased access to schooling beyond basic levels, and teaching and labor market demands may be poorly matched. This pessimistic view receives some support from evidence for negative returns on higher education in Peru and Chile owing to decreased teaching quality and for the consequences of mismatch between secondary schooling and employer demand in Argentina, Brazil, and Chile.[25]

Other economic factors have been more transient. Strong international demand for commodities helped rural workers narrow the wage gap to urban ones but has since abated. Some of the leveling since 2002 simply represented a recovery from a prior temporary surge in inequality that had been triggered by economic crises. The best known case is that of Argentina, where a massive economic meltdown between 1998 and 2002 plunged large parts of the population into poverty. Since then, a steady economic recovery, coupled with a shift to low-skill labor-intensive sectors that has reduced demand for skilled labor and depressed skill premiums, has disproportionately benefited the less affluent half of the population. So, too, have stronger unions and increased government transfers. Colombia, Ecuador, Uruguay, and Venezuela likewise experienced some inequality attenuation from similar recoveries. According to one estimate, if we were to exclude the equalizing effects of the recovery from crisis, the average reduction in income inequality in the first half of the 2000s would be quite modest, on the order of a single Gini point. More generally, the abatement of unfavorable short-term consequences of liberalization in the 1990s exerted a mitigating influence. Strong economic growth, averaging 4 percent per year in real terms or

---

[24] Education and skill premiums: e.g., Lustig, Lopez-Calva, and Ortiz-Juarez 2012: 7–8 (Brazil), 9–10 (Mexico); Alvaredo and Gasparini 2015: 731 (general). Central America: Gindling and Trejos 2013: 12, 16.
[25] Bolivia: Aristázabal-Ramírez, Canavire-Bacarezza, and Jetter 2015: 17. For the importance of falling skill premiums (rather than transfers) for Bolivian leveling, see Hernani-Limarino and Eid 2013. The observed lack of return casts doubt on the notion that increased education has been beneficial (Fortun Vargas 2012). Education quality: Cornia 2014c: 19; Lustig, Lopez-Calva, and Ortiz-Juarez 2014: 11–12, with references.

twice the rate of the previous decades, boosted employment but has been estimated to account for only a small fraction of the observed change in inequality. Moreover, these favorable conditions no longer apply, as annual GDP growth in the region declined for five consecutive years after 2010, from 6 percent in 2010 to a projected 0.9 percent in 2015. At the time of writing, Brazil, by far the largest economy in the region, was said to be enduring its worst recession since the Great Depression. All this casts doubt on the prospects of further leveling.[26]

Finally, expanded government transfers have attracted considerable publicity as a means of combating disposable income inequality. In Brazil, for example, where changes in the size, coverage, and distribution of transfer payments accounted for about half of the decline in inequality in the first decade of this century, the "Bolsa Familia" program has reached 11 million poor families. Nevertheless, compared to that found in developed countries, the actual scale of redistributive transfers in Latin America has remained very low. It is true that the presence of large numbers of impoverished households makes it possible even for relatively modest transfers (on the order of a few tenths of a percentage point of GDP) to make a difference to many people's lives and produce equalizing effects. Yet in Western Europe, gross incomes tend to differ greatly from disposable incomes, whereas in Latin America, they hardly do so at all. Multiple reasons have been invoked. The volume of tax collection relative to GDP is small by international standards, and income taxes are particularly low. At the same time, tax evasion is rife, partly because of distrust in government and partly thanks to the large size of the informal sector. The average exemption level for income tax is about twice mean per capita GDP for the region as a whole, and in several countries, progressive rates apply only at very high income levels. Lack of state revenue thus severely limits the potential for transfers. To make matters worse, some welfare schemes are conducive to net inequality. Pensions and unemployment insurance disproportionately benefit those in the top quintile of the income distribution, primarily urban workers in formal employment arrangements, and discriminate against the rural population and those in

[26] Commodities: see Economic Commission for Latin America and the Caribbean (ECLAC) 2015 for the drastic downturn in foreign demand in recent years. Argentina: Weisbrot, Ray, Montecino, and Kozameh 2011; Lustig, Lopez-Calva, and Ortiz-Juarez 2012: 3–6; Roxana 2014. Other recoveries: Gasparini, Cruces, and Tornarolli 2011: 167–170. One Gini point: 170. Abatement: Alvaredo and Gasparini 2015: 749. Effect of GDP growth: Tsounta and Osueke 2014: 4, 17–18 (maybe an eighth of the overall inequality decline). GDP growth rates: IMF data in https://www.imf.org/external/pubs/ft/reo/2013/whd/eng/pdf/wreo1013 .pdf; http://www.imf.org/external/pubs/ft/survey/so/2015/CAR042915A.htm. Cornia 2014b: 44 identifies several structural obstacles to further leveling.

the informal sector. Only direct cash transfers are different in that they mostly support those in the lower half of the income distribution—but they can do so only to the extent that they are not impeded by revenue constraints and offset by more regressive forms of welfare.[27]

Why is fiscal redistribution in Latin America so feeble? This question takes us back to the central theme of this book, the transformative power of violent shocks. As we have seen, the progressive fiscal systems of the West are firmly rooted in the two world wars, just as redistribution under communist regimes was rooted in other forms of violent upheaval. By contrast, economic development as such is not a useful indicator of the degree of fiscal redistribution. In 1950, when Western nations and Japan were busy taxing the rich and erecting ambitious welfare systems, per capita GDP (in 1990 International Dollars) ranged from $4,000 to $7,000 in Germany, France, the Netherlands, Sweden, the United Kingdom, and Canada, was closer to $2,000 in Japan, and even in the United States was not dramatically higher than in Western Europe. These values are broadly in line with leading South American economies such as Argentina and Venezuela even at that time and with a wider range of Latin American countries today: equivalent mean per capita GDP in the eight most developed substantial countries in the region was $7,800 in 2010 and averaged $6,800 in a much larger sample. By this metric, the average Argentinian, Chilean, and Uruguayan is better off now than the average American was in 1950.[28]

This shows that fiscal restraint in Latin American countries has not been determined by economic performance. Around the world, violent shocks have been an essential precondition for the expansion of fiscal systems, not merely in the first half of the twentieth century but also for hundreds and even thousands of years. Bloody interstate wars and transformative revolutions played a very minor role in the last two centuries of Latin America history. This helps us understand how high levels of inequality have persisted across most of the region. Various features that are specific to the region have been invoked in accounting for this phenomenon, most notably the pernicious influence of

---

[27] Brazil: Gasparini and Lustig 2011: 705-706; Lustig, Lopez-Calva, and Ortiz-Juarez 2012: 7–8. Taxes: Goñi, López, and Servén 2008, esp. 7 fig. 2, 10–14, 18–21; cf. also De Ferranti, Perry, Ferreira, and Walton 2004: 11–12. Low transfers and regressive benefits: Bértola and Ocampo 2012: 254–255; Medeiros and Ferreira de Souza 2013. For low transfers in developing countries more generally, see Alvaredo and Gasparini 2015: 750, who also explain them with reference to low levels of taxation; and see also Besley and Persson 2014 on economic and political reasons for low taxation levels.

[28] GDP measures: Maddison project.

racism and colonial institutions of forced labor and slavery and the persistence of clientelism and oligarchic power. Yet what did *not* happen may be similarly or, arguably, even more important as we attempt to make sense of abiding differences in the sheer scale of inequality between Latin American and most other parts of the world. Against this background, it is highly questionable whether major breakthroughs in income equalization are feasible, let alone plausible.[29]

Policy decisions related to public spending on education, foreign investment, and tax revenues and transfers explain much of the leveling that has occurred in Latin America since the opening years of this century. More purely economic factors contributed in the form of favorable international conditions and recovery from prior crises but have proven to be more short-lived. As recovery has run its course and external demand is diminishing, further leveling would require more aggressive fiscal restructuring to improve education (considering that falling skill premiums are a mixed blessing if they stem from falling demand or poor educational outcomes) and expand redistributive transfers. It is too soon to tell whether the leveling process that commenced more than a decade ago will continue—or rather, in many cases, resume. Five or ten years from now, we will have a better sense of the sustainability of this trend.[30]

I conclude that the Latin American experience offers only very limited evidence for peaceful inequality attenuation and, at least for now, none at all for persistent and substantial leveling in the absence of violent shocks. During the last 150 years, phases of growing inequality have been interspersed with episodic reversals linked to external factors such as Western macroeconomic crises or, in a few cases, aggressive or violent policies. Although it is hard to disagree with Bolivia's president Evo Morales's maxim that "if you combine intellectual and professional capacity with a social conscience, you can change things," the history of Latin America does little to challenge the primacy of leveling by violent means.[31]

[29] Violent shocks and fiscal expansions across world history: Yun-Casalilla and O'Brien 2012; Monson and Scheidel, eds. 2015. Minor role: herein, p. 378. Features: De Ferranti, Perry, Ferreira, and Walton 2004: 5–6 briefly summarize the conventional view, qualified by, e.g., Arroyo Abad 2013; Williamson 2015. Palma 2011: 109–120 emphasizes the resilience and success of Latin American oligarchies in maintaining high income shares. Williamson 2015: 23–25 observes that Latin America missed out on the "Great 20th Century Egalitarian Leveling."

[30] Main causes: Cornia 2014c: 14–15, 17–18; Lustig, Lopez-Calva, and Ortiz-Juarez 2014: 6; Tsounta and Osueke 2014: 18–20. Thernborn 2013: 156 expresses concern about the "long-term political sustainability" of this process.

[31] Quote from http://www.azquotes.com/quote/917097.

What is more, none of the forces discussed in this chapter and the preceding chapter can be shown to have had a consistently dampening effect on material inequality. This is true of peaceful land and debt reform, economic crises, democracy, and economic growth. What all of them have in common is that they sometimes alleviate inequality and sometimes do not: in short, there is no even remotely uniform trend in outcomes. It is true that as modern economic development has caused the importance of human capital to rise relative to that of physical capital and as inequality in the distribution of human capital is primarily a function of the provision of education, equalizing policies regarding the latter may seem particularly promising. Even so, although investment in education, through its effect on wage differentials, may indeed serve as a viable mechanism of nonviolent leveling, it has historically been enmeshed in less peaceful processes: the documented swings in American skill premiums during the twentieth century once again underscore the importance of warfare in shaping social policies and economic payoffs. As we have seen in chapter 5, much the same applies to unionization. Redistributive fiscal and welfare policies do reduce disposable income inequality, but their scale and structure likewise tends to be tied to the legacy of violent shocks and its longer-term repercussions: the contrast between Western and East Asian inequality on the one hand and conditions in Latin America on the other reminds us of this fundamental association. Even after reviewing alternative causes of inequality compression, there is no escaping the fact that violence, actual or latent, has long been a critical catalyst for equalizing policy measures.

Chapter 14

WHAT IF? FROM HISTORY TO COUNTERFACTUALS

"NOTHING NEW UNDER THE SUN?" LESSONS OF HISTORY

How much can history teach us about the dynamics of inequality? My answer is: a lot—but not everything we need to know. Let us begin with the former. Growing imbalances in the distribution of material resources are made possible by intensive economic growth but are not (always) directly caused by it. Although effective inequality could, and for all we can tell frequently did, reach extreme levels even in very underdeveloped economies, nominal inequality was ultimately a function of the size of output above subsistence levels: the more productive an economy, the more concentration of resources in the hands of the few it can support—at least in theory, if not necessarily in practice (a qualification addressed in the appendix). This basic connection between growth and inequality manifested itself in its purest form during humanity's great transition from foraging to domestication, a shift that greatly intensified the uneven distribution of resources by making it generally possible in the first place. It is worth noting that this transition lacked a Kuznetian dimension: we cannot apply a bisectoral model of transient rising inequality unless we are willing to imagine societies that consisted partly of foragers and partly of farmers. Even more importantly, the move toward domestication did not hold out any promise of subsequent equalization. Sedentism, farming, and the expansion of hereditary material assets simply pushed up both potential and actual inequality without providing any mechanism for its reduction short of violent shocks.[1]

Once domestication and agrarian or organic-fuel economies had been established, further transitional shifts remained comparatively modest for

---

[1] In this and the next four paragraphs, I recap some of the basic points first made in the introduction (herein, pp. 5–9) and developed in Parts I–VI.

millennia, limited in the first instance to labor transfers from food production to the urban sector, which tended to add to existing disequalizing pressures. Once again, counterbalancing mechanisms were lacking, as the nonfarming sector could never grow beyond a certain level, making any kind of Kuznetian transition thus unfeasible. Yet economic change was only one factor driving the evolution of inequality. Domestication augmented coercive capacities and encouraged predation on a previously unthinkable scale. Top incomes and fortunes in particular received an enormous boost from state formation and the growing reach, depth, and lopsidedness of political power relations. Under these circumstances, substantial leveling was at best unlikely—and de facto mostly impossible—unless violent disasters temporarily displaced entrenched structures of hierarchy, exploitation, and property ownership. Because redistributive policies arising from mass mobilization warfare or revolution were very rare in premodern history, such shocks primarily took the form of state failure or pandemics. In their absence, inequality would simply have remained high throughout, mediated for any given level of economic development by the vagaries of state building, interstate competition, and the balance of power between rulers and elites.

Surveyed over the long term, the historical record suggests that it is futile to search for a systematic connection between changes in inequality and economic performance beyond the very basic association just outlined. The two principal leveling forces in premodern societies tended to go hand in hand with divergent economic trends. Thus although state failure or systems collapse would usually depress average per capita output, making equalization coincide with greater poverty, major epidemics had the opposite effect, leveling by raising per capita productivity and non-elite consumption as Malthusian constraints were relaxed. We also observe a similar lack of a straightforward relationship between inequality and economic growth for the centuries after the Black Death, when inequality rose in both dynamic and stagnant European economies and when even structurally similar countries such as early modern Spain and Portugal experienced different inequality outcomes. Very broadly speaking, political power relations and demography played a much greater role in the evolution of preindustrial inequality than the finer points of economic development.[2]

---

[2] For early modern Europe, see herein, chapter 3, pp. 97–100. Milanovic 2016: 50 also rejects the notion of a link between inequality and economic growth in preindustrial societies.

The next great transition, from an agrarian to an industrial and from an organic to a fossil-fuel economy, varied in its effects on income and wealth inequality. Although much depended on how far inequality in a particular society had already risen prior to this shift, the Industrial Revolution commonly sustained material disparities or even intensified them further. This state of affairs, which can be observed in industrializing as well as commodity-producing countries of the nineteenth and early twentieth century, was terminated by some of the most violent shocks in recorded history, brought about by mass mobilization warfare and transformative revolution.

Thousands of years of history boil down to a simple truth: ever since the dawn of civilization, ongoing advances in economic capacity and state building favored growing inequality but did little if anything to bring it under control. Up to and including the Great Compression of 1914 to 1950, we are hard pressed to identify reasonably well attested and nontrivial reductions in material inequality that were not associated, one way or another, with violent shocks. As we saw earlier, premodern examples appear to be confined to parts of Portugal from the sixteenth century to the eighteenth century and possibly Japan during its period of isolation from the seventeenth century to the mid-nineteenth century. In the modern world, sudden attenuations in Sweden, Norway, and possibly Germany just a few years before the outbreak of World War I make it hard to tell how trends would have turned out in the longer run. Developments in Italy remain too uncertain to contribute much to this sample. Even if I have overlooked some cases or if new evidence comes to light, there can be no doubt that peaceful leveling used to be an exceedingly rare phenomenon. And although it is true that in many countries, income and especially wealth equalization continued for a generation or so beyond the violent 1940s and also began to make some headway in a number of developing economies, this process is generally hard, if not impossible, to disentangle from its extraordinarily violent roots. Even what just a few years ago would have seemed the most promising candidate for peaceful leveling, Latin America, may yet disappoint.[3]

Inequality in the distribution of (disposable) income cannot rise forever. For any given level of development, it is constrained by ceilings that are sensitive to average per capita output yet also fairly rigid in the long term: I discuss the underlying dynamics in the appendix at the end of this volume. History shows that in the absence of violent leveling events, inequality was commonly quite high relative to its theoretical maximum and could remain high for extended

---

[3] See esp. herein, chapter 3, pp.164–173 and chapter 13, pp. 382–383, 387.

periods of time. Noteworthy increases in the concentration of income and wealth took place during phases of recovery from violent shocks: the High Middle Ages, the centuries from 1500 to 1900 in Europe, shorter periods in the Americas, and, arguably, the past few decades in much of the world. These recurrent trends point to a general norm that has applied across very diverse stages of development—agrarian, industrial, and postindustrial societies and growing as well as stagnant economies. This convergence highlights the need for more ambitious cross-cultural research and theorizing: as I said at the beginning, a proper accounting for the varied forces that repeatedly drove up inequality in the wake of intermittent leveling would require another book of similar or even greater length.

"ONE PRINCIPAL CAUSE WAS THE VAST INEQUALITY OF FORTUNES": FROM INEQUALITY TO VIOLENCE?

Two important questions remain: If violent shocks were crucial in curtailing and reversing inequality, were they bound to happen? Had they not occurred, how would inequality have held up in their absence? The former question is a more traditional one, concerned with historical causation, whereas the latter invites us to consider counterfactual outcomes. I begin with the first problem.

There is no evidence to suggest that preindustrial societies contained within them the seeds for substantial peaceful leveling. But how can we tell whether violent dislocations that upset established hierarchies of power, income, and wealth were random, exogenous events or were generated in significant measure by tensions arising from high inequality? The same elitist policies and power disparities that made most early societies so unequal may also have precipitated their eventual unraveling. This may have been particularly true of large imperial formations that not merely confronted external challengers but also had to check the rapacity of domestic elites eager to siphon off and privatize surplus, thereby depriving rulers of the means to hold together their disparate realms. In the second chapter, I already noted such tendencies in Chinese and Roman history. However, it is not enough to envision homeostatic interactions whereby, in Branko Milanovic's words,

> rising inequality indeed sets in motion forces, often of a destructive nature, that ultimately lead to its decrease but in the process destroy much else, including millions of human lives and huge amounts of

wealth. A very high inequality eventually becomes unsustainable, but it does not go down by itself; rather, it generates processes, like wars, social strife, and revolutions, that lower it.[4]

The casual use of "eventually" highlights a serious weakness of this perspective: if high inequality is a default condition of human civilization, it becomes all too easy to imagine a connection between this condition and almost any violent shock that ever occurred—and rather more difficult to explain the absence of similarly plausible shocks that failed to materialize.

The most ambitious attempt to theorize and endogenize state failure and its equalizing consequences has been undertaken by the population ecologist turned historian Peter Turchin. His synthetic theory of secular cycles delineates an ideal-typical sequence of developments that undermine and restore macrosocial structures within a roughly predictable time frame. Population growth puts pressure on carrying capacity and devalues labor relative to land, a process that is conducive to elite enrichment and rising inequality, which in turn leads to intensifying intra-elite competition and, ultimately, state breakdown. This crisis feeds back into population dynamics by reducing population pressure, exposes established elites to greater hazards, and favors the emergence of a new warrior elite that rebuilds state institutions. Historical case studies to test these predictions highlight the paramount importance of elite behavior and competition over demographic and fiscal factors.[5]

Endogenizing approaches of this kind risks downplaying the importance of largely or entirely exogenous forces such as epidemics whose effects were mediated by social condition, including inequality, but were by no means caused by them. Yet even to the extent that violent shocks can legitimately be endogenized to produce a more homeostatic model of the swings in the concentration of income and wealth, this does not affect the core thesis of this book. Regardless of their root causes, the required shocks were invariably violent in nature. The question is merely how deeply they were rooted in political, social,

---

[4] Quote: Milanovic 2016: 98. In 1790, Noah Webster considered Rome's "vast inequality of fortunes" to be the principal cause for the fall of the Republic ("Miscellaneous remarks on divisions of property . . .," http://press-pubs.uchicago.edu/founders/print_documents/v1ch15s44.html).
[5] The clearest exposition of secular cycle theory can be found in Turchin and Nefedov 2009: 6–21. Cf. also 23–25 for more rapid and elite-centered cycles in polygynous societies, and see 303–314 for the results of existing case studies. Turchin 2016a applies an adapted version of this model to the United States. Motesharrei, Rivas, and Kalnay 2014 present a more abstract model of how elite overconsumption may precipitate the collapse of unequal societies.

and economic imbalances that manifested in material inequality. The more they were—and instances of transformative revolution and state failure provide particularly fertile ground for testing this proposition—the better we would be able to incorporate violent leveling into a coherent analytical narrative of state formation and structural disequalization driven by elite behavior and demography. Serious engagement with this question would require a separate book. For now, I merely want to sound a note of caution. Although it would be relatively easy to cherry-pick suitable examples in support of secular cycle theory or comparable self-contained models, such perspectives ultimately need to be judged in terms of how well they perform across the full sweep of documented history.

Consider the case of France, England, the Netherlands, Spain, and the Spanish colonies in the Americas around 1800. As far as we can tell, inequality had been either high or going up in all these places for some time. The French Revolution might readily be accepted as a textbook case of the violent termination of a cycle of demographic pressure, elite rapacity, and painful inequality. In the Netherlands, which had long been characterized by rising levels of wealth inequality, the antimonarchist faction relied on French armed intervention in declaring the Batavian Republic, the outcome of a long-simmering domestic conflict that can be explained with reference to both internal conditions and exogenous inputs. Spanish inequality had likewise been rising for centuries, yet without precipitating any major crises. Multiple invasions by foreign parties, a largely exogenous series of events, were required to change the distribution of income in a measurable way. This, in turn, triggered uprisings against Spanish rule in South and Central America, a process that can likewise be traced to both domestic tensions and the exogenous trigger of the Peninsular War. Finally, England, which boasted a degree of maldistribution of material resources similar to that found in all these other societies, did not experience any significant domestic upheavals at all. It is tempting to attribute different outcomes to variation in political institutions or performance in war, but the more confounding variables we bring to the table, the more difficult it becomes to apply a coherent endogenizing theory to a wide range of real-life cases. Much work remains to be done.[6]

---

[6] Turchin and Nefedov 2009: 28–29 only briefly acknowledge exogenous factors. This can be a serious problem, most notably in the case of the Black Death in late medieval England, which defies endogenization: 35–80. For the societies mentioned in the text, see herein, chapter 3, pp. 94–101. Note that in a comprehensive survey Albertus 2015: 173–174 finds no connection between particular levels of land inequality and land reform or collective action leading to land reform.

"PEACE FOR OUR TIME": ALTERNATIVE OUTCOMES

This is equally true of my second question. History has its limits. Any historical account of inequality necessarily focuses on what (we think) actually happened and tries to explain why it did. What did not happen is left out of the story. Wearing my historian's hat, I find it easy to be complacent about this. If we take it as the historian's task to explore, in Leopold Ranke's much-quoted words of 1824, "wie es eigentlich gewesen"—that is, what actually happened—the job is done: the historical record shows that violent shocks were the most powerful forces of leveling from ancient times well into the twentieth century and that nonviolent mechanisms commonly failed to produce comparable outcomes. But the more social–scientifically inclined would disagree. Explicit consideration of counterfactuals makes for better history, if only because it helps us identify more confidently the factors that were essential in bringing about observed outcomes. So we must ask another question: what if violent equalizing shocks merely spoiled what might otherwise have been a different story of peaceful corrections?

For most of human history, it is true, this line of inquiry seems a dead end. Had the Roman Empire not fallen, would its aristocrats have shared their fabulous wealth with the downtrodden masses? Had the Black Death not struck, could English laborers have persuaded their employers to double and triple their wages? The answer to these or any similar questions must surely be negative. There were no even remotely plausible alternative, peaceful mechanisms that could have generated equivalent changes. In the very long term, moreover, this is not even a meaningful question. Empires generally did not last forever, and epidemics were bound to occur at some point or another. An endless Roman Empire or a world without plagues are not realistic counterfactuals. If the actual shocks had not occurred, others would eventually have taken their place. In this sense, until quite recently there was no feasible alternative to periodic violent leveling.

But what if modernity somehow changed the rules of the game? This is a more serious question because it is so easy to come up with possible candidates for peaceful equalization, such as mass education, extension of the franchise, organized labor, and any number of other novel features of the industrial age. It is fair to say that the message of this book has been unremittingly bleak. To a more optimistic observer—say, an economist traveling along some latter-day Kuznets curve and a political scientist weaned on the glories of Western-style democracy and other enlightened institutions—the turmoil of the modern Thirty Years'

War and its prolonged fallout may simply have pre-empted peaceful, orderly, and properly endogenized leveling brought about by the manifold blessings of modernity. That history inconveniently refused to serve up this story in its requisite purity does not, strictly speaking, mean that this could not have happened.

Even though we will of course never know for sure, it is nevertheless worth pursuing this particular counterfactual in greater depth. *What if* there had been no world wars and no communist revolutions? An entirely peaceful twentieth century might seem like an exceedingly implausible counterfactual. Considering the balance of power and the characteristics of the main European states and their ruling classes at the time, some kind of industrial-scale war may very well have been inevitable. But that is not necessarily true for the timing of the wars or for their duration and severity—or, least of all, for the renewal of conflict after a Great War had already been completed. Nor was the triumph of Bolshevism or Maoism a foregone conclusion.[7]

Ideally, we would like to be able study two Western worlds, one wrecked by total war and economic depression and the other left unscathed. Only this would allow us to hold constant ecology and institutions and focus on the interplay of economic, social, and political development and its consequences for inequality. No such natural experiment is possible. Inexpediently for us, and tragically for those involved, the world wars owe their label to their extraordinary geographical scope. As a result, real-life approximations of counterfactual development are rare, although not completely absent. The United States and Japan both participated in World War I in a comparatively marginal fashion. At nineteen months of formal participation and a significantly shorter period of campaigning, American involvement was short, and conscription rates remained much lower than in Europe. Japan's contribution was fairly minimal—not only relative to that of other parties but also by the standards of its own high-stakes struggle with Russia a decade earlier. In both countries, unlike among the main European belligerents, a drop in top income shares proved short-lived and was quickly undone by rebounding inequality.

---

[7] I bypass here the debate about the causes behind the outbreak of global conflict in 1914 that has been given a boost by the recent centenary. Suffice it to note that in the most general sense, the world wars were endogenous to modern development in that they would not have been feasible without industrialization, and that mass mobilization was a corollary of the weapons technology available at the time: cf. Scheve and Stasavage 2016: 21–22. But this did not by itself determine the odds of actual war. Milanovic 2016: 94–97 proposes a more specific link between inequality and World War I that would allow the resultant leveling to be "'endogenized' in economic conditions predating the war" (94).

World War II, more expansively global than the first round, offers even fewer alternatives. As I argued in chapter 5, the search for materially uninvolved or unaffected developed countries seems rather hopeless. Switzerland might be our best option, with only muted and temporary dips in top wealth shares during both world wars and a fairly stable top 1 percent income share since reporting commenced in 1933. This leaves us with the most advanced Latin American countries—dubious comparanda, considering their considerable institutional and ecological differences from the West, and yet the best we can hope for. Here it is telling that Argentina (just like South Africa) experienced growing income inequality during World War II and lagged behind developed countries in terms of both leveling and fiscal expansion, which only occurred after 1945 and not without foreign influence. What little evidence we have is thus consistent with the notion that major leveling might not have occurred in the absence of mass mobilization war and revolution.[8]

Needless to say, this conjecture is far from conclusive, and one could very reasonably argue that peaceful leveling in the industrial nations would simply have taken more time. Had that additional time been granted, if we suspend disbelief enough to picture a world without major violent shocks throughout the twentieth century—or, somewhat less implausibly, one in which such wars as did occur were swiftly decided and led to a new durable balance of power—how would global and especially Western inequality have evolved? The only thing we can be sure of is what would *not* have happened: without the destruction and devaluation of capital, aggressive fiscal redistribution, and manifold state interventions in the economic sphere, income and wealth inequality would not have fallen nearly as far as it did between 1914 and the late 1940s. The observed scale of leveling was so dramatic that no even remotely plausible counterfactual mechanism could have produced similar changes within a single generation. But what could have happened instead?

Let us consider four ideal-typical outcomes for the full sweep of the twentieth century (1–4 in Fig. 14.1). The first of these, which we may term the "pessimistic" scenario, is a continuation of the pattern that already characterized the nineteenth century and that dated, in Europe, back to the fading of the Black Death near the end of the Middle Ages and, in the United States, at least to independence—a sequence of successive phases of rising and stabilizing concentration of income

---

[8] World War I: WWID. World War II: for putative bystanders, see herein, chapter 5, pp. 158–164. Switzerland: Dell, Piketty, and Saez 2007: 474; Roine and Waldenström 2015: 534–535, 545; and herein, chapter 5, pp. 158–159. For Argentina, see herein, chapter 5, p. 156.

and wealth. In that world, Western (and Japanese) inequality would have been high but relatively stable, a never-ending Gilded Age dominated by firmly entrenched plutocrats. In some Western societies as well as across Latin America, inequality would have risen even further, flattening out in others where it was already as high as it could be—most notably, in Britain.

This outcome, although perfectly realistic for prolonged periods of stability in premodern history, would seem unduly conservative when it comes to the twentieth century. For several decades prior to 1914, numerous Western countries had already begun to introduce social security legislation and income or estate taxes, extend the franchise, and allow unionization. Although these efforts were modest by the standards of later generations, they laid the institutional and ideational foundations for the massive expansion of redistributive institutions and the welfare state that unfolded over the next two generations or so. In our peaceful counterfactual world, these policies would presumably have also been continued, albeit at a slower pace. This might very well have served to curtail inequality in the long run.

But how far would this have taken us? My second scenario is the most "optimistic" counterfactual. In this version, social policies and mass education would slowly but surely have led to a gradual deconcentration of income and wealth, to the extent that this benign process would by now have more or less caught up with the leveling that in real life had largely or entirely run its course several decades ago, mostly by the 1970s or 1980s. However, there are a number of serious obstacles to the assumption that even without the violent Great Compression, inequality would eventually have been attenuated on a similar scale, merely later. One has to do with the role of capital and capital income. Although ascendant social democracy might well have nibbled at the margins of capital income by adjusting estate taxes and intervening in the market economy, it is hard to see how capital could ever have been destroyed and devalued on a comparable scale in the absence of violent shocks. Inasmuch as twentieth-century leveling was a capital phenomenon, a less disruptive environment would have made it much harder for a comparable decline in overall inequality to occur, regardless of how much time was available.

Other real-life measures were also unlikely to be implemented in our counterfactual world of peace: marginal income tax rates in excess of 90 percent, confiscatory estate taxes, massive state interference in business activity and returns on capital, such as controls of wages, rents, dividends, and much more. Nor would there have been catastrophic bouts of inflation that wiped out rentiers in several countries. We also need to eliminate the equalizing effects of communism, not only in their direct manifestations in Russia after 1917, Central Europe after 1945, and East and Southeast Asia after 1950 but also through their indirect impact as a disciplining device acting on Western and East Asian capitalists. Finally, a peaceful counterfactual world would not have experienced the same hiatus in globalization after 1914 that crimped trade and capital flows and promoted various barriers to trade, including tariffs, quotas, and assorted other controls. In the real world, its consequences were only gradually overcome after World War II by the industrialized market economies and had an even bigger and longer-lasting influence on developing countries. By some measures, globalization did not fully recover until the 1970s. In the absence of violent shocks, we might now be looking back at 150 years of uninterrupted and truly global economic integration, coupled with belated or perhaps still incomplete decolonization and attendant windfalls for elites in both core and periphery.[9]

Considering the counterfactual absence of all these powerful leveling forces, the most plausible outcome would seem to be peaceful leveling on a (much? how much?) smaller scale than that observed in actual history. But even this, my third and "intermediate" scenario, is probably too optimistic. If we assume that technological development in our counterfactual world mirrored that in real life, which seems reasonable in the long run, would not the many disequalizing pressures that harrow contemporary observers today—from resurgent sectoral income differentiation to intensifying globalization made possible by technological progress to computerization—have made themselves felt well before inequality had declined to anywhere near the levels achieved in our own world, and would societies that had not been shaped by the violent shocks of the world wars not have been less capable of withstanding them?

In this fourth and final scenario, inequality might indeed have declined to some extent during the second and third quarters of the twentieth century as social democracy and mass education curtailed wealth accumulation in elite circles but would since have rebounded, much in the way it has been doing in the real world, especially in Anglo-Saxon countries. In this case, perhaps the most plausible of my four counterfactual scenarios, inequality might very well have returned to levels that prevailed a century ago, putting us in a worse spot than the one in which we currently find ourselves (Fig. 14.1).

---

[9] For the disequalizing effects of globalization, see herein, chapter 15, pp. 413–414. British colonies in Africa tended to be quite unequal at the time of independence, even though inequality had in some cases already been declining in the postwar period: see Atkinson 2014b. For the importance of colonial assets for some European wealth elites, see Piketty 2014: 116–117 figs. 3.1–2, 148.

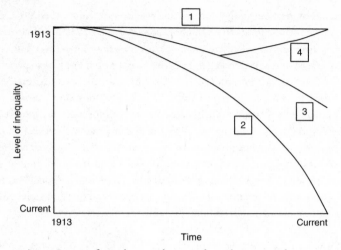

Figure 14.1 Counterfactual inequality trends in the twentieth century

Fruitless though it might be to ponder at greater length the relative merits of these ideal-typical counterfactuals, they help us understand just how much would have had to have been different for substantial leveling to have occurred in the absence of violent shocks. First of all, we have to allow for the feasibility of gradual peaceful leveling under conditions of modernity, even though there is little empirical evidence to support this notion. Second, we have to posit an additional century of relatively peaceful conditions: any counterfactual shocks of comparable severity, regardless of their timing and specifics, would take us back to a close approximation of the real world and simply reinforce the preeminence of violent leveling. Third, we need to assume that the concentration of capital that existed in the early years of the twentieth century could somehow have been undone even without recourse to massive violent dislocations, which arguably entails an even greater stretch of the imagination. And fourth, we have to believe that any such leveling would not have been reversed by the disequalizing forces we have observed over the last generation. The first three conditions must apply for any significant nonviolent leveling to take place at all, and all four are required to approximate levels of inequality in the world we live in today. This is an exceedingly tall order, and it strongly suggests that without major violent shocks, developed countries would currently experience considerably higher levels of income and wealth inequality than they actually do. The only real question is how much higher.

Some might be tempted to dismiss this observation as irrelevant, not merely because it is impossible to verify but above all because that is not the world we actually live in. But this would be a mistake. The counterfactual of peaceful leveling under conditions of modernity is important for a very specific reason: if we cannot tell whether or how much inequality would have been reduced in the absence of the global violence of the Great Compression, how can we judge the prospects of leveling in the present or the future? For all the regional crises that compete for our attention, the world of relative peace and stability and economic integration outlined in my counterfactual is in fact the world that most of humanity inhabits today. How have these conditions shaped current inequalities, and what do they imply for the future of leveling?

Part VII

INEQUALITY REDUX AND THE FUTURE OF LEVELING

Chapter 15

IN OUR TIME

RESURGENT INEQUALITY

The last generation to have lived through the Great Compression is rapidly fading. Ninety-five percent of Americans who served in World War II have passed away, and those who survive are mostly in their nineties. As with people, so with leveling. In developed countries, the massive decline in inequality that commenced in 1914 has long run its course. For about a generation, give or take a decade, income disparities have been growing in all countries for which we have reliable data (Table 15.1 and Fig. 15.1).[1]

In a sample of twenty-six countries, top income shares grew by half between 1980 and 2010, whereas market income inequality rose by 6.5 Gini points—an increase that could only partly be absorbed by an almost universal expansion of redistributive transfers. Statistically, 1983 was a major turning point, with downward trends in inequality reversed in Finland, France, Germany, Italy, Japan, and Switzerland, as well as modally for the entire sample. Anglo-Saxon economies had a head start, mostly in the 1970s: inequality began to rise in 1973 in the United Kingdom, in 1973 or 1976 in the United States, in 1977 in Ireland, in 1978 in Canada, and in 1981 in Australia. American wage dispersion already took off around 1970. Other metrics confirm this picture. Equivalized disposable household income Ginis and the ratios of top to bottom income shares generally increased from the 1970s or 1980s onward. Since the 1980s, the proportion of the population with middling incomes has been retreating relative to those in higher or lower income brackets in a number of OECD countries.[2]

---

[1] Table 15.1 and Fig. 15.1: WWID, SWIID.

[2] See Table 15.1. For the role of transfers in preventing a much steeper increase in disposable income inequality, see, e.g., Adema, Fron, and Ladaique 2014: 17–18 table 2; Morelli, Smeeding, and Thompson 2015: 643–645; and cf. also Wang, Caminada, and Goudswaard 2012. Wage dispersion: Kopczuk, Saez, and Song 2010: 104 fig. I (the wage Gini increased from 0.38 in 1970 to 0.47 in 2004); cf. also Fisher, Johnson, and

Table 15.1 Trends in top income shares and income inequality in select countries, 1980–2010

Country	Metric	1980	1990	2010	Lowest (year)
Australia	Top 1%	4.8	6.3	9.2	4.6 (1981)
	Gini (m)	35.5	38.1	43.3	
	Gini (d)	26.9	30.3	33.3	
Austria	Gini (m)	38.3 (1983)	44.0	42.3	
	Gini (d)	26.6 (1983)	28.4	27.4	
Belgium	Gini (m)	33.0	30.7	33.1	
	Gini (d)	22.6	23.0	25.2	
Canada	Top 1%	8.1	9.4	12.2	7.6 (1978)
	Gini (m)	34.9	37.6	42.2	
	Gini (d)	28.2	23.0	25.2	
Denmark	Top 1%	5.6	5.2	6.4	5.0 (1994)
	Gini (m)	43.1	43.6	46.7	
	Gini (d)	25.5	25.8	25.3	
Finland	Top 1%	4.3	4.6	7.5 (2009)	3.5 (1983)
	Gini (m)	37.5	38.2	45.1	
	Gini (d)	21.7	21.0	25.6	
France	Top 1%	7.6	8.0	8.1	7.0 (1983)
	Gini (m)	36.4	42.6	46.1	
	Gini (d)	29.1	29.1	30.0	
Germany	Top 1%	10.4	10.5 (1989)	13.4 (2008)	9.1 (1983)
	Gini (m)	34.4	42.2	48.2	
	Gini (d)	25.1	26.3	28.6	
Greece	Gini (m)	41.3 (1981)	38.6	43.2	
	Gini (d)	33.0 (1981)	32.7	33.3	
Ireland	Top 1%	6.7	7.3	10.5 (2009)	5.6 (1977)
	Gini (m)	41.3	42.6	45.2	
	Gini (d)	31.1	33.1	29.4	
Italy	Top 1%	6.9	7.8	9.4 (2009)	6.3 (1983)
	Gini (m)	37.0	39.7	47.2	
	Gini (d)	29.1	30.1	32.7	
Japan	Top 1%	7.2	8.1	9.5	6.9 (1983)[a]
	Gini (m)	28.3	31.3	36.3	
	Gini (d)	24.4	25.9	29.4	

Table 15.1 (*Continued*)

Country	Metric	1980	1990	2010	Lowest (year)
Korea	Top 1%	7.5	–	11.8	(6.9 (1995))
Luxembourg	Gini (m)	–	31.3	43.5	
	Gini (d)	–	24.0	26.9	
Netherlands	Top 1%	5.9	5.6	6.5	5.3 (1998)
	Gini (m)	33.8	38.0	39.3	
	Gini (d)	24.8	26.6	27.0	
New Zealand	Top 1%	5.7	8.2	7.4[b]	5.4 (1988)
	Gini (m)	29.7	36.0	35.5	
	Gini (d)	28.1	22.9	23.1	
Norway	Top 1%	4.6	4.3	7.8	4.1 (1989)
	Gini (m)	33.8	36.8	36.9	
	Gini (d)	23.5	22.9	23.1	
Portugal	Top 1%	4.3	7.2	9.8 (2005)	4.0 (1981)
	Gini (m)	33.9	45.1	50.5	
	Gini (d)	22.4	30.8	33.3	
Singapore	Gini (m)	(41.3)	(43.7)	46.9	
	Gini (d)	(38.3)	(40.8)	43.3	
South Africa	Top 1%	10.9	9.9	16.8	8.8 (1987)
Spain	Top 1%	7.5 (1981)	8.4	8.1[b]	7.5 (1981)[c]
	Gini (m)	35.4	35.9	40.9	
	Gini (d)	31.8	30.2	33.3	
Sweden	Top 1%	4.1	4.4	6.9	4.0 (1981)
	Gini (m)	39.3	41.9	48.5	
	Gini (d)	20.0	21.4	25.8	
Switzerland	Top 1%	8.4	8.6–9.2	10.6	8.4 (1983)
	Gini (m)	46.3	39.7	40.7	
	Gini (d)	30.3	32.2	29.8	
Taiwan	Top 1%	6.0	7.8	11.2	5.9 (1981)
	Gini (m)	27.8	29.2	32.4	
	Gini (d)	26.3	27.2	29.6	
UK	Top 1%	5.9–6.7[d]	9.8	12.6	5.7 (1973)
	Gini (m)	37.0	44.4	47.4	
	Gini (d)	26.7	32.8	35.7	

(*Continued*)

Table 15.1 (*Continued*)

Country	Metric	1980	1990	2010	Lowest (year)
U.S.	Top 1%	8.2	13.0	17.5	7.7 (1973)
	Top 1% (cg)	10.0	14.3	19.9	8.9 (1976)
	Gini (m)	38.6	43.3	46.9	
	Gini (d)	30.4	34.2	37.3	
Average	Top 1%[e]	6.7	7.8	10.0	6.1 (1983[f])
	Gini (m)	36.2	38.7	42.7	
	Gini (d)	28.0	28.1	29.8	
	Transfers	8.2	10.6	12.9	

m = market income, d = disposable income, cg = including capital gains
[a] 6.4 in 1945.
[b] See note 3.
[c] No data before 1980.
[d] 1979 and 1981.
[e] Without South Africa. With South Africa: 6.9 (1980), 7.9 (1990), 10.3 (2010), 6.2 (lowest, 1983).
Results based on uncertain data in brackets.
[f] Median and mode.

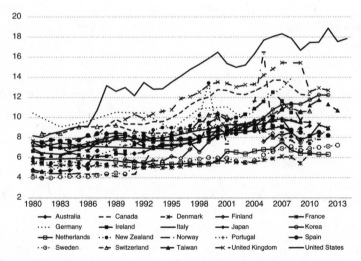

Figure 15.1 Top 1 percent income shares in twenty OECD countries, 1980–2013

Looked at more closely, even partial exceptions to this trend are almost completely absent. Owing to uneven data coverage for top income shares, I use single benchmark years in Table 15.1, a procedure that makes it seem as if inequality slightly fell in Spain and New Zealand and remained unchanged in France. If we apply five-year moving averages instead, it becomes clear that there is not a single country in this group where top income shares have not risen at least minimally since around 1990. If we follow the same method to track Gini coefficients, we find that disposable income inequality increased everywhere except in Austria, Ireland, and Switzerland—and that market inequality grew without any exception at all. And in most cases, the concentration of income has been much more pronounced: in eleven of the twenty-one countries with published top income shares, the portion of all income obtained by the "1 percent" rose between 50 percent and more than 100 percent between 1980 and 2010.[3]

In 2012, inequality in the United States even set several records: in that year, top 1 percent income shares (both with and without capital gains) and the share of private wealth owned by the richest 0.01 percent of households for the first time exceeded the high-water mark of 1929. Moreover, it is very likely that published Gini coefficients of income distribution understate actual levels of inequality, because they are derived from surveys that have trouble capturing information about the most affluent households. For the United States, various adjustments point to significantly higher Gini values, and progressively so over time. Thus, between 1970 and 2010, official Ginis of market income distribution rose from about 0.4 to 0.48 but may actually have been around 0.41 to 0.45 in 1970 and reached as high as 0.52 to 0.58 by 2010. Even the most conservative corrections see this inequality measure as soaring by more than a quarter from

---

Smeeding 2013 for parallel trends in U.S. income and consumption inequality up to 2006. Equivalized Ginis and S80/S20 and P90/P10 ratios: Morelli, Smeeding, and Thompson 2015: 635–640. Hollowing out of the middle class: Milanovic 2016: 194–200, esp. 196 fig. 4.8, for minimal changes in Canada, Germany, and Sweden, modest ones in Spain, and more pronounced shrinkage in Australia, the Netherlands, the United States, and especially the United Kingdom. For further summaries of these trends, see Brandolini and Smeeding 2009: 83, 88, 93–94; OECD 2011: 24 fig. 1, 39 fig. 12; Jaumotte and Osorio Buitron 2015: 10 fig. 1. Wehler 2013 devotes an entire book to rising inequality in Germany, a country that has so far been relatively successful in containing this phenomenon.

[3] In Spain, top 1 percent income shares averaged 8.3 percent from 1988 to 1992 and 8.4 percent from 2008 to 2012; in New Zealand, 7.3 percent from 1988 to 1992 and 8.1 percent from 2008 to 2012; and in France, 8 percent from 1988 to 1992 and 8.5 percent from 2008 to 2012. Between 1980 and 2010, top 1 percent income shares rose 51 percent in Canada, 54 percent in South Africa, 57 percent in Ireland and South Korea, 68 percent in Sweden, 74 percent in Finland, 81 percent in Norway, 87 percent in Taiwan, 92 percent in Australia, about 100 percent in the United Kingdom, and 99 percent to 113 percent in the United States (WWID).

0.41 in 1970 to 0.52 in 2010. Redistribution has only moderately mitigated this trend: from 1979 to 2011, annual income growth for the top 1 percent averaged 3.82 percent before taxes and transfers and 4.05 percent after, compared to 0.46 percent and 1.23 percent, respectively, among the bottom quintile.[4]

This trend has by no means been confined to the countries surveyed in Table 15.1. As I showed in more detail in chapter 7, formally or effectively post-communist societies have witnessed enormous increases in material inequality. This development has been particularly dramatic in China, where the market income Gini more than doubled from 0.23 in 1984 to somewhere around 0.55 in 2014 and the corresponding measure of wealth concentration rapidly rose from 0.45 in 1995 into the 0.7s by the early 2010s, and likewise in Russia, where the market income Gini has hovered above 0.5 since 2008, up from 0.37 in 1991, when the Soviet Union was dissolved, and from an even lower 0.27 in the early 1980s. Some major developing economies have experienced similar shifts: market income Ginis in India rose from 0.44–0.45 in the mid-1970s to 0.5–0.51 in the late 2000s, and top 1 percent income shares doubled between the late 1980s and 1999. Pakistan's market income Gini exploded from the low 0.3s around 1970 to 0.55 in 2010. Yet in much of the developing world, it is difficult to discern coherent long-term trends. In Indonesia, for instance, although it has recovered from a huge surge in income concentration centered on the 1990s, Gini coefficients and top income shares are still higher than they were around 1980. I already noted the complexities of African and Latin American inequality in chapter 13. Between the late 1980s and around 2000, income became more unevenly distributed in all types of economies except in low-income countries—in lower-middle-, upper-middle-, and high-income countries as well as globally. In every part of the world, the income share of the top 20 percent expanded between the 1990s and the early 2000s.[5]

It is striking that a wide variety of countries at different levels of development have come to share in this process of disequalization. To name just two examples,

---

[4] In the United States, excluding capital gains, they stood at 18.4 percent in 1929 and at 18.9 percent in 2012, and at 22.4 and 22.8 percent, respectively, if capital gains are included. The latest available values, for 2014, of 17.9 percent without and 21.2 percent with capital gains are slightly lower (WWID). Top wealth share: Saez and Zucman 2016: Online Appendix table B1. The fact that the wealth share of the richest 1 percent has not (yet) returned to 1929 levels shows that there is now more stratification within elite circles than there was then. Gini corrections: Morelli, Smeeding, and Thompson 2015: 679 and esp. 682 fig. 8.28. Taxes and transfers: Gordon 2016: 611 table 18–2.
[5] For Russia and China, see herein, chapter 7, pp. 222, 227. India, Pakistan, and Indonesia: SWIID, WWID. For Africa and Latin America, see herein, chapter 13, pp. 377–387. Global trends: Jaumotte, Lall, and Papageorgiou 2013: 277 fig. 1, 279 fig. 3.

both Russia and China have experienced a dramatic concentration of income and wealth even though one of them underwent economic collapse while the other enjoyed exceptionally strong growth. As a result, between 1990 and 2010, the extraction rate—the proportion of the theoretically possible maximum degree of inequality that was actually reached—remained largely flat in China as per capita GDP and Gini coefficients climbed in tandem but doubled in Russia, where output failed to outgrow Soviet levels. More generally, income inequality rose in Central and Eastern Europe and in Central Asia as the result of the transition from central planning to market economies but was driven by strong economic growth in East Asia and, up to around 2002, by macroeconomic crises and structural transformations in Latin America. Adding to this mix, a whole range of causes has been blamed for analogous changes in rich Western countries.[6]

With the exception of Latin America, what all of these societies have in common is that they participated in the Great Compression of the 1910s to the 1940s as well as in its more moderately equalizing aftermath. Countries that were directly involved in the world wars currently account for more than three-quarters of global nominal GDP, and when we include European bystanders and significantly affected former colonies, this proportion grows to more than four-fifths. The recent widespread rise in inequality might thus best be understood as an abatement of the equalizing consequences of earlier violent shocks that had pushed it down to unusually, and perhaps unsustainably, low levels.

MARKETS AND POWER

I began this book with an outline of the evolution of income and wealth inequality from the dawn of humanity to the twentieth century. Sampling the historical record across millennia, I was able to trace the concentration of resources in the hands of the few to two principal factors: economic development and predatory behavior by those powerful enough to appropriate wealth well in excess of what their activities might earn them in competitive markets—what economists call rents. These mechanisms remain active to the present day. Reduced to essentials, current debates over the causes of rising inequality tend to revolve around one fundamental question—the relative importance of market forces operating though supply and demand on the one hand and of institutions and

---

[6] Russia and China: Milanovic 2013: 14 fig. 6. Macroregional trends: Alvaredo and Gasparini 2015: 790; and see also Ravaillon 2014: 852–853.

power relations on the other. Although few if any serious observers would deny that all these have significantly contributed to the growing income disparities in advanced economies, the specifics are very much contested. In recent years, institutional and power-based explanations have gained ground just as proponents of supply and demand have been devising ever more sophisticated models that emphasize the centrality of technology, skills, and efficient markets.[7]

A number of observers have traced rising income inequality to higher returns on higher education, especially in the United States. Between 1981 and 2005, the mean earnings gap between high school graduates and those who had continued their education into college doubled from 48 percent to 97 percent. This development goes well beyond mere imbalances in gains: from 1980 to 2012, real earnings of male college graduates rose between 20 percent to 56 percent, with the largest benefits accruing to those with postbaccalaureate degrees, but fell 11 percent for high school graduates and 22 percent for high school dropouts. Roughly two-thirds of the increase in wage dispersion between circa 1980 and the early 2000s have been attributed to the expanded premium commanded by college-educated workers. After the share of college graduates in all hours worked had rapidly grown in the 1960s and 1970s, this increase slowed from about 1982, and premiums rose as demand for skilled labor outpaced supply. Technological change as well as globalization may have played a critical role, substituting automation for routine human labor, shifting manufacturing to overseas producers, and boosting demand for formal education, technical expertise, and cognitive ability more generally. This drove polarization between low-paid, manual-intensive and high-paid, abstract-intensive occupations as mid-level jobs were displaced and the middle tiers of the income distribution hollowed out. In developing countries, technological change may have had even more powerfully disequalizing consequences.[8]

---

[7] Recent surveys of the literature include Bourguignon 2015: 74–116, esp. 85–109; Keister 2014: 359–362; Roine and Waldenström 2015: 546–567; and above all Salverda and Checchi 2015: 1593–1596, 1606–1612. Gordon 2016: 608–624; Lindert and Williamson 2016: 227–241; and Milanovic 2016: 103–112 are the most recent summaries.

[8] Earnings gap: Autor 2014: 846; see also 844 fig. 1 for an increase in the median earnings gap between high school and college graduates from $30,298 to $58,249 in 2012 constant dollars between 1979 and 2012. Real earnings: ibid. 849; the divergence is less extreme among women. Contribution to inequality: 844 with references, esp. Lemieux 2006. Causes: 845–846, 849; for the importance of technological change see also, e.g., Autor, Levy, and Murnane 2003; Acemoglu and Autor 2012. Innovation (proxied by patenting) and top 1 percent income shares in the United States have followed parallel tracks since the 1980s, which suggests that innovation-led growth boosts top incomes: Aghion et al. 2016, esp. 3 figs. 1–2. Polarization: Goos and Manning 2007; Autor and Dorn 2013. Developing countries: Jaumotte, Lall, and Papageorgiou 2013: 300 fig. 7.

Greater investment in education is held up as a solution. Between 2004 and 2012, a renewed increase in the supply of college-educated workers in the United States coincided with flattened premiums (albeit at a high level). Except for the United Kingdom, skill premiums remained fairly flat or even declined in most European and several East Asian countries. Differences between countries are associated with the level of supply of educated workers. In fact, returns on education vary widely across countries: they can be twice as high in America as in Sweden. This is important not least because higher schooling premiums are associated with lower intergenerational earnings mobility.[9]

Even so, critics have pointed out various limitations of this approach. The phenomenon of polarization between high- and low-paid occupations may not be well supported by the evidence, and technological change and automation cannot properly account for the development of wage ratios since the 1990s. Rather, earnings variation within rather than between occupations seems to be a critical driver of inequality. Moreover, the strong rise in top incomes is particularly hard to explain with reference to education, a problem to which I return hereafter. Another twist is added by the observation of a growing mismatch in the United States between education and employment in that workers are increasingly overqualified for the work they do, a process that has also contributed to growing wage dispersion.[10]

Globalization is generally regarded as a potent disequalizing force. Its waxing and waning has long been associated with swings in inequality: whereas the first wave of globalization in the second half of the nineteenth and early twentieth century coincided with rising or stable (and high) inequality—not only in the West but also in Latin America and Japan—it fell during the hiatus from 1914 to the 1940s, which had been induced by war and the Great Depression. A survey of trends in some eighty countries between 1970 and 2005 finds that freedom of international trade and concurrent deregulation significantly raised inequality. Although globalization generally favors economic growth, elites tend to benefit disproportionately in both developed and developing countries. There are several reasons for this imbalance. On one

---

[9] Education as solution: e.g., OECD 2011: 31; Autor 2014: 850. Flattened premiums: Autor 2014: 847–848. Europe: Crivellaro 2014, esp. 37 fig. 3, 39 fig. 5; and see also Ohtake 2008: 93 (Japan); Lindert 2015: 17 (East Asia). Premiums across countries: Hanushek, Schwerdt, Wiederhold, and Woessman 2013. Mobility: Corak 2013: 87 fig. 4, 89 fig. 5.

[10] See now esp. Mishel, Shierholz, and Schmitt 2013. Mismatch: Slonimczyk 2013. For top incomes, see herein, pp. 417–420. Cf. Mollick 2012: 128 for the notion that a general transition to a service economy may be raising inequality.

estimate, China's embrace of capitalism, India's market reforms, and the fall of the Soviet bloc effectively doubled the number of workers in the global economy even as capital failed to increase at the same rate and the proportion of skilled labor in the global workforce declined, thus widening inequality in rich economies. Financial globalization in the form of direct foreign investment puts upward pressure on skill premiums and possibly also on returns to capital, and it raises inequality within higher income brackets. By contrast, competition from low-wage countries through trade in finished goods seems to have had only a modest effect on inequality in the United States. Offsets within global economic integration reduce the overall effect as equalizing consequences of trade globalization compete with disequalizing mobility of capital.[11]

Globalization is also capable of influencing policymaking. Intensified competition, financial liberalization, and the removal of obstacles to the flow of capital may encourage fiscal reforms and economic deregulation. As a result, globalization shifts taxation from corporate and personal to expenditure taxes, which tend to be associated with a less equal distribution of after-tax income. Even so, at least up to this point, international economic integration and competition is in theory expected to constrain only certain types of redistributive policies and in practice has not generally undermined welfare spending.[12]

In rich countries, demographic factors have impinged on the income distribution in different ways. Immigration has had only a small effect on inequality in the United States and has even generated equalizing consequences in some European countries. Conversely, assortative mating—more specifically, the growing economic similarity of marriage partners—has widened gaps between households and has been credited with causing some 25 percent to 30 percent of the overall increase in American earnings inequality between 1967 and 2005, even though this effect may have been largely concentrated in the 1980s.[13]

---

[11] Freeman 2009, Bourguignon 2015: 74–116, and Kanbur 2015 review the relationship between globalization and inequality. Earlier changes: Roine and Waldenström 2015: 548. Country panel: Bergh and Nilsson 2010. Elites: 495; Medeiros and Ferreira de Souza 2015: 884–885. Global workforce: Freeman 2009: 577–579; Alvaredo and Gasparini 2015: 748. Trade and financial globalization: Jaumotte, Lall, and Papageorgiou 2013: 274. Trade competition: Machin 2008: 15–16; Kanbur 2015: 1853. Policies: Bourguignon 2015: 115; Kanbur 2015: 1877.

[12] Taxation: Hines and Summers 2009; Furceri and Karras 2011. Welfare: Bowles 2012a: 73–100 (theory); Hines 2006 (practice).

[13] Immigration to the United States: Card 2009. Europe: Docquier, Ozden, and Peri 2014 (OECD); Edo and Toubal 2015 (France); and cf. also D'Amuri and Peri 2014 (Western Europe). For Latin America, see herein, chapter 13, p. 368 n. 1. Assortative mating: Schwartz 2010, with reference to earlier studies that attribute 17 percent to 51 percent of the overall increase to this factor. 1980s: Larrimore 2014.

Institutional change is another prominent culprit. Falling union membership rates and eroding minimum wages have been contributing to rising income disparities. Government redistribution has been found to be positively correlated with union density and collective wage bargaining. Stronger organized labor and employment protection lower returns to skills. More generally, union membership tends to compress wage inequality by institutionalizing norms of equity. The inverse—deunionization and downward pressure of real minimum wages—has consequently skewed the distribution of earnings: in the United States, a decline in private union membership from 34 percent to 8 percent for men and from 16 percent to 6 percent for women between 1973 and 2007 coincided with an increase in inequality in hourly wages of more than 40 percent and accounted for a sizeable share of overall disequalization in this period, on a scale similar to rising skill premiums. Minimum wages, by comparison, played a much smaller role in this process. At the same time, more equitable labor market institutions in continental Europe were more effective in limiting rising inequality.[14]

Just as labor market institutions help shape the way compensation for labor is allocated, fiscal institutions play a crucial role in determining the distribution of disposable income. During and after World War II, marginal tax rates on income in many developed countries had soared to record highs. This trend was reversed at about the same time when income inequality began to recover: one survey of eighteen OECD countries finds that in all but two of them, top marginal rates have declined since the 1970s or 1980s. Top income shares in particular have been strongly correlated with the burden of taxation: countries that saw significant tax cuts witnessed substantial growth in top incomes even as others did not. The scale of wealth taxation has trended in the same direction: whereas hefty inheritance taxes had hampered the rebuilding of large fortunes in the postwar period, subsequent tax reductions have facilitated renewed accumulation. In the United States, lower taxes on capital income have raised its

---

[14] Salverda and Checchi 2015 provide the most comprehensive survey of this topic. For the importance of unionization and minimum wages, see 1653, 1657, and also, e.g., Koeniger, Leonardi, and Nunziata 2007; and see Autor, Manning, and Smith 2010; Crivellaro 2013: 12 for the role of minimum wages. Visser and Checchi 2009: 245–251 find that coverage and centralization of union bargaining rather than union density per se are critical variables in affecting inequality. Redistribution: Mahler 2010. Unions and premiums: Crivellaro 2013: 3–4; Hanushek, Schwerdt, Wiederhold, and Woessman 2013. Variation between countries: Jaumotte and Osorio Buitron 2015: 26 fig. 7. U.S. unionization rates and wage dispersion: Western and Rosenfeld 2011. U.S. unions and minimum wage: Jaumotte and Osorio Buitron 2015: 26, and, more generally, Salverda and Checchi 2015: 1595–1596.

share of overall after-tax income, and large increases in the relative weight of capital gains and dividends accompanied tax cuts in the 2000s. Between 1980 and 2013, the average income tax rate for the top 0.1 percent of households fell from 42 percent to 27 percent, and average tax on wealth fell from 54 percent to 40 percent. Reduced tax progressivity accounts for about half of recent increases in American wealth dispersion, whereas rising income inequality has largely been driven by divergence in wages. Even though in recent decades the scale of redistribution increased in most OECD countries, taxes and transfers have not kept pace with rising market income inequality and since the mid-1990s have become a less effective means of equalization.[15]

Because taxes, business regulations, immigration laws, and various labor market institutions are determined by policymakers, several of the aforementioned sources of inequality are firmly embedded in the political sphere. I already mentioned that the competitive pressures of globalization may influence legislative outcomes at the national level. But politics and economic disequalization interact in manifold ways. In the United States, both of the dominant parties have shifted toward free-market capitalism. Even though analysis of roll call votes show that since the 1970s, Republicans have drifted farther to the right than Democrats have moved to the left, the latter were instrumental in implementing financial deregulation in the 1990s and focused increasingly on cultural issues such as gender, race, and sexual identity rather than traditional social welfare policies. Political polarization in Congress, which had bottomed out in the 1940s, has been rapidly growing since the 1980s. Between 1913 and 2008, the development of top income shares closely tracked the degree of polarization but with a lag of about a decade: changes in the latter preceded changes in the former but generally moved in the same direction—first down, then up. The same has been true of wages and education levels in the financial sector relative to all other sectors of the American economy, an index that likewise tracks partisan polarization with a time lag. Thus elite incomes in general and those in

---

[15] Tax rates and income inequality: Alvaredo, Atkinson, Piketty, and Saez 2013: 7–9, esp. 8 fig. 4 for top income shares; Piketty 2014: 509. (But cf. Mollick 2012: 140–141.) Downward trends: 499 fig. 14.1, 503 fig. 14.2; Morelli, Smeeding, and Thompson 2015: 661 fig. 8.21 (OECD); Scheve and Stasavage 2016: 101 fig. 4.1 (inheritance taxes); Saez and Zucman 2016: Online Appendix, table B32 (U.S.); and see also herein, chapter 5, pp. 143–144. Capital income: Hungerford 2013: 19–20. Sources of U.S. income and wealth dispersion: Kaymak and Poschke 2016: 1–25. Redistribution: OECD 2011: 37. Higher progressivity offset lower income taxes, Social Security benefits did not become more progressive, and benefits for those out of work contributed to market income inequality (38).

the finance sector in particular have been highly sensitive to the degree of legislative cohesion and have benefited from worsening gridlock.

Moreover, voter participation is strongly biased in favor of affluent households. Since the 1970s, traditionally low turnout among less affluent voters has been amplified by massive immigration of noncitizen low-income workers. In the 2008 and 2010 elections, voter participation was closely correlated with income and characterized by a fairly linear increase from low to high income households: in 2010, only a quarter of the poorest households but more than half of those enjoying incomes in excess of $150,000 cast their ballots. The American "1 percent" are both politically more active and more conservative regarding taxation, regulation, and social welfare than the population as a whole, and this skew is even stronger in the highest tiers of this income bracket. Finally, notwithstanding a huge increase in the number of itemized donations, campaign contributions have become more concentrated over time. The highest-earning 0.01 percent used to contribute 10 percent to 15 percent of all donated campaign funds in the 1980s but accounted for more than 40 percent of the total in 2012. Candidates and parties consequently increasingly rely on very rich donors, a trend that further reinforces a more general observable bias of legislators in favor of the preferences of high-income voters.[16]

All this amply supports the conclusion that shifts in power relations have been instrumental in complementing and exacerbating disequalizing pressures arising from technological change and global economic integration. There is now a growing consensus that changes at the very top of the income and wealth distribution have been particularly sensitive to institutional and political factors, sometimes with dramatic consequences. In the United States, 60 percent of the growth in market income between 1979 and 2007 was absorbed by the "1 percent," whereas only 9 percent of the total increase went to the bottom 90 percent. The same elite group pocketed 38 percent of all growth in after-tax income, compared to 31 percent for the bottom 80 percent. The share of the highest-grossing 0.01 percent of American households more than doubled between the early 1990s and the early 2010s. Dispersion has consistently been concentrated in higher income brackets: although the ratio of U.S. incomes at the ninetieth to those at the fiftieth percentile has continuously grown since

---

[16] I rely here on the excellent summary by Bonica, McCarty, Poole, and Rosenthal 2013, esp. 104–105, 106 fig. 1, 107, 108 fig. 2, 109 fig. 3, 110 fig. 4, 112 fig. 5, 118. See also Bartels 2008; Gilens 2012; Schlozman, Verba, and Brady 2012; Page, Bartels, and Seawright 2013.

the 1970s, the ratio of incomes at the fiftieth to those at the tenth percentiles (i.e., between middling and low levels) has been rather flat since the 1990s. In other words, the well-paid are pulling away from everybody else. This trend has been typical of Anglo-Saxon countries in general but is much weaker or even absent in most other OECD countries. Even so, overall income inequality has universally been sensitive to top income shares in the long run: in a number of countries, the share of the 9 percent of households below the top "1 percent" has been stable (at around 20 percent to 25 percent) from the 1920s to the present day, whereas top shares have been much more volatile. Similar trends have been observed for upper wealth shares. All this shows that the relative size of the largest incomes has been a major determinant of overall inequality and thus merits special attention.[17]

Why have the highest earners outpaced everybody else? Economists and sociologists have put forward many different explanations. Some focus on economic factors such as the relationship between higher executive compensation and the growing value of firms, increased demand for specific managerial skills, the extraction of rents by managers who are adept at manipulating corporate boards, and the growing importance of capital income. Others highlight political reasons such as partisanship and political influence biased in favor of conservative policies, deregulation of the financial sector, and falling tax rates or stress the role of social processes such as benchmarking and the use of upwardly skewed or aspirational samples for setting top salaries and, more generally, changes in social norms and notions of equity. Despite a growing emphasis on institutional causes, explanations that foreground supply and demand have proven resilient. Expanding firm size, expressed in market capitalization, might render even small differences in managerial ability very significant: thus it has been claimed that the sixfold increase in stock market value of large companies between 1980 and

---

[17] Distribution of income growth: Bivens and Mishel 2013: 58; Salverda and Checchi 2015: 1575 fig. 18.11(b). Top 0.01 percent: WWID; including capital shares, those shares rose from about 2.4 percent in 1992 and 1994 to about .5.1 percent in 2012 and 2014; six-year averages produce a steady rise, from 2.7 percent in 1992 and 1997 to 3.9 percent in 1996 and 2001, 4.6 percent in 2002 and 2007, and 4.8 percent in 2008 and 2014; moreover, the final two six-year means understate the scale of growth because they are depressed by the downturns centered on 2002 and 2009: the three-year means for 2005 and 2007 and 2012 and 2014 are 5.5 and 5.1 percent, respectively. Variation among countries: 1581 fig. 18.16, 1584 fig. 18.17, 1592. Top 1 versus 2–10 percent: Roine and Waldenström 2015: 496 fig. 7.3, 497–498; and see 539 fig. 7.20 for only a gentle decline of the top 2 percent to 5 percent wealth share over much of the twentieth century. Morelli, Smeeding, and Thompson 2015: 662–663 stress that the rise in top incomes is a robust trend and cannot be explained by better tax compliance.

2003 can fully account for the concurrent sixfold increase in CEO pay in the United States. Under the premise of winner-takes-all models, growing market size all by itself can be expected to boost compensation at the very top.

However, the correlation between firm size and executive pay does not hold in the longer run, and even in recent decades the disproportionate escalation of top incomes has extended well beyond executives and other "superstars": in the United States, top executives and elite entertainers and athletes account for only about a quarter of top income earners. Explanations that stress managerial power, which is relevant for only a relatively small group of CEOs, have difficulties accounting for similar or even larger relative pay increases for other positions. A combination of the effects of technological change, most notably in information and communications technology, and the increasingly global scale of certain businesses may raise the relative productivity of top performers in line with their swelling income shares.[18]

Yet critics forcefully argue that "affluence is strongly influenced by factors that have little or no association with economic productivity." In the finance sector, compensation levels have been closely tied to deregulation but are higher than can be explained by observable factors alone. Although up to the 1990s American finance workers earned the same education-adjusted wages as those in other sectors, by 2006 they enjoyed a 50 percent premium that rose as high as 250 percent or 300 percent for executives. A substantial portion of this dispersion remains unexplained. Such disproportionate gains for finance professionals as well as corporate executives point to rent-taking, defined as income in excess of what is required to secure services in competitive markets. Between 1978 and 2012, American CEO compensation rose 876 percent in 2012 constant dollars, dramatically outstripping increases of 344 percent and 389 percent for the Standard & Poor and Dow Jones stock market indices. During the 1990s, it also grew quite dramatically in relation to other top incomes or wages.

The supply of education relative to demand has no bearing on these developments and cannot explain the dispersion of incomes within the same

---

[18] Keister 2014 and Keister and Lee 2014 offer recent surveys of the "1 percent." Different types of explanations: Volscho and Kelly 2012; Keister 2014: 359–362; Roine and Waldenström 2015: 557–562. Market forces or not: Blume and Durlauf 2015: 762–764. Firm size: Gabaix and Landier 2008; Gabaix, Landier, and Sauvagnat 2014. Cf. also Rubin and Segal 2015 for the sensitivity of top incomes to stock market performance. Superstar/winner-takes-all models: Kaplan and Rauh 2010, esp. 1046–1048; Kaplan and Rauh 2013; and cf. also Medeiros and Ferreira de Souza 2015: 876–877; Roine and Waldenström 2015: 559–560. See also herein, 412 n. 8, for the effect of innovation-led growth on top incomes.

educational groups. In fact, social skills matter more than formal education in some of the most profitable areas of employment and business activity, and top executives may be valued in large part for their position within nontransferable networks of customers, suppliers, and managers that corporations need to access and control. Knock-on effects also merit attention: although soaring executive compensation and the "financialization" of the economy are directly responsible for only some of the recent growth in top incomes, their influence on other sectors such as law and medicine has amplified their disequalizing effect. Moreover, preferential treatment of well-placed workers also extends beyond private industry into the public sphere, as top income shares have benefited from reductions in marginal top tax rates across OECD countries. Although the creation of large fortunes frequently owes much to political influence and predatory behavior, power relations are even more important in non-Western societies: in the People's Republic of China, CEOs with a background in or strong connections to politics are better compensated than others, mostly for that reason.[19]

Finally—capital. Because wealth is invariably more unevenly distributed and more strongly concentrated among affluent households than income is, any increase in the relative importance of capital income or in the concentration of wealth is likely to push up income inequality. Resurgence of capital is a central theme of Piketty's recent work. This trend is most clearly visible in the recovery of the ratio of national wealth to national income, which had plummeted during the Great Compression. Since then, the relative size of wealth has grown considerably in a number of developed countries and also worldwide. Analogous trends have raised the ratio of private wealth to national income and of private capital to disposable income. The overall impact of this development on inequality remains contested. Critics have argued that much of this increase reflects the rising value of private housing and that adjustments in the way the contribution of housing to capital stocks is calculated point to stable rather than rising capital/income ratios in several major economies since the 1970s. And although the

[19] Quote: Medeiros and Ferreira de Souza 2015: 886. Finance sector: Philippon and Reshef 2012. Rent-taking and CEO pay: Bivens and Mishel 2013, esp. 57, 61 table 2, 69 fig. 2. Education: Roine and Waldenström 2015: 547, 550, 557. Social skills and networks: Medeiros and Ferreira de Souza 2015: 881–882. Financialization and inequality: Lin and Tomaskovic-Devey 2013, and cf. Davis and Kim 2015 for the process in general. Knock-on effects: Bivens and Mishel 2013: 66–67, and cf. Keister 2014: 360. Top tax rates and income shares: Atkinson and Leigh 2013; Piketty, Saez, and Stantcheva 2013; Roine and Waldenström 2015: 565–566. Large fortunes: Villette and Vuillermot 2009, based on thirty-two case studies. Chinese CEOs: Conyon, He, and Zhou 2015.

share of capital income in national income has been going up in a number of OECD countries during this period, the relative weight of income from capital and earnings from wages for those in the highest income brackets has not changed in a consistent fashion between the 1970s and the early 2000s.[20]

Wealth inequality has followed divergent trajectories. Since the 1970s, the share of private wealth held by the richest 1 percent of households has changed little in France, Norway, Sweden, and the United Kingdom; has declined in the Netherlands; and has risen moderately in Finland—and more strongly in Australia and the United States. American wealth has become concentrated even more rapidly than American income has. This process has been particularly pronounced among the very rich: between the late 1970s and 2012, the share of all private wealth held by the "1 percent" slightly less than doubled, but it tripled among the richest 0.1 percent and no less than quintupled among the top 0.01 percent of households. This has had dramatic repercussions for the distribution of capital income. In the same period, the share of the "1 percent" in all taxable capital income roughly doubled from one-third to two-thirds of the national total. In 2012, this group claimed three-quarters of all dividends and taxable interest. The single most spectacular increase concerns the share in all interest earned by the top 0.01 percent of households in this category, which grew thirteenfold from 2.1 percent in 1977 to 27.3 percent in 2012.[21]

These changes have helped drive up wealth inequality across American society: between 2001 and 2010, the Gini coefficient of the distribution of net worth rose from 0.81 to 0.85 and that for financial assets from 0.85 to 0.87. Although the distributions of earned and capital income have become more closely associated, the relative importance of wage income has been gently

---

[20] Piketty 2014: 171–222, esp. 171 fig. 5.3, 181, 195; Piketty and Zucman 2015: 1311 figs. 15.1–2, 1316 fig. 15.6, 1317 fig. 15.8. Housing: Bonnet, Bono, Chapelle, and Wasmer 2014; Rognlie 2015. Capital share in national incomes: Piketty 2014: 222 fig. 6.5. Top income components: Morelli, Smeeding, and Thompson 2015: 676–679, esp. 678 fig. 8.27. Labor income is crucial for the "1 percent" of many countries: Medeiros and Ferreira de Souza 2015: 872.

[21] International variation: Roine and Waldenström 2015: 574–575 table 7.A2; Piketty and Zucman 2015: 1320–1326. With its extensive online datasets, Saez and Zucman 2016 effectively supersedes all prior studies of U.S. wealth distribution. For wealth shares, see ibid. Online Appendix table B1: the top 1 percent wealth share grew from 22 percent in 1978 to 39.5 percent in 2012, the top 0.1 percent share from 6.9 percent in 1976 to 20.8 percent in 2012, and the top 0.01 percent share from 2.2 percent in 1978 to 11.2 percent in 2012. The corresponding shares in 1929, the previous height of American wealth inequality, were 50.6 percent, 24.8 percent, and 10.2 percent. B21–B22: the top 1 percent share in taxable capital income grew from 34 percent in 1978 to 62.9 percent in 2012, excluding capital gains, and from 36.1 percent to 69.5 percent with capital gains. For dividend and interest income shares, see tables B23a–b.

declining among the "1 percent." Since the 1990s, income from investments has become more important for top earners, lower taxes have increased its contribution to after-tax income, and a larger portion of the elite is now entirely dependent on investment income. Between 1991 and 2006, changes in capital gains and dividends were of critical importance in raising after-tax income inequality.[22]

Even if the United States stands out, growing wealth concentration is very much a global phenomenon. Between 1987 and 2013, the wealth of the super-rich—a rarified group defined as the richest 1 in 20 million or 1 in 100 million people on earth—enjoyed mean annual growth of 6 percent, compared to 2 percent for the globally average adult. Moreover, it has been estimated that 8 percent of the world's financial household wealth is currently being held in offshore tax havens and that much of it goes unrecorded. Considering that the rich are bound to disproportionately engage in this practice and that the estimated percentage for U.S. assets (4 percent) is much lower than that for Europe (10 percent), the actual degree of wealth concentration in notionally more egalitarian European countries may well be considerably higher than tax records suggest. Elites in developing countries park an even larger share of their assets overseas—perhaps as much as half of national private wealth, in the case of Russia.[23]

*

The widespread resurgence in income and wealth inequality of the last few decades seamlessly continues the narrative laid out in the opening chapters. Many of the variables reviewed in this section are closely tied to international relations. Globalization of trade and finance, a powerful driver of rising inequality, is predicated on a relatively peaceful and stable international order of the kind that the British Empire had come to ensure when worldwide economic integration first took off in the nineteenth century, was subsequently

---

[22] Wealth Ginis: Keister 2014: 353 fig. 2, 354. For the difficulties of measuring wealth shares, see, most recently, Kopczuk 2015, esp. 50–51 figs. 1–2. Association: Alvaredo, Atkinson, Piketty, and Saez 2013: 16–18. The share of wage income, including pensions, averaged 62 percent in 1979 to 1993, 61 percent in 1994 to 2003, and 56 percent in 2004 to 2013 (WWID). Lin and Tomaskovic-Devey 2013 argue that financialization has accounted for much of the decline in labor's share of income. Investment income: Nau 2013, esp. 452–454. Capital gains and dividends: Hungerford 2013: 19.

[23] Global wealth growth: Piketty 2014: 435 table 12.1. Offshore wealth: Zucman 2013 and esp. 2015: 53 table 1. Cf. also Medeiros and Ferreira de Souza 2015: 885–886.

reestablished under the effective hegemony of the United States, and then was further reinforced by the end of the Cold War. Key mechanisms of equalization such as unionization, public intervention in private-sector wage setting, and highly progressive taxation of income and wealth all first rose to prominence in the context of global war, as did full employment during and after World War II. In the United States, the disequalizing phenomenon of political polarization rapidly abated in the wake of the Great Depression and during World War II. And although ongoing technological change is a given, the counterbalancing provision of education is very much a matter of public policy. In the final analysis, the driving forces behind the disequalizing shifts of the last few decades reflect the evolution of interstate relations and global security since the Great Compression: after violent shocks had disrupted global exchange networks, boosted social solidarity and political cohesion, and sustained aggressive fiscal policies, their abatement has begun to erode these checks on income dispersion and the concentration of wealth.[24]

---

[24] Förster and Tóth 2015: 1804 fig. 19.3 offer a succinct qualitative summary of the multiple causes of inequality and their contrasting effects. In addition to the ones mentioned in the text, they also note assortative mating, single-headed households, voter turnout, partisanship, and female employment. Levy and Temin 2007 offer a synthetic historical account of institutional change since World War II that first contained and later precipitated income inequality. Historically, the role of the stagflation of the 1970s, which provided a powerful impulse for disequalizing economic liberalization, also needs to be taken into account. For a sociological perspective, see Massey 2007.

Chapter 16

WHAT DOES THE FUTURE HOLD?

UNDER PRESSURE

Before we address this question, it is worth recapitulating that across the globe, economic inequality is greater than it may seem if we simply rely on standard metrics. First of all, Gini coefficients, the most widely used means of measuring income inequality, are of limited value in capturing the contribution of the very highest incomes. Adjustments for this deficit point to significantly higher actual levels of inequality overall. Second, if unreported offshore funds could be incorporated into statistics of private household wealth, inequality would turn out to be higher in that category as well. Third, I have followed common practice in focusing on relative indices of income and wealth distribution. However, in terms of absolute inequality—the width of the gap between high and low incomes—even the fairly constant or only gently rising Gini coefficients and top income shares observed in some western European countries translate to growing imbalances in actual incomes (in Euros or other national currencies) when economic growth is taken into account.

This effect has been much stronger in societies, such as the United States, that have experienced both an increasingly skewed distribution of resources and stronger growth rates. In China, where the Gini coefficient of income distribution has more than doubled and average real per capita output has grown sixfold since the 1980s, absolute inequality has gone through the roof. Absolute income gaps have continued to grow even in Latin America, where a recent reduction in relative income inequality coincided with strong economic growth. Worldwide, absolute income inequality has risen to new heights. Between 1988 and 2008, the real incomes of the global top 1 percent posted percentage gains similar to those in the world's fifth, sixth, and seventh deciles but grew about forty times as much in per capita terms. Finally, as I discuss in more detail in the appendix, the maximum degree of income inequality that is theoretically feasible in a given society varies with per capita GDP. When we control for the fact that advanced economies are systemically less tolerant of an extreme maldistribution of resources than their agrarian precursors were, it is not at all clear that the United States today is *effectively* less unequal than it was 100 or 150 years ago.[1]

It is true that the last caveat only applies to modern economies with relatively high levels of nominal inequality. There can be no doubt that in much of continental Europe, where high levels of economic development are coupled with a more equitable distribution of disposable incomes, effective inequality—defined as the proportion of maximum feasible inequality that is actually being achieved—is currently much lower than it had been before the world wars. Even so, although top income shares in those countries tend to be smaller than in the United States, relatively moderate inequality in disposable household incomes is very much the result of massive redistribution that offsets generally high levels of market income inequality. In 2011, the Gini coefficient for market incomes—before taxes and transfers—in five famously redistributive societies—Denmark, Finland, France, Germany, and Sweden—averaged 0.474, a figure virtually indistinguishable from that for the United States (0.465) and the United Kingdom (0.472). It was only their mean Gini for disposable income (0.274) that was much lower than in the United Kingdom (0.355) and the United States (0.372).

Although several European countries enjoy somewhat lower market income inequality than the five cases mentioned here, that the scale of redistribution is, with very few exceptions, higher (and often much higher) than in the United States shows that the more balanced distribution of final incomes that is typical of the Eurozone and Scandinavia primarily depends on the maintenance of an expansive and expensive system of powerfully equalizing state interventions. This arrangement does not bode well for the future of European equality.

---

[1] See herein, chapter 15, pp. 409–410 (Gini adjustments), 422 (offshore wealth), Introduction, p. 13 (absolute inequality); Hardoon, Ayele, and Fuentes-Nieva 2016: 10 fig. 2 (growing absolute income gap between the top 10 percent and the bottom half in Brazil 1988 to 2011). For global inequality, see Milanovic 2016: 11 fig. 1.1, 25 fig. 1.2: real incomes of the global 1 percent rose about two-thirds, comparable to rates of the order of 60 percent to 75 percent between the fortieth and seventieth percentiles of the global income distribution; yet 19 percent of the total gain went to the 1 percent, 25 percent to the next highest 4 centiles, and only 14 percent to those in the middling three deciles. For even larger absolute gains of the global 1 percent relative to the bottom 10 percent, see Hardoon, Ayele, and Fuentes-Nieva 2016: 10–11. Effective inequality: herein, appendix, pp. 452–455.

Social and redistributive public expenditure is already very high in large parts of Europe. In 2014, eleven European countries committed between a quarter and a third of GDP to social spending, and in those countries, central governments absorbed between 44.1 and 57.6 percent of GDP, for a median of 50.9 percent. In view of the negative effect of government size on economic growth, it seems doubtful that this share could grow much further. From the early 1990s to the late 2000s, social spending as a proportion of national output had remained fairly flat in the European Union, in the United States, and across OECD countries, which suggests that a plateau had been reached. In 2009, it rose once again as a correlate of faltering economic performance and in response to increased demand caused by the global financial crisis but has remained at that newly elevated level ever since.[2]

It is an open question how well these high-equilibrium welfare systems will withstand two growing demographic challenges. The aging of European populations is one of them. Fertility rates have long been well below replacement level and will remain so for the foreseeable future. The median age of Europe's population is expected to rise from thirty-nine to forty-nine by 2050, whereas the number of those at working age has already peaked and may decline by about 20 percent between now and then. Between now and 2050 or 2060, the dependency ratio—the proportion of people aged sixty-five or older relative to those aged fifteen to sixty-four—will explode from 0.28 to 0.5 or more, and the share of those aged eighty or older will multiply from 4.1 percent in 2005 to 11.4 percent in 2050. Demand for pensions, health care, and long-term care will increase accordingly, by up to 4.5 percent of GDP. This fundamental restructuring of the age distribution will be accompanied by lower rates of economic growth than in previous decades, variously projected to average 1.2 percent from 2031 to 2050 or 1.4 or 1.5 percent per year from 2020

---

[2] Ginis: SWIID. In 2011 Portugal had an even higher market income Gini (0.502) than the United States. European countries with lower market Ginis include Austria, Belgium, the Netherlands, Norway, Spain, and Switzerland, although Belgium is the only real outlier: see herein, chapter 15, p. 406 table 15.1. In this latter group, only in Belgium and Spain was the gap between market and disposable income Ginis smaller than in the United States. For the redistributive effort required to stem rising market income inequality in Europe, see herein, chapter 15, pp. 406–407. Social spending: OECD 2014: 1 fig. 1 (in descending order, France, Finland, Belgium, Denmark, Italy, Austria, Sweden, Spain, Germany, Portugal, and, a smidgen under 25 percent, the Netherlands). Central government share in GDP: OECD, General government spending (indicator), doi: 10.1787/a31cbd4d-en. Bergh and Henrekson 2011 survey the literature on the relationship between government share of GDP and economic growth in high-income countries. Social spending trends: OECD 2014: 2 fig. 2. For the main components, see 4 fig. 4.

to 2060—and, indeed, much less among the core members of the European Union.[3]

The more modest rate of aging in recent decades has failed to have a significant effect on inequality, but this is likely to change. In principle, the shrinking ratio of retirees to workers is expected to raise inequality, as is the concurrent increase in the share of single-adult households. Private pensions, which are likely to gain in importance, tend to maintain or increase inequality. One study predicts much higher inequality in Germany in 2060 as a result of aging. In Japan, where the foreign-born make up a much smaller proportion of residents than in the European Union or the United States and the dependency ratio has already reached 0.4, rising income inequality has been attributed in large measure to the aging of its population. This is a sobering finding considering that—just as in South Korea and Taiwan—its highly restrictive immigration policy had previously helped maintain a relatively egalitarian distribution of income before taxes and transfers.[4]

All these projections assume a considerable volume of ongoing immigration: without this demographic contribution, the European dependency ratio could be as high as 0.6 by 2050. The arrival of many millions of newcomers will thus merely mitigate the long-term consequences of the secular aging process. At the same time, immigration may test redistributive policies in unprecedented ways. In his pioneering study of what he labels the "Third Demographic Transition," the eminent demographer David Coleman calculates that even on conservative assumptions about immigration rates and the fertility of immigrants, by 2050 the share of the national population that is of foreign origin (a concept whose definition varies by country) will reach between a quarter and a third in

---

[3] European Commission 2007, 2013, and 2015 are key reports on the scale and consequences of aging in Europe. Cf. also briefly United Nations 2015 for global trends. Fertility rates: European Commission 2007: 12 (about 1.5 now, projected to rise to about 1.6 by 2050). Median age and working age population: 13. Dependency ratios: 13 (rise to 53 percent by 2050); European Commission 2013 (rise to 51 percent by 2050) and 2015: 1 (rise to 50.1 percent by 2060). Eighty-year-olds and older: European Commission 2007: 13. Cf. 46 fig. 2.7., 49 fig. 2.9, and Hossmann et al. 2008: 8 on the range of future age pyramids. Growth as share of GDP: 13, with 70 table 3.3 (health care), 72 table 3.4 (long-term care); but contrast European Commission 2015: 4, for an additional 1.8 percent of GDP in spending required by 2060, albeit with great differences among countries (4–5). Economic growth rates: European Commission 2007: 62 (1.3 percent for EU-15 and 0.9 percent for EU-10 in 2031–2050), 2013: 10 (1.2 percent 2031–2050), 2015: 3 (1.4–1.5 percent 2020–2060).

[4] Effects on inequality: Faik 2012, esp. 20–23 for the forecast (Germany); European Commission 2013: 10–11, 16. Japan: Ohtake 2008: 91–93 for the disequalizing consequences of aging in conjunction with an expansion of informal labor relations among the young. Restrictions on immigration and domestic equality: Lindert 2015: 18.

six out of seven countries he reviews: Austria, England and Wales, Germany, the Netherlands, Norway, and Sweden. These countries contain about half of the population of Western Europe, and many others will undergo similar changes. Moreover, the presence of individuals in this category will be much greater among children in education and young workers—in some cases up to half of national totals. Non-Western immigrants are projected to account for up to a sixth of the German and Dutch population. Because there is no compelling reason to assume that these trends will abate by mid-century, the Netherlands and Sweden might turn into countries having majority foreign-origin populations by 2100.[5]

Demographic replacement on this scale not only would be without precedent in the history of that part of the world since the emergence of agriculture but also might influence inequality in unpredictable ways. From an economic perspective, much hinges on the successful integration of immigrants. Their educational attainment is and will continue to be much lower than for European nationals, and employment rates are low in a number of countries, especially for women. The persistence or worsening of these problems may produce disequalizing consequences for the societies in question. Moreover, the growth of communities of first-generation immigrants and those of recent foreign-origin family background has the potential to affect attitudes and policies regarding social welfare and redistributive spending. Alberto Alesina and Edward Glaeser have argued that welfare policies are correlated with ethnic homogeneity, which helps explain why the United States developed a weaker welfare state than European countries. They anticipate that growing immigration will undermine the generosity of European welfare states and that anti-immigrant sentiment may be used to dismantle redistributive policies and "eventually push the continent toward more American levels of redistribution." At least up to this point, this prediction has not been borne out by actual developments. A recent comprehensive survey has found no support for the notion that immigration undermines public support for social policy.[6]

<hr>

[5] Dependency ratio: Lutz and Scherbov 2007: 11 fig. 5. Coleman 2006, esp. 401, 414–416. Even a zero immigration policy would reduce the foreign-origin population by not more than a third to a half by 2050 (417). Children and young workers: European Commission 2015: 27.

[6] Scale of replacement: Coleman 2006: 419–421. Education, employment and integration: European Commission 2007: 15, 2013: 28. Heterogeneity: Alesina and Glaeser 2004: 133–181 (quote: 175). Survey: Brady and Finnigan 2014: 19–23.

But more specific observations show there is cause for concern. Greater heterogeneity and more immigration are in fact associated with less extensive social policy provisions as well as higher levels of poverty and inequality. In European OECD countries, ethnic diversity may be only weakly inversely correlated with levels of public social spending but has a stronger negative effect on attitudes that is mediated by the unemployment rate. Affluent Europeans—who carry much of the fiscal burden—express less support for redistribution if many of the low-income members of their societies belong to ethnic minorities. According to British surveys, redistributive preferences in the context of taxation weaken if ethnic diversity causes the poor to be perceived as different. The sources and dimensions of heterogeneity are of vital importance: immigration and religious heterogeneity have a more powerful adverse effect on welfare state provisions than the presence of ethnoracial minorities. The first two of these factors have already become defining features of the European experience, and the likelihood of persistent migratory pressures from the Middle East and Africa will ensure their continuing and arguably growing relevance. In all of this, it is important to realize that Europe's "Third Demographic Transition," which will transform the composition of national populations in response to subreplacement fertility and immigration, is still in its early stages. Over the course of the next generation, it may alter established patterns of redistribution and inequality in ways impossible to anticipate. Considering the high costs of current systems and the disequalizing pressures exerted by aging, immigration, and growing heterogeneity, these changes are more likely to raise inequality than to hold it in check.[7]

Not all demographic factors are equally likely to have a significant effect on the further evolution of inequality. There is no good evidence that the frequency of assortative mating that might widen income and wealth disparities among households has been growing in the United States in recent years. Likewise, intergenerational mobility in terms of income does not appear to have slowed, although a longer time frame might be needed to generate conclusive findings.

---

[7] Waglé 2013 is now the most detailed analysis, noting throughout the complexities of the relationship between heterogeneity and welfare (esp. 263–275). Ho 2013 argues that ethnic diversity per se does not reduce redistribution once other identities are taken into account. See Huber, Ogorzalek, and Gore 2012 for the different effects of democracy on inequality in homogeneous and heterogeneous countries, and Lindqvist and Östling 2013 for a model that predicts maximization of welfare under ethnic homogeneity. Correlations: Mau and Burkhardt 2009; Waglé 2013: 103–262. Attitudes: Finseraas 2012; Duch and Rueda 2014; and see also European Commission 2007: 15, 104. Immigration and religious heterogeneity: Waglé 2013: 164, 166. Lindert and Williamson 2016: 246 speculate that future immigration might raise European inequality by increasing the labor supply.

Conversely, growing residential segregation by income, which has been on the rise in America, may have a stronger effect on inequality in the long run. Insofar as the income of one's neighbors indirectly affects one's own socioeconomic outcomes and the spatial concentration of specific income groups skews the distribution of locally funded public goods, growing economic imbalances in the physical distribution of the population can be expected to perpetuate—and, indeed, reinforce—inequality in future generations.[8]

Piketty's argument that ongoing accumulation capital will raise both its share in national income and its overall importance relative to national income as rates of return on capital investment exceed economic growth, thereby putting upward pressure on inequality, has attracted a fair amount of criticism and caused its main proponent to stress the uncertainties associated with these predictions. Yet there is no shortage of other economic and technological forces capable of exacerbating existing disparities in the distribution of income and wealth. Globalization, which has been credited with disequalizing effects, especially in developed countries, shows no sign of abating in the near future. Whether this process will create some kind of global super-elite unfettered by the constraints of national policies, exemplified by the much-maligned image of "Davos Man" and heralded in the popular press, remains to be seen. By their very nature, automation and computerization are more open-ended processes that are bound to influence the distribution of returns to labor. According to one estimate, almost half of all employment in 702 occupations across the America labor market is at risk from computerization. Notwithstanding predictions that automation will not indefinitely serve to polarize labor markets between high and low incomes, future breakthroughs in artificial intelligence that would allow machines to catch up with or surpass humans in terms of general intelligence render moot any attempts to forecast long-term outcomes.[9]

---

[8] Greenwood, Guner, Kocharkov, and Santos 2014 find that assortative mating increased in the 1960s and 1970s but not since, whereas Eika, Mogstad, and Zafar 2014 observe its decline among the college-educated and its rise at low education levels. For intergenerational mobility, see herein, in the introduction, p. 20, and esp. Chetty et al. 2014 for stable rates. Residential segregation: Reardon and Bischoff 2011a: 1093, 1140–1141; 2011b: 4–6.

[9] Piketty 2014: 195–196; Piketty and Saez 2014: 840–842; Piketty and Zucman 2015: 1342–1365, esp. 1348 fig. 15.24. For a random sample of critiques, see Blume and Durlauf 2015: 755–760 and Acemoglu and Robinson 2015, the latter with the response by Piketty 2015b: 76–77, who notes the uncertainties involved in his prediction (82, 84). Cf. also Piketty 2015a for responses to other work. For the effects of globalization, see herein, chapter 15, pp. 413–414. Disequalizing trade competition from low-income countries is likely to continue: Lindert and Williamson 2016: 250; cf. Milanovic 2016: 115. Global super-elite: Rothkopf 2008; Freeland 2012. On computerization and labor markets, see now esp. Autor 2015: 22–28, and, more generally, Ford 2015. Estimate: Frey and Osborne 2013. Among many others, Brynjolfsson and McAfee 2014 stress the enormous transformative potential of computerization. For AI, see most recently Bostrom 2014.

Our remaking of the human body will open up new frontiers in the evolution of inequality. The creation of cybernetic organisms and genetic engineering have the potential of expanding disparities among individual persons and even their descendants well beyond their natural endowments and the extrasomatic resources they command, and they may do so in ways that feed back into the future distribution of income and wealth. As advances in nanotechnology greatly expand the use and utility of artificial implants, applications may increasingly shift from restoration of functions to their enhancement. Over the last few years, advances in gene editing have made it possible to delete and insert specific pieces of DNA both in Petri dishes and in living organisms with unprecedented ease. Although the consequences of such interventions may be confined to individual organisms, they can also be made hereditary by manipulating the genetic makeup of sperms, eggs, and small embryos. The results of the first experiment in modifying the genome of (nonviable) human embryos were published in 2015. Recent progress in this field has been extremely rapid and will continue to take us far into uncharted territory. Depending on cost and availability, the affluent may come to enjoy privileged access to some of these biomechatronic and genetic refinements.

There is reason to doubt that political constraints would prove sufficient to suppress these opportunities: unlike public health, enhancements are an upgrade and thus are more amenable to unequal provisioning. Legal restrictions in Western democracies, which are already being proposed, could well precipitate even more unequal outcomes by handing an advantage to those able to afford private treatment in those countries where it will be offered—most likely, in parts of Asia. In the long run, the creation of designer babies for the rich and well-connected might curtail mobility between genetic or cyborg haves and have-nots and even, at least in theory, ultimately result in a bifurcation into two different species—such as the genetic elite of the "GenRich" and the "Naturals," or everybody else, envisioned by Princeton geneticist Lee Silver.[10]

Education has long been the default response to technological change. It may remain so under continuing globalization and—although perhaps only up

---

[10] Center for Genetics and Society 2015 surveys recent advances in genetic techniques, most notably genomic editing by means of CRISPR/Cas9; see esp. 20–25 on germline modification, and 27–28 on ethics and inequality. Liang et al. 2015 report on human embryo gene editing at a Chinese university, which was largely unsuccessful. See also Church and Regis 2014 for the potential of synthetic biology. Harari 2015 makes valuable points about the limits of political constraints. Bostrom 2003 considers the equality outcomes of genetic modifications, while Harris 2010 is sanguine about their ethics and desirability. Speciation: Silver 1997.

to a point—in the event of further breakthroughs in computerization. But after humans become more unequal thanks to genetic engineering or body–machine hybridization—or, most likely, both—this paradigm will be stretched to its breaking point. Would education ever be capable of counteracting entirely new degrees of artificial physical and mental enhancement? But we should not get ahead of ourselves. Long before the time has come to worry about super-robots who do the bidding of superhumans, the world faces the more mundane challenge of existing income and wealth inequality. I now return one last time to the central topic of this book: the reduction of inequality. What, then, are the prospects of leveling?

RECIPES

There is currently no shortage of proposals on how to reduce inequality. Nobel laureates in economics have joined their less decorated but sometimes even better-selling peers and assorted journalists in the lucrative business of publishing long lists of measures designed to rebalance the distribution of income and wealth. Tax reform occupies a prominent position. (Unless noted otherwise, the following refers to conditions in the United States.) Income should be taxed in a more progressive manner; capitals gains should be taxed as ordinary income and higher taxes imposed on capital income in general; regressive payroll taxes should be eliminated. Wealth should be taxed directly and in ways designed to curtail its transmission across generations. Sanctions such as trade tariffs and the creation of a global wealth register would help prevent offshore tax evasion. Corporations should be taxed on their global profits and hidden subsidies ended. French economists have even proposed an annual global tax on wealth, withheld at the source. In addition, a larger one-time levy on capital would reduce public debt and help rebalance the ratio of private to public wealth. The demand-and-supply approach to skills referenced earlier has brought attention to the role of education. Public policy should aim to boost intergenerational mobility by equalizing access to and the quality of schooling. Disconnecting school funding from local property taxes would be one step in that direction. Universal provision of preschool would be helpful, and price controls might be imposed on tertiary education. More generally, improved education would result in "up-skilling" of the workforce in a competitive global environment.

On the expenditure side, public policies should provide forms of insurance that protect the value of the assets of lower-income groups against exogenous shocks, from housing values to worker-owned cooperatives to people's health. Universal health care would buffer against such shocks. It should be easier for the less affluent to secure credit for entrepreneurial activity, and bankruptcy law should be made more forgiving to debtors. Lenders should be offered incentives or otherwise forced to restructure mortgages. More ambitious schemes include a basic minimum income, matching grants for personal savings up to a ceiling, and the provisioning of each child with a minimum endowment of stocks and bonds. Business regulation is another item on the agenda. The market distribution of incomes could be adjusted by changing laws regarding patents, antitrust, and contracts; by curbing monopolies; and by more strictly regulating the financial sector. Corporate taxes might be linked to the ratio of CEO compensation to worker median wage. Rent-seeking behavior of executives should be tackled through corporate governance reform. The standing of shareholders and employees should be shored up by ensuring the latter's representation and voting rights and by compelling companies to share profits with workers. Institutional reforms should revive union power, raise minimum wages, improve access to employment for underrepresented groups, and create federal jobs programs. Immigration policies should favor the import of skilled labor in order to lower skill premiums. The disequalizing impact of globalization could be mitigated by international coordination of labor standards and taxing foreign earnings and corporate profits regardless of the location of production. International capital flows should be regulated—and according to a particularly bold suggestion, the United States might want to require trade partners to institute minimum wages equal to half their respective national median wages. In the political sphere, America should combat inequality by passing campaign finance reform and take measures to raise voter turnout. Intervention in the media might democratize their coverage.[11]

Recent discussions have focused mostly (or even exclusively) on the content of policy measures without paying adequate attention to the likely scale of their costs and benefits and their real-life political feasibility. A few examples will suffice. Francois Bourguignon estimates that the effective tax rate on America's "1 percent" would have to nearly double, from 35 percent to 67.5

---

[11] This is a florilegium of the ideas put forward in OECD 2011: 40–41; Bowles 2012a: 72, 98–99, 157, 161; Noah 2012: 179–195; Bivens and Mishel 2013: 73–74; Corak 2013: 95–97; Stiglitz 2013: 336–363; Piketty 2014: 515–539, 542–544; Blume and Durlauf 2015: 766; Bourguignon 2015: 160–161, 167–175; Collins and Hoxie 2015: 9–15; Kanbur 2015: 1873–1876; Ales, Kurnaz, and Sleet 2015; Reich 2015: 183–217; Zucman 2015: 75–101.

percent, to reduce their share in disposable household income even to the level of 1979—a goal that "does not look entirely feasible from a political viewpoint." Piketty considers a top income tax rate of 80 percent "optimal" in terms of economic costs versus equality benefits but readily concedes that "it seems quite unlikely that any such policy will be adopted anytime soon." Proposals whose success is predicated on effective global policy coordination raise the bar to dizzying heights. Ravi Kanbur advocates the creation of an international body for coordinating labor standards—akin to a miracle weapon in the fight against globalization pressures—"leaving aside the political feasibility or operational practicality of such an agency." Piketty states outright that this proposed "global tax on capital is a utopian idea" but sees "no *technical* reason why" a Europewide wealth tax would not be realistic. Lofty ideas of this kind have been criticized, however, as not only unhelpful but also potentially counterproductive for threatening to divert attention from more feasible measures. In all of this, serious consideration of the means required to mobilize political majorities for implementing any of this advocacy is conspicuous by its absence.[12]

The most detailed and precise equalization program that has been put forward to date, Anthony Atkinson's recent blueprint for how to reduce inequality in the United Kingdom, illustrates the limitations of this policy-oriented approach. Numerous and often ambitious measures add up to a comprehensive reform package: the public sector should seek to influence technological change by "encouraging innovation that increases the employability of workers"; legislators should strive to "reduce market power in consumer markets"

---

[12] Income tax: Bourguignon 2015: 163; Piketty 2014: 512–513 (quote: 513), drawing on Piketty, Saez, and Stantcheva 2013. Global labor standards: Kanbur 2015: 1876. Wealth tax: Piketty 2014: 515, 530 (quotes; my emphasis). Criticism: Piachaud 2014: 703, on the idea of a global wealth; cf. also Blume and Durlauf 2015: 765. Others have criticized Piketty's focus on taxation: 765–766; Auerbach and Hassett 2015: 39–40. Bowles 2012a: 156–157 notes the importance of devising politically viable policy designs. Regarding political action, Levy and Temin 2007: 41 note that "[o]nly a reorientation of government policy can restore the general prosperity of the postwar boom," and Atkinson 2015: 305 reminds us that "[t]here has to be an appetite for action, and this requires political leadership." This begs the question of implementation; Atkinson's reference to the improvements made "in the period of the Second World War and subsequent postwar decades" (308; cf. 55–77 for a historical survey) is very much to the point but offers scant hope for the present. Stiglitz 2013: 359–361, on the prospects of putting his numerous proposals into practice, offers no substantive suggestions. Milanovic 2016: 112–117 voices healthy skepticism regarding the potential of various equalizing forces (political change, education, and an abatement of globalization pressures), placing hope on the slow dissipation of rents over time and the emergence of future technologies that might increase the relative productivity of low-skilled workers. He is particularly pessimistic about the short-term prospects of economic equalization in the United States, where all indicators point to a continuing rise in inequality in the near future (181–190, esp. 190).

and revive the bargaining power of organized labor; firms should share profits with workers in ways that "reflect ethical principles" or be barred from supplying public bodies; the top income tax rate should rise to 65 percent, income from capital should be taxed more aggressively than earnings from labor, taxes on estates and gifts should *inter vivos* be tightened, and property taxes should be set based on up-to-date assessments; national savings bonds should guarantee a "positive (and possibly subsidized) real rate of interest on savings" up to a personal cap; a statutory minimum wage should be "set at a living wage"; every citizen should receive a capital endowment upon reaching maturity or a later date; and "the government should offer guaranteed employment at the living wage to everyone who seeks it" (which Atkinson himself concedes "may seem outlandish"). Possible add-ons include an annual wealth tax and a "global tax regime for personal taxpayers, based on total wealth." In addition, the European Union should be persuaded to introduce "universal basic income for children" as a taxable benefit indexed to median national income.

In his extended discussion of whether this could actually be accomplished, Atkinson focuses on the costs to the economy (which remain unclear); the countervailing pressures of globalization, which he hopes to counter through European or global policy coordination; and fiscal affordability. Unlike other proponents of equalizing reform measures, Atkinson also ventures an estimate of the likely effect of this package: if four major policies were implemented— higher and more progressive income taxes, an earned income discount at low income levels, substantial taxable benefits paid out for each child, and a minimum income for all citizens—the Gini coefficient of equalized disposable income would fall by 5.5 percentage points, thereby narrowing the current inequality gap between Britain and Sweden by a little more than half. More limited changes would translate to correspondingly lesser improvements on the order of 3 or 4 percentage points. To put this in perspective, by his own account, the same British Gini had gone up by 7 percentage points between the late 1970s and 2013. Thus even a combination of several quite radical and historically unprecedented government interventions would reverse the effects of resurgent inequality only partially, and more moderate policies would yield even smaller benefits.[13]

---

[13] Atkinson 2014a and 2015. In addition to Atkinson 2015: 237–238, I quote mostly from the summary version (2014a). For the question "Can it be done?" see 241–299. Gini reduction: 294, with 19 fig. 1.2, 22 fig. 1.3 (and cf. also 299 for a probable reduction of about 4 points). The British income Gini fell by about 7 points during World War II: 19 fig. 1.2.

A WORLD WITHOUT HORSEMEN?

"*Tout cela est-il utopique?*"[14] Even when they are not outright utopian, many of these policy recommendations suffer from a lack of historical awareness. Reforms at the margins are unlikely to have a significant effect on current trends in the distribution of market income and wealth. Atkinson's discussion has the unique merit of considering both the price of an ambitious package of measures and its probable effect on disposable income inequality, which for any realistic policy configuration is relatively modest. More generally, there seems to be surprisingly little interest in how to turn such proposals into reality or even in whether they could ever make a big difference. And yet history teaches us two important things about leveling. One is that radical policy interventions occur in times of crisis. The shocks of the world wars and the Great Depression, to say nothing of assorted communist revolutions, generated equalizing policy measures that owed much to these specific contexts and that may not have been feasible under different circumstances—at the very least, not on the same scale. The second lesson is even more straightforward: policymaking can take us only so far. Time and again the compression of material imbalances within societies was driven by violent forces either that were outside human control or that are now far beyond the scope of any viable political agenda. None of the most effective mechanisms of leveling are operational in the world today: the Four Horsemen have dismounted their steeds. And nobody in his or her right mind would want them to get back on.

Mass mobilization warfare has run its course. The format of military conflict has always been decisively shaped by technology. Sometimes this favored investment in high-value assets such as ancient war chariots or medieval knights, and at other times it gave an edge to massed low-cost infantry. In the West, national mass armies replaced mercenaries when fiscal-military states matured in the early modern period. Popular military mobilization scaled new heights with the French Revolution and culminated in the armies of millions raised to fight the two world wars. Since then, trends have once again moved in the opposite direction—from quantity to quality. In theory, nuclear weapons may have made large-scale conventional war obsolete as early as the late 1940s, although in practice it survived for lower-stakes conflicts and those between or involving powers lacking nuclear capabilities. Conscription has faded, increasingly

---

[14] Piketty 2013: 921 (English translation in Piketty 2014: 561).

replaced by volunteer armies of professionals charged with handling more sophisticated equipment.

In those relatively few developed countries that still engage in military operations, military service has often become detached from mainstream society, and equalizing "mobilization effects" have disappeared. In the United States, 1950 was the last time when tax increases to pay for war were passed without serious debate. Even at a time when the draft was still in place, the Revenue Act of 1964 provided for the largest tax cuts in American history prior to 1981 even as military involvement in Vietnam was expanding. Surges in U.S. military spending in the 1980s and during the invasions of Afghanistan and Iraq in the 2000s were both accompanied by tax cuts as well as rising income and wealth inequality, the inverse of what had happened during the world wars. The same was true of the United Kingdom before and after the Falklands War of 1982.

Although recent conflicts have been relatively modest in scale or—in the case of the Cold War—never actually progressed to open hostilities, bigger wars, were they to break out, would be unlikely to alter this trajectory in coming decades. It is hard to see how the largest imaginable conflict short of thermonuclear conflagration, all-out conventional war between the United States and China, could productively involve very large armies. Even more than seventy years ago, the Pacific War already privileged expensive ships and airpower over massed infantry forces, and any future fighting in this region would primarily involve air and sea power, missiles, satellites, and all manner of cyber warfare, none of which is amenable to mass mobilization. Nor, in extremis, is nuclear warfare. Russia is currently shedding conscripts in favor of volunteers, and a large majority of European Union countries have already abolished the draft altogether. India and Pakistan, two other potential parties to large-scale warfare, likewise rely on volunteers. Even Israel, whose military capabilities dwarf those of its increasingly unstable neighbors, is envisioning an eventual transition of this kind.

Ultimately, it is simply not clear what very large infantry armies would be able to accomplish on twenty-first century battlefields. Current projections of the nature of future combat focus on "robotics, smart munitions, ubiquitous sensing, and extreme networking, along with the potentially massive impact of cyber warfare." There will be fewer but higher-performance human combatants, physically and cognitively augmented with exoskeletons, implants, and eventually perhaps also genetic enhancements. They will share battlefields with robots in all shapes and sizes, as small as insects and as large as vehicles, and might operate directed energy weapons such as lasers and microwave rays, as well as force fields. Weapons miniaturization will allow precision targeting down to the level of specific individuals, replacing more indiscriminate projection of force, and high-speed, high-altitude super-drones may make human pilots redundant. These scenarios are exceedingly remote from earlier forms of industrialized warfare and will further reinforce the separation of the military from the civilian domain. Any equalizing effects of such conflicts are likely to be concentrated in the financial markets, triggering dislocations akin to those of the recent global financial crisis that only temporarily depress elite wealth until it rebounds a few years later.[15]

Much the same would be true of wars that involved the limited tactical use of small-scale nuclear devices. Only all-out thermonuclear war might fundamentally reset the existing distribution of resources. If escalation could be contained at a point where public institutions are still functioning and sufficient amounts of critical infrastructure remain intact, governments and military authorities would freeze wages, prices, and rents; block non-essential withdrawals from banks; impose a comprehensive rationing system for food; requisition needed goods; adopt forms of central planning, including the centralized allocation of scarce resources in favor of the war effort, government operations, and the production of survival items essential to survival; assign housing; and possibly even resort to forced labor. In American planning for the "Day After," the sharing of war losses throughout the economy has long been a key policy goal. Any strategic-level exchange of nuclear warheads between major powers would wipe out physical capital on a vast scale and wreck financial markets. The most likely outcome would be not only a dramatic fall in GDP but also an equalizing rebalancing of the available resources and a shift from capital to labor.

A doomsday scenario of unrestricted nuclear warfare is bound to take leveling far beyond these projected outcomes. It would represent an extreme version of systems collapse, exceeding in severity even the dramatic fall of early civilizations discussed in chapter 9. Although contemporary science fiction accounts of a postapocalyptic world sometimes envision high degrees of inequality between those in control of scarce vital resources and deprived majorities, the experience of the thoroughly impoverished and less stratified postcollapse communities of premodern history might be a better guide to conditions in a future "nuclear winter."

---

[15] Projections: Kott et al. 2015, esp. 1 (quote), 7–11, 16–17, 19–21. For the future use of robots, see also Singer 2009. For the effects of recent economic crises, see herein, chapter 12, p. 364.

But this is unlikely to happen. Although nuclear proliferation may change the rules of the game in regional theaters, the same existential risks that have prevented nuclear war between major powers since the 1950s continue to apply. Moreover, the mere existence of stockpiles of nuclear weapons makes it less likely that core regions such as the United States or China will get massively involved even in conventional warfare and serves to displace conflict into global peripheries, which in turn lowers the odds of severe damage to the world's major economies.[16]

Weapons technology is only part of the story. We must also allow for the possibility that humankind has become more peaceful over time. Various strands of evidence reaching back to the Stone Age strongly suggest that the average probability of a person's death from violent causes has been declining in the very long run of history—and that this trend continues. Although this secular shift appears to be driven by the growing power of the state and attendant cultural adaptations, a more specific factor that has already been mentioned is about to reinforce the pacification of our species. All other things being equal, the aging of populations, which has already begun in the West and which will eventually occur everywhere in the world, can be expected to reduce the overall likelihood of violent conflict. This is particularly relevant for assessments of future relations between the United States and China and among East Asian countries, many of which face a dramatic demographic shift from younger cohorts to the elderly. All of this lends support to Milanovic's hope "that humanity, facing a very similar situation today as one hundred years ago, will not allow the cataclysm of a world war to be the remedy for the ills of inequality."[17]

The next two horsemen of apocalyptic leveling do not require a lot of attention. Transformative revolution has even more thoroughly gone out of fashion than mass mobilization warfare. As I have shown in chapter 8, mere revolts rarely succeed and do not normally achieve substantial equalization. Only

---

[16] See Zuckerman 1984: 2–5, 8–11, 236–237, 283–288 for U.S. government planning for the aftermath of a nuclear war. Forced labor: the U.S. Oath of Allegiance requires that citizens "perform work of national importance under civilian direction when required by the law." See Bracken 2012 on new forms of nuclear conflict and Barrett, Baum, and Hostetler 2013 on the odds of accidental nuclear war. National Military Strategy 2015: 4 assesses the probability of a war between the United States and a major power "to be low but growing," and predicts that its "consequences would be immense." For the displacement effect, see international studies scholar Artyom Lukin's contribution at http://www.huffingtonpost.com/artyom-lukin/world-war-iii_b_5646641.html. Allison 2014 provides an accessible survey of the differences and similarities between 1914 and 2014. Morris 2014: 353–393 considers a range of future outcomes.

[17] Declining violence: Pinker 2011; Morris 2014, esp. 332–340. See Thayer 2009 for a survey of the relationship between demography and war, and Sheen 2013 for the irenic effects of future aging in Northeast Asia. Quote: Milanovic 2016: 102–103.

communist revolutions were capable of greatly leveling imbalances in income and wealth. Yet the massive expansion of communist rule between 1917 and 1950 was rooted in the world wars and has never been repeated. Subsequent communist movements, sponsored by the Soviet Union, only occasionally scored victories—in Cuba, Ethiopia, South Yemen, and, above all, in Southeast Asia up to 1975—before they began to fizzle out. The late 1970s witnessed the final modest takeovers, in Afghanistan, Nicaragua, and Grenada, which proved either ephemeral or politically moderate. Peru's substantial communist insurgencies were largely crushed in the 1990s, and by 2006, the Nepalese Maoists had abjured civil war and joined electoral politics. Market reforms have effectively eroded the socialist underpinnings of all remaining people's republics. Even Cuba and North Korea have been unable to escape this global trend. At this point in time, there are no further leftist revolutions on the horizon, nor has any alternative movement with a comparable potential for violent leveling arrived on the scene.[18]

State failure and systems collapse on the scale discussed in chapter 9 have likewise become extremely rare. Recent instances of state failure tend to be confined to central and eastern Africa and the peripheries of the Middle East. In 2014, the State Fragility Index of the Center for Systemic Peace assigned the world's worst scores to the Central African Republic, South Sudan, the Democratic Republic of Congo, Sudan, Afghanistan, Yemen, Ethiopia, and Somalia. With the single exception of Myanmar, the seventeen next most fragile countries are also located in Africa or the Middle East. Although the dissolution of the Soviet Union and Yugoslavia in the early 1990s as well as ongoing events in Ukraine demonstrate that even industrialized middle-income countries are by no means immune to disintegrative pressures, contemporary developed countries—and, indeed, many developing ones—are highly unlikely to go down the same path. Thanks to modern economic growth and fiscal expansion, state institutions in high-income countries have generally become too powerful and too deeply entrenched in society for a wholesale collapse of governmental structures and concurrent leveling to occur. And even in the most disadvantaged societies, state failure has often been associated with civil war, a type of violent shock that does not normally produce equalizing outcomes.[19]

---

[18] Venezuela's "Bolivarian revolution," a leftist movement with a strong record of income equalization that continues to work through a parliamentary system, has been facing growing domestic resistance and may not survive its mismanagement of the economy.

[19] Index: http://www.systemicpeace.org/inscr/SFImatrix2014c.pdf. For civil war and inequality, see herein, chapter 6, pp. 202–207. I discuss the state failure in Somalia in chapter 9, pp. 283–286.

This leaves us with the fourth and final horseman: severe epidemics. The risk of novel and potentially catastrophic outbreaks is far from negligible. Zoonotic infections that jump from animal hosts to humans are on the rise thanks to population growth and deforestation in tropical countries. Consumption of bush meat also sustains this chain of transmission, and industrial livestock farming makes it easier for microorganisms to adapt to new environments. Pathogen weaponization and bioterrorism are growing concerns. Even so, the same factors that are conducive to the emergence and spread of new infectious diseases— economic development and global interconnectivity—also help us monitor and respond to such threats. Rapid DNA sequencing, the miniaturization of laboratory equipment for use in the field, and the ability to track outbreaks by setting up control centers and exploiting digital resources are powerful weapons in our arsenal.

For the purposes of this study, two points are crucial. First, anything that might approximate the relative scale of the major premodern pandemics discussed in chapters 10 and 11 would require the death of hundreds of millions of people in the world today, which far exceeds the most pessimistic scenarios. Moreover, any future global epidemic may well be largely confined to developing countries. Even a century ago, at a time when existing therapeutic intervention made little or no difference, the death toll of the global influenza pandemic of 1918 to 1920 was strongly mediated by per capita income levels. Today, medical intervention would reduce the overall impact of an outbreak of a comparably severe strain, and mortality outcomes would be even more strongly biased in favor of high-income countries. Extrapolating from the mortality rates reported for the "Spanish flu" to 2004, 96 percent of the projected 50 million to 80 million fatalities worldwide might occur in developing countries. Although sophisticated weaponization might produce a more potent superbug, it would hardly be in the interest of any state-level actors to unleash such an agent. Bioterrorism, on the other hand, may well have only a minimal chance of success and is even less likely to result in genuine mass mortality on a national or wider scale.

The second point concerns the distributional economic consequences of future epidemics. It is far from certain that sudden catastrophic mortality caused by infectious disease would level inequality of income or wealth as it had done in the agrarian era. We cannot even tell whether the global influenza pandemic of 1918 to 1920, which is thought to have killed anywhere from 50 million to 100 million people, or some 3 percent to 5 percent of the world's population at the time, had any significant effect on the distribution of material resources, coinciding as it did with the equalizing fallout of World War I. Although generic infections such as influenza today more severely affect the poor, we cannot simply conjecture a class-specific mortality crisis that would drive up the value of low-skilled labor even as the economy as a whole remained largely intact. For a contemporary epidemic to be truly catastrophic, claiming the lives of hundreds of millions around the world, it would have to be impossible to contain at least in the short term and would have to kill people across national boundaries and the socioeconomic spectrum. In that case, its destructive impact on complex and interconnected modern economies and their highly differentiated labor markets might well outweigh any equalizing effects regarding the labor supply and the valuation of capital stocks. Even in far less integrated agrarian societies, plagues triggered short-term dislocations that hurt people indiscriminately. In the long run, distributional consequences would be shaped by novel ways of substituting capital for labor: in plague-depleted economies, robots might eventually take the place of many of the missing workers.[20]

We cannot be certain that the coming years will be free of the violent shocks that have punctuated history since the dawn of civilization. There is always a chance, however small, that a big war or a new Black Death might shatter the established order and reshuffle the distribution of income and wealth. The best we can do is to identify the most economical prediction, and it is this: the four traditional levelers are gone for now and are unlikely to return any time soon. This casts serious doubt on the feasibility of future leveling. Many factors contribute to historical outcomes, and the history of leveling is no exception: institutional arrangements have been critical in determining the distributional consequences of compressive shocks. Variation in the coercive power of rulers and capital owners allowed plague to raise real wages in some societies but not in others; the world wars flattened the distribution of market incomes in some economies but encouraged ambitious redistributive schemes in others; Mao's revolution wiped out "landlords" but promoted inequalities between cities and countryside.

---

[20] There is no shortage of popular science books describing the emergence of novel infections and considering future threats: see, most recently, Drexler 2009 and Quammen 2013. The best-informed contribution has been made by Stanford-affiliated virologist Nathan Wolfe, who stresses our improved capabilities to monitor and respond: Wolfe 2011. Scale: for what it is worth, Bill Gates reckoning with tens of millions of future deaths: https://www.ted.com/talks/bill_gates_the_next_disaster_we_re_not_ready?language=en. Extrapolation from "Spanish flu": Murray et al. 2006. Bioterrorism: e.g., Stratfor 2013. For pathogens with weaponization potential, see Zubay et al. 2005.

But there was always one Big Reason behind every known episode of substantial leveling. There was one Big Reason why John D. Rockefeller was an entire order of magnitude richer in real terms than his richest compatriots one and two generations later, why the Britain of Downton Abbey gave way to a society known for universal free healthcare and powerful labor unions, why in industrialized nations around the globe the gap between rich and poor was so much smaller in the third quarter of the twentieth century than it had been at its beginning—and, indeed, why a hundred generations earlier ancient Spartans and Athenians had embraced ideals of equality and sought to put them into practice. There was one Big Reason why by the 1950s the Chinese village of Zhangzhuangcun had come to boast a perfectly egalitarian distribution of farmland; one Big Reason why the high and mighty of Lower Egypt 3,000 years ago had to bury their dead with hand-me-downs or in shoddily manufactured coffins, why the remnants of the Roman aristocracy lined up for handouts from the pope and the successors of Maya chiefs subsisted on the same diet as *hoi polloi*; and one Big Reason why humble farmhands in Byzantine and early Islamic Egypt and carpenters in late medieval England and hired workers in early modern Mexico earned more and ate better than their peers before or after. These Big Reasons were not all the same, but they shared one common root: massive and violent disruptions of the established order. Across recorded history, the periodic compressions of inequality brought about by mass mobilization warfare, transformative revolution, state failure, and pandemics have invariably dwarfed any known instances of equalization by entirely peaceful means.

History does not determine the future. Maybe modernity really is different. In the very long run, it may well turn out to be. It may put us on a trajectory toward singularity, a point at which all human beings merge into a globally interconnected hybrid body-machine super-organism and no longer have to worry about inequality. Or perhaps technological advances will instead take inequalities to new extremes by separating a biomechatronically and genetically enhanced elite from ordinary mortals, the latter perpetually kept at bay by the ever more superior capabilities of their overlords. Or, just as likely, none of the above—we may be moving toward outcomes we cannot even yet conceive. But science fiction takes us only so far. For the time being, we are stuck with the minds and bodies we have and with the institutions they have created. This suggests that the prospects of future leveling are poor. It will be a challenge for the social democracies of continental Europe to maintain and adjust elaborate systems of high taxation and extensive redistribution or for the richest democracies of Asia to preserve their unusually equitable allocation of pretax incomes to stem the rising tide of inequality, which can grow only stronger as ongoing globalization and unprecedented demographic transformations add to the pressure. It is doubtful whether they will manage to hold the line: inequality has been inching up everywhere, a trend that undeniably works against the status quo. And if the stabilization of existing distributions of income and wealth will be increasingly difficult to achieve, any attempt to render them more equitable necessarily faces even bigger obstacles.

For thousands of years, history has alternated between long stretches of rising or high and stable inequality interspersed with violent compressions. For six or seven decades from 1914 to the 1970s or 1980s, both the world's rich economies and those countries that had fallen to communist regimes experienced some of most intense leveling in recorded history. Since then, much of the world has entered what could become the next long stretch—a return to persistent capital accumulation and income concentration. If history is anything to go by, peaceful policy reform may well prove unequal to the growing challenges ahead. But what of the alternatives? All of us who prize greater economic equality would do well to remember that with the rarest of exceptions, it was only ever brought forth in sorrow. Be careful what you wish for.

APPENDIX:
THE LIMITS OF INEQUALITY

How far can inequality rise? In one important respect, measurements of income inequality differ from those of wealth inequality. There is no limit to how unequally wealth can be distributed within a given population. In theory, one person could own everything there is to own, with everybody else owning nothing but surviving on income from labor or transfers. This distribution would produce a Gini coefficient of ~1 or a top wealth share of 100 percent. In purely mathematical terms, income Ginis might also run from 0, for perfect equality, to ~1, for complete inequality. However, ~1 can never be reached in practice, because everyone needs a minimum amount of income just to stay alive. To account for this basic requirement, Branko Milanovic, Peter Lindert, and Jeffrey Williamson developed the concept of the "Inequality Possibility Frontier" (IPF), a measure that determines the highest theoretically possible degree of inequality at a given level of average per capita output. The lower the per capita GDP, the smaller the per capita surplus beyond bare subsistence and the more restrictive the Income Possibility Frontier.

Imagine a society in which average per capita GDP equals minimum subsistence. In this case, the income Gini has to be 0, because even small disparities in income would push some members of this group below the level necessary for their survival. Although this is certainly possible—some would get richer while others starved—it would not be sustainable in the long run, because the population would gradually dwindle away. If average per capita GDP amounts to just a little above subsistence—say, 1.05 times in a population of 100 individuals—one person could claim six times subsistence income while everybody else lived precisely at the minimal income level. The Gini coefficient would be 0.047, and the top 1 percent income share would be 5.7 percent. At an average GDP of twice minimum subsistence—a more realistic scenario for a poor real-life economy—with one person hogging all the available surplus, this solitary top earner would claim 50.5 percent of all income, and the Gini coefficient would reach 0.495. The IPF thus rises with growing per capita GDP: at an average per

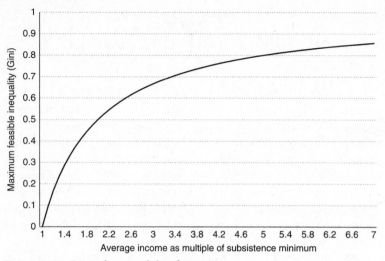

Figure A.1   Inequality possibility frontier

capita output of five times subsistence, the maximum feasible Gini would be close to 0.8 (Fig. A.1).[1]

Fig. A.1 shows that the greatest changes in the IPF occur at very low levels of per capita GDP. Once the latter increases to a large multiple of bare subsistence, which is generally the case in modern developed countries, the IPF is pushed into the high 0.9s and becomes increasingly undistinguishable from the formal ceiling of ~1. For this reason, this basic IPF is of relevance mostly for our understanding of inequality in premodern societies and contemporary low-income countries. If minimum subsistence is defined as an annual income of $300 in 1990 International Dollars—a conventional benchmark, even though somewhat higher levels might be more plausible—economies generating an annual per capita GDP of up to $1,500 are most significantly affected by IPF-based adjustments of their inequality potential. All or virtually all premodern economies fall into this rubric, which means that the range depicted in Fig. A.1 covers most of human history. At the country level, the threshold of five times the subsistence-level income of $300 was first reached in

---

[1] Milanovic, Lindert, and Williamson 2011: 256–259. Fig. A.1 based on their 258 fig. 1. Modalsli 2015: 241–242 is more sanguine about the possibility of human existence below subsistence levels. For the notion of a maximum Gini of ~1 rather than 1, see herein, introduction, p. 12 n. 9.

the Netherlands in the early sixteenth century, in England around 1700, in the United States by 1830, in France and Germany in the mid-nineteenth century, in Japan in the 1910s, and in China as a whole not until 1985—and in India a decade later.[2]

Dividing an observed income Gini coefficient by the maximum possible value (IPF) yields the "extraction rate," which measures the proportion of theoretically possible inequality that was actually extracted by earners of incomes above subsistence. The extraction rate may range from 0 under conditions of perfect equality to 100 percent, when one person absorbs the entire output beyond aggregate per capita subsistence. The smaller the difference between observed Ginis and the IPF, the closer the extraction rate is to 100 percent. Milanovic, Lindert, and Williamson calculate extraction rates for twenty-eight premodern societies from the Roman empire to British India by relying on a combination of social tables that provide a crude index of income distribution—a format that goes back to Gregory King's famous social table for England in 1688 that differentiates among thirty-one classes from lords to paupers—and census information whenever it is available (Fig. A.2).[3]

The mean Gini coefficient of income across these twenty-eight societies is about 0.45, and the extraction rate averages 77 percent. Poorer societies tend to be closer to the IPF than more developed ones are. For those twenty-one societies in the sample having an average per capita GDP below $1,000 in 1990 International Dollars, the mean extraction rate is 76 percent, effectively the same as the mean of 78 percent for seven societies with an average per capita GDP of between $1,000 and $2,000. It declines only once economic performance improves to a per capita level of between four and five times minimum subsistence: the extraction rate for England and Holland or the Netherlands between 1732 and 1808 averages 61 percent. The five highest rates in the sample, ranging from 97 percent to 113 percent, may be an artifact of inadequate data, especially for those cases in which putative Ginis significantly exceed the implied IPF. In real life, actual levels of inequality should never have reached or even have come very close to the IPF, if only because it is difficult to imagine a society in which

---

[2] Maddison project. For a possible ancient forerunner, classical Athens, see herein, chapter 2, pp. 84–85; but note that even fifteenth-century Florentine Tuscany only reached about $1,000.

[3] Milanovic, Lindert, and Williamson 2011: 259–263 for the underlying data and their limitations. Fig. A.2 is based on 265 fig. 2. Recourse to social tables produces a range of possible income distributions; Milanovic, Lindert, and Williamson calculate two: one that minimizes and one that maximizes inequality within each income bracket. In most cases, the differences between such metrics are small.

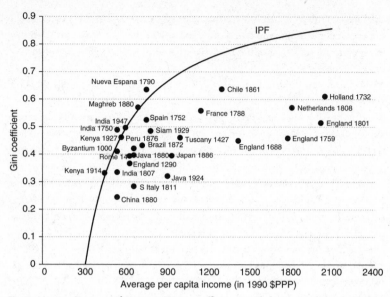

Figure A.2 Estimated income Gini coefficients and the inequality possibility frontier in preindustrial societies

one ruler or a tiny elite would have been able to control a population in which everybody else was reduced to bare subsistence. Even so, it is worth noting that these five societies were ruled by colonial powers or a foreign conquest elite, conditions that might have raised predatory extraction to exceptionally high levels.[4]

Calculation of the IPF and extraction rates offers two important insights. It highlights the fact that early societies tended to be about as unequal as they could possibly be. Only societies in which a wealthy "1 percent" and a few more percent made up of soldiers, administrators, and commercial intermediaries were superimposed on an impoverished agrarian population could have generated extraction rates that were anywhere near the IPF. And yet this appears

---

[4] Milanovic, Lindert, and Williamson 2011: 263 table 2. Modalsli 2015: 230–243 argues that proper accounting of within-group dispersion in social tables leads to substantially higher overall income Ginis for the societies in question: see esp. 237 fig. 2 for the wide dispersion of outcomes. However, the envisioned increases by about 15 percentage points would raise Ginis too close or even beyond the IPF, a problem that could be avoided only by consistently assuming a lower subsistence floor or higher per capita GDP. Most importantly, he notes that these adjustments alter the relative inequality ranking of these societies only rarely (238). See Atkinson 2014b for the mixed effects of decolonization on income inequality as proxied by top income shares.

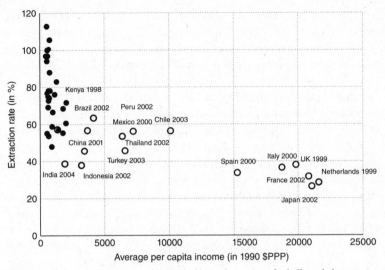

Figure A.3 Extraction rates for preindustrial societies (solid) and their counterpart modern societies (hollow)

to have been a common pattern. We may derive some comfort from the internal consistency of the guesstimates plotted in Fig. A.2: it seems unlikely that all these datasets lead us to err in the same direction and in so doing create a profoundly misleading impression of past levels of inequality. The second important observation is that intensive economic growth eventually reduced extraction rates. The scale of the phenomenon is illustrated by a comparison between the sampled twenty-eight societies and sixteen of the same or partly coextensive countries around 2000 (Fig. A.3).[5]

The observed discontinuity in extraction rates show how misleading it can be to compare income Gini coefficients across very different levels of average per capita GDP. At 0.45 and 0.41, the mean Gini values for the premodern and near-contemporary samples are quite similar. Taken at face value, they would suggest only a mild attenuation of inequality in the course of modernization. However, because average per capita GDP was eleven times as large in the modern sample as in the earlier one, the mean extraction rate was much lower—44 percent compared to 76 percent. On this measure, by 2000, these societies had become

---

[5] Fig. A.3 from Milanovic, Lindert, and Williamson 2011: 268 fig. 4.

far less unequal than they had been in the more distant past. Unadjusted comparison of top income shares can be even more problematic. Recall my example of one well-to-do and ninety-nine poor individuals in a fictitious society with a mean per capita GDP equivalent to 1.05 times minimum subsistence and a top 1 percent income share of 5.7 percent. Precisely this top 1 percent income share was found in Denmark in 2000 when that country's mean per capita GDP was no fewer than seventy-three times as large as in my thought experiment. Dramatically different levels of economic development can translate to superficially similar levels of inequality. The lesson is clear: unadjusted estimates of historical income distributions may cloud our understanding of how what I call "effective inequality"—defined in relation to the degree of inequality that was theoretically feasible—changed over time. Leaving aside the question of the reliability of any of these figures, income Gini coefficients for England of 0.37 around 1290, 0.45 in 1688, 0.46 in 1759, and 0.52 in 1801 suggest a gradual increase in inequality, whereas the extraction rate declined for much of this period as economic output grew—from 0.69 to 0.57 and 0.55 before recovering to 0.61. In Holland or the Netherlands, income Ginis rose from 0.56 in 1561 to 0.61 in 1732 and then fell to 0.57 in 1808 even as extraction rates kept dropping, from 76 percent to 72 percent and 69 percent. Considering the considerable degree of uncertainty surrounding these numbers, it would be unwise to put too much weight on these specific observations. It is the principle that counts: extraction rates give us a better sense of real inequality than Gini coefficients do alone.

Does this mean that conventional inequality measures overstate the extent of real income inequality in modern societies relative to those found in the more distant past or in the poorest developing countries today—and that economic development had thus sustained substantial peaceful leveling after all? The answer to this question very much depends on how we define effective inequality. Contextual adjustments to standard inequality measures open a can of worms. Actual income floors are determined not merely by bare physiological subsistence but also by powerful social and economic factors. Shortly after introducing the concepts of the IPF and the extraction rate, Milanovic refined this approach by taking account of the social dimension of subsistence. A minimum annual income of $300 in 1990 International Dollars is indeed sufficient for physical survival and may even be a viable standard in very low-income societies. Yet subsistence needs rise in relative terms as economies become wealthier and social norms change. Only in the poorest countries today do official poverty lines coincide with conventional minimum subsistence levels. More generous

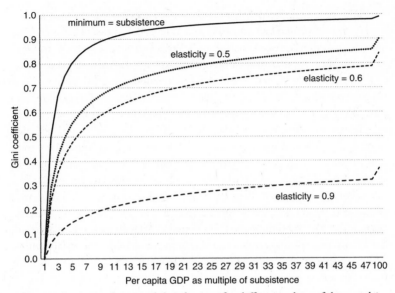

Figure A.4   Inequality possibility frontier for different values of the social
minimum

limits elsewhere are a function of higher per capita GDP. Subjective assessments
of what constitutes socially acceptable minimum subsistence also show some
sensitivity to overall living standards. Adam Smith's definition of minimum
requirements in his own day is a famous example. In his opinion, they include
"not only the commodities which are indispensably necessary for the support
of life, but whatever the custom of the country renders it indecent for credit-
able people, even of the lowest order, to be without," such as—in England—a
linen shirt and leather shoes. However, poverty levels do not change at the same
rate as GDP but rather lag behind: their elasticity relative to mean income is
limited. Reckoning with elasticity of 0.5, Milanovic demonstrates that adjusted
for social minima, the IPF for a given level of average per capita GDP is significantly lower than that determined by bare physiological subsistence needs
alone. For a population with a mean per capita GDP of $1,500, it falls from 0.8
to 0.55, and at $3,000, it drops from 0.9 to 0.68 (Fig. A.4).[6]

---

[6] Adam Smith, *An inquiry into the nature and causes of the wealth of nations* V.ii.k. Fig. A.4 from Milanovic
2013: 9 fig. 3.

With or without accounting for changing social minima, extraction rates held steady in England between 1688 and 1867 and in America between 1774 and 1860. However, if an elasticity of 0.5 of social minima relative to GDP growth is incorporated into the calculation of the IPF, the implied extraction rate is roughly 80 percent for these two periods—much higher than the roughly 60 percent obtained by relating observed inequality to minimum physiological subsistence. By contrast, extraction rates, defined either way, have been much lower since World War II. Effective inequality remained high prior to the twentieth century as elites continued to capture a fairly constant share of the available surplus even while economic output was growing. This suggests that with the exception of periods of violent compression, effective inequality—constrained by socially determined subsistence floors—was generally high not only across premodern history but also during the early stages of industrialization. Measures of nominal inequality, as expressed in Gini coefficients or top income shares and real inequality adjusted for social minima, thus converge in supporting the impression of massive income disparities prior to the Great Compression.[7]

But what about the present? By the end of the first decade of the twenty-first century, with or without an adjustment for social minima, American and British extraction rates stood at around 40 percent, effectively only half as much as back in the 1860s. Does this mean that even after the recent resurgence in inequality, these two countries are now much more egalitarian in real terms than they had been in the past? Not necessarily. The key question is this: in an economy that does not primarily depend on the extraction of fossil fuels but rather on some combination of food production, manufacturing, and services, what is the maximum level of income inequality that is economically feasible at a given level of per capita GDP? The maximum theoretically possible disposable income Gini coefficient for the United States is either 0.99 in a scenario in which one person captures all the surplus above minimum physiological subsistence or approximately 0.9 if that one person merely captures all the surplus above socially determined minimum incomes. Allowing, for the sake of argument, that such a society would somehow be politically viable—even if this might require the monoplutocrat to employ an army of robots to police his 320 million fellow citizens—we must ask whether it could sustain an economy that

---

[7] Milanovic 2013: 12 table 1, 13 fig. 4 (UK and United States). For high inequality up to 1914, see herein, chapter 3, pp. 104–105, 108–110.

generates an average annual per capita GDP of $53,000. The answer must surely be negative: an extravagantly unequal society such as this would be incapable of producing and reproducing the human capital and supporting the volume of domestic consumption (which accounts for almost 70 percent of America's GDP) required to reach these levels of output. The "real" IPF must therefore be considerably lower.[8]

But how much lower? The Gini coefficient for disposable income in the United States is currently close to 0.38. Assume, again merely for the sake of argument, that it could be as high as 0.6, Namibia's score in 2010, without depressing average per capita GDP below existing levels. This would translate to an effective extraction rate of 63 percent. In a different context, Milanovic has argued that even under fairly extreme assumptions about feasible labor and capital income inequality, the Gini coefficient for the overall American income distribution could not rise above 0.6. But even 0.6 might be too high for a U.S.-style economy: Namibia's per capita GDP is only about a seventh of the U.S. figure in real terms, and its economy is highly dependent on mineral exports. If the true ceiling were 0.5, America's current effective extraction rate would be 76 percent, equivalent to the mean computed for the aforementioned twenty-eight premodern societies and close to that of 84 percent for the United States in 1860. In 1929, the country's Gini coefficient for disposable income was not much less than 0.5, and an IPF adjusted for social minima of close to 0.8 implies an extraction rate of about 60 percent. However, even in 1929, when real per capita GDP was less than a quarter of today's, the maximum economically feasible Gini ought to have been less than 0.8, albeit higher than it is now. At this point there is little to be gained from experimenting with different numbers. If it is possible to measure inequality's negative effect on economic growth, then it should also be possible to estimate the level of inequality at which current levels of output could no longer be attained. I hope that economists will address this question.[9]

---

[8] I exclude petrostates because they could, and de facto do, combine high income inequality with high per capita GDP. Economies that depend on other forms of mineral extraction such as Botswana and Namibia are also very unequal but fail to reach high levels of average per capita income. Data for United States and UK: Milanovic 2013: table 1. I control for his use of market income inequality figures for the United States, which are not relevant in this context.

[9] Data: SWIID; Maddison project; Milanovic 2013: 12 table 1, with Atkinson 2015: 18 fig. 1.1. See Milanovic 2015 for an upper limit of 0.55 to 0.6. Only market income Gini figures appear to be available for the United States in 1929, but considering the low levels of taxation and transfers at the time, they would not have been much higher than those for disposable income. For the impact of inequality on growth, see herein, introduction, p. 19.

Over the entire course of history, the potential for income inequality has been delimited by a succession of different factors. At very low levels of economic performance, inequality is constrained in the first instance by the volume of output beyond what is needed to ensure bare physiological subsistence. A Gini coefficient of 0.4—middling by contemporary standards—points to extremely high effective inequality in a society in which average per capita GDP is only twice minimum subsistence and the potential for inequality is capped at an income Gini of around 0.5. At intermediate levels of development, social minima become the principal constraint. For example, in 1860, when mean per capita GDP in the United States had reached seven times minimum subsistence, the highest feasible Gini or IPF implied by social minima was very considerably lower than that determined by bare subsistence alone—0.63 compared to 0.86—and the effective extraction rate was correspondingly higher: 84 percent rather than 62 percent. At that time, the IPF derived from social minima was almost certainly lower than the ceiling imposed by economic complexity as such: at a time when more than half of the population was still engaged in agriculture, the theoretical potential for income inequality would have been quite high. This changed as social minima–based IPF Ginis rose into the 0.7s and 0.8s even as the IPF associated with modern economic development declined. At some point the two frontiers crossed, turning the latter into the most powerful restraint on potential inequality (Fig. A.5).[10]

My model suggests that the IPF remains fairly stable across the full historical spectrum of income distribution. Maximum feasible Ginis in the 0.5s and 0.6s for societies with an average per capita GDP equivalent to two to three times minimum subsistence closely resemble those for more advanced agrarian and early industrializing societies with an average per capita GDP equivalent to between five and ten times minimum subsistence, which in turn need not be very different from those applying to high income economies today that generate the equivalent of a hundred times minimum subsistence per person. What does change is the nature of the key constraint, from bare subsistence to social minima to economic complexity. I call the IPF's counterintuitive lack of sensitivity to economic performance the "development paradox of inequality"—another variation on the theme of *plus ça change, plus c'est la même chose*. This long-term stability is a major boon to comparative assessments of income

---

[10] For the data, see, once again, Milanovic 2013: 12 table 1. My simple model omits other factors that are also bound to play a role—most notably, political institutions.

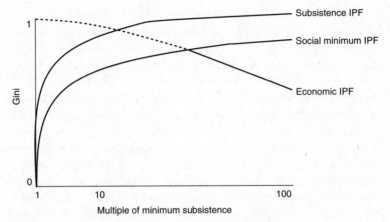

Figure A.5 Different types of inequality possibility frontiers

inequality in the very long run of history: if the IPF does not greatly vary among different stages of economic development, then it is legitimate directly to compare Gini coefficients from antiquity to the present.[11]

Whether the real extraction rate of inequality in the United States or in the United Kingdom today is as high as it was 150 years ago remains an open question, but there can be no doubt that it has not halved or fallen to any even remotely comparable extent between then and now, as calculations based on social minima alone would seem to suggest. Although the current effective extraction rate in America is almost certainly lower than it was in 1929, inequality has been remarkably persistent—or resurgent—in real terms. But not everywhere: Gini coefficients for disposable income in the mid-0.2s such as those found in Scandinavian countries today are necessarily much lower than they were in the more distant past regardless of how we define IPFs. I conclude this technical excursus with a brief illustration of how constraints on potential inequality affect international comparisons. How much more unequally

---

[11] With reference to the study of ancient Roman inequality by Scheidel and Friesen 2009, online media outlets reported that contemporary U.S. income inequality was higher than it had been in the Roman Empire, an observation based on market Gini coefficients that failed to take account of modern postmarket redistribution and the respective IPFs: http://persquaremile.com/2011/12/16/income-inequality-in-the -roman-empire/, partially reported by http://www.huffingtonpost.com/2011/12/19/us-income-inequality -ancient-rome-levels_n_1158926.html. This statement would be correct only if the actual IPF for the current United States were as low as 0.5.

is disposable income distributed in the United States than in Sweden? Given Ginis of around 0.23 and 0.38, American inequality could be said to be about two-thirds higher. This ratio does not change if we impose an IPF to establish a notional maximum: assuming a GDP-related IPF of 0.6 for both countries, the American extraction rate of 63 percent is two-thirds higher than the Swedish rate of 38 percent. However, the potential for income inequality is not merely capped at the top. In market economies, disposable income inequality needs to be significantly above zero in order to sustain high levels of per capita output. Insertion of a minimum feasible Gini of, say, 0.1 in addition to the previous ceiling of 0.6 would create what we might call an Inequality Possibility Space (IPS) of 50 percentage points. Observed Swedish inequality covers about a quarter of this space, as opposed to a little more than half in the United States. This adjustment would make the American distribution of disposable income at least twice as unequal, in real terms, as that of Sweden.

BIBLIOGRAPHY

Aaberge, R., and Atkinson, A. B. 2010. "Top incomes in Norway." In Atkinson and Piketty, eds. 2010: 448–481.

Abdullah, Abdul Jabbar, Doucouliagos, Hristos, and Manning, Elizabeth. 2015. "Is there a Kuznets process in Southeast Asia?" *Singapore Economic Review* 60. doi:10.1142/S0217590815500174.

Abelshauser, Werner. 1998. "Germany: guns, butter, and economic miracles." In Harrison, ed. 1998b: 122–176.

Abelshauser, Werner. 2011. *Deutsche Wirtschaftsgeschichte: von 1945 bis zur Gegenwart*. 2nd ed. Munich: C. H. Beck.

Abul-Magd, Adel Y. 2002. "Wealth distribution in an ancient Egyptian society." *Physical Review E* 66: 057104, 1–3.

Acemoglu, Daron, and Autor, David. 2012. "What does human capital do? A review of Goldin and Katz's *The race between education and technology*." *Journal of Economic Literature* 50: 426–463.

Acemoglu, Daron, Naidu, Suresh, Restrepo, Pascual, and Robinson, James A. 2015. "Democracy, redistribution, and inequality." In Atkinson and Bourguignon, eds. 2015: 1883–1966.

Acemoglu, Daron, and Robinson, James A. 2000. "Why did the West extend the franchise? Democracy, inequality, and growth in historical perspective." *Quarterly Journal of Economics* 115: 1167–1199.

Acemoglu, Daron, and Robinson, James A. 2002. "The political economy of the Kuznets curve." *Review of Development Economics* 6: 183–203.

Acemoglu, Daron, and Robinson, James A. 2015. "The rise and decline of general laws of capitalism." *Journal of Economic Perspectives* 29: 3–28.

Acosta, Pablo, Calderon, Cesar, Fajnzylber, Pablo, and Lopez, Humberto. 2008. "What is the impact of international remittances on poverty and inequality in Latin America?" *World Development* 36: 89–114.

Adam, Hussein. 2008. *From tyranny to anarchy: the Somali experience*. Trenton, NJ: Red Sea Press.

Adams, Robert McC. 1988. "Contexts of civilizational collapse: a Mesopotamian view." In Yoffee and Cowgill, eds. 1988: 20–43.

Addison, Paul. 1994. *The road to 1945: British politics and the Second World War*. Rev. ed. London: Pimlico.

Adema, Willem, Fron, Pauline, and Ladaique, Maxime. 2014. "How much do OECD countries spend on social protection and how redistributive are their tax/benefit systems?" *International Social Security Review* 76: 1–25.

Aftalion, Florin. 1990. *The French Revolution: an economic interpretation*. Cambridge, UK: Cambridge University Press.

Aghion, Philippe, et al. 2016. "Innovation and top income inequality." NBER Working Paper No. 21247.

Aidt, Toke S., and Jensen, Peter S. 2011. "Workers of the world, unite! Franchise extensions and the threat of revolution in Europe, 1820–1938." CESIFO Working Paper 3417.

Albertus, Michael. 2015. *Autocracy and redistribution: the politics of land reform*. New York: Cambridge University Press.

Albuquerque Sant'Anna, André. 2015. "A spectre has haunted the West: did socialism discipline income inequality?" MPRA Paper No. 64756.

Ales, Laurence, Kurnaz, Musab, and Sleet, Christopher. 2015. "Technical change, wage inequality, and taxes." *American Economic Review* 105: 3061–3101.

Alesina, Alberto, and Glaeser, Edward L. 2004. *Fighting poverty in the US and Europe: a world of difference*. New York: Oxford University Press.

Alfani, Guido. 2010. "Wealth inequalities and population dynamics in early modern Northern Italy." *Journal of Interdisciplinary History* 40: 513–549.

Alfani, Guido. 2015. "Economic inequality in northwestern Italy: a long-term view (fourteenth to eighteenth centuries)." *Journal of Economic History* 75: 1058–1096.

Alfani, Guido. 2016. "The rich in historical perspective: evidence for preindustrial Europe (ca. 1300–1800)." Innocenzo Gasparini Institute for Economic Research Working Paper No. 571.

Alfani, Guido, and Ammannati, Francesco. 2014. "Economic inequality and poverty in the very long run: the case of the Florentine state (late thirteenth to nineteenth century)." Dondena Working Paper No. 70, Università Bocconi, Milan.

Alfani, Guido, and di Tullio, Matteo. 2015. "Dinamiche di lungo periodo della disugualianza in Italia settentrionale: una nota di ricerca." Dondena Working Paper No. 71, Università Bocconi, Milan.

Alfani, Guido, and Ryckbosch, Wouter. 2015. "Was there a 'Little Convergence' in inequality? Italy and the Low Countries compared, ca. 1500–1800." Innocenzo Gasparini Institute for Economic Research, Working Paper No. 557.

Alfani, Guido, and Sardone, Sergio. 2015. "Long-term trends in economic inequality in southern Italy. The kingdoms of Naples and Sicily, 16th–18th centuries: first results." Economic History Association 2015 Annual Meeting, Nashville TN, September 11–13, 2015.

Allen, Robert C. 2001. "The great divergence in European wages and prices from the Middle Ages to the First World War." *Explorations in Economic History* 31: 411–447.

Allen, Robert C. 2003. *Farm to factory: a reinterpretation of the Soviet industrial revolution.* Princeton, NJ: Princeton University Press.

Allen, Robert C. 2009. "Engels' pause: technical change, capital accumulation, and inequality in the British industrial revolution." *Explorations in Economic History* 46: 418–435.

Allen, Robert C., Bassino, Jean-Pascal, Ma, Debin, Moll-Murata, Christine, and van Zanden, Jan Luiten. 2011. "Wages, prices, and living standards in China, 1738–1925: in comparison with Europe, Japan, and India." *Economic History Review* 64: S8–S38.

Allison, Graham. 2014. "Just how likely is another world war? Assessing the similarities and differences between 1914 and 2014." *The Atlantic* July 30, 2014. http://www.theatlantic.com/international/archive/2014/07/just-how-likely-is-another-world-war/375320/.

Alvaredo, Facundo. 2010a. "The rich in Argentina over the twentieth century, 1932–2004." In Atkinson and Piketty, eds. 2010: 253–298.

Alvaredo, Facundo. 2010b. "Top incomes and earnings in Portugal, 1936–2005." In Atkinson and Piketty, eds. 2010: 560–624.

Alvaredo, Facundo. 2011. "A note on the relationship between top income shares and the Gini coefficient." *Economics Letters* 110: 274–277.

Alvaredo, Facundo, Atkinson, Anthony B., Piketty, Thomas, and Saez, Emmanuel. 2013. "The top 1 percent in international and historical perspective." *Journal of Economic Perspectives* 27: 3–20.

Alvaredo, Facundo, and Gasparini, Leonardo. 2015. "Recent trends in inequality and poverty in developing countries." In Atkinson and Bourguignon, eds. 2015: 697–806.

Alvaredo, Facundo, and Piketty, Thomas. 2014. "Measuring top incomes and inequality in the Middle East: data limitations and illustration with the case of Egypt." Paris School of Economics Working Paper.

Alvaredo, Facundo, and Saez, Emmanuel. 2010. "Income and wealth concentration in Spain in a historical and fiscal perspective." In Atkinson and Piketty, eds. 2010: 482–559.

Álvarez-Nogal, Carlos, and Prados de la Escosura, Leandro. 2013. "The rise and fall of Spain (1270–1850)." *Economic History Review* 66: 1–37.

Ammannati, Francesco. 2015. "La distribuzione della proprietà nella Lucchesia del tardo Medioevo (sec. XIV–XV)." Dondena Working Paper No. 73, Università Bocconi, Milan.

Anand, Sudhir, and Segal, Paul. 2015. "The global distribution of income." In Atkinson and Bourguignon, eds. 2015: 937–980.

Andermahr, Anna Maria. 1998. *Totus in praediis: senatorischer Grundbesitz in Italien in der frühen und hohen Kaiserzeit.* Bonn, Germany: Habelt.

Anderson, Thomas P. 1971. *Matanza: El Salvador's communist revolt of 1932.* Lincoln: University of Nebraska Press.

Andreski, Stanislav. 1968. *Military organization and society*. 2nd ed. Berkeley: University of California Press.

Andress, David, ed. 2015. *The Oxford handbook of the French Revolution*. Oxford: Oxford University Press.

Andrews, Dan, and Leigh, Andrew. 2009. "More inequality, less social mobility." *Applied Economics Letters* 16: 1489–1492.

Angeles, Luis. 2010. "An alternative test of Kuznets' hypothesis." *Journal of Economic Inequality* 8: 463–473.

Anghelinu, Mircea. 2012. "On Palaeolithic social inequality: the funerary evidence." In Kogalniceanu, Raluca, Curca, Roxana-Gabriela, Gligor, Mihai, and Stratton, Susan, eds., *Homines, funera, astra: proceedings of the international symposium on funeral anthropology 5–8 June 2011 '1 Decembrie 1918' University (Alba Iulia, Romania)*. Oxford: Archaeopress, 31–43.

Aristázabal-Ramírez, María, Canavire-Bacarezza, Gustavo, and Jetter, Michael. 2015. "Income inequality in Bolivia, Colombia, and Ecuador: different reasons." Working paper.

Arroyo Abad, Leticia. 2013. "Persistent inequality? Trade, factor endowments, and inequality in Republican Latin America." *Journal of Economic History* 73: 38–78.

Arroyo Abad, Leticia, Davies, Elwyn, and van Zanden, Jan Luiten. 2012. "Between conquest and independence: real wages and demographic change in Spanish America, 1530–1820." *Explorations in Economic History* 49: 149–166.

Assuncão, Juliano. 2006. "Land reform and landholdings in Brazil." UNI-WIDER Research Paper No. 2006/137.

Atkinson, Anthony B. 2007. "The distribution of top incomes in the United Kingdom 1908–2000." In Atkinson and Piketty, eds. 2007a: 82–140.

Atkinson, Anthony B. 2014a. "After Piketty?" *British Journal of Sociology* 65: 619–638.

Atkinson, Anthony B. 2014b. "The colonial legacy: income inequality in former British African colonies." WIDER Working Paper.

Atkinson, Anthony B. 2015. *Inequality: what can be done?* Cambridge, MA: Harvard University Press.

Atkinson, Anthony B. n.d. "Income distribution and taxation in Mauritius: a seventy-five year history of top incomes." Working paper.

Atkinson, Anthony B., and Bourguignon, Francois, eds. 2000. *Handbook of income distribution*. Vol. 1. Amsterdam: Elsevier.

Atkinson, Anthony B., and Bourguignon, Francois, eds. 2015. *Handbook of income distribution*. Volumes 2A–B. Amsterdam: North-Holland.

Atkinson, Anthony B., and Brandolini, Andrea. 2004. "Global world income inequality: absolute, relative or intermediate?" Working paper. www.iariw.org/papers/2004/brand.pdf.

Atkinson, Anthony B., and Leigh, Andrew. 2013. "The distribution of top incomes in five Anglo-Saxon countries over the long run." *Economic Record* 89 (S1): 31–47.

Atkinson, Anthony B., and Morelli, Salvatore. 2011. "Economic crises and inequality." UNDP Human Development Reports 2011/06.

Atkinson, Anthony B., and Morelli, Salvatore. 2014. "Chartbook of economic inequality." Working Paper No. 324, ECINE: Society for the Study of Economic Inequality. (Also available at http://www .chartbookofeconomicinequality.com.)

Atkinson, Anthony B., and Piketty, T., eds. 2007a. *Top incomes over the twentieth century: a contrast between continental European and English-speaking countries*. Oxford: Oxford University Press.

Atkinson, Anthony B., and Piketty, T. 2007b. "Towards a unified data set on top incomes." In Atkinson and Piketty, eds. 2007a: 531–565.

Atkinson, Anthony B., and Piketty, T., eds. 2010. *Top incomes: a global perspective*. Oxford: Oxford University Press.

Atkinson, Anthony B., and Søgaard, Jakob E. 2016. "The long-run history of income inequality in Denmark." *Scandinavian Journal of Economics* 118: 264–291.

Auerbach, Alan J., and Hassett, Kevin. 2015. "Capital taxation in the twenty-first century." *American Economic Review* 105: 38–42.

Autor, David H. 2014. "Skills, education, and the rise of earnings inequality among the 'other 99 percent.'" *Science* 344: 843–850.

Autor, David H. 2015. "Why are there still so many jobs? The history and future of workplace automation." *Journal of Economic Perspectives* 29: 3–30.

Autor, David, and Dorn, David. 2013. "The growth of low-skill service jobs and the polarization of the U.S. labor market." *American Economic Review* 103: 1553–1597.

Autor, David, Levy, Frank, and Murnane, Richard J. 2003. "The skill content of recent technological change: an empirical exploration." *Quarterly Journal of Economics* 116: 1279–1333.

Autor, David, Manning, Alan, and Smith, Christopher. 2010. "The contribution of the minimum wage to U.S. wage inequality over three decades: a reassessment." NBER Working Paper No. 16533.

Bagchi, Sutirtha, and Svejnar, Jan. 2015. "Does wealth inequality matter for growth? The effect of billionaire wealth, income distribution, and poverty." *Journal of Comparative Economics* 43: 505–530.

Bagnall, Roger S. 1992. "Landholding in late Roman Egypt: the distribution of wealth." *Journal of Roman Studies* 82: 128–149.

Balch, Stephen H. 2014. "On the fragility of the Western achievement." *Society* 51: 8–21.

Banerjee, Abhijit, and Piketty, Thomas. 2010. "Top Indian incomes, 1922–2000." In Atkinson and Piketty, eds. 2010: 1–39.

Bang, Peter F., Bayly, Christopher A., and Scheidel, Walter, eds. Forthcoming. *The Oxford world history of empire*. 2 vols. New York: Oxford University Press.

Bang, Peter F., and Turner, Karen. 2015. "Kingship and elite formation." In Scheidel 2015a: 11–38.

Bank, Steven A., Stark, Kirk J., and Thorndike, Joseph J. 2008. *War and taxes*. Washington, DC: Urban Institute Press.

Barbiera, Irene, and Dalla Zuanna, Gianpiero. 2009. "Population dynamics in Italy in the Middle Ages: new insights from archaeological findings." *Population and Development Review* 35: 367–389.

Barfield, Thomas J. 1989. *The perilous frontier: nomadic empires and China, 221 BC to AD 1757*. Cambridge, MA: Blackwell.

Barker, Graeme. 2006. *The agricultural revolution in prehistory: why did foragers become farmers?* Oxford: Oxford University Press.

Barker, John W. 2004. "Late Byzantine Thessalonike: a second city's challenges and responses." In Alice-Mary Talbot, ed., *Symposium on late Byzantine Thessalonike*. Washington, DC: Dumbarton Oaks Research Library and Collection, 5–33.

Barraclough, Solon L. 1999. "Land reform in developing countries: the role of the state and other actors." UNRISD Discussion Paper No. 101.

Barrett, Anthony M., Baum, Seth D., and Hostetler, Kelly R. 2013. "Analyzing and reducing the risks of inadvertent nuclear war between the United States and Russia." *Science and Global Security* 21: 106–133.

Bartels, Larry M. 2008. *Unequal democracy: the political economy of the new Gilded Age*. Princeton, NJ: Princeton University Press.

Bassino, Jean-Pascal, Fukao, Kyoji, and Takashima, Masanori. 2014. "A first escape from poverty in late medieval Japan: evidence from real wages in Kyoto (1360–1860)." Working paper.

Bassino, Jean-Pascal, Fukao, Kyoji, Settsu, Tokihiko, and Takashima, Masanori. 2014. "Regional and personal inequality in Japan, 1850–1955." Conference paper for "Accounting for the Great Divergence," University of Warwick in Venice, May 22–24, 2014.

Baten, Joerg, and Mumme, Christina. 2013. "Does inequality lead to civil wars? A global long-term study using anthropometric indicators (1816–1999)." *European Journal of Political Economy* 32: 56–79.

Baten, Joerg, and Schulz, Rainer. 2005. "Making profits in wartime: corporate profits, inequality, and GDP in Germany during the First World War." *Economic History Review* 58: 34–56.

Batten, Bruce. 1986. "Foreign threat and domestic reform: the emergence of the Ritsuryo state." *Monumenta Nipponica* 41: 199–219.

Bauer, Michal, et al. 2016. "Can war foster cooperation?" NBER Working Paper No. 22312.

Bekar, Cliff T., and Reed, Clyde G. 2013. "Land markets and inequality: evidence from medieval England." *European Review of Economic History* 17: 294–317.

Bentzel, Ragnar. 1952. *Inkomstfördelningen i Sverige*. Stockholm: Victor Peterssons Bokindustri Aktiebolag.

Bercé, Yves-Marie. 1987. *Revolt and revolution in early modern Europe: an essay on the history of political violence*. Manchester, UK: Manchester University Press.

Bergh, Andreas. 2011. "The rise, fall and revival of the Swedish welfare state: what are the policy lessons from Sweden?" IFN Working Paper No. 871.

Bergh, Andreas, and Henrekson, Magnus. 2011. "Government size and growth: a survey and interpretation of the evidence." *Journal of Economic Surveys* 25: 872–897.

Bergh, Andreas, and Nilsson, Therese. 2010. "Do liberalization and globalization increase income inequality?" *European Journal of Political Economy* 26: 488–505.

Berkowitz, Edward, and McQuaid, Kim. 1988. *Creating the welfare state: the political economy of twentieth-century reform*. 2nd ed. New York: Praeger.

Bernhardt, Kathryn. 1992. *Rents, taxes, and peasant resistance: the Lower Yangzi region, 1840–1950*. Stanford, CA: Stanford University Press.

Bertelsmann Stiftung. 2012. *BTI 2012—Cuba country report*. Gütersloh, Germany: Bertelsmann Stiftung.

Bértola, Luis, Castelnuovo, Cecilia, Rodríguez, Javier, and Willebald, Henry. 2009. "Income distribution in the Latin American Southern Cone during the first globalization boom and beyond." *International Journal of Comparative Sociology* 50: 452–485.

Bértola, Luis, and Ocampo, José Antonio. 2012. *The economic development of Latin America since independence*. Oxford: Oxford University Press.

Besley, Timothy, and Persson, Torsten. 2014. "Why do developing countries tax so little?" *Journal of Economic Perspectives* 28 (4): 99–120.

Beveridge, Sir William. 1942. *Social insurance and allied services*. London: His Majesty's Stationery Office.

Biehl, Peter F., and Marciniak, Arkadiusz. 2000. "The construction of hierarchy: rethinking the Copper Age in southeastern Europe." In Diehl, Michael W., ed., *Hierarchies in action: cui bono?* Center for Archaeological Investigations, Occasional Paper No. 27: 181–209.

Bircan, Cagatay, Brück, Tilman, and Vothknecht, Marc. 2010. "Violent conflict and inequality." DIW Berlin Discussion Paper No. 1013.

Bivens, Josh, and Mishel, Lawrence. 2013. "The pay of corporate executives and financial professionals as evidence of rents in top 1 percent incomes." *Journal of Economic Perspectives* 27: 57–77.

Björklund, Anders, and Jäntti, Markus. 2009. "Intergenerational income mobility and the role of family background." In Salverda, Nolan, and Smeeding, eds. 2009: 491–521.

Blanton, Richard. 1998. "Beyond centralization: steps toward a theory of egalitarian behavior in archaic states." In Feinman, Gary M., and Marcus, Joyce, eds., *Archaic states*. Santa Fe: School of American Research, 135–172.

Blanton, Richard, and Fargher, Lane. 2008. *Collective action in the formation of pre-modern states*. New York: Springer.

Blanton, Richard E., Kowalewski, Stephen A., Feinman, Gary M., and Finsten, Laura M. 1993. *Ancient Mesoamerica: a comparison of change in three regions*. 2nd ed. Cambridge, UK: Cambridge University Press.

Blickle, Peter. 1983. *Die Revolution von 1525*. 2nd ed. Munich: Oldenbourg.

Blickle, Peter. 1988. *Unruhen in der ständischen Gesellschaft 1300–1800*. Munich: Oldenbourg.

Blum, Jerome. 1957. "The rise of serfdom in Eastern Europe." *American Historical Review* 62: 807–836.

Blume, Lawrence E., and Durlauf, Steven N. 2015. "*Capital in the twenty-first century*: a review essay." *Journal of Political Economy* 123: 749–777.

Bodde, Derk. 1986. "The state and empire of Ch'in." In Twitchett and Loewe, eds. 1986: 20–102.

Boehm, Christopher. 1999. *Hierarchy in the forest: the evolution of egalitarian behavior*. Cambridge, MA: Harvard University Press.

Boix, Carles. 2015. *Political order and inequality: their foundation and their consequences for human welfare*. Cambridge, UK: Cambridge University Press.

Boix, Carles, and Rosenbluth, Frances. 2014. "Bones of contention: the political economy of height inequality." *American Political Science Review* 108: 1–22.

Bonica, Adam, McCarty, Nolan, Poole, Keith T., and Rosenthal, Howard. 2013. "Why hasn't democracy slowed rising inequality?" *Journal of Economic Perspectives* 27: 103–123.

Bonnet, Odran, Bono, Pierre-Henri, Chapelle, Guillaume, and Wasmer, Etienne. 2014. "Does housing capital contribute to inequality? A comment on Thomas Piketty's *Capital in the 21st century*." SciencesPo, Department of Economics, Discussion Paper 2014–07.

Bordo, Michael D., and Meissner, Christopher M. 2011. "Do financial crises always raise inequality? Some evidence from history." Working paper.

Borgerhoff Mulder, Monique, et al. 2009. "Intergenerational wealth transmission and the dynamics of inequality in small-scale societies." *Science* 326: 682–688, with supporting online material at www.sciencemag.org/cgi/content/full/326/5953/682/DC1.

Borsch, Stuart J. 2005. *The Black Death in Egypt and England: a comparative study*. Austin: University of Texas Press.

Boserup, Ester. 1965. *The conditions of agricultural growth: the economics of agrarian change under population pressure*. London: Allen and Unwin.

Boserup, Ester. 1981. *Population and technological change: a study of long-term trends*. Chicago: University of Chicago Press.

Bostrom, Nick. 2003. "Human genetic enhancements: a transhumanist perspective." *Journal of Value Inquiry* 37: 493–506.

Bostrom, Nick. 2014. *Superintelligence: paths, dangers, strategies*. Oxford: Oxford University Press.

Bosworth, Barry, Burtless, Gary, and Zhang, Kan. 2016. "Later retirement, inequality in old age, and the growing gap in longevity between rich and poor." Washington, DC: Brookings Institution.

Bourguignon, Francois. 2015. *The globalization of inequality*. Princeton, NJ: Princeton University Press.

Bower, John M. 2001. *The politics of "Pearl": court poetry in the age of Richard II*. Woodbridge, UK: Boydell and Brewer.

Bowles, Samuel. 2006. "Group competition, reproductive leveling and the evolution of human altruism." *Science* 314: 1569–1572.

Bowles, Samuel. 2012a. *The new economics of inequality and redistribution*. Cambridge, UK: Cambridge University Press.

Bowles, Samuel. 2012b. "Warriors, levelers, and the role of conflict in human social evolution." *Science* 336: 876–879.

Bowles, Samuel. 2015. "Political hierarchy, economic inequality & the first Southwest Asian farmers." SFI Working Paper 2015–06–015.

Bowles, Samuel, and Choi, Jung-Kyoo. 2013. "Coevolution of farming and private property during the early Holocene." *Proceedings of the National Academy of Sciences* 110: 8830–8835.

Bowles, Samuel, and Gintis, Herbert. 2002. "The inheritance of inequality." *Journal of Economic Perspectives* 16: 3–30.

Bowman, Alan K. 1985. "Landholding in the Hermopolite nome in the fourth century AD." *Journal of Roman Studies* 75: 137–163.

Bracken, Paul. 2012. *The second nuclear age: strategy, danger, and the new power politics*. New York: Times Books.

Brady, David, and Finnigan, Ryan. 2014. "Does immigration undermine public support for social policy?" *American Sociological Review* 79: 17–42.

Brandolini, Andrea, and Smeeding, Timothy M. 2009. "Income inequality in richer and OECD countries." In Salverda, Nolan, and Smeeding, eds. 2009: 71–100.

Brandolini, Andrea, and Vecchi, Giovanni. 2011. "The well-being of Italians: a comparative historical approach." Quaderni di Storia Economica (Economic History Working Papers), No. 19.

Brandt, Loren, and Sands, Barbara. 1992. "Land concentration and income distribution in Republican China." In Rawski, Thomas G., and Li, Lillian M., eds., *Chinese history in economic perspective*. Berkeley: University of California Press, 179–207.

Brenner, Y. S., Kaelble, Hartmut, and Thomas, Mark, eds. 1991. *Income distribution in historical perspective*. Cambridge, UK: Cambridge University Press.

Briggs, Asa. 1961. "The welfare state in historical perspective." *European Journal of Sociology* 2: 221–258.

Britnell, Richard. 2004. *Britain and Ireland 1050–1500: economy and society*. Oxford: Oxford University Press.

Broadberry, Stephen, and Gupta, Bishnupriya. 2006. "The early modern great divergence: wages, prices and economic development in Europe and Asia, 1500–1800." *Economic History Review* 59: 2–31.

Broadberry, Stephen, and Harrison, Mark, eds. 2005a. *The economics of World War I.* Cambridge, UK: Cambridge University Press.

Broadberry, Stephen, and Harrison, Mark. 2005b. "The economics of World War I: an overview." In Broadberry and Harrison, eds. 2005a: 3–40.

Broadberry, Stephen, and Howlett, Peter. 2005. "The United Kingdom during World War I: business as usual?" In Broadberry and Harrison, eds. 2005a: 206–234.

Brown, Peter. 2012. *Through the eye of a needle: wealth, the fall of Rome, and the making of Christianity in the West, 350–550 AD.* Princeton, NJ: Princeton University Press.

Brown, T. S. 1984. *Gentlemen and officers: imperial administration and aristocratic power in Byzantine Italy A.D. 554–800.* Rome: British School at Rome.

Brown, Kyle S., et al. 2012. "An early and enduring advanced technology originating 71,000 years ago in South Africa." *Nature* 491: 590–593.

Brownlee, W. Elliot. 2004. *Federal taxation in America: a short history.* 2nd ed. Washington, DC: Woodrow Wilson Center Press.

Brueckner, Markus, and Lederman, Daniel. 2015. "Effects of income inequality on aggregate output." World Bank Policy Discussion Paper No. 7317.

Brynjolfsson, Erik, and McAfee, Andrew. 2014. *The second machine age: work, progress, and prosperity in a time of brilliant technologies.* New York: Norton.

Buffett, Warren E. 2011. "Stop coddling the super-rich." *New York Times* August 15, 2011: A21.

Burbank, Jane, and Cooper, Frederick. 2010. *Empires in world history: geographies of power, politics of difference.* Princeton, NJ: Princeton University Press.

Burgers, Peter. 1993. "Taxing the rich: confiscation and the financing of the Claudian Principate (AD 41–54)." *Laverna* 4: 55–68.

Byrne, Joseph P. 2006. *Daily life during the Black Death.* Westport, CT: Greenwood Press.

Campbell, Bruce M. S. 2008. "Benchmarking medieval economic development: England, Wales, Scotland, and Ireland, c. 1290." *Economic History Review* 61: 896–945.

Campos-Vazquez, Raymundo, and Sobarzo, Horacio. 2012. *The development and fiscal effects of emigration on Mexico.* Washington, DC: Migration Policy Institute.

Canbakal, Hülya. 2012. "Wealth and inequality in Ottoman Bursa, 1500–1840." Conference paper for "New perspectives in Ottoman economic history," Yale University, November 9–10, 2012.

Canbakal, Hülya, and Filiztekin, Alpay. 2013. "Wealth and inequality in Ottoman lands in the early modern period." Conference paper for "AALIMS—Rice University conference on the political economy of the Muslim world," April 4–5, 2013.

Card, David. 2009. "Immigration and inequality." *American Economic Review* 99: 1–21.

Carneiro, Robert L. 1970. "A theory of the origin of the state." *Science* 169: 733–738.

Carneiro, Robert L. 1988. "The circumscription theory: challenge and response." *American Behavioral Scientist* 31: 497–511.

Cartledge, Paul, and Spawforth, Antony. 1989. *Hellenistic and Roman Sparta: a tale of two cities.* London: Routledge.

Cederman, Lars-Erik, Weidmann, Nils B., and Skrede, Kristian. 2011. "Horizontal inequalities and ethnonationalist civil war: a global comparison." *American Political Science Review* 105: 478–495.

Center for Genetics and Society. 2015. "Extreme genetic engineering and the human future: reclaiming emerging biotechnologies for the common good." Center for Genetics and Society.

Cerman, Markus. 2012. *Villagers and lords in Eastern Europe, 1300–1800.* Basingstoke, UK: Palgrave Macmillan.

Champlin, Edward. 1980. "The Volcei land register (*CIL* X 407)." *American Journal of Ancient History* 5: 13–18.

Cherry, John F., and Davis, Jack L. 2007. "An archaeological homily." In Galaty and Parkinson, eds. 2007b: 118–127.

Chetty, Raj, et al. 2014. "Is the United States still a land of opportunity? Recent trends in intergenerational mobility." *American Economic Review* 104: 141–147.

Christian, David. 2004. *Maps of time: an introduction to Big History.* Berkeley: University of California Press.

Ch'ü, T'ung-tsu. 1972. *Han social structure.* Seattle: University of Washington Press.

Church, George, and Regis, Ed. 2014. *Regenesis: how synthetic biology will reinvent nature and ourselves.* New York: Basic Books.

Cingano, Federico. 2014. "Trends in income inequality and its impact on economic growth." OECD Social, Employment and Migration Working Papers No. 163.

Cioffi-Revilla, Claudio, Rogers, J. Daniel, Wilcox, Steven P., and Alterman, Jai. 2011. "Computing the steppes: data analysis for agent-based models of polities in Inner Asia." In Brosseder, Ursula, and Miller, Bryan K., eds., *Xiongnu archaeology: multidisciplinary perspectives of the first steppe empire in Inner Asia.* Bonn, Germany: Rheinische Friedrich-Wilhelms-Universität Bonn, 97–110.

Claessen, Henry J. M., and Skalník, Peter. 1978a. "The early state: models and reality." In Claessen and Skalník, eds. 1978b: 637–650.

Claessen, Henry J. M., and Skalník, Peter, eds. 1978b. *The early state.* The Hague: De Gruyter.

Clark, Andrew E., and D'Ambrosio, Conchita. 2015. "Attitudes to income inequality: experimental and survey evidence." In Atkinson and Bourguignon, eds. 2015: 1147–1208.

Clark, Gregory. 2007a. *A farewell to alms: a brief economic history of the world.* Princeton, NJ: Princeton University Press.

Clark, Gregory. 2007b. "The long march of history: farm wages, population, and economic growth, England 1209–1869." *Economic History Review* 60: 97–135.

Clark, Gregory. 2014. *The son also rises: surnames and the history of social mobility.* Princeton, NJ: Princeton University Press.

Clarke, Walter S., and Gosende, Robert. 2003. "Somalia: can a collapsed state reconstitute itself?" In Rotberg, Robert I., ed,. *State failure and state weakness in a time of terror.* Washington, DC: Brookings Institution Press, 129–158.

Clausewitz, Carl von. 1976. *On war.* Trans. Peter Paret and Michael Howard. Princeton, NJ: Princeton University Press.

Cline, Eric C. 2014. *1177 B.C.: the year civilization collapsed.* Princeton, NJ: Princeton University Press.

Cobham, Alex, and Sumner, Andy. 2014. "Is inequality all about the tails? The Palma measure of income inequality." *Significance* 11 (1): 10–13.

Coe, Michael D. 2003. *Angkor and the Khmer civilization.* New York: Thames and Hudson.

Coe, Michael D. 2005. *The Maya.* 7th ed. New York: Thames and Hudson.

Cohen, Joel. 1995. *How many people can the earth support?* New York: W. W. Norton.

Cohen, Ronald. 1978. "State origins: a reappraisal." In Claessen and Skalník, eds. 1978b: 31–75.

Cohn, Samuel K., Jr. 2004. *Popular protest in late medieval Europe: Italy, France, and Flanders.* Manchester, UK: Manchester University Press.

Cohn, Samuel K., Jr. 2006. *Lust for liberty. The politics of social revolt in medieval Europe, 1200–1425: Italy, France, and Flanders.* Cambridge, MA: Harvard University Press.

Coleman, David. 2006. "Immigration and ethnic change in low-fertility countries: a third demographic transition." *Population and Development Review* 32: 401–446.

Collier, Paul, and Hoeffler, Anke. 2004. "Greed and grievance in civil war." *Oxford Economic Papers* 56: 563–595.

Collins, Chuck, and Hoxie, Josh. 2015. "Billionaire bonanza: the Forbes 400 … and the rest of us." Washington, DC: Institute for Policy Studies.

Conyon, Martin J., He, Lerong, and Zhou, Xin. 2015. "Star CEOs or political connections? Evidence from China's publicly traded firms." *Journal of Business Finance and Accounting* 42: 412–443.

Cook, Noble David. 1998. *Born to die: disease and the New World conquest, 1492–1650.* Cambridge, UK: Cambridge University Press.

Cooney, Kathlyn M. 2011. "Changing burial practices at the end of the New Kingdom: defensive adaptations in tomb commissions, coffin commissions, coffin decoration, and mummification." *Journal of the American Research Center in Egypt* 47: 3–44.

Corak, Miles. 2013. "Income inequality, equality of opportunity, and intergenerational mobility." *Journal of Economic Perspectives* 27: 79–102.

Cornia, Giovanni Andrea, ed. 2014a. *Falling inequality in Latin America: policy changes and lessons.* Oxford: Oxford University Press.

Cornia, Giovanni Andrea. 2014b. "Inequality trends and their determinants: Latin America over the period 1990–2010." In Cornia, ed. 2014a: 23–48.

Cornia, Giovanni Andrea. 2014c. "Recent distributive changes in Latin America: an overview." In Cornia, ed. 2014a: 3–22.

Courtois, Stéphane. 1999. "Introduction: the crimes of communism." In Courtois et al. 1999: 1–31.

Courtois, Stéphane, Werth, Nicolas, Panné, Jean-Louis, Paczkowski, Andrzej, Bartosek, Karel, and Margolin, Jean-Louis. 1999. *The black book of communism: crimes, terror, repression.* Cambridge, MA: Harvard University Press.

Cowell, Frank A., and Flachaire, Emmanuel. 2015. "Statistical methods for distributional analysis." In Atkinson and Bourguignon, eds. 2015: 359–465.

Cowen, Deborah. 2008. *Military workfare: the soldier and social citizenship in Canada.* Toronto: University of Toronto Press.

Cowgill, George. 2015. *Ancient Teotihuacan: early urbanism in central Mexico.* New York: Cambridge University Press.

Crafts, Nicholas, and Mills, Terence C. 2009. "From Malthus to Solow: how did the Malthusian economy really end?" *Journal of Macroeconomics* 31: 68–93.

Credit Suisse. 2014. *Global wealth report.* Zurich: Credit Suisse AG.

Credit Suisse. 2015. *Global wealth report.* Zurich: Credit Suisse AG.

Crivellaro, Elena. 2014. "College wage premium over time: trends in Europe in the last 15 years." Ca' Foscari University of Venice, Department of Economics, Working Paper No. 03/WP/2014.

Crone, Patricia. 2003. *Pre-industrial societies: anatomy of the pre-modern world.* 2nd ed. Oxford: Oneworld Publications.

Cronin, James E. 1991. *The politics of state expansion: war, state and society in twentieth-century Britain.* London: Routledge.

Crosby, Alfred. 1972. *The Columbian exchange: biological and cultural consequences of 1492.* Westport, CT: Westview Press.

Crosby, Alfred. 2004. *Ecological imperialism: the biological expansion of Europe, 900–1900.* 2nd ed. Cambridge, UK: Cambridge University Press.

Culbert, T. Patrick, ed. 1973. *The Classic Maya collapse.* Albuquerque: University of New Mexico Press.

Culbert, T. Patrick. 1988. "The collapse of classic Maya civilization." In Yoffee and Cowgill, eds. 1988: 69–101.

Dabla-Norris, Era, et al. 2015. "Causes and consequences of income inequality: a global perspective." IMF Staff Discussion Note.

D'Amuri, Francesco, and Peri, Giovanni. 2014. "Immigration, jobs, and employment protection: evidence from Europe before and after the Great Recession." *Journal of the European Economic Association* 12: 432–464.

Davies, John K. 1971. *Athenian propertied families, 600–300 B.C.* Oxford: Oxford University Press.

Davies, John K. 1981. *Wealth and the power of wealth in classical Athens.* New York: Ayer.

Davies, R. W. 1998. *Soviet economic development from Lenin to Khrushchev.* Cambridge, UK: Cambridge University Press.

Davis, Gerald F., and Kim, Suntae. 2015. "Financialization of the economy." *Annual Review of Sociology* 41: 203–221.

De Ferranti, David, Perry, Guillermo E., Ferreira, Francisco H. G., and Walton, Michael. 2004. *Inequality in Latin America: breaking with history?* Washington, DC: World Bank.

Deger-Jalkotzy, Sigrid. 2008. "Decline, destruction, aftermath." In Shelmerdine, ed. 2008: 387–416.

Deininger, Klaus, and Squire, Lyn. 1998. "New ways of looking at old issues: inequality and growth." *Journal of Development Economics* 57: 259–287.

De Jong, Herman. 2005. "Between the devil and the deep blue sea: the Dutch economy during World War I." In Broadberry and Harrison, eds. 2005a: 137–168.

De Ligt, Luuk, and Garnsey, Peter. 2012. "The album of Herculaneum and a model of the town's demography." *Journal of Roman Archaeology* 24: 69–94.

Dell, Fabien. 2005. "Top incomes in Germany and Switzerland over the twentieth century." *Journal of the European Economic Association* 3: 412–421.

Dell, F. 2007. "Top incomes in Germany throughout the twentieth century: 1891–1998." In Atkinson and Piketty, eds. 2007a: 365–425.

Dell, F., Piketty, F., and Saez, E. 2007. "Income and wealth concentration in Switzerland over the twentieth century." In Atkinson and Piketty, eds. 2007a: 472–500.

Demarest, Arthur A. 2006. *The Petexbatun regional archaeological project: a multidisciplinary study of the Maya collapse.* Nashville, TN: Vanderbilt University Press.

Demarest, Arthur A., Rice, Prudence M., and Rice, Don S., eds. 2004a. "The Terminal Classic in the Maya lowlands: assessing collapse, terminations, and transformations." In Demarest, Rice, and Rice, eds. 2004b: 545–572.

Demarest, Arthur A., Rice, Prudence M., and Rice, Don S., eds. 2004b. *The Terminal Classic in the Maya lowlands: collapse, transition, and transformation.* Boulder: University Press of Colorado.

Deng, Gang. 1999. *The premodern Chinese economy: structural equilibrium and capitalist sterility.* London: Routledge.

Department of State. 1946. *Occupation of Japan: policy and progress.* Washington, DC: U.S. Government Printing Office.

D'Errico, Francesco, and Vanhaeren, Marian. 2016. "Upper Palaeolithic mortuary practices: reflection of ethnic affiliation, social complexity, and cultural turnover." In Renfrew, Colin, Boyd, Michael J., and Morley, Iain, eds., *Death rituals, social order and the archaeology of immortality in the ancient world: "death shall have no dominion."* Cambridge, UK: Cambridge University Press, 45–64.

De Vries, Jan. 1984. *European urbanization, 1500–1800.* London: Methuen.

De Vries, Jan, and Van der Woude, Ad. 1997. *The first modern economy: success, failure, and perseverance of the Dutch economy, 1500–1815.* Cambridge, UK: Cambridge University Press.

Diamond, Jared. 1997. *Guns, germs, and steel: the fates of human societies.* New York: W. W. Norton.

Diamond, Jared. 2005. *Collapse: how societies choose to fail or succeed.* New York: Viking.

Dikötter, Frank. 2013. *The tragedy of liberation: a history of the Chinese revolution, 1945–1957.* New York: Bloomsbury.

Diskin, Martin. 1989. "El Salvador: reform prevents change." In Thiesenheusen, ed. 1989b: 429–450.

Dobado González, Rafael, and García Montero, Héctor. 2010. "Colonial origins of inequality in Hispanic America? Some reflections based on new empirical evidence." *Revista de Historia Económica* 28: 253–277.

Dobson, R. B. 1983. *The peasants' revolt of 1381.* 2nd ed. London: Macmillan.

Docquier, Frederic, Ozden, Caglar, and Peri, Giovanni. 2014. "The labour market effects of immigration and emigration in OECD countries." *Economic Journal* 124: 1106–1145.

Dols, Michael W. 1977. *The Black Death in the Middle East.* Princeton, NJ: Princeton University Press.

Dore, R. P. 1984. *Land reform in Japan.* London: Athlone Press.

Doyle, Michael. 1986. *Empires.* Ithaca: Cornell University Press.

Doyle, William. 2009. *Aristocracy and its enemies in the age of revolution.* Oxford: Oxford University Press.

Draper, Nicholas. 2010. *The price of emancipation: slave-ownership, compensation and British society at the end of slavery.* Cambridge, UK: Cambridge University Press.

Drexler, Madeline. 2009. *Emerging epidemics: the menace of new infections.* New York: Penguin.

Drinkwater, John F. 1992. "The bacaudae of fifth-century Gaul." In Drinkwater, John, and Elton, Hugh, eds., *Fifth-century Gaul: a crisis of identity?* Cambridge, UK: Cambridge University Press, 208–217.

Dubreuil, Benoît. 2010. *Human evolution and the origins of hierarchies: the state of nature.* Cambridge, UK: Cambridge University Press.

Duch, Raymond M., and Rueda, David. 2014. "Generosity among friends: population homogeneity, altruism and insurance as determinants of redistribution?" Working paper.

Dumke, Rolf. 1991. "Income inequality and industrialization in Germany, 1850–1913: the Kuznets hypothesis re-examined." In Brenner, Kaelble, and Thomas, eds. 1991: 117–148.

Duncan-Jones, Richard. 1982. *The economy of the Roman empire: quantitative studies.* 2nd ed. Cambridge, UK: Cambridge University Press.

Duncan-Jones, Richard. 1994. *Money and government in the Roman empire.* Cambridge, UK: Cambridge University Press.

Duncan-Jones, Richard P. 1996. "The impact of the Antonine plague." *Journal of Roman Archaeology* 9: 108–136.

Dunn, Alastair. 2004. *The peasants' revolt: England's failed revolution of 1381.* Stroud: Tempus.

Durevall, Dick, and Henrekson, Magnus. 2011. "The futile quest for a grand explanation of long-run government expenditure." *Journal of Public Economics* 95: 708–722.

Du Rietz, Gunnar, Henrekson, Magnus, and Waldenström, Daniel. 2012. "The Swedish inheritance and gift taxation, 1885–2004." IFN Working Paper 936.

Du Rietz, Gunnar, Johansson, Dan, and Stenkula, Mikael. 2013. "The evolution of Swedish labor income taxation in a 150-year perspective: an in-depth characterization." IFN Working Paper No. 977.

Du Rietz, Gunnar, Johansson, Dan, and Stenkula, Mikael. 2014. "A 150-year perspective on Swedish capital income taxation." IFN Working Paper No. 1004.

Dutton, Paul V. 2002. *Origins of the French welfare state.* Cambridge, UK: Cambridge University Press.

Dyer, Christopher. 1998. *Standards of living in the later Middle Ages: social change in England c. 1200–1520.* Rev. ed. Cambridge, UK: Cambridge University Press.

Easterly, William. 2007. "Inequality does cause underdevelopment: insights from a new instrument." *Journal of Development Economics* 84: 755–776.

Ebrey, Patricia. 1986. "The economic and social history of Later Han." In Twitchett and Loewe, eds. 1986: 608–648.

Economic Commission for Latin America and the Caribbean (ECLAC) 2015. *Latin America and the Caribbean in the world economy, 2015.* Santiago, Chile: United Nations.

Economist Intelligence Unit. 2014. "Economic challenges in Somaliland." http://country.eiu.com/Somalia/ArticleList/Updates/Economy.

Edo, Anthony, and Toubal, Farid. 2015. "Selective immigration policies and wages inequality." *Review of International Economics* 23: 160–187.

Ehrenreich, Robert M., Crumley, Carole L., and Levy, Janet E., eds. 1995. *Heterarchy and the analysis of complex societies.* Washington, DC: American Anthropological Association.

Eidelberg, Philip Gabriel. 1974. *The great Rumanian peasant revolt of 1907: origins of a modern jacquerie.* Leiden, Netherlands: Brill.

Eika, Lasse, Mogstad, Magne, and Zafar, Basit. 2014. "Educational assortative mating and household income inequality." Federal Reserve Bank of New York Staff Report No. 682.

Eisenstadt, Shmuel N. 1993. *The political systems of empires.* Pb. ed. New Brunswick: Transaction Publishers.

Elhaik, Eran, et al. 2014. "The 'extremely ancient' chromosome that isn't: a forensic investigation of Albert Perry's X-degenerate portion of the Y chromosome." *European Journal of Human Genetics* 22: 1111–1116.

Elton, Hugh. 2007. "Military forces." In Sabin, van Wees and Whitby, eds. 2007: 270–309.

Elvin, Mark. 1973. *The pattern of the Chinese past.* Stanford, CA: Stanford University Press.

Esmonde Cleary, Simon. 1989. *The ending of Roman Britain.* London: Routledge.

Estevez-Abe, Margarita. 2008. *Welfare and capitalism in postwar Japan: party, bureaucracy, and business.* Cambridge, UK: Cambridge University Press.

European Commission. 2007. *Europe's demographic future: facts and figures on challenges and opportunities.* Luxembourg: Office for Official Publications of the European Communities.

European Commission. 2013. "Demography and inequality: how Europe's changing population will impact on income inequality." http://europa.eu/epic/studies-reports/docs/eaf_policy_brief_-_demography_and_inequality_final_version.pdf.

European Commission. 2015. *The 2015 aging report: economic and budgetary projections for the 28 EU member states (2013–2060).* Luxembourg: Publications Office of the European Union.

Faik, Jürgen. 2012. "Impacts of an ageing society on macroeconomics and income inequality—the case of Germany since the 1980s." ECINEQ Working Paper 2012–272.

Falkenhausen, Lothar von. 2006. *Chinese society in the age of Confucius (1000–250 BC): the archaeological evidence*. Los Angeles: Cotsen Institute of Archaeology.

Farber, Samuel. 2011. *Cuba since the revolution of 1959: a critical assessment*. Chicago: Haymarket Books.

Farris, William Wayne. 1993. *Heavenly warriors: the evolution of Japan's military, 500–1300*. Cambridge, MA: Harvard University Press.

Fearon, James D., and Laitin, David. 2003. "Ethnicity, insurgency, and civil war." *American Political Science Review* 97: 75–90.

Feinstein, Charles. 1988. "The rise and fall of the Williamson curve." *Journal of Economic History* 48: 699–729.

Ferguson, Niall. 1999. *The pity of war: explaining World War I*. New York: Basic Books.

Fernandez, Eva, and Santiago-Caballero, Carlos. 2013. "Economic inequality in Madrid, 1500–1840." Working paper. http://estructuraehistoria.unizar.es/personal/vpinilla/documents/ Fernandez_Santiago.pdf.

Figes, Orlando. 1997. *A people's tragedy: the Russian revolution 1891–1924*. London: Pimlico.

Findlay, Ronald, and Lundahl, Mats. 2006. "Demographic shocks and the factor proportion model: from the plague of Justinian to the Black Death." In Findlay, Ronald, Henriksson, Rolf G. H., Lindgren, Hakan, and Lundahl, Mats, eds., *Eli Heckscher, international trade, and economic history*. Cambridge, MA: MIT Press, 157–198.

Fine, John V. A. 1987. *The late medieval Balkans: a critical survey from the late twelfth century to the Ottoman conquest*. Ann Arbor: University of Michigan Press.

Finlayson, Bill, and Warren, Graeme M. 2010. *Changing natures: hunter-gatherers, first farmers and the modern world*. London: Duckworth.

Finseraas, Henning. 2012. "Poverty, ethnic minorities among the poor, and preferences for redistribution in European regions." *Journal of European Social Policy* 22: 164–180.

Fisher, Jonathan D., Johnson, David S., and Smeeding, Timothy M. 2013. "Measuring the trends in inequality of individuals and families: income and consumption." *American Economic Review* 103: 184–188.

Fitzgerald, F. Scott. 1926. "The rich boy." *Red Magazine* January/February 1926. http://gutenberg.net.au /fsf/THE-RICH-BOY.html.

Flakierski, Henryk. 1992. "Changes in income inequality in the USSR." In Aslund, Anders, ed., *Market socialism or the restoration of capitalism?* Cambridge, UK: Cambridge University Press, 172–193.

Flannery, Kent, and Marcus, Joyce. 2012. *The creation of inequality: how our prehistoric ancestors set the stage for monarchy, slavery, and empire*. Cambridge, MA: Harvard University Press.

Fochesato, Mattia, and Bowles, Samuel. 2015. "Nordic exceptionalism? Social democratic egalitarianism in world-historic perspective." *Journal of Public Economics* 127: 30–44.

Ford, Martin. 2015. *Rise of the robots: technology and the threat of a jobless future*. New York: Basic Books.

Formicola, Vincenzo. 2007. "From the Sungir children to the Romito dwarf: aspects of the Upper Paleolithic funerary landscape." *Current Anthropology* 48: 446–453.

Förster, Michael F., and Tóth, István György. 2015. "Cross-country evidence of the multiple causes of inequality changes in the OECD area." In Atkinson and Bourguignon, eds. 2015: 1729–1843.

Fortun Vargas, Jonathan M. 2012. "Declining inequality in Bolivia: how and why." MPRA Paper No. 41208.

Foster, Benjamin R. 2016. *The age of Agade: inventing empire in ancient Mesopotamia*. London: Routledge.

Fourquin, Guy. 1978. *The anatomy of popular rebellion in the Middle Ages*. Amsterdam: North-Holland.

Foxhall, Lin. 1992. "The control of the Attic landscape." In Wells, ed. 1992: 155–159.

Foxhall, Lin. 2002. "Access to resources in classical Greece: the egalitarianism of the polis in practice." In Cartledge, Paul, Cohen, Edward E., and Foxhall, Lin, eds., *Money, labour and land: approaches to the economies of ancient Greece*. London: Routledge, 209–220.

Frankema, Ewout. 2012. "Industrial wage inequality in Latin America in global perspective, 1900–2000." *Studies in Comparative International Development* 47: 47–74.

Frankfurt, Harry G. 2015. *On inequality*. Princeton, NJ: Princeton University Press.

Fraser, Derek. 2009. *The evolution of the British welfare state: a history of social policy since the Industrial Revolution*. Basingstoke, UK: Palgrave Macmillan.

Frazer, Garth. 2006. "Inequality and development across and within countries." *World Development* 34: 1459–1481.

Freeland, Chrystia. 2012. *Plutocrats: the rise of the new global super-rich and the fall of everyone else*. New York: Penguin.

Freeman, Richard B. 2009. "Globalization and inequality." In Salverda, Nolan, and Smeeding, eds. 2009: 575–598.

Freu, Christel. 2015. "Labour status and economic stratification in the Roman world: the hierarchy of wages in Egypt." *Journal of Roman Archaeology* 28: 161–177.

Frey, Carl Benedikt, and Osborne, Michael A. 2013. "The future of employment: how susceptible are jobs to computerization?" Oxford Martin School Working Paper.

Frier, Bruce W. 2001. "More is worse: some observations on the population of the Roman empire." In Scheidel, Walter, ed., *Debating Roman demography*. Leiden, Netherlands: Brill, 139–159.

Frydman, Carola, and Molloy, Raven. 2012. "Pay cuts for the boss: executive compensation in the 1940s." *Journal of Economic History* 72: 225–251.

Fuentes-Nieva, Ricardo, and Galasso, Nick. 2014. "Working for the few: political capture and economic inequality." Oxford: Oxfam.

Fuks, Alexander. 1984. *Social conflict in ancient Greece*. Jerusalem: Magnes Press.

Fukuyama, Francis. 2011. *The origins of political order: from prehuman times to the French Revolution*. New York: Farrar, Straus and Giroux.

Furceri, Davide, and Karras, Georgios. 2011. "Tax design in the OECD: a test of the Hines–Summers hypothesis." *Eastern Economic Journal* 37: 239–247.

Fussell, Paul. 1989. *Wartime: understanding and behavior in the Second World War*. New York: Oxford University Press.

Gabaix, Xabier, and Landier, Augustin. 2008. "Why has CEO pay increased so much?" *Quarterly Journal of Economics* 121: 49–100.

Gabaix, Xavier, Landier, Augustin, and Sauvagnat, Julien. 2014. "CEO pay and firm size: an update after the crisis." *Economic Journal* 124: F40–F59.

Galassi, Francesco, and Harrison, Mark. 2005. "Italy at war, 1915–1918." In Broadberry and Harrison, eds. 2005a: 276–309.

Galaty, Michael L., and Parkinson, William A. 2007a. "2007 introduction: Mycenaean palaces rethought." In Galaty and Parkinson, eds. 2007b: 1–17.

Galaty, Michael L., and Parkinson, William A., eds. 2007b. *Rethinking Mycenaean palaces II*. Rev. and exp. 2nd ed. Los Angeles: Cotsen Institute of Archaeology.

Gallagher, Thomas. 1982. *Paddy's lament: Ireland 1846–1847. Prelude to hatred*. San Diego, CA: Harcourt Brace.

García-Montero, Héctor. 2015. "Long-term trends in wealth inequality in Catalonia, 1400–1800: initial results." Dondena Working Paper No. 79.

Gärtner, Svenja, and Prado, Svante. 2012. "Inequality, trust and the welfare state: the Scandinavian model in the Swedish mirror." Working paper.

Gasparini, Leonardo, and Lustig, Nora. 2011. "The rise and fall of income inequality in Latin America." In Ocampo, José Antonio, and Ros, Jaime, eds., *The Oxford handbook of Latin American Economics*. New York: Oxford University Press, 691–714.

Gasparini, Leonardo, Cruces, Guillermo, and Tornarolli, Leopoldo. 2011. "Recent trends in income inequality in Latin America." *Economía* 11 (2): 147–190.

Gat, Azar. 2006. *War in human civilization*. Oxford: Oxford University Press.

Gatrell, Peter. 2005. *Russia's First World War: a social and economic history*. Harlow, UK: Pearson.

Geary, Frank, and Stark, Tom. 2004. "Trends in real wages during the Industrial Revolution: a view from across the Irish Sea." *Economic History Review* 57: 362–395.

Gellner, Ernest. 1983. *Nations and nationalism*. Ithaca, NY: Cornell University Press.

Giannecchini, Monica, and Moggi-Cecchi, Jacopo. 2008. "Stature in archaeological samples from Central Italy: methodological issues and diachronic changes." *American Journal of Physical Anthropology* 135: 284–292.

Giddens, Anthony. 1987. *The nation-state and violence: volume two of a contemporary critique of historical materialism*. Berkeley: University of California Press.

Gilens, Martin. 2012. *Affluence and influence: economic inequality and political power in America.* Princeton, NJ: Princeton University Press.

Gilmour, John. 2010. *Sweden, the swastika and Stalin: the Swedish experience in the Second World War.* Edinburgh: Edinburgh University Press.

Gilmour, John, and Stephenson, Jill, eds. 2013. *Hitler's Scandinavian legacy: the consequences of the German invasion for the Scandinavian countries, then and now.* London: Bloomsbury.

Gindling, T. H., and Trejos, Juan Diego. 2013. "The distribution of income in Central America." IZA Discussion Paper No. 7236.

Goetzmann, William N. 2016. *Money changes everything: how finance made civilization possible.* Princeton, NJ: Princeton University Press.

Goldin, Claudia, and Katz, Lawrence F. 2008. *The race between education and technology.* Cambridge, MA: Harvard University Press.

Goldin, Claudia, and Margo, Robert A. 1992. "The Great Compression: the wage structure in the United States at mid-century." *Quarterly Journal of Economics* 107: 1–34.

Goñi, Edwin, López, J. Humberto, and Servén, Luis. 2008. "Fiscal redistribution and income inequality in Latin America." World Bank Policy Research Paper No. 4487.

Goodin, Robert E., and Dryzek, Jon. 1995. "Justice deferred: wartime rationing and post-war welfare policy." *Politics and Society* 23: 49–73.

Goos, Maarten, and Manning, Alan. 2007. "Lousy and lovely jobs: the rising polarization of work in Britain." *Review of Economics and Statistics* 89: 118–133.

Gordon, Robert J. 2016. *The rise and fall of American growth: the U.S. standard of living since the Civil War.* Princeton, NJ: Princeton University Press.

Gottfried, Robert S. 1983. *The Black Death: natural and human disaster in medieval Europe.* New York: Free Press.

Graeber, David. 2011. *Debt: the first 5,000 years.* Brooklyn, NY: Melville House.

Grant, Oliver Wavell. 2002. "Does industrialisation push up inequality? New evidence on the Kuznets curve from nineteenth-century Prussian tax statistics." University of Oxford Discussion Papers in Economic and Social History, No. 48.

Gray, Lewis C. 1933. *History of agriculture in the southern United States to 1860.* Vol. I. Washington, DC: Carnegie Institution of Washington.

Greenwood, Jeremy, Guner, Nezih, Kocharkov, Georgi, and Santos, Cezar. 2014. "Marry your like: assortative mating and income inequality." *American Economic Review* 104: 348–353.

Gregory, Paul R. 1982. *Russian national income, 1885–1913.* New York: Cambridge University Press.

Grigg, David. 1980. *Population growth and agrarian change: an historical perspective.* Cambridge, UK: Cambridge University Press.

Grimnes, Ole Kristian. 2013. "Hitler's Norwegian legacy." In Gilmour and Stephenson, eds. 2013: 159–177.

Grogger, Jeffrey, and Hanson, Gordon H. 2011. "Income maximization and the selection and sorting of international migrants." *Journal of Development Economics* 95: 42–57.

Gross, Jean-Pierre. 1997. *Fair shares for all: Jacobin egalitarianism in practice.* Cambridge, UK: Cambridge University Press.

Grütter, Alfred. 1968. "Die eidgenössische Wehrsteuer, ihre Entwicklung und Bedeutung." PhD thesis, Zürich.

Guasti, Cesare, ed. 1880. *Il sacco di Prato e il ritorno de' Medici in Firenze nel MDXII.* Bologna, Italy: Gaetano Romagnoli.

Gurven, Michael, et al. 2010. "Domestication alone does not lead to inequality: intergenerational wealth transmission among agriculturalists." *Current Anthropology* 51: 49–64.

Gustafsson, Björn, and Johansson, Mats. 2003. "Steps toward equality: how and why income inequality in urban Sweden changed during the period 1925–1958." *European Review of Economic History* 7: 191–211.

Haas, Ain. 1993. "Social inequality in aboriginal North America: a test of Lenski's theory." *Social Forces* 72: 295–313.

Haber, Stephen. 2006. "The political economy of Latin American industrialization." In Bulmer-Thomas, Victor, Coatsworth, John, and Cortes Conde, Roberto, eds., *The Cambridge economic history of Latin America.* Vol. 2. *The long twentieth century.* Cambridge, UK: Cambridge University Press, 537–584.

Haber, Stephen. 2012. "Climate, technology, and the evolution of political and economic institutions." PERC Working Paper.

Haldon, John F. 1993. *The state and the tributary mode of production.* London: Verso.

Haldon, John F. 1997. *Byzantium in the seventh century: the transformation of a culture.* Rev. ed. Cambridge, UK: Cambridge University Press.

Hamilton, Malcolm B. 1989. *Democratic socialism in Britain and Sweden.* Basingstoke, UK: Macmillan Press.

Haney, Emil B., Jr., and Haney, Wava G. 1989. "The agrarian transition in Highland Ecuador: from precapitalism to agrarian capitalism in Chimborazo." In Thiesenheusen, ed. 1989b: 70–91.

Hansen, Mogens H. 1985. *Demography and democracy: the number of Athenian citizens in the fourth century B.C.* Herning, Denmark: Systime.

Hansen, Mogens H. 1988. *Three studies in Athenian demography.* Copenhagen: Royal Danish Academy of Sciences and Letters.

Hansen, Mogens H., ed. 2000. *A comparative study of thirty city-state cultures: an investigation conducted by the Copenhagen Polis Centre.* Copenhagen: Royal Danish Academy of Sciences and Letters.

Hansen, Mogens H. 2006a. *Polis: an introduction to the ancient Greek city-state.* Oxford: Oxford University Press.

Hansen, Mogens H. 2006b. *The shotgun method: the demography of the ancient Greek city-state culture.* Columbia: University of Missouri Press.

Hansen, Mogens H., and Nielsen, Thomas H., eds. 2004. *An inventory of archaic and classical poleis.* Oxford: Oxford University Press.

Hanus, Jord. 2013. "Real inequality in the early modern Low Countries: the city of 's-Hertogenbosch, 1500–1660." *Economic History Review* 66: 733–756.

Hanushek, Eric A., Schwerdt, Guido, Wiederhold, Simon, and Woessmann, Ludger. 2013. "Returns to skills around the world: evidence from PIAAC." NBER Working Paper No. 19762.

Hara, Akira. 1998. "Japan: guns before rice." In Harrison, ed. 1998b: 224–267.

Hara, Akira. 2003. "Wartime controls." In Nakamura and Odaka, eds. 2003a: 247–286.

Harari, Yuval Noah. 2015. "Upgrading inequality: will rich people become a superior biological caste?" *The World Post* February 4, 2015. http://www.huffingtonpost.com/dr-yuval-noah-harari/inequality-rich-superior-biological_b_5846794.html.

Hardoon, Deborah, Ayele, Sophia, and Fuentes-Nieva, Ricardo. 2016. "An economy for the 1%: how privilege and power in the economy drive extreme inequality and how this can be stopped." Oxford: Oxfam GB.

Harper, Kyle. 2015a. "Landed wealth in the long term: patterns, possibilities, evidence." In Erdkamp, Paul, Verboven, Koenraad, and Zuiderhoek, Arjan, eds., *Ownership and exploitation of land and natural resources in the Roman world.* Oxford: Oxford University Press, 43–61.

Harper, Kyle. 2015b. "Pandemics and passages to late antiquity: rethinking the plague of c. 249–270 described by Cyprian." *Journal of Roman Archaeology* 28: 223–260.

Harris, John. 2010. *Enhancing evolution: the ethical case for making better people.* Princeton, NJ: Princeton University Press.

Harrison, Mark. 1998a. "The economics of World War II: an overview." In Harrison, ed. 1998b: 1–42.

Harrison, Mark, ed. 1998b. *The economics of World War II: six great powers in international comparison.* Cambridge, UK: Cambridge University Press.

Hartung, J. 1898. "Die direkten Steuern und die Vermögensentwicklung in Augsburg von der Mitte des 16. bis zum 18. Jahrhundert." *Jahrbuch für Gesetzgebung, Verwaltung und Volkswirtschaft im Deutschen Reich* 22 (4): 166–209.

Hashim, Alice B. 1997. *The fallen state: dissonance, dictatorship and death in Somalia.* Lanham, MD: University Press of America.

Hashimoto, Jurô. 2003. "The rise of big business." In Nakamura and Odaka, eds. 2003a: 190–222.

Hatzfeld, Jean. 2005. *Machete season: the killers in Rwanda speak.* New York: Farrar, Straus and Giroux.

Hautcoeur, Pierre-Cyrille. 2005. "Was the Great War a watershed? The economics of World War I in France." In Broadberry and Harrison, eds. 2005a: 169–205.

Hayami, Akira. 2004. "Introduction: the emergence of 'economic society.'" In Hayami, Saitô, and Toby, eds. 2004: 1–35.

Hayami, Akira, Saitô, Osamu, and Toby, Ronald P. 2004. *The economic history of Japan: 1600–1990*. Vol. 1. *Emergence of economic society in Japan, 1600–1859*. Oxford: Oxford University Press.

Hegyi, Géza, Néda, Zoltán, and Santos, Maria Augusta. 2005. "Wealth distribution of Pareto's law in the Hungarian medieval society." *arXiv*. http://arxiv.org/abs/physics/0509045.

Henken, Ted A., Celeya, Miriam, and Castellanos, Dimas, eds. 2013. *Cuba*. Santa Barbara, CA: ABC-CLIO.

Henrekson, Magnus, and Waldenström, Daniel. 2014. "Inheritance taxation in Sweden, 1885–2004: the role of ideology, family firms and tax avoidance." IFN Working Paper 1032.

Henshilwood, Christopher S., et al. 2001. "An early bone tool industry from the Middle Stone Age at Blombos Cave, South Africa: implications for the origins of modern human behavior, symbolism and language." *Journal of Human Evolution* 41: 631–678.

Hernani-Limarino, Werner L., and Eid, Ahmed. 2013. "Unravelling declining income inequality in Bolivia: do government transfers matter?" Working paper.

Higham, Tom, et al. 2007. "New perspectives on the Varna cemetery (Bulgaria)—AMS dates and social implications." *Antiquity* 81: 640–654.

Hilton, Rodney. 1973. *Bond men made free: medieval peasant movements and the English rising of 1381*. London: Temple Smith.

Hilton, R. H., and Aston, T. H., eds. 1984. *The English rising of 1381*. Cambridge, UK: Cambridge University Press.

Hines, James R., Jr. 2006. "Will social welfare expenditures survive tax competition?" *Oxford Review of Economic Policy* 22: 330–348.

Hines, James R., Jr., and Summers, Lawrence H. 2009. "How globalization affects tax design." *Tax Policy and the Economy* 23: 123–158.

Hinton, William. 1966. *Fanshen: a documentary of revolution in a Chinese village*. New York: Monthly Review Press.

Ho, Hoang-Anh. 2013. "Not a destiny: ethnic diversity and redistribution examined." MSc thesis, University of Gothenburg.

Hodkinson, Stephen. 2000. *Property and wealth in classical Sparta*. London: Duckworth.

Hoffman, Philip T. 1996. *Growth in a traditional society: the French countryside, 1450–1850*. Princeton, NJ: Princeton University Press.

Hoffman, Philip T., Jacks, David S., Levin, Patricia A., and Lindert, Peter H. 2005. "Sketching the rise of real inequality in early modern Europe." In Allen, Robert C., Bengtsson, Tommy, and Dribe, Martin, eds., *Living standards in the past: new perspectives on well-being in Asia and Europe*. Oxford: Oxford University Press, 131–172.

Hoffner, Harry A. Jr. 1998. *Hittite myths*. 2nd ed. Atlanta: Scholars Press.

Hoggarth, Julie A., et al. 2016. "The political collapse of Chichén Itza in climatic and cultural context." *Global and Planetary Change* 138: 25–42.

Holtermann, Helge. 2012. "Explaining the development-civil war relationship." *Conflict Management and Peace Science* 29: 56–78.

Holtfrerich, Carl-Ludwig. 1980. *Die deutsche Inflation 1914–1923: Ursachen und Folgen in internationaler Perspektive*. Berlin: Walter de Gruyter.

Hooglund, Eric J. 1982. *Land and revolution in Iran, 1960–1980*. Austin: University of Texas Press.

Hopkins, Keith. 1978. *Conquerors and slaves: sociological studies in Roman history 1*. Cambridge, UK: Cambridge University Press.

Hopkins, Keith. 2002. "Rome, taxes, rents, and trade" (1995/96). In Scheidel, Walter, and von Reden, Sitta, eds., *The ancient economy*. Edinburgh: Edinburgh University Press, 190–230.

Horden, Peregrine. 2005. "Mediterranean plague in the age of Justinian." In Mass, Michael, ed. *The Cambridge companion to the age of Justinian*. Cambridge, UK: Cambridge University Press, 134–160.

Horn, Jeff. 2015. "Lasting economic structures: successes, failures, legacies." In Andress, ed. 2015: 607–624.

Horrox, Rosemary, trans. and ed. 1994. *The Black Death*. Manchester, UK: Manchester University Press.

Hossmann, Iris, et al. 2008. "Europe's demographic future: growing imbalances." Berlin: Berlin Institute for Population and Development.

Hsu, Cho-yun. 1965. *Ancient China in transition: an analysis of social mobility, 722–222 B.C.* Stanford, CA: Stanford University Press.

Hsu, Cho-yun. 1980. *Han agriculture: the formation of early Chinese agrarian economy (206 B.C.–A.D. 220)*. Seattle: University of Washington Press.

Huber, John D., Ogorzalek, Thomas K., and Gore, Radhika. 2012. "Democracy, targeted redistribution and ethnic inequality." Working paper.

Hudson, Michael. 1993. "The lost tradition of biblical debt cancellations." http://michael-hudson.com/wp-content/uploads/2010/03/HudsonLostTradition.pdf.

Hudson, Michael. 1996a. "Privatization: a survey of the unresolved controversies." In Hudson and Levine, eds. 1996: 1–32.

Hudson, Michael. 1996b. "The dynamics of privatization, from the Bronze Age to the present." In Hudson and Levine, eds. 1996: 33–72.

Hudson, Michael. 1996c. "Early privatization and its consequences." In Hudson and Levine, eds. 1996: 293–308.

Hudson, Michael, and Levine, Baruch, eds. 1996. *Privatization in the Ancient Near East and classical world*. Cambridge, MA: Peabody Museum of Archaeology and Ethnology, Harvard University.

Hudson, Michael, and Van De Mieroop, Marc, eds. 2002. *Debt and economic renewal in the Ancient Near East*. Bethesda, MD: CDL.

Human development report. 2014. *Human development report 2014. Sustaining human progress: reducing vulnerabilities and building resilience*. New York: United Nations Development Programme.

Hungerford, Thomas L. 2013. "Changes in income inequality among U.S. tax filers between 1991 and 2006: the role of wages, capital income, and taxes." SSRN Working Paper No. 2207372.

Jabbari, Eric. 2012. *Pierre Laroque and the welfare state in post-war France*. Oxford: Oxford University Press.

Jackson, R. V. 1987. "The structure of pay in nineteenth-century Britain." *Economic History Review* 40: 561–570.

Jackson, R. V. 1994. "Inequality of incomes and lifespans in England since 1688." *Economic History Review* 47: 508–524.

Jacobs, Harrison. 2015. "Here's the ridiculous loot that's been found with corrupt Chinese officials." *Business Insider* January 22, 2015.

Janowitz, Morris. 1976. *Social control of the welfare state*. Chicago: University of Chicago Press.

Jäntti, Markus, and Jenkins, Stephen P. 2015. "Income mobility." In Atkinson and Bourguignon, eds. 2015: 807–935.

Jäntti, M., Riihelä, M., Sullström, R., and Tuomala, M. 2010. "Trends in top income shares in Finland." In Atkinson and Piketty, eds. 2010: 371–447.

Janusek, John Wayne. 2004. *Identity and power in the ancient Andes: Tiwanaku cities through time*. New York: Routledge.

Jarvis, Lovell S. 1989. "The unraveling of Chile's agrarian reform, 1973–1986." In Thiesenheusen, ed. 1989b: 240–275.

Jaumotte, Florence, Lall, Subir, and Papageorgiou, Chris. 2013. "Rising income inequality: technology, or trade and financial globalization?" *IMF Economic Review* 61: 271–309.

Jaumotte, Florence, and Osorio Buitron, Carolina. 2015. "Inequality and labor market institutions." IMF Staff Discussion Note 15/14.

Jaworski, Taylor. 2009. "War and wealth: economic opportunity before and after the Civil War, 1850–1870." LSE Working Papers No. 114/09.

Jenkins, Stephen P., Brandolini, Andrea, Micklewright, John, and Nolan, Brian, eds. 2013. *The Great Recession and the distribution of household income*. Oxford: Oxford University Press.

Jenkins, Stephen P., and Van Kerm, Philippe. 2009. "The measurement of economic inequality." In Salverda, Nolan, and Smeeding, eds. 2009: 40–67.

Johnson, Allen W., and Earle, Timothy. 2000. *The evolution of human societies: from foraging group to agrarian state*. 2nd. Stanford, CA: Stanford University Press.

Johnson, Harold B. Jr. 2001. "Malthus confirmed? Being some reflections on the changing distribution of wealth and income in Portugal [1309–1789]." Working paper.

Jongman, Willem. 1988. *The economy and society of Pompeii*. Amsterdam: Gieben.

Jongman, Willem. 2006. "The rise and fall of the Roman economy: population, rents and entitlement." In Bang, Peter F., Ikeguchi, Mamoru, and Ziche, Hartmut G., eds., *Ancient economies, modern methodologies: archaeology, comparative history, models and institutions*. Bari, Italy: Edipuglia, 237–254.

Jordan, William C. 1996. *The great famine: northern Europe in the early fourteenth century*. Princeton, NJ: Princeton University Press.

Jursa, Michael. 2010. *Aspects of the economic history of Babylonia in the first millennium BC*. Münster, Germany: Ugarit-Verlag.

Jursa, Michael. 2015. "Economic growth and growing economic inequality? The case of Babylonia." Conference paper for "The haves and the have-nots: exploring the global history of wealth and income inequality," September 11, 2015, University of Vienna.

Justman, Moshe, and Gradstein, Mark. 1999. "The industrial revolution, political transition, and the subsequent decline in inequality in 19th-century Britain." *Explorations in Economic History* 36: 109–127.

Kaboski, Joseph P. 2005. "Supply factors and the mid-century fall in the skill premium." Working paper.

Kage, Rieko. 2010. "The effects of war on civil society: cross-national evidence from World War II." In Kier and Krebs, eds. 2010: 97–120.

Kaimowitz, David. 1989. "The role of decentralization in the recent Nicaraguan agrarian reform." In Thiesenheusen, ed. 1989b: 384–407.

Kanbur, Ravi. 2015. "Globalization and inequality." In Atkinson and Bourguignon, eds. 2015: 1845–1881.

Kaplan, Steve N., and Rauh, Joshua. 2010. "Watt Street and Main Street: what contributes to the rise in the highest incomes?" *Review of Financial Studies* 23: 1004–1050.

Kaplan, Steven N., and Rauh, Joshua. 2013. "It's the market: the broad-based rise in return to top talent." *Journal of Economic Perspectives* 27 (3): 35–55.

Kapteijns, Lidwien. 2013. *Clan cleansing in Somalia: the ruinous legacy of 1991*. Philadelphia: University of Pennsylvania Press.

Kasza, Gregory J. 2002. "War and welfare policy in Japan." *Journal of Asian Studies* 61: 417–435.

Katajala, Kimmo, ed. 2004. *Northern revolts: medieval and early modern peasant unrest in the Nordic countries*. Helsinki: Finnish Literature Society.

Kautsky, John H. 1982. *The politics of aristocratic empires*. New Brunswick, NJ: Transaction Publishers.

Kawagoe, Toshihiko. 1993. "Land reform in postwar Japan." In Teranishi and Kosai, eds. 1993: 178–204.

Kawagoe, Toshihiko. 1999. "Agricultural land reform in postwar Japan: experiences and issues." World Bank Policy Research Working Paper No. 2111.

Kay, Philip. 2014. *Rome's economic revolution*. Oxford: Oxford University Press.

Kaymak, Baris, and Poschke, Markus. 2016. "The evolution of wealth inequality over half a century: the role of taxes, transfers and technology." *Journal of Monetary Economics* 77: 1–25.

Keister, Lisa A. 2014. "The one percent." *Annual Review of Sociology* 40: 347–367.

Keister, Lisa A., and Lee, Hang Y. 2014. "The one percent: top incomes and wealth in sociological research." *Social Currents* 1: 13–24.

Kelly, Robert L. 2013. *The lifeways of hunter-gatherers: the foraging spectrum*. New York: Cambridge University Press.

Kemp, Barry J. 1983. "Old Kingdom, Middle Kingdom and Second Intermediate Period, c. 2686–1552 BC." In Trigger, Bruce G., Kemp, Barry J., O'Connor, David, and Lloyd, Alan B., *Ancient Egypt: a social history*. Cambridge, UK: Cambridge University Press, 71–182.

Kennett, Douglas J., et al. 2012. "Development and disintegration of Maya political systems in response to climate change." *Science* 338: 788–791.

Kier, Elizabeth, and Krebs, Ronald, R., eds. 2010. *In war's wake: international conflict and the fate of liberal democracy*. Cambridge, UK: Cambridge University Press.

Klausen, Jytte. 1998. *War and welfare: Europe and the United States, 1945 to the present*. New York: St. Martin's Press.

Klein, Richard. 2009. *The human career: human biological and cultural origins*. 3rd ed. Chicago: University of Chicago Press.

Knapp, A. Bernhard, and Manning, Sturt W. 2015. "Crisis in context: the end of the Late Bronze Age in the Eastern Mediterranean." *American Journal of Archaeology* 120: 99–149.

Koeniger, Winfried, Leonardi, Marco, and Nunziata, Luca. 2007. "Labor market institutions and wage inequality." *Industrial and Labor Relations Review* 60: 340–356.

Koepke, Nicola, and Baten, Jörg. 2005. "The biological standard of living in Europe during the last two millennia." *European Review of Economic History* 9: 61–95.

Kolata, Alan. 1993. *The Tiwanaku: portrait of an Andean civilization*. Cambridge, MA: Blackwell.

Komlos, John, Hau, Michel, and Bourguinat, Nicolas. 2003. "An anthropometric history of early-modern France." *European Review of Economic History* 7: 159–189.

Kopczuk, Wojciech. 2015. "What do we know about the evolution of top wealth shares in the United States?" *Journal of Economic Perspectives* 29: 47–66.

Kopczuk, Wojciech, Saez, Emmanuel, and Song, Jae. 2010. "Earnings inequality and mobility in the United States: evidence from Social Security data since 1937." *Quarterly Journal of Economics* 125: 91–128.

Kott, Alexander, et al. 2015. "Visualizing the tactical ground battlefield in the year 2050: workshop report." US Army Research Laboratory ARL-SR-0327.

Kozol, Jonathan. 2005. *The shame of the nation: the restoration of apartheid schooling in America*. New York: Random House.

Kron, Geoffrey. 2011. "The distribution of wealth in Athens in comparative perspective." *Zeitschrift für Papyrologie und Epigraphik* 179: 129–138.

Kron, Geoffrey. 2014. "Comparative evidence and the reconstruction of the ancient economy: Greco-Roman housing and the level and distribution of wealth and income." In Callataÿ, Francois de, ed., *Quantifying the Greco-Roman economy and beyond*. Bari, Italy: Edipuglia, 123–146.

Kršljanin, Nina. 2016. "The land reform of the 1830s in Serbia: the impact of the shattering of the Ottoman feudal system." Conference paper for "Old and new words: the global challenges of rural history," Lisbon, January 27–30, 2016.

Kuehn, John T. 2014. *A military history of Japan: from the age of the Samurai to the 21st century*. Santa Barbara: ABC-CLIO.

Kuhn, Dieter. 2009. *The age of Confucian rule: the Song transformation of China*. Cambridge, MA: Harvard University Press.

Kuhn, Philip A. 1978. "The Taiping Rebellion." In Fairbank, John F., ed., *The Cambridge history of China*. Vol. 10. *Late Ch'ing, 1800–1911, Part I*. Cambridge, UK: Cambridge University Press, 264–317.

Kuhrt, Amélie. 1995. *The ancient Near East c. 3000–330 BC*. 2 vols. London: Routledge.

Kuroda, Masahiro. 1993. "Price and goods control in the Japanese postwar inflationary period." In Teranishi and Kosai, eds. 1993: 31–60.

Kuznets, Simon. 1955. "Economic growth and income inequality." *American Economic Review* 45: 1–28.

Labuda, Damian, Lefebvre, Jean-Francois, Nadeau, Philippe, and Roy-Gagnon, Marie-Hélène. 2010. "Female-to-male breeding ratio in modern humans—an analysis based on historical recombinations." *American Journal of Human Genetics* 86: 353–363.

Lakner, Christoph, and Milanovic, Branko. 2013. "Global income distribution: from the fall of the Berlin Wall to the Great Recession." World Bank Policy Research Working Paper No. 6719.

Larrimore, Jeff. 2014. "Accounting for United States household income inequality trends: the changing importance of household structure and male and female labor earnings inequality." *Review of Income and Wealth* 60: 683–701.

Laybourn, Keith. 1995. *The evolution of British social policy and the welfare state*. Keele, UK: Keele University Press.

Lee, Richard B. 1979. *The !Kung San: men, women, and work in a foraging society*. Cambridge, UK: Cambridge University Press.

Lee, Richard B. 1984. *The Dobe !Kung*. New York: Holt, Rinehart and Winston.

Lee, Ronald D. 1986a. "Malthus and Boserup: a dynamic synthesis." In Coleman, David, and Schofield, Roger, eds., *The state of population theory: forward from Malthus*. Oxford: Blackwell, 96–130.

Lee, Ronald D. 1986b. "Population homeostasis and English demographic history." In Rotberg, Robert I., and Rabb, Theodore K., eds., *Population and economy: population and history from the traditional to the modern world*. Cambridge, UK: Cambridge University Press, 75–100.

Leeson, Peter T. 2007. "Better off stateless: Somalia before and after government collapse." *Journal of Comparative Economics* 35: 689–710.

Leigh, Andrew. 2007. "How closely do top income shares track other measures of inequality?" *Economic Journal* 117: F619–F633.

Leigh, Andrew, Jencks, Christopher, and Smeeding, Timothy M. 2009. "Health and economic inequality." In Salverda, Nolan, and Smeeding, eds. 2009: 384–405.

Leitner, Ulrich. 2011. *Imperium: Geschichte und Theories eines politischen Systems*. Frankfurt, Germany: Campus Verlag.

Lemieux, Thomas. 2006. "Post-secondary education and increasing wage inequality." *American Economic Review* 96: 195–199.

Leonard, Carol S. 2011. *Agrarian reform in Russia: the road to serfdom*. New York: Cambridge University Press.

Le Roy Ladurie, Emmanuel. 1966. *Les paysans de Languedoc*. 2 vols. Paris: Mouton.

Levy, Frank, and Temin, Peter. 2007. "Inequality and institutions in 20th century America." NBER Working Paper No. 13106.

Lewis, Joanna. 2000. *Empire state-building: war and welfare in Kenya 1925–52*. Oxford: James Currey.

Lewis, Mark Edward. 1990. *Sanctioned violence in early China*. Albany: State University of New York Press.

Lewis, Mark Edward. 1999. "Warring States: political history." In Loewe, Michael, and Shaughnessy, Edward L., eds., *The Cambridge history of ancient China: from the origins to 211 B.C.* Cambridge, UK: Cambridge University Press, 587–650.

Lewis, Mark Edward. 2007. *The early Chinese empires: Qin and Han*. Cambridge, MA: Harvard University Press.

Lewis, Mark Edward. 2009a. *China between empires: the Northern and Southern dynasties*. Cambridge, MA: Harvard University Press.

Lewis, Mark Edward. 2009b. *China's cosmopolitan empire: the Tang dynasty*. Cambridge, MA: Harvard University Press.

Li, Feng. 2013. *Early China: a social and cultural history*. Cambridge, UK: Cambridge University Press.

Li, Shi. 2014. "Rising income and wealth inequality in China." http://unsdsn.org/wp-content/uploads /2014/05/TG03-SI-Event-LI-Shi-income-inequality.pdf.

Liang, Puping, et al. 2015. "CRISPR/Cas9-mediated gene editing in human tripronuclear zygotes." *Protein and Cell* 6: 363–372.

Lin, Ken-Hou, and Tomaskovic-Devey, Donald. 2013. "Financialization and US income inequality, 1970–2008." *American Journal of Sociology* 118: 1284–1329.

Lindert, Peter H. 1991. "Toward a comparative history of income and wealth inequality." In Brenner, Kaelble, and Thomas, eds. 1991: 212–231.

Lindert, Peter H. 2000a. "Three centuries of inequality in Britain and America." In Atkinson and Bourguignon, eds. 2000: 167–216.

Lindert, Peter H. 2000b. "When did inequality rise in Britain and America?" *Journal of Income Distribution* 9: 11–25.

Lindert, Peter H. 2004. *Growing public: social spending and economic growth since the eighteenth century*. 2 vols. Cambridge, UK: Cambridge University Press.

Lindert, Peter H. 2015. "Where has modern equality come from? Lucky and smart paths in economic history." Conference paper for "Unequal chances and unequal outcomes in economic history," All-UC Economic History Group/Caltech Conference, February 6–7, 2015.

Lindert, Peter H., and Williamson, Jeffrey G. 2014. "American colonial incomes, 1650–1774." NBER Working Paper 19861.

Lindert, Peter H., and Williamson, Jeffrey G. 2016. *Unequal gains: American growth and inequality since 1700.* Princeton, NJ: Princeton University Press.

Lindqvist, Erik, and Östling, Robert. 2013. "Identity and redistribution." *Public Choice* 155: 469–491.

Lindsay, Craig. 2003. "A century of labour market change: 1900 to 2000." Labour Market Trends 111 (3). www.statistics.gov.uk/downloads/theme_labour/LMT_March03_revised.pdf.

Link, Stefan. 1991. *Landverteilung und sozialer Frieden im archaischen Griechenland.* Stuttgart, Germany: Steiner.

Lipton, Michael. 2009. *Land reform in developing countries: property rights and property wrongs.* Abingdon, UK: Routledge.

Little, Lester K., ed. 2007. *Plague and the end of antiquity: the pandemic of 541–750.* Cambridge, UK: Cambridge University Press.

Livi Bacci, Massimo. 2008. *Conquest: the destruction of the American Indios.* Cambridge, UK: Polity Press.

Lo Cascio, Elio. 2001. "Recruitment and the size of the Roman population from the third to the first century BCE." In Scheidel, Walter, ed., *Debating Roman demography.* Leiden, Netherlands: Brill, 111–137.

Lo Cascio, Elio, ed. 2012. *L'impatto della "peste antonina."* Bari, Italy: Edipuglia.

Lodin, Sven-Olof. 2011. *The making of Swedish tax law: the development of the Swedish tax system.* Trans. Ken Schubert. Uppsala, Sweden: Iustus.

Loewe, Michael. 1986a. "The Former Han dynasty." In Twitchett and Loewe, eds. 1986: 103–222.

Loewe, Michael. 1986b. "Wang Mang, the restoration of the Han dynasty, and Later Han." In Twitchett and Loewe, eds. 1986: 223–290.

Lovejoy, Paul E. 2011. *Transformations in slavery: a history of slavery in Africa.* 3rd ed. New York: Cambridge University Press.

Lowe, Rodney. 1990. "The second world war, consensus, and the foundation of the welfare state." *Twentieth Century British History* 1: 152–182.

Lustig, Nora, Lopez-Calva, Luis F., and Ortiz-Juarez, Eduardo. 2012. "Declining inequality in Latin America in the 2000s: the cases of Argentina, Brazil, and Mexico." World Bank Policy Research Working Paper No. 6248.

Lustig, Nora, Lopez-Calva, Luis F., and Ortiz-Juarez, Eduardo. 2014. "Deconstructing the decline in inequality in Latin America." Working paper.

Lutz, Wolfgang, and Scherbov, Sergei. 2007. "The contribution of migration to Europe's demographic future: projections for the EU-25 to 2050." Laxenburg, Austria: International Institute for Applied Systems Analysis, IR-07-024.

Machin, Stephen. 2008. "An appraisal of economic research on changes in wage inequality." *Labour* 22: 7–26.

Maddison project. "Maddison project." http://www.ggdc.net/maddison/maddison-project/home.htm.

Magness, Phillip W., and Murphy, Robert P. 2015. "Challenging the empirical contribution of Thomas Piketty's *Capital in the twenty-first century*." *Journal of Private Enterprise* 30: 1–34.

Mahler, Vincent A. 2010. "Government inequality reduction in comparative perspective: a cross-national study of the developed world." *Polity* 42: 511–541.

Maisels, Charles K. 1990. *The emergence of civilization: from hunting and gathering to agriculture, cities, and the state in the Near East.* London: Routledge.

Malinen, Tuomas. 2012. "Estimating the long-run relationship between income inequality and economic development." *Empirical Economics* 42: 209–233.

Malthus, T. R. 1992. *An essay on the principle of population; or a view of its past and present effects on human happiness; with an inquiry into our prospects respecting the future removal or mitigation of the evils which it occasions.* Selected and introduced by Donald Winch using the text of the 1803 edition as prepared by Patricia James for the Royal Economic Society, 1990, showing the additions and corrections made in the 1806, 1807, 1817, and 1826 editions. Cambridge, UK: Cambridge University Press.

Mango, Cyril. 1985. *Le développement urbain de Constantinople (IVe-VIIe siècles).* Paris: De Boccard.

Mansfield, Edward D., and Snyder, Jack. 2010. "Does war influence democratization?" In Kier and Krebs, eds. 2010: 23–49.

Mansvelt Beck, B. J. 1986. "The fall of Han." In Twitchett and Loewe, eds. 1986: 317–376.

Marean, Curtis W. 2014. "The origins and significance of coastal resource use in Africa and Western Eurasia." *Journal of Human Evolution* 77: 17–40.

Marean, Curtis W. 2015. "An evolutionary anthropological perspective on modern human origins." *Annual Review of Anthropology* 44: 533–556.

Margolin, Jean-Louis. 1999a. "Cambodia: a country of disconcerting crimes." In Courtois et al. 1999: 577–644.

Margolin, Jean-Louis. 1999b. "China: a long march into night." In Courtois et al. 1999: 463–546.

Markoff, John. 1996a. *The abolition of feudalism: peasants, lords and legislators in the French Revolution.* University Park: Pennsylvania State University Press.

Markoff, John. 1996b. *Waves of democracy: social movements and political change.* Thousand Oaks, CA: Pine Forge Press.

Marlowe, Frank W. 2010. *The Hadza: hunter-gatherers of Tanzania.* Berkeley: University of California Press.

Marwick, Arthur. 1988. "Conclusion." In Marwick, Arthur, ed. 1988. *Total war and social change.* Houndmills, UK: Macmillan Press, 119–125.

Marzagalli, Silvia. 2015. "Economic and demographic developments." In Andress, ed. 2015: 3–20.

Massey, Douglas S. 2007. *Categorically unequal: the American stratification system.* New York: Russell Sage Foundation.

Masson, Marilyn A., and Peraza Lope, Carlos. 2014. *Kukulcan's realm: urban life at ancient Mayapan.* Boulder: University Press of Colorado.

Mau, Steffen, and Burkhardt, Christoph. 2009. "Ethnic diversity and welfare state solidarity in Western Europe." *Journal of European Social Policy* 19: 213–229.

Mayer, Emanuel. 2012. *The ancient middle classes: urban life and aesthetics in the Roman empire, 100 BCE–250 CE.* Cambridge, MA: Harvard University Press.

Mayshar, Joram, Moav, Omer, Neeman, Zvika, and Pascali, Luigi. 2015. "Cereals, appropriability and hierarchy." Barcelona GSE Working Paper No. 842.

McCaa, Robert. 2000. "The peopling of Mexico from origins to revolution." In Haines, Michael R., and Steckel, Richard H., eds., *A population history of North America.* Cambridge, UK: Cambridge University Press, 241–304.

McCormick, Michael. 2015. "Tracking mass death during the fall of Rome's empire (I)." *Journal of Roman Archaeology* 28: 325–357.

McDougall, Ian, Brown, Francis H., and Fleagle, John G. 2005. "Stratigraphic placement and age of modern humans from Kibish, Ethiopia." *Nature* 433: 733–736.

McEvedy, Colin, and Jones, Richard. 1978. *Atlas of world population history.* New York: Penguin.

McKenzie, David, and Rapoport, Hillel. 2007. "Network effects and the dynamics of migration and inequality: theory and evidence from Mexico." *Journal of Development Economics* 84: 1–24.

Medeiros, Marcelo, and Ferreira de Souza, Pedro H. G. 2013. "The state and income inequality in Brazil." IRLE Working Paper No. 153–13.

Medeiros, Marcelo, and Ferreira de Souza, Pedro H. G. 2015. "The rich, the affluent and the top incomes." *Current Sociology Review* 63: 869–895.

Mehrotra, Ajay K. 2013. *Making the modern America fiscal state: law, politics, and the rise of progressive taxation, 1877–1929.* New York: Cambridge University Press.

Meloy, John L. 2004. "The privatization of protection: extortion and the state in the Circassian Mamluk period." *Journal of the Economic and Social History of the Orient* 47: 195–212.

Meyer, Bruce D., and Sullivan, James X. 2013. "Consumption and income inequality and the Great Recession." *American Economic Review* 103: 178–183.

Michelmore, Molly C. 2012. *Tax and spend: the welfare state, tax politics, and the limits of American liberalism.* Philadelphia: University of Pennsylvania Press.

Middleton, Guy D. 2010. *The collapse of palatial society in LBA Greece and the postpalatial period.* Oxford: Archaeopress.

Milanovic, Branko. 1997. *Income, inequality, and poverty during the transition from planned to market economy.* Washington, DC: World Bank.

Milanovic, Branko. 2005. *Worlds apart: measuring international and global inequality.* Princeton, NJ: Princeton University Press.

Milanovic, Branko. 2006. "An estimate of average income and inequality in Byzantium around year 1000." *Review of Income and Wealth* 52: 449–470.

Milanovic, Branko. 2010. "Income level and income inequality in the Euro-Mediterranean region: from the Principate to the Islamic conquest." MPRA Paper No. 46640.

Milanovic, Branko. 2012. "Global inequality recalculated and updated: the effect of new PPP estimates on global inequality and 2005 estimates." *Journal of Economic Inequality* 10: 1–18.

Milanovic, Branko. 2013. "The inequality possibility frontier: extensions and new applications." World Bank Policy Research Paper No. 6449.

Milanovic, Branko. 2015. "A note on 'maximum' US inequality." *globalinequality* December 19, 2015. http://glineq.blogspot.com/2015/12/a-note-on-maximum-us-inequality.html?m=1.

Milanovic, Branko. 2016. *Global inequality: a new approach for the age of globalization.* Cambridge, MA: Harvard University Press.

Milanovic, Branko, Lindert, Peter H., and Williamson, Jeffrey G. 2011. "Pre-industrial inequality." *Economic Journal* 121: 255–272.

Millar, Fergus. 1977. *The emperor in the Roman world (31 BC—AD 337).* London: Duckworth.

Miller, Joseph C. 2012. *The problem of slavery as history: a global approach.* New Haven, CT: Yale University Press.

Millon, René. 1988. "The last years of Teotihuacan dominance." In Yoffee and Cowgill, eds. 1988: 102–164.

Minami, Ryoshin. 1998. "Economic development and income distribution in Japan: as assessment of the Kuznets hypothesis." *Cambridge Journal of Economics* 22: 39–58.

Mishel, Lawrence, Shierholz, Heidi, and Schmitt, John. 2013. "Don't blame the robots: assessing the job polarization explanation of growing wage inequality." Economic Policy Institute—Center for Economic and Policy Research, Working Paper.

Mithen, Steven. 2003. *After the ice: a global human history, 20,000–5000 BC.* Cambridge, MA: Harvard University Press.

Miwa, Ryôchi. 2003. "Postwar democratization and economic reconstruction." In Nakamura and Odaka, eds. 2003a: 333–370.

Miyamoto, Matayo. 2004. "Quantitative aspects of Tokugawa economy." In Hayami, Saitô, and Toby, eds. 2004: 36–84.

Miyazaki, Masayasu, and Itô, Osamu. 2003. "Transformation of industries in the war years." In Nakamura and Odaka, eds. 2003a: 287–332.

Modalsli, Jorgen. 2015. "Inequality in the very long run: inferring inequality from data on social groups." *Journal of Economic Inequality* 13: 225–247.

Moise, Edwin E. 1983. *Land reform in China and North Vietnam: consolidating the revolution at the village level.* Chapel Hill: University of North Carolina Press.

Mokyr, Joel, and Ó Gráda, Cormac. 1988. "Poor and getting poorer? Living standards in Ireland before the famine." *Economic History Review* 41: 209–235.

Mollat, Michel, and Wolff, Philippe. 1973. *The popular revolutions of the late Middle Ages.* London: Allen and Unwin.

Mollick, André Varella. 2012. "Income inequality in the U.S.: the Kuznets hypothesis revisited." *Economic Systems* 36: 127–144.

Monson, Andrew, and Scheidel, Walter, eds. 2015. *Fiscal regimes and the political economy of premodern states.* Cambridge, UK: Cambridge University Press.

Morelli, Salvatore, and Atkinson, Anthony B. 2015. "Inequality and crises revisited." *Economia Politica* 32: 31–51.

Morelli, Salvatore, Smeeding, Timothy, and Thompson, Jeffrey. 2015. "Post-1970 trends in within-country inequality and poverty: rich and middle-income countries." In Atkinson and Bourguignon, eds. 2015: 593–696.

Moriguchi, Chiaki, and Saez, Emmanuel. 2010. "The evolution of income concentration in Japan, 1886–2005: evidence from income tax statistics." In Atkinson and Piketty, eds. 2010: 76–170.

Morris, Ian. 1994. "The Athenian economy twenty years after *The Ancient Economy*." *Classical Philology* 89: 351–366.

Morris, Ian. 2000. *Archaeology as cultural history: words and things in Iron Age Greece*. Malden, MA: Polity.

Morris, Ian. 2004. "Economic growth in ancient Greece." *Journal of Institutional and Theoretical Economics* 160: 709–742.

Morris, Ian. 2010. *Why the West rules—for now: the patterns of history, and what they reveal about the future*. New York: Farrar, Straus and Giroux.

Morris, Ian. 2013. *The measure of civilization: how social development decides the fate of nations*. Princeton, NJ: Princeton University Press.

Morris, Ian. 2014. *War! What is it good for? Conflict and the progress of civilization from primates to robots*. New York: Farrar, Straus and Giroux.

Morris, Ian. 2015. *Foragers, farmers, and fossil fuels: how human values evolve*. Princeton, NJ: Princeton University Press.

Morris, Ian, and Scheidel, Walter, eds. 2009. *The dynamics of ancient empires: state power from Assyria to Byzantium*. New York: Oxford University Press.

Morris, Marc. 2012. *The Norman conquest*. London: Hutchinson.

Morrison, Cécile, and Cheynet, Jean-Claude. 2002. "Prices and wages in the Byzantine world." In Laiou, Angeliki E., ed., *The economic history of Byzantium: from the seventh through the fifteenth century*. Washington, DC: Dumbarton Oaks Research Library and Collection, 815–878.

Morrison, Christian. 2000. "Historical perspectives on income distribution: the case of Europe." In Atkinson and Bourguignon, eds. 2000: 217–260.

Morrisson, Christian, and Snyder, Wayne. 2000. "The income inequality of France in historical perspective." *European Review of Economic History* 4: 59–83.

Moselle, Boaz, and Polak, Benjamin. 2001. "A model of a predatory state." *Journal of Law, Economics and Organization* 17: 1–33.

Motesharrei, Safa, Rivas, Jorge, and Kalnay, Eugenia. 2014. "Human and nature dynamics (HANDY): modeling inequality and the use of resources in the collapse or sustainability of societies." *Ecological Economics* 101: 90–102.

Motyl, Alexander J. 2001. *Imperial ends: the decay, collapse, and revival of empires*. New York: Columbia University Press.

Mouritsen, Henrik. 2015. "Status and social hierarchies: the case of Pompeii." In Kuhn, Annika B., ed., *Social status and prestige in the Graeco-Roman world*. Stuttgart, Germany: Steiner, 87–114.

Mousnier, Roland. 1970. *Peasant uprisings in seventeenth-century France, Russia, and China*. New York: Harper & Row.

Moyo, Sam. 2013. "Land reform and distribution in Zimbabwe since 1980." In Moyo and Chambati, eds. 2013b: 29–77.

Moyo, Sam, and Chambati, Walter. 2013a. "Introduction: roots of the Fast Track Land Reform." In Moyo and Chambati, eds. 2013b: 1–27.

Moyo, Sam, and Chambati, Walter, eds. 2013b. *Land and agrarian reform in Zimbabwe: beyond white-settler capitalism*. Dakar, Senegal: CODESRIA.

Mratschek-Halfmann, Sigrid. 1993. *Divites et praepotentes: Reichtum und soziale Stellung in der Literatur der Prinzipatszeit*. Stuttgart, Germany: Steiner.

Mubarak, Jamil. 1997. "The 'hidden hand' behind the resilience of the stateless economy in Somalia." *World Development* 25: 2027–2041.

Mulligan, Casey B., Gil, Ricard, and Sala-i-Martin, Xavier. 2004. "Do democracies have different public policies than nondemocracies?" *Journal of Economic Perspectives* 18: 51–74.

Murphey, Rhoads. 1999. *Ottoman warfare, 1500–1700*. New Brunswick, NJ: Rutgers University Press.

Murray, Charles. 2012. *Coming apart: the state of white America*. New York: Crown Forum.

Murray, Christopher J. L., et al. 2006. "Estimation of potential global pandemic influenza mortality on the basis of vital registry data from the 1918–20 pandemic: a quantitative analysis." *Lancet* 368: 2211–2218.

Murray, Sarah C. 2013. "Trade, imports, and society in early Greece: 1300–900 B.C.E." PhD thesis, Stanford University.

Nafziger, Steven, and Lindert, Peter. 2013. "Russian inequality on the eve of revolution." Working paper.

Nakamura, Takafusa. 2003. "The age of turbulence: 1937–1954." In Nakamura and Odaka, eds. 2003a: 55–110.

Nakamura, Takafusa, and Odaka, Kônosuke, eds. 2003a. *The economic history of Japan: 1600–1990.* Vol. 3. *Economic history of Japan 1914–1955. A dual structure.* Trans. Noah S. Brannen. Oxford: Oxford University Press.

Nakamura, Takafusa, and Odaka, Kônosuke. 2003b. "The inter-war period: 1914–37, an overview." In Nakamura and Odaka, eds. 2003a: 1–54.

National Military Strategy. 2015. "The national military strategy of the United States of America 2015: the United States' military contribution to national security." http://www.jcs.mil/Portals/36/Documents /Publications/2015_National_Military_Strategy.pdf.

Nau, Michael. 2013. "Economic elites, investments, and income inequality." *Social Forces* 92: 437–461.

Nawar, Abdel-Hameed. 2013. "Poverty and inequality in the non-income multidimensional space: a critical review in the Arab states." Working Paper No. 103. Brasília, Brazil: International Policy Centre for Inclusive Growth.

Neal, Larry, and Williamson, Jeffrey G., eds. 2014. *The Cambridge history of capitalism.* 2 vols. Cambridge, UK: Cambridge University Press.

Nenova, Tatiana, and Harford, Tim. 2005. "Anarchy and invention: how does Somalia's private sector cope without government?" World Bank: Findings No. 254.

Neveux, Hugues. 1997. *Les révoltes paysannes en Europe (XIVe–XVIIe siècle).* Paris: Albin Michel.

Newson, Linda A. 2006. "The demographic impact of colonization." In Bulmer-Thomas, V., Coatsworth, John H., and Conde, Roberto Cortes, eds., *The Cambridge economic history of Latin America.* Cambridge, UK: Cambridge University Press, 143–184.

Nguyen, Ngoc-Luu. 1987. "Peasants, party and revolution: the politics of agrarian transformation in Northern Vietnam, 1930–1975. PhD thesis, Amsterdam.

Nishikawa, Shunsaku, and Amano, Masatoshi. 2004. "Domains and their economic policies." In Hayami, Saitô, and Toby, eds. 2004: 247–267.

Noah, Timothy. 2012. *The great divergence: America's growing inequality crisis and what we can do about it.* New York: Bloomsbury Press.

Nolan, B. 2007. "Long-term trends in top income shares in Ireland." In Atkinson and Piketty, eds. 2007a: 501–530.

North, Douglass C., Wallis, John J., and Weingast, Barry R. 2009. *Violence and social orders: a conceptual framework for interpreting recorded human history.* New York: Cambridge University Press.

Nunn, Nathan, and Qian, Nancy. 2010. "The Columbian exchange: a history of disease, food, and ideas." *Journal of Economic Perspectives* 24: 163–188.

Ober, Josiah. 2015a. *The rise and fall of classical Greece.* Princeton, NJ: Princeton University Press.

Ober, Josiah. 2015b. "Classical Athens." In Monson and Scheidel, eds. 2015: 492–522.

Ober, Josiah. 2016. "Inequality in late-classical democratic Athens: evidence and models." Working paper.

Obinger, Herbert, and Schmitt, Carina. 2011. "Guns and butter? Regime competition and the welfare state during the Cold War." *World Politics* 63: 246–270.

Oded, Bustenay. 1979. *Mass deportations and deportees in the Neo-Assyrian empire.* Wiesbaden, Germany: Reichert.

O'Donnell, Owen, Van Doorslaer, Eddy, and Van Ourti, Tom. 2015. "Health and inequality." In Atkinson and Bourguignon, eds. 2015: 1419–1533.

OECD. 2010. *Economic policy reforms: going for growth.* Paris: OECD Publishing.

OECD. 2011. *Divided we stand: why inequality keeps rising.* Paris: OECD Publishing.

OECD. 2014. "Social expenditure update—social spending is falling in some countries, but in many others it remains at historically high levels." http://www.oecd.org/els/soc/OECD2014-Social-Expenditure -Update-Nov2014–8pages.pdf.

OECD. 2015. *In it together: why less inequality benefits all.* Paris: OECD Publishing.

Oechslin, Hanspeter. 1967. *Die Entwicklung des Bundessteuersystems der Schweiz von 1848 bis 1966.* Einsie-deln, Switzerland: Etzel.

Ó Gráda, Cormac. 1994. *Ireland: a new economic history, 1780–1939*. Oxford: Oxford University Press.

Ohlsson, Henry, Roine, Jesper, and Waldenström, Daniel. 2006. "Long run changes in the concentration of wealth: an overview of recent findings." WIDER Working Paper.

Ohlsson, Henry, Roine, Jesper, and Waldenström, Daniel. 2014. "Inherited wealth over the path of development: Sweden, 1810–2010." IFN Working Paper. 1033.

Ohtake, Fumio. 2008. "Inequality in Japan." *Asian Economic Policy Review* 3: 87–109.

Okazaki, Tetsuji. 1993. "The Japanese firm under the wartime planned economy." *Journal of the Japanese and International Economies* 7: 175–203.

Olson, Jan Marie, and Smith, Michael E. 2016. "Material expressions of wealth and social class at Aztec-period sites in Morelos, Mexico." *Ancient Mesoamerica* 27: 133–147.

Osborne, Robin. 1992. "'Is it a farm?' The definition of agricultural sites and settlements in ancient Greece." In Wells, ed. 1992: 21–27.

Oshima, Takayoshi. 2014. *Babylonian poems of pious sufferers: Ludlul Bel Nemeqi and the Babylonian Theodicy*. Tübingen, Germany: Mohr Siebeck.

Ostby, Gudrun. 2008. "Polarization, horizontal inequalities and violent civil conflict." *Journal of Peace Research* 45: 143–162.

Östling, Johan. 2013. "Realism and idealism. Swedish narratives of the Second World War: historiography and interpretation in the post-war era." In Gilmour and Stephenson, eds. 2013: 179–196.

Ostry, Jonathan D., Berg, Andrew, and Tsangarides, Charalambos G. 2014. "Redistribution, inequality, and growth." IMF Staff Discussion Note.

Özmucur, Süleyman, and Pamuk, Şevket. 2002. "Real wages and standards of living in the Ottoman empire, 1489–1914." *Journal of Economic History* 62: 292–321.

Page, Benjamin I., Bartels, Larry M., and Seawright, Jason. 2013. "Democracy and the policy preferences of wealthy Americans." *Perspectives on Politics* 11: 51–73.

Palma, José Gabriel. 2011. "Homogeneous middles vs. heterogeneous tails, and the end of the 'inverted-U': it's all about the share of the rich." *Development and Change* 42: 87–153.

Palme, Bernhard. 2015. "Shifting income inequality in Roman and late antique Egypt." Conference paper for "The haves and the have-nots: exploring the global history of wealth and income inequality," September 11, 2015, University of Vienna.

Pamuk, Şevket. 2005. "The Ottoman economy in World War I." In Broadberry and Harrison, eds. 2005a: 112–136.

Pamuk, Şevket. 2007. "The Black Death and the origins of the 'Great Divergence' across Europe, 1300–1600." *European Review of Economic History* 11: 289–317.

Pamuk, Şevket. Forthcoming. *Uneven progress: economic history of Turkey since 1820*. Princeton, NJ: Princeton University Press.

Pamuk, Şevket, and Shatzmiller, Maya. 2014. "Plagues, wages, and economic change in the Islamic Middle East, 700–1500." *Journal of Economic History* 74: 196–229.

Parkin, Tim G. 1992. *Demography and Roman society*. Baltimore, MD: Johns Hopkins University Press.

Patlagean, Evelyne. 1977. *Pauvreté économique et pauvreté sociale à Byzance, 4ᵉ–7ᵉ siècles*. Paris: Mouton.

Patterson, Orlando. 1982. *Slavery and social death: a comparative study*. Cambridge, MA: Harvard University Press.

Payne, Richard. 2016. "Sex, death, and aristocratic empire: Iranian jurisprudence in late antiquity." *Comparative Studies in Society and History* 58: 519–549.

Petersen, Michael B., and Skaaning, Svend-Erik. 2010. "Ultimate causes of state formation: the significance of biogeography, diffusion, and Neolithic Revolutions." *Historical Social Research* 35: 200–226.

Pettitt, Paul B., Richards, Michael, Maggi, Roberto, and Formicola, Vincenzo. 2003. "The Gravettian burial known as the Prince ('Il Principe'): new evidence for his age and diet." *Antiquity* 77: 15–19.

Philippon, Thomas, and Reshef, Ariell. 2012. "Wages and human capital in the U.S. finance industry: 1909–2006." *Quarterly Journal of Economics* 127: 1551–1609.

Piachaud, David. 2014. "Piketty's capital and social policy." *British Journal of Sociology* 65: 696–707.

Pigou, A. C. 1918. "A special levy to discharge war debt." *Economic Journal* 28: 135–156.

Piketty, Thomas. 2007. "Income, wage, and wealth inequality in France, 1901–98." In Atkinson and Piketty, eds. 2007a: 43–81.

Piketty, Thomas. 2011. "On the long-run evolution of inheritance: France 1820–1998." *Quarterly Journal of Economics* 126: 1071–1131.

Piketty, Thomas. 2013. *Le capital au XXIe siècle.* Paris: Éditions du Seuil.

Piketty, Thomas. 2014. *Capital in the twenty-first century.* Trans. Arthur Goldhammer. Cambridge, MA: Harvard University Press.

Piketty, Thomas. 2015a. "Vers une économie politique et historique: réflexions sur le capital au XXIe siècle." *Annales: Histoire, Sciences Sociales,* 125–138.

Piketty, Thomas. 2015b. "Putting distribution back at the center of economics: reflections on *Capital in the twenty-first century.*" *Journal of Economic Perspectives* 29: 67–88.

Piketty, Thomas, Postel-Vinay, Gilles, and Rosenthal, Jean-Laurent. 2006. "Wealth concentration in a developing economy: Paris and France, 1807–1994." *American Economic Review* 96: 236–256.

Piketty, Thomas, and Saez, Emmanuel. 2007. "Income and wage inequality in the United States, 1913–2002." In Atkinson and Piketty, eds. 2007a: 141–225.

Piketty, Thomas, and Saez, Emmanuel. 2013. "Top incomes and the Great Recession: recent evolutions and policy implications." *IMF Economic Review* 61: 456–478.

Piketty, Thomas, and Saez, Emmanuel. 2014. "Inequality in the long run." *Science* 344: 838–842.

Piketty, Thomas, Saez, Emmanuel, and Stantcheva, Stefanie. 2013. "Optimal taxation of top incomes: a tale of three elasticities." *American Economic Journal: Economic Policy* 6: 230–271.

Piketty, Thomas, and Zucman, Gabriel. 2015. "Wealth and inheritance in the long run." In Atkinson and Bourguignon, eds. 2015: 1303–1368.

Pines, Yuri. 2009. *Envisioning eternal empire: Chinese political thought of the Warring States era.* Honolulu: University of Hawai'i Press.

Pinker, Steven. 2011. *The better angels of our nature: why violence has declined.* New York: Viking.

Plack, Noelle. 2015. "Challenges in the countryside, 1790–2." In Andress, ed. 2015: 346–361.

Platt, Stephen R. 2012. *Autumn in the heavenly kingdom: China, the West, and the epic story of the Taiping civil war.* New York: Knopf.

Plavcan, J. Michael. 2012. "Sexual size dimorphism, canine dimorphism, and male–male competition in primates." *Human Nature* 23: 45–67.

Ponthieux, Sophie, and Meurs, Dominique. 2015. "Gender inequality." In Atkinson and Bourguignon, eds. 2015: 981–1146.

Porter, Bruce D. 1994. *War and the rise of the state: the military foundations of modern politics.* New York: Free Press.

Postel-Vinay, Gilles. 1989. "À la recherche de la révolution économique dans les campagnes (1789–1815)." *Revue Économique* 40: 1015–1045.

Postles, Dave. 2011. "Inequality of wealth in the early sixteenth centuries." Paper for the 2011 Economic History Society Annual Conference, Cambridge.

Postles, Dave. 2014. *Microcynicon: aspects of early-modern England.* Loughborough, UK: self-published.

Powell, Benjamin, Ford, Ryan, and Nowrasteh, Alex. 2008. "Somalia after state collapse: chaos or improvement?" *Journal of Economic Behavior and Organization* 67: 657–670.

Powelson, John P. 1988. *The story of land: a world history of land tenure and agrarian reform.* Cambridge, MA: Lincoln Institute of Land Policy.

Poznik, G. David, et al. 2013. "Sequencing Y chromosomes resolves discrepancy in time to common ancestor of males versus females." *Science* 341: 562–565.

Pozzi, Luca, et al. 2014. "Primate phylogenetic relationships and divergence dates inferred from complete mitochondrial genomes." *Molecular Phylogenetics and Evolution* 75: 165–183.

Prados de la Escosura, Leandro. 2007. "Inequality and poverty in Latin America: a long-run exploration." In Hatton, Timothy, O'Rourke, Kevin H., and Taylor, Alan M., eds., *The new comparative economic history: essays in honor of Jeffrey G. Williamson.* Cambridge, MA: MIT Press, 291–315.

Prados de la Escosura, Leandro. 2008. "Inequality, poverty and the Kuznets curve in Spain, 1850–2000." *European Review of Economic History* 12: 287–324.

Preiser-Kapeller, Johannes. 2016. "Piketty in Byzanz? Ungleichverteilungen von Vermögen und Einkommen im Mittelalter." Working paper. http://www.dasanderemittelalter.net/news/piketty-in-byzanz-ungleichverteilungen-von-vermogen-und-einkommen-im-mittelalter/.

Prentiss, Anne Marie, et al. 2007. "The emergence of status inequality in intermediate scale societies: a demographic and socio-economic history of the Keatley Creek site, British Columbia." *Journal of Anthropological Archaeology* 26: 299–327.

Prentiss, Anne Marie, et al. 2012. "The cultural evolution of material wealth-based inequality at Bridge River, British Columbia." *American Antiquity* 77: 542–564.

Price, T. Douglas, and Bar-Yosef, Ofer. 2010. "Traces of inequality at the origins of agriculture in the Ancient Near East." In Price, T. Douglas, and Feinman, Gary M., eds., *Pathways to power: new perspectives on the emergence of social inequality*. New York: Springer, 147–168.

Price, T. Douglas, and Bar-Yosef, Ofer. 2011. "The origins of agriculture: new data, new ideas. An introduction to Supplement 4." *Current Anthropology* 52: S163–S174.

Pringle, Heather. 2014. "The ancient roots of the 1%." *Science* 344: 822–825.

Pritchard, David M. 2010. "The symbiosis between democracy and war: the case of ancient Athens." In Pritchard, David M., ed., *War, democracy and culture in classical Athens*. Cambridge, UK: Cambridge University Press, 1–62.

Pritchett, Lant, and Woolcock, Michael. 2002. "Solutions when the solution is the problem: arraying the disarray in development." Center for Global Development Working Paper No. 10.

Psacharopoulos, George, et al. 1995. "Poverty and income inequality in Latin America during the 1980s." *Review of Income and Wealth* 41: 245–264.

Pyzyk, Mark. Forthcoming. "Onerous burdens: liturgies and the Athenian elite."

Quammen, David. 2013. *Spillover: animal infections and the next human pandemic*. New York: W. W. Norton.

Raghavan, Srinath. 2016. *India's war: the making of modern South Asia, 1939–1945*. New York: Basic Books.

Ranis, Gustav, and Kosack, Stephen. 2004. "Growth and human development in Cuba's transition." Miami, FL: University of Miami.

Rankov, Boris. 2007. "Military forces." In Sabin, van Wees, and Whitby, eds. 2007: 30–75.

Ravaillon, Martin. 2014. "Income inequality in the developing world." *Science* 344: 851–855.

Raven, Maarten J. 1991. *The tomb of Iurudef: a Memphite official in the reign of Ramesses II*. London: Egypt Exploration Society.

Raven, Maarten J., et al. 1998. "The date of the secondary burials in the tomb of Iurudef at Saqqara." *Oudheidkundige Mededelingen uit het Rijksmuseum van Oudheden* 78: 7–30.

Raven, Maarten J. Forthcoming. "Third Intermediate Period burials in Saqqara."

Reardon, Sean F., and Bischoff, Kendra. 2011a. "Income inequality and income segregation." *American Journal of Sociology* 116: 1092–1153.

Reardon, Sean F., and Bischoff, Kendra. 2011b. "Growth in the residential segregation of families by income, 1970–2009." US 2010 Project Report.

Reich, Robert B. 2015. *Saving capitalism: for the many, not the few*. New York: Alfred A. Knopf.

Reis, Jaime, Santos Pereira, Alvaro, and Andrade Martins, Conceicão. n.d. "How unequal were the Latins? The "strange" case of Portugal, 1550–1770." Working paper.

Renfrew, Colin. 1979. "Systems collapse as social transformation: catastrophe and anastrophe in early state societies." In Renfrew, Colin, and Cooke, Kenneth L., eds., *Transformations: mathematical approaches to cultural change*. New York: Academic Press, 481–506.

Reno, Philip L., and Lovejoy, C. Owen. 2015. "From Lucy to Kadanuumuu: balanced analyses of Australopithecus afarensis assemblages confirm only moderate skeletal dimorphism." *PeerJ* 3:e925; DOI 10.7717/peerj.925.

Reno, Philip L., McCollum, Melanie A., Meindl, Richard S., and Lovejoy, C. Owen. 2010. "An enlarged postcranial sample confirms *Australopithecus afarensis* dimorphism was similar to modern humans." *Philosophical Transactions of the Royal Society B* 365: 3355–3363.

Rigoulot, Pierre. 1999. "Crimes, terror, and secrecy in North Korea." In Courtois et al. 1999: 547–576.

Ritschl, Albrecht. 2005. "The pity of peace: Germany's economy at war, 1914–1918 and beyond." In Broadberry and Harrison, eds. 2005a: 41–76.

Ritter, Gerhard A. 2010. *Der Sozialstaat: Entstehung und Entwicklung im internationalen Vergleich.* 3rd ed. Munich: Oldenbourg.

Rivaya-Martínez, Joaquín. 2012. "Becoming Comanches: patterns of captive incorporation into Comanche kinship networks, 1820–1875." In Adams, David Wallace, and DeLuzio, Crista, eds., *On the borders of love and power: families and kinship in the intercultural American Southwest.* Berkeley: University of California Press, 47–70.

Roach, Neil T., Venkadesan, Madhusudhan, Rainbow, Michael J., and Lieberman, Daniel E. 2013. "Elastic energy storage in the shoulder and the evolution of high-speed throwing in *Homo.*" *Nature* 498: 483–486.

Rockoff, Hugh. 2005. "Until it's over, over there: the US economy in World War I." In Broadberry and Harrison, eds. 2005a: 310–343.

Rodríguez Weber, Javier E. 2015. "Income inequality in Chile since 1850." Programa de Historian Económica y Social—Unidad Multidisciplinaria—Facultad de Ciencias Sociales—Universidad de la República. Documento On Line No. 36.

Roeck, Bernd. 1989. *Eine Stadt in Krieg und Frieden: Studien zur Geschichte der Reichsstadt Augsburg zwischen Kalenderstreit und Parität.* 2 vols. Göttingen, Germany: Vandenhoeck & Ruprecht.

Rognlie, Matthew. 2015. "Deciphering the fall and rise in the net capital share: accumulation, or scarcity?" Working paper.

Roine, Jesper, and Waldenström, Daniel. 2008. "The evolution of top incomes in an egalitarian society: Sweden, 1903–2004." *Journal of Public Economics* 92: 366–387.

Roine, Jesper, and Waldenström, Daniel. 2010. "Top incomes in Sweden over the twentieth century." In Atkinson and Piketty, eds. 2010: 299–370.

Roine, Jesper, and Waldenström, Daniel. 2015. "Long-run trends in the distribution of income and wealth." In Atkinson and Bourguignon, eds. 2015: 469–592.

Roselaar, Saskia T. 2010. *Public land in the Roman republic: a social and economic history of* ager publicus *in Italy, 396–89 BC.* Oxford: Oxford University Press.

Rosenbloom, Joshua, and Dupont, Brandon. 2015. "The impact of the Civil War on Southern wealth mobility." Paper presented at the annual meeting of the Economic History Association, Nashville.

Rosenbloom, Joshua L., and Stutes, Gregory W. 2008. "Reexamining the distribution of wealth in 1870." In Rosenbloom, Joshua L., ed., *Quantitative economic history: the good of counting.* London: Routledge, 146–169.

Rosenstein, Nathan. 2008. "Aristocrats and agriculture in the Middle and Late Republic." *Journal of Roman Studies* 98: 1–26.

Rossi, Nicola, Toniolo, Gianni, and Vecchi, Giovanni. 2001. "Is the Kuznets curve still alive? Evidence from Italian household budgets, 1881–1961." *Journal of Economic History* 61: 904–925.

Rotberg, Robert I. 2003. "The failure and collapse of nation-states: breakdown, prevention, and repair." In Rotberg, Robert I., ed. *When states fail.* Princeton, NJ: Princeton University Press, 1–25.

Rothkopf, David. 2008. *Superclass: the global power elite and the world they are making.* New York: Farrar, Straus and Giroux.

Roxana, Maurizio. 2014. "Labour formalization and declining inequality in Argentina and Brazil in 2000s [*sic*]." ILO Research Paper No. 9.

Roy, Kaushik. 2016. *Military manpower, armies and warfare in South Asia.* Milton Park, UK: Routledge.

Rubin, Amir, and Segal, Dan. 2015. "The effects of economic growth on income inequality in the US." *Journal of Macroeconomics* 45: 258–273.

Ryckbosch, Wouter. 2010. "Vroegmoderne economische ontwikkeling en sociale repercussies in de zuidelijke Nederlanden." *Tijdschrift voor Sociale en Economische Geschiedenis* 7: 26–55.

Ryckbosch, Wouter. 2014. "Economic inequality and growth before the industrial revolution: a case study of the Low Countries (14th–19th centuries)." Dondena Working Paper No. 67, Università Bocconi, Milan.

Sabin, Philip, van Wees, Hans, and Whitby, Michael, eds. 2007. *The Cambridge history of Greek and Roman warfare.* Vol. II. *Rome from the late Republic to the late Empire.* Cambridge, UK: Cambridge University Press.

Sadao, Nishijima. 1986. "The economic and social history of Former Han." In Twitchett and Loewe, eds. 1986: 545–607.

Sadomba, Zvkanyorwa W. 2013. "A decade of Zimbabwe's land revolution: the politics of the war veteran vanguard." In Moyo and Chambati, eds. 2013b: 79–121.

Saez, Emmanuel, and Veall, Michael R. 2007. "The evolution of high incomes in Canada, 1920–2000." In Atkinson and Piketty, eds. 2007a: 226–308.

Saez, Emmanuel, and Zucman, Gabriel. 2016. "Wealth inequality in the United States since 1913: evidence from capitalized income tax data." *Quarterly Journal of Economics* 131: 519–578.

Saito, Osamu. 2015. "Growth and inequality in the great and little divergence debate: a Japanese perspective." *Economic History Review* 68: 399–419.

Sallares, Robert. 1991. *The ecology of the ancient Greek world.* London: Duckworth.

Salverda, Wiemer, and Atkinson, Anthony B. 2007. "Top incomes in the Netherlands over the twentieth century." In Atkinson and Piketty, eds. 2007a: 426–471.

Salverda, Wiemer, and Checchi, Daniele. 2015. "Labor market institutions and the dispersion of wage earnings." In Atkinson and Bourguignon, eds. 2015: 1535–1727.

Salverda, Wiemer, Nolan, Brian, and Smeeding, Timothy M., eds. 2009. *The Oxford handbook of economic inequality.* Oxford: Oxford University Press.

Samaraweera, Vijaya. 1982. "Land reform in Sri Lanka." *Third World Legal Studies* 1 (7). Valparaiso University Law School.

Sanderson, Stephen K. 1999. *Social transformations: a general theory of historical development.* Exp. ed. Lanham, MD: Rowman and Littlefield.

Sandmo, Angar. 2015. "The principal problem in political economy: income distribution in the history of economic thought." In Atkinson and Bourguignon, eds. 2015: 3–65.

Santiago-Caballero, Carlos. 2011. "Income inequality in central Spain, 1690–1800." *Explorations in Economic History* 48: 83–96.

Sapolsky, Robert M., and Share, Lisa J. 2004. "A pacific culture among wild baboons: its emergence and transmission." *PLoS Biology* 2 (4): e106. doi:10.1371/journal.pbi0.0020106.

Sarris, Peter. 2007. "Bubonic plague in Byzantium: the evidence of non-literary sources." In Little, ed. 2007: 119–132.

Sassaman, Kenneth E. 2004. "Complex hunter-gatherers in evolution and history: a North American perspective." *Journal of Archaeological Research* 12: 227–280.

Scheidel, Walter. 2001. *Death on the Nile: disease and the demography of Roman Egypt.* Leiden, Netherlands: Brill.

Scheidel, Walter. 2002. "A model of demographic and economic change in Roman Egypt after the Antonine plague." *Journal of Roman Archaeology* 15: 97–114.

Scheidel, Walter. 2005a. "Human mobility in Roman Italy, II: the slave population." *Journal of Roman Studies* 95: 64–79.

Scheidel, Walter. 2005b. "Military commitments and political bargaining in classical Greece." Princeton/Stanford Working Papers in Classics.

Scheidel, Walter. 2006. "Stratification, deprivation and quality of life." In Atkins, Margaret, and Osborne, Robin, eds., *Poverty in the Roman world.* Cambridge, UK: Cambridge University Press, 40–59.

Scheidel, Walter. 2007. "A model of real income growth in Roman Italy." *Historia* 56: 322–346.

Scheidel, Walter. 2008. "Roman population size: the logic of the debate." In De Ligt, Luuk, and Northwood, Simon J., eds., *People, land, and politics: demographic developments and the transformation of Roman Italy, 300 BC–AD 14.* Leiden, Netherlands: Brill, 17–70.

Scheidel, Walter. 2009a. "From the 'Great Convergence' to the 'First Great Divergence.'" In Scheidel, Walter, ed. *Rome and China: comparative perspectives on ancient world empires.* New York: Oxford University Press, 11–23.

Scheidel, Walter. 2009b. "Sex and empire: a Darwinian perspective." In Morris and Scheidel 2009: 255–324.

Scheidel, Walter. 2010. "Real wages in early economies: evidence for living standards from 1800 BCE to 1300 CE." *Journal of the Economic and Social History of the Orient* 53: 425–462.

Scheidel, Walter. 2012. "Roman wellbeing and the economic consequences of the Antonine Plague." In Lo Cascio, ed. 2012: 265–295.

Scheidel, Walter. 2013. "Studying the state." In Bang, Peter Fibiger, and Scheidel, Walter, eds., *The Oxford handbook of the state in the ancient Near East and Mediterranean.* New York: Oxford University Press, 5–57.

Scheidel, Walter. 2015a. "The early Roman monarchy." In Monson and Scheidel, eds. 2015: 229–257.

Scheidel, Walter, ed. 2015b. *State power in ancient China and Rome.* New York: Oxford University Press.

Scheidel, Walter. 2015c. "State revenue and expenditure in the Han and Roman empires." In Scheidel 2015b: 150–180.

Scheidel, Walter. 2016. "Empires of inequality: ancient China and Rome." Working paper. http://papers.ssrn .com/abstract=2817173.

Scheidel, Walter, and Friesen, Stephen J. 2009. "The size of the economy and the distribution of income in the Roman empire." *Journal of Roman Studies* 99: 61–91.

Schepartz, Lynne A., Miller-Antonio, Sari, and Murphy, Joanne M. A. 2009. "Differential health among the Mycenaeans of Messenia: status, sex, and dental health at Pylos." In Schepartz, Lynne A., Fox, Sherry C., and Bourbou, Chryssi, eds., *New directions in the skeletal biology of Greece.* Princeton, NJ: American School of Classical Studies at Athens, 155–174.

Scheve, Kenneth, and Stasavage, David. 2009. "Institutions, partisanship, and inequality in the long run." *World Politics* 61: 215–253.

Scheve, Kenneth, and Stasavage, David. 2010. "The conscription of wealth: mass warfare and the demand for progressive taxation." *International Organization* 64: 529–561.

Scheve, Kenneth, and Stasavage, David. 2012. "Democracy, war, and wealth: lessons from two centuries of inheritance taxation." *American Political Science Review* 106: 81–102.

Scheve, Kenneth, and Stasavage, David. 2016. *Taxing the rich: a history of fiscal fairness in the United States and Europe.* Princeton, NJ: Princeton University Press.

Schlozman, Kay L., Verba, Sidney, and Brady, Henry E. 2012. *The unheavenly chorus: unequal political voice and the broken promise of American democracy.* Princeton, NJ: Princeton University Press.

Schmidt-Nowara, Christopher. 2010. "Emancipation." In Paquette, Robert L., and Smith, Mark M., eds., *The Oxford handbook of slavery in the Americas.* Oxford: Oxford University Press, 578–597.

Schmidt-Nowara, Christopher. 2011. *Slavery, freedom, and abolition in Latin America and the Atlantic world.* Albuquerque: University of New Mexico Press.

Schulze, Max-Stephan. 2005. "Austria-Hungary's economy in World War I." In Broadberry and Harrison, eds. 2005a: 77–111.

Schütte, Robert. 2015. *Civilian protection in armed conflicts: evolution, challenges and implementation.* Wiesbaden, Germany: Springer.

Schwartz, Christine. 2010. "Earnings inequality and the changing association between spouses' earnings." *American Journal of Sociology* 115: 1524–1557.

Seidel, Frederick. 2016. *Widening income inequality: poems.* New York: Farrar, Straus and Giroux.

Seker, Sirma Demir, and Jenkins, Stephen P. 2015. "Poverty trends in Turkey." *Journal of Economic Inequality* 13: 401–424.

Sharp, Michael. 1999. "The village of Theadelphia in the Fayyum: land and population in the second century." In Bowman, Alan K., and Rogan, E., eds., *Agriculture in Egypt: from Pharaonic to modern times.* Oxford: British Academy, 159–192.

Shatzman, Israel. 1975. *Senatorial wealth and Roman politics.* Brussels: Latomus.

Shaw, Brent D. 2011. *Sacred violence: African Christians and sectarian hatred in the age of Augustine.* Cambridge, UK: Cambridge University Press.

Sheen, Seongho. 2013. "Northeast Asia's aging population and regional security: 'demographic peace?'" *Asia Survey* 53: 292–318.

Shelmerdine, Cynthia W., ed. 2008. *The Cambridge companion to the Aegean Bronze Age.* Cambridge, UK: Cambridge University Press.

Shennan, Stephen. 2011. "Property and wealth inequality as cultural niche construction." *Philosophical Transactions: Biological Sciences* 366: 918–926.

Shultziner, Doron, et al. 2010. "The causes and scope of political egalitarianism during the Last Glacial: a multi-disciplinary perspective." *Biology and Philosophy* 25: 319–346.

Sidrys, Raymond, and Berger, Rainer. 1979. "Lowland Maya radiocarbon dates and the Classic Maya collapse." *Nature* 277: 269–74.

Silver, Lee M. 1997. *Remaking Eden: cloning and beyond in a brave new world.* New York: Avon Books.

Singer, Peter W. 2009. *Wired for war: the robotics revolution and conflict in the 21st century.* New York: Penguin.

Slonimczyk, Fabián. 2013. "Earnings inequality and skill mismatch in the U.S.: 1973–2002." *Journal of Economic Inequality* 11: 163–194.

Smith, Eric A., et al. 2010a. "Production systems, inheritance, and inequality in premodern societies." *Current Anthropology* 51: 85–94.

Smith, Eric A., et al. 2010b. "Wealth transmission and inequality among hunter-gatherers." *Current Anthropology* 51: 19–34.

Smith, Michael E., et al. 2014. "Quantitative measures of wealth inequality in ancient central Mexican communities." *Advances in Archaeological Practice* 2: 311–323.

Smith, Roger S. 1995. "The personal income tax: average and marginal rates in the post-war period." *Canadian Tax Journal* 43: 1055–1076.

Smolensky, Eugene, and Plotnick, Robert. 1993. "Inequality and poverty in the United States: 1900 to 1990." Institute for Research on Poverty, University of Wisconsin–Madison Discussion Paper No. 998–93.

Snyder, Timothy. 2010. *Bloodlands: Europe between Hitler and Stalin.* New York: Basic Books.

Söderberg, Johan. 1991. "Wage differentials in Sweden, 1725–1950." In Brenner, Kaelble, and Thomas, eds. 1991: 76–95.

Soltow, Lee. 1968. "Long-run changes in British income inequality." *Economic History Review* 21: 17–29.

Soltow, Lee. 1975. *Men and wealth in the United States, 1850–1870.* New Haven, CT: Yale University Press.

Soltow, Lee. 1979. "Wealth distribution in Denmark in 1789." *Scandinavian Economic Review* 27: 121–138.

Soltow, Lee. 1985. "The Swedish census of wealth at the beginning of the 19th century." *Scandinavian Economic Review* 33: 60–70.

Soltow, Lee, and van Zanden, Jan Luiten. 1998. *Income and wealth inequality in the Netherlands 16th–20th century.* Amsterdam: Het Spinhuis.

Spant, Roland. 1981. "The distribution of income in Sweden, 1920–76." In Klevmarken, N. A., and Lybeck J. A., eds., *The statics and dynamics of income.* Clevedon, UK: Tieto, 37–54.

Sparrow, James T. 2011. *Warfare state: World War II Americans and the age of big government.* New York: Oxford University Press.

Speller, Camilla F., Yang, Dongya Y., and Hayden, Brian. 2005. "Ancient DNA investigation of prehistoric salmon resource utilization at Keatley Creek, British Columbia, Canada." *Journal of Archaeological Science* 32: 1378–1389.

Spence, Jonathan D. 1996. *God's Chinese son: the Taiping heavenly kingdom of Hong Xiuquan.* New York: W. W. Norton.

Stanley, Marcus. 2003. "College education and the midcentury GI bills." *Quarterly Journal of Economics* 118: 671–708.

State Council. 2013. "Some opinions on deepening the reform of the system of income distribution." http://www.gov.cn/zwgk/2013–02/05/content_2327531.htm.

Stathakopoulos, Dionysios C. 2004. *Famine and pestilence in late Roman and early Byzantine empire: a systematic survey of subsistence crises and epidemics.* Aldershot, UK: Ashgate.

Steckel, Richard H. 2009. "Heights and human welfare: recent developments and new directions." *Explorations in Economic History* 46: 1–23.

Stenkula, Mikael, Johansson, Dan, and Du Rietz, Gunnar. 2014. "Marginal taxation on labour income in Sweden from 1862 to 2010." *Scandinavian Economic History Review* 62: 163–187.

Stephan, Robert Perry. 2013. "House size and economic growth: Regional trajectories in the Roman world." PhD dissertation, Stanford University.

Stiglitz, Joseph E. 2013. *The price of inequality: how today's divided society endangers our future*. New York: W. W. Norton.

Strasma, John. 1989. "Unfinished business: consolidating land reform in El Salvador." In Thiesenheusen, ed. 1989b: 408–428.

Stratfor. 2013. "Bioterrorism and the pandemic potential." *Security Weekly* March 7, 2013. https://www.stratfor.com/weekly/bioterrorism-and-pandemic-potential.

Stringer, Randy. 1989. "Honduras: toward conflict and agrarian reform." In Thiesenheusen, ed. 1989b: 358–383.

Sullivan, Michael. 1996. *The development of the British welfare state*. London: Prentice Hall.

Sussman, Nathan. 2006. "Income inequality in Paris in the heyday of the commercial revolution." Working paper. http://degit.sam.sdu.dk/papers/degit_11/C011_043.pdf.

Sutherland, Donald M. G. 2003. *The French Revolution and empire: the quest for a civic order*. Malden, MA: Blackwell.

Swann, Nancy Lee. 1950. *Food and money in ancient China: the earliest economic history of China to A.D. 25. Han shu 24 with related texts, Han shu 91 and Shih-chi 129*. Princeton, NJ: Princeton University Press.

SWIID. "The standardized world income inequality database." http://fsolt.org/swiid/.

Taagepera, Rein. 1978. "Size and duration of empires: systematics of size." *Social Science Research* 7: 108–127.

Tackett, Nicolas. 2014. *The destruction of the medieval Chinese aristocracy*. Cambridge, MA: Harvard University Press.

Tainter, Joseph A. 1988. *The collapse of complex societies*. Cambridge, UK: Cambridge University.

Takigawa, Tsutomo. 1972. "Historical background of agricultural land reform in Japan." *The Developing Economies* 10: 290–310.

Tan, James. Forthcoming. *Politics and public finance at Rome (264–49 BCE)*. New York: Oxford University Press.

TeBrake, William H. 1993. *A plague of insurrection: popular politics and peasant revolt in Flanders, 1323–1328*. Philadelphia: University of Pennsylvania Press.

Teranishi, Juro. 1993a. "Inflation stabilization with growth: the Japanese experience, 1945–50." In Teranishi and Kosai, eds. 1993: 61–85.

Teranishi, Juro. 1993b. "Financial sector reform after the war." In Teranishi and Kosai, eds. 1993: 153–177.

Teranishi, Juro, and Kosai, Yutaka, eds. 1993. *The Japanese experience of economic reforms*. Basingstoke, UK: Macmillan.

Thayer, Bradley A. 2009. "Considering population and war: a critical and neglected aspect of conflict studies." *Philosophical Transactions of the Royal Society of London B* 263: 3081–3092.

Therborn, Göran. 2013. *The killing fields of inequality*. Cambridge, UK: Polity.

Thiesenheusen, William C. 1989a. "Conclusions: searching for agrarian reform in Latin America." In Thiesenheusen, ed. 1989b: 483–503.

Thiesenheusen, William C., ed. 1989b. *Searching for agrarian reform in Latin America*. London: Unwin Hyman.

Thomas, Hugh M. 2003. "The significance and fate of the native English landholders of 1086." *English Historical Review* 118: 303–333.

Thomas, Hugh M. 2008. *The Norman conquest: England after William the Conqueror*. Lanham, MD: Rowman and Littlefield.

Thompson, Edward A. 1952. "Peasant revolts in late Roman Gaul and Spain." *Past and Present* 2: 11–23.

Thomson, Henry. 2015. "Rural grievances, landholding inequality and civil conflict." SSRN Working Paper. http://dx.doi.org/10.2139/ssrn.2551186.

Thorp, Rosemary. 1998. *Progress, poverty and exclusion: an economic history of Latin America in the 20th century*. Washington, DC: Inter-American Development Bank.

Ticchi, Davide, and Vindigni, Andrea. 2008. "War and endogenous democracy." IZA Discussion Paper 3397.

Tilly, Charles. 1985. "War making and state making as organized crime." In Evans, Peter B., Rueschemeyer, Dietrich, and Skocpol, Theda, eds., *Bringing the state back in*. Cambridge, UK: Cambridge University Press, 169–191.

Tilly, Charles. 1992. *Coercion, capital, and European states, AD 990–1992*. Cambridge, MA: Blackwell.

Tilly, Charles. 2003. *The politics of collective violence*. Cambridge, UK: Cambridge University Press.

Tinbergen, Jan. 1974. "Substitution of graduate by other labour." *Kyklos* 27: 217–226.

Tinh, V. N., et al. 2011. "Mitochondrial evidence for multiple radiations in the evolutionary history of small apes." *BMC Evolutionary Biology* 10: 74. doi:10.1186/1471-2148-10-74.

Titmuss, Richard M. 1958. "War and social policy." In Titmuss, Richard M., ed., *Essays on the welfare state*. London: George Allen and Unwin, 75–87.

Toynbee, Arnold J. 1946. *A study of history: abridgment of volumes I–VI by David C. Somervell*. Oxford: Oxford University Press.

Treisman, David. 2012. "Inequality: the Russian experience." *Current History* 111: 264–268.

Trigger, Bruce G. 2003. *Understanding early civilizations: a comparative study*. Cambridge, UK: Cambridge University Press.

Trinkaus, Erik, Buzhilova, Alexandra P., Mednikova, Maria B., and Dobrovolskaya, Maria V. 2014. *The people of Sunghir: burials, bodies, and behavior in the Earlier Upper Paleolithic*. Oxford: Oxford University Press.

Tsounta, Evridiki, and Osueke, Anayochukwu I. 2014. "What is behind Latin America's declining income inequality?" IMF Working Paper 14/124.

Tuma, Elias H. 1965. *Twenty-six centuries of agrarian reform: a comparative analysis*. Berkeley: University of California Press.

Turchin, Peter. 2009. "A theory for formation of large empires." *Journal of Global History* 4: 191–217.

Turchin, Peter. 2016a. *Ages of discord: a structural-demographic analysis of American history*. Chaplin, CT: Beresta Books.

Turchin, Peter. 2016b. *Ultrasociety: how 10,000 years of war made humans the greatest cooperators on earth*. Chaplin, CT: Beresta Books.

Turchin, Peter, Currie, Thomas E., Turner, Edward A. L., and Gavrilets, Sergey. 2013. "War, space, and the evolution of Old World complex societies." *Proceedings of the National Academy of Science* 110: 16384–16389.

Turchin, Peter, and Gavrilets, Sergey. 2009. "Evolution of complex hierarchical societies." *Social Evolution and History* 8: 167–198.

Turchin, Peter, and Nefedov, Sergey A. 2009. *Secular cycles*. Princeton, NJ: Princeton University Press.

Turner, Michael. 1996. *After the famine: Irish agriculture, 1850–1914*. Cambridge, UK: Cambridge University Press.

Twitchett, Denis, and Loewe, Michael, eds. 1986. *The Cambridge history of China*. Vol. 1. *The Ch'in and Han empires, 221 B.C.-A.D. 220*. Cambridge, UK: Cambridge University Press.

United Nations. 2015. "World population prospects: the 2015 revision, key findings and advance tables." United Nations, Department of Economic and Social Affairs, Population Division, Working Paper No. ESA/P/WP.241.

United States strategic bombing survey 1946. *Summary report (Pacific war)*. Washington, DC: United States Government Printing Office.

Vanhaeren, Marian, and d'Errico, Francesco. 2005. "Grave goods from the Saint-Germain-la-Rivière burial: evidence for social inequality in the Upper Palaeolithic." *Journal of Anthropological Archaeology* 24: 117–134.

van Praag, Bernard, and Ferrer-i-Carbonell, Ada. 2009. "Inequality and happiness." In Salverda, Nolan, and Smeeding, eds. 2009: 364–383.

van Treeck, Till. 2014. "Did inequality cause the U.S. financial crisis?" *Journal of Economic Surveys* 28: 421–448.

van Wees, Hans. 2004. *Greek warfare: myths and realities*. London: Duckworth.

van Zanden, Jan Luiten. 1995. "Tracing the beginning of the Kuznets curve: western Europe during the early modern period." *Economic History Review* 48: 643–664.

van Zanden, Jan Luiten. 2009. "The skill premium and the 'Great Divergence.'" *European Review of Economic History* 13: 121–153.

Veltmeyer, Henry, and Rushton, Mark. 2012. *The Cuban revolution as socialist human development*. Leiden, Netherlands: Brill.

Verme, Paolo, et al. 2014. *Inside inequality in the Arab Republic of Egypt: facts and perceptions across people, time, and space*. Washington, DC: World Bank.

Villette, Michel, and Vuillermot, Catherine. 2009. *From predators to icons: exposing the myth of the business hero*. Ithaca: Cornell University Press.

Virén, Matti. 2000. "Financing the welfare state in the global economy." Working Paper No. 732, Elinkeinoelämän Tutkimuslaitos, Helsinki.

Visser, Jelle. 1989. *European trade unions in figures*. Deventer, Netherlands: Kluwer.

Visser, Jelle, and Checchi, Danielle. 2009. "Inequality and the labor market: unions." In Salverda, Nolan, and Smeeding, eds. 2009: 230–256.

Voitchovsky, Sarah. 2009. "Inequality and economic growth." In Salverda, Nolan, and Smeeding, eds. 2009: 549–574.

Volscho, Thomas W., and Kelly, Nathan J. 2012. "The rise of the super-rich: power resources, taxes, financial markets, and the dynamics of the top 1 percent, 1949 to 2008." *American Sociological Review* 77: 679–699.

Waglé, Udaya R. 2013. *The heterogeneity link of the welfare state and redistribution: ethnic heterogeneity, welfare state policies, poverty, and inequality in high income countries*. Cham, Switzerland: Springer.

Wagner, David M., et al. 2014. "*Yersinia pestis* and the Plague of Justinian 541–543 AD: a genomic analysis." *The Lancet Infectious Diseases* 14 (4): 319–326.

Waldenström, Daniel. 2015. "Wealth-income ratios in a small, late-industrializing, welfare-state economy: Sweden, 1810–2014." Uppsala Center for Fiscal Studies Working Paper 2015:6.

Walder, Andrew G. 2015. *China under Mao: a revolution derailed*. Cambridge, MA: Harvard University Press.

Wang, Chen, Caminada, Koen, and Goudswaard, Kees. 2012. "The redistributive effect of social transfer programmes and taxes: a decomposition across countries." *International Social Security Review* 65 (3): 27–48.

Ward, Eric E. 1990. *Land reform in Japan 1946–1950, the Allied role*. Tokyo: Nobunkyo.

Watkins, Susan Cotts, and Menken, Jane. 1985. "Famines in historical perspective." *Population and Development Review* 11: 647–675.

Weber, Max. 1950. *General economic history*. New York: Free Press.

Wehler, Hans-Ulrich. 2013. *Die neue Umverteilung: soziale Ungleichheit in Deutschland*. 2nd ed. Munich: Beck.

Weisbrot, Mark, Ray, Rebecca, Montecino, Juan A., and Kozameh, Sara. 2011. "The Argentine success story and its implications." Washington, DC: Center for Economic and Policy Research.

Wells, Berit, ed. 1992. *Agriculture in ancient Greece*. Stockholm: Swedish Institute at Athens.

Wengrow, David, and Graeber, David. 2015. "Farewell to the 'childhood of man': ritual, seasonality, and the origins of inequality." *Journal of the Royal Anthropological Institute* 21: 597–619.

Werth, Nicolas. 1999. "A state against its people: violence, repression, and terror in the Soviet Union." In Courtois et al. 1999: 33–268.

Western, Bruce, and Rosenfeld, Jake. 2011. "Unions, norms, and the rise of U.S. wage inequality." *American Sociological Review* 76: 513–537.

Wickham, Chris. 2005. *Framing the early Middle Ages: Europe and the Mediterranean, 400–800*. Oxford: Oxford University Press.

Wilensky, Harold L. 1975. *The welfare state and equality: structural and ideological roots of public expenditures*. Berkeley: University of California Press.

Willey, Gordon R., and Shimkin, Demitri B. 1973. "The Maya collapse: a summary view." In Culbert, ed. 1973: 457–501.

Williamson, Jeffrey G. 1985. *Did British capitalism breed inequality?* Winchester, MA: Allen and Unwin.

Williamson, Jeffrey G. 1991. "British inequality during the Industrial Revolution: accounting for the Kuznets curve." In Brenner, Kaelble, and Thomas, eds. 1991: 56–75.

Williamson, Jeffrey G. 2009. "History without evidence: Latin American inequality since 1491." National Bureau of Economic Research Working Paper No. 14766.

Williamson, Jeffrey G. 2015. "Latin American inequality: colonial origins, commodity booms, or a missed 20th century leveling?" NBER Working Paper No. 20915.

Wimmer, Andreas. 2014. "War." *Annual Review of Sociology* 40: 173–197.

Windler, Anne, Thiele, Rainer, and Müller, Johannes. 2013. "Increasing inequality in Chalcolithic Southeast Europe: the case of Durankulak." *Journal of Archaeological Science* 40: 204–210.

Winters, Jeffrey A. 2011. *Oligarchy*. New York: Cambridge University Press.

Wolfe, Nathan. 2011. *The viral storm: the dawn of a new pandemic age*. New York: Times Books.

Wolff, Edward N. 1996. "International comparisons of wealth inequality." *Review of Income and Wealth* 42: 433–451.

Wood, Ellen Meiksins. 2003. *Empire of capital*. London: Verso.

Wood, James W. 1988. "A theory of preindustrial population dynamics." *Current Anthropology* 39: 99–135.

World Bank. 2008. *Land reforms in Sri Lanka: a poverty and social impact analysis (PSIA)*. Washington, DC: World Bank.

Wright, Gavin. 2006. *Slavery and American economic development*. Baton Rouge: Louisiana State University Press.

Wright, James C. 2008. "Early Mycenaean Greece." In Shelmerdine, ed. 2008: 230–257.

Wright, Katherine I. 2014. "Domestication and inequality? Households, corporate groups and food processing tools at Neolithic Catalhöyük." *Journal of Anthropological Archaeology* 33: 1–33.

Wright, Lisa. 2006. *Diet, health, and status among the Pasión Maya: a reappraisal of the collapse*. Nashville, TN: Vanderbilt University Press.

Wright, Rita. 2010. *The ancient Indus: urbanism, economy, and society*. New York: Cambridge University Press.

WWID. "The world wealth and income database." http://www.wid.world.

Xie, Y., and Zhou, X. 2014. "Income inequality in today's China." *Proceedings of the National Academy of Sciences* 111: 6928–6933.

Yamada, Shigeo. 2000. *The construction of the Assyrian empire: a historical study of the inscriptions of Shalmaneser III (859–824 BC) relating to his campaigns to the west*. Leiden, Netherlands: Brill.

Yamamoto, Yûzô. 2003. "Japanese empire and colonial management." In Nakamura and Odaka, eds. 2003a: 223–246.

Yaycioglu, Ali. 2012. "Wealth, power and death: capital accumulation and imperial seizures in the Ottoman empire (1453–1839)." Working Paper, Yale Program in Economic History, Yale University.

Yoffee, Norman. 1988. "The collapse of ancient Mesopotamian states and civilization." In Yoffee and Cowgill, eds. 1988: 44–68.

Yoffee, Norman, and Cowgill, George L., eds. 1988. *The collapse of ancient states and civilizations*. Tucson: University of Arizona Press.

Yonekura, Seiichiro. 1993. "Postwar reform in management and labour: the case of the steel industry." In Teranishi and Kosai, eds. 1993: 205–238.

Yoshikawa, Hiroshi, and Okazaki, Tetsuji. 1993. "Postwar hyper-inflation and the Dodge Plan, 1945–50: an overview." In Teranishi and Kosai, eds. 1993: 86–104.

You, Jong-sung. 2015. *Democracy, inequality and corruption: Korea, Taiwan and the Philippines compared*. Cambridge, UK: Cambridge University Press.

You, Jong-sung. n.d. "Inequality and corruption: the role of land reform in Korea, Taiwan, and the Philippines." Working paper.

Yuen, Choy Leng. 1982. "The struggle for land reform in Japan: a study of the major land legislation, 1920–1943." PhD thesis, Harvard University.

Yun-Casalilla, Bartolomé, and O'Brien, Patrick K., with Comín Comín, Francisco, eds. 2012. *The rise of fiscal states: a global history, 1500–1914*. Cambridge, UK: Cambridge University Press.

Zala, Sacha. 2014. "Krisen, Konfrontation, Konsens (1914–1949)." In Kreis, Georg, ed. *Geschichte der Schweiz*. Basel, Switzerland: Schwabe, 490–539.

Zamagni, Vera. 2005. "Italy: how to lose the war and win the peace." In Harrison, ed. 1998b: 177–223.

Zébitch, Milorade. 1917. *La Serbie agricole et sa démocratie*. Paris: Libraire Berger-Levrault.

Ze'evi, Dror, and Buke, Ilkim. 2015. "Banishment, confiscation, and the instability of the Ottoman elite household." In Ze'evi, Dror, and Toledano, Ehud, eds., *Society, law, and culture in the Middle East: "modernities" in the making*. Berlin: De Gruyter, 16–30.

Zelener, Yan. 2012. "Genetic evidence, density dependence and epidemiological models of the 'Antonine Plague.'" In Lo Cascio, ed. 2012: 167–191.

Zelin, Madeleine. 1984. *The magistrate's tael: rationalizing fiscal reform in eighteenth-century Ch'ing China.* Berkeley: University of California Press.

Zeuske, Michael. 2013. *Handbuch der Geschichte der Sklaverei: eine Globalgeschichte von den Anfängen bis zur Gegenwart.* Berlin: De Gruyter.

Zhong, Wei, et al. 2010. "Wealth inequality: China and India." India China Institute collaborative project *Prosperity and inequality in India and China, 2008–2010.* Working paper.

Zubay, Geoffrey, et al. 2005. *Agents of bioterrorism: pathogens and their weaponization.* New York: Columbia University Press.

Zuckerman, Edward. 1984. *The day after World War III.* New York: Avon.

Zucman, Gabriel. 2013. "The missing wealth of nations: are Europe and the US net debtors or net creditors?" *Quarterly Journal of Economics* 128: 1321–1364.

Zucman, Gabriel. 2015. *The hidden wealth of nations: the scourge of tax havens.* Chicago: University of Chicago Press.

INDEX

absolute inequality, 13, 434
Abdullah, Abdul Jabbar, 374
Abul-Magd, Adel Y., 267n13
Adams, Robert McC, 279n32
Akkadians, 56–57, 280
Albertus, Michael, 352n11, 354n13, 357, 359n22,
    394n6
Alexander II, 348
Alexander the Great, 194
Alfani, Guido, 92n9, 98n17, 111n36, 306,
    307n26, 308n27
Alien Landownership Act, 355
Alliance for Peace, 352
American Civil War, 7, 17, 109, 174–75, 176,
    177, 204, 244, 264n8; black suffrage, 168;
    Confederacy, 175, 176; destruction of slavery,
    361; material inequality, 179; mobilization,
    181, 208; Union Army, 175, 176; wealth, 111
Amsterdam, 93–95, 300–1
Anand, Sudhir, 10n7
Angkor, 278
Antonine Plague, 326–30, 329n19, 333
Apiones family, 79
Argentina, 133–34, 144, 156, 380, 382–84,
    386, 397
Argos, 252
Aristophanes, 251
Aristotle, 199n35
Ashur, 200
Ashurbanipal (king), 61
Assyrians, 60–61, 199–200, 270
Athens, 84–85, 192–98, 244, 251
Atkinson, Anthony, 12n9, 13n10, 15n12, 21n18,
    107n30, 108n32, 138n4, 363n27, 434n12,
    435, 436
Augsburg, 93, 201–2, 335–41
Australia, 133, 136, 142, 364, 405–6
Austria, 147, 406, 409, 428
Austro-Hungary, 141–42, 146, 151, 154, 349
Aztec period, 53, 54, 58–59, 82, 103, 103n25,
    241, 315, 317, 319, 319n6

Babylonia, 48, 280, 334–35
Babylonian Theodicy, 59n47
Bagaudae, 245, 245n20

Barfield, Thomas J., 64n5
barter, 218
Baten, Jorg, 151n24
Battle of Britain, 170
Battle of Changping, 184
Battle of Mello, 247
Battle of Nördlingen, 339
Belgium, 154–55, 168, 246–47, 406
Bercé, Yves-Marie, 246n21, 250–51, 253
Bergh, Andreas, 162n41
Berkowitz, Edward, 170
Bertola, Luis, 110n35
Béthune, Maximilien de, 83
Beveridge, William, 171
Beveridge Report, 379
"billionaire class," 3, 4
billionaires, 1, 2, 3, 4, 19n16; China, 2n3; Forbes
    World's Billionaires, 71; Russia, 222
Bischoff, Kendra, 20n17
Black Death, 18, 90, 91n6, 93, 94, 96, 112,
    291–313, 293n2, 333, 335, 341, 375,
    390, 397, 442; Byzantine, 303; cultivation
    patterns, 329; eastern European countries,
    311; elites, 310; end of Middle Ages, 111;
    England, 299, 342, 394n6; Europe, 297;
    famines, 331–32; "First," 326; fourteenth
    century, 319; impact, 297; income, 101;
    initial wave, 332; Italy, 313; Justinianic
    Plague, 325; labor costs, 247, 302; labor
    supply, 248; late medieval Europe, 324,
    336; late medieval pandemic 293–313;
    Lorenz curves, 308; Mamluk Egypt, 312;
    mid-fourteenth century, 314; mortality, 304,
    307–8, 316; New World, 316; Ottoman,
    303; population, 298; real wages, 4, 304;
    Tuscani, 308n28; western Europe, 318, 326,
    330, 341; wheat wages, 324
"bloodlands," 155
Blum, Jerome, 311
Boccaccio, Giovanni, 296
Boehm, Christopher, 26n1, 28n4, 29n6
Boix, Carles, 30n8, 85n36, 267n12
Bolivia, 243, 276–78, 382–84, 387
Bolsheviks, 215, 216, 223, 396
Borgerhoff Mulder, Monique, 37n20

THE PRINCETON ECONOMIC HISTORY OF THE WESTERN WORLD

Joel Mokyr, Series Editor